Probability and Random Processes

GEOFFREY GRIMMETT
School of Mathematics, University of Bristol

DAVID STIRZAKER
St. John's College, Oxford

CLARENDON PRESS · OXFORD · 1982

Oxford University Press, Walton Street, Oxford OX2 6DP

London Glasgow New York Toronto
Delhi Bombay Calcutta Madras Karachi
Kuala Lumpur Singapore Hong Kong Tokyo
Nairobi Dar es Salaam Cape Town
Melbourne Wellington

and associate companies in
Beirut Berlin Ibadan Mexico City

Published in the United States
by Oxford University Press, New York

British Library Cataloguing in Publication Data

Grimmett, Geoffrey
Probability and random processes.
1. Probabilities
I. Title II. Stirzaker, David
519.2 QA273

ISBN 0-19-853184-2
ISBN 0-19-853185-0 Pbk

Filmset and printed in Northern Ireland at The Universities Press (Belfast) Ltd.

Probability and Random Processes

Preface

This is a new textbook about probability theory and random processes. We hope that it attains some of the following targets:

to be suitable for mathematics undergraduates at all levels, and to be a useful reference book for graduate students and others with interests in probability and its applications;

to be a rigorous introduction to probability theory without burdening the reader with a great deal of measure theory;

to discuss random processes in some depth with many examples;

to include certain topics which are suitable for undergraduate courses but which are rarely taught;

to impart to the beginner some flavour of more advanced work.

We assume that the reader has certain fundamental mathematical skills such as a familiarity with elementary set theory and analysis.

The book can be divided broadly into two parts. Chapters 1–5 begin with the foundations of probability theory, move through the elementary properties of random variables, and finish with the weak law of large numbers and the central limit theorem; on route, the reader meets random walks, branching processes, and characteristic functions. This material is suitable for about two lecture courses at a moderately elementary level. The rest of the book is largely concerned with random processes. Chapter 6 deals with Markov chains, treating discrete-time chains in some detail (and including an easy proof of the ergodic theorem for chains with countably infinite state spaces) and continuous-time chains largely by example. Chapter 7 contains the usual general discussion of convergence, together with simple but rigorous accounts of the strong law of large numbers, martingale convergence, and optional stopping. Each of these two chapters could be used as a basis for a lecture course. Chapters 8–11 are more fragmented and provide suitable material for about four shorter lecture courses on stationary processes, diffusion processes, renewal processes, and queueing processes. There is a final appendix which contains a few useful remarks about some of the problems in the text.

The ends of proofs and examples are indicated by the symbols ■ and ● respectively.

We thank those who read and commented upon sections of this work. Brian Davies read an early draft and Tim Brown read large chunks of the final version; both had many valuable ideas about possible improvements.

Sean Collins made many suggestions about our treatment of discrete-time Markov chains; Stephen Suen found too many errors for our liking. We are grateful also to Geoff Eagleson, Professor G. E. H. Reuter, David Green, and Bernard Silverman. Danica Novak typed the whole manuscript with skill and patience.

Finally, we are both especially grateful to Dominic Welsh. He taught us both when we were undergraduates and graduate students, and later gave us the idea for this book. He must take sole responsibility for all serious mathematical errors, details of which may be addressed directly to him.

Bristol and Oxford
April 1981

G. G.
D. S.

Contents

1 Events and their probabilities

1.1 Introduction

Much of our life is based on the belief that the future is largely unpredictable. For example, games of chance such as dice or roulette would have few adherents if their outcomes were known in advance. We express this belief in chance behaviour by the use of words such as 'random' or 'probability', and we seek, by way of gaming and other experience, to assign quantitative as well as qualitative meanings to such usages. Our acquaintance with statements about probability relies on a wealth of concepts, some more reasonable than others. A mathematical theory of probability will incorporate those concepts of chance which are expressed and implicit in common rational understanding. Such a theory will formalize these concepts as a collection of axioms, which should lead directly to conclusions in agreement with practical experimentation. This chapter contains the essential ingredients of this construction.

1.2 Events as sets

Many everyday statements take the form 'the chance (or probability) of A is p', where A is some event (such as 'the sun shining tomorrow', 'Cambridge winning the Boat Race', ...) and p is a number or adjective describing quantity (such as 'one-eighth', 'low', ...). The occurrence or non-occurrence of A depends upon the chain of circumstances involved. This chain is called an *experiment* or *trial*; the result of an experiment is called its *outcome*. In general, we cannot predict with certainty the outcome of an experiment in advance of its completion; we can only list the collection of possible outcomes.

(1) **Definition.** The set of all possible outcomes of an experiment is called the **sample space** and is denoted by Ω.

(2) **Example.** A coin is tossed. There are two possible outcomes, heads (denoted by H) and tails (denoted by T), so that

$$\Omega = \{H, T\}.$$

We may be interested in the possible occurrences of the following events:

(a) the outcome is a head;
(b) the outcome is either a head or a tail;
(c) the outcome is both a head and a tail (this seems very unlikely to occur);
(d) the outcome is not a head. ●

(3) **Example.** A die is thrown once. There are six possible outcomes depending on which of the numbers 1, 2, 3, 4, 5, or 6 is uppermost. Thus

$$\Omega = \{1, 2, 3, 4, 5, 6\}.$$

We may be interested in the following events:

(a) the outcome is the number 1;
(b) the outcome is an even number;
(c) the outcome is even but does not exceed 3;
(d) the outcome is not even. ●

We see immediately that each of the events of these examples can be specified as a subset A of the appropriate sample space Ω. In the first example they can be rewritten as

(a) $A = \{H\}$, (b) $A = \{H\} \cup \{T\}$,

(c) $A = \{H\} \cap \{T\}$, (d) $A = \{H\}^c$,

whilst those of the second example become

(a) $A = \{1\}$, (b) $A = \{2, 4, 6\}$,

(c) $A = \{2, 4, 6\} \cap \{1, 2, 3\}$, (d) $A = \{2, 4, 6\}^c$.

(The *complement* of a subset A of Ω is denoted here and subsequently by A^c; henceforth subsets of Ω containing a single member, such as $\{H\}$, will be written without the containing brackets.)

Henceforth we think of *events* as subsets of the sample space Ω. Whenever A and B are events in which we are interested, then we can reasonably concern ourselves also with the events $A \cup B$, $A \cap B$, and A^c, representing 'A or B', 'A and B', and 'not A' respectively. Events A and B are called *disjoint* if their intersection is the empty set $\varnothing$; $\varnothing$ is called the *impossible event.* The set Ω is called the *certain event,* since some member of Ω will certainly occur.

Thus events are subsets of Ω, but need all the subsets of Ω be events? The answer is in the negative, but some of the reasons for this are too difficult to be discussed here. It suffices for us to think of the collection of events as a subcollection $\mathcal{F}$ of the set of all subsets of Ω. This subcollection should have certain properties in accordance with the earlier discussion:

(a) if $A, B \in \mathcal{F}$ then $A \cup B \in \mathcal{F}$ and $A \cap B \in \mathcal{F}$;
(b) if $A \in \mathcal{F}$ then $A^c \in \mathcal{F}$;
(c) the empty set $\varnothing$ belongs to $\mathcal{F}$.

Any collection $\mathcal{F}$ of subsets of Ω which satisfies these three conditions is called a *field.* It follows from the properties of a field $\mathcal{F}$ that

$$\text{if} \quad A_1, A_2, \ldots, A_n \in \mathcal{F} \quad \text{then} \quad \bigcup_{i=1}^{n} A_i \in \mathcal{F};$$

that is to say, $\mathcal{F}$ is closed under finite unions and hence under finite intersections also (see Problem (1.8.3)). This is fine when Ω is a finite set, but we require slightly more to deal with the common situation when Ω is infinite, as the following example indicates.

(4) **Example.** A coin is tossed repeatedly until the first head turns up; we are concerned with the number of tosses before this happens. The set of all possible outcomes is the set

$$\Omega = \{\omega_1, \omega_2, \omega_3, \ldots\}$$

where ω_i denotes the outcome when the first $i-1$ tosses are tails and the ith toss is a head. We may seek to assign a probability to the event A, that the first head occurs after an even number of tosses:

$$A = \omega_2 \cup \omega_4 \cup \omega_6 \cup \ldots.$$

This is an infinite countable union of members of Ω, and we require that such sets lie in $\mathcal{F}$ in order that we can discuss its probability. ●

Thus we also require that the collection of events be closed under the operation of taking countable unions. Any collection of subsets of Ω with these properties is called a *σ-field.*

(5) **Definition.** A collection $\mathcal{F}$ of subsets of Ω is called a **σ-field** if it satisfies the following conditions:

(a) $\varnothing \in \mathcal{F}$;

(b) if $A_1, A_2, \ldots \in \mathcal{F}$ then $\bigcup_{i=1}^{\infty} A_i \in \mathcal{F}$;

(c) if $A \in \mathcal{F}$ then $A^c \in \mathcal{F}$.

It follows from Problem (1.8.3) that σ-fields are closed under the operation of taking countable intersections. Here are some examples of σ-fields.

(6) **Example.** The smallest σ-field associated with Ω is the collection $\mathcal{F} = \{\varnothing, \Omega\}$.

(7) **Example.** If A is any subset of Ω then $\mathcal{F} = \{\varnothing, A, A^c, \Omega\}$ is a σ-field. ●

(8) **Example.** The *power set* of Ω, which is written $\{0, 1\}^{\Omega}$ and contains all subsets of Ω, is obviously a σ-field. For reasons beyond the scope of this book, it is often too large a collection for probabilities to be assigned reasonably to all its members. ●

To recapitulate, with any experiment we may associate a pair $(\Omega, \mathcal{F})$, where Ω is the set of all possible outcomes or *elementary events* and $\mathcal{F}$ is a σ-field of subsets of Ω which contains all the events in whose occurrences we may be interested; henceforth, to call a set A an *event* is equivalent to asserting that A belongs to the σ-field in question. We usually translate statements about combinations of events into set-theoretic jargon; for example, the event that both A and B occur is written as $A \cap B$. Table 1.1 is a translation chart.

Table 1.1

Typical notation	Set jargon	Probability jargon
Ω	Collection of objects	Sample space
ω	Member of Ω	Elementary event, outcome
A	Subset of Ω	Event that some outcome in A occurs
A^c	Complement of A	Event that no outcome in A occurs
$A\cap B$	Intersection	Both A and B
$A\cup B$	Union	Either A or B, or both
$A\setminus B$	Difference	A, but not B
$A\triangle B$	Symmetric difference	Either A or B, but not both
$A\subseteq B$	Inclusion	If A, then B
$\varnothing$	Empty set	Impossible event
Ω	Whole space	Certain event

1.3 Probability

We wish to be able to discuss the likelihoods of the occurrences of events. Suppose that we repeat an experiment a large number N of times, keeping the initial conditions as equal as possible, and suppose that A is some event which may or may not occur on each repetition. Our experience of most scientific experimentation is that the proportion of times that A occurs settles down to some value as N becomes larger and larger; that is to say, writing $N(A)$ for the number of occurrences of A in the N trials, $N(A)/N$ converges to a constant limit as N increases. We can think of the ultimate value of this ratio as being the probability $\mathbf{P}(A)$ that A occurs on any particular trial†; it may happen that the ratio does not behave in a coherent manner and our intuition fails us at this level, but we shall not discuss this here. Clearly, the ratio is a number between zero and one; if $A=\varnothing$ then $N(\varnothing)=0$ and the ratio is 0, whilst if $A=\Omega$ then $N(\Omega)=N$ and the ratio is 1. Furthermore, suppose that A and B are two disjoint events, each of which may or may not occur at each trial. Then

$$N(A\cup B)=N(A)+N(B)$$

and so the ratio $N(A\cup B)/N$ is the sum of the two ratios $N(A)/N$ and $N(B)/N$. We now think of these ratios as representing the probabilities of the appropriate events. The above relations become

$$\mathbf{P}(A\cup B)=\mathbf{P}(A)+\mathbf{P}(B),\qquad \mathbf{P}(\varnothing)=0,\qquad \mathbf{P}(\Omega)=1.$$

This discussion suggests that the probability function $\mathbf{P}$ should be *finitely additive*, which is to say that

$$\text{if } A_1, A_2, \ldots, A_n \text{ are disjoint events, then } \mathbf{P}\left(\bigcup_{i=1}^{n} A_i\right)=\sum_{i=1}^{n}\mathbf{P}(A_i);$$

a glance at Example (1.2.4) suggests the more extensive property that

† This superficial discussion of probabilities is inadequate in many ways; questioning readers may care to discuss the philosophical and empirical aspects of the subject amongst themselves.

$\mathbf{P}$ be *countably additive*, in that this should hold for countable collections $A_1, A_2, \ldots$ of disjoint events.

These relations are sufficient to specify the desirable properties of a probability function $\mathbf{P}$ applied to the set of events. Any such assignment of likelihoods to the members of $\mathcal{F}$ is called a *probability measure*.

(1) **Definition.** A **probability measure** $\mathbf{P}$ on $(\Omega, \mathcal{F})$ is a function $\mathbf{P}: \mathcal{F} \to [0, 1]$ satisfying

(a) $\mathbf{P}(\varnothing)=0, \qquad \mathbf{P}(\Omega)=1;$

(b) if $A_1, A_2, \ldots$ is a collection of disjoint members of $\mathcal{F}$, so that $A_i \cap A_j = \varnothing$ for all pairs i, j satisfying $i \neq j$, then

$$\mathbf{P}\left(\bigcup_{i=1}^{\infty} A_i\right) = \sum_{i=1}^{\infty} \mathbf{P}(A_i).$$

The triple $(\Omega, \mathcal{F}, \mathbf{P})$, comprising a set Ω, a σ-field $\mathcal{F}$ of subsets of Ω and a probability measure $\mathbf{P}$ on $(\Omega, \mathcal{F})$, is called a **probability space.**

We can associate a probability space $(\Omega, \mathcal{F}, \mathbf{P})$ with any experiment, and all questions associated with the experiment can be reformulated in terms of this space. It may seem natural to ask for the numerical value of the probability $\mathbf{P}(A)$ of some event A. The answer to such questions must be contained in the description of the experiment in question. For example, the assertion that a *fair* coin is tossed once is equivalent to saying that heads and tails have an equal probability of occurring; actually, this is the *definition* of fairness.

(2) **Example.** A coin, possibly biased, is tossed once. We can take $\Omega=\{H, T\}$ and $\mathcal{F}=\{\varnothing, H, T, \Omega\}$, and a possible probability measure $\mathbf{P}: \mathcal{F} \to [0, 1]$ is given by

$$\mathbf{P}(\varnothing)=0, \qquad \mathbf{P}(H)=p, \qquad \mathbf{P}(T)=1-p, \qquad \mathbf{P}(\Omega)=1$$

where p is a fixed real number in the interval $[0, 1]$. If $p=\frac{1}{2}$, then we say that the coin is *fair*, or *unbiased*. ●

(3) **Example.** A die is thrown once. We can take $\Omega=\{1, 2, 3, 4, 5, 6\}$, $\mathcal{F}=\{0, 1\}^{\Omega}$ and the probability measure $\mathbf{P}$ given by

$$\mathbf{P}(A) = \sum_{i \in A} p_i \qquad \text{for any } A \subseteq \Omega$$

where $p_1, p_2, \ldots, p_6$ are specified numbers from the interval $[0, 1]$ with unit sum. The probability that i turns up is p_i. The die is fair if $p_i=\frac{1}{6}$ for each i, in which case

$$\mathbf{P}(A)=|A|/6 \qquad \text{for any } A \subseteq \Omega$$

where $|A|$ denotes the cardinality of A. ●

$(\Omega, \mathcal{F}, \mathbf{P})$ denotes a typical probability space. We now give some of its simple but important properties.

(4) **Lemma.**

(a) $\mathbf{P}(A^c) = 1 - \mathbf{P}(A)$
(b) *if* $B \supseteq A$ *then* $\mathbf{P}(B) = \mathbf{P}(A) + \mathbf{P}(B \setminus A) \geq \mathbf{P}(A)$
(c) $\mathbf{P}(A \cup B) = \mathbf{P}(A) + \mathbf{P}(B) - \mathbf{P}(A \cap B)$
(d) *more generally, if* $A_1, A_2, \ldots, A_n$ *are events then*

$$\mathbf{P}\left(\bigcup_{i=1}^{n} A_i\right) = \sum_i \mathbf{P}(A_i) - \sum_{i<j} \mathbf{P}(A_i \cap A_j) + \sum_{i<j<k} \mathbf{P}(A_i \cap A_j \cap A_k) - \ldots$$
$$+ (-1)^{n+1}\mathbf{P}(A_1 \cap A_2 \cap \ldots \cap A_n)$$

where, for example, $\sum_{i<j}$ *sums over all unordered pairs* (i, j) *for* $i \neq j$.

Proof.

(a) $A \cup A^c = \Omega$ and $A \cap A^c = \varnothing$, so $\mathbf{P}(A \cup A^c) = \mathbf{P}(A) + \mathbf{P}(A^c) = 1$.
(b) $B = A \cup (B \setminus A)$. However, this is the union of disjoint sets and so

$$\mathbf{P}(B) = \mathbf{P}(A) + \mathbf{P}(B \setminus A).$$

(c) $A \cup B = A \cup (B \setminus A)$, which is a disjoint union. So

$$\mathbf{P}(A \cup B) = \mathbf{P}(A) + \mathbf{P}(B \setminus A) = \mathbf{P}(A) + \mathbf{P}(B \setminus (A \cap B))$$
$$= \mathbf{P}(A) + \mathbf{P}(B) - \mathbf{P}(A \cap B)$$

by the result of (b).
(d) The proof is by induction on n, and is left as an *exercise* (see Problem (1.8.10)). ■

In (4b) $B \setminus A$ denotes the set of members of B which are not in A. In order to write down the quantity $\mathbf{P}(B \setminus A)$, we require that $B \setminus A$ is in $\mathcal{F}$, the domain of $\mathbf{P}$; this is always true when A and B are in $\mathcal{F}$ and the proof of this is left until Problem (1.8.3). Notice that each proof proceeded by expressing an event in terms of disjoint unions and then applying $\mathbf{P}$. It is sometimes easier to calculate the probabilities of intersections of events rather than their unions; part (d) of the lemma is useful then, as we shall discover soon. The next property of $\mathbf{P}$ is more technical, and says that $\mathbf{P}$ is a *continuous* set function; this property is essentially equivalent to the condition that $\mathbf{P}$ is countably additive rather than just finitely additive (see Problem (1.8.14) also).

(5) **Lemma.** *Let* $A_1, A_2, \ldots$ *be an increasing sequence of events, so that* $A_1 \subseteq A_2 \subseteq A_3 \subseteq \ldots$, *and write* A *for their limit:*

$$A = \bigcup_{i=1}^{\infty} A_i = \lim A_i.$$

Then $\mathbf{P}(A) = \lim \mathbf{P}(A_i)$.

Similarly, if $B_1, B_2, \ldots$ is a decreasing sequence of events, so that $B_1 \supseteq B_2 \supseteq B_3 \supseteq \ldots$, then

$$B = \bigcap_{i=1}^{\infty} B_i = \lim B_i$$

satisfies $\mathbf{P}(B) = \lim \mathbf{P}(B_i)$.

Proof. $A = A_1 \cup (A_2 \setminus A_1) \cup (A_3 \setminus A_2) \cup \ldots$ is the union of a disjoint family of events. Thus, by Definition (1),

$$\begin{aligned}\mathbf{P}(A) &= \mathbf{P}(A_1) + \sum_{i=1}^{\infty} \mathbf{P}(A_{i+1} \setminus A_i) \\ &= \mathbf{P}(A_1) + \lim_{n\to\infty} \sum_{i=1}^{n-1} \{\mathbf{P}(A_{i+1}) - \mathbf{P}(A_i)\} \\ &= \lim_{n\to\infty} \mathbf{P}(A_n).\end{aligned}$$

To show the result for decreasing families of events, take complements and use the first part (*exercise*). ■

To recapitulate, statements concerning chance are implicitly related to experiments or trials, the outcomes of which are not entirely predictable. With any such experiment we can associate a probability space $(\Omega, \mathcal{F}, \mathbf{P})$ the properties of which are consistent with our shared and reasonable conceptions of the notion of chance.

Here is a final piece of jargon. An event A is called *null* if $\mathbf{P}(A) = 0$. Null events should not be confused with the impossible event $\varnothing$. Null events are happening all around us, even though they have zero probability; after all, what is the chance that a dart strikes the precise centre of the target at which it is thrown? That is, the impossible event is null, but null events need not be impossible.

1.4 Conditional probability: a fundamental lemma

Many statements about chance take the form 'if B occurs, then the probability of A is p', where B and A are events (such as 'it rains tomorrow' and 'the bus being on time' respectively) and p is a quantifier as before. To include this in our theory, we should return briefly to the discussion about proportions at the beginning of the previous section. An experiment is repeated N times, and on each occasion we observe the occurrences or non-occurrences of two events A and B. Now, suppose we only take an interest in those outcomes for which B occurs; all other experiments are disregarded. In this smaller collection of trials the proportion of times that A occurs is $N(A \cap B)/N(B)$, since B occurs at each of them. However,

$$\frac{N(A \cap B)}{N(B)} = \frac{N(A \cap B)/N}{N(B)/N}.$$

If we now think of these ratios as probabilities, we see that the probability that A occurs, given that B occurs, should be reasonably defined as $\mathbf{P}(A \cap B)/\mathbf{P}(B)$.

(1) **Definition.** If $\mathbf{P}(B) > 0$ then the **conditional probability** that A occurs given that B occurs is defined to be

$$\mathbf{P}(A \mid B) = \frac{\mathbf{P}(A \cap B)}{\mathbf{P}(B)}.$$

$\mathbf{P}(A \mid B)$, pronounced 'the probability of A given B', is our notation for this conditional probability. We sometimes speak of $\mathbf{P}(A \mid B)$ as 'the probability of A conditioned on B'.

(2) **Example.** Two fair dice are thrown. Given that the first shows 3, what is the probability that the total exceeds 6? The answer is obviously $\frac{1}{2}$, since the second must show 4, 5, or 6. However, let us labour the point. Clearly $\Omega = \{1, 2, 3, 4, 5, 6\}^2$, the set of all ordered pairs (i, j) for $i, j \in \{1, 2, \ldots, 6\}$ (remember that $A \times B = \{(a, b) : a \in A, b \in B\}$ and that $A \times A = A^2$), and we can take $\mathcal{F}$ to be the set of all subsets of Ω, with $\mathbf{P}(A) = |A|/36$ for any $A \subseteq \Omega$. Let B be the event that the first die shows 3 and A be the event that the total exceeds 6. Then

$$B = \{(3, b) : 1 \leqslant b \leqslant 6\}, \qquad A = \{(a, b) : a + b > 6\}$$

$$A \cap B = \{(3, 4), (3, 5), (3, 6)\}.$$

Thus

$$\mathbf{P}(A \mid B) = \frac{\mathbf{P}(A \cap B)}{\mathbf{P}(B)} = \frac{|A \cap B|}{|B|} = \frac{3}{6}.$$ ●

(3) **Example.** A family has two children. What is the probability that both are boys, given that at least one is a boy? The older and younger child may each be male or female, so there are four possible combinations of sexes, which we assume to be equally likely. Hence we can represent the sample space in the obvious way as

$$\Omega = \{GG, GB, BG, BB\}$$

where $\mathbf{P}(GG) = \mathbf{P}(GB) = \mathbf{P}(BG) = \mathbf{P}(BB) = \frac{1}{4}$. From the definition of conditional probability

$$\begin{aligned}\mathbf{P}(BB \mid \text{one boy at least}) &= \mathbf{P}(BB \mid GB \cup BG \cup BB) \\ &= \frac{\mathbf{P}(BB \cap (GB \cup BG \cup BB))}{\mathbf{P}(GB \cup BG \cup BB)} \\ &= \frac{\mathbf{P}(BB)}{\mathbf{P}(GB \cup BG \cup BB)} = \frac{1}{3}.\end{aligned}$$

A popular but incorrect answer to the question is $\frac{1}{2}$. This is the correct answer to another question: for a family with two children, what is the probability that both are boys given that the younger is a boy? In this case

$$\mathbf{P}(BB \mid \text{younger is a boy}) = \mathbf{P}(BB \mid GB \cup BB)$$
$$= \frac{\mathbf{P}(BB \cap (GB \cup BB))}{\mathbf{P}(GB \cup BB)} = \frac{\mathbf{P}(BB)}{\mathbf{P}(GB \cup BB)} = \frac{1}{2}.$$

The usual dangerous argument contains the assertion

$$\mathbf{P}(BB \mid \text{one child is a boy}) = \mathbf{P}(\text{other child is a boy}).$$

Why is this meaningless? ●

The next lemma is crucially important in probability theory. A family $B_1, B_2, \ldots, B_n$ of events is called a *partition* of Ω if

$$B_i \cap B_j = \varnothing \quad \text{when} \quad i \neq j, \quad \text{and} \quad \bigcup_{i=1}^{n} B_i = \Omega.$$

Each elementary event $\omega \in \Omega$ belongs to exactly one set in a partition of Ω.

(4) **Lemma.** *For any events A and B*

$$\mathbf{P}(A) = \mathbf{P}(A \mid B)\mathbf{P}(B) + \mathbf{P}(A \mid B^c)\mathbf{P}(B^c).$$

More generally, let $B_1, B_2, \ldots, B_n$ be a partition of Ω. Then

$$\mathbf{P}(A) = \sum_{i=1}^{n} \mathbf{P}(A \mid B_i)\mathbf{P}(B_i).$$

Proof. $A = (A \cap B) \cup (A \cap B^c)$. This is a disjoint union and so

$$\mathbf{P}(A) = \mathbf{P}(A \cap B) + \mathbf{P}(A \cap B^c)$$
$$= \mathbf{P}(A \mid B)\mathbf{P}(B) + \mathbf{P}(A \mid B^c)\mathbf{P}(B^c).$$

The second part is similar (see Problem (1.8.10)). ■

(5) **Example.** We are given two urns, each containing a collection of coloured balls. Urn I contains two white and three blue balls, whilst urn II contains three white and four blue balls. A ball is drawn at random from urn I and put into urn II, and then a ball is picked at random from urn II and examined. What is the probability that it is blue? We assume unless otherwise specified that a ball picked randomly from any urn is equally likely to be any of those present. The reader will be relieved to know that we no longer need to describe $(\Omega, \mathcal{F}, \mathbf{P})$ in detail; we are confident that we could do so if necessary. Clearly, the colour of the final ball depends on the colour of the ball picked from urn I. So let us 'condition' on this. Let A be the event that the final ball is blue and B be the event that the first one picked was blue. Then, by Lemma (4),

$$\mathbf{P}(A) = \mathbf{P}(A \mid B)\mathbf{P}(B) + \mathbf{P}(A \mid B^c)\mathbf{P}(B^c).$$

We can easily find all these probabilities:

$$\mathbf{P}(A \mid B) = \mathbf{P}(A \mid \text{urn II contains three white and five blue balls}) = \tfrac{5}{8}$$
$$\mathbf{P}(A \mid B^c) = \mathbf{P}(A \mid \text{urn II contains four white and four blue balls}) = \tfrac{1}{2}$$

$$\mathbf{P}(B) = \tfrac{3}{5}, \qquad \mathbf{P}(B^c) = \tfrac{2}{5}.$$

Hence

$$\mathbf{P}(A) = \tfrac{5}{8} \cdot \tfrac{3}{5} + \tfrac{1}{2} \cdot \tfrac{2}{5} = \tfrac{23}{40}. \qquad \bullet$$

(6) **Example.** Only two factories manufacture zoggles. 20 per cent of the zoggles from factory I and 5 per cent from factory II are defective. Factory I produces twice as many zoggles as factory II each week. What is the probability that a zoggle, randomly chosen from a week's production, is satisfactory? Clearly this satisfaction depends on the factory of origin. Let A be the event that the chosen zoggle is satisfactory and let B be the event that it was made in factory I. Arguing as before,

$$\begin{aligned}\mathbf{P}(A) &= \mathbf{P}(A \mid B)\mathbf{P}(B) + \mathbf{P}(A \mid B^c)\mathbf{P}(B^c) \\ &= \tfrac{4}{5} \cdot \tfrac{2}{3} + \tfrac{19}{20} \cdot \tfrac{1}{3} = \tfrac{51}{60}.\end{aligned}$$

If the chosen zoggle is defective, what is the probability that it came from factory I? In our notation this is just $\mathbf{P}(B \mid A^c)$. However,

$$\begin{aligned}\mathbf{P}(B \mid A^c) &= \frac{\mathbf{P}(B \cap A^c)}{\mathbf{P}(A^c)} \\ &= \frac{\mathbf{P}(A^c \mid B)\mathbf{P}(B)}{\mathbf{P}(A^c)} = \frac{\frac{1}{5} \cdot \frac{2}{3}}{1 - 51/60} = \frac{8}{9}. \qquad \bullet\end{aligned}$$

1.5 Independence

In general, the occurrence of some event B changes the probability that another event A occurs; the original probability $\mathbf{P}(A)$ is replaced by $\mathbf{P}(A \mid B)$. If this probability remains unchanged, that is to say $\mathbf{P}(A \mid B) = \mathbf{P}(A)$, then we call A and B 'independent'. This is well defined only if $\mathbf{P}(B) > 0$. Definition (1.4.1) of conditional probability leads us to the following.

(1) **Definition.** Events A and B are called **independent** if

$$\mathbf{P}(A \cap B) = \mathbf{P}(A)\mathbf{P}(B).$$

More generally, a family $\{A_i : i \in I\}$ is called **independent** if

$$\mathbf{P}\Big(\bigcap_{i \in J} A_i\Big) = \prod_{i \in J} \mathbf{P}(A_i)$$

for all finite subsets J of I.

A common student error is to say that A and B are independent if $A \cap B = \varnothing$; this is clearly false. If the family $\{A_i : i \in I\}$ has the property that

$$\mathbf{P}(A_i \cap A_j) = \mathbf{P}(A_i)\mathbf{P}(A_j) \quad \text{for all } i \neq j$$

then it is called *pairwise independent*. Pairwise independent families are not necessarily independent, as the following example shows.

(2) **Example.** Suppose $\Omega = \{abc, acb, cab, cba, bca, bac, aaa, bbb, ccc\}$, and each of the nine elementary events in Ω occurs with equal probability $\frac{1}{9}$. Let A_k be the event that the kth letter is a. It is left as an *exercise* to show that $\{A_1, A_2, A_3\}$ is pairwise independent but not independent. ●

(3) **Example (1.4.6) revisited.** The events A and B of this example are clearly dependent because

$$\mathbf{P}(A \mid B) = \tfrac{4}{5}, \qquad \mathbf{P}(A) = \tfrac{51}{60}.$$ ●

(4) **Example.** Choose a card at random from a pack of 52 playing cards, each being picked with equal probability 1/52. We claim that the suit of the chosen card is independent of its rank. For example,

$$\mathbf{P}(\text{king}) = 4/52, \qquad \mathbf{P}(\text{king} \mid \text{spade}) = 1/13.$$

Alternatively,

$$\begin{aligned}\mathbf{P}(\text{spade king}) &= 1/52 \\ &= \tfrac{1}{4} \cdot \tfrac{1}{13} = \mathbf{P}(\text{spade})\mathbf{P}(\text{king}).\end{aligned}$$ ●

1.6 Completeness and product spaces

This section should be omitted at the first reading, but we shall require its contents later. It contains only a sketch of complete probability spaces and product spaces; the reader should look elsewhere for a more detailed treatment (see Billingsley 1979). We require the following result.

(1) **Lemma.** *If $\mathscr{F}$ and $\mathscr{G}$ are two σ-fields of subsets of Ω then $\mathscr{F} \cap \mathscr{G}$ is a σ-field also. More generally, if $\{\mathscr{F}_i : i \in I\}$ is a family of σ-fields of subsets of Ω then $\mathscr{I} = \bigcap_{i \in I} \mathscr{F}_i$ is a σ-field also.*

The proof is not difficult and is left as an *exercise*. Note that $\mathscr{F} \cup \mathscr{G}$ may not be a σ-field, although it may be extended to a unique smallest σ-field, written $\sigma(\mathscr{F} \cup \mathscr{G})$, as follows. Let $\{\mathscr{I}_i : i \in I\}$ be the collection of all σ-fields which contain both $\mathscr{F}$ and $\mathscr{G}$ as subsets; this collection is non-empty since it contains the set of all subsets of Ω. Then $\mathscr{I} = \bigcap_{i \in I} \mathscr{I}_i$ is the unique smallest σ-field which contains $\mathscr{F} \cup \mathscr{G}$.

(A) Completeness. Let $(\Omega, \mathscr{F}, \mathbf{P})$ be a probability space. Any event A which has zero probability, that is $\mathbf{P}(A) = 0$, is called *null*. It may seem reasonable to suppose that any subset B of a null set A will itself be null, but this may be without meaning since B may not be an event and thus $\mathbf{P}(B)$ may not be defined.

(2) **Definition.** A probability space $(\Omega, \mathcal{F}, \mathbf{P})$ is called **complete** if all subsets of null sets are events.

Any incomplete space can be completed. Let $\mathcal{N}$ be the collection of all subsets of null sets in $\mathcal{F}$ and let $\mathcal{G} = \sigma(\mathcal{F} \cup \mathcal{N})$ be the smallest σ-field which contains all sets in $\mathcal{F}$ and $\mathcal{N}$. It can be shown that the domain of $\mathbf{P}$ may be extended in an obvious way from $\mathcal{F}$ to $\mathcal{G}$; $(\Omega, \mathcal{G}, \mathbf{P})$ is the *completion* of $(\Omega, \mathcal{F}, \mathbf{P})$.

(B) Product spaces. The probability spaces discussed in this chapter have usually been constructed around the outcomes of one experiment, but instances occur naturally when we need to combine the outcomes of several independent experiments into one space (see (1.2.4) and (1.4.2)). How should we proceed in general?

Suppose two experiments have associated probability spaces $(\Omega_1, \mathcal{F}_1, \mathbf{P}_1)$ and $(\Omega_2, \mathcal{F}_2, \mathbf{P}_2)$ respectively. The sample space of the pair of experiments, considered jointly, is the collection $\Omega_1 \times \Omega_2 = \{(\omega_1, \omega_2) : \omega_1 \in \Omega_1, \omega_2 \in \Omega_2\}$ of ordered pairs. The appropriate σ-field of events is more complicated to construct. Certainly it should contain all subsets of $\Omega_1 \times \Omega_2$ of the form $A_1 \times A_2 = \{(a_1, a_2) : a_1 \in A_1, a_2 \in A_2\}$ where A_1 and A_2 are typical members of $\mathcal{F}_1$ and $\mathcal{F}_2$ respectively. However, the family of all such sets, $\mathcal{F}_1 \times \mathcal{F}_2 = \{A_1 \times A_2 : A_1 \in \mathcal{F}_1, A_2 \in \mathcal{F}_2\}$, is not in general a σ-field. By the discussion after (1), there exists a unique smallest σ-field $\mathcal{G} = \sigma(\mathcal{F}_1 \times \mathcal{F}_2)$ of subsets of $\Omega_1 \times \Omega_2$ which contains $\mathcal{F}_1 \times \mathcal{F}_2$. All we require now is a suitable probability function on $(\Omega_1 \times \Omega_2, \mathcal{G})$. Let $\mathbf{P}_{12} : \mathcal{F}_1 \times \mathcal{F}_2 \to [0, 1]$ be given by

(3) $$\mathbf{P}_{12}(A_1 \times A_2) = \mathbf{P}_1(A_1)\mathbf{P}_2(A_2)$$

for any $A_1 \in \mathcal{F}_1$ and $A_2 \in \mathcal{F}_2$. It can be shown that the domain of $\mathbf{P}_{12}$ can be extended from $\mathcal{F}_1 \times \mathcal{F}_2$ to the whole of $\mathcal{G} = \sigma(\mathcal{F}_1 \times \mathcal{F}_2)$. The ensuing probability space $(\Omega_1 \times \Omega_2, \mathcal{G}, \mathbf{P}_{12})$ is called the *product space* of $(\Omega_1, \mathcal{F}_1, \mathbf{P}_1)$ and $(\Omega_2, \mathcal{F}_2, \mathbf{P}_2)$. Products of larger numbers of spaces are constructed similarly. The measure $\mathbf{P}_{12}$ is sometimes called the 'product measure' since its defining equation (3) assumed that the two experiments are independent. There are of course many other measures that can be applied to $(\Omega_1 \times \Omega_2, \mathcal{G})$.

In many simple cases this technical discussion is unnecessary. Suppose that Ω_1 and Ω_2 are finite, and that their σ-fields contain all their subsets; this is the case in (1.2.4) and (1.4.2). Then $\mathcal{G}$ contains all subsets of $\Omega_1 \times \Omega_2$.

1.7 Worked examples

Here are some more examples to illustrate the ideas of this chapter. The reader is now equipped to try his hand at a substantial number of those problems which exercised the pioneers in probability. These frequently involved experiments having equally likely outcomes, such as dealing whist hands, putting balls of various colours into urns and taking them out again, throwing dice, and so on. In many such instances, the reader will be pleasantly surprised to find that it is not necessary to write down $(\Omega, \mathcal{F}, \mathbf{P})$ explicitly, but only to think of Ω as being a collection $\{\omega_1, \omega_2, \ldots, \omega_N\}$ of possibilities, each of which may occur with probability $1/N$. Thus, $\mathbf{P}(A) = |A|/N$ for any $A \subseteq \Omega$. The basic tools used in such problems are as follows.

(a) Combinatorics: remember that the number of permutations of n objects is $n!$ and that the number of ways of choosing r objects from n is $\binom{n}{r}$.

(b) Set theory: to obtain $\mathbf{P}(A)$ we can compute $\mathbf{P}(A^c) = 1 - \mathbf{P}(A)$ or we can partition A by conditioning on events B_i and use (1.4.4).

(c) Use of independence: problems can then be simplified using (1.5.1).

(1) **Example.** Consider a series of hands dealt at bridge. Let A be the event that in a given deal each player has one ace. Show that the probability that A occurs at least once in seven deals is approximately $\frac{1}{2}$.

Solution. The number of ways of dealing 52 cards into four equal hands is $52!/(13!)^4$. There are 4! ways of distributing the aces so that each hand holds one, and there are $48!/(12!)^4$ ways of dealing the remaining cards. Thus

$$\mathbf{P}(A) = \frac{4!48!/(12!)^4}{52!/(13!)^4} \simeq \frac{1}{10}.$$

Now let B_i be the event that A occurs for the first time on the ith deal. Clearly $B_i \cap B_j = \varnothing$, $i \neq j$. Thus

$$\begin{aligned}\mathbf{P}(A \text{ occurs in seven deals}) &= \mathbf{P}(B_1 \cup \ldots \cup B_7)\\ &= \sum_1^7 \mathbf{P}(B_i) \quad \text{using (1.3.1)}.\end{aligned}$$

Since successive deals are independent, we have

$$\begin{aligned}\mathbf{P}(B_i) &= \mathbf{P}(A^c \text{ occurs on deal 1 and } A^c \text{ occurs on deal } 2 \ldots\\ &\qquad \ldots \text{and } A^c \text{ occurs on deal } i-1 \text{ and } A \text{ occurs on deal } i)\\ &= (\mathbf{P}(A^c))^{i-1}\mathbf{P}(A) \quad \text{using (1.5.1)}\\ &\simeq \left(1 - \frac{1}{10}\right)^{i-1} \frac{1}{10}.\end{aligned}$$

Thus

$$\mathbf{P}(A \text{ occurs in seven deals}) = \sum_1^7 \mathbf{P}(B_i) \simeq \sum_1^7 \left(\frac{9}{10}\right)^{i-1} \frac{1}{10} \simeq \frac{1}{2}.$$ ●

(2) **Example.** There are two roads from A to B and two roads from B to C. Each of the four roads has probability p of being blocked by snow,

independently of all the others. What is the probability that there is an open road from A to C?

Solution.

$$\mathbf{P}(\text{open road}) = \mathbf{P}((\text{open road from A to B}) \cap (\text{open road from B to C}))$$
$$= \mathbf{P}(\text{open road from A to B})\mathbf{P}(\text{open road from B to C})$$

using the independence. However, p is the same for all roads; thus, using (1.3.4),

$$\mathbf{P}(\text{open road}) = (1 - \mathbf{P}(\text{no road from A to B}))^2$$
$$= (1 - \mathbf{P}((\text{first road blocked}) \cap (\text{second road blocked})))^2$$
$$= (1 - \mathbf{P}(\text{first road blocked})\mathbf{P}(\text{second road blocked}))^2$$

using the independence. Thus

(3) $$\mathbf{P}(\text{open road}) = (1 - p^2)^2.$$

Further suppose that there is also a direct road from A to C, which is independently blocked with probability p. Then by (1.4.4),

$$\mathbf{P}(\text{open road}) = \mathbf{P}(\text{open road} \mid \text{direct road blocked}) \,.\, p$$
$$+ \mathbf{P}(\text{open road} \mid \text{direct road open}) \,.\, (1-p)$$
$$= (1-p^2)^2 \,.\, p + 1 \,.\, (1-p)$$

using (3). ●

(4) **Example. Symmetric random walk (or 'Gambler's ruin').** A man is saving up to buy a new Jaguar at a cost of N units of money. He starts with k $(0 < k < N)$ units and tries to win the remainder by the following gamble with his bank manager. He tosses a fair coin repeatedly; if it comes up heads then the manager pays him one unit, but if it comes up tails then he pays the manager one unit. He plays this game repeatedly until one of two events occurs: either he runs out of money and is bankrupted or he wins enough to buy the Jaguar. What is the probability that he is ultimately bankrupted?

Solution. This is one of many problems the solution to which proceeds by the construction of a linear difference equation subject to certain boundary conditions. Let A_k denote the event that he is eventually bankrupted after his initial capital was k units, and let B be the event that the first toss of the coin shows heads. By (1.4.4)

(5) $$\mathbf{P}(A_k) = \mathbf{P}(A_k \mid B)\mathbf{P}(B) + \mathbf{P}(A_k \mid B^c)\mathbf{P}(B^c).$$

We want to find $\mathbf{P}(A_k)$. Consider $\mathbf{P}(A_k \mid B)$. If the first toss is a head then his capital increases to $k+1$ units and the game starts afresh from a different starting point. Thus $\mathbf{P}(A_k \mid B) = \mathbf{P}(A_{k+1})$, and similarly $\mathbf{P}(A_k \mid B^c) = \mathbf{P}(A_{k-1})$. So, writing $p_k = \mathbf{P}(A_k)$, (5) becomes

(6) $$p_k = \tfrac{1}{2}(p_{k+1} + p_{k-1}) \quad \text{if} \quad 0 < k < N,$$

which is a linear difference equation subject to the boundary conditions $p_0 = 1$, $p_N = 0$. The analytical solution to such equations is routine, and we shall return later to the general method of solution. In this case we can proceed directly. We put $b_k = p_k - p_{k-1}$ to obtain $b_k = b_{k-1}$ and hence $b_k = b_1$ for all k. Thus

$$p_k = b_1 + p_{k-1} = 2b_1 + p_{k-2} = \ldots = kb_1 + p_0$$

is the general solution to (6). The boundary conditions imply that $p_0 = 1$, $b_1 = -1/N$, giving

(7) $$\mathbf{P}(A_k) = 1 - k/N.$$

As the price of the Jaguar rises, that is as $N \to \infty$, ultimate bankruptcy becomes very likely. This is the problem of the 'symmetric random walk with two absorbing barriers' to which we shall return in more generality later. ●

Our experience of student calculations leads us to stress that probabilities lie between zero and one; any calculated probability which violates this must be incorrect.

1.8 Problems

1. A traditional fair die is thrown twice. What is the probability that
   (a) a six turns up exactly once?
   (b) both numbers are odd?
   (c) the sum of the scores is 4?
   (d) the sum of the scores is divisible by 3?

2. A fair coin is thrown repeatedly. What is the probability that on the nth throw
   (a) a head appears for the first time?
   (b) the numbers of heads and tails are equal?
   (c) exactly two heads have appeared altogether?
   (d) at least two heads have appeared?

3. Show that if A and B belong to some σ-field $\mathcal{F}$ then $B \setminus A$ belongs to $\mathcal{F}$ also. Use elementary set operations to show that σ-fields are closed under countable intersections; that is, if $A_1, A_2, \ldots$ are in $\mathcal{F}$, then so is $\bigcap_i A_i$.

4. Describe the underlying probability spaces for the following experiments:
   (a) a biased coin is tossed three times;
   (b) two balls are drawn without replacement from an urn which originally contained two ultramarine and two vermilion balls;
   (c) a biased coin is tossed repeatedly until a head turns up.

5. Show that the probability that *exactly* one of the events A and B occurs is $\mathbf{P}(A) + \mathbf{P}(B) - 2\mathbf{P}(A \cap B)$.

6. Prove that $\mathbf{P}(A \cap B \cap C) = \mathbf{P}(A \mid B \cap C)\mathbf{P}(B \mid C)\mathbf{P}(C)$.

7. Prove that if A and B are independent then so are A^c and B.

8. Show that the condition $\mathbf{P}(\varnothing) = 0$ in (1.3.1) is unnecessary, since it is implied by the other conditions.

9. Suppose $(\Omega, \mathcal{F}, \mathbf{P})$ is a probability space and $B \in \mathcal{F}$ satisfies $\mathbf{P}(B)>0$. Let $\mathbf{Q}: \mathcal{F} \to [0, 1]$ be defined by $\mathbf{Q}(A)=\mathbf{P}(A \mid B)$. Show that $(\Omega, \mathcal{F}, \mathbf{Q})$ is a probability space. If $C \in \mathcal{F}$ and $\mathbf{Q}(C)>0$, show that $\mathbf{Q}(A \mid C)=\mathbf{P}(A \mid B \cap C)$; discuss.

10. Complete the proofs of (1.3.4) and (1.4.4).

11. Prove Boole's inequalities

(a) $\mathbf{P}\left(\bigcup_1^n A_i\right) \leq \sum_1^n \mathbf{P}(A_i)$

(b) $\mathbf{P}\left(\bigcap_1^n A_i\right) \geq 1 - \sum_1^n \mathbf{P}(A_i^c)$.

12. Prove Bayes's formula; that is, if $A_1, A_2, \ldots, A_n$ is a partition of Ω, then

$$\mathbf{P}(A_j \mid B) = \frac{\mathbf{P}(B \mid A_j)\mathbf{P}(A_j)}{\sum_1^n \mathbf{P}(B \mid A_i)\mathbf{P}(A_i)}.$$

13. A random number N of dice is thrown. A_i is the event that $N=i$, and $\mathbf{P}(A_i)=2^{-i}$; $i \geq 1$. The sum of the scores is S. Find the probability that:
(a) $N=2$ given $S=4$;
(b) $S=4$ given N is even;
(c) $N=2$ given $S=4$ and the first die showed 1;
(d) the largest number shown by any die is r, when S is unknown.

14. Let $A_1, A_2, \ldots$ be a sequence of events. Define

$$B_n = \bigcup_{m=n}^{\infty} A_m, \qquad C_n = \bigcap_{m=n}^{\infty} A_m.$$

Clearly $C_n \subseteq A_n \subseteq B_n$. The sequences $\{B_n\}$ and $\{C_n\}$ are decreasing and increasing respectively with limits

$$\lim B_n = B = \bigcap_n B_n = \bigcap_n \bigcup_{m \geq n} A_m$$

$$\lim C_n = C = \bigcup_n C_n = \bigcup_n \bigcap_{m \geq n} A_m;$$

B and C are called $\limsup_{n\to\infty} A_n$ and $\liminf_{n\to\infty} A_n$ respectively. Show that
(a) $B=\{\omega \in \Omega: \omega \in A_n$ for infinitely many values of $n\}$,
(b) $C=\{\omega \in \Omega: \omega \in A_n$ for all but finitely many values of $n\}$.
We say that the sequence $\{A_n\}$ converges to a limit $A = \lim A_n$ if B and C are the same set A. Suppose that $A_n \to A$ and show that
(c) A is an event, in that $A \in \mathcal{F}$,
(d) $\mathbf{P}(A_n) \to \mathbf{P}(A)$. See (1.3.5) for help here.

15. Anne, Betty, Chloë, and Daisy were all friends at school. Subsequently each of the $\binom{4}{2}=6$ subpairs meet up; at each of the six meetings the pair involved quarrel with some fixed probability p, or become firm friends with probability $1-p$. Quarrels take place independently of each other. In future, if any of the four

hears a rumour, then she tells it to her firm friends only. If Anne hears a rumour, what is the probability that

(a) Daisy hears it?
(b) Daisy hears it if Anne and Betty have quarrelled?
(c) Daisy hears it if Betty and Chloë have quarrelled?
(d) Daisy hears it if she has quarrelled with Anne?

16. A biased coin is tossed repeatedly. Each time there is probability p of a head turning up. Let p_n be the probability that an even number of heads has occurred after n tosses (zero is an even number). Show that $p_0 = 1$ and that, if $n \geqslant 1$,

$$p_n = p(1-p_{n-1}) + (1-p)p_{n-1}.$$

Can you solve this difference equation?

17. A biased coin is tossed repeatedly. Find the probability that there is a run of r heads in a row before there is a run of s tails, where r and s are positive integers.

18. A bowl contains twenty cherries, exactly fifteen of which have had their stones removed. A greedy pig eats five whole cherries, picked at random, without remarking on the presence or absence of stones. Subsequently, a cherry is picked randomly from the remaining fifteen.

(a) What is the probability that this cherry contains a stone?
(b) Given that this cherry contains a stone, what is the probability that the pig consumed at least one stone?

2 Random variables and their distributions

2.1 Random variables

We shall not always be interested in an experiment itself, but rather in some consequence of its random outcome. For example, many gamblers are more concerned with their losses than with the games which give rise to them. Such consequences, when real valued, may be thought of as functions which map Ω into the real line $\mathbb{R}$, and these functions are called 'random variables'.

(1) **Example.** A fair coin is tossed twice: $\Omega = \{HH, HT, TH, TT\}$. For $\omega \in \Omega$, let $X(\omega)$ be the number of heads, so that

$$X(HH) = 2, \qquad X(HT) = X(TH) = 1, \qquad X(TT) = 0.$$

Now suppose that a gambler wagers his fortune of £1 on the result of this experiment. He gambles cumulatively so that his fortune is doubled each time a head appears and is annihilated on the appearance of a tail. His subsequent fortune W is a random variable given by

$$W(HH) = 4, \qquad W(HT) = W(TH) = W(TT) = 0.$$ ●

After the experiment is done and the outcome $\omega \in \Omega$ is known, a random variable $X : \Omega \to \mathbb{R}$ takes some value. In general this numerical value is more likely to lie in certain subsets of $\mathbb{R}$ than in certain others, depending on the probability space $(\Omega, \mathscr{F}, \mathbf{P})$ and the function X itself. We wish to be able to describe the distribution of the likelihoods of possible values of X. Example (1) above suggests that we might do this through the function $f : \mathbb{R} \to [0, 1]$ defined by

$$f(x) = \text{probability that } X \text{ is equal to } x,$$

but this turns out to be inappropriate in general. Rather, we use the *distribution function* $F : \mathbb{R} \to \mathbb{R}$ defined by

$$F(x) = \text{probability that } X \text{ does not exceed } x.$$

More rigorously, this is

(2) $$F(x) = \mathbf{P}(A(x))$$

where $A(x) \subseteq \Omega$ is given by

$$A(x) = \{\omega \in \Omega : X(\omega) \le x\}.$$

However, $\mathbf{P}$ is a function on the collection $\mathscr{F}$ of events; we cannot discuss $\mathbf{P}(A(x))$ unless $A(x)$ belongs to $\mathscr{F}$, and so we are led to the following definition.

(3) **Definition.** A **random variable** is a function $X:\Omega\to\mathbb{R}$ with the property that $\{\omega\in\Omega: X(\omega)\le x\}\in\mathcal{F}$ for each $x\in\mathbb{R}$.

If the reader so desires, then he may pay no attention to the technical condition in the definition and think of random variables simply as functions mapping Ω into $\mathbb{R}$. (If $\{\omega\in\Omega: X(\omega)\le x\}\in\mathcal{F}$ for each $x\in\mathbb{R}$ then we say that X is $\mathcal{F}$-*measurable*.) We shall always use upper-case letters, like X, Y, and Z, to represent generic random variables, whilst lower-case letters, like x, y, and z, will be used to represent possible numerical values of these variables. Do not confuse this notation in your written work.

Every random variable has a distribution function, given by (2); distribution functions are *very* important and useful.

(4) **Definition.** The **distribution function** of a random variable X is the function $F:\mathbb{R}\to[0,1]$ given by

$$F(x)=\mathbf{P}(X\le x).$$

This is the obvious abbreviation of equation (2). Events written as $\{\omega\in\Omega: X(\omega)\le x\}$ are commonly abbreviated to $\{\omega: X(\omega)\le x\}$ or $\{X\le x\}$. We write F_X where it is necessary to emphasize the role of X.

(5) **Example (1) revisited.** The distribution function F_X of X is given by

$$F_X(x)=\begin{cases}0 & \text{if } x<0\\ \frac{1}{4} & \text{if } 0\le x<1\\ \frac{3}{4} & \text{if } 1\le x<2\\ 1 & \text{if } x\ge 2,\end{cases}$$

and is sketched in Figure 2.1. The distribution function F_W of W is given by

$$F_W(x)=\begin{cases}0 & \text{if } x<0\\ \frac{3}{4} & \text{if } 0\le x<4\\ 1 & \text{if } x\ge 4,\end{cases}$$

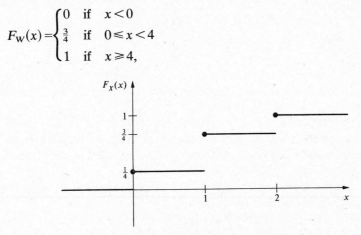

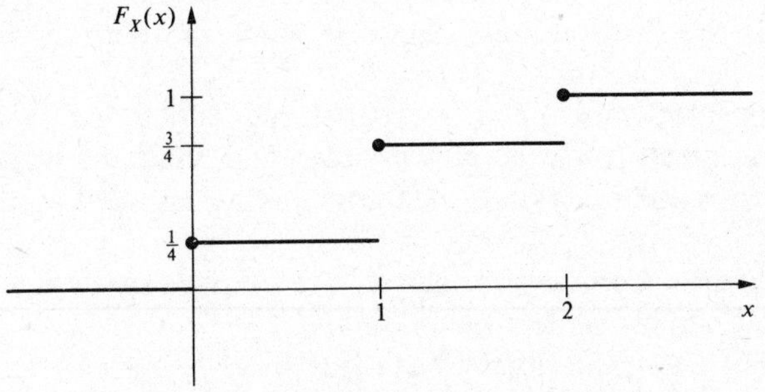

FIG. 2.1 The distribution function F_X of X.

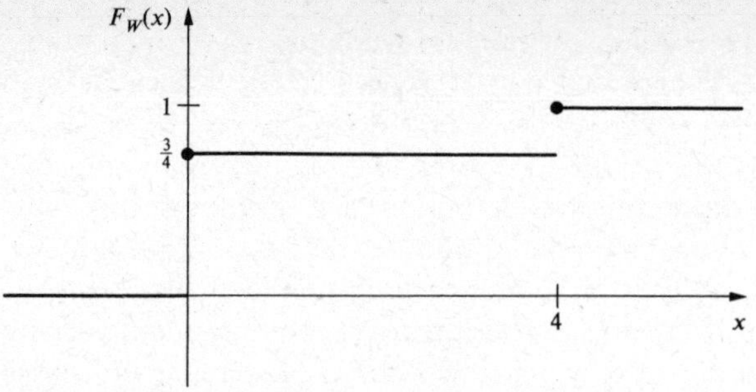

FIG. 2.2 The distribution function F_W of W.

and is sketched in Figure 2.2. This illustrates the important point that the distribution function of a random variable X tells us about the values taken by X and their relative likelihoods, rather than about the sample space and collection of events. ●

(6) **Lemma.** *A distribution function F has the following properties:*

(a) $\lim_{x\to-\infty} F(x)=0, \qquad \lim_{x\to\infty} F(x)=1,$

(b) *if $x<y$ then $F(x)\leq F(y)$,*

(c) *F is right-continuous (that is $F(x+h)\to F(x)$ as $h\downarrow 0$).*

Proof.

(a) Let $B_n=\{\omega\in\Omega: X(\omega)\leq -n\}=\{X\leq -n\}$. Then $B_1, B_2, \ldots$ is a decreasing family of events with the empty set as limit. Thus, by (1.3.5), $\mathbf{P}(B_n)\to\mathbf{P}(\varnothing)=0$. The other part is similar.

(b) Let $A(x)=\{X\leq x\}$, $A(x, y)=\{x<X\leq y\}$. Then $A(y)=A(x)\cup A(x, y)$ is a disjoint union, and so by (1.3.1),

$$\mathbf{P}(A(y))=\mathbf{P}(A(x))+\mathbf{P}(A(x, y))$$

giving

$$F(y)=F(x)+\mathbf{P}(x<X\leq y)\geq F(x).$$

(c) This is an *exercise*. Use (1.3.5). ■

Actually, this lemma characterizes distribution functions. That is to say, F is the distribution function of some random variable if and only if it satisfies (6a), (6b), and (6c).

For the time being we can forget all about probability spaces and concentrate on random variables and their distribution functions. The distribution function F of X contains a great deal of information about X.

(7) **Example. Constant variables.** The simplest random variable takes a constant value on the whole domain Ω.

Let $c\in\mathbb{R}$ and define $X:\Omega\to\mathbb{R}$ by

$$X(\omega)=c \qquad \text{for all } \omega\in\Omega.$$

The distribution function $F(x)=\mathbf{P}(X\leq x)$ is the step function

$$F(x)=\begin{cases}0 & x<c\\ 1 & x\geq c.\end{cases}$$

Slightly more generally, we call X *constant* (*almost surely*) if there exists $c\in\mathbb{R}$ such that

$$\mathbf{P}(X=c)=1. \qquad \bullet$$

(8) **Example. Bernoulli variables.** Consider Example (1.3.2). Let $X:\Omega\to\mathbb{R}$ be given by

$$X(H)=1, \qquad X(T)=0.$$

Then X is the simplest non-trivial random variable, with two possible values, 0 and 1. Its distribution function $F(x)=\mathbf{P}(X\leq x)$ is

$$F(x)=\begin{cases}0 & x<0\\ 1-p & 0\leq x<1\\ 1 & x\geq 1.\end{cases}$$

X is said to have the *Bernoulli distribution*.

(9) **Example. Indicator functions.** A particular class of Bernoulli variables is very useful in probability theory. Let A be an event and let $I_A:\Omega\to\mathbb{R}$ be the *indicator function* of A; that is,

$$I_A(\omega)=\begin{cases}1 & \text{if} \quad \omega\in A\\ 0 & \text{if} \quad \omega\in A^c.\end{cases}$$

Then I_A is a Bernoulli random variable taking the values 1 and 0 with probabilities $\mathbf{P}(A)$ and $\mathbf{P}(A^c)$ respectively. The following is a useful identity. Suppose $\{B_i:i\in I\}$ is a family of disjoint events with $A\subseteq\bigcup_{i\in I}B_i$. Then

(10) $$I_A=\sum_i I_{A\cap B_i}. \qquad \bullet$$

(11) **Lemma.** *Let F be the distribution function of X. Then*

(a) $\mathbf{P}(X>x)=1-F(x)$,

(b) $\mathbf{P}(x<X\leq y)=F(y)-F(x)$,

(c) $\mathbf{P}(X=x)=F(x)-\lim_{y\uparrow x}F(y)$.

Proof. (a) and (b) are *exercises.*

(c) Let $B_n=\{x-1/n<X\leq x\}$ and use the method of proof of Lemma (6). ∎

Note one final piece of jargon for future use. A random variable X

with distribution function F is said to have two 'tails' given by

$$T_1(x) = \mathbf{P}(X > x) = 1 - F(x)$$
$$T_2(x) = \mathbf{P}(X \leqslant -x) = F(-x)$$

where x is large and positive. We shall see later that the rates at which the T's decay to zero as $x \to \infty$ have a substantial effect on the existence or non-existence of certain associated quantities called the 'moments' of the distribution.

2.2 Discrete and continuous variables

Much of the study of random variables is devoted to distribution functions, characterized by (2.1.6). The general theory of distribution functions and their applications is quite difficult and abstract and is best omitted at this stage. It relies on a rigorous treatment of the construction of the Lebesgue–Stieltjes integral; this is sketched in Section 5.6. However, things become much easier if we are prepared to restrict our attention to certain subclasses of random variables specified by properties which make them tractable. We shall consider in depth the collection of 'discrete' random variables and the collection of 'continuous' random variables.

(1) **Definition.** The random variable X is called **discrete** if it takes values in some countable subset $\{x_1, x_2, \ldots\}$, only, of $\mathbb{R}$.

We shall see that the distribution function of a discrete variable has jump discontinuities at the values $x_1, x_2, \ldots$ and is constant in between; such a distribution is called *atomic*. This contrasts sharply with the other important class of distribution functions considered here.

(2) **Definition.** The random variable X is called **continuous** if its distribution function can be expressed as

$$F(x) = \int_{-\infty}^{x} f(u)\, du \qquad x \in \mathbb{R},$$

for some integrable function $f : \mathbb{R} \to [0, \infty)$.

The distribution function of a continuous random variable is certainly continuous (actually it is 'absolutely continuous'). For the moment we are concerned only with discrete variables and continuous variables. There is another sort of random variable, called 'singular', for a discussion of which the reader should look elsewhere. A common example of this phenomenon is based upon the Cantor ternary set (see Billingsley 1979 or Kingman and Taylor 1966). Other variables are 'mixtures' of discrete, continuous, and singular variables.

(3) **Example. Discrete variables.** The variables X and W of Example (2.1.1) take values in the sets $\{0, 1, 2\}$ and $\{0, 4\}$ respectively; they are both discrete. ●

(4) **Example. Continuous variables.** A straight rod is flung down at random onto a horizontal plane and the angle ω between the rod and true north is measured. The result is a number in $\Omega = [0, 2\pi)$. Never mind about $\mathcal{F}$ for the moment; we can suppose that $\mathcal{F}$ contains all nice subsets of Ω, such as the collection of open subintervals like (a, b), where $0 \leq a < b < 2\pi$. The implicit symmetry suggests the probability measure $\mathbf{P}$ which satisfies $\mathbf{P}((a, b)) = (b-a)/(2\pi)$; that is to say, the probability that the angle lies in some interval is directly proportional to the length of the interval. Here are two random variables X and Y:

$$X(\omega) = \omega$$
$$Y(\omega) = \omega^2.$$

Notice that Y is a function of X in that $Y = X^2$. The distribution functions of X and Y are

$$F_X(x) = \begin{cases} 0 & x \leq 0 \\ x/(2\pi) & 0 \leq x < 2\pi \\ 1 & x \geq 2\pi \end{cases}$$

$$F_Y(y) = \begin{cases} 0 & y \leq 0 \\ y^{1/2}/(2\pi) & 0 \leq y < 4\pi^2 \\ 1 & y \geq 4\pi^2. \end{cases}$$

To see this, let $0 \leq x < 2\pi$ and $0 \leq y < 4\pi^2$. Then

$$\begin{aligned} F_X(x) &= \mathbf{P}(\{\omega \in \Omega : 0 \leq X(\omega) \leq x\}) \\ &= \mathbf{P}(\{\omega \in \Omega : 0 \leq \omega \leq x\}) = x/(2\pi), \\ F_Y(y) &= \mathbf{P}(\{\omega : Y(\omega) \leq y\}) \\ &= \mathbf{P}(\{\omega : \omega^2 \leq y\}) = \mathbf{P}(\{\omega : 0 \leq \omega \leq y^{1/2}\}) = \mathbf{P}(X \leq y^{1/2}) \\ &= y^{1/2}/(2\pi). \end{aligned}$$

X and Y are continuous because

$$F_X(x) = \int_{-\infty}^{x} f_X(u)\, du, \qquad F_Y(y) = \int_{-\infty}^{y} f_Y(u)\, du$$

where

$$f_X(u) = \begin{cases} 1/(2\pi) & \text{if } 0 \leq u \leq 2\pi \\ 0 & \text{otherwise} \end{cases}$$

$$f_Y(u) = \begin{cases} u^{-1/2}/(4\pi) & \text{if } 0 \leq u \leq 4\pi^2 \\ 0 & \text{otherwise.} \end{cases}$$ ●

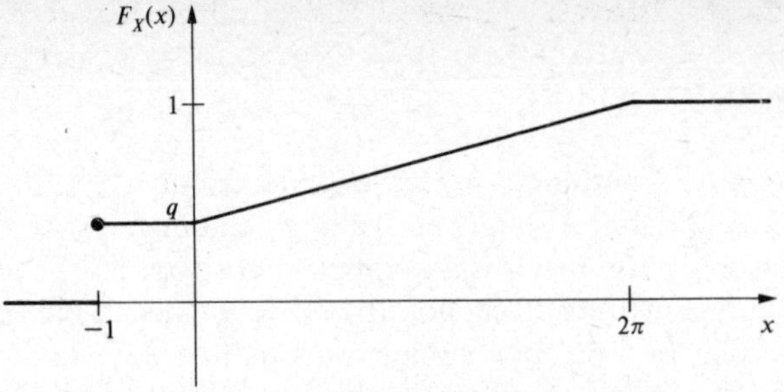

FIG. 2.3 The distribution function F_X of X.

(5) **Example. A random variable which is neither continuous nor discrete.** A coin is tossed, and a head turns up with probability p $(=1-q)$. If a head turns up then a rod is flung on the ground and the angle measured as in Example (4). Then $\Omega=\{T\}\cup\{(H,x):0\leq x<2\pi\}$, in the obvious notation. Let $X:\Omega\to\mathbb{R}$ be given by

$$X(T)=-1, \qquad X((H,x))=x.$$

X takes values in $\{-1\}\cup[0,2\pi)$ (see Figure 2.3 for a sketch of its distribution function). We say that X is continuous, except for a 'point mass (or *atom*) at -1'. ●

2.3 Worked examples

(1) **Example. Darts.** A dart is flung at a circular target of radius 3. We can think of the hitting point as the outcome of a random experiment; we shall suppose for simplicity that the player is guaranteed to hit the target somewhere. Setting the centre of the target at the origin of $\mathbb{R}^2$, we see that the sample space of this experiment is

$$\Omega=\{(x,y):x^2+y^2<9\}.$$

Never mind about the collection $\mathcal{F}$ of events. Let us suppose that, roughly speaking, the probability that the dart lands in some region A is proportional to the area $|A|$ of A. Thus

(2) $$\mathbf{P}(A)=|A|/(9\pi).$$

The scoring system is as follows. The target is partitioned by three concentric circles C_1, C_2, and C_3, centred at the origin with radii 1, 2, and 3. These circles divide the target into three annuli A_1, A_2, and A_3, where

$$A_k=\{(x,y):k-1\leq(x^2+y^2)^{\frac{1}{2}}<k\}.$$

We suppose that the player scores an amount k if and only if his dart hits

A_k. The resulting score X is the random variable given by

$$X(\omega)=k \quad \text{whenever} \quad \omega\in A_k.$$

What is its distribution function?

Solution. Clearly

$$\begin{aligned}\mathbf{P}(X=k)&=\mathbf{P}(A_k)\\ &=|A_k|/(9\pi)\\ &=(2k-1)/9, \qquad \text{for } k=1,2,3,\end{aligned}$$

and so the distribution function of X is given by

$$F_X(r)=\mathbf{P}(X\leqslant r)=\begin{cases}0 & \text{if } \ r<1\\ \lfloor r\rfloor^2/9 & \text{if } \ 1\leqslant r<3\\ 1 & \text{if } \ r\geqslant 3\end{cases}$$

where $\lfloor r\rfloor$ denotes the largest integer not larger than r (see Figure 2.4).

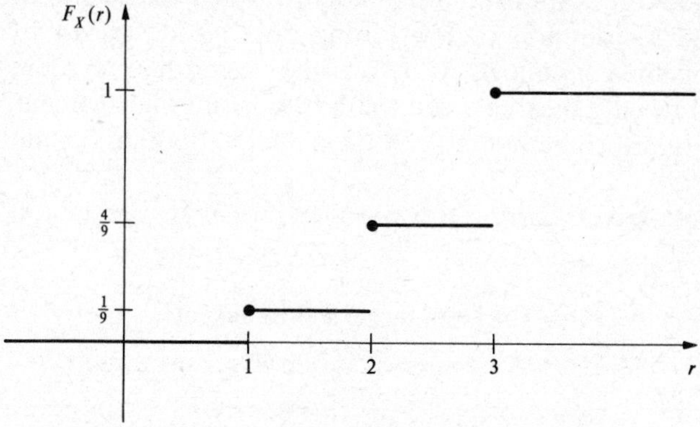

FIG. 2.4 The distribution function F_X of X. ●

(3) **Example. Continuation of (1).** Let us consider a revised method of scoring in which the player scores an amount equal to the distance between the hitting point ω and the centre of the target. This time the score Y is a random variable given by

$$Y(\omega)=(x^2+y^2)^{1/2}, \quad \text{if} \quad \omega=(x,y).$$

What is the distribution function of Y?

Solution. For any real r let C_r denote the disc with centre $(0,0)$ and radius r, that is

$$C_r=\{(x,y):x^2+y^2\leqslant r\}.$$

Then

$$F_Y(r)=\mathbf{P}(Y\leqslant r)=\mathbf{P}(C_r)=r^2/9 \quad \text{if} \quad 0\leqslant r\leqslant 3.$$

This distribution function is sketched in Figure 2.5.

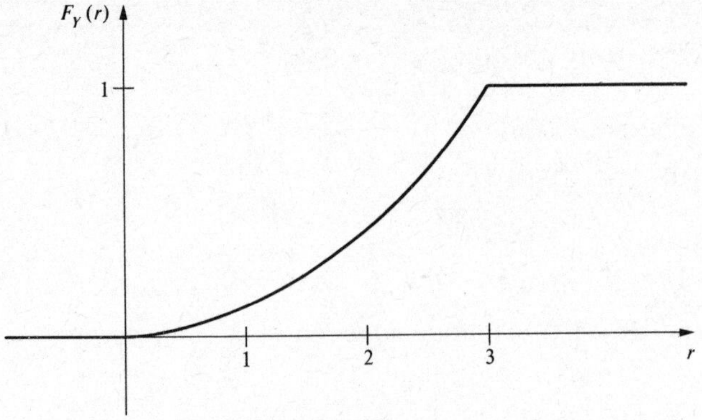

FIG. 2.5 The distribution function F_Y of Y. ●

(4) **Example. Continuation of (1).** Now suppose that the player fails to hit the target with fixed probability p; if he is successful then we suppose that the distribution of the hitting point is described by (2). His score is specified as follows. If he hits the target then he scores an amount equal to the distance between the hitting point and the centre; if he misses the target then he scores 4. What is the distribution function of his score Z?

Solution. Clearly Z takes values in $[0, 4]$. Use (1.4.4) to see that

$$\begin{aligned} F_Z(r) &= \mathbf{P}(Z \leqslant r) \\ &= \mathbf{P}(Z \leqslant r \mid \text{hits target})\mathbf{P}(\text{hits target}) \\ &\quad + \mathbf{P}(Z \leqslant r \mid \text{misses target})\mathbf{P}(\text{misses target}) \\ &= \begin{cases} 0 & \text{if } r < 0 \\ (1-p)F_Y(r) & \text{if } 0 \leqslant r < 4 \\ 1 & \text{if } r \geqslant 4, \end{cases} \end{aligned}$$

where F_Y is given in (3) (see Figure 2.6 for a sketch of F_Z).

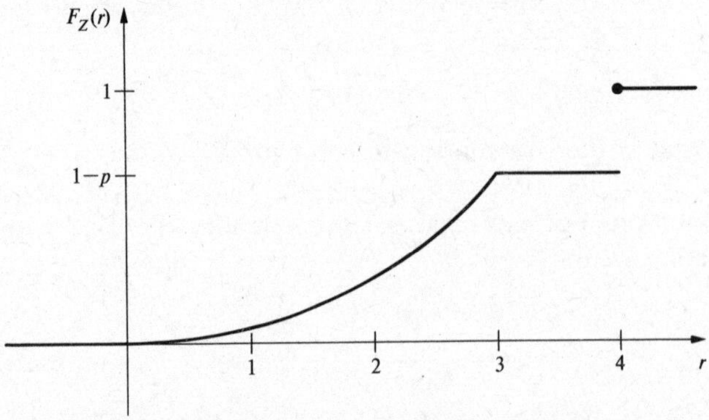

FIG. 2.6 The distribution function F_Z of Z. ●

2.4 Problems

1. Each toss of a coin results in a head with probability p. The coin is tossed until the first head appears. The sample space of this experiment is given in Problem (1.8.4). Let X be the total number of tosses. What is $\mathbf{P}(X>m)$? Find the distribution function of X.

2. Show that any discrete random variable may be written as a linear combination of indicator functions (see (2.1.9)).

3. A random variable X has distribution function F. What is the distribution function of $Y=aX+b$, if a and b are real constants?

4. In Example (2.2.4) find
 (a) $\mathbf{P}(\frac{1}{2}\pi \leqslant X \leqslant \frac{3}{2}\pi)$
 (b) $\mathbf{P}(\pi \leqslant X < 2\pi)$
 (c) $\mathbf{P}(Y \leqslant X)$
 (d) $\mathbf{P}(X \leqslant 2Y)$
 (e) $\mathbf{P}(X+Y \leqslant \frac{3}{4})$
 (f) the distribution function of $Z=\sqrt{X}$.

5. In Example (2.2.5) find
 (a) $\mathbf{P}(X=-1)$
 (b) $\mathbf{P}(X=0)$
 (c) $\mathbf{P}(X \geqslant \pi)$.

6. Buses arrive at ten minute intervals starting at noon. A man arrives at the bus stop a random number X minutes after noon, where X has distribution function

$$\mathbf{P}(X \leqslant x) = \begin{cases} 0 & \text{if } x<0 \\ x/60 & \text{if } 0 \leqslant x \leqslant 60 \\ 1 & \text{if } x>60. \end{cases}$$

 What is the probability that he waits less than five minutes for a bus?

7. Airlines find that each passenger who reserves a seat fails to turn up with probability $\frac{1}{10}$ independently of the other passengers. So Teeny Weeny Airlines always sell 10 tickets for their 9 seat aeroplane while Blockbuster Airways always sell 20 tickets for their 18 seat aeroplane. Which is more often overbooked?

8. A fairground performer claims the power of telekinesis. The crowd throws coins and he wills them to fall heads up. He succeeds five times out of six. What chance would he have of doing at least this well if he had no supernatural powers?

9. Express the distribution functions of

$$X^+ = \max\{0, X\}, \qquad X^- = -\min\{0, X\}, \qquad |X| = X^+ + X^-, \qquad -X$$

 in terms of the distribution function F of the random variable X.

10. Show that $F_X(x)$ is continuous at $x=x_0$ if and only if $\mathbf{P}(X=x_0)=0$.

11. The real number m is called a *median* of the distribution function F whenever $\lim_{y \uparrow m} F(y) \leqslant \frac{1}{2} \leqslant F(m)$. Show that every distribution function F has at least one median, and that the set of medians of F is a closed interval of $\mathbb{R}$.

12. Show that it is not possible to weight two dice in such a way that the sum of the two numbers shown by these loaded dice is equally likely to take any value between 2 and 12.

3 Discrete random variables

3.1 Probability mass functions

Recall that a random variable X is *discrete* if it takes values in some countable set $\{x_1, x_2, \ldots\}$. Its distribution function $F(x)=\mathbf{P}(X\leq x)$ is a jump function; just as important as its distribution function is its mass function.

(1) **Definition.** The **(probability) mass function** of a discrete random variable X is the function $f:\mathbb{R}\to[0,1]$ given by $f(x)=\mathbf{P}(X=x)$.

The distribution and mass functions are related by

$$F(x)=\sum_{i:x_i\leq x} f(x_i), \qquad f(x)=F(x)-\lim_{y\uparrow x} F(y).$$

(2) **Lemma.** *The probability mass function $f:\mathbb{R}\to[0,1]$ satisfies*

(a) $f(x)\neq 0$ *if and only if x belongs to some countable set* $\{x_1, x_2, \ldots\}$

(b) $\sum_i f(x_i)=1$.

Proof. The proof is obvious. ∎

This lemma characterizes probability mass functions.

(3) **Example. Binomial distribution.** A coin is tossed n times, and a head turns up each time with probability p $(=1-q)$. Then $\Omega=\{H, T\}^n$. Let X be the total number of heads. X takes values in the set $\{0, 1, 2, \ldots, n\}$ and is discrete. Its probability mass function $f(x)=\mathbf{P}(X=x)$ satisfies

$$f(x)=0 \quad \text{if} \quad x\notin\{0, 1, 2, \ldots, n\}.$$

Let $0\leq k\leq n$, and consider $f(k)$. Exactly $\binom{n}{k}$ points in Ω give a total of k heads; each of these points occurs with probability $p^k q^{n-k}$, and so

$$f(k)=\binom{n}{k}p^k q^{n-k} \quad \text{if} \quad 0\leq k\leq n.$$

X is said to have the *binomial distribution* with parameters n and p, written $B(n, p)$. It is the sum $X=Y_1+Y_2+\ldots+Y_n$ of n Bernoulli variables (see (2.1.8)). ●

(4) **Example. Poisson distribution.** If a random variable X takes values in the

set $\{0, 1, 2, \ldots\}$ with mass function

$$f(k) = \frac{\lambda^k}{k!} e^{-\lambda}, \qquad k = 0, 1, 2, \ldots,$$

where $\lambda > 0$, then X is said to have the *Poisson distribution* with parameter λ. ●

Exercise. Find some other probability mass functions.

3.2 Independence

Remember that events A and B are called 'independent' if the occurrence of A does not change the subsequent probability of B occurring. More rigorously, A and B are independent if and only if $\mathbf{P}(A \cap B) = \mathbf{P}(A)\mathbf{P}(B)$. Similarly, we say that discrete variables X and Y are 'independent' if the numerical value of X does not affect the distribution of Y. With this in mind we make the following definition.

(1) **Definition.** Discrete variables X and Y are **independent** if the events $\{X = x\}$ and $\{Y = y\}$ are independent for all x and y.

Suppose X takes values in $\{x_1, x_2, \ldots\}$ and Y takes values in $\{y_1, y_2, \ldots\}$. Let

$$A_i = \{X = x_i\}, \qquad B_j = \{Y = y_j\}.$$

Notice (see (2.4.2)) that X and Y are linear combinations of the indicator variables I_{A_i}, I_{B_j}, in that

$$X = \sum_i x_i I_{A_i} \quad \text{and} \quad Y = \sum_j y_j I_{B_j}.$$

X and Y are independent if and only if A_i and B_j are independent for all pairs i, j. A similar definition holds for collections $\{X_1, X_2, \ldots, X_n\}$ of discrete variables.

(2) **Example.** A coin is tossed once and heads turns up with probability $p = 1 - q$. Let X and Y be the numbers of heads and tails respectively. It is no surprise that X and Y are not independent. After all,

$$\mathbf{P}(X = Y = 1) = 0, \qquad \mathbf{P}(X = 1)\mathbf{P}(Y = 1) = p(1 - p).$$

Suppose now that the coin is tossed a random number N of times, where N has the Poisson distribution with parameter λ. It is a remarkable fact that the resulting numbers X and Y of heads and tails *are* independent, for

$$\begin{aligned}\mathbf{P}(X = x, Y = y) &= \mathbf{P}(X = x, Y = y \mid N = x + y)\mathbf{P}(N = x + y) \\ &= \binom{x+y}{x} p^x q^y \frac{\lambda^{x+y}}{(x+y)!} e^{-\lambda} \\ &= \frac{(\lambda p)^x (\lambda q)^y}{x!\, y!} e^{-\lambda}.\end{aligned}$$

But, by (1.4.4)

$$\mathbf{P}(X=x)=\sum_{n\geq x}\mathbf{P}(X=x\mid N=n)\mathbf{P}(N=n)$$

$$=\sum_{n\geq x}\binom{n}{x}p^x q^{n-x}\frac{\lambda^n}{n!}e^{-\lambda}=\frac{(\lambda p)^x}{x!}e^{-\lambda p};$$

a similar result holds for Y, and so

$$\mathbf{P}(X=x, Y=y)=\mathbf{P}(X=x)\mathbf{P}(Y=y).$$ ●

If X is a random variable and $g:\mathbb{R}\to\mathbb{R}$, then $Z=g(X)$, defined by $Z(\omega)=g(X(\omega))$, is a random variable also.

(3) **Theorem.** *If X and Y are independent and g, $h:\mathbb{R}\to\mathbb{R}$, then $g(X)$ and $h(Y)$ are independent also.*

Proof. *Exercise.* See Problem (3.9.1). ■

Independent families of random variables are very much easier to study than dependent families; we shall see many examples of this soon.

3.3 Expectation

Let $x_1, x_2, \ldots, x_N$ be the numerical outcomes of N repetitions of some experiment. The average of these outcomes is

$$m=\frac{1}{N}\sum_i x_i.$$

In advance of performing these experiments we can represent their outcomes by a sequence $X_1, X_2, \ldots, X_N$ of random variables, and we shall suppose that these variables are discrete with a common mass function f. Then, roughly speaking (see the beginning of Section 1.3), for each possible value x, about $Nf(x)$ of the X's will take that value x. So the average m is about

$$m\simeq\frac{1}{N}\sum_x xNf(x)=\sum_x xf(x)$$

where the summation here is over all possible values of the X's. This average is called the 'expectation' or 'mean value' of the underlying distribution with mass function f.

(1) **Definition.** The **mean value,** or **expectation,** or **expected value** of X with mass function f, is defined to be

$$\mathbf{E}(X)=\sum_{x:f(x)>0} xf(x)$$

whenever this sum is absolutely convergent.

We require *absolute* convergence in order that $\mathbf{E}(X)$ be unchanged by re-ordering the x's. We can, for notational convenience, write $\mathbf{E}(X)=\sum_x xf(x)$. This appears to be an uncountable sum; however, all but countably many of its contributions are zero. If the numbers $f(x)$ are regarded as masses $f(x)$ at points x then $\mathbf{E}(X)$ is just the position of the centre of gravity; we can speak of X as having an 'atom' or 'point mass' of size $f(x)$ at x. We sometimes omit the brackets and simply write $\mathbf{E}X$.

(2) **Example (2.1.5) revisited.** The random variables X and W of this example have mean values

$$\mathbf{E}(X)=\sum_x x\mathbf{P}(X=x)=0\,.\,\tfrac{1}{4}+1\,.\,\tfrac{1}{2}+2\,.\,\tfrac{1}{4}=1$$

$$\mathbf{E}(W)=\sum_x x\mathbf{P}(W=x)=0\,.\,\tfrac{3}{4}+4\,.\,\tfrac{1}{4}=1. \qquad \bullet$$

If X is a random variable and $g:\mathbb{R}\to\mathbb{R}$, then $Y=g(X)$, given formally by $Y(\omega)=g(X(\omega))$, is a random variable also. To calculate its expectation we need first to find its probability mass function f_Y. This process can be complicated, and it is avoided by the following lemma (called by some the 'Law of the Unconscious Statistician'!).

(3) **Lemma.** *If X has mass function f and $g:\mathbb{R}\to\mathbb{R}$, then*

$$\mathbf{E}(g(X))=\sum_x g(x)f(x)$$

whenever this sum is absolutely convergent.

Proof. This is Problem (3.9.3). ■

(4) **Example.** Suppose that X takes values $-2,-1,1,3$ with probabilities $\frac{1}{4},\frac{1}{8},\frac{1}{4},\frac{3}{8}$ respectively. Consider the random variable $Y=X^2$; Y takes values $1,4,9$ with probabilities $\frac{3}{8},\frac{1}{4},\frac{3}{8}$ respectively, and so

$$\mathbf{E}(Y)=\sum_x x\mathbf{P}(Y=x)=1\,.\,\tfrac{3}{8}+4\,.\,\tfrac{1}{4}+9\,.\,\tfrac{3}{8}=19/4.$$

Alternatively, use the Law of the Unconscious Statistician to find that

$$\mathbf{E}(Y)=\mathbf{E}(X^2)=\sum_x x^2\mathbf{P}(X=x)=4\,.\,\tfrac{1}{4}+1\,.\,\tfrac{1}{8}+1\,.\,\tfrac{1}{4}+9\,.\,\tfrac{3}{8}=19/4. \qquad \bullet$$

Lemma (3) provides a method for calculating the 'moments' of a distribution; these are defined as follows.

(5) **Definition.** If k is a positive integer, then the kth **moment** m_k of X is

$$m_k=\mathbf{E}(X^k).$$

The kth **central moment** μ_k is

$$\mu_k=\mathbf{E}((X-m_1)^k).$$

The two moments of most use are $m_1 = \mathbf{E}(X)$ and $\mu_2 = \mathbf{E}((X-\mathbf{E}(X))^2)$, called the *mean* (or *expectation*) and *variance* of X. These two quantities are crude measures of the dispersion of X: m_1 is the average value of X, and μ_2 measures the amount by which X tends to deviate from this average. μ_2 is often written as σ^2 or var (X); its positive square root σ is called the *standard deviation*. The central moments $\{\mu_i\}$ can be expressed in terms of the ordinary moments $\{m_i\}$. For example, $\mu_1 = 0$ and

$$\begin{aligned}\mu_2 &= \sum_x (x-m_1)^2 f(x)\\ &= \sum_x x^2 f(x) - 2m_1 \sum_x x f(x) + m_1^2 \sum_x f(x)\\ &= m_2 - m_1^2\end{aligned}$$

or

$$\begin{aligned}\text{var}\,(X) &= \mathbf{E}((X-\mathbf{E}(X))^2)\\ &= \mathbf{E}(X^2) - (\mathbf{E}(X))^2.\end{aligned}$$

Experience with student calculations of variances causes us to stress the following elementary fact: *variances cannot be negative.*

(6) **Example. Bernoulli variables.** Let X be a Bernoulli variable, taking the value 1 with probability $p(=1-q)$. Then

$$\mathbf{E}(X) = \sum_x x f(x) = 0 \,.\, q + 1 \,.\, p = p$$

$$\mathbf{E}(X^2) = \sum_x x^2 f(x) = 0 \,.\, q + 1 \,.\, p = p$$

$$\text{var}\,(X) = \mathbf{E}(X^2) - \mathbf{E}(X)^2 = pq.$$

Thus the indicator variable I_A has expectation $\mathbf{P}(A)$ and variance $\mathbf{P}(A)\mathbf{P}(A^c)$. $\mathbf{E}(X)^2$ means $(\mathbf{E}(X))^2$ and must not be confused with $\mathbf{E}(X^2)$. ●

(7) **Example. Binomial variables.** Let X be $B(n, p)$. Then

$$\mathbf{E}(X) = \sum_{k=0}^{n} k f(k) = \sum_{k=0}^{n} k \binom{n}{k} p^k q^{n-k}.$$

To calculate this, differentiate the identity

$$\sum_{k=0}^{n} \binom{n}{k} x^k = (1+x)^n,$$

multiply by x to obtain

$$\sum_{k=0}^{n} k \binom{n}{k} x^k = nx(1+x)^{n-1},$$

and substitute $x = p/q$ to obtain $\mathbf{E}(X) = np$. A similar argument shows that var $(X) = npq$. ●

We can think of the process of calculating expectations as a linear operator on the space of random variables.

(8) **Theorem.** *The expectation operator* $\mathbf{E}$ *has the following properties:*
(a) *if* $X \geqslant 0$ *then* $\mathbf{E}(X) \geqslant 0$
(b) *if* $a, b \in \mathbb{R}$ *then* $\mathbf{E}(aX+bY) = a\mathbf{E}(X) + b\mathbf{E}(Y)$
(c) *the random variable* 1, *taking the value one always, has expectation* $\mathbf{E}(1) = 1$.

Proof. (a) and (c) are obvious.
(b) Let $A_x = \{X = x\}$, $B_y = \{Y = y\}$. Then

$$aX+bY = \sum_{x,y}(ax+by)I_{A_x \cap B_y}$$

and the solution of the first part of Problem (3.9.3) shows that

$$\mathbf{E}(aX+bY) = \sum_{x,y}(ax+by)\mathbf{P}(A_x \cap B_y).$$

However,

$$\sum_y \mathbf{P}(A_x \cap B_y) = \mathbf{P}\left(A_x \cap \left(\bigcup_y B_y\right)\right)$$
$$= \mathbf{P}(A_x \cap \Omega) = \mathbf{P}(A_x)$$

and similarly $\sum_x \mathbf{P}(A_x \cap B_y) = \mathbf{P}(B_y)$, which gives

$$\mathbf{E}(aX+bY) = \sum_x ax \sum_y \mathbf{P}(A_x \cap B_y) + \sum_y by \sum_x \mathbf{P}(A_x \cap B_y)$$
$$= a\sum_x x\mathbf{P}(A_x) + b\sum_y y\mathbf{P}(B_y)$$
$$= a\mathbf{E}(X) + b\mathbf{E}(Y).$$ ■

It is not in general true that $\mathbf{E}(XY)$ is the same as $\mathbf{E}(X)\mathbf{E}(Y)$.

(9) **Lemma.** *If* X *and* Y *are independent then* $\mathbf{E}(XY) = \mathbf{E}(X)\mathbf{E}(Y)$.

Proof. Let A_x and B_y be as in the proof of (8). Then

$$XY = \sum_{x,y} xyI_{A_x \cap B_y}$$

and so

$$\mathbf{E}(XY) = \sum_{x,y} xy\mathbf{P}(A_x)\mathbf{P}(B_y) \quad \text{by independence}$$
$$= \sum_x x\mathbf{P}(A_x)\sum_y y\mathbf{P}(B_y) = \mathbf{E}(X)\mathbf{E}(Y).$$ ■

(10) **Definition.** X and Y are called **uncorrelated** if $\mathbf{E}(XY) = \mathbf{E}(X)\mathbf{E}(Y)$.

Lemma (9) asserts that independent variables are uncorrelated. The converse is not true, as Problem (3.9.16) indicates.

(11) **Theorem.** *If X and Y are independent then*

(a) *if* $a \in \mathbb{R}$ *then* $\operatorname{var}(aX) = a^2 \operatorname{var}(X)$
(b) $\operatorname{var}(X+Y) = \operatorname{var}(X) + \operatorname{var}(Y)$.

Proof.
(a) Using the linearity of $\mathbf{E}$,

$$\begin{aligned}\operatorname{var}(aX) &= \mathbf{E}((aX - \mathbf{E}(aX))^2)\\ &= \mathbf{E}(a^2(X - \mathbf{E}(X))^2)\\ &= a^2\mathbf{E}((X-\mathbf{E}(X))^2)\\ &= a^2 \operatorname{var}(X).\end{aligned}$$

(b)
$$\begin{aligned}\operatorname{var}(X+Y) &= \mathbf{E}((X+Y-\mathbf{E}(X+Y))^2)\\ &= \mathbf{E}((X-\mathbf{E}(X))^2 + 2(XY - \mathbf{E}(X)\mathbf{E}(Y)) + (Y-\mathbf{E}(Y))^2)\\ &= \operatorname{var}(X) + 2(\mathbf{E}(XY) - \mathbf{E}(X)\mathbf{E}(Y)) + \operatorname{var}(Y)\\ &= \operatorname{var}(X) + \operatorname{var}(Y) \quad \text{by independence.}\end{aligned}$$ ■

Equation (11a) shows that the variance operator 'var' is *not* a linear operator, even when it is applied only to independent variables.

Sometimes the sum $S = \sum xf(x)$ does not converge absolutely, and the mean of the distribution does not exist. If $S = -\infty$ or $S = +\infty$, then we can sometimes speak of the mean as taking these values also. Of course, there exist distributions which do not have a mean value.

(12) **Example. A distribution without a mean.** Let X have mass function

$$f(k) = Ak^{-2} \quad \text{for} \quad k = \pm 1, \pm 2, \ldots$$

where A is chosen so that $\sum f(k) = 1$. The sum

$$\sum kf(k) = A \sum_{k \neq 0} \frac{1}{k}$$

does not converge absolutely, because both the positive and the negative parts diverge. ●

This is a suitable opportunity to point out that we can base probability theory upon the expectation operator $\mathbf{E}$ rather than upon the probability measure $\mathbf{P}$. After all, our intuitions about the notion of 'average' are probably just as well developed as those about quantitative chance. Roughly speaking, the way we proceed is to postulate axioms, such as (a), (b), and (c) of Theorem (8), for a so-called 'expectation operator' $\mathbf{E}$ acting on a space of 'random variables'. The probability of an event can then be recaptured by defining

$$\mathbf{P}(A) = \mathbf{E}(I_A).$$

Whittle (1970) is an able advocate of this approach.

This method can be easily and naturally adapted to deal with probabilistic questions in quantum theory. In this major branch of theoretical physics, questions arise which cannot be formulated entirely within the usual framework of probability theory. However, there still exists an expectation operator **E**, which is applied to linear operators known as observables (such as square matrices) rather than to random variables. There does not exist a sample space Ω, and nor therefore are there any indicator functions, but nevertheless there exist analogues of other concepts in probability theory. For example, the *variance* of an operator X is defined by

$$\operatorname{var}(X)=\mathbf{E}(X^2)-\mathbf{E}(X)^2.$$

Furthermore, it can be shown that

$$\mathbf{E}(X)=\operatorname{tr}(UX)$$

where tr denotes *trace* and U is a non-negative definite operator with unit trace.

3.4 Indicators and matching

This section contains light entertainment, in the guise of some illustrations of the uses of indicator functions. These were defined in (2.1.9) and have appeared occasionally since. Recall that

$$I_A(\omega)=\begin{cases}1 & \text{if } \omega\in A\\ 0 & \text{if } \omega\in A^c\end{cases}$$

and

$$\mathbf{E}I_A=\mathbf{P}(A).$$

(1) **Example. Proofs of (1.3.4c, d).** Note that

$$I_A+I_{A^c}=I_{A\cup A^c}=I_\Omega=1$$

and that $I_{A\cap B}=I_AI_B$. Thus

$$\begin{aligned}I_{A\cup B}&=1-I_{(A\cup B)^c}=1-I_{A^c\cap B^c}\\&=1-I_{A^c}I_{B^c}=1-(1-I_A)(1-I_B)\\&=I_A+I_B-I_AI_B.\end{aligned}$$

Take expectations to obtain

$$\mathbf{P}(A\cup B)=\mathbf{P}(A)+\mathbf{P}(B)-\mathbf{P}(A\cap B).$$

More generally, if $B=\bigcup_{i=1}^n A_i$ then

$$I_B=1-\prod_{i=1}^n(1-I_{A_i});$$

multiply this out and take expectations to obtain

(2) $$\mathbf{P}(B)=\sum_i \mathbf{P}(A_i)-\sum_{i<j}\mathbf{P}(A_i\cap A_j)+\ldots+(-1)^{n+1}\mathbf{P}(A_1\cap\ldots\cap A_n). \qquad \bullet$$

(3) **Example. Matching problem.** A number of melodramatic applications of (2) are available, of which the following is typical. A secretary types n different letters together with matching envelopes, drops the pile down the stairs, and then places the letters randomly into the available envelopes. Each arrangement is equally likely, and we ask for the probability that exactly r letters are in their correct envelopes. Rather than using (2), we shall proceed directly by way of indicator functions.

Solution. Let $L_1, L_2, \ldots, L_n$ denote the letters. Call a letter *good* if it is correctly addressed, and *bad* otherwise; write X for the number of good letters. Let A_i be the event that L_i is good, and I_i be the indicator function of A_i. Let $j_1, \ldots, j_r, k_{r+1}, \ldots, k_n$ be a permutation of the numbers $1, 2, \ldots, n$ and define

(4) $$S=\sum_{\pi} I_{j_1}\ldots I_{j_r}(1-I_{k_{r+1}})\ldots(1-I_{k_n})$$

where the sum is taken over all such permutations π. Then

$$S=\begin{cases} 0 & \text{if } X\neq r\\ r!(n-r)! & \text{if } X=r.\end{cases}$$

To see this, let $L_{i_1}, \ldots, L_{i_m}$ be the good letters. If $m\neq r$ then each summand in (4) equals 0. If $m=r$ then the summand in (4) equals 1 if and only if $j_1, \ldots, j_r$ is a permutation of $i_1, \ldots, i_r$ and $k_{r+1}, \ldots, k_n$ is a permutation of the remaining numbers; there are $r!(n-r)!$ such permutations. It follows that I, given by

(5) $$I=\frac{1}{r!(n-r)!}S,$$

is the indicator function of the event $\{X=r\}$ that exactly r letters are good. We take expectations of (4) and multiply out to obtain

$$\mathbf{E}(S)=\sum_{\pi}\sum_{s=0}^{n-r}(-1)^s\binom{n-r}{s}\mathbf{E}(I_{j_1}\ldots I_{j_r}I_{k_{r+1}}\ldots I_{k_{r+s}})$$

by a symmetry argument. However,

(6) $$\mathbf{E}(I_{j_1}\ldots I_{j_r}I_{k_{r+1}}\ldots I_{k_{r+s}})=\frac{(n-r-s)!}{n!}$$

since there are $n!$ possible permutations only $(n-r-s)!$ of which allocate $L_{j_1}, \ldots, L_{j_r}, L_{k_{r+1}}, \ldots, L_{k_{r+s}}$ to their correct envelopes. We combine (4),

(5), and (6) to obtain

$$\begin{aligned}\mathbf{P}(X=r)=\mathbf{E}(I)&=\frac{1}{r!(n-r)!}\mathbf{E}(S)\\&=\frac{1}{r!(n-r)!}\sum_{s=0}^{n-r}(-1)^s\binom{n-r}{s}n!\frac{(n-r-s)!}{n!}\\&=\frac{1}{r!}\sum_{s=0}^{n-r}(-1)^s\frac{1}{s!}\\&=\frac{1}{r!}\left\{\frac{1}{2!}-\frac{1}{3!}+\ldots+\frac{(-1)^{n-r}}{(n-r)!}\right\}\text{ for } r\leqslant n-2 \text{ and } n\geqslant 2.\end{aligned}$$

In particular, as the number n of letters tends to infinity, we obtain the possibly surprising result that the probability that no letter is put into its correct envelope approaches e^{-1}. It is left as an *exercise* to prove this without using indicators. ●

3.5 Examples of discrete variables

Exercise. Sketch the mass functions and the distribution functions of the variables discussed here.

(1) **Bernoulli trials.** X takes values 1 and 0 with probabilities p and $q(=1-p)$, respectively. Sometimes we think of these values as representing the 'success' or the 'failure' of the trial. The mass function is

$$f(0)=1-p, \qquad f(1)=p,$$

and it follows that $\mathbf{E}X=p$, $\operatorname{var}(X)=p(1-p)$. ●

(2) **Binomial distribution.** We perform n independent Bernoulli trials $X_1, X_2, \ldots, X_n$ and count the total number of successes $Y=X_1+X_2+\ldots+X_n$. As in (3.1.3), the mass function of Y is

$$f(k)=\binom{n}{k}p^k(1-p)^{n-k}, \qquad k=0,1,\ldots,n.$$

Application of (3.3.8) and (3.3.11) yields immediately

$$\mathbf{E}Y=np, \qquad \operatorname{var}(Y)=np(1-p);$$

the method of (3.3.7) provides a more lengthy derivation of this. ●

(3) **Trinomial distribution.** More generally, suppose we conduct n trials, each of which results in one of three outcomes (red, white, or blue, say), where red occurs with probability p, white with probability q, and blue with probability $1-p-q$. Then the probability of r reds, w whites, and $n-r-w$ blues is

$$\frac{n!}{r!w!(n-r-w)!}p^rq^w(1-p-q)^{n-r-w}.$$

This is the *trinomial distribution*, with parameters n, p, and q. The 'multinomial distribution' is the obvious generalization of this distribution to the case of some number, say t, of possible outcomes. ●

(4) **Poisson distribution.** A *Poisson* variable is a random variable with the Poisson mass function

$$f(k)=\frac{\lambda^k}{k!}e^{-k}, \qquad k=0,1,2,\ldots$$

for some $\lambda>0$. It can be obtained in practice in the following way. Let Y be a $B(n, p)$ variable, and suppose that n is very large and p is very small (an example might be the number Y of misprints on the front page of the *Grauniad*, where n is the total number of characters and p is the probability for each character that the typesetter has made an error). Now, let $n\to\infty$ and $p\to 0$ in such a way that $\mathbf{E}(Y)=np$ approaches a non-zero constant λ. Then for $k=0,1,2,\ldots,$

$$\mathbf{P}(Y=k)=\binom{n}{k}p^k(1-p)^{n-k}\simeq\frac{1}{k!}\left(\frac{np}{1-p}\right)^k(1-p)^n\to\frac{\lambda^k}{k!}e^{-\lambda}.$$

Check that both the mean and the variance of this distribution are equal to λ. Now do Problem (2.4.7) again (*exercise*). ●

(5) **Geometric distribution.** A *geometric* variable is a random variable with the geometric mass function

$$f(k)=p(1-p)^{k-1}, \qquad k=1,2,\ldots$$

for some number p in $(0, 1)$. This distribution arises in the following way. Suppose that independent Bernoulli trials (parameter p) are performed at times $1, 2, \ldots$. Let W be the time which elapses before the first success; W is called a *waiting time*. Then

$$\mathbf{P}(W>k)=(1-p)^k$$

and thus

$$\begin{aligned}\mathbf{P}(W=k)&=\mathbf{P}(W>k-1)-\mathbf{P}(W>k)\\&=p(1-p)^{k-1}.\end{aligned}$$

The reader should calculate the mean and the variance. ●

(6) **Negative binomial distribution.** More generally, in the previous example, let W_r be the waiting time for the rth success. Check that W_r has mass function

$$\mathbf{P}(W_r=k)=\binom{k-1}{r-1}p^r(1-p)^{k-r}, \qquad k=r, r+1,\ldots;$$

it is said to have the *negative binomial distribution* with parameters r and p. W_r is the sum of r independent geometric variables. For, let X_1 be the waiting time for the first success, X_2 the *further* waiting time for the second success, X_3 the *further* waiting time for the third success, and so on. Then $X_1, X_2, \ldots$ are independent and geometric, and

$$W_r = X_1 + X_2 + \ldots + X_r.$$

Apply (3.3.8) and (3.3.11) to find the mean and the variance of W_r. ●

3.6 Dependence

Probability theory is largely concerned with families of random variables; these families will not in general consist entirely of independent variables.

(1) **Example.** Suppose that we back three horses to win as an accumulator. If our stake is £1 and the starting prices are α, β, and γ, then our total profit is

$$W = (\alpha+1)(\beta+1)(\gamma+1)I_1 I_2 I_3 - 1$$

where I_i denotes the indicator of a win in the ith race by our horse. (In checking this expression remember that a bet of £B on a horse with starting price α brings a return of £$B(\alpha+1)$, should this horse win.) We lose £1 if some backed horse fails to win. It seems clear that the random variables W and I_1 are *not* independent. If the races are run independently, then

$$\mathbf{P}(W=-1) = \mathbf{P}(I_1 I_2 I_3 = 0),$$

but

$$\mathbf{P}(W=-1 \mid I_1 = 1) = \mathbf{P}(I_2 I_3 = 0)$$

which are different from each other unless the first backed horse is guaranteed victory. ●

We require a tool for studying collections of dependent variables. Knowledge of their individual mass functions is little help by itself. Just as the main tool for studying a random variable is its distribution function, so the study of, say, a pair of random variables is based on its 'joint' distribution function and mass function.

(2) **Definition.** The **joint distribution function** $F: \mathbb{R}^2 \to [0, 1]$ of X and Y, where X and Y are discrete variables, is given by

$$F(x, y) = \mathbf{P}(X \leq x \text{ and } Y \leq y).$$

Their **joint mass function** $f: \mathbb{R}^2 \to [0, 1]$ is given by

$$f(x, y) = \mathbf{P}(X = x \text{ and } Y = y).$$

Joint distribution functions and joint mass functions of larger collections of variables are defined similarly. The functions F and f can be characterized in much the same way ((2.1.6) and (3.1.2)) as the corresponding functions of a single variable. We omit the details. We write $F_{X,Y}$ and $f_{X,Y}$ when we need to stress the role of X and Y. We think of the joint mass function in the following way. If $A_x = \{X = x\}$ and $B_y = \{Y = y\}$, then

$$f(x, y) = \mathbf{P}(A_x \cap B_y).$$

The definition of independence can now be reformulated in a lemma.

(3) **Lemma.** *X and Y are independent if and only if*

(4) $$f_{X,Y}(x, y) = f_X(x) f_Y(y) \quad \textit{for all } x, y \in \mathbb{R}.$$

More generally, X and Y are independent if and only if $f_{X,Y}(x, y)$ can be factorized as the product $g(x)h(y)$ of a function of x alone and a function of y alone.

Proof. This is Problem (3.9.1). ■

Suppose that X and Y have joint mass function $f_{X,Y}$ and we wish to check whether or not (4) holds. First we need to calculate the *marginal mass functions* f_X and f_Y from our knowledge of $f_{X,Y}$. These are found in the following way:

$$f_X(x) = \mathbf{P}(X = x) = \mathbf{P}\left(\bigcup_y (\{X = x\} \cap \{Y = y\})\right)$$

$$= \sum_y \mathbf{P}(X = x, Y = y) = \sum_y f_{X,Y}(x, y),$$

and similarly

$$f_Y(y) = \sum_x f_{X,Y}(x, y).$$

Having found the marginals, it is a trivial matter to see whether (4) holds or not.

(5) **Example. Calculation of marginals.** In Example (3.2.2) we encountered a pair X, Y of variables with a joint mass function

$$f(x, y) = \frac{\alpha^x \beta^y}{x! y!} e^{-(\alpha+\beta)} \quad \text{for} \quad x, y = 0, 1, 2, \ldots$$

where $\alpha, \beta > 0$. The marginal mass function of X is

$$f_X(x) = \sum_y f(x, y) = \frac{\alpha^x}{x!} e^{-\alpha} \sum_{y=0}^{\infty} \frac{\beta^y}{y!} e^{-\beta} = \frac{\alpha^x}{x!} e^{-\alpha}$$

and so X has the Poisson distribution with parameter α. Similarly Y has the Poisson distribution with parameter β, and it is easy to check that (4) holds, giving that X and Y are independent. ●

For any discrete pair X, Y, a real function $g(X, Y)$ is a random variable. We shall often need to find its expectation. To avoid explicit calculation of its mass function, we shall use the following more general form of the Law of the Unconscious Statistician.

(6) **Lemma.** $\mathbf{E}(g(X, Y)) = \sum_{x,y} g(x, y) f_{X,Y}(x, y)$.

Proof. As for (3.3.3). ■

For example, $\mathbf{E}(XY) = \sum_{x,y} xy f_{X,Y}(x, y)$. This formula is particularly useful to statisticians who may need to find simple ways of explaining dependence to laymen. For instance, suppose that the Government wishes to announce that the dependence between defence spending and the cost of living is very small. It should *not* publish an estimate of the joint mass function unless its object is obfuscation alone. Most members of the public would prefer to find that this dependence can be represented in terms of a single number on a prescribed scale. Towards this end we make the following definition.

(7) **Definition.** The **covariance** of X and Y is

$$\operatorname{cov}(X, Y) = \mathbf{E}((X - \mathbf{E}X)(Y - \mathbf{E}Y)).$$

The **correlation (coefficient)** of X and Y is

$$\rho(X, Y) = \frac{\operatorname{cov}(X, Y)}{(\operatorname{var}(X) \,.\, \operatorname{var}(Y))^{1/2}}$$

as long as the variances are non-zero.

Expanding the covariance gives

$$\operatorname{cov}(X, Y) = \mathbf{E}(XY) - \mathbf{E}(X)\mathbf{E}(Y).$$

Remember (3.3.10) that X and Y are called *uncorrelated* if $\operatorname{cov}(X, Y) = 0$. Also, independent variables are always uncorrelated, although the converse is not true. Covariance itself is not a satisfactory measure of dependence because the scale of values which $\operatorname{cov}(X, Y)$ may take contains no points which are clearly interpretable in terms of the relationship between X and Y. The following lemma shows that this is not the case for correlations.

(8) **Lemma.** ρ *satisfies*

$$|\rho(X, Y)| \leq 1$$

with equality if and only if $\mathbf{P}(Y = aX + b) = 1$ *for some* $a, b \in \mathbb{R}$.

The proof is an application of the following important inequality.

(9) **Theorem. Cauchy–Schwarz inequality.** *For any X and Y*

$$\mathbf{E}(XY)^2 \leq \mathbf{E}(X^2)\mathbf{E}(Y^2)$$

with equality if and only if $\mathbf{P}(aX = bY) = 1$ for some real a and b, at least one of which is non-zero.

Proof. We can assume that $\mathbf{E}(X^2)$ and $\mathbf{E}(Y^2)$ are strictly positive, since otherwise the result follows immediately from Problem (3.9.2). For $a, b \in \mathbb{R}$, let $Z = aX - bY$. Then

$$0 \leq \mathbf{E}(Z^2) = a^2\mathbf{E}(X^2) - 2ab\mathbf{E}(XY) + b^2\mathbf{E}(Y^2).$$

Thus the right-hand side is a quadratic in the variable a with at most one real root. Its discriminant must be non-positive. That is to say, if $b \neq 0$,

$$\mathbf{E}(XY)^2 - \mathbf{E}(X^2)\mathbf{E}(Y^2) \leq 0.$$

The discriminant is zero if and only if the quadratic has a real root. This occurs if and only if

$$\mathbf{E}((aX - bY)^2) = 0 \text{ for some } a \text{ and } b,$$

which, by Problem (3.9.2), completes the proof. ■

Proof of (8). Apply (9) to the variables $X - \mathbf{E}X$ and $Y - \mathbf{E}Y$. ■

A more careful treatment than this proof shows that $\rho = +1$ if and only if Y *increases* linearly with X and $\rho = -1$ if and only if Y *decreases* linearly with X.

(10) **Example.** Here is a tedious numerical example of the use of joint mass functions. Let X and Y take values in $\{1, 2, 3\}$ and $\{-1, 0, 2\}$ respectively, with joint mass function f where $f(x, y)$ is the appropriate entry in Table 3.1.

Table 3.1. The joint mass function of X and Y.

	$y=-1$	$y=0$	$y=2$	f_X
$x=1$	$\frac{1}{18}$	$\frac{3}{18}$	$\frac{2}{18}$	$\frac{6}{18}$
$x=2$	$\frac{2}{18}$	0	$\frac{3}{18}$	$\frac{5}{18}$
$x=3$	0	$\frac{4}{18}$	$\frac{3}{18}$	$\frac{7}{18}$
f_Y	$\frac{3}{18}$	$\frac{7}{18}$	$\frac{8}{18}$	

The indicated row and column sums are the marginal mass functions f_X

and f_Y. A quick calculation gives

$$\mathbf{E}(XY)=\sum_{x,y} xyf(x, y)=29/18$$

$$\mathbf{E}(X)=\sum_{x} xf_X(x)=37/18 \qquad \mathbf{E}(Y)=13/18$$

$$\operatorname{var}(X)=\mathbf{E}(X^2)-\mathbf{E}(X)^2=233/324, \qquad \operatorname{var}(Y)=461/324$$

$$\operatorname{cov}(X, Y)=41/324, \qquad \rho(X, Y)=41/(107413)^{1/2}$$

3.7 Conditional distributions and conditional expectation

In Section 1.4 we discussed the conditional probability $\mathbf{P}(B \mid A)$. This may be set in the more general context of the conditional distribution of one variable Y given the value of another variable X; this reduces to the definition of the conditional probabilities of events A and B if $X=I_A$ and $Y=I_B$.

Let X and Y be two discrete variables on $(\Omega, \mathcal{F}, \mathbf{P})$.

(1) **Definition.** The **conditional distribution function** of Y given $X=x$, written $F_{Y|X}(\cdot \mid x)$, is defined by

$$F_{Y|X}(y \mid x)=\mathbf{P}(Y\leq y \mid X=x)$$

for any x such that $\mathbf{P}(X=x)>0$. The **conditional (probability) mass function** of Y given $X=x$, written $f_{Y|X}(\cdot \mid x)$, is defined by

(2) $$f_{Y|X}(y \mid x)=\mathbf{P}(Y=y \mid X=x)$$

for any x such that $\mathbf{P}(X=x)>0$.

Formula (2) is easy to remember as $f_{Y|X}=f_{X,Y}/f_X$. Conditional distribution and mass functions are undefined at values of x for which $\mathbf{P}(X=x)=0$. Clearly X and Y are independent if and only if $f_{Y|X}=f_Y$.

Suppose we are told that $X=x$. Conditional upon this, the new distribution of Y has mass function $f_{Y|X}(y \mid x)$, which we think of as a function of y. The expected value $\sum_y yf_{Y|X}(y \mid x)$ of this distribution is called the *conditional expectation* of Y given $X=x$ and is written $\psi(x)=\mathbf{E}(Y \mid X=x)$. Now, we observe that the conditional expectation depends on the value x taken by X, and can be thought of as a function $\psi(X)$ of X itself.

(3) **Definition.** Let $\psi(x)=\mathbf{E}(Y \mid X=x)$. Then $\psi(X)$ is called the **conditional expectation** of Y given X, written as $\mathbf{E}(Y \mid X)$.

Although 'conditional expectation' sounds like a number, it is actually a random variable! It has the following important property.

(4) **Theorem.** *The conditional expectation* $\psi(X)=\mathbf{E}(Y \mid X)$ *satisfies* $\mathbf{E}(\psi(X))=\mathbf{E}(Y)$.

Proof. By (3.3.3)

$$\begin{aligned}\mathbf{E}(\psi(X)) &= \sum_x \psi(x) f_X(x) = \sum_{x,y} y f_{Y|X}(y \mid x) f_X(x)\\ &= \sum_{x,y} y f_{X,Y}(x, y) = \sum_y y f_Y(y) = \mathbf{E}(Y). \qquad \blacksquare\end{aligned}$$

This is an extremely useful theorem, to which we shall make repeated references. It often provides a useful method for calculating $\mathbf{E}(Y)$, since it asserts that

$$\mathbf{E}(Y) = \sum_x \mathbf{E}(Y \mid X = x)\mathbf{P}(X = x).$$

(5) **Example.** A hen lays N eggs, where N has the Poisson distribution with parameter λ. Each egg hatches with probability $p(=1-q)$ independently of the other eggs. Let K be the number of chicks. Find $\mathbf{E}(K \mid N)$, $\mathbf{E}(K)$, and $\mathbf{E}(N \mid K)$.

Solution. We are given that

$$f_N(n) = \frac{\lambda^n}{n!} e^{-\lambda}, \qquad f_{K|N}(k \mid n) = \binom{n}{k} p^k (1-p)^{n-k}.$$

Therefore

$$\psi(n) = \mathbf{E}(K \mid N = n) = \sum_k k f_{K|N}(k \mid n) = pn.$$

Thus

$$\mathbf{E}(K \mid N) = \psi(N) = pN$$

and

$$\mathbf{E}(K) = \mathbf{E}(\psi(N)) = p\mathbf{E}(N) = p\lambda.$$

To find $\mathbf{E}(N \mid K)$ we need to know the conditional mass function $f_{N|K}$ of N given K. However,

$$\begin{aligned} f_{N|K}(n \mid k) &= \mathbf{P}(N = n \mid K = k)\\ &= \mathbf{P}(K = k \mid N = n)\mathbf{P}(N = n)/\mathbf{P}(K = k)\\ &= \frac{\binom{n}{k} p^k (1-p)^{n-k} (\lambda^n/n!) e^{-\lambda}}{\sum_{m \geq k} \binom{m}{k} p^k (1-p)^{m-k} (\lambda^m/m!) e^{-\lambda}} \quad \text{if} \quad n \geq k\\ &= \frac{(q\lambda)^{n-k}}{(n-k)!} e^{-q\lambda}. \end{aligned}$$

Hence

$$\mathbf{E}(N \mid K=k)=\sum_{n\geq k} n\frac{(q\lambda)^{n-k}}{(n-k)!}e^{-q\lambda}=k+q\lambda,$$

giving

$$\mathbf{E}(N \mid K)=K+q\lambda. \qquad \bullet$$

3.8 Sums of random variables

We shall be very interested later in properties of the sum of a large number of random variables. The first stage is to find a formula for describing the mass function of the sum $Z=X+Y$ of two variables with joint mass function $f(x, y)$.

(1) **Theorem.** $\mathbf{P}(Z=z)=\sum_x f(x, z-x)$.

Proof. $\{Z=z\}=\bigcup_x (\{X=x\}\cap\{Y=z-x\})$.

This is a disjoint union, and at most countably many of its contributors have non-zero probability. Therefore

$$\mathbf{P}(Z=z)=\sum_x \mathbf{P}(X=x, Y=z-x)=\sum_x f(x, z-x). \qquad \blacksquare$$

If X and Y are independent, then

$$\mathbf{P}(Z=z)=f_Z(z)=\sum_x f_X(x)f_Y(z-x)=\sum_y f_X(z-y)f_Y(y).$$

The mass function of Z is called the *convolution* of the mass functions of X and Y, and is written

(2) $$f_Z=f_X * f_Y.$$

(3) **Example (3.5.6) revisited.** Let X_1 and X_2 be independent geometric variables with common mass function

$$f(k)=p(1-p)^{k-1}, \qquad k=1, 2, \ldots.$$

By (2), $Z=X_1+X_2$ has mass function

$$\mathbf{P}(Z=z)=\sum_k \mathbf{P}(X_1=k)\mathbf{P}(X_2=z-k)$$

$$=\sum_{k=1}^{z-1} p(1-p)^{k-1}p(1-p)^{z-k-1}=(z-1)p^2(1-p)^{z-2}, \qquad z=2, 3, \ldots$$

in agreement with (3.5.6). The general formula for the sum of a number, r say, of geometric variables can easily be verified by induction. $\bullet$

3.9 Problems

1. Complete the proofs of (3.2.3) and (3.6.3).

2. Show that if var $(X)=0$ then X is constant; that is, there exists $a\in\mathbb{R}$ such that $\mathbf{P}(X=a)=1$. (First show that if $\mathbf{E}(X^2)=0$ then $\mathbf{P}(X=0)=1$.)

3. Let $A_1, A_2, \ldots$ be a partition of Ω, and suppose that $X(\omega)=a_i$ whenever $\omega\in A_i$. Show that $\mathbf{E}X=\sum_i a_i\mathbf{P}(A_i)$. Prove (3.3.3). If X and Y are independent, show that $\mathbf{E}(g(X)h(Y))=\mathbf{E}(g(X))\mathbf{E}(h(Y))$.

4. Let $\Omega=\{\omega_1, \omega_2, \omega_3\}$, with $\mathbf{P}(\omega_1)=\mathbf{P}(\omega_2)=\mathbf{P}(\omega_3)=\frac{1}{3}$. Define $X, Y, Z:\Omega\to\mathbb{R}$ by

$$\begin{array}{lll} X(\omega_1)=1, & X(\omega_2)=2, & X(\omega_3)=3\\ Y(\omega_1)=2, & Y(\omega_2)=3, & Y(\omega_3)=1\\ Z(\omega_1)=2, & Z(\omega_2)=2, & Z(\omega_3)=1. \end{array}$$

Show that X and Y have the same mass functions. Find the mass functions of $X+Y$, XY and X/Y. Find the conditional mass functions $f_{Y|Z}$ and $f_{Z|Y}$.

5. For what values of k and α is f a mass function, where

   (a) $f(n)=\dfrac{k}{n(n+1)}, \quad n=1, 2, \ldots,$

   (b) $f(n)=kn^\alpha, \quad n=1, 2, \ldots$ (*zeta* or *Zipf* distribution)?

6. Let X and Y be independent Poisson variables with parameters λ and μ. Show that

   (a) $X+Y$ is Poisson, parameter $\lambda+\mu$,

   (b) the conditional distribution of X, given $X+Y=n$, is binomial, and find its parameters.

7. If X is geometric, show that

$$\mathbf{P}(X=n+k\mid X>n)=\mathbf{P}(X=k) \quad \text{for} \quad k\geq 1.$$

Why do you think that this is called the 'lack of memory' property? Does any other distribution on the positive integers have this property?

8. Show that the sum of two independent binomial variables, $B(m, p)$ and $B(n, p)$ respectively, is $B(m+n, p)$.

9. Let N be the number of heads occurring after n tosses of a biased coin. Write down the mass function of N in terms of the probability p of heads turning up on each toss. Prove and utilize the identity

$$\sum_i \binom{n}{2i} x^{2i}y^{n-2i}=\tfrac{1}{2}\{(x+y)^n+(y-x)^n\}$$

in order to calculate the probability p_n that N is even. Compare with Problem (1.8.16).

10. An urn contains N balls, b of which are blue and $r(=N-b)$ of which are red. A random sample of n balls is withdrawn without replacement from the urn. Show that the number B of blue balls in this sample has the mass function

$$\mathbf{P}(B=k)=\binom{b}{k}\binom{N-b}{n-k}\bigg/\binom{N}{n}.$$

This is called the *hypergeometric distribution* with parameters N, b, and n. Show further that if N, b, and r approach ∞ in such a way that $b/N \to p$ and $r/N \to 1-p$, then

$$\mathbf{P}(B=k) \to \binom{n}{k} p^k (1-p)^{n-k}.$$

You have shown that, for small n and large N, the distribution of B barely depends on whether or not the balls are replaced in the urn immediately after their withdrawal.

11. Let X and Y be independent $B(n, p)$ variables, and let $Z = X + Y$. Show that the conditional distribution of X given $Z = N$ is the hypergeometric distribution of Problem (10).

12. Suppose X and Y take values in $\{0, 1\}$, with joint mass function $f(x, y)$. Write

$$f(0,0) = a, \qquad f(0,1) = b, \qquad f(1,0) = c, \qquad f(1,1) = d,$$

and find necessary and sufficient conditions for X and Y to be
(a) uncorrelated
(b) independent.

13. (a) If X takes positive integer values show that $\mathbf{E}X = \sum_{n=0}^{\infty} \mathbf{P}(X > n)$.
(b) An urn contains b blue and r red balls. Balls are removed at random until the first blue ball is drawn. Show that the expected number drawn is $(b+r+1)/(b+1)$.
(c) The balls are replaced and then removed at random until all the remaining balls are of the same colour. Find the expected number remaining in the urn.

14. Let $X_1, X_2, \ldots, X_n$ be independent variables, and suppose that X_k is Bernoulli with parameter p_k. Show that $Y = X_1 + X_2 + \ldots + X_n$ has mean and variance given by

$$\mathbf{E}(Y) = \sum_1^n p_k, \qquad \operatorname{var}(Y) = \sum_1^n p_k(1-p_k).$$

Show that, for $\mathbf{E}(Y)$ fixed, $\operatorname{var}(Y)$ is a maximum when $p_1 = p_2 = \ldots = p_n$. Feller 1968, p. 231 has a striking interpretation of this result, which says roughly that the variation in the sum is greatest when individuals are most alike. Is this contrary to intuition?

15. Let $\mathbf{X} = (X_1, X_2, \ldots, X_n)$ be a vector of random variables. The *covariance matrix* $\mathbf{V}(\mathbf{X})$ of $\mathbf{X}$ is defined to be the symmetric n by n matrix with entries $(v_{ij} : 1 \leq i, j \leq n)$ given by

$$v_{ij} = \operatorname{cov}(X_i, X_j).$$

Show that $|\mathbf{V}(\mathbf{X})| = 0$ if and only if the X's are linearly dependent with probability one, in that

$$\mathbf{P}(a_1 X_1 + a_2 X_2 + \ldots + a_n X_n = b) = 1$$

for some a and b. ($|\mathbf{V}|$ denotes the determinant of $\mathbf{V}$.)

16. Let X and Y be independent Bernoulli random variables with parameter $\frac{1}{2}$. Show that $X + Y$ and $|X - Y|$ are dependent though uncorrelated.

17. **Matching (3.4.3).** Use indicators to prove that the number X of correct matchings in (3.4.3) has mean and variance 1 for all $n \geq 2$. Show that the mass function of X converges to a Poisson mass function as $n \to \infty$.

4 Continuous random variables

4.1 Probability density functions

Recall that a random variable X is *continuous* if its distribution function $F(x)=\mathbf{P}(X\leqslant x)$ can be written as†

(1) $$F(x)=\int_{-\infty}^{x} f(u)\,\mathrm{d}u$$

for some integrable $f:\mathbb{R}\to[0,\infty)$.

(2) **Definition.** f is called the **(probability) density function** of X.

The density function of F is not prescribed uniquely by (1) since two integrable functions which take identical values except at some specific point have the same integrals. However, if F is differentiable at u then we shall normally set $f(u)=F'(u)$. We write $f_X(u)$ to stress the role of X.

(3) **Example (2.2.4) revisited.** X and Y have density functions

$$f_X(x)=\begin{cases}(2\pi)^{-1} & \text{if } 0\leqslant x\leqslant 2\pi\\ 0 & \text{otherwise}\end{cases}$$

$$f_Y(y)=\begin{cases}y^{-1/2}/(4\pi) & \text{if } 0\leqslant y\leqslant 4\pi^2\\ 0 & \text{otherwise.}\end{cases}$$ ●

Continuous variables contrast starkly with discrete variables in that they satisfy $\mathbf{P}(X=x)=0$ for all $x\in\mathbb{R}$; this may seem paradoxical since X needs to take *some* value. Very roughly speaking, the resolution of this paradox lies in the observation that there are uncountably many values which X can take; this number is so large that the probability of X taking any particular value cannot exceed zero.

The numerical value $f(x)$ is *not* a probability. However, we can think of $f(x)\,\mathrm{d}x$ as the element of probability $\mathbf{P}(x<X\leqslant x+\mathrm{d}x)$, since

$$\mathbf{P}(x<X\leqslant x+\mathrm{d}x)=F(x+\mathrm{d}x)-F(x)\simeq f(x)\,\mathrm{d}x.$$

From equation (1), the probability that X takes a value in the interval

† Never mind what type of integral this is, at this stage.

$[a, b]$ is

$$\mathbf{P}(a \leqslant X \leqslant b) = \int_a^b f(x)\,\mathrm{d}x.$$

(Intuitively, to calculate this probability, we simply add up all the small elements of probability which contribute.) More generally, if B is a sufficiently nice subset of $\mathbb{R}$ (such as an interval, or the countable union of intervals, and so on), then it is reasonable to expect that

(4) $$\mathbf{P}(X \in B) = \int_B f(x)\,\mathrm{d}x,$$

and indeed this turns out to be the case.

We have deliberately used the same letter f for mass functions and density functions since these functions perform exactly analogous tasks for the appropriate classes of random variables. In most cases proofs of results for discrete variables can be rewritten for continuous variables by replacing any summation sign by an integral sign, and any probability mass $f(x)$ by the corresponding element of probability $f(x)\,\mathrm{d}x$.

(5) **Lemma.** *If X has density function f then*

(a) $\int_{-\infty}^{\infty} f(x)\,\mathrm{d}x = 1$

(b) $\mathbf{P}(X = x) = 0$ *for all* $x \in \mathbb{R}$

(c) $\mathbf{P}(a \leqslant X \leqslant b) = \int_a^b f(x)\,\mathrm{d}x.$

Proof. *Exercise.* ■

Part (a) of the lemma characterizes those non-negative integrable functions which are density functions of some random variable.

We conclude this section with a technical note for the more critical reader. For what sets B is (4) meaningful, and why does (5a) characterize density functions? Let $\mathcal{J}$ be the collection of all open intervals in $\mathbb{R}$. By the discussion in Section 1.6, $\mathcal{J}$ can be extended to a unique smallest σ-field $\mathcal{B} = \sigma(\mathcal{J})$ which contains $\mathcal{J}$; $\mathcal{B}$ is called the *Borel σ-field* and contains *Borel sets.* Equation (4) holds for all $B \in \mathcal{B}$. Setting $\mathbf{P}_X(B) = \mathbf{P}(X \in B)$, we can check that $(\mathbb{R}, \mathcal{B}, \mathbf{P}_X)$ is a probability space. Secondly, suppose that $f: \mathbb{R} \to [0, \infty)$ is integrable and $\int_{-\infty}^{\infty} f(x)\,\mathrm{d}x = 1$. For any $B \in \mathcal{B}$, we define

$$\mathbf{P}(B) = \int_B f(x)\,\mathrm{d}x.$$

Then $(\mathbb{R}, \mathcal{B}, \mathbf{P})$ is a probability space and f is the density function of the identity random variable $X:\mathbb{R}\to\mathbb{R}$ given by $X(x)=x$ for any $x\in\mathbb{R}$. The assiduous reader will verify the steps of this argument for his own satisfaction (or see Clarke 1975, p. 53).

4.2 Independence

This section contains the counterpart of Section 3.2 for continuous variables, though it contains a definition and theorem which hold for any pair of variables, regardless of their types (continuous, discrete, and so on). We cannot continue to define the independence of X and Y in terms of events like $\{X=x\}$ and $\{Y=y\}$, since these events have zero probability and are trivially independent.

(1) **Definition.** X and Y are called **independent** if

(2) $\{X\leq x\}$ and $\{Y\leq y\}$ are independent events for all $x, y\in\mathbb{R}$.

The reader should verify that discrete variables satisfy (2) if and only if they are independent in the sense of Section 3.2. (1) is the general definition of the independence of any two variables X and Y, regardless of their types. The following general result holds for the independence of functions of random variables. Let X and Y be random variables, and let $g, h:\mathbb{R}\to\mathbb{R}$. Then $g(X)$ and $h(Y)$ are functions which map Ω into $\mathbb{R}$ by

$$g(X)(\omega)=g(X(\omega)),\qquad h(Y)(\omega)=h(Y(\omega))$$

as in (3.2.3). Let us suppose that $g(X)$ and $h(Y)$ are random variables. (This holds if they are $\mathcal{F}$-measurable; it is true for instance if g and h are sufficiently smooth or regular by being, say, continuous or monotonic.) In the rest of this book, *we assume that any term of the form '$g(X)$', where g is a function and X is a random variable, is itself a random variable.*

(3) **Theorem.** *If X and Y are independent, then so are $g(X)$ and $h(Y)$.*

Move immediately to the next section unless you want to prove this.

Proof. Some readers may like to try to prove this on their second reading. The proof does not rely on any property like continuity. The key lies in the requirement (2.1.3) that random variables be $\mathcal{F}$-measurable, and in the observation that $g(X)$ is $\mathcal{F}$-measurable if $g:\mathbb{R}\to\mathbb{R}$ is *Borel measurable*, which is to say that $g^{-1}(B)\in\mathcal{B}$, the Borel σ-field, for all $B\in\mathcal{B}$. Complete the proof yourself (*exercise*). ■

4.3 Expectation

The expectation of a discrete variable X is $\mathbf{E}X=\sum_x x\mathbf{P}(X=x)$. This is an average of the possible values of X, each value being weighted by its probability. For continuous variables, expectations are defined as integrals.

(1) **Definition.** The **expectation** of a continuous variable X with density function f is

$$\mathbf{E}X = \int_{-\infty}^{\infty} xf(x)\,dx$$

whenever this integral exists.

There are various ways of defining the integral of a function $g:\mathbb{R}\to\mathbb{R}$, but it is not appropriate to explore this here. Note that usually we shall allow the existence of $\int g(x)\,dx$ only if $\int |g(x)|\,dx < \infty$.

(2) **Examples (2.2.4) and (4.1.3) revisited.** The random variables X and Y of these examples have mean values

$$\mathbf{E}(X) = \int_0^{2\pi} \frac{x}{2\pi}\,dx = \pi,$$

$$\mathbf{E}(Y) = \int_0^{4\pi^2} \frac{y^{1/2}}{4\pi}\,dy = \tfrac{4}{3}\pi^2.$$

Roughly speaking, the expectation operator $\mathbf{E}$ has the same properties for continuous variables as it has for discrete variables.

(3) **Theorem.** *If X and $g(X)$ are continuous random variables then*

$$\mathbf{E}(g(X)) = \int_{-\infty}^{\infty} g(x)f_X(x)\,dx.$$

We give a simple proof for the case when g takes only non-negative values, and we leave it to the reader to extend this to the general case. Our proof is a corollary of the next lemma.

(4) **Lemma.** *If X has density function f with $f(x)=0$ when $x<0$, and distribution function F, then*

$$\mathbf{E}X = \int_0^{\infty} \{1-F(x)\}\,dx.$$

Proof.

$$\int_0^{\infty} \{1-F(x)\}\,dx = \int_0^{\infty} \mathbf{P}(X>x)\,dx = \int_0^{\infty}\int_{y=x}^{\infty} f(y)\,dy\,dx.$$

Now change the order of integration in the last term. ∎

Proof of (3) when $g \geq 0$. By (4)

$$\mathbf{E}(g(X)) = \int_0^\infty \mathbf{P}(g(X) > x)\,dx = \int_0^\infty \left\{\int_B f_X(y)\,dy\right\} dx$$

where $B = \{y : g(y) > x\}$. We interchange the order of integration here to obtain

$$\mathbf{E}(g(X)) = \int_0^\infty \int_0^{g(y)} dx\, f_X(y)\,dy = \int_0^\infty g(y) f_X(y)\,dy. \qquad \blacksquare$$

(5) **Example (2) continued.** Lemma (4) allows us to find $\mathbf{E}(Y)$ without calculating f_Y, for

$$\mathbf{E}(Y) = \mathbf{E}(X^2) = \int_0^{2\pi} x^2 f_X(x)\,dx$$

$$= \int_0^{2\pi} \frac{x^2}{2\pi}\,dx = \tfrac{4}{3}\pi^2. \qquad \bullet$$

We were careful to describe many characteristics of discrete variables—such as moments, covariance, correlation, and linearity of $\mathbf{E}$ (see Sections 3.3 and 3.6)—in terms of the operator $\mathbf{E}$ itself. Exactly analogous discussion holds for continuous variables. We do not spell out the details here but only indicate some of the less obvious emendations required to establish these results. For example, (3.3.5) defines the kth moment of the discrete variable X to be

(6) $$m_k = \mathbf{E}(X^k);$$

we define the kth moment of a continuous variable X by the same equation. Of course, the moments of X may not exist since the integral

$$\mathbf{E}(X^k) = \int x^k f(x)\,dx$$

may not converge (see (4.4.7) for an instance of when this may occur).

4.4 Examples of continuous variables

Exercise. Sketch all the density and distribution functions which are discussed here, and complete all unfinished calculations of means and variances.

(1) **Uniform distribution.** X is *uniform* on $[a, b]$ if

$$F(x) = \begin{cases} 0 & \text{if } x \leq a \\ (x-a)/(b-a) & \text{if } a < x \leq b \\ 1 & \text{if } x > b. \end{cases}$$

Roughly speaking, X takes any value between a and b with equal probability. Example (2.2.4) describes a uniform variable X. ●

(2) **Exponential distribution.** X is *exponential* with parameter λ (>0), if

(3) $$F(x) = 1 - e^{-\lambda x}, \qquad x \geq 0.$$

This arises as the 'continuous limit' of the waiting time distribution of (3.5.5) and very often occurs in practice as a description of the time elapsing between unpredictable events (such as telephone calls, earthquakes, emissions of radioactive particles, and arrivals of buses, girls, and so on). Suppose, as in (3.5.5), that a sequence of Bernoulli trials is performed at time epochs $\delta, 2\delta, 3\delta, \ldots$ and let W be the waiting time for the first success. Then

$$\mathbf{P}(W > k\delta) = (1-p)^k \quad \text{and} \quad \mathbf{E}W = \delta/p.$$

Now fix a time t. By this time, roughly $k = t/\delta$ trials have been made. We shall let $\delta \downarrow 0$. In order that the limiting distribution $\lim_{\delta \downarrow 0} \mathbf{P}(W > t)$ be non-trivial, we shall need to assume that $p \downarrow 0$ also and p/δ approaches some positive constant λ. Then

$$\mathbf{P}(W > t) = \mathbf{P}\left(W > \left(\frac{t}{\delta}\right)\delta\right) \simeq (1 - \lambda\delta)^{t/\delta} \to e^{-\lambda t}$$

which yields (3).

The exponential distribution (3) has mean

$$\mathbf{E}X = \int_0^\infty \{1 - F(x)\}\, dx = \lambda^{-1}.$$

Further properties of the exponential distribution will be discussed in Section 4.7 and Problem (4.10.5); this distribution proves to be the cornerstone of the theory of Markov processes in continuous time which will be discussed later. ●

(4) **Normal distribution.** Probably the most important continuous distribution is the *normal* (or *Gaussian*) distribution, which has two parameters μ and σ^2 and density function

$$f(x) = \frac{1}{\sqrt{(2\pi\sigma^2)}} \exp\left\{-\frac{(x-\mu)^2}{2\sigma^2}\right\} \qquad -\infty < x < \infty, \ \sigma > 0.$$

It is denoted by $N(\mu, \sigma^2)$. If $\mu = 0$ and $\sigma^2 = 1$ then

$$f(x) = \frac{1}{\sqrt{(2\pi)}} \exp\left(-\tfrac{1}{2}x^2\right)$$

is the density of the *standard* normal distribution. It is an *exercise* in analysis (Problem (4.10.1)) to show that f satisfies (4.1.5a), and is indeed therefore a density function.

The normal distribution arises in many ways. In particular it can be obtained as a continuous limit of the binomial distribution $B(n, p)$ as $n \to \infty$ (this is the de Moivre–Laplace limit theorem). This result is a special case of the Central Limit Theorem to be discussed in Chapter 5; it transpires that in many cases the sum of a large number of independent (or at least not too dependent) random variables is approximately normally distributed. The binomial random variable has this property because it is the sum of Bernoulli variables (see (3.5.2)).

Let X be $N(\mu, \sigma^2)$ and let

(5) $$Y = (X-\mu)/\sigma.$$

For the distribution of Y,

$$\begin{aligned}\mathbf{P}(Y \leq y) &= \mathbf{P}((X-\mu)/\sigma \leq y) = \mathbf{P}(X \leq y\sigma + \mu)\\ &= \frac{1}{\sigma\sqrt{(2\pi)}}\int_{-\infty}^{y\sigma+\mu} \exp\left\{-\frac{(x-\mu)^2}{2\sigma^2}\right\} dx\\ &= \frac{1}{\sqrt{(2\pi)}}\int_{-\infty}^{y} \exp(-\tfrac{1}{2}v^2)\, dv \quad \text{by substituting } x = v\sigma + \mu\end{aligned}$$

where σ is the positive square root of σ^2. Thus Y is $N(0, 1)$. Routine integrations (see Problem (4.10.1)) show that

$$\mathbf{E}Y = 0, \qquad \operatorname{var}(Y) = 1$$

and it follows immediately from (5), (3.3.8), and (3.3.11) that the mean and variance of the $N(\mu, \sigma^2)$ distribution are μ and σ^2 respectively, thus explaining the notation.

Traditionally we denote the distribution function of Y by Φ:

$$\Phi(y) = \mathbf{P}(Y \leq y) = \int_{-\infty}^{y} \frac{1}{\sqrt{(2\pi)}} \exp(-\tfrac{1}{2}v^2)\, dv. \qquad \bullet$$

(6) **Gamma distribution.** X has the *gamma* distribution with parameters $\lambda, t > 0$, denoted† by $\Gamma(\lambda, t)$, if it has density

$$f(x) = \frac{1}{\Gamma(t)}\lambda^t x^{t-1} e^{-\lambda x}, \qquad x \geq 0.$$

Here, $\Gamma(t)$ is the *gamma function*

$$\Gamma(t) = \int_0^{\infty} x^{t-1} e^{-x}\, dx.$$

If $t = 1$ then X is exponentially distributed with parameter λ. We remark

† Do not confuse the order of the parameters. Some authors denote this distribution by $\Gamma(t, \lambda)$.

that if $\lambda = \frac{1}{2}$, $t = \frac{1}{2}d$, for some integer d, then X is said to have the *chi-squared distribution* $\chi^2(d)$ with d degrees of freedom (see Problem (4.10.10)). ●

(7) **Cauchy distribution.** X is *Cauchy* if

$$f(x) = \frac{1}{\pi(1+x^2)}, \qquad -\infty < x < \infty.$$

This distribution is notable for having no moments and for its frequent appearances in counter-examples (but see Problem (4.10.4)). ●

(8) **Beta distribution.** X is *beta*, parameters $a, b > 0$, if

$$f(x) = \frac{1}{B(a, b)} x^{a-1}(1-x)^{b-1}, \qquad 0 \leq x \leq 1.$$

The constant

$$B(a, b) = \int_0^1 x^{a-1}(1-x)^{b-1}\,dx$$

ensures that f has total integral equal to one. You may care to prove that

$$B(a, b) = \frac{\Gamma(a)\Gamma(b)}{\Gamma(a+b)}.$$

If $a = b = 1$ then X is uniform on $[0, 1]$. ●

(9) **Weibull distribution.** X is *Weibull*, parameters $\alpha, \beta > 0$, if

$$F(x) = 1 - \exp(-\alpha x^{\beta}), \qquad x \geq 0.$$

Differentiate to find that

$$f(x) = \alpha\beta x^{\beta-1} \exp(-\alpha x^{\beta}), \qquad x \geq 0.$$

Set $\beta = 1$ to obtain the exponential distribution. ●

4.5 Dependence

Many interesting probabilistic statements about a pair X, Y of variables concern the way X and Y vary together as functions on the same domain Ω.

(1) **Definition.** The **joint distribution function** of X and Y is the function $F:\mathbb{R}^2 \to [0, 1]$ given by

$$F(x, y) = \mathbf{P}(X \leq x, Y \leq y).$$

If X and Y are continuous then we cannot talk of their joint mass function (see (3.6.2)) since this is identically zero. Instead we need another density function.

(2) **Definition.** X and Y are **(jointly) continuous** with **joint (probability) density function** $f:\mathbb{R}^2 \to [0, \infty)$ if

$$F(x, y) = \int_{-\infty}^{y} \int_{-\infty}^{x} f(u, v)\, du\, dv \quad \text{for each } x, y \in \mathbb{R}.$$

If F has both its partial derivatives at the point (x, y), then we normally specify

$$f(x, y) = \frac{\partial^2}{\partial x\, \partial y} F(x, y).$$

The properties of joint distribution and density functions are very much the same as those of the corresponding functions of a single variable, and the reader is left to find them. We note the following facts. Let X and Y have joint distribution function F and joint density function f. (Sometimes we write $F_{X,Y}$ and $f_{X,Y}$ to stress the roles of X and Y.)

(3) **Probabilities.**

$$\mathbf{P}(a \leqslant X \leqslant b, c \leqslant Y \leqslant d) = F(b, d) - F(a, d) - F(b, c) + F(a, c)$$

$$= \int_{c}^{d} \int_{a}^{b} f(x, y)\, dx\, dy.$$

Think of $f(x, y)\, dx\, dy$ as the element of probability $\mathbf{P}(x < X \leqslant x + dx, y < Y \leqslant y + dy)$, so that if B is a sufficiently nice subset of $\mathbb{R}^2$ (such as a rectangle or a union of rectangles and so on) then

(4) $$\mathbf{P}((X, Y) \in B) = \iint_{B} f(x, y)\, dx\, dy.$$

We can think of (X, Y) as a point chosen randomly from the plane; then $\mathbf{P}((X, Y) \in B)$ is the probability that the outcome of this random choice lies in B.

(5) **Marginal distributions.** The *marginal distribution functions* of X and Y are

$$F_X(x) = \mathbf{P}(X \leqslant x) = F(x, \infty), \qquad F_Y(y) = \mathbf{P}(Y \leqslant y) = F(\infty, y)$$

($F(x, \infty)$ is shorthand for $\lim_{y \to \infty} F(x, y)$); now

$$F_X(x) = \int_{-\infty}^{x} \left(\int_{-\infty}^{\infty} f(u, y)\, dy \right) du$$

and it follows that the *marginal density function* of X is

$$f_X(x) = \int_{-\infty}^{\infty} f(x, y)\, dy.$$

Similarly, the *marginal density function* of Y is

$$f_Y(y) = \int_{-\infty}^{\infty} f(x, y)\, dx.$$

(6) **Expectation.** If $g:\mathbb{R}^2 \to \mathbb{R}$ is a sufficiently nice function (see the proof of (4.2.3) for an idea of what this means) then

$$\mathbf{E}(g(X, Y)) = \int_{-\infty}^{\infty} \int_{-\infty}^{\infty} g(x, y) f(x, y)\, dx\, dy;$$

in particular, setting $g(x, y) = ax + by$,

$$\mathbf{E}(aX + bY) = a\mathbf{E}X + b\mathbf{E}Y.$$

(7) **Independence.** X and Y are *independent* if and only if

$$F(x, y) = F_X(x)F_Y(y) \quad \text{for all } x, y \in \mathbb{R},$$

or if and only if

$$f(x, y) = f_X(x) f_Y(y)$$

whenever F is differentiable at (x, y) (see Problem (4.10.6) also).

(8) **Example. Buffon's needle.** A plane is ruled by the lines $y = n$ $(n = 0, \pm 1, \pm 2, \ldots)$ and a needle of unit length is cast randomly onto the plane. What is the probability that it intersects any line? We suppose that the needle shows no preference for position or direction.

Solution. Let (X, Y) be the coordinates of the centre of the needle and let Θ be the angle, modulo π, made by the needle and the x-axis. Denote the distance from the needle's centre and the nearest line beneath it by Z $(= Y - \lfloor Y \rfloor$, where $\lfloor Y \rfloor$ is the greatest integer not greater than $Y)$. We need to interpret the statement 'a needle is cast randomly', and do this by assuming that

(a) Z is uniformly distributed on $[0, 1]$, so that $f_Z(z) = 1$ if $0 \leq z \leq 1$,
(b) Θ is uniformly distributed on $[0, \pi]$, so that $f_\Theta(\theta) = 1/\pi$ if $0 \leq \theta \leq \pi$,
(c) Z and Θ are independent, so that $f_{Z,\Theta}(z, \theta) = f_Z(z) f_\Theta(\theta)$.

Thus the pair Z, Θ has joint density function

$$f(z, \theta) = \frac{1}{\pi} \quad \text{if} \quad 0 \leq z \leq 1,\ 0 \leq \theta \leq \pi.$$

Draw a diagram to see that an intersection occurs if and only if $(Z, \Theta) \in B$ where $B \subseteq [0, 1] \times [0, \pi]$ is given by

$$B = \{(z, \theta) : z \leq \tfrac{1}{2} \sin \theta \quad \text{or} \quad 1 - z \leq \tfrac{1}{2} \sin \theta\}.$$

Hence

$$\mathbf{P}(\text{intersection}) = \iint_B f(z, \theta)\,dz\,d\theta$$

$$= \frac{1}{\pi}\int_0^{\pi}\left(\int_0^{\frac{1}{2}\sin\theta} dz + \int_{1-\frac{1}{2}\sin\theta}^{1} dz\right)d\theta$$

$$= \frac{2}{\pi}.$$

Buffon designed the experiment in order to estimate the numerical value of π. Try it if you have time. ●

(9) **Example. Bivariate normal distribution.** Let $f:\mathbb{R}^2 \to \mathbb{R}$ be given by

(10) $$f(x, y) = \frac{1}{2\pi\sqrt{(1-\rho^2)}}\exp\left\{-\frac{1}{2(1-\rho^2)}(x^2 - 2\rho xy + y^2)\right\}$$

where ρ is a constant satisfying $-1 < \rho < 1$. Check that f is a joint density function by verifying that

$$f(x, y) \geq 0, \qquad \int_{-\infty}^{\infty}\int_{-\infty}^{\infty} f(x, y)\,dx\,dy = 1;$$

f is called the *standard bivariate normal* density function of some pair X and Y. Calculation of its marginals shows that X and Y are $N(0, 1)$ variables (*exercise*). Furthermore, the covariance

$$\text{cov}(X, Y) = \mathbf{E}(XY) - \mathbf{E}(X)\mathbf{E}(Y)$$

is given by

$$\text{cov}(X, Y) = \int_{-\infty}^{\infty}\int_{-\infty}^{\infty} xyf(x, y)\,dx\,dy = \rho;$$

check this. Remember that independent variables are uncorrelated, but the converse is not true in general. In this case, however, if $\rho = 0$ then

$$f(x, y) = \left\{\frac{1}{\sqrt{(2\pi)}}\exp(-\tfrac{1}{2}x^2)\right\}\left\{\frac{1}{\sqrt{(2\pi)}}\exp(-\tfrac{1}{2}y^2)\right\} = f_X(x)f_Y(y)$$

and so X and Y are independent. We reach the following important conclusion. *Standard bivariate normal variables are independent if and only if they are uncorrelated.*

The general bivariate normal distribution is more complicated. We say that the pair X, Y has the bivariate normal distribution with means μ_1 and μ_2, variances σ_1^2 and σ_2^2, and correlation ρ if their joint density function is

$$f(x, y) = \frac{1}{2\pi\sigma_1\sigma_2\sqrt{(1-\rho^2)}}\exp\{-\tfrac{1}{2}Q(x, y)\}$$

where $\sigma_1, \sigma_2 > 0$ and Q is the following quadratic form:

$$Q(x, y) = \frac{1}{(1-\rho^2)} \left\{ \left(\frac{x-\mu_1}{\sigma_1} \right)^2 - 2\rho \left(\frac{x-\mu_1}{\sigma_1} \right) \left(\frac{y-\mu_2}{\sigma_2} \right) + \left(\frac{y-\mu_2}{\sigma_2} \right)^2 \right\}.$$

Routine integrations (*exercise*) show that

(a) X is $N(\mu_1, \sigma_1^2)$ and Y is $N(\mu_2, \sigma_2^2)$,
(b) the correlation between X and Y is ρ,
(c) *X and Y are independent if and only if* $\rho = 0$.

Finally, here is a hint about calculating integrals associated with normal density functions. It is an analytical exercise (Problem (4.10.1)) to show that

$$\int_{-\infty}^{\infty} \exp(-\tfrac{1}{2}x^2)\, dx = \sqrt{(2\pi)}$$

and hence that

$$f(x) = \frac{1}{\sqrt{(2\pi)}} \exp(-\tfrac{1}{2}x^2)$$

is indeed a density function. Similarly, a change of variables in the integral shows that the more general function

$$f(x) = \frac{1}{\sigma\sqrt{(2\pi)}} \exp\left\{ -\frac{1}{2}\left(\frac{x-\mu}{\sigma} \right)^2 \right\}$$

is itself a density function. This knowledge can often be used to shorten calculations. For example, let X and Y have joint density function given by (10). Then, by completing the square in the exponent of the integrand, we see that

$$\begin{aligned} \operatorname{cov}(X, Y) &= \iint xyf(x, y)\, dx\, dy \\ &= \int y \frac{1}{\sqrt{(2\pi)}} \exp(-\tfrac{1}{2}y^2) \left\{ \int xg(x, y)\, dx \right\} dy \end{aligned}$$

where

$$g(x, y) = \frac{1}{\sqrt{\{2\pi(1-\rho^2)\}}} \exp\left\{ -\frac{1}{2} \frac{(x-\rho y)^2}{(1-\rho^2)} \right\}$$

is the density function of the $N(\rho y, 1-\rho^2)$ distribution. Therefore $\int xg(x, y)\, dx$ is the mean, ρy, of this distribution, giving

$$\operatorname{cov}(X, Y) = \rho \int y^2 \frac{1}{\sqrt{(2\pi)}} \exp(-\tfrac{1}{2}y^2)\, dy.$$

However, the integral here is, in turn, the variance of the $N(0, 1)$ distribution, and so

$$\operatorname{cov}(X, Y) = \rho$$

as was asserted previously. ●

(11) **Example.** Here is another example of how to manipulate density functions. Let X and Y have joint density function

$$f(x, y) = \frac{1}{y} \exp\left(-y - \frac{x}{y}\right), \qquad 0 < x, y < \infty.$$

Find the marginal density function of Y.

Solution.

$$f_Y(y) = \int_{-\infty}^{\infty} f(x, y)\, dx$$

$$= \int_0^{\infty} \frac{1}{y} \exp\left(-y - \frac{x}{y}\right) dx = e^{-y}, \qquad y > 0$$

and hence Y is exponentially distributed. ●

Following the final paragraph of Section 4.3, we should note that the expectation operator $\mathbf{E}$ has similar properties when applied to a family of continuous variables as when applied to discrete variables. Consider just one example of this.

(12) **Theorem. Cauchy–Schwarz inequality.** *For any pair X, Y of jointly continuous variables, we have that*

$$\mathbf{E}(XY)^2 \leq \mathbf{E}(X^2)\mathbf{E}(Y^2),$$

with equality if and only if $\mathbf{P}(aX = bY) = 1$ for some real a and b, at least one of which is non-zero.

Proof. Exactly as for (3.6.9). ■

4.6 Conditional distributions and conditional expectation

Suppose that X and Y have joint density function f. We wish to discuss the conditional distribution of Y given that X takes the value x. However, the probability $\mathbf{P}(Y \leq y \mid X = x)$ is undefined since (see (1.4.1)) we may only condition on events which have strictly positive probability. We proceed as follows. If $f_X(x) > 0$ then, by (4.5.4),

$$\mathbf{P}(Y \leq y \mid x \leq X \leq x + dx) = \frac{\mathbf{P}(Y \leq y, x \leq X \leq x + dx)}{\mathbf{P}(x \leq X \leq x + dx)}$$

$$\simeq \frac{\int_{v=-\infty}^{y} f(x, v)\, dx\, dv}{f_X(x)\, dx}$$

$$= \int_{v=-\infty}^{y} \frac{f(x, v)}{f_X(x)}\, dv.$$

As $dx \downarrow 0$, the left-hand side of this equation approaches our intuitive notion of the probability that $Y \leq y$ given $X = x$, and it is appropriate to make the following definition.

(1) **Definition.** The **conditional distribution function** of Y given $X = x$, written $F_{Y|X}(y \mid x)$ or $\mathbf{P}(Y \leq y \mid X = x)$, is defined to be

$$F_{Y|X}(y \mid x) = \int_{v=-\infty}^{y} \frac{f(x, v)}{f_X(x)}\, dv$$

for any x such that $f_X(x) > 0$.

Remembering that distribution functions are integrals of density functions, we are led to the following definition.

(2) **Definition.** The **conditional density function** of $F_{Y|X}$, written $f_{Y|X}$, is given by

$$f_{Y|X}(y \mid x) = \frac{f(x, y)}{f_X(x)}$$

for any x such that $f_X(x) > 0$.

Of course,

$$f_X(x) = \int_{-\infty}^{\infty} f(x, y)\, dy,$$

and so

$$f_{Y|X}(y \mid x) = \frac{f(x, y)}{\int_{-\infty}^{\infty} f(x, y)\, dy}.$$

Definition (2) is easily remembered as $f_{Y|X} = f_{X,Y}/f_X$. Here is an example of a conditional density function in action.

(3) **Example.** Let X and Y have joint density function

$$f_{X,Y}(x, y) = \frac{1}{x}, \qquad 0 \leq y \leq x \leq 1.$$

Show for yourself (*exercise*) that

$$f_X(x) = 1, \quad \text{if} \quad 0 \leq x \leq 1, \quad f_{Y|X}(y \mid x) = \frac{1}{x}, \quad \text{if} \quad 0 \leq y \leq x \leq 1,$$

which is to say that X is uniformly distributed on $[0, 1]$ and, conditional on the event $\{X = x\}$, Y is uniform on $[0, x]$. To calculate probabilities such as $\mathbf{P}(X^2 + Y^2 \leq 1 \mid X = x)$, say, we proceed as follows. If $x > 0$, define

$$A(x) = \{y \in \mathbb{R} : 0 \leq y \leq x,\ x^2 + y^2 \leq 1\};$$

clearly $A(x)=[0, \min\{x, (1-x^2)^{1/2}\}]$. Also,

$$\begin{aligned}\mathbf{P}(X^2+Y^2\leqslant 1 \mid X=x) &= \int_{A(x)} f_{Y|X}(y\mid x)\,dy\\ &= \frac{1}{x}\min\{x, (1-x^2)^{1/2}\}\\ &= \min\{1, (x^{-2}-1)^{1/2}\}.\end{aligned}$$

Next, let us calculate $\mathbf{P}(X^2+Y^2\leqslant 1)$. Let

$$A=\{(x, y): 0\leqslant y\leqslant x\leqslant 1,\ x^2+y^2\leqslant 1\}.$$

Then

(4) $$\begin{aligned}\mathbf{P}(X^2+Y^2\leqslant 1) &= \iint_A f_{X,Y}(x, y)\,dx\,dy\\ &= \int_{x=0}^{1} f_X(x) \int_{y\in A(x)} f_{Y|X}(y\mid x)\,dy\,dx\\ &= \int_0^1 \min\{1, (x^{-2}-1)^{1/2}\}\,dx = \log(1+\sqrt{2}).\end{aligned}$$ ●

From Definitions (1) and (2) it is easy to see that the *conditional expectation* of Y given X can be defined as in Section 3.7 by

$$\mathbf{E}(Y\mid X)=\psi(X)$$

where

$$\psi(x)=\mathbf{E}(Y\mid X=x)=\int_{-\infty}^{\infty} y f_{Y|X}(y\mid x)\,dy;$$

once again, $\mathbf{E}(Y\mid X)$ has the following important property.

(5) **Theorem.** *The conditional expectation* $\psi(X)=\mathbf{E}(Y\mid X)$ *satisfies*

$$\mathbf{E}(\psi(X))=\mathbf{E}(Y).$$

We shall use this result repeatedly; it is normally written as

$$\mathbf{E}(\mathbf{E}(Y\mid X))=\mathbf{E}(Y),$$

and it provides a useful method for calculating $\mathbf{E}(Y)$ since it asserts that

$$\mathbf{E}(Y)=\int_{-\infty}^{\infty} \mathbf{E}(Y\mid X=x) f_X(x)\,dx.$$

The proof of (5) proceeds exactly as for discrete variables (see (3.7.4)); indeed the theorem holds for all pairs of random variables, regardless of their types. For example, in the special case when X is continuous and Y

is the discrete random variable I_B, the indicator function of an event B, the theorem asserts that

(6) $$\mathbf{P}(B)=\mathbf{E}(\psi(X))=\int_{-\infty}^{\infty}\mathbf{P}(B\mid X=x)f_X(x)\,dx$$

(see equation (4) above for an application of (6)).

(7) **Example.** Let X and Y have the standard bivariate normal distribution of (4.5.9). Then

$$\begin{aligned}f_{Y|X}(y\mid x)&=f_{X,Y}(x,y)/f_X(x)\\&=\frac{1}{\sqrt{\{2\pi(1-\rho^2)\}}}\exp\left\{-\frac{(y-\rho x)^2}{2(1-\rho^2)}\right\}\end{aligned}$$

is the density function of a $N(\rho x, 1-\rho^2)$ distribution. Thus $\mathbf{E}(Y\mid X=x)=\rho x$, giving that $\mathbf{E}(Y\mid X)=\rho X$. ●

(8) **Example.** Continuous and discrete variables have mean values, but what can we say about variables which are neither continuous nor discrete, such as X in Example (2.2.5)? In that example, let A be the event that a tail turns up. Then

$$\begin{aligned}\mathbf{E}(X)&=\mathbf{E}(\mathbf{E}(X\mid I_A))\\&=\mathbf{E}(X\mid I_A=1)\mathbf{P}(I_A=1)+\mathbf{E}(X\mid I_A=0)\mathbf{P}(I_A=0)\\&=\mathbf{E}(X\mid \text{tail})\mathbf{P}(\text{tail})+\mathbf{E}(X\mid \text{head})\mathbf{P}(\text{head})\\&=-1\,.\,q+\pi\,.\,p=\pi p-q\end{aligned}$$

since X is uniformly distributed on $[0, 2\pi]$ if a head turns up. ●

(9) **Example (3) revisited.** Suppose, in the notation of (3), that we wish to calculate $\mathbf{E}(Y)$. Use (5) to obtain

$$\begin{aligned}\mathbf{E}(Y)&=\int_0^1\mathbf{E}(Y\mid X=x)f_X(x)\,dx\\&=\int_0^1\tfrac{1}{2}x\,dx=\tfrac{1}{4}\end{aligned}$$

since, conditional on $\{X=x\}$, Y is uniformly distributed on $[0, x]$. ●

4.7 Functions of random variables

Let X be a random variable with density function f, and let $g:\mathbb{R}\to\mathbb{R}$ be a sufficiently nice function (in the sense of the discussion after (4.2.3)). Then $Y=g(X)$ is a random variable also. To calculate the distribution of

Y, proceed thus:†

$$\mathbf{P}(Y \leqslant y) = \mathbf{P}(g(X) \leqslant y) = \mathbf{P}(g(X) \in (-\infty, y])$$
$$= \mathbf{P}(X \in g^{-1}(-\infty, y]) = \int_{g^{-1}(-\infty, y]} f(x)\,dx.$$

Example (2.2.4) contains an instance of this calculation, when $g(x) = x^2$.

(1) **Example.** Let X be $N(0, 1)$ and let $g(x) = x^2$. Then $Y = g(X) = X^2$ has distribution function

$$\mathbf{P}(Y \leqslant y) = \mathbf{P}(X^2 \leqslant y) = \mathbf{P}(-\sqrt{y} \leqslant X \leqslant +\sqrt{y})$$
$$= \Phi(\sqrt{y}) - \Phi(-\sqrt{y}) = 2\Phi(\sqrt{y}) - 1 \qquad \text{if } y \geqslant 0,$$

by the fact that $\Phi(x) = 1 - \Phi(-x)$. Differentiate to obtain

$$f_Y(y) = 2\frac{d}{dy}\Phi(\sqrt{y}) = y^{-1/2}\Phi'(\sqrt{y}) = \frac{1}{\sqrt{(2\pi y)}}\exp(-\tfrac{1}{2}y)$$

for $y \geqslant 0$. Compare with (4.4.6) to see that X^2 is $\Gamma(\frac{1}{2}, \frac{1}{2})$, or chi-squared with one degree of freedom. See Problem (4.10.10) also. ●

(2) **Example.** Let $g(x) = ax + b$ for fixed $a, b \in \mathbb{R}$. Then $Y = g(X) = aX + b$ has distribution function

$$\mathbf{P}(Y \leqslant y) = \mathbf{P}(aX + b \leqslant y) = \begin{cases} \mathbf{P}(X \leqslant (y-b)/a) & \text{if } a > 0 \\ \mathbf{P}(X \geqslant (y-b)/a) & \text{if } a < 0. \end{cases}$$

Differentiate to obtain $f_Y(y) = |a|^{-1} f_X((y-b)/a)$. ●

More generally, if X_1 and X_2 have joint density function f and $g, h : \mathbb{R}^2 \to \mathbb{R}$, then what is the joint density function of the pair $Y_1 = g(X_1, X_2)$, $Y_2 = h(X_1, X_2)$? Recall how to change variables within an integral. Let $y_1 = y_1(x_1, x_2)$, $y_2 = y_2(x_1, x_2)$ be a one–one mapping $T : (x_1, x_2) \mapsto (y_1, y_2)$ taking some domain $D \subseteq \mathbb{R}^2$ onto some range $R \subseteq \mathbb{R}^2$. The transformation can be inverted as $x_1 = x_1(y_1, y_2)$, $x_2 = x_2(y_1, y_2)$; the *Jacobian* of this inverse is defined to be the determinant

$$J = \begin{vmatrix} \dfrac{\partial x_1}{\partial y_1} & \dfrac{\partial x_2}{\partial y_1} \\ \dfrac{\partial x_1}{\partial y_2} & \dfrac{\partial x_2}{\partial y_2} \end{vmatrix} = \frac{\partial x_1}{\partial y_1}\frac{\partial x_2}{\partial y_2} - \frac{\partial x_1}{\partial y_2}\frac{\partial x_2}{\partial y_1}$$

which we express as a function $J = J(y_1, y_2)$. We assume that these partial derivatives are continuous and that J is finite on R.

† If $A \subseteq \mathbb{R}$ then $g^{-1}(A) = \{x \in \mathbb{R} : g(x) \in A\}$.

(3) **Theorem.** *If* $g:\mathbb{R}^2\to\mathbb{R}$, *and* T *maps the set* $A\subseteq D$ *onto the set* $B\subseteq R$ *then*

$$\iint_A g(x_1,x_2)\,dx_1\,dx_2=\iint_B g(x_1(y_1,y_2),x_2(y_1,y_2))\,|J(y_1,y_2)|\,dy_1\,dy_2.$$

(4) **Corollary.** *If* X_1, X_2 *have joint density function* f, *then the pair* Y_1, Y_2 *given by* $(Y_1,Y_2)=T(X_1,X_2)$ *has joint density function*

$$f_{Y_1,Y_2}(y_1,y_2)=\begin{cases} f(x_1(y_1,y_2),x_2(y_1,y_2))\,|J(y_1,y_2)| & \text{if } (y_1,y_2) \text{ is in the range of } T\\ 0 & \text{otherwise.}\end{cases}$$

A similar result holds for mappings of $\mathbb{R}^n$ into $\mathbb{R}^n$. This technique is sometimes referred to as the method of *change of variables*.

Proof of Corollary. Let $A\subseteq D$, $B\subseteq R$ be typical sets such that $T(A)=B$. Then $(X_1,X_2)\in A$ if and only if $(Y_1,Y_2)\in B$. Thus

$$\mathbf{P}((Y_1,Y_2)\in B)=\mathbf{P}((X_1,X_2)\in A)=\iint_A f(x_1,x_2)\,dx_1\,dx_2$$

$$=\iint_B f(x_1(y_1,y_2),x_2(y_1,y_2))\,|J(y_1,y_2)|\,dy_1\,dy_2$$

by (4.5.4) and (3). Compare this with the definition of the joint density function of Y_1 and Y_2,

$$\mathbf{P}((Y_1,Y_2)\in B)=\iint_B f_{Y_1,Y_2}(y_1,y_2)\,dy_1\,dy_2 \qquad \text{for suitable sets } B\subseteq\mathbb{R}^2,$$

to obtain the result. ■

(5) **Example.** Suppose that

$$X_1=aY_1+bY_2$$
$$X_2=cY_1+dY_2$$

and $ad-bc\neq 0$. Check that

$$f_{Y_1,Y_2}(y_1,y_2)=|ad-bc|\,f_{X_1,X_2}(ay_1+by_2,\,cy_1+dy_2).$$ ●

(6) **Example.** If X and Y have joint density function f, show that the density function of $U=XY$ is

$$f_U(u)=\int_{-\infty}^{\infty} f(x,u/x)\,|x|^{-1}\,dx.$$

Solution. Let T map (x, y) onto (u, v) by

$$u = xy, \qquad v = x.$$

The inverse T^{-1} maps (u, v) onto (x, y) by

$$x = v, \qquad y = u/v$$

and the Jacobian is

$$J(u, v) = \begin{vmatrix} \dfrac{\partial x}{\partial u} & \dfrac{\partial y}{\partial u} \\ \dfrac{\partial x}{\partial v} & \dfrac{\partial y}{\partial v} \end{vmatrix} = -v^{-1}.$$

Thus $f_{U,V}(u, v) = f(v, u/v)\,|v|^{-1}$. Integrate over v to obtain the result. ●

(7) **Example.** Let X_1 and X_2 be independent exponential variables, parameter λ. Find the joint density function of

$$Y_1 = X_1 + X_2, \qquad Y_2 = X_1/X_2$$

and show that they are independent.

Solution. Let T map (x_1, x_2) onto (y_1, y_2) by

$$y_1 = x_1 + x_2, \qquad y_2 = x_1/x_2, \qquad x_1, x_2, y_1, y_2 \geqslant 0.$$

The inverse T^{-1} maps (y_1, y_2) onto (x_1, x_2) by

$$x_1 = y_1 y_2/(1 + y_2), \qquad x_2 = y_1/(1 + y_2)$$

and the Jacobian is

$$J(y_1, y_2) = -y_1/(1 + y_2)^2,$$

giving

$$f_{Y_1,Y_2}(y_1, y_2) = f_{X_1,X_2}(y_1 y_2/(1 + y_2), y_1/(1 + y_2))\,|y_1|/(1 + y_2)^2.$$

However, X_1 and X_2 are independent and exponential, so that

$$\begin{aligned} f_{X_1,X_2}(x_1, x_2) &= f_{X_1}(x_1) f_{X_2}(x_2) \\ &= \lambda^2 \exp\{-\lambda(x_1 + x_2)\} \quad \text{if} \quad x_1, x_2 \geqslant 0. \end{aligned}$$

Thus

$$f_{Y_1,Y_2}(y_1, y_2) = \lambda^2 \exp(-\lambda y_1) y_1/(1 + y_2)^2 \quad \text{if} \quad y_1, y_2 \geqslant 0$$

is the joint density function of Y_1 and Y_2. However,

$$f_{Y_1,Y_2}(y_1, y_2) = \{\lambda^2 y_1 \exp(-\lambda y_1)\}(1 + y_2)^{-2}$$

factorizes as the product of a function of y_1 and a function of y_2; therefore, by Problem (4.10.6) they are independent. Suitable normalization of the functions in this product gives

$$f_{Y_1}(y_1) = \lambda^2 y_1 \exp(-\lambda y_1),$$
$$f_{Y_2}(y_2) = (1 + y_2)^{-2}.$$

●

(8) **Example.** Let X_1 and X_2 be given by the previous example and let

$$X = X_1, \qquad S = X_1 + X_2.$$

By (4), X and S have joint density function

$$f(x, s) = \lambda^2 e^{-\lambda s} \quad \text{if} \quad 0 \leq x \leq s.$$

This may look like the product of a function of x with a function of s, implying that X and S are independent; a glance at the domain of f shows this to be false. Suppose we know that $S = s$. What now is the conditional distribution of X, given $S = s$?

Solution.

$$\begin{aligned}\mathbf{P}(X \leq x \mid S = s) &= \int_{-\infty}^{x} f(u, s)\, du \Big/ \int_{-\infty}^{\infty} f(u, s)\, du \\ &= x\lambda^2 e^{-\lambda s}/(s\lambda^2 e^{-\lambda s}) \\ &= x/s \quad \text{if} \quad 0 \leq x \leq s.\end{aligned}$$

So, conditional on $S = s$, X is uniformly distributed on $[0, s]$. This result, and its later generalization, is of great interest to statisticians. ●

(9) **Example. Multivariate normal distribution.** This example is of even greater interest to statisticians. A *quadratic form* is a function $Q : \mathbb{R}^n \to \mathbb{R}$ of the form

(10) $$Q(\boldsymbol{x}) = \sum_{1 \leq i,j \leq n} a_{ij} x_i x_j = \boldsymbol{x}\mathbf{A}\boldsymbol{x}'$$

where $\boldsymbol{x} = (x_1, x_2, \ldots, x_n)$, $\boldsymbol{x}'$ is the transpose of $\boldsymbol{x}$, and $\mathbf{A} = (a_{ij})$ is a real symmetric matrix with non-zero determinant. A well-known theorem about diagonalizing matrices states that there exists an orthogonal matrix $\boldsymbol{B}$ such that

(11) $$\mathbf{A} = \boldsymbol{B}\boldsymbol{\Lambda}\boldsymbol{B}'$$

where $\boldsymbol{\Lambda}$ is the diagonal matrix with the eigenvalues $\lambda_1, \lambda_2, \ldots, \lambda_n$ of $\mathbf{A}$ on its diagonal. Substitute (11) into (10) to obtain

(12) $$Q(\boldsymbol{x}) = \boldsymbol{y}\boldsymbol{\Lambda}\boldsymbol{y}' = \sum_i \lambda_i y_i^2$$

where $\boldsymbol{y} = \boldsymbol{x}\boldsymbol{B}$. Q (respectively $\mathbf{A}$) is called a *positive definite quadratic form* (respectively *matrix*) if $Q(\boldsymbol{x}) > 0$ for all vectors $\boldsymbol{x}$ with some non-zero co-ordinate, and we write $Q > 0$ (respectively $\mathbf{A} > 0$) if this holds. From (12), $Q > 0$ if and only if $\lambda_i > 0$ for all i. This is all elementary matrix theory. We are concerned with the following question: when is the function $f : \mathbb{R}^n \to \mathbb{R}$ given by

$$f(\boldsymbol{x}) = K \exp(-\tfrac{1}{2}Q(\boldsymbol{x})), \qquad \boldsymbol{x} \in \mathbb{R}^n$$

the joint density function of some collection of n random variables? See

(4.5.9) for a hint about the reason for asking this question. It is necessary and sufficient that

(a) $f(\mathbf{x}) \geq 0$ for all $\mathbf{x} \in \mathbb{R}^n$

(b) $\int_{\mathbb{R}^n} f(\mathbf{x})\,\mathrm{d}\mathbf{x} = 1$

(this integral is shorthand for $\int \ldots \int f(x_1, \ldots, x_n)\,\mathrm{d}x_1 \ldots \mathrm{d}x_n$).

It is clear that (a) holds whenever $K > 0$. Next we investigate (b). First note that Q must be positive definite, since otherwise f has an infinite integral. If $Q > 0$,

$$\int_{\mathbb{R}^n} f(\mathbf{x})\,\mathrm{d}\mathbf{x} = \int_{\mathbb{R}^n} K \exp(-\tfrac{1}{2}Q(\mathbf{x}))\,\mathrm{d}\mathbf{x}$$

$$= \int_{\mathbb{R}^n} K \exp\left(-\tfrac{1}{2}\sum_i \lambda_i y_i^2\right)\mathrm{d}\mathbf{y}$$

by (3) and (12), since $|J| = 1$ for orthogonal transformations

$$= K \prod_i \int_{-\infty}^{\infty} \exp(-\tfrac{1}{2}\lambda_i y_i^2)\,\mathrm{d}y_i$$

$$= K\{(2\pi)^n/(\lambda_1\lambda_2 \ldots \lambda_n)\}^{1/2} = K\{(2\pi)^n/|\mathbf{A}|\}^{1/2}$$

where $|\mathbf{A}|$ denotes the determinant of $\mathbf{A}$. Hence (b) holds whenever $K = \{(2\pi)^{-n}\,|\mathbf{A}|\}^{1/2}$.

We have seen that

$$f(\mathbf{x}) = \{(2\pi)^{-n}\,|\mathbf{A}|\}^{1/2} \exp(-\tfrac{1}{2}\mathbf{x}\mathbf{A}\mathbf{x}'), \qquad \mathbf{x} \in \mathbb{R}^n$$

is a joint density function if and only if $\mathbf{A}$ is positive definite. Suppose that $\mathbf{A} > 0$ and that $\mathbf{X} = (X_1, \ldots, X_n)$ is a sequence of variables with density function f. It is easy to see that each X_i has zero mean; just note that

$$f(\mathbf{x}) = f(-\mathbf{x})$$

and so $(X_1, \ldots, X_n)$ and $(-X_1, \ldots, -X_n)$ are identically distributed random vectors; however, $\mathbf{E}|X_i| < \infty$ and so $\mathbf{E}(X_i) = \mathbf{E}(-X_i)$, giving $\mathbf{E}(X_i) = 0$. $\mathbf{X}$ is said to have the *multivariate normal distribution* with zero means. More generally, if $\mathbf{Y} = (Y_1, \ldots, Y_n)$ is given by

$$\mathbf{Y} = \mathbf{X} + \boldsymbol{\mu}$$

for some vector $\boldsymbol{\mu} = (\mu_1, \ldots, \mu_n)$ of constants, then $\mathbf{Y}$ is said to have the *multivariate normal distribution*.

(13) **Definition.** $\mathbf{X} = (X_1, \ldots, X_n)$ has the **multivariate normal distribution** (or **multinormal distribution**), written $N(\boldsymbol{\mu}, \mathbf{V})$, if its joint density function is

$$f(\mathbf{x}) = \{(2\pi)^n\,|\mathbf{V}|\}^{-1/2} \exp\{-\tfrac{1}{2}(\mathbf{x}-\boldsymbol{\mu})\mathbf{V}^{-1}(\mathbf{x}-\boldsymbol{\mu})'\}$$

where $\mathbf{V}$ is a positive definite symmetric matrix.

We have replaced $\mathbf{A}$ by $\mathbf{V}^{-1}$ in this definition. The reason for this is part (b) of the following theorem.

(14) **Theorem.** *If* $\mathbf{X}$ *is* $N(\boldsymbol{\mu}, \mathbf{V})$ *then*

(a) $\mathbf{E}(\mathbf{X}) = \boldsymbol{\mu}$, *which is to say that* $\mathbf{E}(X_i) = \mu_i$ *for all* i,
(b) $\mathbf{V} = (v_{ij})$ *is called the* ***covariance matrix***, *because* $v_{ij} = \text{cov}(X_i, X_j)$.

Proof. Part (a) follows by the argument before (13). We defer the proof of (b) until (5.8.6). ■

We often write

$$\mathbf{V} = \mathbf{E}((\mathbf{X} - \boldsymbol{\mu})'(\mathbf{X} - \boldsymbol{\mu}))$$

since $(\mathbf{X} - \boldsymbol{\mu})'(\mathbf{X} - \boldsymbol{\mu})$ is a matrix with (i, j)th entry $(X_i - \mu_i)(X_j - \mu_j)$.

A very important property of this distribution is its invariance of type under linear changes of variables.

(15) **Theorem.** *If* $\mathbf{X} = (X_1, X_2, \ldots, X_n)$ *is* $N(\mathbf{0}, \mathbf{V})$ *and* $\mathbf{Y} = (Y_1, Y_2, \ldots, Y_m)$ *is given by* $\mathbf{Y} = \mathbf{XD}$ *for some matrix* $\mathbf{D}$ *of rank* $m \leq n$, *then* $\mathbf{Y}$ *is* $N(\mathbf{0}, \mathbf{D}'\mathbf{V}\mathbf{D})$.

Proof when $m = n$. The mapping $T: \mathbf{x} \mapsto \mathbf{y} = \mathbf{xD}$ is non-singular and can be inverted as $T^{-1}: \mathbf{y} \mapsto \mathbf{x} = \mathbf{yD}^{-1}$. Use this change of variables in (3) to show that, if $A, B \subseteq \mathbb{R}^n$ and $B = T(A)$, then

$$\begin{aligned}\mathbf{P}(\mathbf{Y} \in B) &= \int_A f(\mathbf{x})\,\mathrm{d}\mathbf{x} = \int_A \{(2\pi)^n\,|\mathbf{V}|\}^{-1/2} \exp(-\tfrac{1}{2}\mathbf{x}\mathbf{V}^{-1}\mathbf{x}')\,\mathrm{d}\mathbf{x} \\ &= \int_B \{(2\pi)^n\,|\mathbf{W}|\}^{-1/2} \exp(-\tfrac{1}{2}\mathbf{y}\mathbf{W}^{-1}\mathbf{y}')\,\mathrm{d}\mathbf{y}\end{aligned}$$

where $\mathbf{W} = \mathbf{D}'\mathbf{V}\mathbf{D}$ as required. The proof for values of m strictly smaller than n is more difficult and is omitted (but see Kingman and Taylor 1966, p. 372). ■

A similar result holds for linear transformations of $N(\boldsymbol{\mu}, \mathbf{V})$ variables. ●

4.8 Sums of random variables

This section contains an important result which is a very simple application of the change of variable technique.

(1) **Theorem.** *If X and Y have joint density function f then $Z = X + Y$ has density function*

$$f_Z(z) = \int_{-\infty}^{\infty} f(x, z - x)\,\mathrm{d}x.$$

Proof. Let $A=\{(x, y): x+y\leqslant z\}$. Then

$$\mathbf{P}(Z\leqslant z)=\iint_A f(u, v)\,du\,dv=\int_{u=-\infty}^{\infty}\int_{v=-\infty}^{z-u} f(u, v)\,dv\,du$$

$$=\int_{x=-\infty}^{\infty}\int_{y=-\infty}^{z} f(x, y-x)\,dy\,dx$$

by the substitution $x=u$, $y=v+u$. Reverse the order of integration to obtain the result. ■

If X and Y are independent, the result becomes

$$f_{X+Y}(z)=\int_{-\infty}^{\infty} f_X(x)f_Y(z-x)\,dx=\int_{-\infty}^{\infty} f_X(z-y)f_Y(y)\,dy.$$

f_{X+Y} is called the *convolution* of f_X and f_Y, and is written

(2) $$f_{X+Y}=f_X * f_Y.$$

(3) **Example.** Let X and Y be independent $N(0, 1)$ variables. Then $Z=X+Y$ has density function

$$f_Z(z)=\frac{1}{2\pi}\int_{-\infty}^{\infty}\exp\{-\tfrac{1}{2}x^2-\tfrac{1}{2}(z-x)^2\}\,dx$$

$$=\frac{1}{2\sqrt{\pi}}\exp(-\tfrac{1}{4}z^2)\int_{-\infty}^{\infty}\frac{1}{\sqrt{(2\pi)}}\exp(-\tfrac{1}{2}v^2)\,dv$$

by the substitution $v=(x-\tfrac{1}{2}z)\sqrt{2}$. Therefore

$$f_Z(z)=\frac{1}{2\sqrt{\pi}}\exp(-\tfrac{1}{4}z^2)$$

showing that Z is $N(0, 2)$. More generally, if X is $N(\mu_1, \sigma_1^2)$ and Y is $N(\mu_2, \sigma_2^2)$, and X and Y are independent, then $Z=X+Y$ is $N(\mu_1+\mu_2, \sigma_1^2+\sigma_2^2)$. You should check this. ●

(4) **Example (4.6.3) revisited.** You must take great care in applying (1) when the domain of f depends on x and y. For example, in the notation of (4.6.3)

$$f_{X+Y}(z)=\int_A \frac{1}{x}\,dx, \qquad 0\leqslant z\leqslant 2,$$

where $A=\{x: 0\leqslant z-x\leqslant x\leqslant 1\}=[\tfrac{1}{2}z, \min\{z, 1\}]$. Thus

$$f_{X+Y}(z)=\begin{cases}\log 2 & 0\leqslant z\leqslant 1\\ \log(2/z) & 1\leqslant z\leqslant 2.\end{cases}$$ ●

4.9 Distributions arising from the normal distribution

This section contains some distributional results which have applications in statistics. The reader may omit it without prejudicing his understanding of the rest of the book.

Statisticians are frequently faced with a collection $X_1, X_2, \ldots, X_n$ of random variables arising from a sequence of experiments. They might be prepared to make a general assumption about the unknown distributions of these variables without specifying the numerical values of certain parameters. Commonly they might suppose that $X_1, \ldots, X_n$ is a collection of independent $N(\mu, \sigma^2)$ variables for some fixed but unknown values for μ and σ^2; this assumption is often a very close approximation to reality. They might then proceed to estimate the values of μ and σ^2 by using functions of $X_1, \ldots, X_n$. For reasons which are explained in statistics textbooks, they will commonly use the *sample mean*

$$\bar{X} = \frac{1}{n}\sum_1^n X_i$$

as a guess at the value of μ, and the *sample variance*†

$$S^2 = \frac{1}{n-1}\sum_1^n (X_i - \bar{X})^2$$

as a guess at the value of σ^2; these at least have the property that $\mathbf{E}(\bar{X}) = \mu$ and $\mathbf{E}(S^2) = \sigma^2$. The pair $\bar{X}$, S^2 are related in a striking and important way.

(1) **Theorem.** *If $X_1, X_2, \ldots$ are independent $N(\mu, \sigma^2)$ variables then $\bar{X}$ and S^2 are independent. $\bar{X}$ is $N(\mu, \sigma^2/n)$ and $(n-1)S^2/\sigma^2$ is $\chi^2(n-1)$.*

Remember (4.4.6) that $\chi^2(d)$ denotes the chi-squared distribution with d degrees of freedom.

Proof. Define $Y_i = (X_i - \mu)/\sigma$, and

$$\bar{Y} = \frac{1}{n}\sum_1^n Y_i = \frac{\bar{X} - \mu}{\sigma}.$$

From (4.4.5) Y_i is $N(0, 1)$, and clearly

$$\sum_1^n (Y_i - \bar{Y})^2 = (n-1)S^2/\sigma^2.$$

The joint density function of $Y_1, \ldots, Y_n$ is

$$f(\mathbf{y}) = (2\pi)^{-\frac{1}{2}n} \exp\left(-\tfrac{1}{2}\sum_1^n y_i^2\right).$$

f has spherical symmetry in the sense that if $\mathbf{A} = (a_{ij})$ is an orthogonal

† In some texts the sample variance is defined with n in place of $(n-1)$.

rotation of $\mathbb{R}^n$ so that

(2) $$Y_i = \sum_{j=1}^{n} Z_j a_{ji} \quad \text{and} \quad \sum_1^n Y_i^2 = \sum_1^n Z_i^2,$$

then $Z_1, Z_2, \ldots, Z_n$ are independent $N(0, 1)$ variables also. Now choose

(3) $$Z_1 = n^{-1/2} \sum_1^n Y_i = n^{1/2} \bar{Y}.$$

It is left to the reader to check that Z_1 is $N(0, 1)$. Then let $Z_2, \ldots, Z_n$ be any collection of variables such that (2) holds, where $\mathbf{A}$ is orthogonal. From (2) and (3)

(4) $$\sum_2^n Z_i^2 = \sum_1^n Y_i^2 - \frac{1}{n}\left(\sum_1^n Y_i\right)^2$$
$$= \sum_1^n Y_i^2 - \frac{2}{n} \sum_{i=1}^n \sum_{j=1}^n Y_i Y_j + \frac{1}{n^2} \sum_{i=1}^n \left(\sum_{j=1}^n Y_j\right)^2$$
$$= \sum_{i=1}^n \left(Y_i - \frac{1}{n} \sum_1^n Y_j\right)^2 = \frac{(n-1)S^2}{\sigma^2}.$$

Now, Z_1 is independent of $Z_2, \ldots, Z_n$, and so by (3) and (4), $\bar{Y}$ is independent of $(n-1)S^2/\sigma^2$. By (3) and (4.4.4), $\bar{Y}$ is $N(0, 1/n)$ and so $\bar{X}$ is $N(\mu, \sigma^2/n)$. Finally, $(n-1)S^2/\sigma^2$ is the sum of the squares of $n-1$ independent $N(0, 1)$ variables, and the result of Problem (4.10.10) completes the proof. ■

We may observe that σ is only a scaling factor for $\bar{X}$ and S $(=\sqrt{S^2})$. That is to say

$$U = \frac{n-1}{\sigma^2} S^2 \quad \text{is} \quad \chi^2(n-1)$$

which does not depend on σ, and

$$V = \frac{n^{1/2}}{\sigma} (\bar{X} - \mu) \quad \text{is} \quad N(0, 1)$$

which does not depend on σ. Hence the random variable

$$T = \frac{V}{\{U/(n-1)\}^{1/2}}$$

has a distribution which does not depend on σ. T is the ratio of two independent random variables, the numerator being $N(0, 1)$ and the denominator the square root of $(n-1)^{-1}$ times a $\chi^2(n-1)$ variable; T is said to have the *t-distribution* with $n-1$ degrees of freedom, written $t(n-1)$. It is sometimes called 'Student's t-distribution' in honour of a famous experimenter at the Guinness factory in Dublin. Let us calculate its density function. The joint density of U and V is

$$f(u, v) = \frac{(\frac{1}{2})^r e^{-\frac{1}{2}u} u^{\frac{1}{2}r-1}}{\Gamma(\frac{1}{2}r)} \frac{1}{\sqrt{(2\pi)}} \exp(-\tfrac{1}{2}v^2)$$

where $r=n-1$. Then map (u, v) onto (s, t) by

$$s=u, \qquad t=v(u/r)^{-1/2}.$$

Use (4.7.4) to obtain

$$f_{U,T}(s,t)=\left(\frac{s}{r}\right)^{1/2} f\left(s, t\left(\frac{s}{r}\right)^{1/2}\right)$$

and integrate over s to obtain

$$f_T(t)=\frac{\Gamma(\frac{1}{2}(r+1))}{(\pi r)^{1/2}\Gamma(\frac{1}{2}r)}\left(1+\frac{t^2}{r}\right)^{-\frac{1}{2}(r+1)} \qquad -\infty<t<\infty$$

as the density function of the $t(r)$ distribution.

Another important distribution in statistics is the F distribution which arises as follows. Let U and V be independent variables with the $\chi^2(r)$ and $\chi^2(s)$ distributions respectively. Then

$$F=\frac{U/r}{V/s}$$

is said to have the *F distribution* with r and s degrees of freedom, written $F(r, s)$. The following properties are obvious:

(a) F^{-1} is $F(s, r)$,
(b) T^2 is $F(1, r)$ if T is $t(r)$.

As an *exercise* in the techniques of Section 4.7, show that the density function of the $F(r, s)$ distribution is

$$f(x)=\frac{r\Gamma(\frac{1}{2}(r+s))}{s\Gamma(\frac{1}{2}r)\Gamma(\frac{1}{2}s)}\frac{(rx/s)^{\frac{1}{2}r-1}}{\{1+(rx/s)\}^{\frac{1}{2}(r+s)}}, \qquad x>0.$$

4.10 Problems

1. (a) Show that $\int_{-\infty}^{\infty}\exp(-x^2)\,dx=\sqrt{\pi}$, and deduce that

$$f(x)=\frac{1}{\sigma\sqrt{(2\pi)}}\exp\left\{-\frac{(x-\mu)^2}{2\sigma^2}\right\}, \qquad -\infty<x<\infty$$

is a density function.

(b) Calculate the mean and variance of a standard normal variable.

(c) Show that the $N(0, 1)$ distribution function Φ satisfies

$$(x^{-1}-x^{-3})\exp(-\tfrac{1}{2}x^2)<(2\pi)^{1/2}\{1-\Phi(x)\}<x^{-1}\exp(-\tfrac{1}{2}x^2), \qquad x>0.$$

These bounds are of interest because Φ has no closed form.

2. Let X be continuous with density function

$$f(x)=C(x-x^2) \qquad \alpha<x<\beta \qquad C>0.$$

(a) What are the possible values of α and β?
(b) What is C?

3. Let X be a random variable which takes non-negative values only. Let $A_i = \{i-1 \leqslant X < i\}$ and show that

$$\sum_1^\infty (i-1)I_{A_i} \leqslant X < \sum_1^\infty iI_{A_i}.$$

Deduce directly that

$$\sum_{i=1}^\infty \mathbf{P}(X \geqslant i) \leqslant \mathbf{E}(X) < 1 + \sum_{i=1}^\infty \mathbf{P}(X \geqslant i).$$

4. (a) Let X have a continuous distribution function F. Show that
   (i) $F(X)$ is uniformly distributed on $[0, 1]$,
   (ii) $-\log F(X)$ is exponentially distributed.

(b) A straight line ℓ touches a circle with unit diameter at the point P which is diametrically opposed on the circle to another point Q. A straight line QR joins Q to some point R on ℓ. If the angle $P\hat{Q}R$ between the lines PQ and QR is a random variable with the uniform distribution on $[-\pi/2, \pi/2]$, show that the length of PR has the Cauchy distribution (this length is measured positive or negative depending upon which side of P the point R lies).

5. Let X be exponential. Show that

$$\mathbf{P}(X > s + x \mid X > s) = \mathbf{P}(X > x), \qquad x, s \geqslant 0.$$

This is the 'lack of memory' property again. Show that the exponential distribution is the only continuous distribution with this property. You may need to use the fact that the only non-negative right-continuous solutions of the functional equation

$$g(s+t) = g(s)g(t), \qquad s, t \geqslant 0$$

with $g(0) = 1$, are of the form $g(s) = e^{\lambda s}$. Can you prove this?

6. Show that X and Y are independent continuous variables if and only if their joint density function f factorizes as the product $f(x, y) = g(x)h(y)$ of functions of the single variables x and y alone.

7. Let X and Y have joint density function

$$f(x, y) = 2e^{-x-y} \qquad 0 < x < y < \infty.$$

Are they independent? Find their marginal density functions and their covariance.

8. Let $X_1, X_2, \ldots, X_n$ be independent exponential variables, parameter λ. Show by induction that

$$S = X_1 + X_2 + \ldots + X_n$$

has the $\Gamma(\lambda, n)$ distribution.

9. Let X and Y be independent variables, $\Gamma(\lambda, m)$ and $\Gamma(\lambda, n)$ respectively.
   (a) Use the result of (8) to show that $X + Y$ is $\Gamma(\lambda, m+n)$ when m and n are integral.
   (b) Find the joint density function of $X + Y$ and $X/(X+Y)$ and deduce that they are independent.
   (c) If Z is Poisson with parameter λt and m is integral, show that

$$\mathbf{P}(Z < m) = \mathbf{P}(X > t).$$

10. Let $X_1, X_2, \ldots, X_n$ be independent $N(0, 1)$ variables. Show that $Z = X_1^2 + X_2^2$ is $\chi^2(2)$ by expressing its distribution function as an integral and changing to polar co-ordinates. More generally, show that $X_1^2 + X_2^2 + \ldots + X_n^2$ is $\chi^2(n)$.

11. Let X and Y have the bivariate normal distribution with means μ_1, μ_2, variances σ_1^2, σ_2^2, and correlation ρ (see (4.5.9)). Show that

(a) $\mathbf{E}(X \mid Y) = \mu_1 + \rho \dfrac{\sigma_1}{\sigma_2}(Y - \mu_2)$,

(b) the variance of the conditional density function $f_{X|Y}$ is

$$\operatorname{var}(X \mid Y) = \sigma_1^2(1 - \rho^2).$$

12. Let X and Y have joint density function f. Find the density function of Y/X.

13. Let X and Y be independent $N(0, 1)$ variables, and think of (X, Y) as a random point in the plane. Change to polar co-ordinates (R, Θ) given by

$$R^2 = X^2 + Y^2 \qquad \tan \Theta = Y/X;$$

show that R^2 is $\chi^2(2)$, $\tan \Theta$ has the Cauchy distribution, and R and Θ are independent. Find the density of R.

14. If X and Y are independent show that $U = \min\{X, Y\}$ and $V = \max\{X, Y\}$ have distribution functions

$$F_U(u) = 1 - \{1 - F_X(u)\}\{1 - F_Y(u)\}, \qquad F_V(v) = F_X(v)F_Y(v).$$

Let X and Y be independent exponential variables, parameter 1. Show that

(a) U is exponential, parameter 2,

(b) V has the same distribution as $X + \frac{1}{2}Y$. Hence find the mean and variance of V.

15. **Order statistics.** Let $X_1, X_2, \ldots, X_n$ be independent identically distributed variables with a common density function f. Such a collection is called a *random sample*. For each $\omega \in \Omega$, arrange the sample values $X_1(\omega), \ldots, X_n(\omega)$ in non-decreasing order $X_{(1)}(\omega) \leq X_{(2)}(\omega) \leq \ldots \leq X_{(n)}(\omega)$, where $(1), (2), \ldots, (n)$ is a permutation of $1, 2, \ldots, n$. The new variables $X_{(1)}, X_{(2)}, \ldots, X_{(n)}$ are called the *order statistics*. Show, by a symmetry argument, that the joint distribution function of $X_{(1)}, \ldots, X_{(n)}$ satisfies

$$\mathbf{P}(X_{(1)} \leq y_1, \ldots, X_{(n)} \leq y_n) = n!\,\mathbf{P}(X_1 \leq y_1, \ldots, X_n \leq y_n, X_1 < X_2 < \ldots < X_n)$$

$$= \int \cdots \int_{\substack{x_1 \leq y_1 \\ \vdots \\ x_n \leq y_n}} L(x_1, \ldots, x_n)\, n!\, f(x_1) \ldots f(x_n)\, dx_1 \ldots dx_n$$

where L is given by

$$L(x_1, \ldots, x_n) = \begin{cases} 1 & \text{if } x_1 < x_2 < \ldots < x_n \\ 0 & \text{otherwise.} \end{cases}$$

Compare with (4.5.2) to deduce that the joint density function of $X_{(1)}, \ldots, X_{(n)}$ is

$$g(y_1, \ldots, y_n) = n!\,L(y_1, \ldots, y_n) f(y_1) \ldots f(y_n).$$

16. Find the marginal density function of the kth order statistic $X_{(k)}$ of a sample size n

(a) by integrating the result of (15),

(b) directly.

17. Find the joint density function of the order statistics of n independent uniform variables on $[0, T]$.

18. Let X, Y be a pair of jointly continuous variables.
(a) **Hölder's inequality.** Show that if $p, q>1$ and $p^{-1}+q^{-1}=1$ then

$$\mathbf{E}|XY|\leq(\mathbf{E}|X^p|)^{1/p}(\mathbf{E}|Y^q|)^{1/q}.$$

Set $p=q=2$ to deduce the Cauchy–Schwarz inequality (4.5.12).
(b) **Minkowski's inequality.** Show that if $p\geq 1$ then

$$(\mathbf{E}(|X+Y|^p))^{1/p}\leq(\mathbf{E}|X^p|)^{1/p}+(\mathbf{E}|Y^p|)^{1/p}.$$

Note that in both cases your proofs do not depend on the continuity of X and Y; deduce that the same inequalities hold for discrete variables.

19. Let Z be a random variable with $\mathbf{E}|Z^p|<\infty$ for all $p\geq 0$. Choose X and Y appropriately in the Cauchy–Schwarz inequality to show that

$$g(p)=\log\mathbf{E}|Z^p|$$

is a convex function of p. Deduce that

$$(\mathbf{E}|Z^r|)^{1/r}\geq(\mathbf{E}|Z^s|)^{1/s}$$

whenever $r\geq s>0$. You have shown that if Z has finite rth moment then Z has finite sth moment for all positive $s\leq r$.

20. Show that, using the obvious notation,

$$\mathbf{E}(\mathbf{E}(X\mid Y, Z)\mid Y)=\mathbf{E}(X\mid Y).$$

21. Motor cars of unit length park randomly in a street in such a way that the centre of each car, in turn, is positioned uniformly at random in the available space. Let $m(x)$ be the expected number of cars which are able to park in a street of length x. Show that

$$m(x+1)=\frac{1}{x}\int_0^x(m(y)+m(x-y)+1)\,dy.$$

It is possible to deduce that $m(x)$ is about as big as $\frac{3}{4}x$ when x is large.

22. **Buffon's needle revisited (4.5.8).**
(a) The plane is ruled by the lines $y=nd$ $(n=0, \pm 1, \ldots)$ and the needle has length $L<d$. The problem is otherwise unchanged; show that the probability of an intersection is $2L/(\pi d)$.
(b) Now fix the needle and let C be a circle diameter d centred at the midpoint of the needle. Let λ be a line whose direction and distance from the centre of C are independently and uniformly distributed on $[0, 2\pi]$ and $[0, d/2]$ respectively. This is equivalent to 'casting the ruled plane at random'; show that the probability of an intersection between the needle and λ is $2L/(\pi d)$.
(c) Let S be a curve within C having finite length $L(S)$. Use indicators to show that the expected number of intersections between S and λ is $2L(S)/(\pi d)$.

This type of result is used in stereology, which seeks knowledge of the contents of a cell by studying its cross-sections.

5 Generating functions and their applications

5.1 Probability generating functions

Recall that the *generating function* of a sequence $\{a_i: i=0,1,2,\ldots\}$ of real numbers is the sum

(1) $$A(s)=\sum_i a_i s^i$$

where s is a real variable. Such sums have the following important properties.

(2) **Convergence.** There exists a *radius of convergence* $R \geqslant 0$ such that the sum converges absolutely if $|s|<R$ and diverges if $|s|>R$. The sum is uniformly convergent on sets like $\{|s| \leqslant R'\}$ for any $R'<R$.

(3) **Differentiation.** $A(s)$ can be differentiated or integrated term by term any number of times when $|s|<R$.

(4) **Abel's theorem.** If $a_i \geqslant 0$ for all i then

$$\lim_{s\uparrow 1} A(s)=\sum_i a_i$$

whether this sum is finite or equals $+\infty$.

(5) **Uniqueness.** If $R>0$ then the a_i are uniquely determined by knowledge of A, since $a_i=A^{(i)}(0)/i!$, where $A^{(i)}(s)$ is the ith derivative of $A(s)$.

Generating functions provide a simple way of handling certain properties of sequences of real numbers. Here are two examples.

(6) **An identity.** The combinatorial formula

$$\sum_i \binom{n}{i}^2=\binom{2n}{n}$$

is obtained directly by equating the coefficients of s^0 in the identity

$$(1+s)^n(1+s^{-1})^n=s^{-n}(1+s)^{2n}.$$

(7) **Convolution.** If $c_n=a_0b_n+a_1b_{n-1}+\ldots+a_nb_0$ for sequences $a=\{a_i\}$ and $b=\{b_i\}$, then their generating functions satisfy

$$\left(\sum c_i s^i\right)=\left(\sum a_i s^i\right)\left(\sum b_i s^i\right).$$

The sequence $c=\{c_i\}$ is called the *convolution* of a and b, written $c=a*b$ (see (3.8.2) and (4.8.2) also).

Now, suppose that X is a discrete random variable taking values in the non-negative integers $\{0,1,2,\ldots\}$. Its distribution is specified by the sequence of probabilities $f(i)=\mathbf{P}(X=i)$.

(8) **Definition.** The **(probability) generating function** of X is defined to be the generating function

$$G(s) = \mathbf{E}(s^X)$$

of its probability mass function.

Note that G does indeed generate the sequence $\{f(i)\}$ since

$$\mathbf{E}(s^X) = \sum_i s^i \mathbf{P}(X = i)$$

by (3.3.3). We write G_X when we wish to stress the role of X. Note that the series which defines G converges for $|s| \leq 1$.

(9) **Examples.** Here are some examples of generating functions.

(a) **Constant variables.** If $\mathbf{P}(X = c) = 1$ then $G(s) = \mathbf{E}(s^X) = s^c$.
(b) **Geometric distribution.** If X is geometrically distributed with parameter $\frac{1}{2}$ then

$$G(s) = \mathbf{E}(s^X) = \sum_{k=1}^{\infty} s^k (\tfrac{1}{2})^k = \frac{s}{(2-s)}.$$

(c) **Poisson distribution.** If X is Poisson distributed with parameter λ then

$$G(s) = \mathbf{E}(s^X) = \sum_{k=0}^{\infty} s^k \frac{\lambda^k}{k!} e^{-\lambda} = \exp\{\lambda(s-1)\}.$$ ●

G_X is defined only when X takes values in the non-negative integers. Later in this chapter we shall see how to construct another function, called a 'characteristic function', which is very closely related to G_X but which exists for all random variables regardless of their types.

It is a simple operation to calculate the moments of a distribution from knowledge of its generating function.

(10) **Theorem.** *If X has generating function $G(s)$ then*

(a) $G(1) = 1$ *and* $G(0) = \mathbf{P}(X = 0)$
(b) $\mathbf{E}(X) = G'(1)$
(c) *more generally,* $\mathbf{E}(X(X-1)\dots(X-k+1)) = G^{(k)}(1)$.

Of course, $G^{(k)}(1)$ is shorthand for $\lim_{s \uparrow 1} G^{(k)}(s)$ whenever the radius of convergence of G is 1.

Proof of (c). Take $s < 1$ and calculate the kth derivative of G to obtain

$$G^{(k)}(s) = \sum_i s^{i-k} i(i-1)\dots(i-k+1)f(i)$$
$$= \mathbf{E}(s^{X-k} X(X-1)\dots(X-k+1)).$$

Let $s \uparrow 1$ and use Abel's theorem (4) to obtain

$$G^{(k)}(s) \to \sum_i i(i-1)\ldots(i-k+1)f(i) = \mathbf{E}(X(X-1)\ldots(X-k+1)).$$ ■

To calculate the variance of X in terms of G, we proceed as follows:

(11)
$$\begin{aligned}\operatorname{var}(X) &= \mathbf{E}(X^2) - \mathbf{E}(X)^2 \\ &= \mathbf{E}(X(X-1)+X) - \mathbf{E}(X)^2 \\ &= \mathbf{E}(X(X-1)) + \mathbf{E}(X) - \mathbf{E}(X)^2 \\ &= G''(1) + G'(1) - G'(1)^2.\end{aligned}$$

Exercise. Find the means and variances of the distributions in (9) by this method.

(12) **Example.** Recall the hypergeometric distribution (3.9.10) with mass function

$$f(k) = \binom{b}{k}\binom{N-b}{n-k}\bigg/\binom{N}{n}.$$

Then $G(s) = \sum_k s^k f(k)$, which can be recognized as the coefficient of x^n in

$$Q(s, x) = (1+sx)^b(1+x)^{N-b}\bigg/\binom{N}{n}.$$

Hence the mean $G'(1)$ is the coefficient of x^n in

$$\frac{\partial Q}{\partial s}(1, x) = xb(1+x)^{N-1}\bigg/\binom{N}{n}$$

and so $G'(1) = bn/N$. Now calculate the variance yourself. ●

Much of probability theory is concerned with sums of random variables. To study such a sum we need a useful way of describing its distribution in terms of the distributions of its summands, and generating functions prove to be an invaluable asset in this respect. The formula (3.8.1) for the mass function of the sum of two independent discrete variables

$$\mathbf{P}(X+Y=u) = \sum_x \mathbf{P}(X=x)\mathbf{P}(Y=u-x)$$

involves a complicated calculation; the corresponding generating functions provide a more economical way of specifying the distribution of this sum.

(13) **Theorem.** *If X and Y are independent then*

$$G_{X+Y}(s) = G_X(s)G_Y(s).$$

Proof. $g(X) = s^X$ and $h(Y) = s^Y$ are independent by (3.2.3), and so $\mathbf{E}(g(X)h(Y)) = \mathbf{E}(g(X))\mathbf{E}(h(Y))$. ■

(14) **Example. Binomial distribution.** Let $X_1, X_2, \ldots, X_n$ be independent Bernoulli variables, parameter p, with sum $S = X_1 + \ldots + X_n$. Each X_i has generating function $G(s) = qs^0 + ps^1 = q + ps$. Apply (13) repeatedly to find that the $B(n, p)$ variable S has generating function

$$G_S(s) = \{G(s)\}^n = (q + ps)^n.$$

The sum $S_1 + S_2$ of two independent variables, $B(n, p)$ and $B(m, p)$ respectively, has generating function

$$G_{S_1+S_2}(s) = G_{S_1}(s)G_{S_2}(s) = (q + ps)^{m+n}$$

and is thus $B(m + n, p)$. This was Problem (3.9.8). You should do Problem (3.9.6a) again by this method (*exercise*). ●

Theorem (13) tells us that the sum

$$S = X_1 + X_2 + \ldots + X_n$$

of independent variables taking values in the non-negative integers has generating function given by

$$G_S = G_{X_1} G_{X_2} \ldots G_{X_n}.$$

If n is itself the outcome of a random experiment then the answer is not quite so simple.

(15) **Theorem.** *If $X_1, X_2, \ldots$ is a sequence of independent identically distributed variables with common generating function G_X, and N (≥ 1) is a random variable which is independent of the X's and has generating function G_N, then*

$$S = X_1 + X_2 + \ldots + X_N$$

has generating function given by

(16) $$G_S(s) = G_N(G_X(s)).$$

This has many important applications, one of which we shall meet in Section 5.4. It is an example of a process known as 'compounding' with respect to a parameter. Formula (16) is easily remembered; possible confusion about the order in which the functions G_N and G_X are compounded is avoided by remembering that if $\mathbf{P}(N = n) = 1$ then $G_N(s) = s^n$ and $G_S(s) = (G_X(s))^n$.

Proof. Use conditional expectation and (3.7.4) to find that

$$\begin{aligned} G_S(s) &= \mathbf{E}(s^S) = \mathbf{E}(\mathbf{E}(s^S \mid N)) \\ &= \sum_n \mathbf{E}(s^S \mid N = n)\mathbf{P}(N = n) \end{aligned}$$

$$= \sum_n \mathbf{E}(s^{X_1+\dots+X_n})\mathbf{P}(N=n)$$

$$= \sum_n \mathbf{E}(s^{X_1})\dots\mathbf{E}(s^{X_n})\mathbf{P}(N=n) \quad \text{by independence}$$

$$= \sum_n (G_X(s))^n\mathbf{P}(N=n) = G_N(G_X(s)). \qquad \blacksquare$$

(17) **Example (3.7.5) revisited.** A hen lays N eggs, where N is Poisson distributed with parameter λ. Each egg hatches with probability p, independently of all other eggs. Let K be the number of chicks. Then

$$K = X_1 + X_2 + \dots + X_N$$

where $X_1, X_2, \dots$ are independent Bernoulli variables with parameter p. How is K distributed? Clearly

$$G_N(s) = \sum_{n=0}^{\infty} s^n \frac{\lambda^n}{n!} e^{-\lambda} = \exp\{\lambda(s-1)\}$$

$$G_X(s) = q + ps$$

and so

$$G_K(s) = G_N(G_X(s)) = \exp\{\lambda p(s-1)\}$$

which, by comparison with G_N, we see to be the generating function of a Poisson variable with parameter λp. ●

Just as information about a mass function can be encapsulated in a generating function, so may joint mass functions be similarly described.

(18) **Definition.** The **joint (probability) generating function** of variables X_1 and X_2 taking values in the non-negative integers is defined by

$$G_{X_1,X_2}(s_1, s_2) = \mathbf{E}(s_1^{X_1} s_2^{X_2}).$$

There is a similar definition for the joint generating function of an arbitrary family of random variables. Joint generating functions also have important uses, one of which is the following characterization of independence.

(19) **Theorem.** *X_1 and X_2 are independent if and only if*

$$G_{X_1,X_2}(s_1, s_2) = G_{X_1}(s_1)G_{X_2}(s_2) \quad \textit{for all } s_1 \textit{ and } s_2.$$

Proof. If X_1 and X_2 are independent then so are $g(X_1) = s_1^{X_1}$ and $h(X_2) = s_2^{X_2}$; then proceed as in the proof of (13). To prove the converse, equate the coefficients of terms like $s_1^i s_2^j$ to deduce after some manipulation that

$$\mathbf{P}(X_1 = i, X_2 = j) = \mathbf{P}(X_1 = i)\mathbf{P}(X_2 = j). \qquad \blacksquare$$

So far we have only considered random variables X which always take finite values, and consequently their generating functions G_X satisfy $G_X(1)=1$. In the near future we shall encounter variables which can take the value $+\infty$ (see the first passage time T_{00} of Section 5.3 for example). For such variables X we note that $G_X(s)=\mathbf{E}(s^X)$ converges so long as $|s|<1$, and

(20) $$\lim_{s\uparrow 1} G_X(s)=\sum_k \mathbf{P}(X=k)=1-\mathbf{P}(X=\infty).$$

We can no longer find the moments of X in terms of G_X; of course, they all equal $+\infty$. If $\mathbf{P}(X=\infty)>0$ then we say that X is 'defective' with defective distribution function F_X.

5.2 Simple random walk

At any instant of time a particle inhabits one of the integer points of the real line. At time 0 it starts from some specified point, and at each subsequent epoch of time $1, 2, \ldots$ it moves from its current position to a new position according to the following law. With probability p it moves one step to the right and with probability $q=1-p$ it moves one step to the left; moves are independent of each other. The walk is called *symmetric* if $p=q=\frac{1}{2}$. Example (1.7.4) was of a symmetric random walk with 'absorbing' barriers at the points 0 and N. In general, let S_n denote the position of the particle after n moves, and set $S_0=a$. Then

(1) $$S_n=a+\sum_1^n X_i$$

where $X_1, X_2, \ldots$ is a sequence of independent Bernoulli variables taking values $+1$ and -1 (rather than $+1$ and 0 as before) with probabilities p and q.

We record the motion of the particle as the sequence $\{(n, S_n): n\geq 0\}$ of cartesian coordinates of points in the plane. This collection of points, joined by solid lines between neighbours, is called the *path* of the

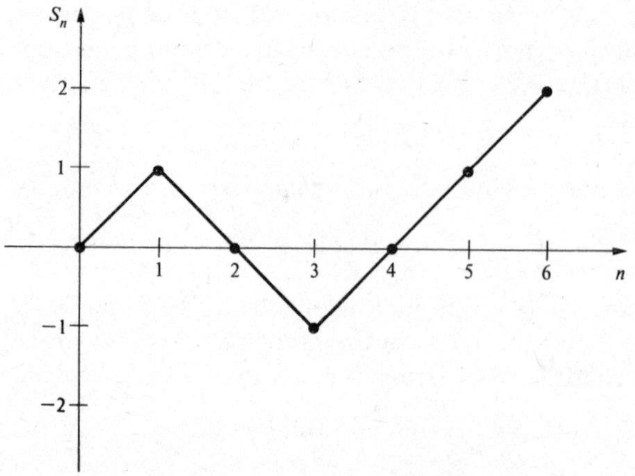

FIG. 5.1 A random walk S_n.

particle. In the example shown in Figure 5.1, the particle has visited the points 0, 1, 0, −1, 0, 1, 2 in succession. This representation has a confusing aspect in that the direction of the particle's steps is parallel to the y-axis, whereas we have previously been specifying the movement in the traditional way as to the right or to the left. In future, any reference to the x-axis or the y-axis will pertain to a diagram of its path as exemplified by Figure 5.1.

The sequence (1) of partial sums has three important properties.

(2) **Lemma.** *The simple random walk is* ***spatially homogeneous****; that is*

$$\mathbf{P}(S_n = j \mid S_0 = a) = \mathbf{P}(S_n = j + b \mid S_0 = a + b).$$

Proof. Both sides equal $\mathbf{P}(\sum_1^n X_i = j - a)$. ■

(3) **Lemma.** *The simple random walk is* ***temporally homogeneous****; that is*

$$\mathbf{P}(S_n = j \mid S_0 = a) = \mathbf{P}(S_{n+m} = j \mid S_m = a).$$

Proof. The left- and right-hand sides satisfy

$$\text{LHS} = \mathbf{P}\left(\sum_1^n X_i = j - a\right) = \mathbf{P}\left(\sum_{m+1}^{m+n} X_i = j - a\right) = \text{RHS}. \quad ■$$

(4) **Lemma.** *The simple random walk has the* ***Markov property****; that is*

$$\mathbf{P}(S_{n+m} = j \mid S_0, S_1, \ldots, S_n) = \mathbf{P}(S_{n+m} = j \mid S_n).$$

Statements like $\mathbf{P}(S = j \mid X, Y) = \mathbf{P}(S = j \mid X)$ are to be interpreted in the obvious way as meaning

$$\mathbf{P}(S = j \mid X = x, Y = y) = \mathbf{P}(S = j \mid X = x) \quad \text{for all } x \text{ and } y.$$

Proof.

$$\begin{aligned}
\mathbf{P}(S_{n+m} &= j \mid S_0, S_1, \ldots, S_{n-1}, \text{ and } S_n = a) \\
&= \mathbf{P}\left(\sum_{n+1}^{n+m} X_i = j - a\right) \\
&= \mathbf{P}\left(\sum_{n+1}^{n+m} X_i = j - a \mid S_n = a\right) \\
&= \mathbf{P}(S_{n+m} = j \mid S_n = a). \quad ■
\end{aligned}$$

This 'Markov property' is often expressed approximately by saying that, conditional upon knowing the value of the process at the nth step, its values *after* the nth step do not depend on its values *before* the nth step, or more colloquially, conditional upon the present, the future does not depend on the past.

(5) **Absorbing barriers.** Let us revisit (1.7.4) for general values of p. Equation (1.7.5) gives us the following difference equation for the probabilities $\{p_k\}$ where p_k is the probability of ultimate ruin starting from k:

(6) $$p_k = pp_{k+1} + qp_{k-1} \quad \text{if} \quad 1 \leqslant k \leqslant N-1$$

with boundary conditions $p_0 = 1$, $p_N = 0$. the solution of such a difference equation proceeds as follows. Look for a solution of the form $p_k = \theta^k$. Substitute this into (6) and cancel out the power θ^{k-1} to obtain

$$p\theta^2 - \theta + q = 0$$

which has roots $\theta_1 = 1$, $\theta_2 = q/p$. If $p \neq \frac{1}{2}$ then these roots are distinct and the general solution of (6) is

$$p_k = A_1\theta_1^k + A_2\theta_2^k$$

for arbitrary constants A_1 and A_2. Use the boundary conditions to obtain

$$p_k = \frac{(q/p)^k - (q/p)^N}{1-(q/p)^N}.$$

If $p = \frac{1}{2}$ then $\theta_1 = \theta_2$ and the general solution to (6) is

$$p_k = (A_1 + A_2k)\theta_1^k.$$

Use the boundary conditions to obtain

$$p_k = 1 - \frac{k}{N}.$$

A more complicated equation is obtained for the mean number D_k of steps before the particle hits one of the absorbing barriers, starting from k. In this case we use conditional expectations and (3.7.4) to find that

(7) $$D_k = p(1 + D_{k+1}) + q(1 + D_{k-1}) \quad \text{if} \quad 1 \leqslant k \leqslant N-1$$

with the boundary conditions $D_0 = D_N = 0$. Try solving this; you need to find a general solution and a particular solution, as in the solution of second-order linear differential equations. ●

(8) **Reflecting barriers.** In (1.7.4), suppose that the Jaguar buyer has a rich uncle who will guarantee all his losses. Then the random walk does not end when the particle hits zero, although it cannot visit a negative integer. Instead

$$\mathbf{P}(S_{n+1} = 0 \mid S_n = 0) = q, \quad \mathbf{P}(S_{n+1} = 1 \mid S_n = 0) = p.$$

The origin is said to have a 'reflecting' barrier. ●

In such examples the techniques of 'conditioning' are supremely useful. The idea is that in order to calculate a probability $\mathbf{P}(A)$ or expectation $\mathbf{E}(Y)$ we condition either on some partition of Ω (and use (1.4.4)) or on the outcome of some random variable (and use (3.7.4) or (4.6.5)). In this section this technique yielded (6) and (7). In later sections the same idea will yield differential equations, integral equations, and functional equations, some of which can be solved.

5.3 First passage times and the reflection principle

Consider the simple random walk starting at the origin. Natural questions of interest concern the sequence of random times at which the particle subsequently returns to the origin. To describe this sequence we need only find the distribution of the time until the particle returns for the first time, since subsequent times between consecutive visits to the origin are independent copies of this.

Let $p_0(n)=\mathbf{P}(S_n=0)$ be the probability of being at the origin after n steps, and let $f_0(n)=\mathbf{P}(S_1\neq 0,\ldots,S_{n-1}\neq 0, S_n=0)$ be the probability that the first return occurs after n steps. Denote the generating functions of these sequences by

$$P_0(s)=\sum_0^\infty p_0(n)s^n \qquad F_0(s)=\sum_1^\infty f_0(n)s^n.$$

F_0 is the probability generating function of the random time T_{00} until the particle makes its first return to the origin. That is

$$F_0(s)=\mathbf{E}(s^{T_{00}}).$$

Take care here; T_{00} may be defective and (5.1.20) may apply.

(1) **Theorem.**

(a) $P_0(s)=1+P_0(s)F_0(s)$
(b) $P_0(s)=(1-4pqs^2)^{-1/2}$
(c) $F_0(s)=1-(1-4pqs^2)^{1/2}$.

Proof. (a) Let A be the event that $S_n=0$, and let B_k be the event that the first return to the origin happens at the kth step. Clearly the B_k's are disjoint and so, by (1.4.4),

$$\mathbf{P}(A)=\sum_1^n \mathbf{P}(A\mid B_k)\mathbf{P}(B_k).$$

However, $\mathbf{P}(B_k)=f_0(k)$ and

$$\mathbf{P}(A\mid B_k)=p_0(n-k) \quad \text{by temporal homogeneity (5.2.3),}$$

giving

(2) $$p_0(n)=\sum_{k=1}^n p_0(n-k)f_0(k) \quad \text{if} \quad n\geq 1.$$

Multiply (2) by s^n, sum over n remembering that $p_0(0)=1$, and use (5.1.7) to obtain

$$P_0(s)=1+P_0(s)F_0(s).$$

(b) $S_n=0$ if and only if the particle takes equal numbers of steps to the left and to the right during its first n steps. The number of ways in which it can do this is $\binom{n}{\frac{1}{2}n}$ and each such way occurs with probability $(pq)^{n/2}$, giving

(3) $$p_0(n)=\binom{n}{\frac{1}{2}n}(pq)^{n/2}.$$

Of course $p_0(n)=0$ if n is odd. This sequence (3) has generating function

$$P_0(s)=(1-4pqs^2)^{-1/2}.$$

(c) This follows immediately from (a) and (b). ■

(4) **Corollary.** (a) *The probability that the particle ever returns to the origin is*

$$\sum_1^{\infty} f_0(n)=F_0(1)=1-|p-q|.$$

(b) *If eventual return is certain, that is* $F_0(1)=1$ *and* $p=\frac{1}{2}$, *then the expected time to the first return is*

$$\sum_1^{\infty} nf_0(n)=F_0'(1)=\infty.$$

We call the process *persistent* (or *recurrent*) if eventual return to the origin is certain; otherwise it is called *transient*. It is immediately obvious from (4a) that the process is persistent if and only if $p=\frac{1}{2}$. This is consistent with our intuition, which suggests that if $p>\frac{1}{2}$ or $p<\frac{1}{2}$, then the particle tends to stray a long way to the right or to the left of the origin respectively. Even when $p=\frac{1}{2}$ the time until first return has infinite mean.

Proof. (a) Let $s\uparrow 1$ in (1c), and remember (5.1.20).

(b) Eventual return is certain if and only if $p=\frac{1}{2}$. But then the generating function of the time T_{00} to the first return is $F_0(s)=1-(1-s^2)^{1/2}$ and

$$\mathbf{E}(T_{00})=\lim_{s\uparrow 1} F_0'(s)=\infty.$$ ■

Now let us consider the times of visits to the point r. Define $f_r(n)=\mathbf{P}(S_1\neq r,\ldots,S_{n-1}\neq r, S_n=r)$ to be the probability that the first such visit occurs at the nth step, with generating function

$$F_r(s)=\sum_1^{\infty} f_r(n)s^n.$$

(5) **Theorem.** (a) $F_r(s)=\{F_1(s)\}^r$ *if* $r\geq 1$.

(b) $F_1(s)=\{1-(1-4pqs^2)^{1/2}\}/(2qs)$.

Proof. (a) The same argument which yields (2) also shows that

$$f_r(n)=\sum_{k=1}^{n-1} f_{r-1}(n-k)f_1(k) \quad \text{if} \quad r>1.$$

Multiply by s^n and sum over n to obtain

$$F_r(s) = F_{r-1}(s)F_1(s) = \{F_1(s)\}^r.$$

We could have written this out in terms of random variables instead of probabilities, and then used (5.1.13). For, let $T_{0r} = \min\{n : S_n = r\}$ be the number of steps taken before the particle reaches r for the first time (T_{0r} may equal $+\infty$ if $r>0$ and $p<\frac{1}{2}$ or if $r<0$ and $p>\frac{1}{2}$). In order to visit r, the particle must first visit the point 1; this requires T_{01} steps. After visiting 1 the particle requires a further number, T_{1r} say, of steps to reach r; T_{1r} is distributed like $T_{0,r-1}$ by the spatial homogeneity (5.2.2). Thus

$$T_{0r} = \begin{cases} \infty & \text{if} \quad T_{01} = \infty \\ T_{01} + T_{1r} & \text{if} \quad T_{01} < \infty, \end{cases}$$

and the result follows from (5.1.13). Some difficulties arise from the possibility that $T_{01} = \infty$, but these are resolved fairly easily (*exercise*).

(b) Condition on X_1 to obtain, for $n>1$,

$$\begin{aligned} \mathbf{P}(T_{01} = n) &= \mathbf{P}(T_{01} = n \mid X_1 = 1)p + \mathbf{P}(T_{01} = n \mid X_1 = -1)q \\ &= 0 \,.\, p + \mathbf{P}(\text{first visit to 1 takes } n-1 \text{ steps} \mid S_0 = -1) \,.\, q \\ &\qquad\qquad \text{by temporal homogeneity} \\ &= \mathbf{P}(T_{02} = n-1)q \quad \text{by spatial homogeneity} \\ &= qf_2(n-1). \end{aligned}$$

Therefore $f_1(n) = qf_2(n-1)$ if $n>1$, and $f_1(1) = p$. Multiply by s^n and sum to obtain

$$F_1(s) = ps + qsF_2(s) = ps + qs\{F_1(s)\}^2$$

by (a). Solve this quadratic to find its two roots. Only one can be a probability generating function; why? (Hint: $F_1(0) = 0$.) ■

(6) **Corollary.** *The probability that the walk ever visits the positive part of the real axis is*

$$F_1(1) = (1 - |p-q|)/(2q).$$

Knowledge of Theorem (5) enables us to calculate $F_0(s)$ directly without recourse to (1). The method of doing this relies upon a symmetry within the collection of paths which may be followed by a random walk. Condition on the value of X_1 as usual to obtain

$$f_0(n) = qf_1(n-1) + pf_{-1}(n-1)$$

and thus

$$F_0(s) = qsF_1(s) + psF_{-1}(s).$$

We need to find $F_{-1}(s)$. Consider any possible path π that the particle may have taken to arrive at the point -1 and replace each step in the path by its mirror image, positive steps becoming negative and negative becoming positive, to obtain a path π^* which ends at $+1$. This operation of reflection provides a one–one correspondence between the collection of paths ending at -1 and the collection of paths ending at $+1$. If $\mathbf{P}(\pi; p, q)$ is the probability that the particle follows π when each step is to the right with probability p, then $\mathbf{P}(\pi; p, q) = \mathbf{P}(\pi^*; q, p)$; thus

$$F_{-1}(s) = \{1-(1-4pqs^2)^{1/2}\}/(2ps),$$

giving that $F_0(s) = 1-(1-4pqs^2)^{1/2}$ as before. This principle of reflection will be most useful when the walk is symmetric, so that $p = q = \frac{1}{2}$. Its usual formulation is in terms of the path $\{(n, S_n): n \geq 0\}$ of the random walk. Suppose we know that $S_0 = a$ and $S_n = b$. The random walk may or may not have visited the origin in between times 0 and n. Let $N_n(a, b)$ be the number of possible paths from $(0, a)$ to (n, b), and let $N_n^0(a, b)$ be the number of such paths which contain some point $(k, 0)$ on the x-axis.

(7) **Theorem. The reflection principle.** *If* $a, b > 0$ *then*

$$N_n^0(a, b) = N_n(-a, b).$$

Proof. Each path from $(0, -a)$ to (n, b) intersects the x-axis at some earliest point $(k, 0)$. Reflect the segment of the path with $0 \leq x \leq k$ in the x-axis to obtain a path joining $(0, a)$ to (n, b) which intersects the x-axis (see Figure 5.2). This operation gives a one–one correspondence between the collections of such paths, and the theorem is proved. ■

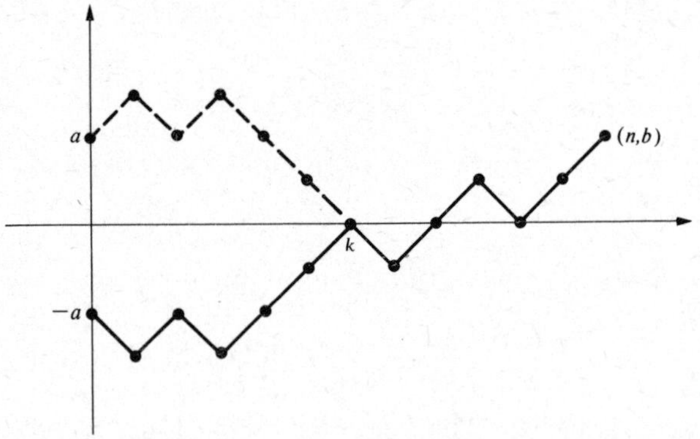

FIG. 5.2 A random walk; the dashed line is the reflection of the first segment of the walk.

(8) **Lemma.** $N_n(a, b) = \binom{n}{\frac{1}{2}(n+b-a)}$.

Proof. Choose a path from $(0, a)$ to (n, b) and let α and β be the number of positive and negative steps, respectively, in this path. Then

$$\alpha + \beta = n \quad \text{and} \quad \alpha - \beta = b - a$$

so that $\alpha = \frac{1}{2}(n+b-a)$. The number of such paths is the number of ways of picking α positive steps from the n available. That is

$$N_n(a,b)=\binom{n}{\alpha}=\binom{n}{\frac{1}{2}(n+b-a)}. \qquad \blacksquare$$

(9) **Corollary.** *If $b>0$ then the number of paths from $(0,0)$ to (n,b) which do not revisit the x-axis equals*

$$\binom{n-1}{\frac{1}{2}(n+b-2)}-\binom{n-1}{\frac{1}{2}(n+b)}.$$

Proof. The first step of all such paths is to $(1,1)$, and so the number of such paths is

$$N_{n-1}(1,b)-N^0_{n-1}(1,b)=N_{n-1}(1,b)-N_{n-1}(-1,b)$$

and the answer follows from (8). $\blacksquare$

We now return to the symmetric random walk, and a remarkable equality dealing with the probability $\mathbf{P}(S_1\neq 0,\ldots,S_{2n}\neq 0)$ (or $\mathbf{P}(S_1S_2\ldots S_{2n}\neq 0)$) that the walk does not revisit its starting point in the first $2n$ steps.

(10) **Theorem.** *If $p=\frac{1}{2}$ and $S_0=0$ then*

$$\mathbf{P}(S_1S_2\ldots S_{2n}\neq 0)=\mathbf{P}(S_{2n}=0)=\binom{2n}{n}\left(\frac{1}{2}\right)^{2n}.$$

That is to say the probability that no return to the origin occurs in the first $2n$ steps is the same as the probability of returning at the $2n$th step.

Proof. The walk must have some value at the $2n$th step, and by symmetry $\mathbf{P}(S_{2n}=r)=\mathbf{P}(S_{2n}=-r)$. Thus

$$\mathbf{P}(S_1S_2\ldots S_{2n}\neq 0)=2\sum_{r=1}^{n}\mathbf{P}(S_1>0,S_2>0,\ldots,S_{2n-1}>0,S_{2n}=2r).$$

However, all paths with $2n$ steps are equally likely, and so by (9)

$$\begin{aligned}\mathbf{P}(S_1S_2\ldots S_{2n}\neq 0)&=2\left(\frac{1}{2}\right)^{2n}\sum_{r=1}^{n}\left(\binom{2n-1}{n+r-1}-\binom{2n-1}{n+r}\right)\\&=2\left(\frac{1}{2}\right)^{2n}\binom{2n-1}{n}=\binom{2n}{n}\left(\frac{1}{2}\right)^{2n}.\end{aligned}$$

By (3), this is the value of $\mathbf{P}(S_{2n}=0)$ also. $\blacksquare$

Finally, here is another extraordinary result. It is obtained by using a one–one correspondence between certain families of paths; this can be thought of as a cumulative reflection in both the x-axis and the y-axis.

If the first n steps of the original random walk are

$$\{0, S_1, S_2, \ldots, S_n\} = \left\{0, X_1, X_1 + X_2, \ldots, \sum_1^n X_i\right\}$$

then the steps of the *reversed* walk, denoted by $0, T_1, \ldots, T_n$, are given by

$$\{0, T_1, T_2, \ldots, T_n\} = \left\{0, X_n, X_n + X_{n-1}, \ldots, \sum_1^n X_i\right\}.$$

Draw a diagram to see how the two walks correspond to each other. The X's are independent and identically distributed, and it follows that the two walks have identical distributions even if $p \neq \frac{1}{2}$. Notice that the addition of an extra step to the original walk changes *every* step of the reversed walk.

(11) **Theorem.** *If* $p = \frac{1}{2}$, $S_0 = 0$ *and* r *is any non-zero integer, then the expected number of visits which the walk makes to the point* r *before returning to the origin equals* 1.

Proof. Let I_n be the indicator function of the event $\{S_1 > 0, S_2 > 0, \ldots, S_{n-1} > 0, S_n = r\}$ that the walk visits $r(>0)$ on the nth step but has not yet revisited the origin. The mean number of such visits is

$$\mathbf{E}\left(\sum_{n=1}^{\infty} I_n\right) = \sum_{n=1}^{\infty} \mathbf{P}(S_1 > 0, S_2 > 0, \ldots, S_{n-1} > 0, S_n = r).$$

Draw another diagram of the reversed walk to see that

$$\begin{aligned}
&\mathbf{P}(S_1 > 0, S_2 > 0, \ldots, S_{n-1} > 0, S_n = r)\\
&\quad = \mathbf{P}(T_1 > 0, T_2 > 0, \ldots, T_{n-1} > 0, T_n = r)\\
&\quad = \mathbf{P}(S_1 < r, S_2 < r, \ldots, S_{n-1} < r, S_n = r) \qquad \text{by reversal}\\
&\quad = f_r(n).
\end{aligned}$$

Deduce that the mean number of visits in question is

$$\begin{aligned}
\sum_{n=1}^{\infty} f_r(n) &= F_r(1)\\
&= (F_1(1))^r \qquad \text{by (5).}
\end{aligned}$$

This holds for any p and $r > 0$. If $p = \frac{1}{2}$ then $F_1(1) = 1$; the result holds for $r < 0$ also, by symmetry. ■

These last results can also be proved by routine enumerations and considerable industry. They are only a small selection of the available results about random walks, which have been chosen to illustrate the idea of reflection. We shall use similar ideas when we study the theory of queues.

5.4 Branching processes

Besides gambling, many probabilists have been interested in reproduction. Accurate models for the evolution of a population are notoriously difficult to handle, but there are simpler non-trivial models which are both tractable and mathematically interesting. The branching process is such a model. Suppose that a population evolves in generations, and let Z_n be the number of members of the nth generation. Each member of the nth generation gives birth to a family, possibly empty, of members of the $(n+1)$th generation; the size of this family is a random variable. We shall make the following assumptions about these family sizes:

(a) the family sizes of the individuals of the branching process form a collection of independent random variables;
(b) all family sizes have the same probability mass function f and generating function G.

These assumptions, together with information about the distribution of the number Z_0 of founding members, specify the random evolution of the process. We assume here that $Z_0 = 1$. There is nothing notably human about this model, which may be just as suitable a description for the growth of a population of cells, or for the increase of neutrons in a reactor, or for the spread of an epidemic in some population.

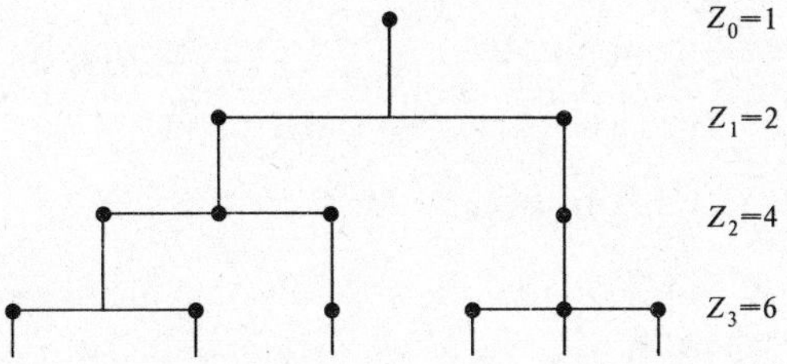

FIG. 5.3 The family tree of a branching process.

We are interested in the random sequence $Z_0, Z_1, \ldots$ of generation sizes. Let $G_n(s) = \mathbf{E}(s^{Z_n})$ be the generating function of Z_n.

(1) **Theorem.** *$G_{m+n}(s) = G_m(G_n(s))$, and thus $G_n(s) = G(G(\ldots(G(s))\ldots))$ is the n-fold iterate of G.*

Proof. Each member of the $(m+n)$th generation has a unique ancestor in the mth generation. Thus

$$Z_{m+n} = X_1 + X_2 + \ldots + X_{Z_m}$$

where X_i is the number of members of the $(m+n)$th generation which stem from the ith member of the mth generation. This is the sum of a random number Z_m of variables. These variables are independent by assumption (a); furthermore, by assumption (b) they are identically distributed with the same distribution as the number Z_n of nth-generation offspring of the first individual in the process. Now use (5.1.15) to obtain $G_{m+n}(s)=G_m(G_{X_1}(s))$ where $G_{X_1}(s)=G_n(s)$. Iterate this relation to obtain

$$G_n(s)=G_1(G_{n-1}(s))=G_1(G_1(G_{n-2}(s)))=G_1(G_1(\ldots(G_1(s))\ldots))$$

and notice that $G_1(s)$ is what we called $G(s)$. ■

In principle, (1) tells us all about Z_n and its distribution, but in practice $G_n(s)$ may be hard to evaluate. The moments of Z_n, at least, may be routinely computed in terms of the moments of a typical family size Z_1. For example:

(2) **Lemma.** *Let* $\mu=\mathbf{E}(Z_1)$, $\sigma^2=\operatorname{var}(Z_1)$. *Then*

$$\mathbf{E}(Z_n)=\mu^n$$

$$\operatorname{var}(Z_n)=\begin{cases} n\sigma^2 & \text{if } \mu=1 \\ \sigma^2(\mu^n-1)\mu^{n-1}(\mu-1)^{-1} & \text{if } \mu\neq 1. \end{cases}$$

Proof. Differentiate $G_n(s)=G(G_{n-1}(s))$ once at $s=1$ to obtain

$$\mathbf{E}(Z_n)=\mu\mathbf{E}(Z_{n-1})$$

and iterate to obtain $\mathbf{E}(Z_n)=\mu^n$. Differentiate twice to obtain

$$G_n''(1)=G''(1)(G_{n-1}'(1))^2+G'(1)G_{n-1}''(1)$$

and use (5.1.11) to obtain the second result. ■

(3) **Example.** Suppose that each family size has the mass function $f(k)=qp^k$ $(k\geq 0)$ where $q=1-p$. Then $G(s)=q(1-ps)^{-1}$, and each family size is one member less than a geometric variable. We can show by induction that

$$G_n(s)=\begin{cases} \dfrac{n-(n-1)s}{n+1-ns} & \text{if } p=q=\tfrac{1}{2} \\[2ex] \dfrac{q(p^n-q^n-ps(p^{n-1}-q^{n-1}))}{p^{n+1}-q^{n+1}-ps(p^n-q^n)} & \text{if } p\neq q. \end{cases}$$

This result can be useful in providing inequalities for more general distributions. What can we say about the behaviour of this process after many generations? In particular, does it eventually become extinct, or, conversely, do all generations have non-zero size? For this example, we can answer this question from a position of strength since we know all about $G_n(s)$. In fact

$$\mathbf{P}(Z_n=0)=G_n(0)=\begin{cases} \dfrac{n}{n+1} & \text{if } p=q \\[2ex] \dfrac{q(p^n-q^n)}{p^{n+1}-q^{n+1}} & \text{if } p\neq q. \end{cases}$$

Let $n \to \infty$ to obtain

$$\mathbf{P}(Z_n = 0) \to \mathbf{P}(\text{ultimate extinction}) = \begin{cases} 1 & \text{if} \quad p \leqslant q \\ q/p & \text{if} \quad p > q. \end{cases}$$

We have used (1.3.5) here surreptitiously, since

(4) $$\{\text{ultimate extinction}\} = \bigcup_n \{Z_n = 0\}$$

and $A_n = \{Z_n = 0\}$ satisfies $A_n \subseteq A_{n+1}$. ●

We saw in this example that extinction is certain if and only if $\mu = \mathbf{E}(Z_1) = p/q$ satisfies $\mathbf{E}(Z_1) \leqslant 1$. This is a very natural condition; it seems reasonable that if $\mathbf{E}(Z_n) = \{\mathbf{E}(Z_1)\}^n \leqslant 1$ then $Z_n = 0$ sooner or later. Actually this result holds in general.

(5) **Theorem.** $\mathbf{P}(Z_n = 0) \to \mathbf{P}$(*ultimate extinction*) $= \eta$, *say, where* η *is the smallest non-negative root of the equation* $s = G(s)$. *Also,* $\eta = 1$ *if and only if* $\mu \leqslant 1$.

Proof. Let $\eta_n = \mathbf{P}(Z_n = 0)$. Then, by (1),

$$\eta_n = G_n(0) = G(G_{n-1}(0)) = G(\eta_{n-1}).$$

In the light of the remarks about equation (4) we know that $\eta_n \uparrow \eta$, and the continuity of G guarantees that

$$\eta = G(\eta).$$

We show that if e is any non-negative root of the equation $s = G(s)$ then $\eta \leqslant e$. For, G is non-decreasing on $[0, 1]$ and so

$$\eta_1 = G(0) \leqslant G(e) = e.$$

Similarly

$$\eta_2 = G(\eta_1) \leqslant G(e) = e$$

and hence, by induction, $\eta_n \leqslant e$ for all n, giving $\eta \leqslant e$. Thus η is the smallest non-negative root of the equation $s = G(s)$.

To verify the second assertion of the theorem, we need the fact that G is convex on $[0, 1]$. This holds because

$$G''(s) = \mathbf{E}(Z_1(Z_1 - 1)s^{Z_1 - 2}) \geqslant 0 \text{ if } s \geqslant 0.$$

So G is convex and non-decreasing on $[0, 1]$ with $G(1) = 1$. We can verify that the two curves $y = G(s)$ and $y = s$ generally have two intersections in $[0, 1]$, and these occur at $s = \eta$ and $s = 1$. A glance at Figure 5.4 (and a more analytical verification) tells us that these intersections are coincident

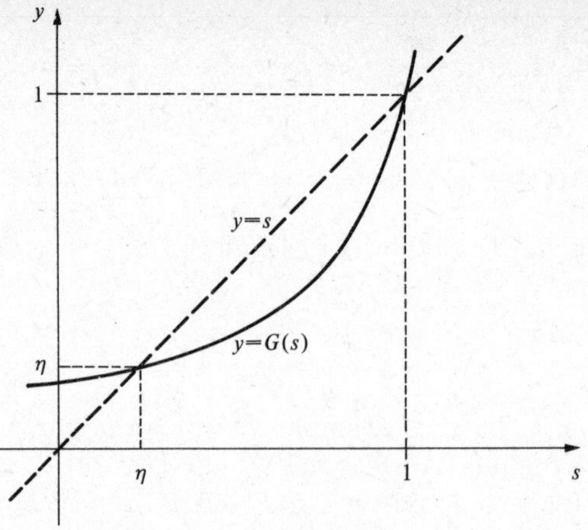

FIG. 5.4 A sketch of $G(s)$ showing the roots of the equation $G(s)=s$.

if and only if $G'(1)\leq 1$, which completes the proof. ■

We have seen that, for large n, the nth generation is empty with probability approaching η. However, what if the process does *not* die out? If $\mathbf{E}(Z_1)>1$ then $\eta<1$ and extinction is not certain. Indeed $\mathbf{E}(Z_n)$ grows geometrically as $n\to\infty$, and it can be shown that

$$\mathbf{P}(Z_n\to\infty \mid \text{non-extinction})=1$$

when this conditional probability is suitably interpreted. To see just how fast Z_n grows, we define

$$W_n=Z_n/\mathbf{E}(Z_n)$$

where $\mathbf{E}(Z_n)=\mu^n$ and suppose that $\mu>1$. Easy calculations show that $\mathbf{E}(W_n)=1$, $\text{var}\,(W_n)=\sigma^2(1-\mu^{-n})(\mu^2-\mu)^{-1}\to\sigma^2(\mu^2-\mu)^{-1}$, and it seems that W_n may have some non-trivial limit, called W say. (Actually we are asserting that the sequence $\{W_n\}$ of variables converges to a limit variable W. The convergence of random variables is a complicated topic and is described later. Neglect the details for the moment.) To study W, define

$$g_n(s)=\mathbf{E}(s^{W_n}).$$

Then

$$g_n(s)=\mathbf{E}(s^{Z_n\mu^{-n}})=G_n(s^{\mu^{-n}})$$

and (1) shows that g_n satisfies the functional recurrence relation

$$g_n(s)=G(g_{n-1}(s^{1/\mu})).$$

Now, as $n\to\infty$, $W_n\to W$, $g_n(s)\to g(s)=\mathbf{E}(s^W)$, and we obtain

(6) $$g(s)=G(g(s^{1/\mu}))$$

by abandoning many of our current notions of mathematical rigour. This functional equation can be established properly and has various uses. For example, although we cannot solve it for g, we can reach such conclusions as 'if $\mathbf{E}(Z_1^2)<\infty$ then W is continuous, apart from a point mass at zero'.

We have made considerable progress with the theory of branching processes. They are reasonably tractable because they satisfy the Markov condition (see (5.2.4)). Can you formulate and prove this property?

5.5 Age-dependent branching processes

Here is a more general model for the growth of a population. It incorporates the observation that generations are not contemporaneous in most populations, with individuals in the same generation giving birth to families at different times. To model this we attach another random variable, called 'age', to each individual; we shall suppose that the collection of all ages is a set of variables which are independent of each other and of all family sizes, and which are continuous, positive, and have the common density function f_T. We specify that each individual lives for a period of time, T say, where T denotes its age, before it gives birth to its family of next generation descendants as before.

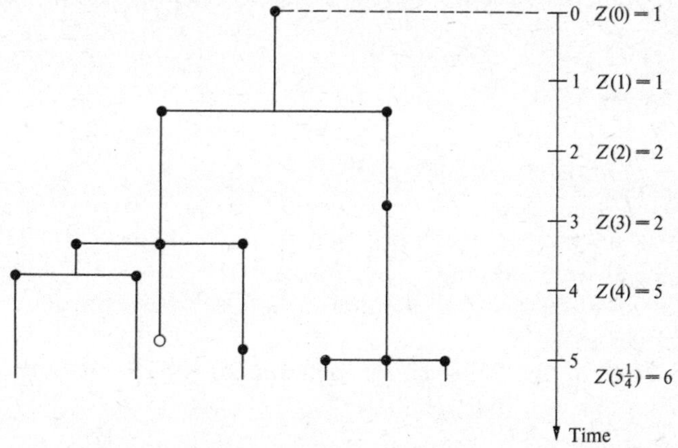

FIG. 5.5 The family tree of an age-dependent branching process; • indicates the birth of an individual, and ○ indicates the death of an individual which has no descendants.

Let $Z(t)$ denote the size of the population at time t; we shall assume that $Z(0)=1$. The population-size generating function $G_t(s)=\mathbf{E}(s^{Z(t)})$ is now a function of t as well. As usual, we hope to find an expression involving G_t by conditioning on some suitable event. In this case we condition on the age of the initial individual in the population.

(1) **Theorem.** $G_t(s)=\displaystyle\int_0^t G(G_{t-u}(s))f_T(u)\,du+\int_t^\infty sf_T(u)\,du.$

Proof. Let T be the age of the initial individual. By the use of conditional expectation

(2) $$G_t(s) = \mathbf{E}(s^{Z(t)}) = \mathbf{E}(\mathbf{E}(s^{Z(t)} \mid T))$$
$$= \int_0^\infty \mathbf{E}(s^{Z(t)} \mid T = u) f_T(u)\, du.$$

If $T = u$, then at time u the initial individual dies and is replaced by a random number N of offspring, where N has generating function G. Each of these offspring behaves in the future as their ancestor did in the past, and the effect of their ancestor's death is to replace the process by the sum of N independent copies of the process displaced in time by an amount u. Now if $u > t$ then $Z(t) = 1$ and $\mathbf{E}(s^{Z(t)} \mid T = u) = s$, whilst if $u < t$ then $Z(t) = Y_1 + Y_2 + \ldots + Y_N$ is the sum of N independent copies of $Z(t-u)$ and so $\mathbf{E}(s^{Z(t)} \mid T = u) = G(G_{t-u}(s))$ by (5.1.15). Substitute into (2) to obtain the result. ∎

Unfortunately we cannot solve equation (1) except in certain special cases. Possibly the most significant case with which we can make some progress arises when the ages are exponentially distributed. Then

$$f_T(t) = \lambda e^{-\lambda t} \quad \text{for} \quad t \geq 0$$

and the reader may show (*exercise*) that

$$\frac{\partial}{\partial t} G_t(s) = \lambda\{G(G_t(s)) - G_t(s)\}.$$

It is no mere coincidence that this case is more tractable. In this very special instance, and in no other, $Z(t)$ satisfies a Markov condition; it is called a Markov process, and we shall return to the general theory of such processes later.

Some information about the moments of $Z(t)$ is fairly readily available from (1). For example,

$$m(t) = \mathbf{E}(Z(t)) = \lim_{s \uparrow 1} \frac{\partial}{\partial s} G_t(s)$$

satisfies the integral equation

(3) $$m(t) = \mu \int_0^t m(t-u) f_T(u)\, du + \int_t^\infty f_T(u)\, du \quad \text{where} \quad \mu = G'(1).$$

We can find the general solution to this equation only by numerical or series methods. It is reasonably amenable to Laplace transform methods and produces a closed expression for the Laplace transform of m. Later we shall use renewal theory arguments (see (10.4.22)) to show that there exist $\delta > 0$ and $\beta > 0$ such that $m(t) \sim \delta e^{\beta t}$ as $t \to \infty$ whenever $\mu > 1$.

Finally observe that, in some sense, the age-dependent process $Z(t)$ contains the old process Z_n. We say that Z_n is 'imbedded' in $Z(t)$ in that we can recapture Z_n by aggregating the generation sizes of $Z(t)$. This imbedding enables us to use properties of Z_n to derive corresponding properties of the less tractable $Z(t)$. For instance, $Z(t)$ dies out if and only if Z_n dies out, and so (5.4.5) provides us immediately with the extinction probability of the age-dependent process. This technique has uses elsewhere as well. With any non-Markovian process we can try to find an imbedded Markovian process which provides information about the original process. We consider examples of this later.

5.6 Expectation revisited

This section is divided into Parts A and B. All readers must read A before they proceed to the next section; B is for people with a keener appreciation of detailed technique. We are about to extend the definition of probability generating functions to more general types of variables than those concentrated on the non-negative integers, and it is a suitable moment to insert some discussion of the expectation of an arbitrary random variable regardless of its type (discrete, continuous, and so on). Up to now we have made only guarded remarks about such variables.

(A) Notation

Remember that the expectations of discrete and continuous variables are given respectively by

(1) $$\mathbf{E}X = \sum xf(x) \qquad \text{if } X \text{ has mass function } f$$

(2) $$\mathbf{E}X = \int xf(x)\,\mathrm{d}x \qquad \text{if } X \text{ has density function } f.$$

We require a single piece of notation which incorporates both these cases. Suppose X has distribution function F. Subject to a trivial and unimportant condition, (1) and (2) can be rewritten

(3) $$\mathbf{E}X = \sum x\,\mathrm{d}F(x) \text{ where } \mathrm{d}F(x) = F(x) - \lim_{y \uparrow x} F(y) = f(x)$$

(4) $$\mathbf{E}X = \int x\,\mathrm{d}F(x) \text{ where } \mathrm{d}F(x) = \frac{\mathrm{d}F}{\mathrm{d}x}\mathrm{d}x = f(x)\,\mathrm{d}x.$$

This suggests that we denote $\mathbf{E}X$ by

(5) $$\mathbf{E}X = \int x\,\mathrm{d}F \quad \text{or} \quad \int x\,\mathrm{d}F(x)$$

whatever the type of X, where (5) is interpreted as (3) for discrete variables and as (4), of course, for continuous variables. We adopt this notation forthwith. Those readers who fail to conquer an aversion to this notation should read $\mathrm{d}F$ as $f(x)\,\mathrm{d}x$. Previous properties of expectation received two statements and proofs which can now be unified. For instance (3.3.3) and (4.3.3) become

(6) $$\text{if } g:\mathbb{R} \to \mathbb{R} \text{ then } \mathbf{E}(g(X)) = \int g(x)\,\mathrm{d}F.$$

(B) Abstract integration

The expectation of a random variable X is specified by its distribution function F. But F itself is describable in terms of X and the underlying probability space and it follows that $\mathbf{E}X$ can be thus described also. This part contains a brief sketch of how to integrate on a probability space $(\Omega, \mathcal{F}, \mathbf{P})$. It contains no details, and the reader is left to check up on his intuition elsewhere (see Clarke 1975 for example). Let $(\Omega, \mathcal{F}, \mathbf{P})$ be some probability space.

(7) The random variable $X:\Omega\to\mathbb{R}$ is called *simple* if it takes only finitely many distinct values. Simple variables can be written

$$X=\sum_{i=1}^{n} x_i I_{A_i}$$

for some partition $A_1, A_2, \ldots, A_n$ of Ω; we define the *integral* of X, written $\mathbf{E}(X)$, to be

$$\mathbf{E}(X)=\sum_{i=1}^{n} x_i \mathbf{P}(A_i).$$

(8) Any non-negative random variable $X:\Omega\to[0,\infty)$ is the limit of some increasing sequence $\{X_n\}$ of simple variables. That is, $X_n(\omega)\uparrow X(\omega)$ for all $\omega\in\Omega$. We define the *integral* of X, written $\mathbf{E}(X)$, to be

$$\mathbf{E}(X)=\lim_{n\to\infty}\mathbf{E}(X_n).$$

This is well defined in the sense that two increasing sequences of simple functions, both converging to X, have the same limit for their sequences of integrals. $\mathbf{E}(X)$ can be $+\infty$.

(9) Any random variable $X:\Omega\to\mathbb{R}$ can be written as the difference $X=X^+-X^-$ of non-negative random variables

$$X^+(\omega)=\max\{X(\omega),0\},\qquad X^-(\omega)=-\min\{X(\omega),0\}.$$

If at least one of $\mathbf{E}(X^+)$ and $\mathbf{E}(X^-)$ is finite, then we define the *integral* of X, written $\mathbf{E}(X)$, to be

$$\mathbf{E}(X)=\mathbf{E}(X^+)-\mathbf{E}(X^-).$$

(10) Thus, $\mathbf{E}(X)$ is well defined, at least for any variable X such that

$$\mathbf{E}|X|=\mathbf{E}(X^++X^-)<\infty.$$

(11) In the language of measure theory $\mathbf{E}(X)$ is denoted by

$$\mathbf{E}(X)=\int_\Omega X(\omega)\,\mathrm{d}\mathbf{P}\quad\text{or}\quad\int_\Omega X(\omega)\,\mathbf{P}(\mathrm{d}\omega).$$

The *expectation operator* $\mathbf{E}$ defined in this way has all the properties which were described in detail for discrete and continuous variables.

(12) **Continuity of E.** Important further properties are the following. If $\{X_n\}$ is

a sequence of variables with $X_n(\omega) \to X(\omega)$ for all $\omega \in \Omega$ then

(a) (*monotone convergence*) *if* $X_n(\omega) \geqslant 0$ *and* $X_n(\omega) \leqslant X_{n+1}(\omega)$ *for all* n *and* ω, *then* $\mathbf{E}(X_n) \to \mathbf{E}(X)$,
(b) (*dominated convergence*) *if* $|X_n(\omega)| \leqslant Y(\omega)$ *for all* n *and* ω, *and* $\mathbf{E}|Y| < \infty$ *then* $\mathbf{E}(X_n) \to \mathbf{E}(X)$,
(c) (*bounded convergence*) this is a special case of dominated convergence; *if* $|X_n(\omega)| \leqslant c$ *for some constant* c *and all* n *and* ω *then* $\mathbf{E}(X_n) \to \mathbf{E}(X)$.

(13) **Lebesgue–Stieltjes integral.** Let X have distribution function F. F gives rise to a probability measure μ_F on the Borel sets of $\mathbb{R}$ as follows:

(a) define $\mu_F((a, b]) = F(b) - F(a)$,
(b) as in the discussion after (4.1.5), the domain of μ_F can be extended to include the Borel σ-field $\mathscr{B}$, which is the smallest σ-field containing all half open intervals $(a, b]$.

So $(\mathbb{R}, \mathscr{B}, \mu_F)$ is a probability space; its completion (see Section 1.6) is denoted by $(\mathbb{R}, \mathscr{L}_F, \mu_F)$, where $\mathscr{L}_F$ is the smallest σ-field containing $\mathscr{B}$ and all subsets of μ_F-null sets. If $g:\mathbb{R} \to \mathbb{R}$ (is $\mathscr{L}_F$-measurable) then the abstract integral

$$\int g \, d\mu_F$$

is called the *Lebesgue–Stieltjes integral* of g with respect to μ_F, and we normally denote it by

$$\int g(x)\, dF \quad \text{or} \quad \int g(x)\, dF(x).$$

Think of it as a special case of the abstract integral (11). The purpose of this discussion is the assertion that if $g:\mathbb{R} \to \mathbb{R}$ (and g is suitably measurable) then $g(X)$ is a random variable and

$$\mathbf{E}(g(X)) = \int g(x)\, dF,$$

and we adopt this forthwith as the official notation for expectation. Here is a final word of caution. If $g(x) = I_B(x)h(x)$ where I_B is the indicator function of some $B \subseteq \mathbb{R}$ then

$$\int g(x)\, dF = \int_B h(x)\, dF.$$

We do not in general obtain the same result when we integrate over $B_1 = [a, b]$ and $B_2 = (a, b)$ unless F is continuous at a and b, and so we do not use the notation

$$\int_a^b h(x)\,dF$$

unless there is no danger of ambiguity.

5.7 Characteristic functions

Probability generating functions proved to be very useful in handling non-negative integral random variables. For more general variables X it is natural to make the substitution $s = e^t$ in the quantity $G_X(s) = \mathbf{E}(s^X)$.

(1) **Definition.** The **moment generating function** of a variable X is a function $M: \mathbb{R} \to [0, \infty)$ given by

$$M(t) = \mathbf{E}(e^{tX}).$$

Moment generating functions are related to Laplace transforms, since

$$M(t) = \int e^{tx}\,dF(x) = \int e^{tx} f(x)\,dx$$

if X is continuous with density function f. They have properties similar to those of probability generating functions. For example, if $M(t) < \infty$ on some open interval containing the origin then

(a) $\mathbf{E}X = M'(0)$, $\mathbf{E}(X^k) = M^{(k)}(0)$,

(b) (*Taylor's theorem*)

$$M(t) = \sum_k \frac{\mathbf{E}(X^k)}{k!} t^k;$$

that is, M is the 'exponential generating function' of the sequence of moments of X.

(c) (*Laplace convolution theorem*) If X and Y are independent then

$$M_{X+Y}(t) = M_X(t) M_Y(t).$$

This is essentially the assertion that the Laplace transform of a convolution (see (4.8.2)) is the product of the Laplace transforms.

Moment generating functions provide a very useful technique but suffer the disadvantage that the integrals which define them may not always be finite. Rather than explore their properties in detail we move on immediately to another class of functions which are equally useful and whose finiteness is guaranteed.

(2) **Definition.** The **characteristic function** of X is the function $\phi: \mathbb{R} \to \mathbb{C}$ defined by

$$\phi(t) = \mathbf{E}(e^{itX}) \quad \text{where} \quad i = \sqrt{(-1)}.$$

Characteristic functions are related to Fourier transforms, since

$$\phi(t)=\int e^{itx}\,dF(x).$$

In the notation of Section 5.6, ϕ is the abstract integral of a complex-valued random variable. It is well defined in the terms of Section 5.6 by

$$\phi(t)=\mathbf{E}(\cos tX)+i\mathbf{E}(\sin tX).$$

Furthermore, $\phi(t)$ is better behaved than $M(t)$.

(3) **Theorem.** *The characteristic function ϕ satisfies*

(a) $\phi(0)=1$, $|\phi(t)|\leqslant 1$ *for all* t
(b) ϕ *is uniformly continuous on* $\mathbb{R}$
(c) ϕ *is non-negative definite, which is to say that*

$$\sum_{j,k}\phi(t_j-t_k)z_j\bar{z}_k\geqslant 0$$

for all real $t_1,\dots,t_n$ *and complex* $z_1,\dots,z_n$.

Proof.

(a) $\phi(0)=\mathbf{E}(1)=1$.

$$|\phi(t)|\leqslant\int|e^{itx}|\,dF=\int dF=1.$$

(b)
$$\begin{aligned}|\phi(t+h)-\phi(t)|&=|\mathbf{E}(e^{i(t+h)X}-e^{itX})|\\&\leqslant\mathbf{E}\,|e^{itX}(e^{ihX}-1)|=\mathbf{E}(Y(h))\end{aligned}$$

where $Y(h)=|e^{ihX}-1|$. However, $|Y(h)|\leqslant 2$ and $Y(h)\to 0$ as $h\to 0$ and so $\mathbf{E}(Y(h))\to 0$ (by bounded convergence (5.6.12)).

(c)
$$\begin{aligned}\sum_{j,k}\phi(t_j-t_k)z_j\bar{z}_k&=\sum_{j,k}\int\{z_j\exp(it_jx)\}\{\bar{z}_k\exp(-it_kx)\}\,dF\\&=\mathbf{E}\left\{\left|\sum_j z_j\exp(it_jX)\right|^2\right\}\geqslant 0.\end{aligned}$$ ■

Actually, (3) characterizes characteristic functions in the sense that ϕ is a characteristic function if and only if it satisfies (a), (b), and (c). This is Bochner's theorem, for which we offer no proof. Many of the properties of characteristic functions rely for their proofs on a knowledge of complex analysis. This is a textbook on probability theory, and will not include such proofs unless they indicate some essential technique. We have asserted that the method of characteristic functions is very useful; however, we warn the reader that we shall not make use of them until Section 5.10. In the meantime we shall establish some of their properties.

First and foremost, from a knowledge of ϕ_X we can recapture the distribution of X. The full power of this statement is deferred until the next section; here we concern ourselves only with the moments of X.

Many of the interesting characteristic functions are not very well behaved, and we must move carefully.

(4) **Theorem.**

(a) *If* $\phi^{(k)}(0)$ *exists then* $\begin{cases} \mathbf{E}|X^k|<\infty & \text{if } k \text{ is even} \\ \mathbf{E}|X^{k-1}|<\infty & \text{if } k \text{ is odd.} \end{cases}$

(b) *If* $\mathbf{E}|X^k|<\infty$ *then*†

$$\phi(t)=\sum_{j=0}^{k}\frac{\mathbf{E}(X^j)}{j!}(it)^j+o(t^k),$$

and so $\phi^{(k)}(0)=i^k\mathbf{E}(X^k)$.

Proof. This is essentially Taylor's theorem for a function of a complex variable. For the proof, see Moran 1968 and Kingman and Taylor 1966. ■

One of the useful properties of characteristic functions is that they enable us to handle sums of independent variables with the minimum of fuss.

(5) **Theorem.** *If X and Y are independent then*

$$\phi_{X+Y}(t)=\phi_X(t)\phi_Y(t).$$

Proof.

$$\phi_{X+Y}(t)=\mathbf{E}(e^{it(X+Y)})=\mathbf{E}(e^{itX}e^{itY}).$$

Expand each exponential term into cosines and sines, multiply out, use independence, and put back together to obtain the result. ■

(6) **Theorem.** *If* $a, b\in\mathbb{R}$ *and* $Y=aX+b$ *then*

$$\phi_Y(t)=e^{itb}\phi_X(at).$$

Proof.

$$\phi_Y(t)=\mathbf{E}(e^{it(aX+b)})=\mathbf{E}(e^{itb}e^{i(at)X})$$
$$=e^{itb}\mathbf{E}(e^{i(at)X})=e^{itb}\phi_X(at).$$ ■

We shall make repeated use of these last two theorems. We sometimes need to study collections of variables which may be dependent.

(7) **Definition.** The **joint characteristic function** of X and Y is the function $\phi:\mathbb{R}^2\to\mathbb{R}$ given by

$$\phi(s,t)=\mathbf{E}(e^{isX}e^{itY}).$$

† See Subsection (10) of Appendix I for a reminder about Landau's O–o notation

Notice that $\phi(s, t) = \phi_{sX+tY}(1)$. As usual we shall be interested mostly in independent variables.

(8) **Theorem.** *X and Y are independent if and only if*

$$\phi_{X,Y}(s, t) = \phi_X(s)\phi_Y(t) \quad \textit{for all } s \textit{ and } t.$$

Proof. If X and Y are independent then the result follows by the argument of (5). The converse is proved by extending the inversion theorem of the next section to deal with joint distributions and showing that the joint distribution function factorizes. ■

Note particularly that for X and Y to be independent it is not sufficient that

(9) $$\phi_{X,Y}(t, t) = \phi_X(t)\phi_Y(t), \qquad \text{for all } t.$$

Exercise. Can you find an example of dependent variables which satisfy (9)?

We have seen (4) that it is an easy calculation to find the moments of X by differentiating its characteristic function $\phi_X(t)$ at $t=0$. A similar calculation gives the 'joint moments' $\mathbf{E}(X^jY^k)$ of two variables from a knowledge of their joint characteristic function $\phi_{X,Y}(s, t)$ (see Problem (5.11.23) for details).

The properties of moment generating functions are closely related to those of characteristic functions. In the rest of the text we shall use the latter whenever possible, but it will be appropriate to use the former for any topic whose analysis employs Laplace transforms; for example this is the case for the queueing theory of Chapter 11.

5.8 Examples of characteristic functions

Those who feel daunted by $\sqrt{(-1)}$ should find it a useful exercise to work through this section using $M(t) = \mathbf{E}(e^{tX})$ in place of $\phi(t) = \mathbf{E}(e^{itX})$. Many calculations here are left as *exercises*.

(1) **Example. Bernoulli distribution.** If X is Bernoulli parameter p then

$$\phi(t) = \mathbf{E}(e^{itX}) = e^{it0}\,.\,q + e^{it1}\,.\,p = q + pe^{it}. \qquad ●$$

(2) **Example. Binomial distribution.** If X is $B(n, p)$ then X has the same distribution as the sum of n independent Bernoulli variables $Y_1, Y_2, \ldots, Y_n$. Thus

$$\phi_X(t) = \phi_{Y_1}(t) \ldots \phi_{Y_n}(t) = (q + pe^{it})^n. \qquad ●$$

(3) **Example. Exponential distribution.** If $f(x) = \lambda e^{-\lambda x}$ for $x \geq 0$ then

$$\phi(t) = \int_0^\infty e^{itx}\lambda e^{-\lambda x}\,dx.$$

This is a complex integral and its solution relies on a knowledge of how to integrate around contours in $\mathbb{R}^2$ (the appropriate contour is a sector). If you know about this then do it. Do not fall into the trap of treating i as if it were a real number, even though this malpractice yields the correct answer in this case:

$$\phi(t)=\frac{\lambda}{\lambda-it}.$$ ●

(4) **Example. Cauchy distribution.** If $f(x)=\{\pi(1+x^2)\}^{-1}$ then

$$\phi(t)=\frac{1}{\pi}\int_{-\infty}^{\infty}\frac{e^{itx}}{1+x^2}\,dx.$$

Treating i as a real number will not help you to avoid the contour integral this time. The answer is

$$\phi(t)=e^{-|t|}.$$

Those who are interested should try integrating around a semicircle with diameter $[-R, R]$ on the real axis. ●

(5) **Example. Normal distribution.** If X is $N(0, 1)$ then

$$\phi(t)=\mathbf{E}(e^{itX})=\int_{-\infty}^{\infty}\frac{1}{\sqrt{(2\pi)}}\exp\left(itx-\tfrac{1}{2}x^2\right)dx.$$

Again, do not treat i as a real number. Consider instead the moment generating function of X

$$M(s)=\mathbf{E}(e^{sX})=\int_{-\infty}^{\infty}\frac{1}{\sqrt{(2\pi)}}\exp\left(sx-\tfrac{1}{2}x^2\right)dx.$$

Complete the square in the integrand and use the hint at the end of Example (4.5.9) to obtain

$$M(s)=e^{s^2/2}.$$

We may not substitute $s=it$ without justification. In this particular instance the theory of analytic continuation of functions of a complex variable provides this justification, and we deduce that

$$\phi(t)=e^{-t^2/2}.$$

By (5.7.6), the characteristic function of the $N(\mu, \sigma^2)$ variable $Y=\sigma X+\mu$ is

$$\phi_Y(t)=e^{it\mu}\phi_X(\sigma t)=\exp\left(i\mu t-\tfrac{1}{2}\sigma^2t^2\right).$$ ●

(6) **Example. Multivariate normal distribution.** If $X_1, \ldots, X_n$ has the multivariate normal distribution $N(\mathbf{0}, \mathbf{V})$ then its joint density function is

$$f(\mathbf{x})=\{(2\pi)^n\,|\mathbf{V}|\}^{-1/2}\exp\left(-\tfrac{1}{2}\mathbf{x}\mathbf{V}^{-1}\mathbf{x}'\right).$$

The joint characteristic function of $X_1, \ldots, X_n$ is

$$\phi(\boldsymbol{t}) = \mathbf{E}(e^{i\boldsymbol{t}\mathbf{X}'})$$

where $\boldsymbol{t} = (t_1, \ldots, t_n)$ and $\mathbf{X} = (X_1, \ldots, X_n)$. Thus

(7) $$\phi(\boldsymbol{t}) = \int_{\mathbb{R}^n} \{(2\pi)^n\,|\mathbf{V}|\}^{-1/2} \exp\left(i\boldsymbol{t}\boldsymbol{x}' - \tfrac{1}{2}\boldsymbol{x}\mathbf{V}^{-1}\boldsymbol{x}'\right) d\boldsymbol{x}.$$

As in the discussion of (4.7.9), there is a linear transformation $\boldsymbol{y} = \boldsymbol{x}\boldsymbol{B}$ such that

$$\boldsymbol{x}\mathbf{V}^{-1}\boldsymbol{x}' = \sum_j \lambda_j y_j^2$$

just as in (4.7.12). Make this transformation in (7) to see that the integrand factorizes into the product of functions of the single variables $y_1, y_2, \ldots, y_n$. Then use (5) to obtain

$$\phi(t) = \exp\left(-\tfrac{1}{2}\boldsymbol{t}\mathbf{V}\boldsymbol{t}'\right).$$

It is now an easy *exercise* to prove Theorem (4.7.14), that $\mathbf{V}$ is the covariance matrix of $\mathbf{X}$, by using the result of Problem (5.11.23). ●

(8) **Example. Gamma distribution.** If X is $\Gamma(\lambda, s)$ then

$$\phi(t) = \int_0^\infty \frac{1}{\Gamma(s)} \lambda^s x^{s-1} \exp(itx - \lambda x)\, dx.$$

As for the exponential distribution (3), routine methods of complex analysis give

$$\phi(t) = \left(\frac{\lambda}{\lambda - it}\right)^s.$$

Why is this similar to the result of (3)? This example includes the chi-squared distribution because a $\chi^2(d)$ variable is $\Gamma(\frac{1}{2}, \frac{1}{2}d)$ and thus has characteristic function

$$\phi(t) = (1 - 2it)^{-d/2}.$$

You may try to prove this from the result of Problem (4.10.10). ●

5.9 Inversion and continuity theorems

This section contains two major reasons why characteristic functions are useful. The first of these states that the distribution of a random variable is specified by its characteristic function. That is to say, if X and Y have the same characteristic function then they have the same distribution. Furthermore, there is a formula which tells us how to recapture the distribution function F corresponding to the characteristic function ϕ. Here is a special case first.

(1) **Theorem.** *If X is continuous with density function f and characteristic function ϕ then*

$$f(x)=\frac{1}{2\pi}\int_{-\infty}^{\infty} e^{-itx}\phi(t)\,dt$$

at every point x at which f is continuous.

Proof. This is the Fourier inversion theorem and can be found in any introduction to Fourier transforms. If the integral fails to converge absolutely then we interpret it as its principal value (see Apostol 1957, p. 487). ■

A sufficient, but not necessary, condition that ϕ be the characteristic function of a continuous variable is that

$$\int_{-\infty}^{\infty} |\phi(t)|\,dt<\infty.$$

The general case is more complicated, and is contained in the next theorem.

(2) **Inversion Theorem.** *Let X have distribution function F and characteristic function ϕ. Define $\bar{F}:\mathbb{R}\to[0,1]$ by*

$$\bar{F}(x)=\tfrac{1}{2}\{F(x)+\lim_{y\uparrow x}F(y)\}.$$

Then

$$\bar{F}(b)-\bar{F}(a)=\lim_{N\to\infty}\int_{-N}^{N}\frac{e^{-iat}-e^{-ibt}}{2\pi it}\phi(t)\,dt.$$

Proof. See Kingman and Taylor 1966. ■

(3) **Corollary.** *X and Y have the same characteristic function if and only if they have the same distribution function.*

Proof. If $\phi_X=\phi_Y$ then, by (2),

$$\bar{F}_X(b)-\bar{F}_X(a)=\bar{F}_Y(b)-\bar{F}_Y(a).$$

Let $a\to-\infty$ to obtain

$$\bar{F}_X(b)=\bar{F}_Y(b);$$

now, for any fixed $x\in\mathbb{R}$, let $b\downarrow x$ and use right-continuity (2.1.6c) to obtain

$$F_X(x)=F_Y(x).$$ ■

Exactly similar results hold for jointly distributed random variables.

For example, if X and Y have joint density function f and joint characteristic function ϕ then

$$f(x, y) = \frac{1}{4\pi^2} \iint_{\mathbb{R}^2} e^{-isx} e^{-ity} \phi(s, t)\, ds\, dt$$

and (5.7.8) follows straight away for this special case.

The second result of this section deals with a sequence $X_1, X_2, \ldots$ of random variables. Roughly speaking it asserts that if the distribution functions $F_1, F_2, \ldots$ of the sequence approach some limit F then the characteristic functions $\phi_1, \phi_2, \ldots$ of the sequence approach the characteristic function of the distribution function F.

(4) **Definition.** We say that the sequence $F_1, F_2, \ldots$ of distribution functions **converges** to the distribution function F, written $F_n \to F$, if $F(x) = \lim_{n\to\infty} F_n(x)$ at each point x where F is continuous.

The reason for the condition of continuity of F at x is indicated by the following. Define the distribution functions F_n and G_n by

$$F_n(x) = \begin{cases} 0 & \text{if } x < \dfrac{1}{n} \\ 1 & \text{if } x \geqslant \dfrac{1}{n} \end{cases} \qquad G_n(x) = \begin{cases} 0 & \text{if } x < -\dfrac{1}{n} \\ 1 & \text{if } x \geqslant -\dfrac{1}{n}. \end{cases}$$

As $n \to \infty$

$$F_n(x) \to F(x) \quad \text{if } x \neq 0,\ F_n(0) \to 0$$

$$G_n(x) \to F(x) \quad \text{for all } x$$

where $F(x)$ is the distribution function of a random variable which is constantly zero. Indeed $\lim_{n\to\infty} F_n(x)$ is not even a distribution function since it is not right-continuous at zero. It is intuitively reasonable to demand that the sequences $\{F_n\}$ and $\{G_n\}$ have the same limit, and so we drop the requirement that $F_n(x) \to F(x)$ at the point of discontinuity of F.

(5) **Continuity Theorem.** *Suppose that $F_1, F_2, \ldots$ is a sequence of distribution functions with corresponding characteristic functions $\phi_1, \phi_2, \ldots$.*

(a) *If $F_n \to F$ for some distribution function F with characteristic function ϕ, then $\phi_n(t) \to \phi(t)$ for all t.*

(b) *Conversely, if $\phi(t) = \lim_{n\to\infty} \phi_n(t)$ exists and is continuous at $t = 0$, then ϕ is the characteristic function of some distribution function F and $F_n \to F$.*

Proof. As for (5.9.2). But see (5.11.30). ■

5.10 Two limit theorems

We are now in a position to prove two very celebrated theorems in probability theory, the 'Law of Large Numbers' and the 'Central Limit Theorem'. The first of these explains the remarks of Sections 1.1 and 1.3, where we discussed a heuristic foundation of probability theory. Part of our intuition about chance is that if we perform many repetitions of an experiment which has numerical outcomes then the average of all the outcomes settles down to some fixed number. This observation deals once again in the convergence of sequences of random variables, the general theory of which is dealt with later. Here it suffices to introduce only one new definition.

(1) **Definition.** If $X_1, X_2, \ldots, X$ is a collection of random variables with distribution functions $F_1, F_2, \ldots, F$, then we say that X_n **converges in distribution** to X, written $X_n \xrightarrow{D} X$, if $F_n \to F$.

This is just (5.9.4) rewritten in terms of random variables.

(2) **Theorem. Law of Large Numbers.** *Let $X_1, X_2, \ldots$ be a sequence of independent identically distributed random variables with finite means μ. Their partial sums*

$$S_n = X_1 + X_2 + \ldots + X_n$$

satisfy

$$\frac{1}{n} S_n \xrightarrow{D} \mu \quad \textit{as} \quad n \to \infty.$$

Proof. The theorem asserts that

$$\mathbf{P}(S_n \leq x) \to \begin{cases} 0 \text{ if } x < \mu \\ 1 \text{ if } x > \mu \end{cases} \quad \text{as} \quad n \to \infty.$$

The method of proof is clear. By the Continuity Theorem (5.9.5) we need to show that the characteristic function of S_n approaches the characteristic function of the constant random variable μ. This is easy. Let ϕ_X be the common characteristic function of the X's, and let ϕ_n be the characteristic function of $(1/n)S_n$. By (5.7.5) and (5.7.6),

(3) $$\phi_n(t) = \{\phi_X(t/n)\}^n.$$

The behaviour of $\phi_X(t/n)$ for large n is given by (5.7.4):

$$\phi_X(t) = 1 + it\mu + o(t).$$

Substitute into (3) to obtain

$$\phi_n(t) = \left(1 + \frac{i\mu t}{n} + o\left(\frac{t}{n}\right)\right)^n \to e^{i\mu t} \quad \text{as} \quad n \to \infty.$$

However, this limit is the characteristic function of the constant μ and the result is proved. ∎

So, for large n, S_n is about as big as $n\mu$. What can we say about the difference $S_n - n\mu$? There is an extraordinary answer to this question so long as the X's have finite variance:

(a) $S_n - n\mu$ is about as big as $n^{1/2}$,
(b) the distribution of $n^{-1/2}(S_n - n\mu)$ approaches the normal distribution as $n \to \infty$ *irrespective* of the distribution of the X's.

(4) **Central Limit Theorem.** *Let $X_1, X_2, \ldots$ be a sequence of independent identically distributed random variables with finite means μ and finite non-zero variances σ^2, and let*

$$S_n = X_1 + X_2 + \ldots + X_n.$$

Then

$$\frac{S_n - n\mu}{\sqrt{(n\sigma^2)}} \xrightarrow{D} N(0, 1) \quad as \quad n \to \infty.$$

Note that the assertion of the theorem is an abuse of notation, since $N(0, 1)$ is a distribution and not a random variable; it is admissible because convergence in distribution involves only the corresponding distribution functions. The method of proof is the same as for the Law of Large Numbers.

Proof. First, write $Y_i = (X_i - \mu)/\sigma$, and let ϕ_Y be the characteristic function of the Y's. By (5.7.4)

$$\phi_Y(t) = 1 - \tfrac{1}{2}t^2 + o(t^2).$$

Also, the characteristic function ψ_n of

$$U_n = \frac{S_n - n\mu}{\sqrt{(n\sigma^2)}} = \frac{1}{\sqrt{n}} \sum_1^n Y_i$$

satisfies, by (5.7.5) and (5.7.6),

$$\begin{aligned}\psi_n(t) &= \{\phi_Y(tn^{-1/2})\}^n \\ &= \left\{1 - \frac{t^2}{2n} + o\left(\frac{t^2}{n}\right)\right\}^n \\ &\to e^{-t^2/2} \quad \text{as} \quad n \to \infty.\end{aligned}$$

However, this is the characteristic function of the $N(0, 1)$ distribution and the Continuity Theorem (5.9.5) completes the proof. ∎

Numerous generalizations of the Law of Large Numbers and the Central Limit Theorem are available. For example, in Chapter 7 we shall meet two stronger versions of (2), involving weaker assumptions on the

X's, and more powerful conclusions. The Central Limit Theorem can be generalized in several directions, two of which deal with dependent variables and differently distributed variables respectively. Some of these are within the reader's grasp. Here is an example.

(5) **Theorem.** *Let $X_1, X_2, \ldots$ be independent variables satisfying*

$$\mathbf{E}X_j = 0, \qquad \operatorname{var}(X_j) = \sigma_j^2, \qquad \mathbf{E}|X_j^3| < \infty$$

and such that

$$\frac{1}{\sigma(n)^3} \sum_{j=1}^{n} \mathbf{E}|X_j^3| \to 0 \quad as \quad n \to \infty$$

where

$$\sigma(n)^2 = \operatorname{var}\left(\sum_1^n X_j\right) = \sum_1^n \sigma_j^2.$$

Then

$$\frac{1}{\sigma(n)} \sum_1^n X_j \xrightarrow{D} N(0, 1).$$

Proof. See Loève 1977, p. 287. ■

The roots of Central Limit Theory are at least 250 years old. The first proof of (4) was found by de Moivre around 1733 for the special case of Bernoulli variables with $p = \frac{1}{2}$. General values of p were treated later by Laplace. Their methods involved the direct estimation of sums like

$$\sum_{k \leq np + x\sqrt{(npq)}} \binom{n}{k} p^k q^{n-k} \quad \text{where} \quad p + q = 1.$$

The first rigorous proof of (4) was discovered by Lyapunov around 1901, thereby confirming a less rigorous proof of Laplace. A glance at these old proofs confirms that the method of characteristic functions is outstanding in its elegance and brevity.

5.11 Problems

1. A die is thrown ten times. What is the probability that the sum of the scores is 27?

2. A coin is tossed repeatedly, heads appearing with probability p on each toss.
(a) Let X be the number of tosses until the first occasion by which three heads have appeared successively. Write down a difference equation for $f(k) = \mathbf{P}(X = k)$ and solve it. Now write down an equation for $\mathbf{E}(X)$ using conditional expectation, and solve it. Finally, find $G_X(s)$ directly using conditional expectation. (Try the same thing for the first occurrence of HTH.)
(b) Let N be the number of heads after n tosses of the coin. Write down $G_N(s)$. Hence find the probability that
   (i) N is divisible by 2 (remember the result of Problem (3.9.9))
   (ii) N is divisible by 3.

3. Find the generating function of the negative binomial distribution (3.5.6). Deduce the mean and variance.

4. In the simple random walk of Section 5.2, show that the probability $p_0(2n)$ that the particle has returned to the origin after $2n$ steps satisfies

$$p_0(2n) \simeq \frac{(4pq)^n}{\sqrt{(\pi n)}},$$

and use this to explain why the walk is persistent if and only if $p = \frac{1}{2}$. You will need *Stirling's formula:*

$$n! \simeq \sqrt{(2\pi)} n^{n+1/2} e^{-n}.$$

5. The symmetric random walk in two dimensions is a sequence of points $\{(X_n, Y_n) : n \geq 0\}$ which evolves in the following way: if $(X_n, Y_n) = (x, y)$ then (X_{n+1}, Y_{n+1}) is one of the four points $(x \pm 1, y)$, $(x, y \pm 1)$, each being picked with equal probability $\frac{1}{4}$. If $(X_0, Y_0) = (0, 0)$
   (a) show that $\mathbf{E}(X_n^2 + Y_n^2) = n$,
   (b) find the probability $p_0(2n)$ that the particle is at the origin after $2n$ steps and deduce that the probability of ever returning to the origin is 1.

6. Consider the one-dimensional random walk $\{S_n\}$ where

$$S_{n+1} = \begin{cases} S_n + 2 & \text{with probability } p \\ S_n - 1 & \text{with probability } q = 1 - p. \end{cases}$$

What is the probability of ever reaching the origin starting from $S_0 = a$?

7. **Ballot Theorem.** Suppose that, in a ballot, candidate A scores p votes and candidate B scores q votes, where $p > q$. We wish to calculate the probability that candidate A was always ahead of candidate B throughout the counting of the votes. Under plausible assumptions about voting habits, translate this question into the following. Show, in the notation of Section 5.3, that the number of paths joining $(0, 0)$ to (x, y), where $y > 0$, which meet the x-axis at the origin only, is equal to $yN_x(0, y)/x$. Deduce that the answer to the original question is $(p - q)/(p + q)$.

8. Complete the proof of (5.4.2).

9. Show that the generating function H_n of the *total* number of individuals in the first n generations of a branching process satisfies

$$H_n(s) = sG(H_{n-1}(s)).$$

10. Show that the number Z_n of individuals in the nth generation of a branching process satisfies

$$\mathbf{P}(Z_n > N \mid Z_m = 0) \leq (G_m(0))^N \quad \text{for} \quad n < m.$$

11. (a) A hen lays N eggs where N is Poisson with parameter λ. The weight of the nth egg is W_n, where $W_1, W_2, \ldots$ are independent identically distributed variables with common probability generating function $G(s)$. Show that the generating function G_W of the total weight $W = \sum_{i=1}^{N} W_i$ is given by

$$G_W(s) = \exp\{-\lambda + \lambda G(s)\}.$$

W is said to have a *compound Poisson distribution.* Show further that $\{G_W(s)\}^{1/n}$ is

the probability generating function of some random variable for any positive integral value of n; W is said to be *infinitely divisible.*
(b) Show that if $H(s)$ is the probability generating function of some infinitely divisible distribution then

$$H(s) = \exp\{-\lambda + \lambda G(s)\}$$

for some probability generating function $G(s)$.

12. If X and Y have joint probability generating function

$$G_{X,Y}(s, t) = \mathbf{E}(s^X t^Y) = \frac{\{1-(p_1+p_2)\}^n}{\{1-(p_1 s + p_2 t)\}^n}$$

find the marginal mass functions of X, Y, and $X+Y$. Find also the conditional probability generating function

$$G_{X|Y}(s \mid y) = \mathbf{E}(s^X \mid Y = y)$$

of X given that $Y = y$. The pair X, Y is said to have the *bivariate negative binomial distribution.*

13. If X and Y have joint probability generating function

$$G_{X,Y}(s, t) = \exp\{\alpha(s-1) + \beta(t-1) + \gamma(st-1)\}$$

find the marginal distributions of X, Y, and $X+Y$, showing that X and Y have the Poisson distribution but that $X+Y$ does not unless $\gamma = 0$.

14. Define $I(a, b) = \int_0^\infty \exp(-a^2u^2 - b^2u^{-2})\,du$ for $a, b > 0$. Show that

(a) $I(a, b) = a^{-1} I(1, ab)$

(b) $\dfrac{\partial I}{\partial b} = -2I(1, ab)$

(c) $I(a, b) = \dfrac{\sqrt{\pi}}{2a} e^{-2ab}$.

(d) If X has density function $(d/\sqrt{x}) \exp(-c/x)$ for $x > 0$ then

$$\mathbf{E}(e^{-tX}) = d(\pi/t)^{1/2} \exp(-2(ct)^{1/2}) \qquad t \geq 0.$$

(e) If X has density function

$$\frac{1}{\sqrt{(2\pi x^3)}} \exp\left(-\frac{1}{2x}\right)$$

for $x > 0$ then

$$\mathbf{E}(e^{-tX}) = \exp\{-(2t)^{1/2}\} \qquad t \geq 0.$$

15. Let X, Y, Z be independent $N(0, 1)$ variables. Use characteristic functions and moment generating functions to find the distributions of

(a) $U = X/Y$

(b) $V = X^{-2}$

(c) $W = \dfrac{XYZ}{\sqrt{(X^2Y^2 + Y^2Z^2 + X^2Z^2)}}$.

16. Show that if $\int_{-\infty}^{\infty} |\phi(t)|\,dt < \infty$ then (5.9.2) reduces to (5.9.1).

17. A random variable X is called *symmetric* if X and $-X$ are identically distributed. Show that X is symmetric if and only if the imaginary part of its characteristic function is identically zero.

18. Let X and Y be independent identically distributed variables with means 0 and variances 1. Let $\phi(t)$ be their common characteristic function, and suppose that $X+Y$ and $X-Y$ are independent. Show that

$$\phi(2t)=\{\phi(t)\}^3\phi(-t)$$

and deduce that X and Y are $N(0, 1)$ variables.

19. Show that the average

$$Z=\frac{1}{n}\sum_{i=1}^{n}X_i$$

of n independent Cauchy variables has the Cauchy distribution too. Why does this not violate the Law of Large Numbers?

20. Let $X_1, X_2, \ldots, X_n$ be independent variables with characteristic functions $\phi_1, \phi_2, \ldots, \phi_n$. Describe random variables which have the following characteristic functions:

(a) $\phi_1(t)\phi_2(t)\ldots\phi_n(t)$
(b) $|\phi_1(t)|^2$
(c) $\sum_1^n p_j\phi_j(t)$ where $p_j\geq 0$ and $\sum_1^n p_j=1$
(d) $(2-\phi_1(t))^{-1}$
(e) $\int_0^\infty \phi_1(ut)e^{-u}\,du$.

21. Which of the following are characteristic functions:

(a) $\phi(t)=\begin{cases}1-|t| & \text{if } |t|\leq 1\\ 0 & \text{otherwise}\end{cases}$
(b) $\phi(t)=(1+t^4)^{-1}$
(c) $\phi(t)=\exp(-t^4)$
(d) $\phi(t)=\cos t$?

22. Show that $|1-\phi_X(t)|\leq \mathbf{E}\,|tX|$.

23. Suppose X and Y have joint characteristic function $\phi(s, t)$. Show that, subject to the appropriate conditions of differentiability,

$$i^{m+n}\mathbf{E}(X^mY^n)=\left.\frac{\partial^{m+n}\phi}{\partial s^m\,\partial t^n}\right|_{s=t=0}$$

for any positive integers m and n.

24. If X has distribution function F and characteristic function ϕ, show that for $u>0$

(a) $$\int_{[-t^{-1},t^{-1}]} x^2\,dF\leq\frac{3}{t^2}\{1-\text{Re}\,\phi(t)\}$$

(b) $$\mathbf{P}\left(|X|\geq\frac{1}{t}\right)\leq\frac{7}{t}\int_0^t\{1-\text{Re}\,\phi(v)\}\,dv.$$

25. Let $X_1, X_2, \ldots$ be independent variables which are uniformly distributed on $[0, 1]$. Let $M_n = \max\{X_1, X_2, \ldots, X_n\}$ and show that

$$n(1-M_n) \xrightarrow{D} X$$

where X is exponentially distributed with parameter 1. You need *not* use characteristic functions.

26. If X is either
   (a) Poisson with parameter λ, or
   (b) $\Gamma(1, \lambda)$,
show that the distribution of $(X - \mathbf{E}X)(\text{var } X)^{-1/2}$ approaches the $N(0, 1)$ distribution as $\lambda \to \infty$.
   (c) Show that

$$e^{-n}\left(1+n+\frac{n^2}{2!}+\ldots+\frac{n^n}{n!}\right) \to \frac{1}{2} \quad \text{as} \quad n \to \infty.$$

27. Theorem (5.9.5b) requires that the limit of a sequence of characteristic functions be continuous at the origin in order that the limit function itself be a characteristic function. Show that this condition may not be relaxed.

28. Use generating functions to show that it is not possible to load two dice in such a way that the sum of the values which they show is equally likely to take any value between 2 and 12. Compare with your method for (2.4.12).

29. A biased coin is tossed N times, where N is a random variable which is Poisson distributed with parameter λ. Find the probability generating function of the number of heads shown. Prove that the total number of heads shown is independent of the total number of tails. Show conversely that N must be Poisson for this to hold.

30. **Continuity theorem (5.9.5).** Let $X_1, X_2, \ldots$ be a sequence of continuous random variables with density functions $f_1, f_2, \ldots$ and characteristic functions $\phi_1, \phi_2, \ldots$ Suppose that, as $n \to \infty$, $\phi_n \to \phi$ where $\phi(t)$ is continuous at zero, and that for all n, $|X_n| \leq a < \infty$.
   (a) Prove that $\phi(t)$ is uniformly continuous.
   (b) Prove that as $n \to \infty$, $\phi_n \to \phi$ uniformly for $-N \leq t \leq N < \infty$.
   (c) Deduce that $f_n(x) \to f(x)$ where $f(x)$ is a density function with characteristic function $\phi(t)$. (Use (5.9.1).)
   (d) Now do the same for arbitrary uniformly bounded random variables $X_1, X_2, \ldots$. (Use (5.9.2).)

31. **Normal sample.** Let $X_1, X_2, \ldots, X_n$ be independently, identically and normally distributed. Define $\bar{X} = \sum_1^n X_i/n$ and $Z_i = X_i - \bar{X}$. Find the joint characteristic function of $\bar{X}, Z_1, Z_2, \ldots, Z_n$, and hence prove (4.9.1).

32. Use the Continuity Theorem (5.9.5) to show that as $n \to \infty$
   (a) if X_n is $B(n, \lambda/n)$ then the distribution of X_n converges to a Poisson distribution.
   (b) if Y_n is geometric with $p = \lambda/n$ then the distribution of Y_n/n converges to an exponential distribution.
This provides more esoteric derivations of the corresponding results in (3.5.4) and (4.4.2).

6 Markov chains

6.1 Markov processes

The simple random walk (5.2) and the branching process (5.4) are two examples of collections of random variables, $\{S_0, S_1, \ldots\}$ and $\{Z_0, Z_1, \ldots\}$ respectively, which evolve in some random but prescribed manner. Such collections are called† 'random processes'. A typical random process X is a family $\{X_t : t \in T\}$ of random variables indexed by some set T. In the above examples $T = \{0, 1, 2, \ldots\}$ and we call the process a 'discrete-time' process; in other important examples $T = \mathbb{R}$ or $T = [0, \infty)$ and we call these 'continuous-time' processes. In either case we think of a random process as a family of variables which evolve as time passes. These variables may even be independent of each other, but then the evolution is not very surprising and this very special case is of little interest to us in this chapter. Rather, we are concerned with more general, and we hope realistic, models for random evolution. Simple random walks and branching processes shared the following property: conditional on their values at the nth step, their future values did not depend on their previous values. This property proved to be very useful in their analysis, and it is to the general theory of processes with this property that we turn our attention now.

Until further notice we shall be interested in discrete-time processes. Let $\{X_0, X_1, \ldots\}$ be a sequence of random variables‡ which take values in some countable set S, called the *state space*. Each X_n is a discrete random variable which takes one of N possible values, where $N = |S|$ (N may equal $+\infty$).

(1) **Definition.** The process X is a **Markov chain** if it satisfies the **Markov property**

$$\mathbf{P}(X_n = s \mid X_0, X_1, \ldots, X_{n-1}) = \mathbf{P}(X_n = s \mid X_{n-1})$$

for all $n \geq 1$ and $s \in S$.

A proof that the random walk is a Markov chain was given in (5.2.4). The reader can check that the Markov property is equivalent to each of

† Such collections are often called 'stochastic' processes; the verbal form of the greek stem of the word 'stochastic' means 'to get at' or 'to aim at with an arrow'.

‡ There is, of course, an underlying probability space $(\Omega, \mathcal{F}, \mathbf{P})$, and each X_n is an $\mathcal{F}$-measurable function which maps Ω into S.

the stipulations (2) and (3) below: for each $s \in S$

(2) $$\mathbf{P}(X_{n+1}=s \mid X_{n_1}, X_{n_2}, \dots, X_{n_k}) = \mathbf{P}(X_{n+1}=s \mid X_{n_k}) \quad \text{for any } n_1 < n_2 < \dots < n_k \leq n$$

(3) $$\mathbf{P}(X_{n+m}=s \mid X_0, X_1, \dots, X_n) = \mathbf{P}(X_{n+m}=s \mid X_n) \quad \text{for any } m, n \geq 0.$$

We have assumed that X takes values in some *countable* set S. The reason for this is essentially the same as the reason for treating discrete and continuous variables separately. Since S is assumed countable, it can be put in one–one correspondence with some subset S' of the integers, and without loss of generality we can assume that S *is* this set S' of integers. If $X_n = i$, then we say that the chain is in the 'ith state at the nth step'; we can also talk of the chain as 'having the value i', 'visiting i', or 'being in state i', depending upon the context of the remark.

The evolution of a chain is described by its 'transition probabilities' $\mathbf{P}(X_{n+1}=j \mid X_n = i)$; it can be quite complicated in general since these probabilities depend upon the three quantities n, i, and j. We shall restrict our attention to the case when they do not depend on n but only upon i and j.

(4) **Definition.** The chain X is called **homogeneous** if

$$\mathbf{P}(X_{n+1}=j \mid X_n = i) = \mathbf{P}(X_1 = j \mid X_0 = i)$$

for all n, i, j. The **transition matrix** $\boldsymbol{P} = (p_{ij})$ is the $|S| \times |S|$ matrix of **transition probabilities**

$$p_{ij} = \mathbf{P}(X_{n+1}=j \mid X_n = i).$$

Some authors write p_{ji} in place of p_{ij} here, so beware; sometimes we write $p_{i,j}$ for p_{ij}. Henceforth, *all Markov chains are assumed homogeneous* unless otherwise specified; we assume that the process X is a Markov chain, and we denote the transition matrix of such a chain by $\boldsymbol{P}$.

(5) **Theorem.** $\boldsymbol{P}$ *is a* **stochastic matrix**, *which is to say that*

(a) $\boldsymbol{P}$ *has non-negative entries, or* $p_{ij} \geq 0$
(b) $\boldsymbol{P}$ *has row sums equal to one, or* $\sum_j p_{ij} = 1$.

Proof. An easy *exercise*. ∎

We can easily see that (5) characterizes transition matrices.

Broadly speaking, we are interested in the evolution of X over two different time scales, the 'short term' and the 'long term'. In the short term the random evolution of X is described by $\boldsymbol{P}$, whilst long-term changes are described in the following way.

(6) **Definition.** The ***n*-step transition matrix** $\boldsymbol{P}_n = (p_{ij}(n))$ is the matrix of ***n*-step**

transition probabilities

$$p_{ij}(n) = \mathbf{P}(X_{m+n} = j \mid X_m = i).$$

Of course, $\boldsymbol{P}_1 = \boldsymbol{P}$.

(7) **Theorem. Chapman–Kolmogorov equations.**

$$p_{ij}(m+n) = \sum_k p_{ik}(m) p_{kj}(n).$$

Hence $\boldsymbol{P}_{m+n} = \boldsymbol{P}_m \boldsymbol{P}_n$, *and so* $\boldsymbol{P}_n = \boldsymbol{P}^n$, *the nth power of* $\boldsymbol{P}$.

Proof.

$$\begin{aligned} p_{ij}(m+n) &= \mathbf{P}(X_{m+n} = j \mid X_0 = i) \\ &= \sum_k \mathbf{P}(X_{m+n} = j, X_m = k \mid X_0 = i) \\ &= \sum_k \mathbf{P}(X_{m+n} = j \mid X_m = k, X_0 = i)\mathbf{P}(X_m = k \mid X_0 = i) \\ &= \sum_k \mathbf{P}(X_{m+n} = j \mid X_m = k)\mathbf{P}(X_m = k \mid X_0 = i) \end{aligned}$$

as required, where we have used the result of Problem (1.8.6.),

$$\mathbf{P}(A \cap B \mid C) = \mathbf{P}(A \mid B \cap C)\mathbf{P}(B \mid C)$$

and the Markov property (2). The rest of the theorem follows immediately. ■

This theorem relates long-term development to short-term development, and tells us how X_n depends on the initial variable X_0. Let $\mu_i^{(n)} = \mathbf{P}(X_n = i)$ be the mass function of X_n, and write $\boldsymbol{\mu}^{(n)}$ for the row vector with entries $(\mu_i^{(n)} : i \in S)$.

(8) **Lemma.** $\boldsymbol{\mu}^{(m+n)} = \boldsymbol{\mu}^{(m)} \boldsymbol{P}_n$, *and hence* $\boldsymbol{\mu}^{(n)} = \boldsymbol{\mu}^{(0)} \boldsymbol{P}^n$.

Proof.

$$\begin{aligned} \mu_j^{(m+n)} &= \mathbf{P}(X_{m+n} = j) = \sum_i \mathbf{P}(X_{m+n} = j \mid X_m = i)\mathbf{P}(X_m = i) \\ &= \sum_i \mu_i^{(m)} p_{ij}(n) = (\boldsymbol{\mu}^{(m)} \boldsymbol{P}_n)_j \end{aligned}$$

and the result follows from (7). ■

Thus we reach the important conclusion that the random evolution of the chain is determined by the transition matrix $\boldsymbol{P}$ and the initial mass function $\boldsymbol{\mu}^{(0)}$. Many questions about the chain can be expressed in terms of these quantities, and the study of the chain is thus largely reducible to the study of algebraic properties of matrices.

(9) **Example. Simple random walk.** $S=\{0, \pm 1, \pm 2, \ldots\}$ and

$$p_{ij}=\begin{cases} p & \text{if } j=i+1 \\ q=1-p & \text{if } j=i-1 \\ 0 & \text{otherwise.} \end{cases}$$

The argument of (5.3.3) shows that

$$p_{ij}(n)=\begin{cases} \binom{n}{\frac{1}{2}(n+j-i)} p^{\frac{1}{2}(n+j-i)} q^{\frac{1}{2}(n-j+i)} & \text{if } n+j-i \text{ is even} \\ 0 & \text{otherwise.} \end{cases}$$

●

(10) **Example. Branching process (5.4).** $S=\{0, 1, 2, \ldots\}$ and p_{ij} is the coefficient of s^j in $(G(s))^i$. Also $p_{ij}(n)$ is the coefficient of s^j in $(G_n(s))^i$. ●

(11) **Example. Gene frequencies.** One of the most interesting and extensive applications of probability theory is to genetics, and particularly to the study of gene frequencies. The problem may be inadequately and superficially described as follows. For definiteness suppose the population is human. Genetic information is contained in chromosomes, which are strands of chemicals grouped in cell nuclei. In humans ordinary cells carry 46 chromosomes, 44 of which are homologous pairs. For our purposes a chromosome can be regarded as an ordered set of n sites, the states of which can be thought of as a sequence of random variables $C_1, C_2, \ldots, C_n$. The possible values of each C_i are certain combinations of chemicals, and these values influence (or determine) some characteristic of the owner such as hair colour or leg length.

Now, suppose that A is a possible value of C_1, say, and let X_n be the number of individuals in the nth generation for which C_1 has the value A. What is the behaviour of the sequence $X_1, X_2, \ldots, X_n, \ldots$? The first important (and obvious) point is that the sequence is random, because of the following factors.

(a) The value A for C_1 may affect the owner's chances of contributing to the next generation. If A gives you short legs, you stand a better chance of being caught by a sabre-toothed tiger. The breeding population is randomly selected from those born, but there may be bias for or against the gene A.

(b) The breeding population is randomly combined into pairs to produce offspring. Each parent contributes 23 chromosomes to its offspring, but here again, if A gives you short legs you may have a smaller (or larger) chance of catching a mate.

(c) Sex cells having half the normal complement of chromosomes are produced by a special and complicated process called 'meiosis'. We shall not go into details, but essentially the homologous pairs of the parent are shuffled to produce new and different chromosomes for offspring. The sex cells from each parent (with 23 chromosomes) are then combined to give a new cell (with 46 chromosomes).

(d) Since meiosis involves a large number of complex chemical operations it is hardly surprising that things go wrong occasionally, producing a new value for C_1, $\hat{A}$ say. This is a 'mutation'.

The reader can now see that if generations are segregated (in a laboratory, say), then we can suppose that $X_1, X_2, \ldots$ is a Markov chain with a finite state space. If generations are not segregated and $X(t)$ is the frequency of A in the population at time t, then $X(t)$ may be a continuous-time Markov chain.

For a simple example, suppose that the population size is N, a constant. If $X_n = i$, then it may seem reasonable that any member of the $(n+1)$th generation carries A with probability i/N, independently of the others. Then

$$p_{ij} = \mathbf{P}(X_{n+1} = j \mid X_n = i) = \binom{N}{j}\left(\frac{i}{N}\right)^j\left(1-\frac{i}{N}\right)^{N-j}.$$

Even more simply, suppose that at each stage exactly one individual dies and is replaced by a new individual; each individual is picked for death with probability $1/N$. If $X_n = i$, we assume that the probability that the replacement carries A is i/N. Then

$$p_{ij} = \begin{cases} \dfrac{i(N-i)}{N^2} & \text{if } j = i \pm 1 \\[2ex] 1 - 2\dfrac{i(N-i)}{N^2} & \text{if } j = i \\[2ex] 0 & \text{otherwise.} \end{cases}$$

●

6.2 Classification of states

We can think of the development of the chain as the motion of a notional particle which jumps between the states of S at each epoch of time. As in Section 5.3, we may be interested in the (possibly infinite) time which elapses before the particle returns to its starting point. We saw there that it sufficed to find the distribution of the length of time until the particle returns for the first time since other interarrival times are merely independent copies of this. However, need the particle ever return to its starting point? With this question in mind we make the following definition.

(1) **Definition.** State i is called **persistent** (or **recurrent**) if

$$\mathbf{P}(X_n = i \text{ for some } n \geq 1 \mid X_0 = i) = 1,$$

which is to say that the probability of eventual return to i, having started from i, is 1. If this probability is strictly less than 1, i is called **transient**.

As in Section 5.3, we are interested in the *first passage times* of the chain. Let

$$f_{ij}(n) = \mathbf{P}(X_1 \neq j, X_2 \neq j, \ldots, X_{n-1} \neq j, X_n = j \mid X_0 = i)$$

be the probability that the first visit to state j, starting from i, takes place at the nth step. Define

(2) $$f_{ij} = \sum_{n=1}^{\infty} f_{ij}(n)$$

to be the probability that the chain ever visits j, starting from i. Of course, j is persistent if and only if $f_{jj} = 1$. We seek a criterion for a state to be persistent in terms of the n-step transition probabilities. Following our random walk experience, define the generating functions

$$P_{ij}(s) = \sum_n s^n p_{ij}(n), \qquad F_{ij}(s) = \sum_n s^n f_{ij}(n),$$

with the conventions that $p_{ij}(0) = \delta_{ij}$, the Kronecker delta, and $f_{ij}(0) = 0$ for all i and j. Clearly $f_{ij} = F_{ij}(1)$.

(3) **Theorem.**

(a) $P_{ii}(s) = 1 + F_{ii}(s)P_{ii}(s)$

(b) $P_{ij}(s) = F_{ij}(s)P_{jj}(s)$ *if* $i \neq j$.

Proof. As for (5.3.1). ■

(4) **Corollary.**

(a) *j is persistent if $\sum_n p_{jj}(n) = \infty$, and if this holds then $\sum_n p_{ij}(n) = \infty$ for all i such that $f_{ij} > 0$.*

(b) *j is transient if $\sum_n p_{jj}(n) < \infty$, and if this holds then $\sum_n p_{ij}(n) < \infty$ for all i.*

Proof. First we show that j is persistent if and only if $\sum_n p_{jj}(n) = \infty$. From (3a), $P_{jj}(s) = \{1 - F_{jj}(s)\}^{-1}$ if $|s| < 1$. Hence, as $s \uparrow 1$, $P_{jj}(s) \to \infty$ if and only if $f_{jj} = F_{jj}(1) = 1$. Now use Abel's theorem to obtain $\lim_{s \uparrow 1} P_{jj}(s) = \sum_n p_{jj}(n)$ and our claim is shown. Use (3b) to complete the proof. ■

(5) **Corollary.** *If j is transient then $p_{ij}(n) \to 0$ as $n \to \infty$ for all i.*

Proof. This is immediate from (4). ■

An application of (4) to the random walk is given in Problem (5.11.4).

Thus each state is either persistent or transient. It is intuitively clear that the number $N(i)$ of times which the chain visits its starting point i satisfies

(6) $$\mathbf{P}(N(i) = \infty) = \begin{cases} 1 & \text{if } i \text{ is persistent} \\ 0 & \text{if } i \text{ is transient,} \end{cases}$$

since after each such visit, subsequent return is assured if and only if $f_{ii}=1$ (see Problem (6.13.5) for a more detailed argument).

Here is another important classification of states. Given that $X_0=i$, let

$$T_{ij}=\min\{n\geqslant 1: X_n=j\}$$

be the time of the first visit to j, with the convention that $T_{ij}=\infty$ if this visit never occurs; T_{ii} is defective if and only if i is transient, and in this case $\mathbf{E}(T_{ii})=\infty$.

(7) **Definition.** The **mean recurrence time** μ_i of a state i is defined as

$$\mu_i=\mathbf{E}(T_{ii})=\begin{cases}\sum_n nf_{ii}(n) & \text{if } i \text{ is persistent.}\\ \infty & \text{if } i \text{ is transient.}\end{cases}$$

μ_i may be infinite even if i is persistent.

(8) **Definition.**

The persistent state i is called $\begin{cases}\textbf{null} & \text{if } \mu_i=\infty\\ \textbf{non-null} \text{ (or } \textbf{positive}) & \text{if } \mu_i<\infty.\end{cases}$

There is a simple criterion for nullity in terms of the transition probabilities.

(9) **Theorem.** *A persistent state i is null if and only if $p_{ii}(n)\to 0$ as $n\to\infty$; if this holds then $p_{ji}(n)\to 0$ for all j.*

Proof. We defer this until Note (a) after (6.4.16). ■

Finally, for technical reasons we shall sometimes be interested in the epochs of time at which return to the starting point is possible.

(10) **Definition.** The **period** $d(i)$ of a state i is defined by

$$d(i)=\gcd\{n: p_{ii}(n)>0\},$$

the greatest common divisor of the epochs at which return is possible. We call i **periodic** if $d(i)>1$ and **aperiodic** if $d(i)=1$.

That is to say, $p_{ii}(n)=0$ unless n is a multiple of $d(i)$.

(11) **Definition.** A state is called **ergodic** if it is persistent, non-null, and aperiodic.

(12) **Example. Random walk.** (5.3.4) and (5.11.4) show that the states of the random walk are all

(a) transient, if $p\neq\frac{1}{2}$

(b) null persistent, if $p=\frac{1}{2}$.

All states have period $d=2$. ●

(13) **Example. Branching process.** Consider the branching process of Section 5.4 and suppose that $\mathbf{P}(Z_1=0)>0$. Then 0 is called an *absorbing* state, because the chain never leaves it once it has visited it; all other states are transient. ●

6.3 Classification of chains

Next, we consider the way in which the states of a Markov chain are related to each other. This investigation will help us to achieve a full classification of the states in the language of the previous section.

(1) **Definition.** We say i **communicates with** j, written $i \to j$, if the chain may ever visit state j with positive probability, starting from i. That is, $i \to j$ if $p_{ij}(m)>0$ for some $m \geq 0$. We say i and j **intercommunicate** if $i \to j$ and $j \to i$, in which case we write $i \leftrightarrow j$.

If $i \neq j$, then $i \to j$ if and only if $f_{ij}>0$. Clearly $i \to i$ since $p_{ii}(0)=1$, and it follows that $\leftrightarrow$ is an equivalence relation (*exercise*: if $i \leftrightarrow j$ and $j \leftrightarrow k$, show that $i \leftrightarrow k$). The state space S can be partitioned into the equivalence classes of $\leftrightarrow$. Within each equivalence class all states are of the same type.

(2) **Theorem.** *If $i \leftrightarrow j$ then*

(a) *i and j have the same period*
(b) *i is transient if and only if j is transient*
(c) *i is null persistent if and only if j is null persistent.*

Proof. (b) If $i \leftrightarrow j$ then there exist $m, n \geq 0$ such that

$$\alpha = p_{ij}(m)p_{ji}(n)>0.$$

By the Chapman–Kolmogorov equations (6.1.7),

$$p_{ii}(m+r+n) \geq p_{ij}(m)p_{jj}(r)p_{ji}(n)=\alpha p_{jj}(r),$$

for any non-negative integer r. Now sum over r to obtain

$$\sum_r p_{jj}(r)<\infty \quad \text{if} \quad \sum_r p_{ii}(r)<\infty.$$

Thus, by (6.2.4), j is transient if i is transient. The converse holds similarly and (b) is shown.

(a) This proof is similar and proceeds by way of (6.2.10).

(c) We defer this until the next section. A possible route is by way of (6.2.9), but we prefer to proceed differently in order to avoid the danger of using a circular argument. ■

(3) **Definition.** A set C of states is called

(a) **closed** if $p_{ij}=0$ for all $i \in C$, $j \notin C$
(b) **irreducible** if $i \leftrightarrow j$ for all $i, j \in C$.

Once the chain takes a value in a closed set C of states then it never leaves C subsequently. A closed set containing exactly one state is called *absorbing*; for example, the state 0 is absorbing for the branching process. It is clear that the equivalence classes of $\leftrightarrow$ are irreducible. We call an irreducible set C *aperiodic* (or *persistent, null* and so on) if all the states in C have this property; (6.3.2) ensures that this is meaningful. If the whole state space S is irreducible, then we speak of the chain itself as having the property in question.

(4) **Decomposition Theorem.** *The state space S can be partitioned uniquely as*

$$S = T \cup C_1 \cup C_2 \cup \dots$$

where T is the set of transient states, and the C's are irreducible closed sets of persistent states.

Proof. Let $C_1, C_2, \dots$ be the persistent equivalence classes of $\leftrightarrow$. We need only show that each C_r is closed. Suppose $i \in C_r$ and $i \to j$. There is positive probability of going from i to j without revisiting i on the way (see Problem (6.13.10)). If $j \nrightarrow i$ then return to i is impossible which contradicts the fact that i is persistent. ■

The Decomposition Theorem clears the air a little. For, if $X_0 \in C_r$, say, then the chain never leaves C_r and we might as well take C_r to be the whole state space. On the other hand, if $X_0 \in T$ then the chain either stays in T for ever or moves eventually to one of the C's where it subsequently remains. Thus, either the chain always takes values in the set of transient states or it lies eventually in some irreducible closed set of persistent states. For the special case when S is finite the first of these possibilities cannot occur.

(5) **Lemma.** *If S is finite, then at least one state is persistent and all persistent states are non-null.*

Proof. If all states are transient, then take the limit through the summation sign to obtain the contradiction

$$1 = \lim_{n\to\infty} \sum_j p_{ij}(n) = 0$$

by (6.2.5). The same contradiction arises by (6.2.9) for the closed set of all null persistent states, should this set be non-empty. ■

(6) **Example.** Let $S = \{1, 2, 3, 4, 5, 6\}$ and

$$\mathbf{P} = \begin{pmatrix} \frac{1}{2} & \frac{1}{2} & 0 & 0 & 0 & 0 \\ \frac{1}{4} & \frac{3}{4} & 0 & 0 & 0 & 0 \\ \frac{1}{4} & \frac{1}{4} & \frac{1}{4} & \frac{1}{4} & 0 & 0 \\ \frac{1}{4} & 0 & \frac{1}{4} & \frac{1}{4} & 0 & \frac{1}{4} \\ 0 & 0 & 0 & 0 & \frac{1}{2} & \frac{1}{2} \\ 0 & 0 & 0 & 0 & \frac{1}{2} & \frac{1}{2} \end{pmatrix}.$$

$\{1, 2\}$ and $\{5, 6\}$ are irreducible closed sets and therefore contain persistent non-null states. States 3 and 4 are transient because $3 \to 4 \to 6$ but return from 6 is impossible. All states have period 1 because $p_{ii}(1) > 0$ for all i. Hence, 3 and 4 are transient, and 1, 2, 5, and 6 are ergodic. Easy calculations give

$$f_{11}(n) = \begin{cases} p_{11} = \frac{1}{2} & \text{if } n = 1 \\ p_{12}(p_{22})^{n-2} p_{21} = \frac{1}{2}(\frac{3}{4})^{n-2} \frac{1}{4} & \text{if } n \geq 2 \end{cases}$$

and hence $\mu_1 = \sum_n n f_{11}(n) = 3$. Other mean recurrence times can be found similarly. The next section gives another way of finding the μ's which usually requires less computation. ●

6.4 Stationary distributions and the limit theorem

How does X_n behave after a long time n has elapsed? The sequence $\{X_n\}$ cannot generally, of course, converge to some particular state s since it enjoys the inherent random fluctuation which is specified by the transition matrix. However, we might hold out some hope that the *distribution* of X_n settles down. Indeed, subject to certain conditions this turns out to be the case. The classical study of limiting distributions proceeds by algebraic manipulation of the generating functions of (6.2.3); we shall avoid this here, contenting ourselves for the moment with results which are not quite the best possible but which have attractive probabilistic proofs. This section is in two parts, which deal with stationary distributions and limit theorems respectively.

(A) Stationary distributions. We shall see that the existence of a limiting distribution for X_n, as $n \to \infty$, is closely bound up with the existence of so-called 'stationary distributions'.

(1) **Definition.** The vector $\boldsymbol{\pi}$ is called a **stationary distribution** of the chain if $\boldsymbol{\pi}$ has entries $(\pi_j : j \in S)$ such that

(a) $\pi_j \geq 0$ for all j, and $\sum_j \pi_j = 1$

(b) $\boldsymbol{\pi} = \boldsymbol{\pi} \mathbf{P}$, which is to say that $\pi_j = \sum_i \pi_i p_{ij}$ for all j.

Such a distribution is called stationary for the following reason. Iterate (1b) to obtain

$$\boldsymbol{\pi}\mathbf{P}^2 = (\boldsymbol{\pi}\mathbf{P})\mathbf{P} = \boldsymbol{\pi}\mathbf{P} = \boldsymbol{\pi}$$

and so

(2) $$\boldsymbol{\pi}\mathbf{P}^n = \boldsymbol{\pi} \quad \text{for all } n \geq 0.$$

Now use (6.1.8) to see that if X_0 has distribution $\boldsymbol{\pi}$ then X_n has distribution $\boldsymbol{\pi}$ for all n, showing that the distribution of X_n is 'stationary' as time passes; in such a case, of course, $\boldsymbol{\pi}$ is also the limiting distribution of X_n as $n \to \infty$.

Following the discussion after the Decomposition Theorem (6.3.4), we shall assume henceforth that the chain is irreducible and shall investigate the existence of stationary distributions.

(3) **Theorem.** *An irreducible chain has a stationary distribution* $\boldsymbol{\pi}$ *if and only if all the states are non-null persistent; in this case,* $\boldsymbol{\pi}$ *is the unique stationary distribution and is given by* $\pi_i = \mu_i^{-1}$ *for each* $i \in S$, *where* μ_i *is the mean recurrence time of* i.

Here are two lemmas, preliminary to the proof of (3).

(4) **Lemma.** *If* $\boldsymbol{\pi}$ *is a stationary distribution of an irreducible chain, then* $\pi_i > 0$ *for all* $i \in S$.

Proof. If $\pi_i = 0$ then

$$0 = \pi_i = \sum_j \pi_j p_{ji}(n) \geq \pi_j p_{ji}(n) \quad \text{for all } j \text{ and } n,$$

and so $\pi_j = 0$ whenever $j \to i$. Thus $\pi_j = 0$ for all j, which contradicts (1a). ■

The second lemma exhibits a stationary distribution explicitly for an irreducible chain with a non-null persistent state k. Let $\rho_i(k)$ be the mean number of visits of the chain to state i between two successive visits to state k; that is, if $X_0 = k$, then

$$\begin{aligned}\rho_i(k) &= \mathbf{E}\left(\sum_{n=0}^{\infty} I_{\{X_n = i\} \cap \{T_{kk} > n\}}\right)\\ &= \sum_{n=0}^{\infty} \mathbf{P}(X_n = i, T_{kk} > n \mid X_0 = k)\end{aligned}$$

where T_{kk} is the time of the first return to state k, as before.

(5) **Lemma.** *If* k *is a non-null state of an irreducible persistent chain, then there exists a stationary distribution* $\boldsymbol{\pi}$ *with entries* $\pi_i = \rho_i(k)/\mu_k$.

Proof. Certainly $\rho_i(k) < \infty$ because $\rho_i(k) \leq \mathbf{E}(T_{kk}) < \infty$. First check that the row vector $\boldsymbol{\rho}(k)$ with entries $(\rho_i(k) : i \in S)$ satisfies $\boldsymbol{\rho}(k) = \boldsymbol{\rho}(k)\mathbf{P}$. For $j \neq k$ we have that

$$\begin{aligned}\rho_j(k) &= \sum_{n=1}^{\infty} \mathbf{P}(X_n = j, T_{kk} > n \mid X_0 = k)\\ &= \sum_{n=1}^{\infty} \mathbf{P}(X_n = j, T_{kk} > n-1 \mid X_0 = k) \quad \text{because} \quad j \neq k\\ &= \sum_{n=1}^{\infty} \sum_i \mathbf{P}(X_n = j, X_{n-1} = i, T_{kk} > n-1 \mid X_0 = k)\\ &= \sum_{n=1}^{\infty} \sum_i p_{ij} \mathbf{P}(X_{n-1} = i, T_{kk} > n-1 \mid X_0 = k) \quad \text{by the Markov property}\\ &= \sum_i p_{ij} \sum_{m=0}^{\infty} \mathbf{P}(X_m = i, T_{kk} > m \mid X_0 = k) \quad \text{putting } m = n-1\\ &= \sum_i \rho_i(k) p_{ij}.\end{aligned}$$

For the case $j=k$, note first that $\rho_k(k)=1$. Then

$$\begin{aligned}\rho_k(k)=1&=\sum_{n=1}^{\infty}\mathbf{P}(T_{kk}=n\mid X_0=k)\quad\text{because } k \text{ is persistent}\\&=\sum_{n=1}^{\infty}\sum_i \mathbf{P}(X_{n-1}=i,\, T_{kk}=n\mid X_0=k)\\&=\sum_{n=1}^{\infty}\sum_i p_{ik}\mathbf{P}(X_{n-1}=i,\, T_{kk}>n-1\mid X_0=k)\\&=\sum_i \rho_i(k)p_{ik}\end{aligned}$$

as before. Thus

$$\rho_j(k)=\sum_i \rho_i(k)p_{ij}\quad\text{for all } j\in S,$$

and so $\pi_j=\rho_j(k)/\mu_k$ satisfies $\boldsymbol{\pi}=\boldsymbol{\pi}\mathbf{P}$. Certainly $\pi_j\geqslant 0$ for all j, and the proof is completed by the observation that

$$\begin{aligned}\mu_k&=\sum_{n=0}^{\infty}\mathbf{P}(T_{kk}>n\mid X_0=k)\quad\text{from Problem (3.9.13)}\\&=\sum_j\sum_{n=0}^{\infty}\mathbf{P}(X_n=j,\, T_{kk}>n\mid X_0=k)\\&=\sum_j \rho_j(k).\end{aligned}$$

■

Proof of (3). Suppose that $\boldsymbol{\pi}$ is a stationary distribution of the chain. If all states are transient then $p_{ij}(n)\to 0$, as $n\to\infty$, for all i and j by (6.2.5). From (2),

(6) $$\pi_j=\sum_i \pi_i p_{ij}(n)\to 0\quad\text{as}\quad n\to\infty,\quad\text{for all } i \text{ and } j,$$

which contradicts (1a). Thus all states are persistent. To see the limit in (6)†, let F be a finite subset of S and write

$$\begin{aligned}\sum_i \pi_i p_{ij}(n)&\leqslant\sum_{i\in F}\pi_i p_{ij}(n)+\sum_{i\notin F}\pi_i\\&\to\sum_{i\notin F}\pi_i\quad\text{as}\quad n\to\infty\\&\to 0\qquad\text{as}\quad F\uparrow S.\end{aligned}$$

We show next that the existence of $\boldsymbol{\pi}$ implies that all states are non-null and that $\pi_i=\mu_i^{-1}$ for each i. Suppose that X_0 has distribution $\boldsymbol{\pi}$, so that $\mathbf{P}(X_0=i)=\pi_i$ for each i. Then, by (3.9.13),

$$\begin{aligned}\pi_j\mu_j&=\sum_{n=1}^{\infty}\mathbf{P}(T_{jj}\geqslant n\mid X_0=j)\mathbf{P}(X_0=j)\\&=\sum_{n=1}^{\infty}\mathbf{P}(T_{jj}\geqslant n,\, X_0=j).\end{aligned}$$

† Actually this argument is a form of the bounded convergence theorem (5.6.12) applied to sums instead of to integrals. We shall make repeated use of this technique.

However, $\mathbf{P}(T_{jj}\geq 1, X_0=j)=\mathbf{P}(X_0=j)$, and for $n\geq 2$

$$\begin{aligned}\mathbf{P}(T_{jj}\geq n, X_0=j)&=\mathbf{P}(X_0=j, X_m\neq j \text{ for } 1\leq m\leq n-1)\\&=\mathbf{P}(X_m\neq j \text{ for } 1\leq m\leq n-1)\\&\qquad -\mathbf{P}(X_m\neq j \text{ for } 0\leq m\leq n-1)\\&=\mathbf{P}(X_m\neq j \text{ for } 0\leq m\leq n-2)\\&\qquad -\mathbf{P}(X_m\neq j \text{ for } 0\leq m\leq n-1) \quad \text{by homogeneity}\\&=a_{n-2}-a_{n-1}\end{aligned}$$

where $a_n=\mathbf{P}(X_m\neq j \text{ for } 0\leq m\leq n)$. Sum over n to obtain

$$\pi_j\mu_j=\mathbf{P}(X_0=j)+\mathbf{P}(X_0\neq j)-\lim_{n\to\infty} a_n=1-\lim_{n\to\infty} a_n.$$

However,

$$\lim_{n\to\infty} a_n=\mathbf{P}(X_m\neq j \text{ for all } m)=0$$

by the persistence of j. We have shown that

(7) $$\pi_j\mu_j=1,$$

implying that $\mu_j=\pi_j^{-1}<\infty$ by (4), so that all the states of the chain are non-null. Furthermore, (7) specifies π_j uniquely as μ_j^{-1}.

Thus, if $\boldsymbol{\pi}$ exists then it is unique and all the states of the chain are non-null persistent. Conversely, if the states of the chain are non-null persistent then the chain has a stationary distribution given by (5). ■

We may now complete the proof of (6.3.2c).

Proof of (6.3.2c). Let $C(i)$ be the irreducible closed equivalence class of states which contains the non-null persistent state i. Suppose that $X_0\in C(i)$. Then $X_n\in C(i)$ for all n, and (5) and (3) combine to tell us that all states in $C(i)$ are non-null. ■

(8) **Example (6.3.6) revisited.** To find μ_1 and μ_2 consider the irreducible closed set $C=\{1, 2\}$. If $X_0\in C$, then solve the equation $\boldsymbol{\pi}=\boldsymbol{\pi}\mathbf{P}_C$ for $\boldsymbol{\pi}=(\pi_1, \pi_2)$ in terms of

$$\mathbf{P}_C=\begin{pmatrix}\frac{1}{2} & \frac{1}{2}\\ \frac{1}{4} & \frac{3}{4}\end{pmatrix}$$

to find the unique stationary distribution $\boldsymbol{\pi}=(\frac{1}{3}, \frac{2}{3})$, giving that

$$\mu_1=\pi_1^{-1}=3, \qquad \mu_2=\pi_2^{-1}=\tfrac{3}{2}.$$

Now find the other mean recurrence times yourself (*exercise*). ●

Theorem (3) provides a useful criterion for deciding whether or not an irreducible chain is non-null persistent: just look for a stationary distribution. There is a similar criterion for the transience of irreducible chains.

(9) **Theorem.** *Let $s \in S$ be any state of an irreducible chain. The chain is transient if and only if there exists a non-zero solution $\{y_j : j \neq s\}$ to the equations*

(10) $$y_i = \sum_{j \neq s} p_{ij} y_j, \qquad i \neq s,$$

such that $|y_j| \leq 1$ for all j.

Proof. The chain is transient if and only if s is transient. First suppose s is transient and define

(11) $$\begin{aligned}\tau_i(n) &= \mathbf{P}(\text{no visit to } s \text{ in first } n \text{ steps} \mid X_0 = i)\\ &= \mathbf{P}(X_m \neq s, 1 \leq m \leq n \mid X_0 = i).\end{aligned}$$

Then

$$\tau_i(1) = \sum_{j \neq s} p_{ij}, \qquad \tau_i(n+1) = \sum_{j \neq s} p_{ij} \tau_j(n).$$

Furthermore, $\tau_i(n) \geq \tau_i(n+1)$, and so

$$\tau_i = \lim_{n \to \infty} \tau_i(n) = \mathbf{P}(\text{no visit to } s \text{ ever} \mid X_0 = i) = 1 - f_{is}$$

satisfies (10). (Can *you* prove this? Use the method of proof of (6).) Also $\tau_i > 0$ for some i, since otherwise $f_{is} = 1$ for all $i \neq s$, and so

$$f_{ss} = p_{ss} + \sum_{i \neq s} p_{si} f_{is} = \sum_i p_{si} = 1$$

by conditioning on X_1; this contradicts the transience of s.

Conversely, let $\boldsymbol{y}$ satisfy (10) with $|y_i| \leq 1$. Then

$$|y_i| \leq \sum_{j \neq s} p_{ij} |y_j| \leq \sum_{j \neq s} p_{ij} = \tau_i(1)$$

$$|y_i| \leq \sum_{j \neq s} p_{ij} |\tau_j(1)| = \tau_j(2),$$

and so on, where the $\tau_i(n)$ are given by (11). Thus

$$|y_i| \leq \tau_i(n) \quad \text{for all } n.$$

Let $n \to \infty$ to show that

$$\tau_i = \lim_{n \to \infty} \tau_i(n) > 0$$

for some i, which shows that s is transient by the result of (6.13.10). ■

This theorem provides a necessary and sufficient condition for persistence: an irreducible chain is persistent if and only if the only bounded solution to (10) is the zero solution. This combines with (3) to give a condition for null persistence. Another condition is the following (see Cox and Miller 1965, p. 113 for a proof); a corresponding result holds for any countably infinite state space S.

(12) **Theorem.** *Let $s \in S$ be any state of an irreducible chain on $S = \{0, 1, 2, \ldots\}$. The chain is persistent if there exists a solution $\{y_j : j \neq s\}$ to the inequalities*

(13) $$y_i \geq \sum_{j \neq s} p_{ij} y_j, \qquad i \neq s,$$

such that $y_i \to \infty$ *as* $i \to \infty$.

(14) **Example. Random walk with reflecting barrier.** A particle performs a random walk on the non-negative integers with a reflecting barrier at 0. The transition probabilities are

$$p_{i,i+1} = p \quad \text{if} \quad i \geq 0$$

$$p_{0,0} = q, \qquad p_{i,i-1} = q \quad \text{if} \quad i \geq 1$$

where $p + q = 1$. Let $\rho = p/q$.

(a) If $q < p$, take $s = 0$ to see that $y_j = 1 - \rho^{-j}$ satisfies (10), and so the chain is transient.
(b) Solve the equation $\boldsymbol{\pi} = \boldsymbol{\pi} \mathbf{P}$ to find that there exists a stationary distribution, with $\pi_j = \rho^j(1-\rho)$, if and only if $q > p$. Thus the chain is non-null persistent if and only if $q > p$.
(c) If $q = p = \frac{1}{2}$, take $s = 0$ in (12) and check that $y_j = j$ $(j \geq 1)$ solves (13). Thus the chain is null persistent.

These conclusions match our intuitions well. ●

(B) Limit theorems. Next we explore the link between the existence of a stationary distribution and the limiting behaviour of the probabilities $p_{ij}(n)$ as $n \to \infty$. The following example indicates a difficulty which arises from periodicity.

(15) **Example.** If $S = \{1, 2\}$ and $p_{12} = p_{21} = 1$, then

$$p_{11}(n) = p_{22}(n) = \begin{cases} 0 & \text{if} \quad n \text{ is odd} \\ 1 & \text{if} \quad n \text{ is even.} \end{cases}$$

Clearly $p_{ii}(n)$ does not converge as $n \to \infty$; the reason is that both states are periodic with period 2. ●

Until further notice we shall deal only with irreducible *aperiodic* chains. The principal result is the following theorem.

(16) **Theorem.** *For an irreducible aperiodic chain, we have that*

$$p_{ij}(n) \to \frac{1}{\mu_j} \quad \textit{as} \quad n \to \infty, \quad \textit{for all } i \textit{ and } j.$$

We make the following remarks.

(a) If the chain is *transient* or *null persistent* then $p_{ij}(n) \to 0$ for all i and j, since $\mu_j = \infty$. Now we can prove (6.2.9). Let $C(i)$ be the irreducible closed set of states which contains the persistent state i.

If $C(i)$ is aperiodic then the result is an immediate consequence of (16); the periodic case can be treated similarly, but with slightly more difficulty (see Note (d) following).

(b) If the chain is *non-null persistent* then $p_{ij}(n) \to \pi_j = \mu_j^{-1}$, where $\boldsymbol{\pi}$ is the unique stationary distribution by (3).

(c) It follows from (16) that the limit probability, $\lim_{n\to\infty} p_{ij}(n)$, does not depend on the starting point $X_0 = i$; that is, the chain forgets its origin. It is now easy to check that

$$\mathbf{P}(X_n = j) = \sum_i \mathbf{P}(X_0 = i) p_{ij}(n) \to \frac{1}{\mu_j} \quad \text{as} \quad n \to \infty$$

by (6.1.8), irrespective of the distribution of X_0.

(d) If $X = \{X_n\}$ is an irreducible chain with period d, then $Y = \{Y_n = X_{nd} : n \geq 0\}$ is an aperiodic chain, and it follows that

$$p_{jj}(nd) = \mathbf{P}(Y_n = j \mid Y_0 = j) \to \frac{d}{\mu_j} \quad \text{as} \quad n \to \infty.$$

Proof. If the chain is transient then the result holds from (6.2.5). The persistent case is treated by an important technique known as 'coupling'. Construct a 'coupled chain' $Z = (X, Y)$, being an ordered pair $X = \{X_n : n \geq 0\}$, $Y = \{Y_n : n \geq 0\}$ of *independent* Markov chains, each with transition matrix $\mathbf{P}$. Then $Z = \{Z_n = (X_n, Y_n) : n \geq 0\}$ takes values in $S \times S$, and it is easy to check that Z is a Markov chain with transition probabilities

$$\begin{aligned} p_{ij,kl} &= \mathbf{P}(Z_{n+1} = (k, l) \mid Z_n = (i, j)) \\ &= \mathbf{P}(X_{n+1} = k \mid X_n = i)\mathbf{P}(Y_{n+1} = l \mid Y_n = j) \quad \text{by independence} \\ &= p_{ik} p_{jl}. \end{aligned}$$

Since X is irreducible and aperiodic, for any states i, j, k, l there exists $N = N(i, j, k, l)$ such that

$$p_{ik}(n) p_{jl}(n) > 0 \quad \text{for all } n \geq N;$$

thus Z also is irreducible (see Problem (6.13.4); *only here* do we require that X be aperiodic).

Suppose that X is non-null persistent. Then X has a unique stationary distribution $\boldsymbol{\pi}$, by (3), and it is easy to see that Z has a stationary distribution $\boldsymbol{\nu} = (\nu_{ij} : i, j \in S)$ given by $\nu_{ij} = \pi_i \pi_j$; thus Z is also non-null persistent, by (3). Now, suppose that $X_0 = i$ and $Y_0 = j$, so that $Z_0 = (i, j)$. Choose any state $s \in S$ and let

$$T = \min\{n \geq 1 : Z_n = (s, s)\}$$

denote the time of the first passage of Z to (s, s); from Problem (6.13.10) and the persistence of Z, $\mathbf{P}(T < \infty) = 1$. The central idea of the proof is the following observation. If $m \leq n$ and $X_m = Y_m$, then X_n and Y_n are identically distributed since the distributions of X_n and Y_n depend only upon the shared transition matrix $\mathbf{P}$ and upon the shared value of the chains at the mth stage. Thus, conditional on $\{T \leq n\}$, X_n and Y_n have the same distribution. We shall use this fact, together with the finiteness of T, to show that the ultimate distributions of X and Y are independent of their starting points. More precisely, starting from $Z_0 = (X_0, Y_0) = (i, j)$,

$$\begin{aligned} p_{ik}(n) &= \mathbf{P}(X_n = k) \\ &= \mathbf{P}(X_n = k, T \leq n) + \mathbf{P}(X_n = k, T > n) \\ &= \mathbf{P}(Y_n = k, T \leq n) + \mathbf{P}(X_n = k, T > n) \\ &\quad \text{because, given that } T \leq n,\ X_n \text{ and } Y_n \text{ are identically distributed} \\ &\leq \mathbf{P}(Y_n = k) + \mathbf{P}(T > n) \\ &= p_{jk}(n) + \mathbf{P}(T > n). \end{aligned}$$

This, and the related inequality with i and j interchanged, yields

$$|p_{ik}(n) - p_{jk}(n)| \leq \mathbf{P}(T > n) \to 0 \quad \text{as} \quad n \to \infty$$

because $\mathbf{P}(T < \infty) = 1$; therefore

(17) $$p_{ik}(n) - p_{jk}(n) \to 0 \quad \text{as} \quad n \to \infty \quad \text{for all } i, j, \text{ and } k.$$

Thus, if $\lim_{n\to\infty} p_{ik}(n)$ exists, then it does not depend on i. To show that it exists, write

(18) $$\pi_k - p_{jk}(n) = \sum_i \pi_i (p_{ik}(n) - p_{jk}(n)) \to 0 \quad \text{as} \quad n \to \infty,$$

giving the result. To see that the limit in (18) follows from (17), use the bounded convergence argument in the proof of (6), noting that $|p_{ik}(n) - p_{jk}(n)| \leq 2$.

Finally, suppose that X is null persistent; the argument is a little trickier in this case. If Z is transient, then from (6.2.5)

$$\mathbf{P}(Z_n = (j, j) \mid Z_0 = (i, i)) = p_{ij}(n)^2 \to 0 \quad \text{as} \quad n \to \infty$$

and the result holds. If Z is non-null persistent then, starting from $Z_0 = (i, i)$, the epoch T_{ii}^z of the first return of Z to (i, i) is no smaller than the epoch T_{ii} of the first return of X to i; however, $\mathbf{E}(T_{ii}) = \infty$ and $\mathbf{E}(T_{ii}^z) < \infty$ which is a contradiction. Lastly, suppose that Z is null persistent. The argument which leads to (17) still holds, and we wish to deduce that

(19) $$p_{ij}(n) \to 0 \quad \text{as} \quad n \to \infty \quad \text{for all } i \text{ and } j.$$

If (19) does not hold then there exists a subsequence $n_1, n_2, \ldots$ along which

(20) $$p_{ij}(n_r) \to \alpha_j \quad \text{as} \quad r \to \infty \quad \text{for all } i \text{ and } j,$$

for some $\boldsymbol{\alpha}$, where the α_j's are not all zero and are independent of i by (17); this is an application of the principle of 'diagonal selection' (see Billingsley 1979, p. 292, or Feller 1968, p. 336). For any finite set F of states,

$$\sum_{j \in F} \alpha_j = \lim_{r\to\infty} \sum_{j \in F} p_{ij}(n_r) \leq 1$$

and so $\alpha = \sum_j \alpha_j$ satisfies $0 < \alpha \leq 1$. Furthermore

$$\sum_{k \in F} p_{ik}(n_r) p_{kj} \leq p_{ij}(n_r + 1) = \sum_k p_{ik} p_{kj}(n_r);$$

let $r \to \infty$ here to deduce from (20) and bounded convergence (as used in the proof of (18)) that

$$\sum_{k \in F} \alpha_k p_{kj} \leq \sum_k p_{ik} \alpha_j = \alpha_j,$$

and so, letting $F \uparrow S$, we obtain $\sum_k \alpha_k p_{kj} \leq \alpha_j$ for each $j \in S$. But equality must hold here, since if strict inequality holds for some j then

$$\sum_k \alpha_k = \sum_{k,j} \alpha_k p_{kj} < \sum_j \alpha_j,$$

which is a contradiction. Therefore

$$\sum_k \alpha_k p_{kj} = \alpha_j \quad \text{for each } j \in S,$$

giving that $\boldsymbol{\pi} = \{\alpha_j / \alpha : j \in S\}$ is a stationary distribution for X; this contradicts the nullity of X by (3). ■

The original and more general version of the ergodic theorem (16) for Markov chains does *not* assume that the chain is irreducible. We state it here; it is proved in (10.4.20).

(21) **Theorem.** *For any aperiodic state j of a Markov chain,*

$$p_{jj}(n) \to \frac{1}{\mu_j} \quad \text{as} \quad n \to \infty.$$

Furthermore, if i is any other state then

$$p_{ij}(n) \to \frac{1}{\mu_j} f_{ij} \quad \text{as} \quad n \to \infty.$$

(22) **Corollary.** *Let*

$$\tau_{ij}(n) = \frac{1}{n} \sum_{m=1}^{n} p_{ij}(m)$$

be the mean proportion of elapsed time up to the nth step during which the chain was in state j, starting from i. Then, if j is aperiodic,

$$\tau_{ij}(n) \to \frac{1}{\mu_j} f_{ij} \quad \text{as } n \to \infty.$$

Proof. *Exercise*: prove and use the fact that, as $n \to \infty$,

$$\frac{1}{n} \sum_{1}^{n} x_i \to x \quad \text{if} \quad x_n \to x.$$

■

6.5 Time-reversibility

Most laws of physics have the property that they would make the same assertions if the universal clock were reversed and time were made to run backwards. It may be thought to be implausible that nature works in such ways (have *you* ever seen the fragments of a shattered teacup re-assemble themselves on the table from which they fell?), and so one might postulate a non-decreasing quantity called 'entropy'. However, never mind such objections; let us think about the reversal of the time scale of a Markov chain.

Suppose that $\{X_n : -\infty < n < \infty\}$ is an irreducible non-null persistent Markov chain, with transition matrix $\mathbf{P}$ and unique stationary distribution $\boldsymbol{\pi}$. Suppose further that X_n has distribution $\boldsymbol{\pi}$ for every $n \in (-\infty, \infty)$. (In order that this hold, it is *not* sufficient to assume that X_0 has distribution $\boldsymbol{\pi}$; certainly in this case X_n has distribution $\boldsymbol{\pi}$ for all $n \geqslant 0$, by (6.1.8), but it does not follow that X_{-1} has distribution $\boldsymbol{\pi}$ also.) Define the 'reversed chain' Y by

$$Y_n = X_{-n}, \quad -\infty < n < \infty.$$

It is not difficult to show that Y is a Markov chain also, and of course Y_n has distribution $\boldsymbol{\pi}$ for each n.

(1) **Definition.** X is called **time-reversible** if the transition matrices of X and Y are the same.

(2) **Theorem.** *X is time-reversible if and only if*

$$\pi_i p_{ij} = \pi_j p_{ji} \quad \textit{for all } i, j \in S.$$

Proof. The transition probabilities of Y are

$$\begin{aligned} q_{ij} &= \mathbf{P}(Y_{n+1} = j \mid Y_n = i) \\ &= \mathbf{P}(X_{-n-1} = j \mid X_{-n} = i) \\ &= \mathbf{P}(X_m = i \mid X_{m-1} = j)\mathbf{P}(X_{m-1} = j)/\mathbf{P}(X_m = i) \text{ where } m = -n \\ &= p_{ji}\frac{\pi_j}{\pi_i} \end{aligned}$$

by the identity

$$\mathbf{P}(A \mid B) = \mathbf{P}(B \mid A)\mathbf{P}(A)/\mathbf{P}(B).$$

Thus $p_{ij} = q_{ij}$ if and only if $\pi_i p_{ij} = \pi_j p_{ji}$. ■

The equations (2) of time-reversibility provide a useful way of finding the stationary distributions of some chains.

(3) **Theorem.** *For an irreducible chain, if there exists $\boldsymbol{\pi}$ such that*

$$0 \leqslant \pi_i \leqslant 1, \qquad \sum_i \pi_i = 1, \qquad \pi_i p_{ij} = \pi_j p_{ji} \quad \textit{for all } i, j,$$

then the chain is time-reversible and non-null persistent, with stationary distribution $\boldsymbol{\pi}$.

Proof. Suppose that $\boldsymbol{\pi}$ satisfies the conditions of the theorem. Then

$$\sum_i \pi_i p_{ij} = \sum_i \pi_j p_{ji} = \pi_j \sum_i p_{ji} = \pi_j$$

and so $\boldsymbol{\pi} = \boldsymbol{\pi}\mathbf{P}$ and the result follows from (6.4.3). ■

(4) **Example. Ehrenfest model of diffusion.** Two containers A and B are placed adjacently to each other and gas is allowed to pass through a small aperture joining them. A total of m gas molecules is distributed between the containers. We assume that at each epoch of time one molecule, picked uniformly at random from the m available, passes through this aperture. Let X_n be the number of molecules in container A after n units of time have passed. Clearly $\{X_n\}$ is a Markov chain with transition matrix

$$p_{i,i+1} = 1 - \frac{i}{m}, \qquad p_{i,i-1} = \frac{i}{m} \quad \text{if} \quad 0 \leq i \leq m.$$

Rather than solve the equation $\boldsymbol{\pi} = \boldsymbol{\pi}\mathbf{P}$ to find the stationary distribution, we note that such a reasonable diffusion model should be time-reversible. Look for solutions of

$$\pi_i p_{ij} = \pi_j p_{ji}$$

to obtain $\pi_i = \binom{m}{i}(\frac{1}{2})^m$ ●

6.6 Chains with finitely many states

The theory of Markov chains is much simplified by the condition that S be finite. By (6.3.5), if S is irreducible then it is necessarily non-null persistent. It may even be possible to calculate the n-step transition probabilities explicitly. Of central importance here is the following algebraic theorem, in which $i = \sqrt{(-1)}$. Let N denote the cardinality of S.

(1) **Theorem. (Perron–Frobenius).** *If* $\mathbf{P}$ *is the transition matrix of a finite irreducible chain with period d then*

(a) $\lambda_1 = 1$ *is an eigenvalue of* $\mathbf{P}$
(b) *the d complex roots of unity*

$$\lambda_1 = \omega^0, \lambda_2 = \omega^1, \ldots, \lambda_d = \omega^{d-1} \text{ where } \omega = \exp(2\pi i/d)$$

are eigenvalues of $\mathbf{P}$
(c) *the remaining eigenvalues* $\lambda_{d+1}, \ldots, \lambda_N$ *satisfy* $|\lambda_j| < 1$.

If the eigenvalues $\lambda_1, \ldots, \lambda_N$ are distinct then it is well known that there exists a matrix $\mathbf{B}$ such that

$$\mathbf{P} = \mathbf{B}^{-1}\mathbf{\Lambda}\mathbf{B}$$

where $\boldsymbol{\Lambda}$ is the diagonal matrix with entries $\lambda_1, \ldots, \lambda_N$. Thus

$$\boldsymbol{P}^n = \boldsymbol{B}^{-1}\boldsymbol{\Lambda}^n\boldsymbol{B} = \boldsymbol{B}^{-1}\begin{pmatrix} \lambda_1^n & & 0 \\ & \ddots & \\ 0 & & \lambda_N^n \end{pmatrix}\boldsymbol{B}.$$

The rows of $\boldsymbol{B}$ are left eigenvectors of $\boldsymbol{P}$. We can use the Perron–Frobenius Theorem to explore the properties of $\boldsymbol{P}^n$ for large n. For example, if the chain is aperiodic then $d = 1$ and

$$\boldsymbol{P}^n \to \boldsymbol{B}^{-1}\begin{pmatrix} 1 & & & 0 \\ & 0 & & \\ & & \ddots & \\ 0 & & & 0 \end{pmatrix}\boldsymbol{B} \quad \text{as} \quad n \to \infty.$$

When the eigenvalues of $\boldsymbol{P}$ are not distinct, then $\boldsymbol{P}$ cannot be reduced to the diagonal canonical form in this way. The best we can do is to rewrite $\boldsymbol{P}$ in its 'Jordan canonical form'

$$\boldsymbol{P} = \boldsymbol{B}^{-1}\boldsymbol{M}\boldsymbol{B}$$

where

$$\boldsymbol{M} = \begin{pmatrix} \boldsymbol{J}_1 & & & 0 \\ & \boldsymbol{J}_2 & & \\ & & \boldsymbol{J}_3 & \\ 0 & & & \ddots \end{pmatrix}$$

and $\boldsymbol{J}_1, \boldsymbol{J}_2, \ldots$ are square matrices given as follows. Let $\lambda_1, \lambda_2, \ldots, \lambda_m$ be the distinct eigenvalues of $\boldsymbol{P}$ and let k_i be the multiplicity of λ_i. Then

$$\boldsymbol{J}_i = \begin{pmatrix} \lambda_i & 1 & 0 & 0 & \cdots \\ 0 & \lambda_i & 1 & 0 & \cdots \\ 0 & 0 & \lambda_i & 1 & \cdots \\ \vdots & \vdots & \vdots & \vdots & \end{pmatrix}$$

is a $k_i \times k_i$ matrix with each diagonal term λ_i, each superdiagonal term 1, and all other terms 0. Once again we have that $\boldsymbol{P}^n = \boldsymbol{B}^{-1}\boldsymbol{M}^n\boldsymbol{B}$, where $\boldsymbol{M}^n$ has quite a simple form (see Cox and Miller 1965, p. 118 *et seq.* for more details).

(2) **Example. Inbreeding.** Consider the genetic model described in (6.1.11c) and suppose that C_1 can take the values A or a on each of two homologous chromosomes. Then the possible types of individuals can be denoted by

$$AA,\ Aa(\equiv aA),\ aa,$$

and mating between types is denoted by

$AA \times AA$, $AA \times Aa$, and so on.

As described in (6.1.11c), meiosis selects the offspring's chromosomes randomly from each parent; in the simplest case (since there are two choices for each of two places) each outcome has probability $\frac{1}{4}$. Thus for the offspring of $AA \times Aa$ the four possible outcomes are

AA, Aa, AA, Aa

and

$$\mathbf{P}(AA) = \mathbf{P}(Aa) = \tfrac{1}{2}.$$

For the cross $Aa \times Aa$,

$$\mathbf{P}(AA) = \mathbf{P}(aa) = \tfrac{1}{2}\mathbf{P}(Aa) = \tfrac{1}{4}.$$

Clearly the offspring of $AA \times AA$ can only be AA, and those of $aa \times aa$ can only be aa.

We now construct a Markov chain by mating an individual with itself, then crossing a single resulting offspring with itself, and so on. (This scheme is possible with plants.) Then the genetic types of this sequence of individuals constitute a Markov chain with three states, AA, Aa, aa. In view of the above discussion, the transition matrix is

$$\mathbf{P} = \begin{pmatrix} 1 & 0 & 0 \\ \frac{1}{4} & \frac{1}{2} & \frac{1}{4} \\ 0 & 0 & 1 \end{pmatrix}$$

and the reader can verify that

$$\mathbf{P}^n = \begin{pmatrix} 1 & 0 & 0 \\ \frac{1}{2} - (\frac{1}{2})^{n+1} & (\frac{1}{2})^n & \frac{1}{2} - (\frac{1}{2})^{n+1} \\ 0 & 0 & 1 \end{pmatrix} \to \begin{pmatrix} 1 & 0 & 0 \\ \frac{1}{2} & 0 & \frac{1}{2} \\ 0 & 0 & 1 \end{pmatrix} \quad \text{as} \quad n \to \infty.$$

Thus, ultimately, inbreeding produces a pure (AA or aa) line for which all subsequent offspring have the same type. In like manner one can consider the progress of many different breeding schemes which include breeding with rejection of unfavourable genes, back-crossing to encourage desirable genes, and so on. ●

6.7 Branching processes revisited

The foregoing general theory is an attractive and concise account of the evolution through time of a Markov chain. Unfortunately, it is an inadequate description of many specific Markov chains. Consider for example a branching process $\{Z_0, Z_1, \ldots\}$ where $Z_0 = 1$. If there is strictly positive probability $\mathbf{P}(Z_1 = 0)$ that each family is empty then 0 is an absorbing state. Hence 0 is persistent non-null, and all other states are transient. The chain is not irreducible but there exists a unique stationary distribution $\boldsymbol{\pi}$ given by $\pi_0 = 1$, $\pi_i = 0$ if $i > 0$. These facts tell us next to nothing about the behaviour of the process, and we must look elsewhere for detailed information. The difficulty is that the process may behave in one of various qualitatively different ways depending, for instance, on whether or not it ultimately becomes extinct. One way of approaching the problem is to study the behaviour of the process *conditional* upon the occurrence of some event, like extinction, or the value of some random variable, such as the total number $\sum_i Z_i$ of progeny. This section contains an outline of such a method.

Let f and G be the mass function and generating function of a typical family size Z_1:

$$f(k) = \mathbf{P}(Z_1 = k), \qquad G(s) = \mathbf{E}(s^{Z_1}).$$

Let

$$T = \begin{cases} \inf\{n : Z_n = 0\} & \text{if extinction occurs} \\ \infty & \text{otherwise} \end{cases}$$

be the time until extinction. Roughly speaking, if $T = \infty$ then the process will grow beyond all possible bounds, whilst if $T < \infty$ then the size of the process never becomes very large and subsequently reduces to zero. Think of $\{Z_n\}$ as a fluctuating sequence which either becomes so large that it escapes to ∞ or is absorbed at 0 during one of its fluctuations. From Section 5.4, the probability $\mathbf{P}(T < \infty)$ of ultimate extinction is the smallest non-negative root of the equation $s = G(s)$. Now let

$$E_n = \{n < T < \infty\}$$

be the event that extinction occurs at some time after n. We shall study the distribution of Z_n conditional upon the occurrence of E_n. Let

$${}_0p_j^{(n)} = \mathbf{P}(Z_n = j \mid E_n)$$

be the conditional *taboo probability* that $Z_n = j$ given the future extinction of Z. We are interested in the limiting value

$${}_0\pi_j = \lim_{n \to \infty} {}_0p_j(n),$$

if this limit exists. To avoid certain trivial cases we assume henceforth that

$$0 < f(0) + f(1) < 1, \qquad f(0) > 0;$$

these conditions imply for example that $0 < \mathbf{P}(E_n) < 1$ and that the probability η of ultimate extinction satisfies $0 < \eta \leq 1$.

(1) **Lemma.** *If* $\mathbf{E}(Z_1) < \infty$ *then* $\lim_{n \to \infty} {}_0p_j(n) = {}_0\pi_j$ *exists. The generating function*

$$G^{\pi}(s) = \sum_j {}_0\pi_j s^j$$

satisfies the functional equation

(2) $$G^{\pi}(\eta^{-1}G(s\eta)) = mG^{\pi}(s) + 1 - m$$

where η *is the probability of ultimate extinction and* $m = G'(\eta)$.

Note that if $\mu = \mathbf{E}Z_1 \leq 1$ then $\eta = 1$ and $m = \mu$. Thus (2) reduces to

$$G^\pi(G(s)) = G^\pi(s) + 1 - \mu.$$

Whatever the value of μ, we have that $G'(\eta) \leq 1$, with equality if and only if $\mu = 1$.

Proof. For $s \in [0, 1)$, let

$$\begin{aligned} G_n^\pi(s) &= \mathbf{E}(s^{Z_n} \mid E_n) = \sum_j {}_0p_j(n)s^j \\ &= \sum_j s^j \frac{\mathbf{P}(Z_n = j, E_n)}{\mathbf{P}(E_n)} \\ &= \frac{G_n(s\eta) - G_n(0)}{\eta - G_n(0)} \end{aligned}$$

where $G_n(s) = \mathbf{E}(s^{Z_n})$ as before, since

$$\begin{aligned} \mathbf{P}(Z_n = j, E_n) &= \mathbf{P}(Z_n = j \text{ and all subsequent lines die out}) \\ &= \mathbf{P}(Z_n = j)\eta^j \quad \text{if} \quad j \geq 1, \end{aligned}$$

and

$$\mathbf{P}(E_n) = \mathbf{P}(T < \infty) - \mathbf{P}(T \leq n) = \eta - G_n(0).$$

Let

$$H_n(s) = \frac{\eta - G_n(s)}{\eta - G_n(0)}, \qquad h(s) = \frac{\eta - G(s)}{\eta - s}, \qquad 0 \leq s < \eta,$$

so that

(3) $$G_n^\pi(s) = 1 - H_n(s\eta).$$

Note that H_n has domain $[0, \eta)$ and G_n^π has domain $[0, 1)$. By (5.4.1),

$$\frac{H_n(s)}{H_{n-1}(s)} = \frac{h(G_{n-1}(s))}{h(G_{n-1}(0))}.$$

However, G_{n-1} is non-decreasing, and h is non-decreasing because G is convex on $[0, \eta)$, giving that

$$H_n(s) \geq H_{n-1}(s) \quad \text{for} \quad s < \eta.$$

Hence, by (3),

$$\lim_{n\to\infty} G_n^\pi(s) = G^\pi(s) \quad \text{and} \quad \lim_{n\to\infty} H_n(s\eta) = H(s\eta)$$

exist for $s \in [0, 1)$ and satisfy

(4) $$G^\pi(s) = 1 - H(s\eta) \quad \text{if} \quad 0 \leq s < 1.$$

Thus the coefficient ${}_0\pi_j$ of s^j in $G^\pi(s)$ exists for all j as required.

Furthermore, if $0 \leqslant s < \eta$,

(5) $$H_n(G(s)) = \frac{\eta - G_n(G(s))}{\eta - G_n(0)} = \frac{\eta - G(G_n(0))}{\eta - G_n(0)} \frac{\eta - G_{n+1}(s)}{\eta - G_{n+1}(0)}$$
$$= h(G_n(0))H_{n+1}(s).$$

As $n \to \infty$, $G_n(0) \uparrow \eta$ and so

$$h(G_n(0)) \to \lim_{s \uparrow \eta} \frac{\eta - G(s)}{\eta - s} = G'(\eta).$$

Let $n \to \infty$ in (5) to obtain

(6) $$H(G(s)) = G'(\eta)H(s) \quad \text{if} \quad 0 \leqslant s < \eta$$

and (2) follows from (4). ■

(7) **Corollary.** *If* $\mu \neq 1$ *then* $\sum_j {}_0\pi_j = 1$.
If $\mu = 1$ *then* ${}_0\pi_j = 0$ *for all* j.

Proof. $\mu = 1$ if and only if $G'(\eta) = 1$. If $\mu \neq 1$ then $G'(\eta) \neq 1$ and letting s increase to η in (6) gives

$$\lim_{s \uparrow \eta} H(s) = 0;$$

so, from (4), $\lim_{s \uparrow 1} G^\pi(s) = 1$, or

$$\sum_j {}_0\pi_j = 1.$$

If $\mu = 1$ then $G'(\eta) = 1$ and (2) becomes

$$G^\pi(G(s)) = G^\pi(s).$$

However, $G(s) > s$ for all $s < 1$ and so

$$G^\pi(s) = G^\pi(0) = 0 \quad \text{for all } s < 1.$$

Thus ${}_0\pi_j = 0$ for all j. ■

So long as $\mu \neq 1$, the distribution of Z_n, conditional on future extinction, converges as $n \to \infty$ to some limit $\{{}_0\pi_j\}$ which is a proper distribution. The so-called 'critical' branching process with $\mu = 1$ is more difficult in that, for $j \geqslant 1$,

$\mathbf{P}(Z_n = j) \to 0$ because extinction is certain

$\mathbf{P}(Z_n = j \mid E_n) \to 0$ because $Z_n \to \infty$, conditional on E_n.

However, it is possible to show, in the spirit of the discussion at the end of Section 5.4, that the distribution of

$$Y_n = \frac{Z_n}{n\sigma^2} \quad \text{where} \quad \sigma^2 = \operatorname{var} Z_1,$$

conditional on E_n, converges as $n \to \infty$.

(8) **Theorem.** *If* $\mu=1$ *and* $G''(1)<\infty$ *then*

$$\mathbf{P}(Y_n \leq y \mid E_n) \to 1-\exp(-2y), \quad \text{as } n\to\infty.$$

Proof. See Athreya and Ney 1972, p. 20. ■

So, if $\mu=1$, then the distribution of Y_n, given E_n, is asymptotically exponential with parameter 2. In this case, the branching process is called *critical*; the cases $\mu<1$ and $\mu>1$ are called *subcritical* and *supercritical* respectively. See Athreya and Ney 1972 for further details.

6.8 Birth processes and the Poisson process

Many processes in nature may change their values at any instant of time rather than at certain specified epochs only. Such a process is a family $\{X(t):t\geq 0\}$ of random variables taking values in a state space S. Depending on the underlying random mechanism, X may or may not be a Markov process. Before attempting to study any general theory of continuous-time processes we explore one simple but non-trivial example in detail.

Given the right equipment, we should have no difficulty in observing that the process of emission of particles from a radioactive source seems to behave in a manner which is not totally predictable. If we switch on our Geiger counter at time zero, then the reading $N(t)$ which it shows at a later time t is the outcome of some random process. This process $\{N(t):t\geq 0\}$ has certain obvious properties, such as

(a) $N(0)=0$, $N(t)\in\{0,1,2,\ldots\}$
(b) if $s<t$ then $N(s)\leq N(t)$,

but it is not so easy to specify more detailed properties. We might use the following description. In the time interval $(t, t+h)$ there may or may not be some emissions. If h is small then the likelihood of an emission is roughly proportional to h; it is not very likely that two or more emissions will occur in a small interval. More formally, we make the following definition.

(1) **Definition.** A **Poisson process with intensity** λ is a process $N=\{N(t):t\geq 0\}$ taking values in $S=\{0,1,2,\ldots\}$ such that

(a) $N(0)=0$; if $s<t$ then $N(s)\leq N(t)$

(b) $$\mathbf{P}(N(t+h)=n+m \mid N(t)=n)=\begin{cases}\lambda h+o(h) & \text{if } m=1\\ o(h) & \text{if } m>1\\ 1-\lambda h+o(h) & \text{if } m=0\end{cases}$$

(c) if $s<t$ then the number $N(t)-N(s)$ of emissions in the interval $(s,t]$ is independent of all emissions prior to s.

We speak of $N(t)$ as the number of 'arrivals' or 'occurrences', or in this example 'emissions', of the process by time t. N is called a 'counting process' and is one of the simplest examples of continuous-time Markov chains. We shall consider the general theory of such processes in the next section; here we study special properties of Poisson processes and their generalizations.

We are interested first in the distribution of $N(t)$.

(2) **Theorem.** *$N(t)$ has the Poisson distribution with parameter λt; that is to say*

$$\mathbf{P}(N(t)=j)=\frac{(\lambda t)^j}{j!}e^{-\lambda t}, \quad j=0,1,2,\ldots.$$

Proof. Condition $N(t+h)$ on $N(t)$ to obtain

$$\begin{aligned}\mathbf{P}(N(t+h)=j)&=\sum_i \mathbf{P}(N(t)=i)\mathbf{P}(N(t+h)=j \mid N(t)=i)\\&=\sum_i \mathbf{P}(N(t)=i)\mathbf{P}((j-i)\text{ arrivals in }(t,t+h])\\&=\mathbf{P}(N(t)=j-1)\mathbf{P}(\text{one arrival})\\&\quad+\mathbf{P}(N(t)=j)\mathbf{P}(\text{no arrivals})+o(h).\end{aligned}$$

Thus $p_j(t)=\mathbf{P}(N(t)=j)$ satisfies

$$p_j(t+h)=\lambda h p_{j-1}(t)+(1-\lambda h)p_j(t)+o(h) \quad \text{if} \quad j\neq 0$$
$$p_0(t+h)=(1-\lambda h)p_0(t)+o(h).$$

Subtract $p_j(t)$ from each side of the first of these equations, divide by h, and let $h\downarrow 0$ to obtain

(3) $$p_j'(t)=\lambda p_{j-1}(t)-\lambda p_j(t) \quad \text{if} \quad j\neq 0;$$

likewise

(4) $$p_0'(t)=-\lambda p_0(t).$$

The boundary condition is

(5) $$p_j(0)=\delta_{j0}.$$

These form a collection of differential–difference equations for the $p_j(t)$. Here are two methods of solution, both of which have applications elsewhere.

Method A. Induction. Solve (4) subject to the condition $p_0(0)=1$ to obtain

$$p_0(t)=e^{-\lambda t}.$$

Substitute into (3) with $j=1$ to obtain

$$p_1(t)=\lambda t e^{-\lambda t}$$

and continue, to prove

$$p_j(t) = \frac{(\lambda t)^j}{j!} e^{-\lambda t}$$

by induction.

Method B. Generating functions. Define the generating function

$$G(s, t) = \sum_{j=0}^{\infty} p_j(t) s^j = \mathbf{E}(s^{N(t)}).$$

Multiply (3) by s^j and sum over j to obtain

$$\frac{\partial G}{\partial t} = \lambda(s-1)G$$

with the boundary condition $G(s, 0) = 1$. The solution is

$$G(s, t) = \exp\{\lambda(s-1)t\} = e^{-\lambda t} \sum_{j=0}^{\infty} \frac{(\lambda t)^j}{j!} s^j$$

as required. ■

This result seems very like the account (3.5.4) that the binomial $B(n, p)$ distribution approaches the Poisson distribution if $n \to \infty$ and $np \to \lambda$. Why is this no coincidence?

It is clear from the definition (1) of N that the following property holds.

(6) **Weak Markov Property.** Fix $T > 0$. Then

$$N'(t) = N(t+T) - N(T), \qquad t \geq 0$$

is a process which is independent of the collection $\{N(s) : s < T\}$ by (1c). {The so-called 'Strong Markov Property' holds whenever this is true in the case when T is a 'stopping time' with respect to $\{N(t)\}$ (see (7.9.1) for a definition of 'stopping times with respect to sequences of random variables'; a similar definition holds with respect to continuous-time processes). Do you think that N satisfies this?} Furthermore, by the temporal homogeneity of (1b), N' and N are processes with identical distributional laws. It follows that the continuous-time Markov chain $N(t)$ has transition probabilities

$$\begin{aligned} p_{ij}(t) &= \mathbf{P}(N(t+T) = j \mid N(T) = i) \\ &= \mathbf{P}(N'(t) = j - i) \\ &= \frac{(\lambda t)^{j-i}}{(j-i)!} e^{-\lambda t}, \quad j \geq i. \end{aligned}$$

There is an important alternative and equivalent formulation of a Poisson process which provides much insight into its behaviour. Let $T_0, T_1, \ldots$ be given by

(7) $$T_0 = 0, \qquad T_n = \inf\{t : N(t) = n\}.$$

Then T_n is the time of the nth arrival. The *inter-arrival times* are the random variables $X_1, X_2, \ldots$ given by

(8) $$X_n = T_n - T_{n-1}.$$

From knowledge of N, we can find the values of $X_1, X_2, \ldots$ by (7) and (8). Conversely, we can reconstruct N from a knowledge of the X's by

(9) $$T_n = \sum_1^n X_i, \quad N(t) = \max\{n : T_n \leq t\}.$$

Figure 6.1 is an illustration of this.

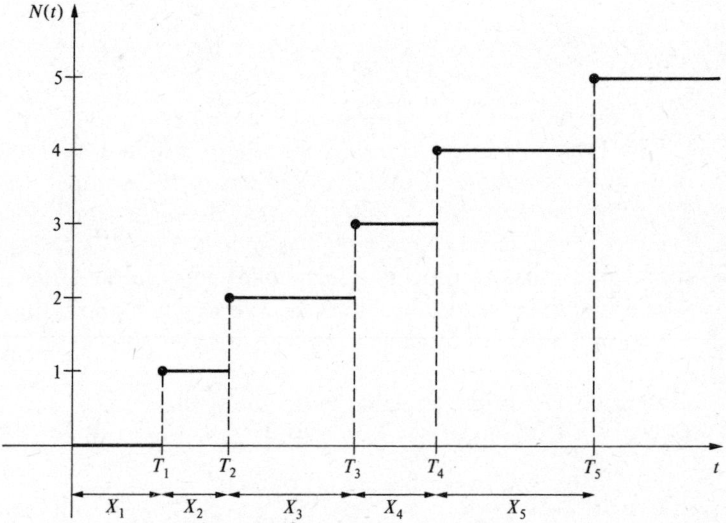

FIG. 6.1 A typical realization of a Poisson process $N(t)$.

(10) **Theorem.** $X_1, X_2, \ldots$ *are independent exponential random variables with parameter* λ.

There is an important generalization of this result to arbitrary continuous-time Markov chains with countable state space. We shall investigate this in the next section.

Proof. First consider X_1:

$$\mathbf{P}(X_1 > t) = \mathbf{P}(N(t) = 0) = e^{-\lambda t}$$

and so X_1 is exponential. Now, conditional on X_1,

$$\mathbf{P}(X_2 > t \mid X_1 = t_1) = \mathbf{P}(N(t + t_1) = 1 \mid N(t_1) = 1) = e^{-\lambda t}$$

from (6), giving that X_2 is independent of X_1 with the same distribution. Show similarly that X_3 is independent of X_1 and X_2, and complete the proof by the obvious induction. ■

Following the previous discussion, the process $N(t)$, constructed by (9) from a sequence $X_1, X_2, \ldots$, is a Poisson process if and only if the X's are independent identically distributed exponential variables. For, suppose the X's satisfy the conclusion of (10). Then $T_n = \sum_1^n X_i$ is $\Gamma(\lambda, n)$ and $N(t)$ is specified by the useful remark that

$$N(t) \geq j \quad \text{if and only if } T_j \leq t.$$

Therefore

$$\begin{aligned}\mathbf{P}(N(t)=j) &= \mathbf{P}(T_j \leq t < T_{j+1}) \\ &= \mathbf{P}(T_j \leq t) - \mathbf{P}(T_{j+1} \leq t) \\ &= \frac{(\lambda t)^j}{j!} e^{-\lambda t}\end{aligned}$$

using the properties of gamma variables and integration by parts.

The Poisson process is a very satisfactory model for radioactive emissions from a sample of uranium-235 since this isotope has a half-life of 7×10^8 years and decays fairly slowly. However, for a newly produced sample of strontium-92, which has a half-life of 2.7 hours, we need a more sophisticated process which takes into account the retardation in decay rate over short time intervals. We might suppose that the rate λ at which emissions are detected depends on the number detected already.

(11) **Definition.** A **birth process with intensities** $\lambda_0, \lambda_1, \ldots$ is a process $\{N(t) : t \geq 0\}$ taking values in $S = \{0, 1, 2, \ldots\}$ such that

(a) $N(0) = 0$; if $s < t$ then $N(s) \leq N(t)$

(b) $\mathbf{P}(N(t+h) = n+m \mid N(t) = n) = \begin{cases} \lambda_n h + o(h) & \text{if } m = 1 \\ o(h) & \text{if } m > 1 \\ 1 - \lambda_n h + o(h) & \text{if } m = 0 \end{cases}$

(c) if $s < t$ then $N(t) - N(s)$ is independent of all arrivals prior to s.

Here are some interesting special cases.

(a) **Poisson process.** $\lambda_n = \lambda$ for all n. ●

(b) **Simple birth.** $\lambda_n = n\lambda$. This models the growth of a population in which each living individual may give birth to a new individual with probability $\lambda h + o(h)$ in the interval $(t, t+h)$. No individuals may die. The number M of births in the interval $(t, t+h)$ satisfies

$$\begin{aligned}\mathbf{P}(M = m \mid N(t) = n) &= \binom{n}{m} (\lambda h)^m (1-\lambda h)^{n-m} + o(h) \\ &= \begin{cases} 1 - n\lambda h + o(h) & \text{if } m = 0 \\ n\lambda h + o(h) & \text{if } m = 1 \\ o(h) & \text{if } m > 1. \end{cases}\end{aligned}$$ ●

(c) **Simple birth with immigration.** $\lambda_n = n\lambda + \nu$. This models a simple birth process which experiences immigration at constant rate ν from elsewhere. ●

Suppose that $\{N(t)\}$ is a birth process with positive intensities $\lambda_0, \lambda_1, \ldots$. Let us proceed as for the Poisson process. Define the transition probabilities

$$\begin{aligned} p_{ij}(t) &= \mathbf{P}(N(s+t)=j \mid N(s)=i) \\ &= \mathbf{P}(N(t)=j \mid N(0)=i); \end{aligned}$$

now condition $N(t+h)$ on $N(t)$ and let $h \downarrow 0$ as we did for (3) and (4), to obtain the so-called

(12) **Forward system of equations**

$$p'_{ij}(t) = \lambda_{j-1} p_{i,j-1}(t) - \lambda_j p_{ij}(t), \quad j \geq i$$

with the convention that $\lambda_{-1}=0$, and the boundary condition $p_{ij}(0)=\delta_{ij}$. Alternatively we might condition $N(t+h)$ on $N(h)$ and let $h \downarrow 0$ to obtain the so-called

(13) **Backward system of equations**

$$p'_{ij}(t) = \lambda_i p_{i+1,j}(t) - \lambda_i p_{ij}(t), \quad j \geq i$$

with the boundary condition $p_{ij}(0)=\delta_{ij}$.

Can we solve these equations as we did for the Poisson process?

(14) **Theorem.** *The forward system has a unique solution, which satisfies the backward system.*

Proof. Solve the forward equation with $j=i$ to obtain

$$p_{ii}(t) = \exp(-\lambda_i t).$$

Substitute into the forward equation with $j=i+1$ to find $p_{i,i+1}(t)$. Continue this operation to deduce that the forward system has a unique solution. To obtain more information about this solution, define the Laplace transforms†

$$\hat{p}_{ij}(\theta) = \int_0^\infty \exp(-\theta t) p_{ij}(t)\, dt.$$

Transform the forward system to obtain

$$(\theta + \lambda_j)\hat{p}_{ij}(\theta) = \delta_{ij} + \lambda_{j-1}\hat{p}_{i,j-1}(\theta);$$

this is a difference equation which is readily solved to give

(15) $$\hat{p}_{ij}(\theta) = \frac{1}{\lambda_j} \frac{\lambda_i}{\theta+\lambda_i} \frac{\lambda_{i+1}}{\theta+\lambda_{i+1}} \cdots \frac{\lambda_j}{\theta+\lambda_j} \quad \text{for} \quad j \geq i.$$

This determines $p_{ij}(t)$ uniquely by the inversion theorem for Laplace transforms.

† See Appendix I for some properties of Laplace transforms.

To see that this solution satisfies the backward system, transform this system similarly to obtain that any solution $\pi_{ij}(t)$ to the backward equation, with Laplace transform

$$\hat{\pi}_{ij}(\theta) = \int_0^\infty \exp(-\theta t)\pi_{ij}(t)\,\mathrm{d}t,$$

satisfies

$$(\theta + \lambda_i)\hat{\pi}_{ij}(\theta) = \delta_{ij} + \lambda_i \hat{\pi}_{i+1,j}(\theta).$$

The $\hat{p}_{ij}$, given by (15), satisfy this equation, and so the p_{ij} satisfy the backward system. ■

We have not been able to show that the backward system has a unique solution, for the very good reason that this may not be true. All we can show is that it has a minimal solution.

(16) **Theorem.** *If* $\{p_{ij}(t)\}$ *is the unique solution of the forward system, then any solution* $\{\pi_{ij}(t)\}$ *of the backward system satisfies*

$$p_{ij}(t) \leq \pi_{ij}(t) \quad \textit{for all } i, j, t.$$

Proof. See Feller 1968, pp. 475–477. ■

There is something wrong here, because the condition

(17) $$\sum_j p_{ij}(t) = 1$$

in conjunction with the result of (16) would constrain $\{p_{ij}(t)\}$ to be the *unique* solution of the backward system which is a proper distribution. The point is that (17) fails to hold in general.

(18) **Definition.** We call N **honest** if $\mathbf{P}(N(t) < \infty) = 1$ for all t.
N is honest if and only if (17) holds for all t.

(19) **Theorem.** *N is honest if and only if* $\sum_n \frac{1}{\lambda_n} = \infty$.

This attractive theorem asserts that if the birth rates are small enough then the process is always finite, but if they are so large that $\sum \lambda_n^{-1}$ converges then births occur so frequently that there is positive probability of infinitely many births occurring in a finite interval of time. Thus $N(t)$ may take the value $+\infty$ instead of a non-negative integer. Think of the deficit $1 - \sum_j p_{ij}(t)$ as the probability of escaping to infinity in time t, starting from i. The condition of (19) is a very natural one for the following reason. Arguing as we did for the inter-arrival times of the Poisson process, it is easy to see that if

$$T_0 = 0, \quad T_n = \inf\{t : N(t) = n\}, \quad X_n = T_n - T_{n-1}$$

then $X_1, X_2, \ldots$ are independent exponential variables and X_i has parameter λ_{i-1}. Thus the mean time until the nth arrival is

$$\mathbf{E}(T_n) = \sum_1^n \mathbf{E}(X_i) = \sum_0^{n-1} \frac{1}{\lambda_i}$$

which tends to infinity as $n \to \infty$ if and only if this sum diverges.

Proof of (19). Sum the forward system over j to obtain

$$\sum_{j=i}^n p'_{ij}(t) = -\lambda_n p_{in}(t);$$

take Laplace transforms and use (15) to obtain

$$\theta \sum_{j=i}^n \hat{p}_{ij}(\theta) = 1 - \lambda_n \hat{p}_{in}(\theta)$$

$$= 1 - \prod_{j=i}^n \left(1 + \frac{\theta}{\lambda_j}\right)^{-1}.$$

Now let $n \to \infty$ for suitable values of θ to find that†

$$\sum_{j=i}^n \hat{p}_{ij}(\theta) \to \frac{1}{\theta} \text{ if and only if } \sum_0^\infty \frac{1}{\lambda_j} = \infty.$$

Invert the first relation to obtain

$$\sum_j p_{ij}(t) = 1 \quad \text{if and only if} \quad \sum_0^\infty \frac{1}{\lambda_j} = \infty. \qquad \blacksquare$$

In summary, we have considered several random processes, indexed by continuous time, which model phenomena occurring in nature. However, certain dangers arise unless we take care in the construction of such processes. They may even find a way to the so-called 'boundary' of the state space by exploding in finite time.

6.9 Continuous-time Markov chains

Let $X = \{X(t) : t \geq 0\}$ be a family of random variables taking values in some countable state space S and indexed by the half-line $[0, \infty)$. As before, we shall assume that S is a subset of the integers. X is called a (continuous-time) *Markov chain* if it satisfies the following condition.

(1) **Definition.** X satisfies the **Markov property** if

$$\mathbf{P}(X(t_n) = j \mid X(t_1), \ldots, X(t_{n-1})) = \mathbf{P}(X(t_n) = j \mid X(t_{n-1}))$$

for any $j \in S$ and any sequence $t_1 < t_2 < \ldots < t_n$ of times.

† See Subsection (8) of Appendix I for some notes about infinite products.

The evolution of continuous-time Markov chains can be described in very much the same terms as those used for discrete-time processes. Various difficulties may arise in the analysis, especially when S is infinite. The way out of these difficulties is too difficult to describe in detail here, and the reader should look elsewhere (see Chung 1960, or Freedman 1971 for example). The general scheme is as follows. For discrete-time processes we wrote the n-step transition probabilities in matrix form and expressed them in terms of the one-step matrix $\mathbf{P}$. In continuous time there is no exact analogue for $\mathbf{P}$ since there is no implicit unit length of time. The infinitesimal calculus enables us to plug this gap; we shall see that there exists a matrix $\mathbf{G}$, called the *generator* of the chain, which takes over the role of $\mathbf{P}$.

(2) **Definition.** The **transition probability** $p_{ij}(s, t)$ is defined to be

$$p_{ij}(s, t) = \mathbf{P}(X(t) = j \mid X(s) = i) \quad \text{for} \quad s \leq t.$$

The chain is called **homogeneous** if

$$p_{ij}(s, t) = p_{ij}(0, t-s) \quad \text{for all } i, j, s, t,$$

and we write $p_{ij}(t-s)$ for $p_{ij}(s, t)$.

Henceforth we suppose that X is a homogeneous chain, and we write $\mathbf{P}_t$ for the $|S| \times |S|$ matrix with entries $p_{ij}(t)$.

(3) **Theorem.** *The family $\{\mathbf{P}_t : t \geq 0\}$ is a* **stochastic semigroup**; *that is, it satisfies the following*:

(a) $\mathbf{P}_0 = \mathbf{I}$, *the identity matrix*;

(b) $\mathbf{P}_t$ *is stochastic, that is* $\mathbf{P}_t$ *has non-negative entries and row sums* 1;

(c) *the* **Chapman–Kolmogorov equations,** $\mathbf{P}_{s+t} = \mathbf{P}_s\mathbf{P}_t$ *if* $s, t \geq 0$.

Proof.

(a) Obvious.

(b) Let $\mathbf{1}$ denote a row vector of 1's.

$$(\mathbf{P}_t\mathbf{1}')_i = \sum_j p_{ij}(t) = \mathbf{P}\Big(\bigcup_j \{X(t) = j\} \mid X(0) = i\Big) = 1.$$

(c)
$$\begin{aligned} p_{ij}(t+s) &= \mathbf{P}(X(t+s) = j \mid X(0) = i) \\ &= \sum_k \mathbf{P}(X(t+s) = j \mid X(s) = k)\mathbf{P}(X(s) = k \mid X(0) = i) \\ &= \sum_k p_{ik}(s)p_{kj}(t) \quad \text{as for (6.1.7).} \end{aligned}$$
■

As before, the evolution of $X(t)$ is specified by the stochastic semigroup $\{\mathbf{P}_t\}$ and the distribution of $X(0)$. Most questions about X can be rephrased in terms of these matrices and their properties.

Many readers will not be very concerned with the general theory of these processes, but will be much more interested in specific examples and their stationary distributions. Therefore, we present only a broad outline of the theory in the remaining part of this section and hope that it is sufficient for most applications. Technical conditions are usually omitted, with the consequence that *some of the statements which follow are false in general*; such statements are marked with an asterisk. Indications of how to fill in the details are given in the next section. We shall always suppose that the transition probabilities are continuous.

(4) **Definition.** The semigroup $\{\mathbf{P}_t\}$ is called **standard** if

$$\mathbf{P}_t \to \mathbf{I} \quad \text{as} \quad t \downarrow 0,$$

which is to say that $p_{ii}(t) \to 1$ and $p_{ij}(t) \to 0$ for $i \neq j$ as $t \downarrow 0$.

Note that the semigroup is standard if and only if its elements $p_{ij}(t)$ are continuous functions of t. For, it is not difficult to see that $p_{ij}(t)$ is continuous for all t whenever the semigroup is standard; we just use the Chapman–Kolmogorov equations (3c) (see Problem (6.13.12)). Henceforth we consider only Markov chains with standard semigroups of transition probabilities.

Suppose that the chain is in state $X(t) = i$ at time t. Various things may happen in the small time interval $(t, t+h)$:

(a) nothing may happen, with probability $p_{ii}(h) + o(h)$, the error term taking into account the possibility that the chain moves out of i and back to i in the interval;
(b) the chain may move to a new state j with probability

$$p_{ij}(h) + o(h).$$

We are assuming here that the probability of two or more transitions in the interval $(t, t+h)$ is $o(h)$; this can be proved. Following (a) and (b), we are interested in the behaviour of $p_{ij}(h)$ for small h; it turns out that $p_{ij}(h)$ is approximately linear in h when h is small. That is, there exist constants $\{g_{ij} : i, j \in S\}$ such that

(5)
$$\boxed{p_{ij}(h) \simeq g_{ij}h \quad \text{if} \quad i \neq j, \quad p_{ii}(h) \simeq 1 + g_{ii}h.}$$

Clearly $g_{ij} \geq 0$ for $i \neq j$ and $g_{ii} \leq 0$ for all i; the matrix $\mathbf{G} = (g_{ij})$ is called the *generator* of the chain and takes over the role of the transition matrix $\mathbf{P}$ for discrete-time chains. Combine (5) with (a) and (b) above to find that, starting from $X(t) = i$,

(a) nothing happens in $(t, t+h)$ with probability $1 + g_{ii}h + o(h)$,
(b) the chain jumps to state $j(\neq i)$ with probability $g_{ij}h + o(h)$.

Of course, $\sum_j p_{ij}(t) = 1$, and so we expect that

$$1 = \sum_j p_{ij}(h) \simeq 1 + h \sum_j g_{ij}$$

giving that

(6)* $$\sum_j g_{ij} = 0 \quad \text{for all } i, \quad \text{or} \quad \mathbf{G1}' = \mathbf{0}',$$

where **1** and **0** are row vectors of ones and zeros. Treat (6) with discretion; there are some chains for which it fails to hold.

(7) **Example. Birth process (6.8.11).** From the definition of this process, it is clear that

$$g_{ii} = -\lambda_i, \quad g_{i,i+1} = \lambda_i, \quad g_{ij} = 0 \quad \text{if} \quad j < i \quad \text{or} \quad j > i+1.$$

Thus

$$\mathbf{G} = \begin{pmatrix} -\lambda_0 & \lambda_0 & 0 & 0 & 0 & \cdots \\ 0 & -\lambda_1 & \lambda_1 & 0 & 0 & \cdots \\ 0 & 0 & -\lambda_2 & \lambda_2 & 0 & \cdots \\ \vdots & \vdots & \vdots & \vdots & \vdots & \end{pmatrix}.$$

Relation (5) is usually written as

(8) $$\lim_{h \, 0} \frac{1}{h}(\mathbf{P}_h - \mathbf{I}) = \mathbf{G},$$

and amounts to saying that $\mathbf{P}_t$ is differentiable at $t = 0$. It is clear that $\mathbf{G}$ can be found from knowledge of $\{\mathbf{P}_t\}$. The converse also is usually true. We argue roughly as follows. Suppose that $X(0) = i$, and condition $X(t+h)$ on $X(t)$ to find that

$$\begin{aligned} p_{ij}(t+h) &= \sum_k p_{ik}(t) p_{kj}(h) \\ &\simeq p_{ij}(t)(1 + g_{jj}h) + \sum_{k \neq j} p_{ik}(t) g_{kj} h \quad \text{by (5)} \\ &= p_{ij}(t) + h \sum_k p_{ik}(t) g_{kj}, \end{aligned}$$

giving that

$$\frac{1}{h}(p_{ij}(t+h) - p_{ij}(t)) \simeq \sum_k p_{ik}(t) g_{kj} = (\mathbf{P}_t \mathbf{G})_{ij}.$$

Let $h \downarrow 0$ to obtain the

(9)* **forward equations:** $p'_{ij}(t) = \sum_k p_{ik}(t) g_{kj}$, or $\mathbf{P}'_t = \mathbf{P}_t \mathbf{G}$,

where $\mathbf{P}'_t$ denotes the matrix with entries $p'_{ij}(t)$.

A similar argument, by conditioning $X(t+h)$ on $X(h)$, yields the

(10)* **backward equations:** $p'_{ij}(t) = \sum_k g_{ik} p_{kj}(t)$, or $\mathbf{P}'_t = \mathbf{G}\mathbf{P}_t$.

These equations are general forms of (6.8.12) and (6.8.13) and relate $\{\mathbf{P}_t\}$ to $\mathbf{G}$. Subject to the boundary condition $\mathbf{P}_0 = \mathbf{I}$, they often have a unique solution given by the infinite sum

(11)* $$\mathbf{P}_t = \sum_{n=0}^{\infty} \frac{t^n}{n!} \mathbf{G}^n$$

of powers of matrices (remember that $\mathbf{G}^0 = \mathbf{I}$). (11) is deducible from (9) or (10) in very much the same way as we might show that the function of a single variable $p(t) = e^{gt}$ solves the differential equation $p'(t) = gp(t)$. The representation (11) for $\{\mathbf{P}_t\}$ is very useful and is usually written as

(12)* $$\mathbf{P}_t = e^{t\mathbf{G}} \quad \text{or} \quad \mathbf{P}_t = \exp(t\mathbf{G}),$$

where $e^{\mathbf{A}}$ is the natural abbreviation for $\sum_{n=0}^{\infty} \left(\frac{1}{n!}\right) \mathbf{A}^n$ whenever $\mathbf{A}$ is a square matrix.

So, subject to certain technical conditions, a continuous-time chain has a generator $\mathbf{G}$ which specifies the transition probabilities. Several examples of such generators are given in Section 6.11. In the last section we saw that a Poisson process (this is Example (7) with $\lambda_i = \lambda$ for all $i \geq 0$) can be described in terms of its inter-arrival times; an equivalent remark holds here. Suppose that the chain is in state $X(t) = i$ at time t. The future development of $X(t+s)$, for $s \geq 0$, goes roughly as follows. Let

$$T = \inf\{s \geq 0 : X(t+s) \neq i\}$$

be the further time until the chain changes its state; T is called a 'holding time'.

(13)* **Claim.** *T is exponentially distributed with parameter $-g_{ii}$.*

This is a remarkable result which explains all earlier remarks about the importance of the exponential distribution.

Sketch Proof. The distribution of T has the 'lack of memory' property (see Problem (4.10.5)) because

$$\begin{aligned}\mathbf{P}(T > x + y \mid T > x) &= \mathbf{P}(T > x + y \mid X(t+x) = i) \\ &= \mathbf{P}(T > y) \quad \text{if} \quad x, y \geq 0\end{aligned}$$

by the Markov property and the homogeneity of the chain. It follows that the distribution function F_T of T satisfies

$$1 - F_T(x+y) = \{1 - F_T(x)\}\{1 - F_T(y)\}$$

and so

$$1 - F_T'(x) = \exp(-\lambda x)$$

where $\lambda = F_T'(0) = -g_{ii}$. ■

Therefore, if $X(t) = i$, then the chain remains in state i for an exponentially distributed time T, after which it jumps to some other state j.

(14)* **Claim.** *The probability that the chain jumps to j ($\neq i$) is $-g_{ij}/g_{ii}$.*

Sketch Proof. Roughly speaking, suppose that $x < T \leq x+h$ and suppose that the chain jumps only once in $(x, x+h]$. Then

$$\mathbf{P}(\text{jumps to } j \mid \text{it jumps}) \simeq \frac{p_{ij}(h)}{1-p_{ii}(h)} \to -\frac{g_{ij}}{g_{ii}} \quad \text{as } h \downarrow 0. \quad \blacksquare$$

(15) **Example.** Consider a two-state chain X with $S = \{1, 2\}$; $X(t)$ jumps between 1 and 2 as time passes. There are two equivalent ways of describing the chain, depending on whether we specify $\mathbf{G}$ or we specify the holding times:

(a) X has generator $\mathbf{G} = \begin{pmatrix} -\alpha & \alpha \\ \beta & -\beta \end{pmatrix}$.

(b) If the chain is in state 1 (or 2), then it stays in this state for a length of time which is exponentially distributed with parameter α (or β) before jumping to 2 (or 1).

The forward equations (9), $\mathbf{P}'_t = \mathbf{P}_t\mathbf{G}$, take the form

$$p'_{11}(t) = -\alpha p_{11}(t) + \beta p_{12}(t)$$

and are easily solved to find the transition probabilities of the chain (*exercise*). ●

We move on to the classification of states; this is not such a chore as it was for discrete-time chains. It turns out that for any pair i, j of states

(16) either $p_{ij}(t) = 0$ for all $t > 0$, or $p_{ij}(t) > 0$ for all $t > 0$,

and this leads to a definition of irreducibility.

(17) **Definition.** The chain is called **irreducible** if for any pair i, j of states we have that $p_{ij}(t) > 0$ for some t.

Any time $t > 0$ will suffice in (17), because of (16). The birth process is *not* irreducible, since it is non-decreasing. See Problem (6.13.13) for a condition for irreducibility in terms of the generator $\mathbf{G}$ of the chain.

As before, the asymptotic behaviour of $X(t)$ for large t is closely bound up with the existence of stationary distributions. Compare their definition with (6.4.1).

(18) **Definition.** The vector $\boldsymbol{\pi}$ is a **stationary distribution** of the chain if $\pi_j \geq 0$, $\sum_j \pi_j = 1$ and $\boldsymbol{\pi} = \boldsymbol{\pi}\mathbf{P}_t$ for all $t \geq 0$.

If $X(0)$ has distribution $\boldsymbol{\mu}^{(0)}$ then the distribution $\boldsymbol{\mu}^{(t)}$ of $X(t)$ is given by

(19) $\boldsymbol{\mu}^{(t)} = \boldsymbol{\mu}^{(0)}\mathbf{P}_t$.

If $\boldsymbol{\mu}^{(0)} = \boldsymbol{\pi}$, a stationary distribution, then $X(t)$ has distribution $\boldsymbol{\pi}$ for all t.

For discrete-time chains we found stationary distributions by solving the equations $\boldsymbol{\pi} = \boldsymbol{\pi}\boldsymbol{P}$; the corresponding equations $\boldsymbol{\pi} = \boldsymbol{\pi}\boldsymbol{P}_t$ for continuous-time chains may seem complicated but they amount to a simple condition relating $\boldsymbol{\pi}$ and $\boldsymbol{G}$.

(20)* **Claim.** $\boldsymbol{\pi} = \boldsymbol{\pi}\boldsymbol{P}_t$ *for all t if and only if* $\boldsymbol{\pi}\boldsymbol{G} = \boldsymbol{0}$.

Sketch Proof. From (12),

$$\boldsymbol{\pi}\boldsymbol{G} = \boldsymbol{0} \Leftrightarrow \boldsymbol{\pi}\boldsymbol{G}^n = \boldsymbol{0} \quad \text{for all } n \geqslant 1$$

$$\Leftrightarrow \sum_1^\infty \frac{t^n}{n!}\boldsymbol{\pi}\boldsymbol{G}^n = \boldsymbol{0} \quad \text{for all } t$$

$$\Leftrightarrow \boldsymbol{\pi} \sum_0^\infty \frac{t^n}{n!}\boldsymbol{G}^n = \boldsymbol{\pi} \quad \text{for all } t$$

$$\Leftrightarrow \boldsymbol{\pi}\boldsymbol{P}_t = \boldsymbol{\pi} \quad \text{for all } t.$$ ■

This provides a useful collection of equations which specify stationary distributions, whenever they exist. The ergodic theorem for continuous-time chains is as follows; it holds exactly as stated, and requires no extra conditions.

(21) **Theorem.** *Let X be irreducible with a standard semigroup* $\{\boldsymbol{P}_t\}$ *of transition probabilities.*

(a) *If there exists a stationary distribution* $\boldsymbol{\pi}$ *then it is unique and*

$$p_{ij}(t) \to \pi_j \quad \text{as} \quad t \to \infty, \quad \text{for all } i \text{ and } j.$$

(b) *If there is no stationary distribution then* $p_{ij}(t) \to 0$ *as* $t \to \infty$, *for all i and j.*

Sketch Proof. Fix $h > 0$ and let $Y_n = X(nh)$. Then $Y = \{Y_n\}$ is an irreducible aperiodic discrete-time Markov chain; Y is called a *skeleton* of X. If Y is non-null persistent, then it has a unique stationary distribution $\boldsymbol{\pi}^h$ and $p_{ij}(nh) = \mathbf{P}(Y_n = j \mid Y_0 = i) \to \pi_j^h$ as $n \to \infty$; otherwise $p_{ij}(nh) \to 0$ as $n \to \infty$. Use this argument for two rational values h_1 and h_2 of h and observe that the sequences $\{nh_1 : n \geqslant 0\}$, $\{nh_2 : n \geqslant 0\}$ have infinitely many points in common to deduce that $\boldsymbol{\pi}^{h_1} = \boldsymbol{\pi}^{h_2}$ in the non-null persistent case. Thus the limit of $p_{ij}(t)$ exists along all sequences $\{nh : n \geqslant 0\}$ of times, for rational h; now use the continuity of $p_{ij}(t)$ to fill in the gaps. The proof is essentially complete. ■

6.10 Uniform semigroups

This section is not for lay readers and may be omitted; it indicates where some of the difficulties lie in the heuristic discussion of the last section (see Chung 1960 or Freedman 1971 for the proofs of the following results).

Perhaps the most important claim is (6.9.5), that $p_{ij}(h)$ is approximately linear in h when h is small.

(1) **Theorem.** *If* $\{\boldsymbol{P}_t\}$ *is a standard stochastic semigroup then there exists an* $|S|\times|S|$ *matrix* $\boldsymbol{G}=(g_{ij})$ *such that, as* $t\downarrow 0$

(a) $p_{ij}(t)=g_{ij}t+o(t)$ *if* $i\neq j$
(b) $p_{ii}(t)=1+g_{ii}t+o(t)$.

Also, $0\leqslant g_{ij}<\infty$ *if* $i\neq j$, *and* $0\geqslant g_{ii}\geqslant -\infty$. $\boldsymbol{G}$ *is called the* **generator** *of* $\{\boldsymbol{P}_t\}$.

(1b) is fairly easy to demonstrate (see Problem (6.13.12)); the proof of (1a) is considerably more difficult. $\boldsymbol{G}$ is a matrix with non-negative entries off the diagonal and non-positive entries (*which may be* $-\infty$) on the diagonal. We normally write

(2) $$\boldsymbol{G}=\lim_{t\downarrow 0}\frac{1}{t}(\boldsymbol{P}_t-\boldsymbol{I}).$$

If S is finite then

$$\boldsymbol{G}\mathbf{1}'=\lim_{t\downarrow 0}\frac{1}{t}(\boldsymbol{P}_t-\boldsymbol{I})\mathbf{1}'=\lim_{t\downarrow 0}\frac{1}{t}(\boldsymbol{P}_t\mathbf{1}'-\mathbf{1}')=\mathbf{0}'$$

from (6.9.3b), and so the row sums of $\boldsymbol{G}$ equal 0. If S is infinite, all we can assert is that

$$\textstyle\sum_j g_{ij}\leqslant 0.$$

In the light of (6.9.13), states i with $g_{ii}=-\infty$ are called *instantaneous*, since the chain leaves them at the same instant that it arrives in them. Otherwise, state i is called *stable* if $0>g_{ii}>-\infty$ and *absorbing* if $g_{ii}=0$.

We cannot proceed much further unless we impose a stronger condition on $\{\boldsymbol{P}_t\}$ than that it be standard.

(3) **Definition.** We call $\{\boldsymbol{P}_t\}$ **uniform** if

$$\boldsymbol{P}_t\rightarrow\boldsymbol{I}\quad\text{as}\quad t\downarrow 0 \text{ uniformly,}$$

which is to say that

(4) $$p_{ii}(t)\rightarrow 1\quad\text{as}\quad t\downarrow 0,\text{ uniformly in } i\in S.$$

Clearly (4) implies that $p_{ij}(t)\rightarrow 0$ for $i\neq j$, since $p_{ij}(t)\leqslant 1-p_{ii}(t)$. A uniform semigroup is standard; the converse is not generally true, but holds if S is finite. The uniformity of the semigroup depends upon the sizes of the diagonal elements of its generator $\boldsymbol{G}$.

(5) **Theorem.** $\{\boldsymbol{P}_t\}$ *is uniform if and only if* $\sup_i\{-g_{ii}\}<\infty$.

We consider uniform semigroups only for the rest of this section; they are so well behaved as to be rather dull. Here is the main result, which vindicates (6.9.9), (6.9.10), and (6.9.11).

(6) **Theorem. Kolmogorov's equations.** *If* $\{\mathbf{P}_t\}$ *is a uniform semigroup with generator* $\mathbf{G}$, *then it is the unique solution to the*

(7) ***forward equation:*** $\mathbf{P}_t' = \mathbf{P}_t\mathbf{G}$

(8) ***backward equation:*** $\mathbf{P}_t' = \mathbf{G}\mathbf{P}_t$

subject to the boundary condition $\mathbf{P}_0 = \mathbf{I}$. *Furthermore,*

(9) $$\mathbf{P}_t = \exp(t\mathbf{G}) \quad \text{and} \quad \mathbf{G}\mathbf{1}' = \mathbf{0}'.$$

The backward equation is more fundamental than the forward equation since it can be derived subject to the condition that $\mathbf{G}\mathbf{1}' = \mathbf{0}'$, which is a weaker condition than that the semigroup be uniform. This remark has some bearing on the discussion of dishonesty in Section 6.8. (Of course, a dishonest birth process is not even a Markov chain in our sense, unless we augment the state space $\{0, 1, 2, \ldots\}$ by adding on the point $\{\infty\}$.) You can prove (6) yourself. Just use the argument which established (6.9.9) and (6.9.10) with an eye to rigour; then show that (9) gives a solution to (7) and (8), and finally prove uniqueness.

Thus uniform semigroups are characterized by their generators; but which matrices are generators of uniform semigroups? Let $\mathcal{M}$ be the collection of $|S| \times |S|$ matrices $\mathbf{A} = (a_{ij})$ for which

$$\|\mathbf{A}\| = \sup_i \sum_{j \in S} |a_{ij}| < \infty.$$

(10) **Theorem.** $\mathbf{A} \in \mathcal{M}$ *is the generator of a uniform semigroup* $\mathbf{P}_t = \exp(t\mathbf{A})$ *if and only if*

$$a_{ij} \geq 0 \quad \text{for} \quad i \neq j, \quad \text{and} \quad \sum_j a_{ij} = 0 \quad \text{for all } i.$$

Next we discuss irreducibility. Observation (6.9.16) amounts to the following.

(11) **Theorem.** *If* $\{\mathbf{P}_t\}$ *is standard (but not necessarily uniform) then*

(a) $p_{ii}(t) > 0$ *for all* $t \geq 0$.
(b) ***Lévy dichotomy:*** *If* $i \neq j$ *then*
either (i) $p_{ij}(t) = 0$ *for all* $t > 0$
or (ii) $p_{ij}(t) > 0$ *for all* $t > 0$.

Partial proof. (a) $\{\mathbf{P}_t\}$ is assumed standard, so $p_{ii}(t) \to 1$ as $t \downarrow 0$. Pick $h > 0$ such that $p_{ii}(s) > 0$ for all $s \leq h$. For any real t pick n large enough so that $t \leq hn$. By the Chapman–Kolmogorov equations

$$p_{ii}(t) \geq \{p_{ii}(t/n)\}^n > 0 \quad \text{because} \quad t/n \leq h.$$

(b) The proof of this is quite difficult, though the method of (a) can easily be adapted to show that if

$$\alpha = \inf\{t : p_{ij}(t) > 0\}$$

then $p_{ij}(t)>0$ for all $t>\alpha$. The full result asserts that either $\alpha=0$ or $\alpha=\infty$. ■

(12) **Example (6.9.15) revisited.** If $\alpha>0$, $\beta>0$, and $S=\{1,2\}$, then

$$\boldsymbol{G}=\begin{pmatrix}-\alpha & \alpha\\ \beta & -\beta\end{pmatrix}$$

is the generator of a uniform stochastic semigroup $\{\boldsymbol{P}_t\}$ given by the following calculation. Diagonalize $\boldsymbol{G}$ to obtain $\boldsymbol{G}=\boldsymbol{B\Lambda B}^{-1}$ where

$$\boldsymbol{B}=\begin{pmatrix}\alpha & 1\\ -\beta & 1\end{pmatrix},\qquad \boldsymbol{\Lambda}=\begin{pmatrix}-(\alpha+\beta) & 0\\ 0 & 0\end{pmatrix}.$$

Therefore

$$\begin{aligned}\boldsymbol{P}_t&=\sum_0^\infty\frac{t^n}{n!}\boldsymbol{G}^n=\boldsymbol{B}\left(\sum_0^\infty\frac{t^n}{n!}\boldsymbol{\Lambda}^n\right)\boldsymbol{B}^{-1}\\ &=\boldsymbol{B}\begin{pmatrix}h(t) & 0\\ 0 & 1\end{pmatrix}\boldsymbol{B}^{-1}\quad\text{since}\quad\boldsymbol{\Lambda}^0=\boldsymbol{I}\\ &=\frac{1}{\alpha+\beta}\begin{pmatrix}\alpha h(t)+\beta & \alpha\{1-h(t)\}\\ \beta\{1-h(t)\} & \alpha+\beta h(t)\end{pmatrix}.\end{aligned}$$

where $h(t)=\exp\{-t(\alpha+\beta)\}$. Let $t\to\infty$ to obtain

$$\boldsymbol{P}_t\to\begin{pmatrix}1-\rho & \rho\\ 1-\rho & \rho\end{pmatrix}\quad\text{where}\quad\rho=\alpha/(\alpha+\beta)$$

and so

$$\mathbf{P}(X(t)=i)\to\begin{cases}1-\rho & \text{if}\quad i=1\\ \rho & \text{if}\quad i=2\end{cases}$$

irrespective of the initial distribution of $X(0)$. This shows that $\boldsymbol{\pi}=(1-\rho,\rho)$ is the limiting distribution. Check that $\boldsymbol{\pi G}=\mathbf{0}$. The method of (6.9.15) provides an alternative and easier route to these results. ●

(13) **Example. Birth process.** Recall the birth process of (6.8.11), and suppose that $\lambda_i>0$ for all i. The process is uniform if and only if

$$\sup_i\{-g_{ii}\}=\sup_i\{\lambda_i\}<\infty$$

and this is a sufficient condition for both the forward and backward equations to have unique solutions. We saw in Section 6.8 that the weaker condition

$$\sum_i\frac{1}{\lambda_i}=\infty$$

is a necessary and sufficient condition for this to hold. ●

6.11 Birth–death processes and imbedding

A birth process is a non-decreasing Markov chain for which the probability of moving from state n to state $n+1$ in the time interval $(t, t+h)$ is $\lambda_n h + o(h)$. More realistic continuous-time models for population growth incorporate death also. Suppose then that the number $X(t)$ of individuals alive in some population at time t evolves in the following way:

(a) X is a Markov chain taking values in $\{0, 1, 2, \dots\}$
(b) the infinitesimal transition probabilities are given by

(1)
$$\mathbf{P}(X(t+h)=n+m \mid X(t)=n)=\begin{cases}\lambda_n h+o(h) & \text{if } m=1\\ \mu_n h+o(h) & \text{if } m=-1\\ o(h) & \text{if } |m|>1\end{cases}$$

(c) deaths and births occur independently of each other, where the 'birth rates' $\lambda_0, \lambda_1, \dots$ and the 'death rates' $\mu_0, \mu_1, \dots$ satisfy

$$\lambda_i \geq 0, \quad \mu_i \geq 0, \quad \mu_0 = 0.$$

Then X is called a *birth–death process*. It has generator $\mathbf{G}=(g_{ij}: i, j \geq 0)$ given by

$$\mathbf{G}=\begin{pmatrix} -\lambda_0 & \lambda_0 & 0 & 0 & 0 & \cdots \\ \mu_1 & -(\lambda_1+\mu_1) & \lambda_1 & 0 & 0 & \cdots \\ 0 & \mu_2 & -(\lambda_2+\mu_2) & \lambda_2 & 0 & \cdots \\ 0 & 0 & \mu_3 & -(\lambda_3+\mu_3) & \lambda_3 & \cdots \\ \vdots & \vdots & \vdots & \vdots & \vdots & \end{pmatrix}.$$

It is uniform if and only if $\sup_i \{\lambda_i + \mu_i\} < \infty$. In many particular cases we have that $\lambda_0 = 0$, and then 0 is an absorbing state and the chain is not irreducible. Here are some examples.

(2) **Example. Pure birth.** $\mu_n = 0$ for all n. ●

(3) **Example. Simple death with immigration.** Let us model a population which evolves in the following way. At time zero the size $X(0)$ of the population equals I. Individuals do not reproduce, but new individuals immigrate into the population at the arrival times of a Poisson process with intensity $\lambda > 0$. Each individual may die in the time interval $(t, t+h)$ with probability $\mu h + o(h)$, where $\mu > 0$. The transition probabilities of $X(t)$ satisfy

$$\begin{aligned} p_{ij}(h) &= \mathbf{P}(X(t+h)=j \mid X(t)=i) \\ &= \begin{cases}\mathbf{P}(j-i \text{ arrivals, no deaths})+o(h) & \text{if } j \geq i\\ \mathbf{P}(i-j \text{ deaths, no arrivals})+o(h) & \text{if } j < i\end{cases}\end{aligned}$$

since the probability of two or more changes occurring in $(t, t+h)$ is $o(h)$.

Therefore

$$p_{i,i+1}(h) = \lambda h(1-\mu h)^i + o(h) = \lambda h + o(h)$$
$$p_{i,i-1}(h) = i(\mu h)(1-\mu h)^{i-1}(1-\lambda h) + o(h) = (i\mu)h + o(h)$$
$$p_{ij}(h) = o(h) \text{ if } |j-i| > 1$$

and we recognize $X(t)$ as a birth–death process with parameters

$$\lambda_n = \lambda, \quad \mu_n = n\mu.$$

It is an irreducible continuous-time Markov chain; (6.10.5) shows that it is not uniform. We may ask for the distribution of $X(t)$ and for the limiting distribution of the chain as $t \to \infty$. The former question is answered by solving the forward equations; this is Problem (6.13.16). The latter question is answered by the following.

(4) **Theorem.** *$X(t)$ is asymptotically Poisson distributed with parameter $\rho = \lambda/\mu$. That is*

$$\mathbf{P}(X(t) = n) \to \frac{\rho^n}{n!} e^{-\rho}, \qquad n = 0, 1, 2, \ldots .$$

Proof. X has generator

$$\mathbf{G} = \begin{pmatrix} -\lambda & \lambda & 0 & 0 & \cdots \\ \mu & -(\mu+\lambda) & \lambda & 0 & \cdots \\ 0 & 2\mu & -(2\mu+\lambda) & \lambda & \cdots \\ \vdots & \vdots & \vdots & \vdots & \end{pmatrix}.$$

There is a unique stationary distribution $\boldsymbol{\pi}$ satisfying $\boldsymbol{\pi}\mathbf{G} = \mathbf{0}$, and it is easy to check that

$$\pi_n = \frac{\rho^n}{n!} e^{-\rho}.$$

The result follows from (6.9.21). ■●

(5) **Example. Simple birth–death.** Assume that each individual who is alive in the population at time t either dies in the interval $(t, t+h)$ with probability $\mu h + o(h)$ or splits into two in the interval with probability $\lambda h + o(h)$. The transition probabilities satisfy equations like

$$\begin{aligned} p_{i,i+1}(h) &= \mathbf{P}(\text{one birth, no deaths}) + o(h) \\ &= i(\lambda h)(1-\lambda h)^{i-1}(1-\mu h)^i + o(h) \\ &= (i\lambda)h + o(h) \end{aligned}$$

and it is easy to check that the number $X(t)$ of living individuals at time t satisfies (1) with

$$\lambda_n = n\lambda, \quad \mu_n = n\mu.$$

We shall explore this model in detail. The chain $X=\{X(t)\}$ is standard but not uniform. We shall assume that $X(0)=I>0$; 0 is an absorbing state. We find the distribution of $X(t)$ through its generating function.

(6) **Theorem.** *The generating function of* $X(t)$ *is*

$$G(s,t)=\mathbf{E}(s^{X(t)})=\begin{cases}\left(\dfrac{\lambda t(1-s)+s}{\lambda t(1-s)+1}\right)^I & \text{if } \mu=\lambda\\[2ex] \left(\dfrac{\mu(1-s)-(\mu-\lambda s)\exp(-t(\lambda-\mu))}{\lambda(1-s)-(\mu-\lambda s)\exp(-t(\lambda-\mu))}\right)^I & \text{if } \mu\neq\lambda.\end{cases}$$

Proof. This is like Proof B of (6.8.2). Write $p_j(t)=\mathbf{P}(X(t)=j)$ and condition $X(t+h)$ on $X(t)$ to obtain the forward equations

$$p_j'(t)=\lambda(j-1)p_{j-1}(t)-(\lambda+\mu)jp_j(t)+\mu(j+1)p_{j+1}(t) \quad \text{if} \quad j\geq 1$$
$$p_0'(t)=\mu p_1(t).$$

Multiply the jth equation by s^j and sum to obtain

$$\sum_0^\infty s^j p_j'(t)=\lambda s^2\sum_1^\infty (j-1)s^{j-2}p_{j-1}(t)-(\lambda+\mu)s\sum_0^\infty js^{j-1}p_j(t)$$
$$+\mu\sum_0^\infty (j+1)s^j p_{j+1}(t).$$

Put $G(s,t)=\sum_0^\infty s^j p_j(t)=\mathbf{E}(s^{X(t)})$ to obtain

(7)
$$\frac{\partial G}{\partial t}=\lambda s^2\frac{\partial G}{\partial s}-(\lambda+\mu)s\frac{\partial G}{\partial s}+\mu\frac{\partial G}{\partial s}$$
$$=(\lambda s-\mu)(s-1)\frac{\partial G}{\partial s}$$

with boundary condition $G(s,0)=s^I$. The solution to this partial differential equation is given by (6); to see this either solve (7) by standard methods (see Hildebrand 1962, Chapter 8), or substitute the conclusion of (6) into (7). ■

Note that X is honest for all λ and μ since $G(1,t)=1$ for all t. To find the mean and variance of $X(t)$, differentiate G:

$$\mathbf{E}(X(t))=Ie^{(\lambda-\mu)t}$$

$$\operatorname{var}(X(t))=\begin{cases}2I\lambda t & \text{if } \lambda=\mu\\ I\dfrac{\lambda+\mu}{\lambda-\mu}e^{(\lambda-\mu)t}(e^{(\lambda-\mu)t}-1) & \text{if } \lambda\neq\mu.\end{cases}$$

Write $\rho=\lambda/\mu$ and notice that

$$\mathbf{E}(X(t))\to\begin{cases}0 & \text{if } \rho<1\\ \infty & \text{if } \rho>1.\end{cases}$$

(8) **Corollary.** *The extinction probabilities* $\eta(t) = \mathbf{P}(X(t)=0)$ *satisfy*

$$\eta(t) \to \begin{cases} 1 & \text{if } \rho \leq 1 \\ \rho^{-I} & \text{if } \rho > 1 \end{cases} \quad \text{as} \quad t \to \infty.$$

Proof. $\eta(t) = G(0, t)$. Substitute $s = 0$ in $G(s, t)$ to find $\eta(t)$ explicitly. ■

The observant reader will have noticed that these results are almost identical to those obtained for the branching process, except in that they pertain to a process in continuous time. There are (at least) two discrete Markov chains imbedded in X.

(A) *Imbedded random walk.* We saw in (6.9.13) and (6.9.14) that if $X(t) = n$, say, then the length of time

$$T = \inf\{s > 0 : X(t+s) \neq n\}$$

until the next birth or death is exponentially distributed with parameter $-g_{nn} = n(\lambda + \mu)$. When this time is up, X moves from state n to state $n + M$ where

$$\mathbf{P}(M = 1) = -g_{n,n+1}/g_{nn} = \frac{\lambda}{\lambda + \mu}$$

$$\mathbf{P}(M = -1) = \frac{\mu}{\lambda + \mu}.$$

Think of this transition as the movement of a particle from the integer n to the new integer $n + M$, where $M = \pm 1$. Such a particle performs a simple random walk with parameter $p = \lambda/(\lambda + \mu)$ and initial position I. We know already (see (5.2.5)) that the probability of ultimate absorption at 0 is given by (8). Other properties of random walks (see Sections 5.2 and 5.3) are applicable also.

(B) *Imbedded branching process.* We can think of the birth–death process in the following way. After birth an individual lives for a certain length of time which is exponentially distributed with parameter $\lambda + \mu$. When this period is over it dies, leaving behind it either no individuals, with probability $\mu/(\lambda + \mu)$, or two individuals, with probability $\lambda/(\lambda + \mu)$. This is just an age-dependent branching process with age density function

(9) $$f_T(u) = (\lambda + \mu)e^{-(\lambda+\mu)u}, \qquad u \geq 0$$

and family size generating function

(10) $$G(s) = \frac{\mu + \lambda s^2}{\mu + \lambda}$$

in the notation of Section 5.5 (do not confuse G in (10) with $G(s, t) = \mathbf{E}(s^{X(t)})$). Thus if $I = 1$, the generating function $G(s, t) = \mathbf{E}(s^{X(t)})$ satisfies the differential equation

(11) $$\frac{\partial G}{\partial t} = \lambda G^2 - (\lambda + \mu)G + \mu.$$

After (7), this is the *second* differential equation for $G(s, t)$. Needless to say, (11) is really just the backward equation of the process; the reader should check this and verify that it has the same solution as the forward equation (7). Suppose we lump together the members of each generation of this age-dependent branching process. Then we obtain an ordinary branching process with family size generating function $G(s)$ given by (10). From the general theory, the extinction probability of the process is the smallest non-negative root of the equation $s = G(s)$, and we can verify easily that this is given by (8) with $I = 1$. ●

(12) **Example. A more general branching process.** Finally, we consider a more general type of age-dependent branching process than that above, and investigate its honesty. Suppose that each individual in a population lives for an exponentially distributed time with parameter λ say. After death it leaves behind it a (possibly empty) family of offspring: the size N of this family has mass function $f(k) = \mathbf{P}(N = k)$ and generating function G_N. Let $X(t)$ be the size of the population at time t; we assume that $X(0) = 1$. From Section 5.5 the backward equation for $G(s, t) = \mathbf{E}(s^{X(t)})$ is just

$$\frac{\partial G}{\partial t} = \lambda(G_N(G) - G)$$

with boundary condition $G(s, 0) = s$; the solution is given by

(13)
$$\int_s^{G(s,t)} \frac{du}{G_N(u) - u} = \lambda t$$

provided that $G_N(u) - u$ has no zeros within the domain of the integral. There are many interesting questions about this process; for example, is it honest in the sense that

$$\sum_{j=0}^{\infty} \mathbf{P}(X(t) = j) = 1?$$

(14) **Theorem.** *X is honest if and only if*

(15)
$$\int_{1-\epsilon}^{1} \frac{du}{G_N(u) - u} \quad \textit{diverges for all } \epsilon > 0.$$

Proof. See Harris 1963, p. 107. ■

If condition (15) fails then the population size may explode to $+\infty$ in finite time.

(16) **Corollary.** *X is honest if* $\mathbf{E}(N) < \infty$.

Proof. Expand $G_N(u) - u$ about $u = 1$ to find that

$$G_N(u) - u = \{\mathbf{E}(N) - 1\}(u - 1) + o(u - 1) \quad \text{as} \quad u \uparrow 1.$$ ■●

6.12 Special processes

There are many more general formulations of the processes which we modelled in Sections 6.8 and 6.11. Here is a very small selection of some of them, with some details of the areas in which they have been found useful.

(1) **Non-homogeneous chains.** Relax the assumption that the transition probabilities $p_{ij}(s, t) = \mathbf{P}(X(t) = j \mid X(s) = i)$ satisfy

$$p_{ij}(s, t) = p_{ij}(0, t - s).$$

This leads to some very difficult problems. We may make some progress in the special case when $X(t)$ is the simple birth–death process of the previous section, for which

$$\lambda_n = n\lambda, \qquad \mu_n = n\mu.$$

The parameters λ and μ are now assumed to be non-constant functions of t. (After all, most populations have birth and death rates which vary from season to season.) It is easy to check that the forward equation (6.11.7) remains unchanged:

$$\frac{\partial G}{\partial t} = \{\lambda(t)s - \mu(t)\}(s-1)\frac{\partial G}{\partial s}.$$

The solution is

$$G(s, t) = \left(1 + \left[\frac{\exp\{r(t)\}}{s-1} - \int_0^t \lambda(u)\exp\{r(u)\}\,du\right]^{-1}\right)^I$$

where $I = X(0)$ and

$$r(t) = \int_0^t \{\mu(u) - \lambda(u)\}\,du.$$

The extinction probability of $X(t)$ is the coefficient of s^0 in $G(s, t)$, and it is left as an *exercise* for the reader to prove the next result.

(2) **Theorem.** $\mathbf{P}(X(t) = 0) \to 1$ *if and only if*

$$\int_0^T \mu(u)\exp\{r(u)\}\,du \to \infty \quad \textit{as} \quad T \to \infty. \qquad \bullet$$

(3) **A bivariate branching process.** We advertised the branching process as a feasible model for the growth of cell populations; we should also note one of its inadequacies in this role. Even the age-dependent process cannot meet the main objection, which is that the time of division of a cell may

depend rather more on the *size* of the cell than on its *age*. So here is a model for the growth and degradation of long-chain polymers†.

A population comprises *particles*. Let $N(t)$ be the number of particles present at time t, and suppose that $N(0)=1$. We suppose that the $N(t)$ particles are divided into $W(t)$ groups of size $N_1, N_2, \ldots, N_W$, $\{\sum_1^{W(t)} N_i = N(t)\}$, such that the particles in each group are aggregated into a *cell*. Think of the cells as a collection of $W(t)$ polymers, containing $N_1, N_2, \ldots, N_W$ particles respectively. As time progresses each cell grows and divides. We suppose that each cell can accumulate one particle from outside the system with probability $\lambda h + o(h)$ in the time interval $(t, t+h)$. As cells become larger they are more likely to divide. We assume that the probability that a cell of size N divides into two cells of sizes M and $N-M$, for some $0<M<N$, in the interval $(t, t+h)$ is $\mu(N-1)h+o(h)$. The assumption that the probability of division is a *linear* function of the cell size N is reasonable for polymer degradation since the particles are strung together in a line and any of the $N-1$ 'links' between pairs of particles may sever. At time t there are $N(t)$ particles and $W(t)$ cells, and the process is said to be in state $X(t)=(N(t), W(t))$. In the interval $(t, t+h)$ various transitions for $X(t)$ are possible. Either some cell grows or some cell divides, or more than one such event occurs. The probability that some cell grows is $\lambda Wh+o(h)$ since there are W chances of this happening; the probability of a division is $\mu(N_1+\ldots+N_W-W)h+o(h)=\mu(N-W)h+o(h)$ since there are $N-W$ links in all; the probability of more than one such occurrence is $o(h)$. Putting this information together gives a Markov chain $X(t)=(N(t), W(t))$ with state space $\{1, 2, \ldots\}^2$ and transition probabilities

$$\mathbf{P}(X(t+h)=(n, w)+\boldsymbol{\epsilon} \mid X(t)=(n, w)) = \begin{cases} \lambda wh + o(h) & \text{if } \boldsymbol{\epsilon}=(1,0) \\ \mu(n-w)h+o(h) & \text{if } \boldsymbol{\epsilon}=(0,1) \\ 1-(w(\lambda-\mu)+\mu n)h+o(h) & \text{if } \boldsymbol{\epsilon}=(0,0) \\ o(h) & \text{otherwise.} \end{cases}$$

Write down the forward equations as usual to obtain that the joint generating function

$$G(x, y; t) = \mathbf{E}(x^{N(t)} y^{W(t)})$$

satisfies the partial differential equation

$$\frac{\partial G}{\partial t} = \mu x(y-1)\frac{\partial G}{\partial x} + y\{\lambda(x-1)-\mu(y-1)\}\frac{\partial G}{\partial y}$$

† In physical chemistry, a *polymer* is a chain of molecules, neighbouring pairs of which are joined by bonds.

with $G(x, y; 0) = xy$. The joint moments of N and W are easily derived from this equation. More sophisticated techniques show that $N(t) \to \infty$, $W(t) \to \infty$, and $N(t)/W(t)$ approaches some constant as $t \to \infty$.

Unfortunately, most cells in nature are irritatingly non-Markovian! ●

(4) **A non-linear epidemic.** Consider a population of constant size $N+1$, and watch the spread of a disease about its members. Let $X(t)$ be the number of healthy individuals at time t and suppose that $X(0) = N$. We assume that if $X(t) = n$ then the probability of a new infection in $(t, t+h)$ is proportional to the number of possible encounters between ill folk and healthy folk. That is,

$$\mathbf{P}(X(t+h) = n-1 \mid X(t) = n) = \lambda n(N+1-n)h + o(h).$$

Nobody ever gets better. In the usual way, the reader can show that

$$G(s, t) = \mathbf{E}(s^{X(t)}) = \sum_{n=0}^{N} s^n \mathbf{P}(X(t) = n)$$

satisfies

$$\frac{\partial G}{\partial t} = \lambda(1-s)\left(N\frac{\partial G}{\partial s} - s\frac{\partial^2 G}{\partial s^2}\right)$$

with $G(s, 0) = s^N$. There is no simple way of solving this equation, though a lot of information is available about approximate solutions. ●

(5) **Birth–death with immigration.** We saw in Example (6.11.3) that populations are not always closed and that there is sometimes a chance that a new process will be started by an arrival from outside. This may be due to mutation (if we are counting genes), or leakage (if we are counting neutrons), or irresponsibility (if we are counting cases of rabies).

Suppose that there is one individual in the population at time zero; this individual is the founding member of some birth–death process $N(t)$ with fixed but unspecified parameters. Suppose further that other individuals immigrate into the population like a Poisson process $I(t)$ with intensity ν. Each immigrant starts a new birth–death process which is an independent identically distributed copy of the original process N but displaced in time according to its time of arrival. Let $T_0 (=0)$, $T_1, T_2, \ldots$ be the times at which immigrants arrive, and let $X_1, X_2, \ldots$ be the inter-arrival times

$$X_n = T_n - T_{n-1}.$$

The total population at time t is the aggregate of the processes generated by the $I(t)+1$ immigrants up to time t. Call this total $Y(t)$ to obtain

(6) $$Y(t) = \sum_{i=0}^{I(t)} N_i(t - T_i)$$

where $N_1, N_2, \ldots$ are independent copies of $N = N_0$. The problem is to find how the distribution of Y depends on the typical process N and the immigration rate ν; this is an example of the problem of compounding discussed in (5.1.15).

First we prove an interesting result about order statistics. Remember that $I(t)$ is a Poisson process and $T_n = \inf\{t : I(t) = n\}$ is the time of the nth immigration.

(7) **Theorem.** *The conditional joint distribution of* $T_1, T_2, \ldots, T_n$, *conditional on the event* $\{I(t) = n\}$, *is the same as the joint distribution of the order statistics of a family of n independent variables which are uniformly distributed on* $[0, t]$.

This is something of a mouthful, and asserts that if we know that n immigrants have arrived by time t then their actual arrival times are indistinguishable from a collection of n points chosen uniformly at random in the interval $[0, t]$.

Proof. We want the conditional density function of $\mathbf{T} = (T_1, \ldots, T_n)$ given $I = I(t) = n$. First note that $X_1, \ldots, X_n$ are independent exponential variables with parameter ν so that

$$f_{\mathbf{X}}(\boldsymbol{x}) = \nu^n \exp\left(-\nu \sum_1^n x_i\right).$$

Make the transformation $\mathbf{X} \to \mathbf{T}$ and use the change of variable formula (4.7.4) to find that

$$f_{\mathbf{T}}(\boldsymbol{t}) = \nu^n \exp(-\nu t_n) \quad \text{if} \quad t_1 < t_2 < \ldots < t_n.$$

Let $C \subset \mathbb{R}^n$. Then

$$\mathbf{P}(\mathbf{T} \in C \mid I = n) = \frac{\mathbf{P}(I = n \text{ and } \mathbf{T} \in C)}{\mathbf{P}(I = n)}, \tag{8}$$

but

$$\begin{aligned} \mathbf{P}(I = n \text{ and } \mathbf{T} \in C) &= \int_C \mathbf{P}(I = n \mid \mathbf{T} = \boldsymbol{t}) f_{\mathbf{T}}(\boldsymbol{t})\, d\boldsymbol{t} \\ &= \int_C \mathbf{P}(I = n \mid T_n = t_n) f_{\mathbf{T}}(\boldsymbol{t})\, d\boldsymbol{t} \end{aligned} \tag{9}$$

and

$$\mathbf{P}(I = n \mid T_n = t_n) = \mathbf{P}(X_{n+1} > t - t_n) = \exp\{-\nu(t - t_n)\} \tag{10}$$

so long as $t_n \leq t$. Substitute (10) into (9) and (9) into (8) to obtain

$$\mathbf{P}(\mathbf{T} \in C \mid I = n) = \int_C L(\boldsymbol{t}) n!\, t^{-n}\, d\boldsymbol{t}$$

where

$$L(\boldsymbol{t}) = \begin{cases} 1 & \text{if} \quad t_1 < t_2 < \ldots < t_n \\ 0 & \text{otherwise.} \end{cases}$$

We recognize $g(\mathbf{t}) = L(\mathbf{t})n!t^{-n}$ from the result of Problem (4.10.17) as the joint density function of the order statistics of n independent uniform variables on $[0, t]$. ■

We are now ready to describe $Y(t)$ in terms of the constituent processes N_i.

(11) **Theorem.** *If $N(t)$ has generating function $G_N(s, t) = \mathbf{E}(s^{N(t)})$ then the generating function $G(s, t) = \mathbf{E}(s^{Y(t)})$ of $Y(t)$ satisfies*

$$G(s, t) = G_N(s, t) \exp\left\{\nu \int_0^t (G_N(s, u) - 1)\,du\right\}.$$

Proof. Let $U_1, U_2, \ldots$ be a sequence of independent uniform variables on $[0, t]$. By (6),

$$\mathbf{E}(s^{Y(t)}) = \mathbf{E}(s^{N_0(t) + N_1(t - T_1) + \ldots + N_I(t - T_I)})$$

where $I = I(t)$. By independence, conditional expectation, and (7),

(12)
$$\begin{aligned}\mathbf{E}(s^{Y(t)}) &= \mathbf{E}(s^{N_0(t)})\mathbf{E}(\mathbf{E}(s^{N_1(t-T_1)+\ldots+N_I(t-T_I)} \mid I))\\ &= G_N(s, t)\mathbf{E}(\mathbf{E}(s^{N_1(t-U_1)+\ldots+N_I(t-U_I)} \mid I))\\ &= G_N(s, t)\mathbf{E}((\mathbf{E}(s^{N_1(t-U_1)}))^I).\end{aligned}$$

However,

(13)
$$\begin{aligned}\mathbf{E}(s^{N_1(t-U_1)}) &= \mathbf{E}(\mathbf{E}(s^{N_1(t-U_1)} \mid U_1))\\ &= \int_0^t \frac{1}{t} G_N(s, t-u)\,du = H(s, t), \text{ say,}\end{aligned}$$

and

(14)
$$\mathbf{E}(H^I) = \sum_{k=0}^{\infty} H^k \frac{(\nu t)^k}{k!} e^{-\nu t} = \exp\{\nu t(H - 1)\}.$$

Substitute (13) and (14) into (12) to obtain the result. ■●

(15) **Branching random walk.** Another characteristic of many interesting populations is their distribution about the space which they inhabit. We introduce this spatial aspect gently, by assuming that each individual lives at some point on the real line. (With the help of our imagination, this may seem to be a fair description of a sewer, river, or hedge.) Let us suppose that the evolution proceeds as follows. After its birth, a typical individual inhabits a randomly determined spot X in $\mathbb{R}$ for a random time T. After this time has elapsed he dies, leaving behind a family containing N offspring which he distributes at points $X + Y_1, X + Y_2, \ldots, X + Y_N$ where $Y_1, Y_2, \ldots$ are independent and identically distributed. These individuals then behave as their ancestor did, producing the next generation offspring after random times at points $X + Y_i + Y_{ij}$, where Y_{ij} is the

displacement of the jth offspring of the ith individual, and the Y's are independent and identically distributed. We shall be interested in the way that living individuals are distributed about $\mathbb{R}$ at some time t.

Suppose that the process begins with a single newborn individual at the point 0. We require some notation. Write $G_N(s)$ for the generating function of a typical family size N and let F be the distribution function of a typical Y. Let $Z(x, t)$ be the number of living individuals at points in the interval $(-\infty, x]$ at time t. We shall study the generating function

$$G(s; x, t) = \mathbf{E}(s^{Z(x,t)}).$$

Let T be the lifetime of the initial individual, N its family size, and $Y_1, Y_2, \ldots, Y_N$ the positions of its offspring. We shall condition Z on all these variables to obtain a type of backward equation. We must be careful about the order in which we do this conditioning, for the length of the sequence $Y_1, Y_2, \ldots$ depends on N. Hold your breath, and note from (4.10.20) that $G(s; x, t) = \mathbf{E}(\mathbf{E}(\mathbf{E}(\mathbf{E}(s^Z \mid T, N, \mathbf{Y}) \mid T, N) \mid T))$ or

$$G(s; x, t) = \mathop{\mathbf{E}}_T\left(\mathop{\mathbf{E}}_N\left(\mathop{\mathbf{E}}_{\mathbf{Y}}\{\mathbf{E}(s^Z \mid T, N, \mathbf{Y}) \mid N\}\right)\right)$$

where $\mathop{\mathbf{E}}_T$, for example, denotes the operation of averaging over the variable T. Clearly

$$Z(x, t) = \begin{cases} Z(x, 0) & \text{if } T > t \\ \sum_{i=1}^{N} Z_i(x - Y_i, t - T) & \text{if } T \leq t \end{cases}$$

where the processes $Z_1, Z_2, \ldots$ are independent copies of Z. Hence

$$\mathbf{E}(s^Z \mid T, N, \mathbf{Y}) = \begin{cases} G(s; x, 0) & \text{if } T > t \\ \prod_{i=1}^{N} G(s; x - Y_i, t - T) & \text{if } T \leq t. \end{cases}$$

Thus, if $T \leq t$ then

$$\mathop{\mathbf{E}}_N\left(\mathop{\mathbf{E}}_{\mathbf{Y}}(\mathbf{E}(s^Z \mid T, N, \mathbf{Y}) \mid N)\right) = \mathop{\mathbf{E}}_N\left(\left(\int_{-\infty}^{\infty} G(s; x - y, t - T)\, dF(y)\right)^N\right)$$

$$= G_N\left(\int_{-\infty}^{\infty} G(s; x - y, t - T)\, dF(y)\right).$$

Now breathe again. We consider here only the Markovian case when T is exponentially distributed with some parameter μ. Then

$$G(s; x, t) = \int_0^t \mu e^{-\mu u} G_N\left\{\int_{-\infty}^{\infty} G(s; x - y, t - u)\, dF(y)\right\} du + e^{-\mu t} G(s; x, 0).$$

Substitute $v = t - u$ inside the integral and differentiate with respect to t

to obtain

$$\frac{\partial G}{\partial t}+\mu G=\mu G_N\left\{\int_{-\infty}^{\infty} G(s; x-y, t)\,dF(y)\right\}.$$

It is not immediately clear that this is useful. However, differentiate with respect to s at $s=1$ to find that

$$m(x, t)=\mathbf{E}(Z(x, t))$$

satisfies

$$\frac{\partial m}{\partial t}+\mu m=\mu\mathbf{E}(N)\int_{-\infty}^{\infty} m(x-y, t)\,dF(y)$$

which is approachable by Laplace transform techiques. Such results can easily be generalized to higher dimensions. ●

(16) **Spatial growth.** Here is a simple model for skin cancer. Suppose that each point (x, y) of the two-dimensional square lattice $\{(x, y): x, y=0, \pm1, \pm2, \ldots\}$ is a skin cell. There are two types of cell, called b-cells (*benign* cells) and m-cells (*malignant* cells). Each cell lives for an exponentially distributed period of time, parameter β for b-cells and parameter μ for m-cells, after which it splits into two similar cells, one of which remains at the point of division and the other displaces one of the four nearest neighbours, each chosen at random with probability $\frac{1}{4}$. The displaced cell moves out of the system. Thus there are two competing types of cell. We assume that m-cells divide at least as fast as b-cells; the ratio

$$\kappa=\mu/\beta\geq 1$$

is the 'carcinogenic advantage'.

Suppose that there is only one m-cell initially and that all other cells are benign. What happens to the resulting tumour of malignant cells?

(17) **Theorem.** *If $\kappa=1$ then the m-cells die out with probability one, but the mean time until extinction is infinite. If $\kappa>1$ then there is probability κ^{-1} that the m-cells die out, and probability $1-\kappa^{-1}$ that their number grows beyond all bounds.*

Thus there is strictly positive probability of the malignant cells becoming significant if and only if the carcinogenic advantage exceeds one.

Proof. Let $X(t)$ be the number of m-cells at time t, and let $T_0(=0)$, $T_1, T_2, \ldots$ be the sequence of times at which X changes its value. Consider the imbedded discrete-time process $X=\{X_n\}$, where

$$X_n=X(T_n+)$$

is the number of m-cells just after the nth transition; X is a Markov chain taking values in $\{0, 1, 2, \ldots\}$. Remember the imbedded random walk of the birth–death process (6.11.5); in the case under consideration a little thought shows that X has transition probabilities

$$p_{i,i+1} = \frac{\mu}{\mu+\beta} = \frac{\kappa}{\kappa+1}, \qquad p_{i,i-1} = \frac{1}{\kappa+1} \quad \text{if} \quad i \neq 0, \qquad p_{0,0} = 1.$$

Therefore X_n is just a random walk with parameter $p = \kappa/(\kappa+1)$ and with an absorbing barrier at 0. The probability of ultimate extinction from the starting point $X(0) = 1$ is κ^{-1}. The walk is symmetric null persistent if $\kappa = 1$ and all non-zero states are transient if $\kappa > 1$. ■

If $\kappa = 1$ then the same argument shows that the m-cells certainly die out whenever there is a finite number of them to start with. However, suppose that they are distributed initially at the points of some (possibly infinite) set. It is possible to decide what happens after a long length of time; roughly speaking this depends on the relative densities of benign and malignant cells over large distances. One striking result is the following.

(18) **Theorem.** *If* $\kappa = 1$, *the probability that a specified finite collection of points contains only one type of cell approaches one as* $t \to \infty$.

Sketch proof. If two cells have a common ancestor then they are of the same type. Since offspring displace any neighbour with equal probability, the line of ancestors of any cell performs a symmetric random walk in two dimensions stretching backwards in time. Therefore, given any two cells at time t, the probability that they have a common ancestor is the probability that two symmetric and independent random walks S_1 and S_2 which originate at these points have met by time t. The difference $S_1 - S_2$ is also a type of symmetric random walk, and the argument of Problem (5.11.5) can be used to show that $S_1 - S_2$ almost certainly visits the origin sooner or later, showing that $\mathbf{P}(S_1(t) = S_2(t) \text{ for some } t) = 1$. ■

These large connected groups of cells of the same type are called 'empires'. ●

(19) **Simple queue.** Here is a simple model for a queueing system. Customers enter a shop like a Poisson process, parameter λ. They are served in the order of their arrival by a single assistant; each service period is a random variable which we assume to be exponential with parameter μ and which is independent of all other considerations. Let $X(t)$ be the length of the waiting line at time t. It is easy to see that X is a birth–death process with parameters

$$\lambda_n = \lambda \ (n \geq 0), \qquad \mu_n = \mu \ (n \geq 1).$$

The server would be very unhappy indeed if the queue length $X(t)$ were to tend to infinity as $t \to \infty$, since then he would have very few tea breaks. It is not difficult to see that the distribution of $X(t)$ settles down to a limit distribution, as $t \to \infty$, if and only if $\lambda < \mu$, which is to say that arrivals occur more slowly than departures on average (see Problem (6.13.20)). We consider this process in detail in Chapter 11, together with other more complicated queueing models. The techniques of this chapter find many applications there. ●

6.13 Problems

1. Classify the states of the discrete-time Markov chain with state space $S = \{1, 2, 3, 4, 5\}$ and transition matrix

$$\text{(a)} \begin{pmatrix} \frac{1}{3} & \frac{2}{3} & 0 & 0 \\ \frac{1}{2} & \frac{1}{2} & 0 & 0 \\ \frac{1}{4} & 0 & \frac{1}{4} & \frac{1}{2} \\ 0 & 0 & 0 & 1 \end{pmatrix} \quad \text{(b)} \begin{pmatrix} 0 & \frac{1}{2} & \frac{1}{2} & 0 \\ \frac{1}{3} & 0 & 0 & \frac{2}{3} \\ 1 & 0 & 0 & 0 \\ 0 & 0 & 1 & 0 \end{pmatrix}.$$

In case (a), calculate $f_{34}(n)$, and deduce that the probability of ultimate absorption in state 4, starting from 3, equals $\frac{2}{3}$. Find the mean recurrence times of the states in case (b).

2. A transition matrix is called *doubly stochastic* if all its column sums equal 1; that is, if $\sum_i p_{ij} = 1$ for all $j \in S$.

   (a) Show that if a finite chain is doubly stochastic then all its states are non-null persistent, and that if it is irreducible and aperiodic then $p_{ij}(n) \to N^{-1}$ as $n \to \infty$, where N is the number of states.

   (b) Show that, if an infinite irreducible chain is doubly stochastic then its states are either all null persistent or all transient.

3. Prove that intercommunicating states of a Markov chain have the same period.

4. Show that for each pair i, j of states of an irreducible aperiodic chain, there exists $N = N(i, j)$ such that $p_{ij}(n) > 0$ for all $n \geq N$. Deduce that the coupled chain $Z = (X, Y)$ in the proof of (6.4.16) is irreducible and aperiodic. Give an example of how the coupled chain Z may fail to be irreducible if X and Y are periodic.

5. Suppose $\{X_n : n \geq 0\}$ is a discrete-time Markov chain with $X_0 = i$. Let N be the total number of visits made subsequently by the chain to the state j. Show that

$$\mathbf{P}(N = n) = \begin{cases} 1 - f_{ij} & \text{if } n = 0 \\ f_{ij}(f_{jj})^{n-1}(1 - f_{jj}) & \text{if } n \geq 1, \end{cases}$$

and deduce that $\mathbf{P}(N = \infty) = 1$ if and only if $f_{ij} = f_{jj} = 1$.

6. Consider the symmetric random walk in three dimensions on the points $\{(x, y, z) : x, y, z = 0, \pm 1, \pm 2, \ldots\}$; this process is a sequence $\{\mathbf{X}_n : n \geq 0\}$ of points such that

$$\mathbf{P}(\mathbf{X}_{n+1} = \mathbf{X}_n + \boldsymbol{\varepsilon}) = \tfrac{1}{6} \quad \text{for} \quad \boldsymbol{\varepsilon} = (\pm 1, 0, 0),\ (0, \pm 1, 0),\ (0, 0, \pm 1).$$

Suppose that $\mathbf{X}_0=(0,0,0)$. Show that

$$\mathbf{P}(\mathbf{X}_{2n}=(0,0,0))=\left(\frac{1}{6}\right)^{2n}\sum_{i+j+k=n}\frac{(2n)!}{(i!j!k!)^2}$$
$$=\left(\frac{1}{2}\right)^{2n}\binom{2n}{n}\sum_{i+j+k=n}\left(\frac{n!}{3^n i!j!k!}\right)^2$$

and deduce by Stirling's formula (see (5.11.4)) that the origin is a transient state.

7. Consider the three-dimensional version of the cancer model (6.12.16). If $\kappa=1$, are the empires inevitable in this case?

8. Let X_n be a discrete-time Markov chain with state space $S=\{1,2\}$, and transition matrix

$$\mathbf{P}=\begin{pmatrix}1-\alpha & \alpha\\ \beta & 1-\beta\end{pmatrix}.$$

Classify the states of the chain. If $\alpha\beta>0$ find the n-step transition probabilities and show directly that they converge to the unique stationary distribution as $n\to\infty$. For what values of α and β is the chain time-reversible?

9. *Another diffusion model.* N black balls and N white balls are placed in two urns so that each contains N balls. After each unit of time one ball is selected at random from each urn, and the two balls thus selected are interchanged. Let the number of black balls in the first urn denote the state of the system. Write down the transition matrix of this Markov chain and find the unique stationary distribution. Is the chain time-reversible?

10. Let i and j be two states of a discrete-time Markov chain. Show that if i communicates with j, then there is positive probability of reaching j from i without revisiting i in the meantime. Deduce that if the chain is irreducible and persistent, then the probability f_{ij} of ever reaching j from i equals 1 for all i and j.

11. If $\{p_i : i\geqslant 0\}$ is a sequence of positive numbers and for $z\in\mathbb{C}$

$$\sum_0^\infty p_i z^i=P(z)=\{1-F(z)\}^{-1}$$

where $F(z)$ is analytic at $z=1$, show that

$$\lim_{i\to\infty} p_i=\left(\sum_1^\infty if_i\right)^{-1}.$$

How might we use this result in the theory of discrete-time Markov chains?

12. Let X be a continuous-time Markov chain with countable state space S and standard semigroup $\{\mathbf{P}_t\}$. Show that $p_{ij}(t)$ is a continuous function of t. Let

$$g(t)=-\log p_{ii}(t);$$

show that g is a continuous function, $g(0)=1$, and

$$g(s+t)\leqslant g(s)+g(t).$$

g is called 'subadditive', and a well-known theorem gives the result that

$$\lim_{t\downarrow 0}\frac{g(t)}{t}=\lambda \text{ exists and } \lambda=\sup_{t>0}\frac{g(t)}{t}\leqslant\infty.$$

Deduce that $g_{ii}=\lim_{t\downarrow 0}\frac{1}{t}\{p_{ii}(t)-1\}$ exists, but may be $-\infty$.

13. Let X be a continuous-time Markov chain with generator $\boldsymbol{G}=(g_{ij})$ and suppose that (6.9.12) holds. Show that X is irreducible if and only if for any pair i, j of states there exists a sequence $k_1, k_2, \ldots, k_n$ of states such that

$$g_{i,k_1}g_{k_1,k_2}\cdots g_{k_n,j}\neq 0.$$

14. Let $X=\{X(t):-\infty<t<\infty\}$ be a Markov chain with stationary distribution $\boldsymbol{\pi}$, and suppose that $X(0)$ has distributions $\boldsymbol{\pi}$. We call X *time-reversible* if X and Y have the same distributions, where $Y(t)=X(-t)$. If the transition semigroup $\{\boldsymbol{P}_t\}$ of X is standard with generator $\boldsymbol{G}$, show that

$$\pi_i g_{ij}=\pi_j g_{ji} \quad \text{for all } i \text{ and } j$$

is a necessary condition for X to be time-reversible. If $\{\boldsymbol{P}_t\}$ is uniform, show that $X(t)$ has distribution $\boldsymbol{\pi}$ for all t and that the above condition is sufficient for the chain to be time-reversible. Finally, show that the chain of Examples (6.9.15) and (6.10.12) is time-reversible when $X(0)$ has the stationary distribution. Compare with the result of Problem (8).

15. Show that not every discrete-time Markov chain can be imbedded in a continuous-time chain. More precisely, let

$$\boldsymbol{P}=\begin{pmatrix}\alpha & 1-\alpha\\ 1-\alpha & \alpha\end{pmatrix} \quad \text{for some } 0<\alpha<1$$

be a transition matrix. Show that there exists a uniform semigroup $\{\boldsymbol{P}_t\}$ of continuous-time transition probabilities such that $\boldsymbol{P}_1=\boldsymbol{P}$ if and only if $\frac{1}{2}<\alpha<1$. In this case show that $\{\boldsymbol{P}_t\}$ is unique and calculate it in terms of α.

16. Consider the immigration–death process $X(t)$ of (6.11.3). Show that its generating function $G(s, t)=\mathbf{E}(s^{X(t)})$ is given by

$$G(s, t)=[\{1+(s-1)e^{-\mu t}\}\exp\{\rho(s-1)(1-e^{-\mu t})\}]^I$$

where $\rho=\lambda/\mu$ as before. Deduce the result of (6.11.4).

17. A *non-homogeneous* Poisson process is a process $N(t)$ which is defined in the same way as a Poisson process except in that the likelihood of an arrival in $(t, t+h)$ is $\lambda(t)h+o(h)$ where $\lambda(t)$ varies with t. Write down the forward and backward equations for N and solve them.

18. Let N be a Poisson process and let $Y_1, Y_2, \ldots$ be independent and identically distributed random variables. The process

$$N^*(t)=\sum_{n=1}^{N(t)} Y_n$$

is called a *compound* Poisson process. Y_n is the change in the value of N^* at the nth arrival of the Poisson process N. Think of it like this. A 'random alarm clock' rings at the arrival times of a Poisson process. At the nth ring the process N^*

accumulates an extra quantity Y_n. Write down the forward and backward equations for N^* and hence find the characteristic function of $N^*(t)$. Can you see directly why it has the form which you have found?

19. If the intensity function $\lambda(t)$ of a non-homogeneous Poisson process N is itself a random process, then N is called a *doubly stochastic* Poisson process. Consider the case when $\lambda(t)=\Lambda$ for all t, and Λ is a random variable taking either of two values λ_1 or λ_2, each being picked with equal probability $\frac{1}{2}$. Find $\mathbf{E}(N(t))$ and var $(N(t))$.

20. Consider the general birth–death process $X(t)$ of Section 6.11, with strictly positive parameters $\lambda_0, \lambda_1, \ldots, \mu_1, \mu_2, \ldots$. Show that there is a stationary distribution if and only if

$$\sum_0^\infty \nu_j < \infty$$

where

$$\nu_j = \frac{\lambda_0\lambda_1 \ldots \lambda_{j-1}}{\mu_1\mu_2 \ldots \mu_j} \quad \text{for} \quad j \geqslant 1, \quad \text{and} \quad \nu_0 = 1,$$

and find it. Let η_i be the probability that $X(t)$ ever takes the value 0 starting from $X(0)=i$. Show that

$$\lambda_j\eta_{j+1} - (\lambda_j + \mu_j)\eta_j + \mu_j\eta_{j-1} = 0 \quad \text{for} \quad j \geqslant 1$$

and deduce that $\eta_i = 1$ for all i if

$$\sum_1^\infty e_j = \infty$$

where

$$e_j = \frac{\mu_1\mu_2 \ldots \mu_j}{\lambda_1\lambda_2 \ldots \lambda_j}.$$

21. Find a good necessary condition and a good sufficient condition for the birth–death process $X(t)$ of Problem (20) to be honest.

22. Consider the epidemic model (6.12.4) and let T be the length of time required until every member of the population has succumbed to the illness. Show that

$$\mathbf{E}(T) = \frac{1}{\lambda}\sum_{k=1}^{N} \frac{1}{k(N+1-k)}$$

and deduce that

$$\mathbf{E}(T) = \frac{2(\log N + \gamma)}{\lambda(N+1)} + O(N^{-2})$$

where γ is Euler's constant. $\mathbf{E}(T)$ decreases with N, for large N!

23. Let $X_1, X_2, \ldots, X_n$ be independent exponential variables with parameter λ, and let $X_{(1)} \leqslant \cdots \leqslant X_{(n)}$ be their order statistics. Show that

$$Y_1 = nX_{(1)}, \qquad Y_r = (n+1-r)(X_{(r)} - X_{(r-1)}), \qquad 1 < r \leqslant n$$

are also independent and have the same common distribution as the X's.

24. Let $X_{(1)}, \ldots, X_{(n)}$ be the order statistics of a family of independent variables with common continuous distribution function F. Show that

$$Y_1 = \{F(X_{(n)})\}^n, \qquad Y_r = \left\{\frac{F(X_{(r-1)})}{F(X_{(r)})}\right\}^{r-1}, \qquad 1 < r \leq n$$

are independent and uniformly distributed on $[0, 1]$. This is a generalization of (23). Why?

25. Consider a particle which performs a random walk on the set $S = \{0, 1, 2, \ldots\}$ with transition probabilities

$$p_{i,i+1} = a_i, \qquad p_{i,0} = 1 - a_i, \qquad i \geq 0$$

where $\{a_i\}$ is a sequence of constants which satisfy $0 < a_i < 1$ for all i. Let $b_0 = 1$, $b_i = a_0 a_1 \ldots a_{i-1}$ for $i \geq 1$. Show that the walk is

(a) persistent if and only if $b_i \to 0$ as $i \to \infty$
(b) non-null persistent if and only if $\sum_i b_i < \infty$,

and write down the stationary distribution if the latter condition holds.

Let A and β be positive constants and suppose that

$$a_i = 1 - Ai^{-\beta}$$

for all large i. Show that the chain is

(a) non-null persistent if $\beta < 1$
(b) transient if $\beta > 1$.

Finally, if $\beta = 1$ show that the chain is

(a) non-null persistent if $A > 1$
(b) null persistent if $A \leq 1$.

7 Convergence of random variables

7.1 Introduction

Expressions such as 'in the long run' and 'on the average' are commonplace in everyday usage, and express our faith that the averages of the results of repeated experimentation show less and less random fluctuation as they settle down to some limit.

(1) **Example. Buffon's needle (4.5.8).** In order to estimate the numerical value of π, Buffon devised the following experiment. Fling a needle a large number n of times onto a ruled plane and count the number S_n of times that the needle meets a line. In accordance with the result of (4.5.8), the proportion S_n/n of intersections is indeed found to be near to the probability $2/\pi$. Thus $X_n = 2n/S_n$ is a plausible estimate for π; this estimate converges as $n \to \infty$, and it seems reasonable to write

$$X_n \to \pi \quad \text{as} \quad n \to \infty. \qquad \bullet$$

(2) **Example.** Any number y satisfying $0 \leq y < 1$ has a decimal expansion

$$y = 0 \,.\, y_1 y_2 \ldots = \sum_{j=1}^{\infty} y_j 10^{-j},$$

where each y_j takes some value in $\{0, 1, 2, \ldots, 9\}$. Now think of y_j as the outcome of a random variable Y_j where $\{Y_j\}$ is a family of independent variables each of which may take any value in $\{0, 1, 2, \ldots, 9\}$ with equal probability $\frac{1}{10}$. The quantity

$$Y = \sum_{j=1}^{\infty} Y_j 10^{-j}$$

is a random variable taking values in $[0, 1]$. It seems likely that Y is uniformly distributed on $[0, 1]$, and this turns out to be the case (see Problem (7.10.4)). More rigorously, this amounts to asserting that the sequence $\{X_n\}$ given by

$$X_n = \sum_{j=1}^{n} Y_j 10^{-j}$$

converges in some sense as $n \to \infty$ to a limit Y, and that this limit random variable is uniform on $[0, 1]$. $\bullet$

In both these examples we encountered a sequence $\{X_n\}$ of random variables together with the assertion that

(3) $$X_n \to X \quad \text{as} \quad n \to \infty$$

for some other random variable X. However, random variables are real-valued functions on some sample space, and so (3) is a statement about the convergence of a sequence of *functions*. It is not immediately clear how such convergence is related to our experience of the theory of convergence of sequences $\{x_n\}$ of real numbers, and so we digress briefly to discuss sequences of functions.

Suppose for example that $f_1(\cdot), f_2(\cdot), \ldots$ is a sequence of functions mapping $[0, 1]$ into $\mathbb{R}$. In what manner may they converge to some limit function f?

(4) **Convergence pointwise.** If, for all $x \in [0, 1]$, the sequence $\{f_n(x)\}$ of real numbers satisfies

$$f_n(x) \to f(x) \quad \text{as} \quad n \to \infty,$$

then we say that $f_n \to f$ *pointwise.* ●

(5) **Norm convergence.** Let V be a collection of functions mapping $[0, 1]$ into $\mathbb{R}$. Subject to certain conditions on the members of V, we can endow V with a function $\|\cdot\|: V \to \mathbb{R}$ satisfying

(a) $\|f\| \geq 0$ for all $f \in V$
(b) $\|f\| = 0$ if and only if f is the zero function (or equivalent to it, in some sense to be specified)
(c) $\|af\| = |a| \, \|f\|$ for all $a \in \mathbb{R}$, $f \in V$
(d) $\|f + g\| \leq \|f\| + \|g\|$ (this is called the *triangle inequality*).

The function $\|\cdot\|$ is called a *norm.* If $\{f_n\}$ is a sequence of members of V then we say that $f_n \to f$ *with respect to this norm* if

$$\|f_n - f\| \to 0 \quad \text{as} \quad n \to \infty.$$

Certain special and important norms are given by

$$\|g\|_p = \left\{ \int_0^1 |g(x)|^p \, dx \right\}^{1/p}$$

for $p \geq 1$ and any suitable function g. ●

(6) **Convergence in measure.** Let $\epsilon > 0$ be prescribed, and define the 'distance' between two functions g and h by

$$d_\epsilon(g, h) = \int_E dx$$

where $E = \{u \in [0, 1]: |g(u) - h(u)| > \epsilon\}$. We say that $f_n \to f$ *in measure* if

$$d_\epsilon(f_n, f) \to 0 \quad \text{as} \quad n \to \infty \quad \text{for all } \epsilon > 0.$$ ●

The convergence of $\{f_n\}$ according to one definition does not necessarily imply its convergence according to another. For example, we shall see later that

(a) if $f_n \to f$ pointwise then $f_n \to f$ in measure, but the converse is not generally true

(b) there exist sequences which converge pointwise but not with respect to $\|\cdot\|_1$, and vice versa.

In this chapter we shall see how to adapt these modes of convergence to suit families of *random variables*. Major applications of the ensuing theory include the study of the sequence

(7) $$S_n = X_1 + X_2 + \ldots + X_n$$

of partial sums of an independent identically distributed sequence $\{X_i\}$; the Law of Large Numbers of Section 5.10 will appear as a special case.

It will be clear, from our discussion and the reader's experience, that probability theory is indispensable in descriptions of many processes which occur naturally in the world. Often in such cases we are interested in the future values of the process, and thus in the long-term behaviour of the mathematical model; this is why we need to prove limit theorems for sequences of random variables. Many of these sequences are generated by less tractable operations than, say, the partial sums in (7), and general results such as the Law of Large Numbers may not be useful. It turns out that many other types of sequence are guaranteed to converge; in particular we shall consider later the remarkable theory of 'martingales' which has important applications throughout the field of applied probability. This chapter ends with a simple account of the convergence theorem for martingales, together with some examples of its use; these include the asymptotic behaviour of the branching process and provide rigorous derivations of certain earlier remarks (such as (5.4.6)).

All readers should follow the chapter up to and including Section 7.4. The subsequent material is more difficult and may be omitted at the first reading.

7.2 Modes of convergence

There are four principal ways of interpreting the statement '$X_n \to X$ as $n \to \infty$'. Three of these are related to (7.1.4), (7.1.5), and (7.1.6), and the fourth is already familiar to us.

(1) **Definition.** Let $X_1, X_2, \ldots, X$ be random variables on some probability space $(\Omega, \mathcal{F}, \mathbf{P})$. We say that

(a) $X_n \to X$ **almost surely**, written $X_n \xrightarrow{\text{a.s.}} X$, if

$$\{\omega \in \Omega : X_n(\omega) \to X(\omega) \text{ as } n \to \infty\} \text{ is an event whose probability is } 1$$

(b) $X_n \to X$ **in rth mean**, where $r \geq 1$, written $X_n \xrightarrow{r} X$, if

$$\mathbf{E}(|X_n - X|^r) \to 0 \quad \text{as} \quad n \to \infty$$

(c) $X_n \to X$ **in probability**, written $X_n \xrightarrow{P} X$, if

$$\mathbf{P}(|X_n - X| > \epsilon) \to 0 \quad \text{as} \quad n \to \infty \quad \text{for all } \epsilon > 0$$

(d) $X_n \to X$ **in distribution**, written† $X_n \xrightarrow{D} X$, if

$$\mathbf{P}(X_n \leqslant x) \to \mathbf{P}(X \leqslant x) \quad \text{as} \quad n \to \infty$$

for all points x at which $F_X(x) = \mathbf{P}(X \leqslant x)$ is continuous.

It is appropriate to make some remarks about the four sections of this potentially bewildering definition.

(a) The natural adaptation of (7.1.4) is to say that $X_n \to X$ *pointwise* if the set $A = \{\omega \in \Omega : X_n(\omega) \to X(\omega) \text{ as } n \to \infty\}$ satisfies

$$A = \Omega.$$

Such a condition is of little interest to probabilists since it contains no reference to probabilities. In part (a) of (1) we do not require that A is the whole of Ω, but rather that its complement A^c is a null set. There are several notations for this mode of convergence, and we shall use these later. They include

$X_n \to X$ *almost everywhere*, or $X_n \xrightarrow{\text{a.e.}} X$

$X_n \to X$ *with probability one*, or $X_n \to X$ w.p.1.

(b) It is easy to check by Minkowski's inequality (4.10.18) that

$$\|Y\|_r = (\mathbf{E}|Y^r|)^{1/r} = \left(\int |y|^r \, dF_Y\right)^{1/r}$$

defines a norm on the collection of random variables with finite rth moment, for any value of $r \geqslant 1$. Rewrite (7.1.5) with this norm to obtain Definition (1b). Here we shall only consider positive integral values of r, though the subsequent theory can be extended without difficulty to deal with any real r not smaller than 1. Of most use are the values $r = 1$ and $r = 2$, in which cases we write respectively

$X_n \xrightarrow{1} X$, or $X_n \to X$ *in mean*, or l.i.m. $X_n = X$

and

$X_n \xrightarrow{2} X$, or $X_n \to X$ *in mean square*, or $X_n \xrightarrow{\text{m.s.}} X$.

(c) The functions of (7.1.6) had a common domain [0, 1]; the X's have a common domain Ω, and the distance function d_ϵ is naturally adapted to

† Many authors avoid this notation since convergence in distribution pertains only to the *distribution function* of X and not to the variable X itself. We use it here for the sake of uniformity of notation, but refer the reader to Note (d) below.

become

$$d_\epsilon(Y,Z) = \mathbf{P}(|Y-Z|>\epsilon) = \int_E d\mathbf{P}$$

where $E = \{\omega \in \Omega : |Y(\omega) - Z(\omega)| > \epsilon\}$. This notation will be familiar to those readers with knowledge of the abstract integral of Section 5.6.

(d) We have seen this already in Section 5.9 where we discussed the continuity condition. Further examples of convergence in distribution are to be found in Chapter 6, where we saw, for example, that an irreducible ergodic Markov chain converges in distribution to its unique stationary distribution. Note that if $X_n \xrightarrow{D} X$ then $X_n \xrightarrow{D} X'$ for any X' which has the same distribution as X.

It is no surprise to learn that the four modes of convergence are not equivalent to each other. You may guess after some reflection that convergence in distribution is the weakest, since it is a condition only on the *distribution functions* of the X's; it contains no reference to the *sample space* Ω and no information about, say, the dependence or independence of the X's. The following example is a partial confirmation of this.

(2) **Example.** Let X be a Bernoulli variable taking values 0 and 1 with equal probability $\frac{1}{2}$. Let $X_1, X_2, \ldots$ be identical random variables given by

$$X_n = X \quad \text{for all } n.$$

The X's are certainly not independent, but $X_n \xrightarrow{D} X$. Let $Y = 1 - X$. Clearly $X_n \xrightarrow{D} Y$ also, since X and Y have the same distribution. However, X_n cannot converge to Y in any other mode because $|X_n - Y| = 1$ always. ●

Here is the chart of implications between the modes of convergence. Learn it well. Statements like

$$(X_n \xrightarrow{P} X) \Rightarrow (X_n \xrightarrow{D} X)$$

mean that any sequence which converges in probability also converges in distribution to the same limit.

(3) **Theorem.** *The following implications hold:*

$$\begin{array}{l} (X_n \xrightarrow{\text{a.s.}} X) \\ \qquad\qquad \searrow \\ \qquad\qquad\quad (X_n \xrightarrow{P} X) \Rightarrow (X_n \xrightarrow{D} X) \\ \qquad\qquad \nearrow \\ (X_n \xrightarrow{r} X) \end{array}$$

for any $r \geq 1$. Also, if $r > s \geq 1$ then

$$(X_n \xrightarrow{r} X) \Rightarrow (X_n \xrightarrow{s} X).$$

No other implications hold in general.†

† But see (14).

The four basic implications of this theorem are of the general form 'if A holds, then B holds'. The converse implications are false in general, but become true if certain extra conditions are imposed; such partial converses take the form 'if B holds together with C, then A holds'. These two types of statement are sometimes said to be of the 'Abelian' and 'Tauberian' types, respectively; these titles are derived from the celebrated theory of the summability of series. Usually, there are many possible choices for appropriate sets C of extra conditions, and it is often difficult to establish attractive 'corrected converses'.

(4) **Theorem.**
(a) *If* $X_n \xrightarrow{\text{D}} c$, *where* c *is constant, then* $X_n \xrightarrow{\text{P}} c$.
(b) *If* $X_n \xrightarrow{\text{P}} X$ *and* $\mathbf{P}(|X_n| \leq k) = 1$ *for all* n *and some* k, *then* $X_n \xrightarrow{r} X$ *for all* $r \geq 1$.
(c) *If* $P_n(\epsilon) = \mathbf{P}(|X_n - X| > \epsilon)$ *satisfies* $\sum_n P_n(\epsilon) < \infty$ *for all* $\epsilon > 0$, *then* $X_n \xrightarrow{\text{a.s.}} X$.

You should become well acquainted with Theorems (3) and (4). The proofs follow as a series of lemmas. These lemmas contain some other relevant and useful results.

Consider briefly the first and principal part of Theorem (3). We may already anticipate some way of showing that convergence in probability implies convergence in distribution, since both modes involve probabilities of the form $\mathbf{P}(Y \leq y)$ for some random variable Y and real y. The other two implications require intermediate steps. Specifically, the relation between convergence in rth mean and convergence in probability requires a link between expectations and distributions. We have to move very carefully in this context; even apparently 'natural' statements may be false. For example, if $X_n \xrightarrow{\text{a.s.}} X$ (and therefore $X_n \xrightarrow{\text{P}} X$ also) then it does *not* necessarily follow that $\mathbf{E}X_n \to \mathbf{E}X$ (see (9) for an instance of this); the result of Problem (7.10.1) is as strong as is available here. The proof of the appropriate stage of Theorem (3) requires Markov's Inequality (7).

(5) **Lemma.** *If* $X_n \xrightarrow{\text{P}} X$ *then* $X_n \xrightarrow{\text{D}} X$. *The converse assertion fails in general.*†

Proof. Suppose $X_n \xrightarrow{\text{P}} X$ and write

$$F_n(x) = \mathbf{P}(X_n \leq x), \qquad F(x) = \mathbf{P}(X \leq x)$$

for the distribution functions of X_n and X respectively. Then, if $\epsilon > 0$,

$$\begin{aligned} F_n(x) = \mathbf{P}(X_n \leq x) &= \mathbf{P}(X_n \leq x, X \leq x + \epsilon) + \mathbf{P}(X_n \leq x, X > x + \epsilon) \\ &\leq F(x+\epsilon) + \mathbf{P}(|X_n - X| > \epsilon). \end{aligned}$$

Similarly

$$\begin{aligned} F(x-\epsilon) = \mathbf{P}(X \leq x - \epsilon) &= \mathbf{P}(X \leq x - \epsilon, X_n \leq x) + \mathbf{P}(X \leq x - \epsilon, X_n > x) \\ &\leq F_n(x) + \mathbf{P}(|X_n - X| > \epsilon). \end{aligned}$$

† But see (14).

Thus

$$F(x-\epsilon)-\mathbf{P}(|X_n-X|>\epsilon)\leqslant F_n(x)\leqslant F(x+\epsilon)+\mathbf{P}(|X_n-X|>\epsilon).$$

Let $n\to\infty$ to obtain

$$F(x-\epsilon)\leqslant \liminf_{n\to\infty} F_n(x)\leqslant \limsup_{n\to\infty} F_n(x)\leqslant F(x+\epsilon)$$

for all $\epsilon>0$. If F is continuous at x then

$$F(x-\epsilon)\uparrow F(x) \quad \text{and} \quad F(x+\epsilon)\downarrow F(x) \quad \text{as} \quad \epsilon\downarrow 0,$$

and the result is proved.

Example (2) shows that the converse is false. ■

(6) **Lemma.**

(a) *If* $r>s\geqslant 1$ *and* $X_n\xrightarrow{r} X$ *then* $X_n\xrightarrow{s} X$.

(b) *If* $X_n\xrightarrow{1} X$ *then* $X_n\xrightarrow{P} X$.

The converse assertions fail in general.

This includes the fact that convergence in rth mean implies convergence in probability. Here is a useful inequality which we shall use in the proof of this lemma.

(7) **Lemma. Markov's inequality.** *If X is any random variable with finite mean then*

$$\mathbf{P}(|X|\geqslant a)\leqslant\frac{\mathbf{E}|X|}{a} \quad \textit{for any } a>0.$$

Proof. Let $A=\{|X|\geqslant a\}$. Then

$$|X|\geqslant aI_A$$

where I_A is the indicator function of A. Take expectations to obtain the result. ■

Proof of Lemma (6).

(a) By the result of Problem (4.10.19),

$$\{\mathbf{E}(|X_n-X|^s)\}^{1/s}\leqslant\{\mathbf{E}(|X_n-X|^r)\}^{1/r}$$

and the result follows immediately. To see that the converse fails, define an independent sequence $X_1, X_2, \ldots$ by

(8) $$X_n=\begin{cases} n & \text{with probability } n^{-(r+s)/2} \\ 0 & \text{with probability } 1-n^{-(r+s)/2}. \end{cases}$$

It is an easy *exercise* to check that

$$\mathbf{E}|X_n^s|=n^{(s-r)/2}\to 0, \qquad \mathbf{E}|X_n^r|=n^{(r-s)/2}\to\infty.$$

(b) By Markov's inequality (7)

$$\mathbf{P}(|X_n-X|>\epsilon)\leqslant\frac{\mathbf{E}|X_n-X|}{\epsilon} \quad \text{for all } \epsilon>0$$

and the result follows immediately. To see that the converse fails, define an independent sequence $\{X_n\}$ by

(9) $$X_n = \begin{cases} n^3 & \text{with probability } n^{-2} \\ 0 & \text{with probability } 1-n^{-2}. \end{cases}$$

Then $\mathbf{P}(|X_n|>\epsilon)=n^{-2}$ for all large n, and so $X_n \xrightarrow{P} 0$. However, $\mathbf{E}|X_n| = n \to \infty$. ■

(10) **Lemma.** *Let* $A_n(\epsilon)=\{|X_n - X|>\epsilon\}$ *and* $B_m(\epsilon)= \bigcup_{n\geq m} A_n(\epsilon)$. *Then*

(a) $X_n \xrightarrow{\text{a.s.}} X$ *if and only if* $\mathbf{P}(B_m(\epsilon))\to 0$ *as* $m\to\infty$, *for all* $\epsilon>0$

(b) $X_n \xrightarrow{\text{a.s.}} X$ *if* $\sum_n \mathbf{P}(A_n(\epsilon))<\infty$ *for all* $\epsilon>0$

(c) *if* $X_n \xrightarrow{\text{a.s.}} X$ *then* $X_n \xrightarrow{P} X$, *but the converse fails in general.*

Proof.

(a) Let $C=\{\omega\in\Omega: X_n(\omega)\to X(\omega) \text{ as } n\to\infty\}$ and let

$$A(\epsilon)=\{\omega\in\Omega:\omega\in A_n(\epsilon) \text{ for infinitely many values of } n\}.$$

Then $\mathbf{P}(C)=1$ if and only if $\mathbf{P}(A(\epsilon))=0$ for all $\epsilon>0$. However, $\{B_m(\epsilon)\}$ is a decreasing sequence of events with limit $\lim_{m\to\infty} B_m(\epsilon)=A(\epsilon)$ (see Problem (1.8.14)), and so $\mathbf{P}(A(\epsilon))=0$ if and only if $\mathbf{P}(B_m(\epsilon))\to 0$.

(b) From the definition of $B_m(\epsilon)$

$$\mathbf{P}(B_m(\epsilon))\leq \sum_{n=m}^{\infty} \mathbf{P}(A_n(\epsilon))$$

and so $\mathbf{P}(B_m(\epsilon))\to 0$ as $m\to\infty$ whenever

$$\sum_n \mathbf{P}(A_n(\epsilon))<\infty.$$

(c) $A_n(\epsilon)\subseteq B_n(\epsilon)$ and so $\mathbf{P}(|X_n-X|>\epsilon)=\mathbf{P}(A_n(\epsilon))\to 0$ whenever $\mathbf{P}(B_n(\epsilon))\to 0$. To see that the converse fails, define an independent sequence $\{X_n\}$ by

(11) $$X_n = \begin{cases} 1 & \text{with probability } n^{-1} \\ 0 & \text{with probability } 1-n^{-1}. \end{cases}$$

Clearly $X_n \xrightarrow{P} 0$. However, if $0<\epsilon<1$,

$$\begin{aligned} \mathbf{P}(B_m(\epsilon)) &= 1-\lim_{r\to\infty}\mathbf{P}(X_n=0 \quad \text{for all } n \text{ such that } m\leq n\leq r) \text{ by (1.3.5)} \\ &= 1-\left(1-\frac{1}{m}\right)\left(1-\frac{1}{m+1}\right)\cdots \quad \text{by independence} \\ &= 1 \quad \text{for all } m, \text{ by Theorem (9) of Appendix I,} \end{aligned}$$

and so $\{X_n\}$ does not converge almost surely. ■

(12) **Lemma.** *There exist sequences which*

(a) *converge almost surely but not in mean*
(b) *converge in mean but not almost surely.*

Proof.

(a) Consider example (9). Use (10b) to show that $X_n \xrightarrow{\text{a.s.}} 0$.
(b) Consider example (11). ■

This completes the proof of Theorem (3), and we move to Theorem (4).

Proof of Theorem (4).

(a) $$\mathbf{P}(|X_n - c| > \epsilon) = \mathbf{P}(X_n < c - \epsilon) + \mathbf{P}(X_n > c + \epsilon) \to 0 \quad \text{if} \quad X_n \xrightarrow{\text{D}} c.$$

(b) If $X_n \xrightarrow{\text{P}} X$ and $\mathbf{P}(|X_n| \le k) = 1$ then

$\mathbf{P}(|X| \le k) = 1$ also, since

$$\mathbf{P}(|X| \le k + \epsilon) = \lim_{n\to\infty} \mathbf{P}(|X_n| \le k + \epsilon) = 1$$

for all $\epsilon > 0$. Now, let $A_n(\epsilon) = \{|X_n - X| > \epsilon\}$, with complement $A_n^c(\epsilon)$. Then

$$|X_n - X|^r \le \epsilon^r I_{A_n^c(\epsilon)} + (2k)^r I_{A_n(\epsilon)}$$

with probability one. Take expectations to obtain

$$\mathbf{E}(|X_n - X|^r) \le \epsilon^r + \{(2k)^r - \epsilon^r\}\mathbf{P}(A_n(\epsilon)) \to \epsilon^r \quad \text{as} \quad n \to \infty.$$

Let $\epsilon \downarrow 0$ to obtain that $X_n \xrightarrow{r} X$.
(c) This is just (10b). ■

Note that any sequence $\{X_n\}$ which satisfies $X_n \xrightarrow{\text{P}} X$ contains a subsequence $\{X_{n_i} : 1 \le i < \infty\}$ which converges almost surely.

(13) **Theorem.** *If $X_n \xrightarrow{\text{P}} X$ then there exists a non-random increasing sequence of integers $n_1, n_2, \ldots$ such that $X_{n_i} \xrightarrow{\text{a.s.}} X$ as $i \to \infty$.*

Proof. Since $X_n \xrightarrow{\text{P}} X$, we have that

$$\mathbf{P}(|X_n - X| > \epsilon) \to 0 \quad \text{as} \quad n \to \infty, \quad \text{for all } \epsilon > 0.$$

Pick an increasing sequence $n_1, n_2, \ldots$ of positive integers such that

$$\mathbf{P}\left(|X_{n_i} - X| > \frac{1}{i}\right) \le \frac{1}{i^2}.$$

Then, for any $\epsilon > 0$

$$\sum_{i > \epsilon^{-1}} \mathbf{P}(|X_{n_i} - X| > \epsilon) \le \sum_{i > \epsilon^{-1}} \mathbf{P}(|X_{n_i} - X| > i^{-1}) < \infty$$

and the result follows from (10b). ■

We have seen that convergence in distribution is the weakest mode of convergence since it involves distribution functions only and makes no reference to an underlying probability space (see (5.9.4) for an equivalent formulation of convergence in distribution which involves distribution functions alone). However, assertions of the form '$X_n \xrightarrow{D} X$' (or equivalently '$F_n \to F$', where F_n and F are the distribution functions of X_n and X) have important and useful representations in terms of almost sure convergence.

(14) **Skorokhod's Representation Theorem.** *If $\{X_n\}$ and X, with distribution functions $\{F_n\}$ and F, are such that*

$$X_n \xrightarrow{D} X \text{ (or, equivalently, } F_n \to F) \text{ as } n \to \infty,$$

then there exists a probability space $(\Omega', \mathcal{F}', \mathbf{P}')$ and random variables $\{Y_n\}$ and Y, which map Ω' into $\mathbb{R}$, such that

(a) *$\{Y_n\}$ and Y have distribution functions $\{F_n\}$ and F*

(b) $Y_n \xrightarrow{\text{a.s.}} Y$ *as* $n \to \infty$.

Therefore although X_n may fail to converge to X in any mode other than in distribution, there exists a sequence $\{Y_n\}$, distributed identically to $\{X_n\}$, which converges almost surely to a copy of X. The proof is elementary, but may be omitted.

Proof. Let $\Omega' = (0, 1)$, $\mathcal{F}'$ be the Borel σ-field generated by the intervals of Ω' (see the discussion at the end of Section 4.1) and let $\mathbf{P}'$ be the probability measure induced on $\mathcal{F}'$ by the requirement that, for any interval $I = (a, b) \subseteq \Omega'$, $\mathbf{P}'(I) = (b - a)$; $\mathbf{P}'$ is called *Lebesgue measure.* For $\omega \in \Omega'$, define

$$Y_n(\omega) = \inf\{x : \omega \leq F_n(x)\}$$
$$Y(\omega) = \inf\{x : \omega \leq F(x)\}.$$

Note that Y_n and Y are essentially the inverse functions of F_n and F since

(15)
$$\omega \leq F_n(x) \Leftrightarrow Y_n(\omega) \leq x$$
$$\omega \leq F(x) \Leftrightarrow Y(\omega) \leq x.$$

It follows immediately that Y_n and Y satisfy (14a) since, for example, from (15)

$$\mathbf{P}'(Y \leq y) = \mathbf{P}'((0, F(y)]) = F(y).$$

To show (14b), proceed as follows. Given $\epsilon > 0$ and $\omega \in \Omega'$, pick a point x of continuity of F such that

$$Y(\omega) - \epsilon < x < Y(\omega).$$

By (15), $F(x) < \omega$, but $F_n(x) \to F(x)$ as $n \to \infty$ and so $F_n(x) < \omega$ for all large n, giving that

$$Y(\omega)-\epsilon<x<Y_n(\omega) \quad \text{for all large } n;$$

now let $n\to\infty$ and $\epsilon\downarrow 0$ to obtain

(16) $$\liminf_{n\to\infty} Y_n(\omega)\geq Y(\omega) \quad \text{for all } \omega.$$

Finally, if $\omega<\omega'<1$, pick a point x of continuity of F such that

$$Y(\omega')<x<Y(\omega')+\epsilon.$$

By (15), $\omega<\omega'\leq F(x)$ and so $\omega<F_n(x)$ for all large n, giving that

$$Y_n(\omega)\leq x<Y(\omega')+\epsilon \quad \text{for all large } n;$$

now let $n\to\infty$ and $\epsilon\downarrow 0$ to obtain

(17) $$\limsup_{n\to\infty} Y_n(\omega)\leq Y(\omega') \quad \text{whenever } \omega<\omega'.$$

Combine this with (16) to see that $Y_n(\omega)\to Y(\omega)$ for all points ω of continuity of Y. However, Y is monotone non-decreasing and so the set D of discontinuities of Y is countable; thus $\mathbf{P}'(D)=0$ and the proof is complete. ■

We complete this section with an elementary application of the representation theorem (14). The result in question is standard, but the usual classical proof is tedious.

(18) **Theorem.** *If* $X_n\xrightarrow{D} X$ *and* $g:\mathbb{R}\to\mathbb{R}$ *is continuous then* $g(X_n)\xrightarrow{D} g(X)$.

Proof. Let $\{Y_n\}$ and Y be given as in (14). By the continuity of g

$$\{\omega: g(Y_n(\omega))\to g(Y(\omega))\}\supseteq\{\omega: Y_n(\omega)\to Y(\omega)\},$$

and so $g(Y_n)\xrightarrow{\text{a.s.}} g(Y)$ as $n\to\infty$. Therefore $g(Y_n)\xrightarrow{D} g(Y)$; however, $\{g(Y_n)\}$ and $g(Y)$ have the same distributions as $\{g(X_n)\}$ and $g(X)$. ■

Other applications of (14) are given in Problems (7.10.2), (7.10.3), and (7.10.8).

7.3 Some ancillary results

Next we shall develop some refinements of the methods of the last section; these will prove to be of great value later. There are two areas of interest. The first deals with inequalities and generalizes Markov's inequality (7.2.7). The second deals with infinite families of events and the Borel–Cantelli lemmas; it is related to the result of (7.2.4c).

Markov's inequality is easily generalized.

(1) **Theorem.** *Let* $h:\mathbb{R}\to[0,\infty)$ *be a non-negative function. Then*

$$\mathbf{P}(h(X)\geq a)\leq\frac{\mathbf{E}(h(X))}{a} \quad \textit{for all } a>0.$$

Proof. Let $A=\{h(X)\geqslant a\}$. Then

$$h(X)\geqslant aI_A.$$

Take expectations to obtain the result. ■

Note some special cases of this.

(2) **Example. Markov's inequality.** Set $h(x)=|x|$. ●

(3) **Example†. Chebyshov's inequality.** Set $h(x)=x^2$ to obtain

$$\mathbf{P}(|X|\geqslant a)\leqslant\frac{\mathbf{E}(X^2)}{a^2} \quad \text{if} \quad a>0.$$

This inequality was also discovered by Bienaymé and others. ●

(4) **Example.** More generally, let $g:[0,\infty)\to[0,\infty)$ be a strictly increasing non-negative function, and set $h(x)=g(|x|)$ to obtain

$$\mathbf{P}(|X|\geqslant a)\leqslant\frac{\mathbf{E}(g(|X|))}{g(a)} \quad \text{if} \quad a>0.$$ ●

Theorem (1) provides an upper bound for the probability $\mathbf{P}(h(X)\geqslant a)$. Lower bounds are harder to find in general, but pose no difficulty in the case when h is a uniformly bounded function.

(5) **Theorem.** *If $h:\mathbb{R}\to[0,M]$ is a non-negative function taking values bounded by some number M, then*

$$\mathbf{P}(h(X)\geqslant a)\geqslant\frac{\mathbf{E}(h(X))-a}{M-a} \quad \textit{whenever} \quad 0\leqslant a<M.$$

Proof. Let $A=\{h(X)\geqslant a\}$ as before and note that

$$h(X)\leqslant MI_A+aI_{A^c}.$$ ■

The reader is left to apply this result to the special cases (2), (3), and (4). This is an appropriate moment to note three other important inequalities. Let X and Y be random variables.

(6) **Theorem. Hölder's inequality.** *If $p,q>1$ and $p^{-1}+q^{-1}=1$ then*

$$\mathbf{E}|XY|\leqslant(\mathbf{E}|X^p|)^{1/p}(\mathbf{E}|Y^q|)^{1/q}.$$

(7) **Theorem. Minkowski's inequality.** *If $p\geqslant1$ then*

$$\{\mathbf{E}(|X+Y|^p)\}^{1/p}\leqslant(\mathbf{E}|X^p|)^{1/p}+(\mathbf{E}|Y^p|)^{1/p}.$$

Proof of (6) and (7). You did these for Problem (4.10.18). ■

† Our transliteration of Чебышёв (Chebyshov) is at odds with common practice, but dispenses with the need for clairvoyance in pronunciation.

(8) **Theorem.** *$\mathbf{E}(|X+Y|^p) \leq C_p(\mathbf{E}|X^p| + \mathbf{E}|Y^p|)$ where $p>0$ and*

$$C_p = \begin{cases} 1 & \text{if } 0<p\leq 1 \\ 2^{p-1} & \text{if } p>1. \end{cases}$$

Proof. It is not difficult to show that

$$|x+y|^p \leq C_p(|x|^p + |y|^p)$$

for all $x, y \in \mathbb{R}$ and $p>0$. Now complete the details. ■

Of course, (6) and (7) assert that

$$\|XY\|_1 \leq \|X\|_p \, \|Y\|_q \qquad \text{if} \quad p^{-1}+q^{-1}=1$$

$$\|X+Y\|_p \leq \|X\|_p + \|Y\|_p \qquad \text{if} \quad p \geq 1$$

where $\|\cdot\|_p$ is given by

$$\|X\|_p = (\mathbf{E}|X^p|)^{1/p}.$$

Here is an application of these inequalities. It is related to the fact that if $x_n \to x$ and $y_n \to y$ then $x_n + y_n \to x+y$.

(9) **Theorem.**

(a) *If $X_n \xrightarrow{\text{a.s.}} X$ and $Y_n \xrightarrow{\text{a.s.}} Y$ then $X_n + Y_n \xrightarrow{\text{a.s.}} X+Y$.*
(b) *If $X_n \xrightarrow{r} X$ and $Y_n \xrightarrow{r} Y$ then $X_n + Y_n \xrightarrow{r} X+Y$.*
(c) *If $X_n \xrightarrow{P} X$ and $Y_n \xrightarrow{P} Y$ then $X_n + Y_n \xrightarrow{P} X+Y$.*
(d) *It is not in general true that $X_n + Y_n \xrightarrow{D} X+Y$ if $X_n \xrightarrow{D} X$ and $Y_n \xrightarrow{D} Y$.*

Proof. *You* do it. You will need either (7) or (8) to prove part (b). ■

Theorem (7.2.4) contains a criterion for a sequence to converge almost surely. It is a special case of two very useful results called the 'Borel–Cantelli lemmas'. Let $A_1, A_2, \ldots$ be an infinite sequence of events from some probability space $\{\Omega, \mathcal{F}, \mathbf{P}\}$. We shall often be interested in finding out how many of the A's occur. Recall (Problem (1.8.14)) that the event that infinitely many of the A's occur, sometimes written $\{A_n$ infinitely often$\}$ or $\{A_n$ i.o.$\}$, satisfies

$$\{A_n \text{ i.o.}\} = \limsup_{n\to\infty} A_n = \bigcap_n \bigcup_{m=n}^{\infty} A_m.$$

(10) **Theorem. Borel–Cantelli lemmas.** *Let $A = \bigcap_n \bigcap_{m=n}^{\infty} A_m$ be the event that infinitely many of the A's occur. Then*

(a) *$\mathbf{P}(A)=0$ if $\sum_n \mathbf{P}(A_n)<\infty$*

(b) *$\mathbf{P}(A)=1$ if $\sum_n \mathbf{P}(A_n)=\infty$ and $A_1, A_2, \ldots$ are independent events.*

It is easy to see that the following assertion, similar to (b),

$$\mathbf{P}(A)=1 \quad \text{if} \quad \sum_n \mathbf{P}(A_n)=\infty,$$

is false unless we impose an extra condition, such as independence. Just consider some event E with $0<\mathbf{P}(E)<1$ and define

$$A_n = E \quad \text{for all } n.$$

Then $A=E$ and $\mathbf{P}(A)=\mathbf{P}(E)$.

Proof.

(a) For any n

$$A \subseteq \bigcup_{m=n}^{\infty} A_m$$

and so

$$\mathbf{P}(A) \leqslant \sum_{m=n}^{\infty} \mathbf{P}(A_m) \to 0 \quad \text{as} \quad n\to\infty$$

whenever $\sum_n \mathbf{P}(A_n)<\infty$.

(b) It is an easy *exercise* in set theory to check that

$$A^c = \bigcup_n \bigcap_{m=n}^{\infty} A_m^c.$$

However,

$$\begin{aligned}
\mathbf{P}\left(\bigcap_{m=n}^{\infty} A_m^c\right) &= \lim_{r\to\infty} \mathbf{P}\left(\bigcap_{m=n}^{r} A_m^c\right) \quad \text{by (1.3.5)} \\
&= \prod_{m=n}^{\infty} \{1-\mathbf{P}(A_m)\} \quad \text{by independence} \\
&\leqslant \prod_{m=n}^{\infty} \exp\{-\mathbf{P}(A_m)\} \quad \text{since} \quad 1-x \leqslant e^{-x} \quad \text{if} \quad x\geqslant 0 \\
&= \exp\left\{-\sum_{m=n}^{\infty} \mathbf{P}(A_m)\right\} \\
&= 0
\end{aligned}$$

whenever $\sum_n \mathbf{P}(A_n)=\infty$. Thus

$$\mathbf{P}(A^c) = \lim_{n\to\infty} \mathbf{P}\left(\bigcap_{m=n}^{\infty} A_m^c\right) = 0,$$

giving $\mathbf{P}(A)=1$ as required. ■

(11) **Example. Markov chains.** Let $\{X_n\}$ be a Markov chain with $X_0=i$ for some state i. Let

$$A_n = \{X_n = i\}$$

be the event that the chain returns to i after n steps. State i is persistent if and only if

$$\mathbf{P}(A_n \text{ i.o.}) = 1.$$

By the first Borel–Cantelli lemma

$$\mathbf{P}(A_n \text{ i.o.}) = 0 \quad \text{if} \quad \sum_n \mathbf{P}(A_n) < \infty$$

and it follows that

$$i \text{ is transient if } \sum_n p_{ii}(n) < \infty$$

which is part of an earlier result (6.2.4). We cannot establish the converse by this method since the A's are not independent. ●

The remaining part of this section may be omitted without sustaining too much damage.

If the events $A_1, A_2, \ldots$ of (10) are independent then $\mathbf{P}(A)$ is either 0 or 1 depending on whether or not $\sum \mathbf{P}(A_n)$ converges. This is an example of a general theorem called a 'zero–one law'. There are many such results, of which the following is a simple example.

(12) **Theorem. Zero–one law.** *Let $A_1, A_2, \ldots$ be a collection of events, and let $\mathscr{A}$ be the smallest σ-field of subsets of Ω which contains all of them. If $A \in \mathscr{A}$ is an event which is independent of the finite collection $A_1, A_2, \ldots, A_n$ for each value of n, then*

$$\textit{either } \mathbf{P}(A) = 0 \textit{ or } \mathbf{P}(A) = 1.$$

Proof. Roughly speaking, the assertion that A is in $\mathscr{A}$ means that A is definable in terms of $A_1, A_2, \ldots$. Examples of such events include B_1, B_2, and B_3 defined by

$$B_1 = A_7 \backslash A_9, \qquad B_2 = A_3 \cup A_6 \cup A_9 \cup \ldots, \qquad B_3 = \bigcup_n \bigcap_{m=n}^{\infty} A_m.$$

A standard result of measure theory asserts that if $A \in \mathscr{A}$ then there exists a sequence of events $\{C_n\}$ such that

(13) $$C_n \in \mathscr{A}_n \quad \text{and} \quad C_n \to A$$

where $\mathscr{A}_n$ is the smallest σ-field which contains the finite collection $A_1, A_2, \ldots, A_n$. But A is independent of this collection, and so is independent of C_n for all n. From (13)

$$A \cap C_n \to A$$

and so

(14) $$\mathbf{P}(A \cap C_n) \to \mathbf{P}(A).$$

However, by independence,

$$\mathbf{P}(A \cap C_n) = \mathbf{P}(A)\mathbf{P}(C_n) \to \mathbf{P}(A)^2$$

which combines with (14) to give

$$\mathbf{P}(A)=\mathbf{P}(A)^2$$

and so $\mathbf{P}(A)$ is 0 or 1. ■

Read on for a more useful zero–one law. Let $X_1, X_2, \ldots$ be a collection of random variables on the probability space $(\Omega, \mathscr{F}, \mathbf{P})$. For any subcollection $\{X_i : i \in I\}$, write $\sigma(X_i : i \in I)$ for the smallest σ-field with respect to which each of the variables X_i $(i \in I)$ is measurable. This σ-field exists by the argument of Section 1.6. It contains events which are 'defined in terms of $\{X_i : i \in I\}$'. Let

$$\mathscr{H}_n = \sigma(X_{n+1}, X_{n+2}, \ldots).$$

Then $\mathscr{H}_n \supseteq \mathscr{H}_{n+1} \supseteq \ldots$; write

$$\mathscr{H}_\infty = \bigcap_n \mathscr{H}_n.$$

$\mathscr{H}_\infty$ is called the *tail σ-field* of the X's and contains events like

$$\{X_n > 0 \text{ i.o.}\}, \quad \left\{\limsup_{n\to\infty} X_n = \infty\right\}, \quad \left\{\sum_n X_n \text{ converges}\right\}$$

the definitions of which need never refer to any finite subcollection such as $\{X_1, X_2, \ldots, X_n\}$.

(15) **Theorem. Kolmogorov's zero–one law.** *If $X_1, X_2, \ldots$ are independent variables then all events $H \in \mathscr{H}_\infty$ satisfy either $\mathbf{P}(H)=0$ or $\mathbf{P}(H)=1$.*

Such a σ-field $\mathscr{H}_\infty$ is called *trivial* since it contains only null events and their complements. You may try to prove this theorem using the techniques in the proof of (12); it is not difficult.

(16) **Example.** Let $X_1, X_2, \ldots$ be independent random variables and let

$$H_1 = \left\{\omega \in \Omega : \sum_n X_n(\omega) \text{ converges}\right\}$$

$$H_2 = \left\{\omega \in \Omega : \limsup_{n\to\infty} X_n(\omega) = \infty\right\}.$$

Each H_i $(i=1, 2)$ has either probability 0 or probability 1. ●

We can associate many other random variables with the sequence $X_1, X_2, \ldots$; these include

$$Y_1 = \tfrac{1}{2}(X_3 + X_6), \quad Y_2 = \limsup_{n\to\infty} X_n, \quad Y_3 = Y_1 + Y_2.$$

We call such a variable Y a *tail function* if it is $\mathscr{H}_\infty$-measurable, where $\mathscr{H}_\infty$ is the tail σ-field of the X's. Roughly speaking, Y is a tail function if its definition includes no reference to any finite subsequence $X_1, X_2, \ldots, X_n$. Y_1 and Y_3 are *not* tail functions; can you see why Y_2 *is* a tail function?

More rigorously (see the discussion after (2.1.3)) Y is a tail function if and only if

$$\{\omega \in \Omega : Y(\omega) \leq y\} \in \mathcal{H}_\infty \quad \text{for all } y \in \mathbb{R}.$$

Thus, if $\mathcal{H}_\infty$ is trivial then the distribution function

$$F_Y(y) = \mathbf{P}(Y \leq y)$$

takes the values 0 and 1 only. Such a function is the distribution function of a random variable which is constant (see (2.1.7)), and we have shown the following useful result.

(17) **Theorem.** *Let Y be a tail function of the independent sequence $X_1, X_2, \ldots$. Then there exists a real number k ($-\infty \leq k \leq \infty$) such that*

$$\mathbf{P}(Y = k) = 1.$$

Proof. Let $k = \inf\{y : \mathbf{P}(Y \leq y) = 1\}$, with the convention that the infimum of an empty set is $+\infty$. Then

$$\mathbf{P}(Y \leq y) = \begin{cases} 0 & \text{if } y < k \\ 1 & \text{if } y \geq k. \end{cases}$$ ■

(18) **Example.** Let $X_1, X_2, \ldots$ be independent variables, with partial sums $S_n = \sum_{i=1}^n X_i$. Then

$$Z_1 = \liminf_{n\to\infty} \frac{1}{n} S_n, \qquad Z_2 = \limsup_{n\to\infty} \frac{1}{n} S_n$$

are almost surely constant (but possibly infinite). To see this, note that if $m \leq n$ then

$$\frac{1}{n} S_n = \frac{1}{n} \sum_{i=1}^{m} X_i + \frac{1}{n} \sum_{i=m+1}^{n} X_i = S(1) + S(2), \text{ say.}$$

However, $S(1) \to 0$ pointwise as $n \to \infty$, and so Z_1 and Z_2 depend in no way upon the values of $X_1, \ldots, X_m$. It follows that the event

$$\left\{\frac{1}{n} S_n \text{ converges}\right\} = \{Z_1 = Z_2\}$$

has either probability 1 or probability 0. That is, $n^{-1}S_n$ converges either almost everywhere or almost nowhere; this was, of course, deducible from (15) since $\{Z_1 = Z_2\} \in \mathcal{H}_\infty$. ●

7.4 Laws of large numbers

Let $\{X_n\}$ be a sequence of random variables with partial sums

$$S_n = \sum_{1}^{n} X_i.$$

We are interested in the asymptotic behaviour of S_n as $n \to \infty$; this long-term behaviour depends crucially upon the original sequence of X's. The general problem may be described as follows. Under what conditions does the following convergence occur?

(1) $$\frac{S_n}{b_n} - a_n \to S \quad \text{as} \quad n \to \infty$$

where $a = \{a_n\}$ and $b = \{b_n\}$ are sequences of real numbers, S is a random variable and the convergence takes place in some mode to be specified.

(2) **Example.** Let $X_1, X_2, \ldots$ be independent identically distributed variables with mean μ and variance σ^2. By (5.10.2) and (5.10.4) we have that

$$\frac{S_n}{n} \xrightarrow{\text{D}} \mu \quad \text{and} \quad \frac{S_n}{\sigma n^{1/2}} - \frac{\mu}{\sigma} n^{1/2} \xrightarrow{\text{D}} N(0, 1).$$

So there may not be a *unique* collection a, b, S such that (1) occurs. ●

The convergence problem (1) can often be simplified by setting $a_n = 0$ for all n, whenever the X's have finite means. Just rewrite the problem in terms of

$$X_i' = X_i - \mathbf{E}X_i, \quad S_n' = S_n - \mathbf{E}S_n.$$

The general theory of relations like (1) is well established and extensive. We shall restrict our attention here to a small but significant part of the theory when the X's are independent and identically distributed random variables. Suppose for the moment that this is true. We saw in Example (2) that (at least) two types of convergence may be established for such sequences, so long as they have finite second moments. The Law of Large Numbers admits stronger forms than that given in (2). For example, notice that $n^{-1}S_n$ converges in distribution to a constant limit, and use (7.2.4) to see that $n^{-1}S_n$ converges in probability also. Perhaps we can strengthen this further to include convergence in rth mean, for some r, or almost sure convergence. Indeed, this turns out to be possible when suitable conditions are imposed on the common distribution of the X's. We shall not use the method of characteristic functions of Chapter 5, preferring to approach the problem more directly in the spirit of Section 7.2.

We shall say that the sequence $\{X_n\}$ obeys the 'Weak Law of Large Numbers' if there exists a constant μ such that

$$\frac{1}{n} S_n \xrightarrow{\text{P}} \mu.$$

If the stronger result

$$\frac{1}{n} S_n \xrightarrow{\text{a.s.}} \mu$$

holds, then we call it the 'Strong Law of Large Numbers'. We seek sufficient, and if possible necessary, conditions on the common distribution of the X's for the Weak and Strong Laws to hold. As the title suggests, the Weak Law is implied by the Strong Law, since convergence in probability is implied by almost sure convergence. A sufficient condition for the Strong Law is given by the following theorem.

(3) **Theorem.** *Let $X_1, X_2, \ldots$ be independent identically distributed random variables with $\mathbf{E}(X_1^2) < \infty$. Then*

$$\frac{1}{n}\sum_{i=1}^{n} X_i \to \mu \text{ almost surely and in mean square,}$$

where $\mu = \mathbf{E}X_1$.

So the Strong Law holds whenever the X's have finite second moment. The proof of mean square convergence is very easy; almost sure convergence is harder to demonstrate (but see Problem (7.10.6) for an easy proof of almost sure convergence subject to the stronger condition that $\mathbf{E}(X_1^4) < \infty$).

Proof. To show mean square convergence, calculate

$$\begin{aligned}\mathbf{E}\left(\left(\frac{1}{n}S_n - \mu\right)^2\right) &= \mathbf{E}\left(\frac{1}{n^2}(S_n - \mathbf{E}S_n)^2\right)\\ &= \frac{1}{n^2}\operatorname{var}\left(\sum_1^n X_i\right)\\ &= \frac{1}{n^2}\sum_1^n \operatorname{var}(X_i) \quad \text{by independence and (3.3.11)}\\ &= \frac{1}{n}\operatorname{var}(X_1) \to 0 \quad \text{as} \quad n \to \infty,\end{aligned}$$

since $\operatorname{var}(X_1) < \infty$ by virtue of the assumption that $\mathbf{E}(X_1^2) < \infty$.

Next we show almost sure convergence. We saw in (7.2.13) that there necessarily exists a subsequence $n_1, n_2, \ldots$ along which $n^{-1}S_n$ converges to μ almost surely; we can find such a subsequence explicitly. Write $n_i = i^2$ and use Chebyshov's inequality (7.3.3) to find that

$$\mathbf{P}\left(\frac{1}{i^2}|S_{i^2} - i^2\mu| > \epsilon\right) \leq \frac{\operatorname{var}(S_{i^2})}{i^4\epsilon^2} = \frac{\operatorname{var}(X_1)}{i^2\epsilon^2}.$$

Sum over i and use (7.2.4c) to find that

(4) $$\frac{1}{i^2}S_{i^2} \xrightarrow{\text{a.s.}} \mu \quad \text{as} \quad i \to \infty.$$

We need to fill in the gaps in this limit process. Suppose for the moment that the X's are *non-negative*. Then $\{S_n\}$ is monotonic non-decreasing, and so

$$S_{i^2} \leq S_n \leq S_{(i+1)^2} \quad \text{if} \quad i^2 \leq n \leq (i+1)^2.$$

Divide by n to find that

$$\frac{1}{(i+1)^2} S_{i^2} \leq \frac{1}{n} S_n \leq \frac{1}{i^2} S_{(i+1)^2} \quad \text{if} \quad i^2 \leq n \leq (i+1)^2;$$

now let $n \to \infty$ and use (4), remembering that $i^2/(i+1)^2 \to 1$ as $i \to \infty$, to deduce that

(5) $$\frac{1}{n} S_n \xrightarrow{\text{a.s.}} \mu \quad \text{as} \quad n \to \infty$$

as required, whenever the X's are non-negative. Finally, we lift the non-negativity condition. For general X's, define random variables X_n^+, X_n^- by

$$X_n^+(\omega) = \max\{X_n(\omega), 0\}, \qquad X_n^-(\omega) = -\min\{X_n(\omega), 0\};$$

then X_n^+ and X_n^- are non-negative and

$$X_n = X_n^+ - X_n^-, \qquad \mathbf{E}(X_n) = \mathbf{E}(X_n^+) - \mathbf{E}(X_n^-).$$

Furthermore, $X_n^+ \leq |X_n|$ and $X_n^- \leq |X_n|$, so that $\mathbf{E}((X_1^+)^2) < \infty$ and $\mathbf{E}((X_1^-)^2) < \infty$. Now apply (5) to the sequences $\{X_n^+\}$ and $\{X_n^-\}$ to find that

$$\frac{1}{n} S_n = \frac{1}{n}\left(\sum_1^n X_i^+ - \sum_1^n X_i^-\right)$$

$$\xrightarrow{\text{a.s.}} \mathbf{E}(X_1^+) - \mathbf{E}(X_1^-) = \mathbf{E}(X_1) \quad \text{as} \quad n \to \infty,$$

by (7.3.9a). ■

Is the result of Theorem (3) as sharp as possible? It is not difficult to see that the condition that $\mathbf{E}(X_1^2) < \infty$ is both necessary and sufficient for mean square convergence to hold. For almost sure convergence the weaker condition that

(6) $$\mathbf{E}|X_1| < \infty$$

will turn out to be necessary and sufficient, but the proof of this is slightly more difficult and is deferred until the next section. There exist sequences which satisfy the Weak Law but not the Strong Law. Indeed, the characteristic function technique (see Section 5.10) can be used to prove the following necessary and sufficient condition for the Weak Law. We offer no proof (but see Laha and Rohatgi 1979, p. 320, and Feller 1971, p. 565).

(7) **Theorem.** *The independent identically distributed sequence $\{X_n\}$, with shared distribution function F, satisfies*

$$\frac{1}{n} \sum_{i=1}^n X_i \xrightarrow{\text{P}} \mu$$

for some constant μ, if and only if one of the following conditions (8) *or* (9) *holds:*

(8) $$n\mathbf{P}(|X_1|>n)\to 0 \text{ and } \int_{[-n,n]} x\,dF \to \mu \text{ as } n\to\infty$$

(9) *the characteristic function $\phi(t)$ of the X's is differentiable at $t=0$ and $\phi'(0)=i\mu$.*

Of course, the integral in (8) can be rewritten as

$$\int_{[-n,n]} x\,dF = \mathbf{E}(X_1 \mid |X_1|\leq n)\mathbf{P}(|X_1|\leq n) = \mathbf{E}(X_1 I_{\{|X_1|\leq n\}}).$$

Thus, a sequence satisfies the Weak Law but not the Strong Law whenever (8) holds without (6); as an example of this, suppose the X's are symmetric (so that X_1 and $-X_1$ have the same distribution) but their distribution function F satisfies

$$F(x)\simeq 1-(x\log x)^{-1} \quad \text{as} \quad x\to\infty.$$

Some distributions fail even to satisfy (8).

(10) **Example.** Let the X's have the Cauchy distribution with density function

$$f(x)=\frac{1}{\pi(1+x^2)}.$$

Then the first part of (8) is violated. Indeed, the characteristic function of $U_n = n^{-1}S_n$ is

$$\phi_{U_n}(t) = \phi_{X_1}\left(\frac{t}{n}\right)\cdots\phi_{X_n}\left(\frac{t}{n}\right)$$
$$= \left\{\exp\left(-\frac{|t|}{n}\right)\right\}^n = \exp(-|t|)$$

and so U_n itself has the Cauchy distribution for all values of n. In particular, (1) holds with $b_n = n$, $a_n = 0$, where S is Cauchy, and the convergence is in distribution. ●

7.5 The strong law

This section is devoted to the proof of the Strong Law of Large Numbers.

(1) **Theorem. Strong Law of Large Numbers.** *Let $X_1, X_2, \ldots$ be independent identically distributed random variables. Then*

$$\frac{1}{n}\sum_{i=1}^{n} X_i \to \mu \text{ almost surely, as } n\to\infty,$$

for some constant μ, if and only if $\mathbf{E}|X_1|<\infty$. *In this case* $\mu = \mathbf{E}X_1$.

The traditional proof of this theorem is long and difficult, and proceeds by a generalization of Chebyshov's inequality. We avoid that here, and give a relatively elementary proof which is an adaptation of the method used to prove (7.4.3). We need only one new technique, called the method of *truncation.*

Proof.† Suppose first that the X's are *non-negative* random variables with $\mathbf{E}|X_1| = \mathbf{E}(X_1) < \infty$, and write $\mu = \mathbf{E}(X_1)$. We 'truncate' the X's to obtain a new sequence $\{Y_n\}$ given by

(2) $$Y_n = X_n I_{\{X_n < n\}} = \begin{cases} X_n & \text{if } X_n < n \\ 0 & \text{if } X_n \geqslant n. \end{cases}$$

Note that

$$\sum_n \mathbf{P}(X_n \neq Y_n) = \sum_n \mathbf{P}(X_n \geqslant n) \leqslant \mathbf{E}(X_1) < \infty$$

by the result of (4.10.3). Of course, $\mathbf{P}(X_n \geqslant n) = \mathbf{P}(X_1 \geqslant n)$ since the X's are identically distributed. By the first Borel–Cantelli lemma (7.3.10a), $\mathbf{P}(X_n \neq Y_n$ for infinitely many values of $n) = 0$, and so

(3) $$\frac{1}{n}\sum_{i=1}^{n}(X_i - Y_i) \xrightarrow{\text{a.s.}} 0 \quad \text{as} \quad n \to \infty;$$

thus it will suffice to show that

(4) $$\frac{1}{n}\sum_{i=1}^{n} Y_i \xrightarrow{\text{a.s.}} \mu \quad \text{as} \quad n \to \infty.$$

We shall need the following elementary observation. If $\alpha > 1$ and $\beta_k = \lfloor \alpha^k \rfloor$, the integer part of α^k, then there exists $A > 0$ such that

(5) $$\sum_{k=m}^{\infty} \frac{1}{\beta_k^2} \leqslant \frac{A}{\beta_m^2} \quad \text{for} \quad m \geqslant 1.$$

This holds because, for large m, the convergent series on the left-hand side is 'nearly' geometric with first term β_m^{-2}. Note also that

(6) $$\beta_{k+1}/\beta_k \to \alpha \quad \text{as} \quad k \to \infty.$$

Write $S_n' = \sum_{i=1}^{n} Y_i$. For $\alpha > 1$, $\epsilon > 0$, use Chebyshov's inequality to find that

(7) $$\begin{aligned}\sum_{n=1}^{\infty} \mathbf{P}\left(\frac{1}{\beta_n}|S'_{\beta_n} - \mathbf{E}(S'_{\beta_n})| > \epsilon\right) &\leqslant \frac{1}{\epsilon^2}\sum_{n=1}^{\infty}\frac{1}{\beta_n^2}\operatorname{var}(S'_{\beta_n}) \\ &= \frac{1}{\epsilon^2}\sum_{n=1}^{\infty}\frac{1}{\beta_n^2}\sum_{i=1}^{\beta_n}\operatorname{var}(Y_i) \quad \text{by independence} \\ &\leqslant \frac{A}{\epsilon^2}\sum_{i=1}^{\infty}\frac{1}{i^2}\mathbf{E}(Y_i^2)\end{aligned}$$

by changing the order of summation and using (5).

† This method was found by N. Etemadi.

For a fixed but typical value of i, let $B_j = \{j-1 \leq X_i < j\}$, and note that

$$\text{(8)} \qquad \sum_{i=1}^{\infty} \frac{1}{i^2} \mathbf{E}(Y_i^2) = \sum_{i=1}^{\infty} \frac{1}{i^2} \sum_{j=1}^{i} \mathbf{E}(Y_i^2 I_{B_j}) \quad \text{by (2)}$$

$$\leq \sum_{i=1}^{\infty} \frac{1}{i^2} \sum_{j=1}^{i} j^2 \mathbf{P}(B_j)$$

$$\leq \sum_{j=1}^{\infty} j^2 \mathbf{P}(B_j) \frac{2}{j} \leq 2\{\mathbf{E}(X_1)+1\} < \infty.$$

Combine (7) and (8) and use (7.2.4c) to deduce that

$$\text{(9)} \qquad \frac{1}{\beta_n}\{S'_{\beta_n} - \mathbf{E}(S'_{\beta_n})\} \xrightarrow{\text{a.s.}} 0 \quad \text{as} \quad n \to \infty.$$

Also,

$$\mathbf{E}(Y_n) = \mathbf{E}(X_n I_{\{X_n < n\}}) = \mathbf{E}(X_1 I_{\{X_1 < n\}}) \to \mathbf{E}(X_1) = \mu$$

as $n \to \infty$, by monotone convergence (5.6.12). Thus

$$\frac{1}{\beta_n} \mathbf{E}(S'_{\beta_n}) = \frac{1}{\beta_n} \sum_{i=1}^{\beta_n} \mathbf{E}(Y_i) \to \mu \quad \text{as} \quad n \to \infty$$

(remember the hint in the proof of (6.4.22)), yielding from (9) that

$$\text{(10)} \qquad \frac{1}{\beta_n} S'_{\beta_n} \xrightarrow{\text{a.s.}} \mu \quad \text{as} \quad n \to \infty;$$

this is a partial demonstration of (4). To fill in the gaps, use the fact that the Y's are non-negative, implying that the sequence $\{S'_n\}$ is monotonic non-decreasing, to deduce that

$$\text{(11)} \qquad \frac{1}{\beta_{n+1}} S'_{\beta_n} \leq \frac{1}{m} S'_m \leq \frac{1}{\beta_n} S'_{\beta_{n+1}} \quad \text{if} \quad \beta_n \leq m \leq \beta_{n+1}.$$

Let $m \to \infty$ in (11) and remember (6) to find that

$$\text{(12)} \qquad \alpha^{-1}\mu \leq \liminf_{m\to\infty} \frac{1}{m} S'_m \leq \limsup_{m\to\infty} \frac{1}{m} S'_m \leq \alpha\mu \text{ almost surely.}$$

But this holds for all $\alpha > 1$; let $\alpha \downarrow 1$ to obtain (4), and deduce by (3) that

$$\text{(13)} \qquad \frac{1}{n} \sum_{i=1}^{n} X_i \xrightarrow{\text{a.s.}} \mu \quad \text{as} \quad n \to \infty$$

whenever the X's are non-negative. Now proceed exactly as in the proof of (7.4.3) in order to lift the non-negativity condition. Note that we have proved the main part of the theorem without using the full strength of the independence assumption; we have used only the fact that the X's are *pairwise* independent.

To prove the converse, suppose that

$$\frac{1}{n} \sum_{i=1}^{n} X_i \xrightarrow{\text{a.s.}} \mu.$$

Then $n^{-1}X_n \xrightarrow{\text{a.s.}} 0$ by the theory of convergent real series, and the second Borel–Cantelli lemma (7.3.10b) gives

$$\sum_n \mathbf{P}(|X_n| \geqslant n) < \infty,$$

since the divergence of this sum would imply that $\mathbf{P}(n^{-1}|X_n| \geqslant 1$ infinitely often$) = 1$ (only here do we use the full assumption of independence). But (4.10.3) shows that

$$\mathbf{E}|X_1| \leqslant 1 + \sum_{n=1}^{\infty} \mathbf{P}(|X_1| \geqslant n) = 1 + \sum_{n=1}^{\infty} \mathbf{P}(|X_n| \geqslant n),$$

and hence $\mathbf{E}|X_1| < \infty$, which completes the proof of the theorem. ■

7.6 The law of the iterated logarithm

Let S_n be the partial sum

$$S_n = \sum_{i=1}^{n} X_i$$

of independent identically distributed variables, as usual, and suppose further that $\mathbf{E}(X_i) = 0$ and $\text{var}(X_i) = 1$ for all i. To date, we have two results about the growth rate of $\{S_n\}$.

Law of Large Numbers: $\frac{1}{n} S_n \to 0$ a.s. and in mean square.

Central Limit Theorem: $\frac{1}{\sqrt{n}} S_n \xrightarrow{\text{D}} N(0, 1)$.

Thus the sequence

$$U_n = \frac{1}{\sqrt{n}} S_n$$

enjoys a random fluctuation which is asymptotically regularly distributed. Apart from this long-term trend towards the normal distribution, the sequence $\{U_n\}$ may suffer some large but rare fluctuations. The Law of the Iterated Logarithm is an extraordinary result which tells us exactly how big these fluctuations are. First note that, in the language of Section 7.3 (if you have read this),

$$U = \limsup_{n \to \infty} \frac{U_n}{\sqrt{(2 \log \log n)}}$$

is a tail function of the sequence of X's. The zero–one law (7.3.17) tells us that there exists a number k, possibly infinite, such that

$$\mathbf{P}(U = k) = 1.$$

The next theorem asserts that $k = 1$!

(1) **Theorem. Law of the Iterated Logarithm.** *If* $\mathbf{E}(X_1^2) < \infty$ *then*

$$\mathbf{P}\left(\limsup_{n\to\infty} \frac{S_n}{\sqrt{(2n \log\log n)}} = 1\right) = 1.$$

The proof is long and difficult and is omitted (but see the discussion in Billingsley 1979 or Laha and Rohatgi 1979). The theorem amounts to the assertion that

$$A_n = \{S_n \geq c(2n \log\log n)^{1/2}\}$$

occurs for infinitely many values of n if $c < 1$ and for only finitely many values of n if $c > 1$, with probability one. It is an immediate corollary of (1) that

$$\mathbf{P}\left(\liminf_{n\to\infty} \frac{S_n}{(2n \log\log n)^{1/2}} = -1\right) = 1;$$

just apply (1) to the sequence $-X_1, -X_2, \ldots$

7.7 Martingales

Many probabilists specialize in limit theorems, and much of applied probability is devoted to finding such results. The accumulated literature is vast and the techniques multifarious. One of the most useful skills for establishing such results is that of martingale divination, because the convergence of martingales is guaranteed.

(1) **Example.** It is appropriate to discuss an example of the use of the word 'martingale' which pertains to gambling, a favourite source of probabilistic illustrations. We are all familiar with the following gambling strategy. A gambler has a large fortune. He wagers £1 on an evens bet. If he loses then he wagers £2 on the next play. If he loses on the nth play then he wagers £2^n on the next. Each sum is calculated so that his inevitable ultimate win will cover his lost stakes and profit him by £1. This strategy is called a 'martingale'. Nowadays casinos do not allow its use, and croupiers have instructions to refuse the bets of those who are seen to practise it. Thackeray's advice was to avoid its use at all costs, and his reasoning may have had something to do with the following calculation. Suppose the gambler wins for the first time at the Nth play. N is a random variable with mass function

$$\mathbf{P}(N = n) = (\tfrac{1}{2})^n$$

and so $\mathbf{P}(N < \infty) = 1$; the gambler is almost surely guaranteed a win in the long run. However, by this time he will have lost an amount £L with mean value

$$\mathbf{E}(L) = \sum_{n=1}^{\infty} (\tfrac{1}{2})^n (1 + 2 + \ldots + 2^{n-2}) = \infty.$$

He must be prepared to lose a lot of money! And so, of course, must the proprietor of the casino. ●

In the spirit of this diversion, suppose a gambler wagers repeatedly with an initial capital S_0, and let S_n be his capital after n plays. We shall think of $S_0, S_1, \ldots$ as a sequence of dependent random variables. Before his $(n+1)$th wager the gambler knows the numerical values of $S_0, S_1, \ldots, S_n$, but can only guess at the future $S_{n+1}, \ldots$. If the game is fair then, conditional upon the past information, he will expect no change in his present capital on average. That is,

(2)† $$\mathbf{E}(S_{n+1} \mid S_0, S_1, \ldots, S_n) = S_n.$$

Most casinos need to pay at least their overheads, and will find a way of changing this equation to

$$\mathbf{E}(S_{n+1} \mid S_0, S_1, \ldots, S_n) \leqslant S_n.$$

The gambler is fortunate indeed if this inequality is reversed. Sequences satisfying (2) are called 'martingales', and they have very special and well studied properties of convergence. They may be discovered within many probabilistic models, and their general theory may be used to establish limit theorems. We shall now abandon the gambling example, and refer disappointed readers to *How to gamble if you must* by L. Dubins and L. Savage, where they may find an account of the Gamblers' Ruin Theorem.

(3) **Definition.** A sequence $\{S_n : n \geqslant 1\}$ is a **martingale** with respect to the sequence $\{X_n : n \geqslant 1\}$ if, for all $n \geqslant 1$,

(a) $\mathbf{E}|S_n| < \infty$

(b) $\mathbf{E}(S_{n+1} \mid X_1, X_2, \ldots, X_n) = S_n$.

Equation (2) shows that the sequence of gambler's fortunes is a martingale with respect to itself. The extra generality, introduced by the sequence $\{X_n\}$ in (3), is useful for martingales which arise in the following way. A specified sequence $\{X_n\}$ of random variables, such as a Markov chain, may itself *not* be a martingale. However, it is often possible to find some function ϕ such that $\{S_n = \phi(X_n) : n \geqslant 1\}$ *is* a martingale. In this case, the martingale property (2) becomes the assertion that, given the values of $X_1, X_2, \ldots, X_n$, the mean value of $S_{n+1} = \phi(X_{n+1})$ is just $S_n = \phi(X_n)$; that is

(4) $$\mathbf{E}(S_{n+1} \mid X_1, \ldots, X_n) = S_n.$$

Of course, condition (b) of (3) is without meaning unless S_n is some

† Such conditional expectations appear often in this section. Make sure you understand their meanings. This one is the mean value of S_{n+1}, calculated as though $S_0, \ldots, S_n$ were already known. Clearly this mean value depends on $S_0, \ldots, S_n$; so it is a *function* of $S_0, \ldots, S_n$. Assertion (2) is that it has the value S_n. Any detailed account of conditional expectations would probe into the guts of measure theory. We shall avoid that here, but describe some important properties at the end of this section.

function, say ϕ_n, of $X_1, \ldots, X_n$ (that is, $S_n = \phi_n(X_1, \ldots, X_n)$) since the conditional expectation in (3) is itself a function of $X_1, \ldots, X_n$. We shall often omit reference to the underlying sequence $\{X_n\}$, asserting merely that $\{S_n\}$ is a martingale.

(5) **Example. Branching processes–two martingales.** Let Z_n be the size of the nth generation of a branching process. Recall that the probability η that the process ultimately becomes extinct is the smallest non-negative root of the equation

$$s = G(s)$$

where G is the probability generating function of Z_1. There are two martingales associated with the process. First, conditional on $Z_n = z_n$, Z_{n+1} is the sum of z_n independent family sizes, and so

$$\mathbf{E}(Z_{n+1} \mid Z_n = z_n) = z_n\mu$$

where $\mu = G'(1)$ is the mean family size. Thus, by the Markov property,

$$\mathbf{E}(Z_{n+1} \mid Z_1, Z_2, \ldots, Z_n) = Z_n\mu.$$

Now define

$$W_n = Z_n/\mathbf{E}(Z_n)$$

and remember that $\mathbf{E}(Z_n) = \mu^n$ to obtain

$$\mathbf{E}(W_{n+1} \mid Z_1, \ldots, Z_n) = W_n,$$

and so $\{W_n\}$ is a martingale (with respect to $\{Z_n\}$). It is not the only martingale which arises from the branching process. Let

$$V_n = \eta^{Z_n}$$

where η is the probability of ultimate extinction. Surprisingly perhaps, $\{V_n\}$ is a martingale also. For, as in the proof of (5.4.1), write

$$Z_{n+1} = X_1 + \ldots + X_{Z_n}$$

in terms of the family sizes of the members of the nth generation to obtain

$$\begin{aligned}\mathbf{E}(V_{n+1} \mid Z_1, \ldots, Z_n) &= \mathbf{E}(\eta^{(X_1+\ldots+X_{Z_n})} \mid Z_1, \ldots, Z_n)\\ &= \prod_{i=1}^{Z_n} \mathbf{E}(\eta^{X_i} \mid Z_1, \ldots, Z_n) \quad \text{by independence}\\ &= \prod_{i=1}^{Z_n} \mathbf{E}(\eta^{X_i})\\ &= \prod_{i=1}^{Z_n} G(\eta) = \eta^{Z_n} = V_n,\end{aligned}$$

since $\eta = G(\eta)$. These facts are very significant in the study of the long-term behaviour of the branching process. ●

(6) **Example.** Let $X_1, X_2, \ldots$ be independent variables with zero means. We claim that the sequence of partial sums

$$S_n = X_1 + \ldots + X_n$$

is a martingale (with respect to $\{X_n\}$). For

$$\begin{aligned}\mathbf{E}(S_{n+1} \mid X_1, \ldots, X_n) &= \mathbf{E}(S_n + X_{n+1} \mid X_1, \ldots, X_n)\\ &= \mathbf{E}(S_n \mid X_1, \ldots, X_n) + \mathbf{E}(X_{n+1} \mid X_1, \ldots, X_n)\\ &= S_n + 0, \quad \text{by independence.}\end{aligned}$$

●

(7) **Example. Markov chains.** Let $X_0, X_1, \ldots$ be a discrete-time Markov chain taking values in some countable state space S with transition matrix $\boldsymbol{P}$. Suppose that $\psi: S \to \mathbb{R}$ is a bounded function which satisfies

(8) $$\sum_{j \in S} p_{ij}\psi(j) = \psi(i) \quad \text{for all } i \in S.$$

We claim that $S_n = \psi(X_n)$ constitutes a martingale (with respect to $\{X_n\}$). For,

$$\begin{aligned}\mathbf{E}(S_{n+1} \mid X_1, \ldots, X_n) &= \mathbf{E}(\psi(X_{n+1}) \mid X_1, \ldots, X_n)\\ &= \mathbf{E}(\psi(X_{n+1}) \mid X_n) \quad \text{by the Markov property}\\ &= \sum_{j \in S} p_{X_n, j}\psi(j)\\ &= \psi(X_n) = S_n \text{ by (8).}\end{aligned}$$

●

(9) **Example.** Let $X_1, X_2, \ldots$ be independent variables with zero means, finite variances, and partial sums $S_n = \sum_{i=1}^n X_i$. Define

$$T_n = S_n^2 = \left(\sum_{i=1}^n X_i\right)^2.$$

Then

$$\begin{aligned}\mathbf{E}(T_{n+1} \mid X_1, \ldots, X_n) &= \mathbf{E}(S_n^2 + 2S_nX_{n+1} + X_{n+1}^2 \mid X_1, \ldots, X_n)\\ &= T_n + 2\mathbf{E}(X_{n+1})\mathbf{E}(S_n \mid X_1, \ldots, X_n) + \mathbf{E}(X_{n+1}^2) \quad \text{by independence}\\ &= T_n + \mathbf{E}(X_{n+1}^2) \geqslant T_n.\end{aligned}$$

$\{T_n\}$ is not a martingale, since it only satisfies (4) with $\geqslant$ in place of $=$; it is called a 'submartingale', and has properties similar to those of a martingale. ●

These examples show that martingales are all around us. They are extremely useful because, subject to a condition on their moments, they always converge; this is 'Doob's Convergence Theorem' and is the main result of the next section.

Finally, here are some properties of conditional expectation. Do not read them straightaway, but refer back to them when necessary. Recall that the conditional expectation of X given Y is defined by

$$\mathbf{E}(X \mid Y) = \psi(Y) \quad \text{where} \quad \psi(y) = \mathbf{E}(X \mid Y = y)$$

is the mean of the conditional distribution of X given that $Y = y$. Most of the conditional expectations in this chapter take the form $\mathbf{E}(X \mid \boldsymbol{Y})$, the mean value of X conditional on the values of the variables in the random vector $\boldsymbol{Y} = (Y_1, Y_2, \ldots, Y_n)$. We stress that $\mathbf{E}(X \mid \boldsymbol{Y})$ is a function of $\boldsymbol{Y}$ alone. Expressions like '$\mathbf{E}(X \mid Y) = Z$' should sometimes be qualified by 'almost surely'; we omit this qualification always.

(10) **Lemma.**

(a) $\mathbf{E}(X_1 + X_2 \mid \boldsymbol{Y}) = \mathbf{E}(X_1 \mid \boldsymbol{Y}) + \mathbf{E}(X_2 \mid \boldsymbol{Y})$
(b) $\mathbf{E}(Xg(\boldsymbol{Y}) \mid \boldsymbol{Y}) = g(\boldsymbol{Y})\mathbf{E}(X \mid \boldsymbol{Y})$ *for nice functions* $g : \mathbb{R}^n \to \mathbb{R}$
(c) $\mathbf{E}(X \mid h(\boldsymbol{Y})) = \mathbf{E}(X \mid \boldsymbol{Y})$ *if* $h : \mathbb{R}^n \to \mathbb{R}^n$ *is one–one.*

Proof.
(a) This depends on the linearity of expectation only.
(b) $\mathbf{E}(Xg(\boldsymbol{Y}) \mid \boldsymbol{Y} = \boldsymbol{y}) = g(\boldsymbol{y})\mathbf{E}(X \mid \boldsymbol{Y} = \boldsymbol{y})$.
(c) Roughly speaking, knowledge of $\boldsymbol{Y}$ is interchangeable with knowledge of $h(\boldsymbol{Y})$, in that

$$\boldsymbol{Y}(\omega) = \boldsymbol{y} \text{ if and only if } h(\boldsymbol{Y}(\omega)) = h(\boldsymbol{y}), \quad \text{for any } \omega \in \Omega. \qquad \blacksquare$$

(11) **Lemma.** $\mathbf{E}(\mathbf{E}(X \mid \boldsymbol{Y}_1, \boldsymbol{Y}_2) \mid \boldsymbol{Y}_1) = \mathbf{E}(X \mid \boldsymbol{Y}_1)$.

Proof. Just write down these expectations as integrals involving conditional distributions to see that the result holds. It is a more general version of Problem (4.10.20). ■

Sometimes we consider the mean value $\mathbf{E}(X \mid A)$ of a random variable X conditional upon the occurrence of some event A. This is just the mean of the corresponding distribution function

$$F_{X \mid A}(x) = \mathbf{P}(X \leq x \mid A).$$

We can think of $\mathbf{E}(X \mid A)$ as a constant random variable with domain $A \subseteq \Omega$; it is undefined at points $\omega \in A^c$. The following result is an application of (1.4.4).

(12) **Lemma.** *If* $\{B_i : 1 \leq i \leq n\}$ *is a partition of* A *then*

$$\mathbf{E}(X \mid A)\mathbf{P}(A) = \sum_{i=1}^{n} \mathbf{E}(X \mid B_i)\mathbf{P}(B_i).$$

You may prefer the following proof:

$$\mathbf{E}(XI_A) = \mathbf{E}\left(X \sum_i I_{B_i}\right) = \sum_i \mathbf{E}(XI_{B_i}).$$

Sometimes we consider mixtures of these two types of conditional expectation. These are of the form $\mathbf{E}(X \mid \boldsymbol{Y}, A)$ where $X, Y_1, \ldots, Y_n$ are random variables and A is an event. Such quantities are defined in the obvious way and have the usual properties. For example, (11) becomes

(13) $$\mathbf{E}(X \mid A) = \mathbf{E}(\mathbf{E}(X \mid \boldsymbol{Y}, A) \mid A).$$

We shall make some use of the following fact soon. If, in (13), A is an event which is defined in terms of the Y's (such as $A=\{Y_1 \leqslant 1\}$ or $A=\{|Y_2Y_3-Y_4|>2\}$) then it is not difficult to see that

(14) $$\mathbf{E}(\mathbf{E}(X \mid \boldsymbol{Y}) \mid A)=\mathbf{E}(\mathbf{E}(X \mid \boldsymbol{Y}, A) \mid A);$$

just note that evaluating the random variable $\mathbf{E}(X \mid \boldsymbol{Y}, A)$ at a point $\omega \in \Omega$ yields

$$\mathbf{E}(X \mid \boldsymbol{Y}, A)(\omega)\begin{cases} =\mathbf{E}(X \mid \boldsymbol{Y})(\omega) & \text{if} \quad \omega \in A \\ \text{is undefined} & \text{if} \quad \omega \notin A. \end{cases}$$

The sequences $\{S_n\}$ of this section satisfy

(15) $$\mathbf{E}\,|S_n|<\infty, \qquad \mathbf{E}(S_{n+1} \mid X_1, \dots, X_n)=S_n.$$

(16) **Lemma.** *If $\{S_n\}$ satisfies (15) then*
(a) $\mathbf{E}(S_{n+m} \mid X_1, \dots, X_n)=S_n$ *for all n, $m \geqslant 1$*
(b) $\mathbf{E}(S_n)=\mathbf{E}(S_1)$ *for all n.*

Proof.

(a) Use (11) with $X=S_{n+m}$, $\mathbf{Y}_1=(X_1, \dots, X_n)$ and $\mathbf{Y}_2=(X_{n+1}, \dots, X_{n+m-1})$ to obtain

$$\begin{aligned}\mathbf{E}(S_{n+m} \mid X_1, \dots, X_n) &= \mathbf{E}(\mathbf{E}(S_{n+m} \mid X_1, \dots, X_{n+m-1}) \mid X_1, \dots, X_n) \\ &= \mathbf{E}(S_{n+m-1} \mid X_1, \dots, X_n)\end{aligned}$$

and iterate to obtain the result.

(b) $\mathbf{E}(S_n)=\mathbf{E}(\mathbf{E}(S_n \mid X_1))=\mathbf{E}(S_1)$ by (a). ∎

7.8 Martingale convergence theorem

This section is devoted to the proof and subsequent applications of the following theorem. It receives a section to itself by virtue of its wealth of applications.

(1) **Theorem.** *If $\{S_n\}$ is a martingale with $\mathbf{E}(S_n^2)<M<\infty$ for some M and all n, then there exists a random variable S such that $S_n \xrightarrow{\text{a.s.}} S$.*

This result has a more general version which, amongst other things,

(i) deals with submartingales
(ii) imposes weaker moment conditions
(iii) explores convergence in mean also

but the proof of this is long and difficult. On the other hand, the proof of (1) is within our grasp, and is only slightly more difficult than the proof of the Strong Law (7.5.1) for independent sequences; it mimics the traditional proof of the Strong Law and begins with a generalization of Chebyshov's inequality.

(2) **Theorem. Doob–Kolmogorov inequality.** *If $\{S_n\}$ is a martingale with respect to $\{X_n\}$ then*

$$\mathbf{P}\left(\max_{1\leq i\leq n}|S_i|\geq\epsilon\right)\leq\frac{1}{\epsilon^2}\mathbf{E}(S_n^2)\quad\textit{whenever}\quad\epsilon>0.$$

Proof of (2). Let $A_0=\Omega$, $A_k=\{|S_i|<\epsilon$ for all $i\leq k\}$, and let $B_k=A_{k-1}\cap\{|S_k|\geq\epsilon\}$ be the event that $|S_i|\geq\epsilon$ for the first time when $i=k$. Then

$$A_k\cup\left(\bigcup_{i=1}^{k}B_i\right)=\Omega.$$

Therefore

(3)
$$\begin{aligned}\mathbf{E}(S_n^2)&=\sum_{i=1}^{n}\mathbf{E}(S_n^2I_{B_i})+\mathbf{E}(S_n^2I_{A_n})\\&\geq\sum_{i=1}^{n}\mathbf{E}(S_n^2I_{B_i}).\end{aligned}$$

However,

$$\begin{aligned}\mathbf{E}(S_n^2I_{B_i})&=\mathbf{E}((S_n-S_i+S_i)^2I_{B_i})\\&=\mathbf{E}((S_n-S_i)^2I_{B_i})+2\mathbf{E}((S_n-S_i)S_iI_{B_i})+\mathbf{E}(S_i^2I_{B_i})\\&=\alpha+\beta+\gamma,\text{ say.}\end{aligned}$$

Note that $\alpha\geq0$ and $\gamma\geq\epsilon^2\mathbf{P}(B_i)$, because $|S_i|\geq\epsilon$ if B_i occurs. To deal with β, note that

$$\begin{aligned}\mathbf{E}((S_n-S_i)S_iI_{B_i})&=\mathbf{E}(S_iI_{B_i}\mathbf{E}(S_n-S_i\mid X_1,\dots,X_i))\text{ by (7.7.10b)}\\&=0\text{ by (7.7.16a),}\end{aligned}$$

since B_i concerns $X_1,\dots,X_i$ only, by the discussion after (7.7.4). Thus (3) becomes

$$\mathbf{E}(S_n^2)\geq\sum_{i=1}^{n}\epsilon^2\mathbf{P}(B_i)=\epsilon^2\mathbf{P}\left(\max_{1\leq i\leq n}|S_i|\geq\epsilon\right)$$

and the result is shown. ■

Proof of (1). First note that S_m and $(S_{m+n}-S_m)$ are uncorrelated whenever $m,n\geq1$; for,

$$\mathbf{E}(S_m(S_{m+n}-S_m))=\mathbf{E}(S_m\mathbf{E}(S_{m+n}-S_m\mid X_1,\dots,X_m))=0$$

by (7.7.16). Thus

(4)
$$\mathbf{E}(S_{m+n}^2)=\mathbf{E}(S_m^2)+\mathbf{E}((S_{m+n}-S_m)^2).$$

It follows that $\{\mathbf{E}(S_n^2)\}$ is a non-decreasing sequence, which is bounded above, by the assumption in (1); hence we may suppose that the constant M is chosen such that

$$\mathbf{E}(S_n^2)\uparrow M\quad\text{as}\quad n\to\infty.$$

The rest of the proof is a simple application of the Doob–Kolmogorov inequality. It is easy to check that, for any choice of m, the sequence $\{S_{m,n} : n \geq 1\}$, given by $S_{m,n} = S_{m+n} - S_m$, is a martingale with respect to itself. For, if $\{S_n\}$ is a martingale with respect to $\{X_n\}$ then

$$\begin{aligned}\mathbf{E}(S_{m,n+1} \mid S_{m,1}, \ldots, S_{m,n}) &= \mathbf{E}(\mathbf{E}(S_{m,n+1} \mid X_1, \ldots, X_{m+n}) \mid S_{m,1}, \ldots, S_{m,n}) \\ &= \mathbf{E}(S_{m,n} \mid S_{m,1}, \ldots, S_{m,n}) \\ &= S_{m,n},\end{aligned}$$

by (7.7.11), the martingale property, and the properties of conditional expectations. Now apply (2) to this martingale to deduce that

$$\mathbf{P}\left(\max_{m \leq i \leq m+n} |S_i - S_m| \geq \epsilon\right) \leq \frac{1}{\epsilon^2} \mathbf{E}((S_{m+n} - S_m)^2).$$

Let $n \to \infty$ and use (4) to obtain

$$\mathbf{P}\left(\sup_{i \geq m} |S_i - S_m| \geq \epsilon\right) \leq \frac{1}{\epsilon^2} (M - \mathbf{E}(S_m^2));$$

let $m \to \infty$ to obtain

$\mathbf{P}(|S_i - S_m| \geq \epsilon$ for infinitely many $i, m) = 0$, for all $\epsilon > 0$.

Thus $\{S_n(\omega)\}$ is Cauchy convergent for all ω in some event which has probability 1 (see Problem (7.10.25)). On this event $\{S_n(\omega)\}$ converges to a limit $S(\omega)$ and the result is proved. ■

Here are some applications of the martingale convergence theorem.

(5) **Example. Branching processes.** Recall (7.7.5). By (5.4.2),

$$W_n = Z_n / \mathbf{E}(Z_n)$$

has second moment

$$\mathbf{E}(W_n^2) = 1 + \frac{\sigma^2(1 - \mu^{-n})}{\mu(\mu - 1)} \quad \text{if} \quad \mu \neq 1$$

where $\sigma^2 = \text{var}(Z_1)$. Thus, if $\mu \neq 1$, there exists a random variable W such that

$$W_n \xrightarrow{\text{a.s.}} W$$

and so $W_n \xrightarrow{\text{D}} W$ also; their characteristic functions satisfy

$$\phi_{W_n}(t) \to \phi_W(t)$$

by (5.9.5). This makes the discussion at the end of Section 5.4 fully rigorous, and we can rewrite (5.4.6) as

$$\phi_W(\mu t) = G(\phi_W(t)).$$ ●

(6) **Example. Markov chains.** Suppose that the chain $X_0, X_1, \ldots$ of (7.7.7) is irreducible and persistent, and let ψ be a bounded function mapping S into $\mathbb{R}$ which satisfies (7.7.8). Then the sequence $\{S_n\}$, given by $S_n = \psi(X_n)$, is a martingale and satisfies the condition

$$\mathbf{E}(S_n^2) \leq M$$

for some M, by the boundedness of ψ. For any state i, the event $\{X_n = i\}$ occurs for infinitely many values of n with probability 1. However, $\{S_n = \psi(i)\} \supseteq \{X_n = i\}$ and so

$$S_n \xrightarrow{\text{a.s.}} \psi(i) \quad \text{for all } i,$$

which is clearly impossible unless $\psi(i)$ is the same for all i. We have shown that any bounded solution of (7.7.8) is constant. ●

(7) **Example. Genetic model.** Recall Example (6.1.11), which dealt with gene frequencies in the evolution of a population. We encountered there a Markov chain $X_0, X_1, \ldots$ taking values in $\{0, 1, \ldots, N\}$ with transition probabilities given by

(8)
$$p_{ij} = \mathbf{P}(X_{n+1} = j \mid X_n = i) = \binom{N}{j}\left(\frac{i}{N}\right)^j\left(1 - \frac{i}{N}\right)^{N-j}.$$

Then

$$\begin{aligned}\mathbf{E}(X_{n+1} \mid X_0, \ldots, X_n) &= \mathbf{E}(X_{n+1} \mid X_n) \quad \text{by the Markov property}\\ &= \sum_j j p_{X_n, j} = X_n\end{aligned}$$

by (8). Thus $X_0, X_1, \ldots$ is a martingale. Also, let Y_n be defined by

$$Y_n = X_n(N - X_n),$$

and suppose that $N > 1$. Then

$$\mathbf{E}(Y_{n+1} \mid X_0, \ldots, X_n) = \mathbf{E}(Y_{n+1} \mid X_n) \quad \text{by the Markov property}$$

and

$$\mathbf{E}(Y_{n+1} \mid X_n = i) = \sum_j j(N-j)p_{ij} = i(N-i)(1 - N^{-1})$$

by (8). Thus

(9)
$$\mathbf{E}(Y_{n+1} \mid X_0, \ldots, X_n) = Y_n(1 - N^{-1}),$$

and we see that $\{Y_n\}$ is not itself a martingale. However, set $S_n = Y_n/(1 - N^{-1})^n$ to obtain from (9) that

$$\mathbf{E}(S_{n+1} \mid X_0, \ldots, X_n) = S_n;$$

deduce that $\{S_n\}$ is a martingale.

The martingale $\{X_n\}$ has uniformly bounded second moments, and so there exists an X such that

$$X_n \xrightarrow{\text{a.s.}} X.$$

Unlike the previous example, this chain is not irreducible. In fact, 0 and N are absorbing states, and X takes these values only. Can you find the probability $\mathbf{P}(X = 0)$ that the chain is ultimately absorbed at 0? The results of the next section will help you with this.

Finally, what happens when we apply the convergence theorem to $\{S_n\}$? ●

7.9 Optional stopping and Wald's identity

The cunning gambler will not gamble for ever; rather, he will devise a rule for stopping at some time which he thinks advantageous. Possible rules include

(a) stop after 100 plays
(b) stop as soon as a net profit exists for the session
(c) stop just before the play which brings bankruptcy.

Let S_n be the gambler's fortune after the nth play and let T be the (possibly random) time at which he intends to stop. These rules become

(a) $T=100$
(b) $T=\min\{n: S_n > S_0\}$
(c) $T=\min\{n: S_{n+1} \leqslant 0\}$;

after he has stopped, his fortune totals S_T. The last rule is hard to apply in practice since its operation requires a knowledge of the future; we eliminate such rules from our reckoning. On the other hand, the first two rules are feasible and are examples of 'stopping times'. After n plays the gambler knows $S_0, \ldots, S_n$ only, and is left to guess at the values of $S_{n+1}, \ldots$. Roughly speaking, we call T a stopping time if at each stage n the gambler can tell from his current knowledge whether or not T has arrived. That is to say, T is a stopping time if the event $\{T=n\}$ is describable in terms of $S_0, \ldots, S_n$ without reference to $S_{n+1}, S_{n+2}, \ldots$.

(1) **Definition.** The random variable T, taking values in $\{1, 2, \ldots, \infty\}$, is a **stopping time** for the sequence $\{X_n\}$ if

$$\{T=n\} \in \mathscr{F}_n \quad \text{for all } n \geqslant 1$$

where $\mathscr{F}_n$ is the smallest σ-field of events with respect to which $X_1, X_2, \ldots, X_n$ are measurable.

That is to say, anyone who knows the values of $X_0, \ldots, X_n$ also knows whether or not T has been reached. Clearly $\mathbf{P}(T=n \mid X_0, \ldots, X_n)$ is a function of $(X_1, \ldots, X_n)$ and takes the values 0 and 1 only.

(2) **Example. Symmetric random walk.** A fair coin is tossed repeatedly. Each head credits the player with £1; each tail debits him £1. Let S_n be his fortune after n tosses and suppose $S_0=0$; we allow negative fortunes. A plausible strategy for the player is to continue the game until a time T given by

$$T=\min\{n: S_n=1\}.$$

Certainly T is a stopping time for $\{S_n\}$, and $\mathbf{P}(T<\infty)=1$ because the symmetric random walk is persistent. This seems to be a cunning strategy, but is marred by our knowledge that

$$\mathbf{E}T = \infty$$

since the symmetric random walk is also null. ●

We have already encountered many examples of stopping times in the theory of Markov chains. Let $X_0, X_1, \ldots$ be a Markov chain taking values in some set S. Then the first passage times

$$T_i = \min\{n : X_n = i\}$$

are stopping times; they may take the value $+\infty$ if the chain is not irreducible and persistent. The concept of stopping times has proved to be immensely useful in the theory of stochastic processes generally, and particularly for processes which evolve continuously in time and space. We are not able to describe their full power in this book, but close this chapter with an account of a theorem which leads to remarkably speedy derivations of results which are often quite complicated to show by more basic methods. To use the gambling analogy for the last time, this 'Optional Stopping Theorem' asserts that, subject to certain conditions, whichever stopping time T is adopted by the gambler, he cannot improve his expected gain. You will see that Example (2) violates the third condition of the theorem.

(3) **Optional Stopping Theorem.** *Let $\{S_n\}$ be a martingale with respect to $\{X_n\}$ and let T be a stopping time for $\{X_n\}$ such that*

(a) $\mathbf{P}(T < \infty) = 1$
(b) $\mathbf{E}\,|S_T| < \infty$
(c) $\mathbf{E}(S_n \mid T > n)\mathbf{P}(T > n) \to 0$ *as* $n \to 0$.

Then $\mathbf{E}(S_T) = \mathbf{E}(S_1)$.

Henceforth, if $\{S_n\}$ is a martingale with respect to $\{X_n\}$ and T is a stopping time for $\{X_n\}$, then we call T a 'stopping time for the martingale'.

If T is almost surely constant then the result follows from (7.7.16), since

$$\mathbf{E}(S_n) = \mathbf{E}(\mathbf{E}(S_n \mid X_1)) = \mathbf{E}(S_1).$$

First we state and prove a preliminary lemma. For any real x and y define

$$x \wedge y = \min\{x, y\}.$$

(4) **Lemma.** *Let T be a stopping time for the martingale $\{S_n\}$. Then*

$$\mathbf{E}(S_{T \wedge n}) = \mathbf{E}(S_1) \quad \text{for all } n \leqslant 1.$$

This is another example of the use of truncation, a technique used in the proof of the Strong Law (7.5.1) and having many other applications elsewhere.

Proof. Use (7.7.12)–(7.7.14) to obtain

$$\begin{aligned}
\mathbf{E}(S_1) &= \mathbf{E}(S_n)\\
&= \sum_{i=1}^{n} \mathbf{E}(S_n \mid T=i)\mathbf{P}(T=i) + \mathbf{E}(S_n \mid T>n)\mathbf{P}(T>n)\\
&= \sum_{i=1}^{n} \mathbf{E}(\mathbf{E}(S_n \mid X_1, \ldots, X_i, T=i) \mid T=i)\mathbf{P}(T=i)\\
&\qquad\qquad + \mathbf{E}(S_n \mid T>n)\mathbf{P}(T>n)\\
&= \sum_{i=1}^{n} \mathbf{E}(\mathbf{E}(S_n \mid X_1, \ldots, X_i) \mid T=i)\mathbf{P}(T=i) + \mathbf{E}(S_n \mid T>n)\mathbf{P}(T>n)\\
&\quad \text{by (7.7.14), since } T \text{ is a stopping time}\\
&= \sum_{i=1}^{n} \mathbf{E}(S_i \mid T=i)\mathbf{P}(T=i) + \mathbf{E}(S_n \mid T>n)\mathbf{P}(T>n)\\
&\quad \text{since } \{S_n\} \text{ is a martingale}\\
&= \mathbf{E}(S_T \mid T\leq n)\mathbf{P}(T\leq n) + \mathbf{E}(S_n \mid T>n)\mathbf{P}(T>n)\\
&= \mathbf{E}(S_{T\wedge n}).
\end{aligned}$$

■

Proof of (3).

$$\begin{aligned}
\mathbf{E}(S_T) &= \mathbf{E}(S_T \mid T\leq n)\mathbf{P}(T\leq n) + \mathbf{E}(S_T \mid T>n)\mathbf{P}(T>n)\\
&= \mathbf{E}(S_{T\wedge n}) - \mathbf{E}(S_n \mid T>n)\mathbf{P}(T>n) + \mathbf{E}(S_T \mid T>n)\mathbf{P}(T>n)
\end{aligned}$$

by the last two lines in the proof of (4). However, as $n \to \infty$

$$\mathbf{E}(S_n \mid T>n)\mathbf{P}(T>n) \to 0$$

by assumption (3c), and, by (3a),

$$\begin{aligned}
|\mathbf{E}(S_T \mid T>n)\mathbf{P}(T>n)| &\leq \sum_{i=n+1}^{\infty} \mathbf{E}(|S_T| \,\big|\, T=k)\mathbf{P}(T=k)\\
&\to 0 \quad \text{as} \quad n\to\infty
\end{aligned}$$

because the summation is the tail of the convergent series

$$\mathbf{E}\,|S_T| = \sum_{i=1}^{\infty} \mathbf{E}(|S_T| \,\big|\, T=k)\mathbf{P}(T=k) < \infty$$

by assumption (3b). ■

Here are some examples of the use of the Optional Stopping Theorem.

(5) **Example. Symmetric random walk.** Let S_n be the position of the particle after n steps and suppose that $S_0 = 0$. Then

$$S_n = \sum_{i=1}^{n} X_i$$

where $X_1, X_2, \ldots$ are independent and equally likely to take each of the values $+1$ and -1. It is easy to see that $\{S_n\}$ is a martingale. Let a and b be positive integers and let

$$T = \min\{n : S_n = -a \text{ or } S_n = b\}$$

be the earliest time at which the walk visits either $-a$ or b. Certainly T is a stopping time and satisfies the conditions of (3). Let p_a be the probability that the particle visits $-a$ before it visits b. By the Optional Stopping Theorem

(6) $$\begin{aligned}\mathbf{E}(S_T) &= (-a)p_a + b(1-p_a)\\ &= \mathbf{E}(S_1) = 0;\end{aligned}$$

thus

$$p_a = \frac{b}{a+b}$$

which agrees with the earlier result (1.7.7) when the notation is translated suitably. $\{S_n\}$ is not the only martingale available. Let $\{Y_n\}$ be given by

$$Y_n = S_n^2 - n;$$

then $\{Y_n\}$ is a martingale also. Apply (3) with T given as before to obtain

$$\mathbf{E}(T) = ab.$$

●

(7) **Example. Wald's equation.** Related to the previous example is the following, which deals with the partial sums of variables with more general distributions. Let $X_1, X_2, \ldots$ be independent identically distributed variables which are not constant and which have finite means μ and partial sums

$$S_n = \sum_{i=1}^{n} X_i.$$

It is easy to see (Example (7.7.6)) that $\{S'_n\}$ is a martingale, where

$$S'_n = S_n - n\mu.$$

If T is a stopping time with finite mean, then it can be shown that the Optional Stopping Theorem is applicable (see Laha and Rohatgi 1979, p. 426). Thus

$$\mathbf{E}(S'_T) = \mathbf{E}(S'_1) = 0,$$

which is equivalent to *Wald's equation:*

(8) $$\mathbf{E}(S_T) = \mu\mathbf{E}(T).$$

This asserts that the mean of the sum of a random number T of random variables is the obvious linear combination whenever T is a stopping time, and is related to the similar statement, derivable from (5.1.15), that this holds when T is independent of the X's. ●

(9) **Example. Wald's identity.** This time, let $X_1, X_2, \ldots$ be independent identically distributed variables which are not constant and such that their moment generating function

$$M(t) = \mathbf{E}\{\exp(tX_1)\}$$

satisfies $M(t) < \infty$ in some open interval containing the origin. If $a, b > 0$, define

$$T = \min\{n : S_n \leqslant -a \text{ or } S_n \geqslant b\}$$

to be the 'first exit time' of $\{S_n\}$ from the interval $(-a, b)$. Next we need to find a martingale. Fix t such that $M(t) < \infty$ and define

$$Y_n = \{M(t)\}^{-n} \exp(tS_n);$$

now perform the calculation

$$\begin{aligned}\mathbf{E}(Y_{n+1} \mid X_1, \ldots, X_n) &= \mathbf{E}(Y_n\{M(t)\}^{-1} \exp(tX_{n+1}) \mid X_1, \ldots, X_n)\\ &= Y_n\{M(t)\}^{-1}\mathbf{E}(\exp(tX_{n+1})) \quad \text{by independence}\\ &= Y_n\end{aligned}$$

to see that $\{Y_n\}$ is a martingale. Of course, Y_n depends on the choice of t. It can be shown that T and $\{Y_n\}$ satisfy the conditions of the Optional Stopping Theorem whenever

$$1 \leqslant M(t) < \infty$$

(see Karlin and Taylor 1975, p. 264). Subject to this condition, (3) gives that

(10) $$\mathbf{E}(\{M(t)\}^{-T} \exp(tS_T)) = 1,$$

an equation which is known as *Wald's identity*. For this choice of T, Wald's equation (8) follows immediately so long as $\mathbf{E}(X_1) < \infty$. Just differentiate (10) at $t = 0$ to obtain

$$\mathbf{E}(S_T) = \mathbf{E}(X_1)\mathbf{E}(T).$$

Our particular choice for T does not seem to have been very significant in the derivation of (10). Indeed (10) holds in greater generality (see Breiman 1968, p. 100, for example). ●

(11) **Example. Asymmetric random walk.** A particle performs a random walk $\{S_n\}$ on the integers, moving one step to the right with probability p and one step to the left with probability $q = 1 - p$ at each stage. Let a and b be positive integers and let

$$T = \min\{n : S_n = -a \text{ or } S_n = b\}$$

as usual. Apply Wald's identity (10) to obtain

(12) $$e^{-at}P_1(\{M(t)\}^{-1}) + e^{bt}P_2(\{M(t)\}^{-1}) = 1$$

where

$$M(t) = pe^t + qe^{-t}$$

and

$$P_1(s)=\mathbf{E}(s^T \mid S_T=-a)\mathbf{P}(S_T=-a)=\mathbf{E}(s^T I_{\{S_T=-a\}})$$
(13)
$$P_2(s)=\mathbf{E}(s^T \mid S_T=b)\mathbf{P}(S_T=b)=\mathbf{E}(s^T I_{\{S_T=b\}}).$$

We proceed to find P_1 and P_2. Invert the substitution

$$s=\{M(t)\}^{-1}$$

to obtain

$$e^t=\lambda_1(s) \text{ or } e^t=\lambda_2(s)$$

where

$$\lambda_1(s)=\frac{1+(1-4pqs^2)^{1/2}}{2ps}$$

$$\lambda_2(s)=\frac{1-(1-4pqs^2)^{1/2}}{2ps}.$$

Substitute these into (12) to obtain two linear equations in P_1 and P_2 with solution

$$P_1(s)=\frac{\lambda_1^a\lambda_2^a(\lambda_1^b-\lambda_2^b)}{\lambda_1^{a+b}-\lambda_2^{a+b}}$$

$$P_2(s)=\frac{\lambda_1^a-\lambda_2^a}{\lambda_1^{a+b}-\lambda_2^{a+b}}$$

and add together to obtain the probability generating function of T,

$$\mathbf{E}(s^T)=P_1(s)+P_2(s).$$

Suppose we let $a\to\infty$, so that T becomes the time until the first passage to the point b. From (13),

$$P_1(s)\to 0 \quad \text{as} \quad a\to\infty \quad \text{if} \quad 0<s<1$$

and a quick calculation gives

$$P_2(s)\to\left\{\frac{1-(1-4pqs^2)^{1/2}}{2qs}\right\}^b$$

in agreement with (5.3.5). Notice that

$$P_2(1)\begin{cases}=1 & \text{if } p\geqslant q\\ <1 & \text{if } p<q\end{cases}$$

in agreement with the previous observation that the walk may never visit the point $b>0$ if its steps are biased in the leftwards direction. ●

7.10 Problems

1. Show that $\mathbf{E}(X_n^r)\to\mathbf{E}(X^r)$ if $X_n\xrightarrow{r}X$.
2. Prove Theorem (7.3.9). Show also that if $X_n\xrightarrow{\text{a.s.}}X$ and $Y_n\xrightarrow{\text{a.s.}}Y$ then $X_nY_n\xrightarrow{\text{a.s.}}XY$.
   Does the corresponding result hold for the other modes of convergence?

3. Let $g:\mathbb{R}\to\mathbb{R}$ be continuous. Show that
   (a) $g(X_n)\xrightarrow{\text{P}} g(X)$ if $X_n\xrightarrow{\text{P}} X$
   (b) $\mathbf{E}(g(X_n))\to\mathbf{E}(g(X))$ if $X_n\xrightarrow{\text{D}} X$ and g is bounded.

4. Let $Y_1, Y_2, \ldots$ be independent identically distributed variables, each of which can take any value in $\{0, 1, \ldots, 9\}$ with equal probability $\frac{1}{10}$. Let

$$X_n=\sum_{j=1}^{n} Y_j 10^{-j}.$$

Show by the use of characteristic functions that $\{X_n\}$ converges in distribution to the uniform distribution on $[0, 1]$. Deduce that $X_n \xrightarrow{\text{a.s.}} Y$ for some Y which is uniformly distributed on $[0, 1]$.

5. Let $N(t)$ be a Poisson process.
   (a) Prove that N is continuous in probability, which is to say that $\mathbf{P}(|N(t+h)-N(t)|>\epsilon)\to 0$ as $h\to 0$ for all $\epsilon>0$.
   (b) Find the covariance of $N(s)$ and $N(t)$.
   (c) Deduce that N is continuous in mean square, which is to say that $\mathbf{E}(\{N(t+h)-N(t)\}^2)\to 0$ as $h\to 0$.
   (d) Show that N is differentiable in probability but not in mean square.

6. Use Lemma (7.2.10) to show that

$$\frac{1}{n}\sum_{i=1}^{n} X_i \xrightarrow{\text{a.s.}} 0$$

whenever the X's are independent identically distributed variables with zero means and such that $\mathbf{E}(X_1^4)<\infty$.

7. Show that $X_n \xrightarrow{\text{a.s.}} X$ whenever

$$\sum_n \mathbf{E}(|X_n-X|^r)<\infty \quad \text{for some } r>0.$$

8. Show that if $X_n\xrightarrow{\text{D}} X$ then

$$aX_n+b\xrightarrow{\text{D}} aX+b$$

for any real a and b.

9. If X has zero mean and variance σ^2, show that

$$\mathbf{P}(X\geqslant t)\leqslant\frac{\sigma^2}{\sigma^2+t^2}, \quad \text{for} \quad t>0.$$

10. Show that $X_n\xrightarrow{\text{P}} 0$ if and only if

$$\mathbf{E}\left(\frac{|X_n|}{1+|X_n|}\right)\to 0 \quad \text{as} \quad n\to\infty.$$

11. The sequence $\{X_n\}$ is called *mean square Cauchy convergent* if

$$\mathbf{E}((X_n-X_m)^2)\to 0 \quad \text{as} \quad m, n\to\infty.$$

Show that $\{X_n\}$ converges in mean square to some limit X if and only if it is mean square Cauchy convergent. Does the corresponding result hold for the other modes of convergence?

12. Suppose that $\{X_n\}$ is a sequence of identically distributed variables with zero means and such that $\mathbf{E}(X_1^2)<\infty$. Show that

$$\frac{1}{n}\sum_{i=1}^{n} X_i \xrightarrow{\text{m.s.}} 0$$

if the X's are uncorrelated.

13. Let $X_1, X_2, \ldots$ be independent identically distributed random variables with the shared distribution function $F(x)$, and suppose that $F(x)<1$ for all x. Let

$$M_n = \max\{X_1, X_2, \ldots, X_n\}$$

and suppose that there exists a sequence $a_1<a_2<\ldots<a_n$, with $a_n\to\infty$, such that

$$\mathbf{P}\left(\frac{M_n}{a_n}\leqslant x\right)\to H(x)$$

for some distribution function H. Let us assume that H is continuous with $0<H(1)<1$; substantially weaker conditions suffice but introduce extra difficulties.

(a) Show that $n(1-F(a_n x))\to -\log H(x)$ as $n\to\infty$ and deduce that

$$\frac{1-F(a_n x)}{1-F(a_n)}\to\frac{\log H(x)}{\log H(1)} \quad \text{if} \quad x>0.$$

(b) Deduce that if $x>0$

$$\frac{1-F(tx)}{1-F(t)}\to\frac{\log H(x)}{\log H(1)} \quad \text{as} \quad t\to\infty.$$

(c) Set $x=x_1x_2$ and make the substitution

$$g(x)=\frac{\log H(e^x)}{\log H(1)}$$

to find that

$$g(x+y)=g(x)g(y).$$

(d) Use the hint of Problem (4.10.5) to deduce that

$$H(x)=\begin{cases}\exp(-\alpha x^{-\beta}) & \text{if} \quad x\geqslant 0\\ 0 & \text{if} \quad x<0\end{cases}$$

for some non-negative constants α and β. We have shown that H is the distribution function of Y^{-1}, where Y has the Weibull distribution.

14. (a) Use Taylor's Theorem to show that

$$f(y)=\frac{\pi}{2}-\tan^{-1}(y^{-1})$$

satisfies

$$f(y)=y+o(y) \text{ when } y \text{ is small and positive.}$$

(b) In Problem (13), suppose the X's have the Cauchy distribution with density function

$$f(x)=\frac{1}{\pi(1+x^2)}.$$

Suppose further that $a_n = n/\pi$ and show that

$$H(x)=\begin{cases} e^{-x^{-1}} & \text{if } x \geq 0 \\ 0 & \text{if } x<0. \end{cases}$$

15. A bag contains red and green balls. A ball is drawn from the bag, its colour noted, and then it is returned to the bag together with a new ball of the same colour. Initially the bag contained one ball of each colour. If R_n denotes the number of red balls in the bag after n additions, show that

$$S_n=\frac{R_n}{n+2}$$

is a martingale. Deduce that the ratio of red to green balls converges almost surely to some limit as $n \to \infty$. Let T be the number of balls drawn until the first green ball appears. Show that

$$\mathbf{E}\left(\frac{1}{T+2}\right)=\tfrac{1}{4}.$$

16. Let $X_1, X_2, \ldots$ be independent identically distributed variables which are not constant, and suppose there exists $t>0$ such that

$$M(t)=\mathbf{E}\{\exp(tX_1)\}=1.$$

Show that the partial sums $\{S_n\}$ satisfy

$$\mathbf{P}(S_n \geq x \text{ for some } n) \leq e^{-tx}$$

for all $x>0$.

17. Let £Y_n be the assets of an insurance company after n years of trading. During each year it receives a total income of £P in premiums. During the nth year it pays out a total of £C_n in claims. Thus

$$Y_{n+1}=Y_n+P-C_{n+1}.$$

Suppose that $C_1, C_2, \ldots$ are independent $N(\mu, \sigma^2)$ variables and show that the probability of ultimate bankruptcy satisfies

$$\mathbf{P}(Y_n<0 \text{ for some } n) \leq \exp\{-2(P-\mu)Y_0/\sigma^2\}.$$

18. **Jensen's inequality.** A function $u:\mathbb{R} \to \mathbb{R}$ is called *convex* if for all real a there exists λ, depending on a, such that

$$u(x) \geq u(a)+\lambda(x-a) \quad \text{for all } x.$$

(Draw a diagram to illustrate this definition.) Show that, if X is a random variable with finite mean, then

$$\mathbf{E}(u(X)) \geq u(\mathbf{E}(X)).$$

19. Let $\{S_n\}$ be a martingale with respect to $\{X_n\}$ and let $u:\mathbb{R}\to\mathbb{R}$ be a convex function. Use Jensen's inequality to show that $\{u(S_n)\}$ is a submartingale with respect to $\{X_n\}$, whenever $\mathbf{E}\,|u(S_n)|<\infty$ for all n. Deduce that, subject to the

appropriate moment condition,
(a) $\{S_n^2\}$ is a submartingale
(b) $\{\max(0, S_n)\}$ is a submartingale.

20. If $\{S_n\}$ is a positive submartingale with $\mathbf{E}(S_n^2) < M$ for all n, show that $S_n \to S$ almost surely, as $n \to \infty$, for some S.

21. Suppose that $\{X_n\}$ is a sequence of independent variables such that

$$S_n = \sum_{i=1}^{n} X_i \xrightarrow{D} S \quad \text{as} \quad n \to \infty$$

for some variable S. Let $\phi_n(t)$ be the characteristic function of S_n and write

$$Z_n = \frac{\exp(itS_n)}{\phi_n(t)}.$$

Show that $\{Z_n\}$ is a (complex-valued) martingale with respect to $\{X_n\}$ for all sufficiently small t. Deduce that $\{Z_n\}$ converges almost surely to some limit Z as n tends to infinity, when t is small. Can you see why this shows that the sequence $\{S_n\}$ converges almost surely as well as in distribution?

22. Let $\{X_n\}$ be a sequence of independent identically distributed variables with $\mathbf{E}\,|X_1| < \infty$. If

$$S_n = X_1 + \ldots + X_n$$

as usual, show that $T_n = n^{-1} S_n$ satisfies

$$\mathbf{E}\,|T_n| < \infty, \qquad \mathbf{E}(T_n \mid S_{n+1}, S_{n+2}, \ldots) = T_{n+1}.$$

$\{T_n\}$ is called a *backward* (or *reversed*) *martingale* with respect to $\{S_n\}$. Backward martingales converge as $n \to \infty$, which is to say that

$$T_n \xrightarrow{\text{a.s.}} T \quad \text{as} \quad n \to \infty$$

for some T. Use the zero–one law (7.3.17) to show that T is a.s. constant. In fact $T = \mathbf{E}(X_1)$ with probability one, and we have proved the Strong Law of Large Numbers.

23. Let $\{N(t): t \geq 0\}$ be a Poisson process with parameter λ. Show that S_1, S_2, and S_3, given by

$$S_1(t) = N(t) - \lambda t$$
$$S_2(t) = S_1(t)^2 - \lambda t$$
$$S_3(t) = \exp\{-\theta N(t) + \lambda t(1 - e^{-\theta})\}, \quad -\infty < \theta < \infty$$

each satisfy the *continuous martingale condition*

$$\mathbf{E}(S(t+u) \mid \{N(u): u \leq t\}) = S(t) \text{ for all } u, t > 0.$$

24. Problem (5.11.2) asked for the mean number of tosses of a coin before the first appearance of the sequence *HHH*. Here is a martingale approach to the question. A large casino contains infinitely many gamblers $G_1, G_2, \ldots$, each with an initial fortune of \$1. A croupier tosses a coin repeatedly. For each n, gambler G_n bets as follows. Just before the nth toss he stakes his \$1 on the event that the nth toss shows heads. The game is assumed fair, so that he receives a total of $\$p^{-1}$ if he

wins, where p is the probability of heads. If he wins this gamble, then he *repeatedly* stakes his entire current fortune on heads, at the same odds as his first gamble. At the first subsequent tail he loses his fortune and leaves the casino, penniless. Let S_n be the casino's profit (losses count negative) after the nth toss. Show that S_n is a martingale. Let T be the number of tosses before the first appearance of HHH; show that T is a stopping time and hence find $\mathbf{E}(T)$.

Now adapt this scheme to calculate the mean time to the first appearance of the sequence HTH.

25. Suppose that the sequence $\{X_n\}$ of random variables satisfies

$$\mathbf{P}(|X_n - X_m| > \epsilon \text{ for infinitely many pairs } (m, n)) = 0$$

for all $\epsilon > 0$. Show that $X_n \xrightarrow{\text{a.s.}} X$ for some X.

26. **Stirling's formula.**

(a) Let $a(k, n) = n^k/(k-1)!$ for $1 \leq k \leq n+1$. Use the fact that $1 - x \leq e^{-x}$ if $x \geq 0$ to show that

$$\frac{a(n-k, n)}{a(n+1, n)} \leq \exp\left(-\frac{k^2}{2n}\right) \quad \text{if } k \geq 0.$$

(b) Let $X_1, X_2, \ldots$ be independent Poisson variables with parameter 1, and let $S_n = X_1 + \ldots + X_n$. Define the function $g: \mathbb{R} \to \mathbb{R}$ by

$$g(x) = \begin{cases} 0 & \text{if } x > 0 \\ -x & \text{if } 0 \geq x \geq -M \\ -M & \text{if } x < -M \end{cases}$$

where M is large and positive. Show that, for large n,

$$\mathbf{E}\left(g\left\{\frac{S_n - n}{\sqrt{n}}\right\}\right) = \frac{e^{-n}}{\sqrt{n}}\{a(n+1, n) - a(n-k, n)\}$$

where $k = \lfloor Mn^{1/2} \rfloor$. Now use the Central Limit Theorem, (7.10.3b), and (a) above, to deduce Stirling's formula:

$$\frac{n! e^n}{n^{n+1/2}\sqrt{(2\pi)}} \to 1 \quad \text{as } n \to \infty.$$

8 Random Processes

8.1 Introduction

Recall that a 'random process' X is a family $\{X_t : t \in T\}$ of random variables which map the sample space Ω into some set S. There are many possible choices for the index set T and the state space S; the characteristics of the process depend strongly upon these choices. For example, in Chapter 6 we studied discrete-time ($T = \{0, 1, 2, \ldots\}$) and continuous-time ($T = [0, \infty)$) Markov chains which took values in some countable set S. Other possible choices for T include $\mathbb{R}^n$ and $\mathbb{Z}^n$, whilst S might be an uncountable set, such as $\mathbb{R}$. The mathematical analysis of a random process varies greatly depending on whether S and T are countable or uncountable, just as discrete random variables are distinguishable from continuous variables. The main differences are indicated by those cases in which

(a) $T = \{0, 1, 2, \ldots\}$ or $T = [0, \infty)$,
(b) $S = \mathbb{Z}$ or $S = \mathbb{R}$.

There are two levels at which we can observe the evolution of a random process X.

(a) Each X_t is a function which maps Ω into S. For any fixed $\omega \in \Omega$, there is a corresponding collection $\{X_t(\omega) : t \in T\}$ of members of S; this is called the *realization* or *sample path* of X at ω. We can study properties of sample paths.

(b) The X's are not independent in general. If $S \subseteq \mathbb{R}$ and $\mathbf{t} = (t_1, t_2, \ldots, t_n)$ is a vector of members of T, then the vector $(X_{t_1}, X_{t_2}, \ldots, X_{t_n})$ has joint distribution function $F_{\mathbf{t}} : \mathbb{R}^n \to [0, 1]$ given by

$$F_{\mathbf{t}}(\mathbf{x}) = \mathbf{P}(X_{t_1} \leq x_1, \ldots, X_{t_n} \leq x_n).$$

The collection $\{F_{\mathbf{t}}\}$, as $\mathbf{t}$ ranges over all vectors of members of T of any finite length, is called the collection of *finite-dimensional distributions* (abbreviated to *fdds*) of X, or the *name* of X, and it contains all the information which is available about X from the distributions of its constituent variables X_t. We can study the distributional properties of X by using its fdds.

It is not generally the case that these two approaches yield the same information about the process in question, since knowledge of its fdds does not yield complete information about the properties of its sample paths. We shall see an example of this in the final section of this chapter.

We are not concerned here with the general theory of random processes, but prefer to study certain specific collections of processes which are characterized by one or more special properties. This is not a new approach for us. In Chapter 6 we devoted our attention to processes which satisfy the Markov property, whilst large parts of Chapter 7 were devoted to sequences $\{S_n\}$ which were either martingales or the partial sums of independent sequences. In this short chapter we introduce certain other types of process and their characteristic properties. These can be divided broadly under three headings, covering 'stationary processes and diffusions', 'renewal processes', and 'queues'; their detailed analysis is left for Chapters 9, 10, and 11 respectively.

We shall only be concerned with the cases when T is one of the sets $\mathbb{Z}$, $\{0, 1, 2, \dots\}$, $\mathbb{R}$, or $[0, \infty)$ here. If T is an uncountable subset of $\mathbb{R}$, representing continuous-time say, then we shall write $X(t)$ rather than X_t for ease of notation. Evaluation of $X(t)$ at some $\omega \in \Omega$ yields a point in S, which we shall denote by $X(t; \omega)$.

The final section contains a technical discussion about the construction of a process with specified fdds; it may be omitted without prejudicing your understanding of the rest of the book.

8.2 Stationary processes

Many important processes have the property that their finite-dimensional distributions are invariant under time shifts (or space shifts if T is a subset of some Euclidean space $\mathbb{R}^n$, say).

(1) **Definition.** The process $X = \{X(t) : t \geq 0\}$, taking values in $\mathbb{R}$, is called **strongly stationary** if the families

$$\{X(t_1), X(t_2), \dots, X(t_n)\} \quad \text{and} \quad \{X(t_1+h), X(t_2+h), \dots, X(t_n+h)\}$$

have the same joint distribution for all $t_1, t_2, \dots, t_n$ and $h > 0$.

Note that, if X is strongly stationary, then the distribution of $X(t)$ is the same for all times t.

We saw in Section 3.6 that the covariance of two random variables X and Y contains some information, albeit incomplete, about their joint distribution. With this in mind we formulate another stationarity property for processes with $\text{var}(X(t)) < \infty$; it is weaker than (1).

(2) **Definition.** $X = \{X(t) : t \geq 0\}$ is **weakly** (or **second-order** or **covariance**) **stationary** if

$$\mathbf{E}(X(t_1)) = \mathbf{E}(X(t_2))$$

and

$$\text{cov}(X(t_1), X(t_2)) = \text{cov}(X(t_1+h), X(t_2+h))$$

for all t_1, t_2, and $h > 0$.

Thus, X is weakly stationary if and only if it has constant means and the *autocovariance function*

(3) $$c(t, t+h) = \text{cov}\,(X(t), X(t+h))$$

satisfies

$$c(t, t+h) = c(0, h) \quad \text{for all } t, h \geq 0.$$

Definitions similar to (1) and (2) hold for processes with $T = \mathbb{R}$ and for discrete-time processes $X = \{X_n : n \geq 0\}$; the autocovariance function of a weakly stationary discrete-time process X is just a sequence $\{c(0, m) : m \geq 0\}$ of real numbers.

Weak stationarity interests us more than strong stationarity for two reasons. First, the condition of strong stationarity is often too restrictive for certain applications; secondly, many substantial and useful properties of stationary processes are derivable from weak stationarity alone. Thus, the assertion that X is *stationary* should be interpreted to mean that X is *weakly stationary*. Of course, there exist processes which are stationary but not strongly stationary (see Example (5)).

(4) **Example. Markov chains.** Let $X = \{X(t) : t \geq 0\}$ be an irreducible Markov chain taking values in some countable subset S of $\mathbb{R}$ and with a unique stationary distribution $\boldsymbol{\pi}$. Then (see (6.9.21))

$$\mathbf{P}(X(t) = j \mid X(0) = i) \to \pi_j \quad \text{as} \quad n \to \infty$$

for all $i, j \in S$. The fdds of X depend on the initial distribution $\boldsymbol{\mu}^{(0)}$ of $X(0)$, and it is not generally true that X is stationary (in either sense). Suppose, however, that $\boldsymbol{\mu}^{(0)} = \boldsymbol{\pi}$. Then the distribution $\boldsymbol{\mu}^{(t)}$ of $X(t)$ satisfies

$$\boldsymbol{\mu}^{(t)} = \boldsymbol{\pi}\boldsymbol{P}_t = \boldsymbol{\pi}$$

from (6.9.19), where $\{\boldsymbol{P}_t\}$ is the transition semigroup of the chain. Thus $X(t)$ has distribution $\boldsymbol{\pi}$ for all t. Furthermore, if $0 < s < s+t$ and $h > 0$, then the pairs

$$\{X(s), X(s+t)\} \quad \text{and} \quad \{X(s+h), X(s+t+h)\}$$

have the same joint distribution since

(a) $X(s)$ and $X(s+h)$ are identically distributed,
(b) the distribution of $X(s+h)$ (respectively $X(s+t+h)$) depends only on the distribution of $X(s)$ (respectively $X(s+t)$) and on the transition matrix $\boldsymbol{P}_h$.

A similar argument holds for collections of the X's which contain more than two elements, and we have shown that X is strongly stationary. ●

(5) **Example.** Let A and B be uncorrelated (but not necessarily independent) random variables, each of which has mean 0 and variance 1. Fix a number $\lambda \in [0, \pi]$ and define

(6) $$X_n = A\cos(\lambda n) + B\sin(\lambda n).$$

Then $\mathbf{E}X_n = 0$ for all n and $X = \{X_n\}$ has autocovariance function

$$\begin{aligned} c(n, n+m) &= \mathbf{E}(X_n X_{n+m}) \\ &= \mathbf{E}(\{A\cos(\lambda n) + B\sin(\lambda n)\}[A\cos\{\lambda(n+m)\} \\ &\qquad\qquad + B\sin\{\lambda(n+m)\}]) \\ &= \mathbf{E}(A^2\cos(\lambda n)\cos\{\lambda(n+m)\} + B^2\sin(\lambda n)\sin\{\lambda(n+m)\}) \\ &= \cos(\lambda m) \end{aligned}$$

Since $\mathbf{E}(AB) = 0$. Thus $c(n, n+m)$ depends on m alone and so X is stationary. In general X is not strongly stationary unless extra conditions are imposed on the joint distribution of A and B; to see this for the case $\lambda = \frac{1}{2}\pi$, simply calculate that

$$\{X_0, X_1, X_2, X_3, \ldots\} = \{A, B, -A, -B, \ldots\}$$

which is strongly stationary if and only if the pairs (A, B), $(B, -A)$, and $(-A, -B)$ have the same joint distributions. It can be shown that X is strongly stationary for any λ if A and B are $N(0, 1)$ variables. The reason for this lies in (4.5.9), where we saw that normal variables are independent whenever they are uncorrelated. ●

Two major results in the theory of stationary processes are the 'Spectral Theorem' and the 'Ergodic Theorem'; we close this section with a short discussion of these. First, recall the theory of Fourier analysis. Any function $f: \mathbb{R} \to \mathbb{R}$ which

(a) is periodic with period 2π (that is, $f(x+2\pi) = f(x)$ for all x),
(b) is continuous, and
(c) has bounded variation

has a unique Fourier expansion

$$f(x) = \tfrac{1}{2}a_0 + \sum_{n=1}^{\infty} \{a_n\cos(nx) + b_n\sin(nx)\}$$

which expresses f as the sum of varying proportions of regular oscillations. In some sense to be specified, a stationary process X is similar to a periodic function since its autocovariances are invariant under time shifts. The Spectral Theorem asserts that, subject to certain conditions, stationary processes can be decomposed in terms of regular underlying oscillations whose magnitudes are random variables; the set of frequencies of oscillations which contribute to this combination is called the 'spectrum' of the process. For example, the process X in (5) is specified precisely in these terms by (6). In spectral theory it is convenient to allow the processes in question to take values in the complex plane. In this case (6) can be rewritten as

(7) $$X_n = \operatorname{Re}(Y_n) \quad \text{where} \quad Y_n = Ce^{i\lambda n};$$

here C is a complex-valued random variable and $i=\sqrt{(-1)}$. $Y=\{Y_n\}$ is stationary also whenever

$$\mathbf{E}(C)=0 \quad \text{and} \quad \mathbf{E}(C\bar{C})<\infty$$

where $\bar{C}$ is the complex conjugate of C (but see (9.1.1)).

The Ergodic Theorem deals with the partial sums of a stationary sequence $X=\{X_n : n\geqslant 0\}$. Consider first the following two extreme examples of stationarity.

(8) **Example. Independent sequences.** Let $X=\{X_n : n\geqslant 0\}$ be a sequence of independent identically distributed variables with zero means and unit variances. Certainly X is stationary, and its autocovariance function is given by

$$c(n, n+m)=\mathbf{E}(X_n X_{n+m})=\begin{cases}1 & \text{if} \quad m=0\\ 0 & \text{if} \quad m\neq 0.\end{cases}$$

The Strong Law of Large Numbers asserts that

$$\frac{1}{n}\sum_{j=1}^{n} X_j \xrightarrow{\text{a.s.}} 0. \qquad \bullet$$

(9) **Example. Identical sequences.** Let Y be a random variable with zero mean and unit variance, and let $X=\{X_n : n\geqslant 0\}$ be the stationary sequence given by

$$X_n = Y \quad \text{for all } n.$$

X has autocovariance function

$$c(n, n+m)=\mathbf{E}(X_n X_{n+m})=1 \quad \text{for all } m.$$

It is clear that

$$\frac{1}{n}\sum_{j=1}^{n} X_j \xrightarrow{\text{a.s.}} Y$$

since each term in the sum is Y itself. $\bullet$

These two examples are, in some sense, extreme examples of stationarity since the first deals with independent variables and the second deals with identical variables. In both examples, however, the averages $n^{-1}\sum_{j=1}^{n} X_j$ converge as $n\to\infty$. In the first case the limit is constant, whilst in the second the limit is a random variable. This indicates a shared property of nice stationary processes, and we shall see that any stationary sequence $X=\{X_n : n\geqslant 0\}$ satisfies

$$\frac{1}{n}\sum_{j=1}^{n} X_j \xrightarrow{\text{a.s.}} Y$$

for some random variable Y. This result is called the Ergodic Theorem for stationary sequences. A similar result holds for continuous-time stationary processes.

The theory of stationary processes is important and useful in statistics. Many sequences $\{x_n : 0 \leq n \leq N\}$ of observations, indexed by the time at which they were taken, are suitably modelled by random processes, and statistical problems such as the estimation of unknown parameters and the prediction of the future values of the sequence are often studied in this context. Such sequences are called 'time series' and they include many examples which are well known to us already, such as the successive values of the Financial Times Share Index, or the frequencies of sunspots in successive years. Statisticians and politicians often seek to find some underlying structure in such sequences, and to this end they may study 'moving average' processes Y, which are smoothed versions of a stationary sequence X,

$$Y_n = \sum_{i=0}^{r} \alpha_i X_{n-i},$$

where $\alpha_0, \alpha_1, \ldots, \alpha_r$ are constants. Alternatively, they may try to fit a model to their observations, and may typically consider 'autoregressive schemes' Y, defined by

$$Y_n = \sum_{i=1}^{r} \alpha_i Y_{n-i} + Z_n$$

where $\{Z_n\}$ is a sequence of uncorrelated variables with zero means and constant finite variance.

An introduction to the theory of stationary processes is given in Chapter 9.

8.3 Renewal processes

We are often interested in the successive occurrences of events such as the emission of radioactive particles, the failures of light bulbs, or the incidences of earthquakes.

(1) **Example. Light bulb failures.** This is the archetype of renewal processes. A room is lit by a single light bulb. When this bulb fails it is replaced immediately by an apparently identical copy. Let X_i be the (random) lifetime of the ith bulb, and suppose that the first bulb is installed at time $t=0$. Then

$$T_n = X_1 + \ldots + X_n$$

is the time until the nth failure (where, by convention, we set $T_0 = 0$), and

$$N(t) = \max\{n : T_n \leq t\}$$

is the number of bulbs which have failed by time t. It is natural to assume that the X's are independent and identically distributed random variables. ●

(2) **Example. Markov chains.** Let $\{Y_n : n \geq 0\}$ be a Markov chain, and choose

some state i. We are interested in the time epochs at which the chain is in the state i. The times $0 < T_1 < T_2 < \dots$ of successive visits to i are given by

$$T_1 = \min\{n \geq 1 : Y_n = i\}$$

$$T_{m+1} = \min\{n > T_m : Y_n = i\} \quad \text{for} \quad m \geq 1;$$

they may be defective unless the chain is irreducible and persistent. Let $\{X_m : m \geq 1\}$ be given by

$$X_m = T_m - T_{m-1} \quad \text{for } m \geq 1,$$

where we set $T_0 = 0$ by convention. It is clear that the X's are independent, and that $X_2, X_3, \dots$ are identically distributed since each is the elapsed time between two successive visits to i. On the other hand, X_1 does *not* have this shared distribution in general, unless the chain began in the state $Y_0 = i$. The number of visits to i which have occurred by time t is given by

$$N(t) = \max\{n : T_n \leq t\}. \quad \bullet$$

Both these examples contain a continuous-time random process $N = \{N(t) : t \geq 0\}$, where $N(t)$ represents the number of occurrences of some event in the time interval $[0, t]$. Such a process N is called a 'renewal' or 'counting' process for obvious reasons; the Poisson process of Section 6.8 provides another example of a renewal process.

(3) **Definition.** A **renewal process** $N = \{N(t) : t \geq 0\}$ is a process for which

$$N(t) = \max\{n : T_n \leq t\}$$

where

$$T_0 = 0, \quad T_n = X_1 + \dots + X_n \quad \text{for} \quad n \geq 1,$$

and the X's are independent identically distributed non-negative random variables.

This definition describes N in terms of an underlying sequence $\{X_n\}$. In the absence of knowledge about this sequence we can construct it from N; just define

(4) $$T_n = \inf\{t : N(t) = n\}, \qquad X_n = T_n - T_{n-1}.$$

Note that the finite-dimensional distributions of a renewal process N are specified by the distribution of the X's. For example, if the X's are exponentially distributed then N is a Poisson process. We shall try to use the notation of (3) consistently in Chapter 10, in the sense that $\{N(t)\}$, $\{T_n\}$, and $\{X_n\}$ will always denote variables satisfying (4).

It is sometimes appropriate to allow X_1 to have a different distribution from the shared distribution of $X_2, X_3, \dots$; in this case N is called a *delayed* (or *modified*) renewal process. The process N in (2) is a delayed renewal process whatever the initial Y_0; if $Y_0=i$ then N is an ordinary renewal process.

Those readers who paid attention to (6.9.13) will be able to prove the following little result, which relates renewal processes to Markov chains.

(5) **Theorem.** *Poisson processes are the only renewal process which are Markov chains.*

If you like, think of renewal processes as a generalization of Poisson processes in which we have dropped the condition that inter-arrival times be exponentially distributed.

There are two principal areas of interest concerning renewal processes. First, suppose that we interrupt a renewal process N at some specified time s. By this time $N(s)$ occurrences have already taken place and we are waiting for the $(N(s)+1)$th. That is, s belongs to the random interval

$$I_s=[T_{N(s)},T_{N(s)+1}).$$

Here are three random variables of interest.

(6) The **excess** (or **residual**) **lifetime** of I_s: $E(s)=T_{N(s)+1}-s$.

(7) The **current lifetime** (or **age**) of I_s: $C(s)=s-T_{N(s)}$.

(8) The **total lifetime** of I_s: $D(s)=E(s)+C(s)$.

We shall be interested in the distributions of these random variables; they are illustrated in Figure 8.1.

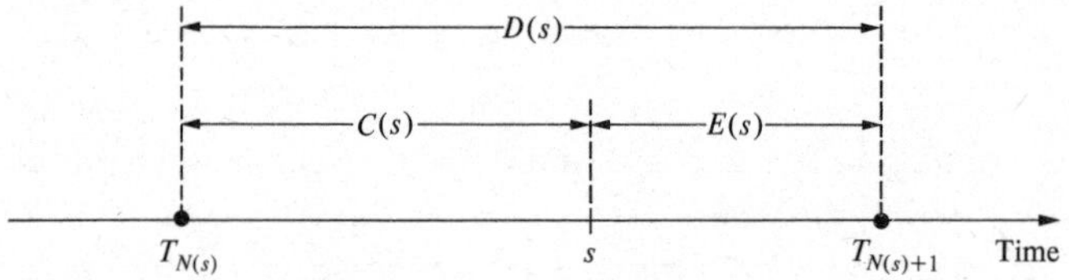

FIG. 8.1 Excess, current, and total lifetimes at time s.

It will come as no surprise to the reader to learn that the other principal topic concerns the asymptotic behaviour of a renewal process N as $t\to\infty$. Here we turn our attention to the *renewal function* $m(t)$ given by

(9) $$m(t)=\mathbf{E}(N(t)).$$

For a Poisson process N with intensity λ, (6.8.2) shows that

$$m(t)=\lambda t.$$

In general m is *not* a linear function of t; however, it is not too difficult to show that m is asymptotically linear, in that

$$\frac{1}{t}m(t)\to\frac{1}{\mu} \quad \text{as} \quad t\to\infty, \quad \text{where} \quad \mu=\mathbf{E}(X_1).$$

The 'Renewal Theorem' is a refinement of this result and asserts that

$$m(t+h)-m(t)\to\frac{h}{\mu} \quad \text{as} \quad t\to\infty$$

subject to a certain condition on X_1.

An introduction to the theory of renewal processes is given in Chapter 10.

8.4 Queues

The theory of queues is attractive and popular for two main reasons. First, queueing models are easily described and draw strongly from our intuitions about activities such as shopping or dialling the telephone operator. Secondly, even the solutions to the simplest models use much of the apparatus which we have developed in this book. Queues are, in general, non-Markovian, non-stationary, and quite difficult to study. Subject to certain conditions, however, their analysis uses ideas related to imbedded Markov chains, convergence of sequences of random variables, martingales, stationary processes, and renewal processes. We present a broad account of their theory in Chapter 11.

Customers arrive at a service point or counter at which a number of servers are stationed. An arriving customer may have to wait until one of these servers becomes available. Then he moves to the head of the queue and is served; he leaves the system on the completion of his service. We must specify a number of details about this queueing system before we are able to model it adequately. For example,

(a) in what manner do customers enter the system?
(b) in what order are they served?
(c) how long are their service times?

For the moment we shall suppose that the answers to these questions are as follows.

(a) The number $N(t)$ of customers who have entered by time t is a renewal process. That is, if T_n is the time of arrival of the nth customer (with the convention that $T_0=0$) then the *inter-arrival times*

$$X_n=T_n-T_{n-1}$$

are independent and identically distributed.

(b) Arriving customers join the end of a single line of people who receive attention on a 'first come, first served' basis. There are a certain number of servers. When a server becomes free, he turns his attention to the customer at the head of the waiting line. We shall usually suppose that the queue has a single server only.

(c) Service times are independent identically distributed random variables. That is, if S_n is the service time of the nth customer to arrive, then $\{S_n\}$ is a sequence of independent identically distributed non-negative random variables which do not depend on the arriving stream N of customers.

It requires only a little imagination to think of various other systems. Here are some examples.

(1) *Queues with baulking.* If the line of waiting customers is long then an arriving customer may, with a certain probability, decide not to join it.

(2) *Continental queueing.* In the absence of queue discipline, unoccupied servers pick a customer at random from the waiting mêlée.

(3) *Post Office queues.* The waiting customers divide into several lines, one for each server. The servers themselves enter and leave the system at random, causing the attendant customers to change lines as necessary.

(4) *Last come, first served.* No explanation is necessary.

(5) *Group service.* Waiting customers are served in batches. This is appropriate for lift queues and bus queues.

(6) *Student discipline.* Arriving customers jump the queue, joining it where a friend is standing.

Specific examples of some of these occur in the problems at the end of Chapter 11. Henceforth we shall consider only single-server queues described by (a), (b), and (c) above. Such queues are specified by the distribution of a typical inter-arrival time and the distribution of a typical service time; the method of analysis depends partly upon how much information we have about these quantities.

The state of the queue at time t is described by the number $Q(t)$ of waiting customers ($Q(t)$ *includes* customers who are in the process of being served at this time). It would be unfortunate if $Q(t) \to \infty$ as $t \to \infty$, and we devote special attention to finding out when this occurs. We call a queue *stable* if the distribution of $Q(t)$ settles down as $t \to \infty$ in some well-behaved way; otherwise we call it *unstable*. We choose not to define stability more precisely at this stage, wishing only to distinguish between such extremes as

(a) queues which either grow beyond all bounds or enjoy large wild fluctuations in length,

(b) queues whose lengths, say, converge in distribution, as $t \to \infty$, to some 'equilibrium distribution'.

Let S and X be a typical service time and a typical inter-arrival time, respectively; the ratio

$$\rho = \frac{\mathbf{E}(S)}{\mathbf{E}(X)}$$

is called the *traffic density*.

(7) **Theorem.** *Let Q be a queue with a single server and traffic density ρ.*

(a) *If $\rho < 1$ then Q is stable.*

(b) *If $\rho > 1$ then Q is unstable.*

(c) *If $\rho = 1$ and at least one of S and X has strictly positive variance then Q is unstable.*

The conclusions of this theorem are intuitively very attractive. Why?

A more satisfactory account of this theorem is given in Section 11.5.

8.5 What is in a name?

In our discussions of the properties of random variables, only scanty reference has been made to the underlying probability space $(\Omega, \mathcal{F}, \mathbf{P})$; indeed we have felt some satisfaction and relief from this omission. We have often made assumptions about hypothetical random variables without even checking that such variables exist. For example, we are in the habit of making statements such as 'let $X_1, X_2, \ldots$ be independent variables with common distribution function F', but we have made no effort to show that there exists some probability space on which such variables can be constructed. The foundations of such statements require examination. It is the purpose of this section to indicate that our assumptions are fully justified. Move immediately to the next chapter if you are prepared to take our word for this and require no further insight.

First, suppose that $(\Omega, \mathcal{F}, \mathbf{P})$ is a probability space and that $X = \{X_t : t \in T\}$ is some collection of random variables mapping Ω into $\mathbb{R}$. We saw in Section 8.1 that to any vector $\boldsymbol{t} = (t_1, t_2, \ldots, t_n)$ containing members of T and of finite length there corresponds a joint distribution function $F_{\boldsymbol{t}}$; the collection of such functions $F_{\boldsymbol{t}}$, as $\boldsymbol{t}$ ranges over all possible vectors of any length, is called the set of *fdds* (or *name*) of X. It is clear that these distribution functions satisfy the two *Kolmogorov consistency conditions:*

(1) $$F_{(t_1,\ldots,t_n,t_{n+1})}(x_1, \ldots, x_n, x_{n+1}) \to F_{(t_1,\ldots,t_n)}(x_1, \ldots, x_n) \quad \text{as} \quad x_{n+1} \to \infty;$$

(2) if π is a permutation of $(1, 2, \ldots, n)$ and $\pi\boldsymbol{y}$ denotes the vector

$$\pi\boldsymbol{y} = (y_{\pi(1)}, \ldots, y_{\pi(n)})$$

for any n-vector $\boldsymbol{y}$, then

$$F_{\pi\boldsymbol{t}}(\pi\boldsymbol{x}) = F_{\boldsymbol{t}}(\boldsymbol{x}) \quad \text{for all } \boldsymbol{x}, \boldsymbol{t}, \pi, \text{ and } n.$$

Condition (1) is just a higher-dimensional form of (2.1.6a), and condition (2) says that the operation of permuting the X's has the obvious corresponding effect on their joint distributions. So fdds always satisfy (1) and (2); furthermore (1) and (2) characterize fdds.

(3) **Theorem.** *Let T be any set, and suppose that to each vector $\boldsymbol{t} = (t_1, \ldots, t_n)$, containing members of T and of finite length, there corresponds a joint distribution function $F_{\boldsymbol{t}}$. If the collection $\{F_{\boldsymbol{t}}\}$ satisfies the Kolmogorov consistency conditions then there exists a probability space $(\Omega, \mathcal{F}, \mathbf{P})$ and a collection $X = \{X_t : t \in T\}$ of random variables on this space such that $\{F_{\boldsymbol{t}}\}$ is the set of fdds of X.*

The proof of this result lies in the heart of measure theory, as the following sketch indicates.

Sketch proof. Let $\Omega = \mathbb{R}^T$, the product of T copies of $\mathbb{R}$; the points of Ω are collections $\mathbf{y} = \{y_t : t \in T\}$ of real numbers. Let $\mathcal{F} = \mathcal{B}^T$, the product σ-field of T copies of the σ-field $\mathcal{B}$ of Borel subsets of $\mathbb{R}$. It is a fundamental result in measure theory that there exists a probability measure $\mathbf{P}$ on $(\Omega, \mathcal{F})$ such that

$$\mathbf{P}(\{\mathbf{y} \in \Omega : y_{t_1} \leq x_1, y_{t_2} \leq x_2, \ldots, y_{t_n} \leq x_n\}) = F_{\mathbf{t}}(\mathbf{x})$$

for all $\mathbf{t}$ and $\mathbf{x}$; this follows by an extension of the argument of Section 1.6. Then $(\Omega, \mathcal{F}, \mathbf{P})$ is the required space. Define $X_t : \Omega \to \mathbb{R}$ by

$$X_t(\mathbf{y}) = y_t$$

to obtain the required family $\{X_t\}$. ■

We have seen that fdds are characterized by the consistency conditions (1) and (2). But how much do they tell us about the sample paths of the corresponding process X? A simple example is enough to indicate some of the dangers here.

(4) **Example.** Let U be a random variable which is uniformly distributed on $[0, 1]$. Define two processes $X = \{X_t : 0 \leq t \leq 1\}$ and $Y = \{Y_t : 0 \leq t \leq 1\}$ by

$$X_t = 0 \quad \text{for all } t, \qquad Y_t = \begin{cases} 1 & \text{if } U = t \\ 0 & \text{otherwise.} \end{cases}$$

Clearly X and Y have the same fdds, since

$$\mathbf{P}(U = t) = 0 \quad \text{for all } t.$$

But X and Y are different processes. In particular

$$\mathbf{P}(X_t = 0 \quad \text{for all } t) = 1$$
$$\mathbf{P}(Y_t = 0 \quad \text{for all } t) = 0.$$

●

The resolution of this paradox lies deep in the theory of the sample paths of random processes, and we avoid it here, leaving you with some points to ponder about Example (4).

(a) Is $\{\omega \in \Omega : Y_t = 0 \text{ for all } t\}$ an event? After all, it is an *uncountable* intersection.

$$\bigcap_{0 \leq t \leq 1} \{Y_t = 0\},$$

and property (1.8.3) of σ-fields is not applicable.

(b) The difficulty of (a) would be avoided if all sample paths of Y were continuous, since then

$$\{Y_t = 0 \text{ for all } t\} = \bigcap_{\substack{\text{rational } t \\ 0 \leq t \leq 1}} \{Y_t = 0\}$$

which is a *countable* intersection. Such observations as this led J. L. Doob to a discussion of the continuity properties of sample paths and the theory of 'separable' processes (see Billingsley 1979, p. 467 for more details).

8.6 Problems

1. Let $\{Z_n\}$ be a sequence of uncorrelated real-valued variables with zero means and unit variances, and define the 'moving average'

$$Y_n = \sum_{i=0}^{r} \alpha_i Z_{n-i},$$

for constants $\alpha_0, \alpha_1, \ldots, \alpha_r$. Show that Y is stationary and find its autocovariance function.

2. Let $\{Z_n\}$ be as in Problem (1). Suppose that $\{Y_n\}$ is an 'autoregressive' stationary sequence in that it satisfies

$$Y_n = \alpha Y_{n-1} + Z_n, \qquad -\infty < n < \infty$$

for some real α satisfying $|\alpha| < 1$. Show that Y has autocovariance function

$$c(m) = \frac{\alpha^{|m|}}{(1-\alpha^2)}.$$

3. Let $\{X_n\}$ be independent identically distributed Bernoulli variables, each taking values 0 and 1 with probabilities $1-p$ and p respectively. Find the mass function of the renewal process $N(t)$ with inter-arrival times $\{X_n\}$. Find the distribution of the total lifetime at time t.

4. Customers arrive in a shop like a Poisson process with parameter λ. There are infinitely many servers, and each service time is exponentially distributed with parameter μ. Show that the number $Q(t)$ of waiting customers at time t constitutes a birth–death process. Find the stationary distribution.

5. In a Prague teashop (U Myšáka) customers queue at the entrance for a blank bill. In the shop there are separate counters for coffee, sweetcakes, pretzels, milk drinks, and ice cream, and queues form at each of these. At each service point the customers' bills are marked appropriately. There is a restricted number N of seats, and departing customers have to queue in order to pay their bills. If inter-arrival times and service times are exponentially distributed and the process is in equilibrium, find how much longer a greedy customer must wait if he insists on sitting down. Answers on a postcard to the authors, please.

9 Stationarity and diffusion

9.1 Introduction

Recall that a process X is *strongly stationary* whenever its *finite-dimensional distributions* are invariant under time shifts; it is (*weakly*) *stationary* whenever it has constant means and its *autocovariance function* is invariant under time shifts. Section 8.2 contains various examples of such processes. Next, we shall explore the consequences of stationarity and see how they include the Spectral Theorem and the Ergodic Theorem†.

A special class of random processes comprises those processes whose joint distributions are multivariate normal; these are called 'Gaussian processes'. Section 9.5 contains a brief account of some of the properties of such processes. In general, a Gaussian process is not stationary, but it is easy to characterize those which are.

It is a classical problem in probability theory to model certain erratic and apparently disordered motions such as the movement of a particle suspended in a fluid or the motion of a star in a stellar cluster. Such models are called 'diffusion processes', and they include the Wiener process, a Gaussian process whose increments enjoy a certain stationarity property. The chapter closes with a short description of this and other diffusion processes. We are only able to scratch the surface of their theory here; any more profound account would be considerably more complicated.

We shall be interested mostly in continuous-time processes $X = \{X(t): -\infty < t < \infty\}$, indexed by the whole real line, and will indicate any necessary variations for processes with other index sets, such as discrete-time processes. It is convenient to suppose that X takes values in the complex plane $\mathbb{C}$. This entails few extra complications and provides the natural setting for the theory. No conceptual difficulty is introduced by this generalization, since any complex-valued process X can be decomposed as

$$X = X_1 + iX_2$$

where X_1 and X_2 are real-valued processes. However, we must take care when discussing the fdds of X since the distribution function of a complex-valued random variable $C = R + iI$ is no longer a function of a single real variable. Thus, our definition of strong stationarity requires revision; we leave this to the reader. The concept of weak stationarity concerns covariances; we must note an important amendment to the real-valued

† The word 'ergodic' has several meanings, and probabilists tend to use it rather carelessly. We conform to this custom here.

theory in this context. As before, the expectation operator $\mathbf{E}$ is well defined by

$$\mathbf{E}(R+iI)=\mathbf{E}(R)+i\mathbf{E}(I).$$

(1) **Definition.** The **covariance** of two complex-valued random variables C_1 and C_2 is defined to be

$$\operatorname{cov}(C_1, C_2)=\mathbf{E}((C_1-\mathbf{E}C_1)\overline{(C_2-\mathbf{E}C_2)})$$

where $\bar{z}$ denotes the complex conjugate of z.

This reduces to the usual definition (3.6.7) when C_1 and C_2 are real. Note that the operator 'cov' is not symmetrical in its arguments, since

$$\operatorname{cov}(C_2, C_1)=\overline{\operatorname{cov}(C_1, C_2)}.$$

Variances are defined as follows.

(2) **Definition.** The **variance** of a complex-valued random variable C is defined to be

$$\operatorname{var}(C)=\operatorname{cov}(C, C).$$

Decompose C into its real and imaginary parts

$$C=R+iI$$

and apply (2) to obtain

$$\operatorname{var}(C)=\operatorname{var}(R)+\operatorname{var}(I).$$

We can write

$$\operatorname{var}(C)=\mathbf{E}(|C-\mathbf{E}C|^2).$$

We do not generally speak of complex random variables as being 'uncorrelated', preferring to use a word which emphasizes the geometrical properties of the complex plane.

(3) **Definition.** Complex-valued random variables C_1 and C_2 are called **orthogonal** if $\operatorname{cov}(C_1, C_2)=0$.

If $X=X_1+iX_2$ is a complex-valued process with real part X_1 and imaginary part X_2 then $\bar{X}$ denotes the complex conjugate process of X:

$$\bar{X}=X_1-iX_2.$$

9.2 Autocovariances and spectra

Let $X=\{X(t):-\infty<t<\infty\}$ be a (weakly) stationary process which takes values in $\mathbb{C}$. It has autocovariance function c given by

$$c(s, s+t)=\operatorname{cov}(X(s), X(s+t)) \quad \text{for} \quad s, t\in\mathbb{R}$$

where $c(s, s+t)$ depends on t alone. We think of c as a complex-valued function of the single variable t, and abbreviate it to

$$c(t) = c(s, s+t) \quad \text{for any } s.$$

Notice that the variance of $X(t)$ is constant for all t since

(1) $$\text{var}\,(X(t)) = \text{cov}\,(X(t), X(t)) = c(0).$$

We shall sometimes assume that the mean value $\mathbf{E}(X(t))$ of X equals zero; if this is not true, then define $X'(t) = X(t) - \mathbf{E}(X(t))$ to obtain another stationary process with zero means and the same autocovariance function c.

Autocovariances have the following properties.

(2) **Theorem.**

(a) $c(-t) = \overline{c(t)}$

(b) *c is a non-negative definite function, which is to say that*

$$\sum_{j,k} c(t_k - t_j) z_j \bar{z}_k \geq 0$$

for all real $t_1, \ldots, t_n$ and all complex $z_1, \ldots, z_n$.

Proof.

(a) $$\begin{aligned} c(-t) &= \text{cov}\,(X(t), X(0)) \\ &= \overline{\text{cov}\,(X(0), X(t))} = \overline{c(t)}. \end{aligned}$$

(b) This is like the proof of (5.7.3c). Just write

$$\begin{aligned} \sum_{j,k} c(t_k - t_j) z_j \bar{z}_k &= \sum_{j,k} \text{cov}\,(z_j X(t_j), z_k X(t_k)) \\ &= \text{cov}\,(Z, Z) \geq 0 \end{aligned}$$

where

$$Z = \sum_j z_j X(t_j).$$ ■

Of more interest than the autocovariance function is the 'autocorrelation function' (see (3.6.7)).

(3) **Definition.** The **autocorrelation function** of a weakly stationary process X with autocovariance function c is defined by

$$\rho(t) = \frac{\text{cov}\,(X(0), X(t))}{\{\text{var}\,(X(0))\,\text{var}\,(X(t))\}^{1/2}} = \frac{c(t)}{c(0)}$$

whenever $c(0) = \text{var}\,(X(t)) > 0$.

Of course, $\rho(t)$ is just the correlation between $X(s)$ and $X(s+t)$, for any s.

Following the discussion in Section 8.2, we seek to assess the incidence of certain regular oscillations within the random fluctuation of X. For a weakly stationary process this is often a matter of studying regular oscillations in its autocorrelation function.

(4) **Theorem. Spectral theorem for autocorrelation functions.** *The autocorrelation function $\rho(t)$ of a weakly stationary process X with strictly positive variance is the characteristic function of some distribution function F whenever $\rho(t)$ is continuous at $t=0$. That is to say,*

(5)
$$\rho(t)=\int_{-\infty}^{\infty} e^{it\lambda}\,dF(\lambda).$$

Proof. This follows immediately from the discussion after (5.7.3), and is a simple application of Bochner's Theorem. Following (2), we need only show that ρ is uniformly continuous. Without loss of generality we can suppose that $\mathbf{E}(X(t))=0$ for all t. Let c be the autocovariance function of X, and use the Cauchy–Schwarz inequality (3.6.9) to obtain

$$\begin{aligned}|c(t+h)-c(t)| &= |\mathbf{E}(X(0)\{X(t+h)-X(t)\})|\\ &\leq \mathbf{E}(|X(0)|\,|X(t+h)-X(t)|)\\ &\leq \{\mathbf{E}(|X(0)|^2)\mathbf{E}(|X(t+h)-X(t)|^2)\}^{1/2}\\ &= \{c(0)(2c(0)-c(h)-c(-h))\}^{1/2}\end{aligned}$$

whenever $c(h)$ is continuous at $h=0$. Thus ρ is uniformly continuous, and the result follows. ■

Think of equation (5) as follows. With any real λ we may associate a complex-valued oscillating function g_λ which has period $2\pi/|\lambda|$ and some non-negative amplitude f_λ, say:

$$g_\lambda(t)=f_\lambda \exp(it\lambda);$$

in the less general real-valued theory we might consider oscillations such as

$$g'_\lambda(t)=f_\lambda \cos(t\lambda)$$

(see (8.2.6) and (8.2.7)). With any collection $\lambda_1, \lambda_2, \ldots$ of frequencies we can associate a mixture

(6)
$$g_{\boldsymbol{\lambda}}(t)=\sum_j f_j \exp(it\lambda_j)$$

of pure oscillations, where the f's indicate the relative strengths of the various components. As the number of component frequencies in (6) grows, the summation may approach an integral

(7)
$$g(t)=\int_{-\infty}^{\infty} f(\lambda)\exp(it\lambda)\,d\lambda$$

where f is some non-negative function which assigns weights to the λ's. The progression from (6) to (7) is akin to the construction of the abstract integral (see Section 5.6). We have seen many expressions which are similar to (7), but in which f is the density function of some continuous random variable. Just as continuous variables are only a special subclass of the larger family of all random variables, so (7) is not the most general limiting form for (6); the general form is

(8) $$g(t) = \int_{-\infty}^{\infty} \exp(it\lambda)\, dF(\lambda)$$

where F is a function which maps $\mathbb{R}$ into $[0, \infty)$ and which is right-continuous, non-decreasing, and such that $F(-\infty) = 0$; we omit the details of this, which are very much the same as in Part B of Section 5.6. It is easy to see that F is a distribution function if and only if $g(0) = 1$. Theorem (4) asserts that ρ enjoys a decomposition in the form of (8), as a mixture of pure oscillations.

There is an alternative view of (5) which differs slightly from this. If Λ is a random variable with distribution function F, then

$$g_\Lambda(t) = \exp(it\Lambda)$$

is a pure oscillation with a random frequency. Theorem (4) asserts that ρ is the mean value of this random oscillation for some special distribution F. Of course, by the uniqueness theorem (5.9.3) there is a unique distribution function F such that (5) holds.

(9) **Definition.** If the autocorrelation function ρ satisfies

$$\rho(t) = \int_{-\infty}^{\infty} e^{it\lambda}\, dF(\lambda)$$

then F is called the **spectral distribution function** of the process. The **spectral density function** is the density function which corresponds to the distribution function F whenever this density exists.

For a given autocorrelation function ρ, we can find the spectral distribution function by the inversion techniques of Section 5.9.

In general, there may be certain frequency bands which make no contribution to (5). For example, if the spectral distribution function F satisfies

$$F(\lambda) = 0 \quad \text{for all } \lambda \leq 0,$$

then only positive frequencies make non-trivial contributions. If the frequency band $(\lambda - \epsilon, \lambda + \epsilon)$ makes a non-trivial contribution to (5) for all $\epsilon > 0$, then we say that λ belongs to the 'spectrum' of the process.

(10) **Definition.** The **spectrum** of X is the set of all real numbers λ with the property that

$$F(\lambda+\epsilon)-F(\lambda-\epsilon)>0 \quad \text{for all } \epsilon>0$$

where F is the spectral distribution function.

If X is a discrete-time process then the above account is inadequate, since the autocorrelation function ρ now maps $\mathbb{Z}$ into $\mathbb{C}$ and cannot be a characteristic function unless its domain is extended. Theorem (4) remains broadly true, but asserts now that ρ has a representation

(11) $$\rho(n)=\int_{-\infty}^{\infty} e^{in\lambda}\,\mathrm{d}F(\lambda)$$

for some distribution function F and all integral n. No condition of continuity is appropriate here. This representation (11) is not unique because the integrand

$$g_\lambda(n)=e^{in\lambda}$$

is periodic in λ:

$$g_{\lambda+2\pi}(n)=g_\lambda(n) \quad \text{for all } n.$$

In this case it is customary to rewrite (11) as

$$\rho(n)=\sum_{k=-\infty}^{\infty}\int_{((2k-1)\pi,(2k+1)\pi]} e^{in\lambda}\,\mathrm{d}F(\lambda),$$

yielding the usual statement of the Spectral Theorem for discrete-time processes

$$\rho(n)=\int_{(-\pi,\pi]} e^{in\lambda}\,\mathrm{d}\tilde{F}(\lambda)$$

for some appropriate distribution function $\tilde{F}$ obtained from F and satisfying

$$\tilde{F}(-\pi)=0, \qquad \tilde{F}(\pi)=1.$$

How may we find the spectral distribution which corresponds to a particular ρ? We may no longer use the Inversion Theorem of Section 5.9 since ρ is defined on the integers only. Here, we consider only the case when $\sum_n |\rho(n)|<\infty$, and give no proof.

(12) **Theorem.** *If* $\sum_{n=-\infty}^{\infty} |\rho(n)|<\infty$ *then there exists a spectral density function* f *given by*

$$f(\lambda)=\frac{1}{2\pi}\sum_{n=-\infty}^{\infty} e^{-in\lambda}\rho(n), \qquad -\pi\leq\lambda\leq\pi.$$

Sketch proof. By the spectral theorem $\rho(n)$ is proportional to the nth Fourier coefficient of f. The result of (12) is merely the statement that the Fourier series converges to the correct limit. ■

If the stationary process X is real-valued, then so is its autocorrelation function ρ. In this case the spectral distribution of ρ is symmetric.

(13) **Example. Independent sequences.** Let $X=\{X_n : n\geq 0\}$ be a sequence of independent variables with zero means and unit variances. In (8.2.8) we found that the autocorrelation function is given by

$$\rho(n)=\begin{cases}1 & \text{if} \quad n=0\\ 0 & \text{if} \quad n\neq 0.\end{cases}$$

To find the spectral density function, either use (12) or recognise that

$$\rho(n)=\frac{1}{2\pi}\int_{-\pi}^{\pi} e^{in\lambda}\, d\lambda$$

to see that the spectral density function is the uniform density function on $[-\pi, \pi]$. The spectrum of X is $[-\pi, \pi]$. ●

(14) **Example. Identical sequences.** Let Y be a random variable with zero mean and unit variance, and let $X=\{X_n : n\geq 0\}$ be the stationary sequence given by

$$X_n = Y \quad \text{for all } Y.$$

In (8.2.9) we calculated the autocorrelation function as

$$\rho(n)=1 \quad \text{for all } n$$

and we recognise this as the characteristic function of a distribution which is concentrated at 0. The spectrum of X is the set $\{0\}$. ●

(15) **Example. Two-state Markov chains.** Let $X=\{X(t): t\geq 0\}$ be a Markov chain with state space $S=\{1, 2\}$. Suppose, as in Example (6.9.15), that the times spent in states 1 and 2 are exponentially distributed with parameters α and β respectively where $\alpha\beta>0$. That is to say, X has generator $\mathbf{G}$ given by

$$\mathbf{G}=\begin{pmatrix}-\alpha & \alpha\\ \beta & -\beta\end{pmatrix}.$$

In our solution to (6.9.15) we wrote down the Kolmogorov forward equations and found that the transition probabilities

$$p_{ij}(t)=\mathbf{P}(X(t)=j \mid X(0)=i), \qquad 1\leq i, j\leq 2$$

are given by

$$p_{11}(t) = 1 - p_{12}(t) = \frac{\beta}{\alpha+\beta} + \frac{\alpha}{\alpha+\beta} e^{-t(\alpha+\beta)}$$

$$p_{22}(t) = 1 - p_{21}(t) = \frac{\alpha}{\alpha+\beta} + \frac{\beta}{\alpha+\beta} e^{-t(\alpha+\beta)}$$

in agreement with (6.10.12). Let $t \to \infty$ to find that the chain has a stationary distribution $\boldsymbol{\pi}$ given by

$$\pi_1 = \frac{\beta}{\alpha+\beta}, \qquad \pi_2 = \frac{\alpha}{\alpha+\beta}.$$

Suppose now that $X(0)$ has distribution $\boldsymbol{\pi}$. As in (8.2.4), X is a strongly stationary process. We are going to find its spectral representation. First, find the autocovariance function. If $t \geq 0$, then a short calculation yields

$$\begin{aligned} \mathbf{E}(X(0)X(t)) &= \sum_i i\mathbf{E}(X(t) \mid X(0) = i)\pi_i \\ &= \sum_{i,j} ij p_{ij}(t)\pi_i \\ &= \frac{(2\alpha+\beta)^2}{(\alpha+\beta)^2} + \frac{\alpha\beta}{(\alpha+\beta)^2} e^{-t(\alpha+\beta)} \end{aligned}$$

and so the autocovariance function c is given by

$$\begin{aligned} c(t) &= \mathbf{E}(X(0)X(t)) - \mathbf{E}(X(0))\mathbf{E}(X(t)) \\ &= \frac{\alpha\beta}{(\alpha+\beta)^2} e^{-t(\alpha+\beta)} \quad \text{if} \quad t \geq 0. \end{aligned}$$

Hence

$$c(0) = \frac{\alpha\beta}{(\alpha+\beta)^2}$$

and the autocorrelation function ρ is given by

$$\rho(t) = \frac{c(t)}{c(0)} = e^{-t(\alpha+\beta)} \quad \text{if} \quad t \geq 0.$$

X is real and so ρ is symmetric; thus

(16) $$\rho(t) = e^{-|t|(\alpha+\beta)}.$$

The Spectral Theorem asserts that ρ is the characteristic function of some distribution. We may use the inversion theorem (5.9.2) to find this distribution; however, this method is long and complicated and we prefer to rely on our experience. Compare (16) with the result of (5.8.4), where we saw that if Y is a random variable with the Cauchy density function

$$f(\lambda) = \frac{1}{\pi(1+\lambda^2)}, \qquad -\infty < \lambda < \infty$$

then Y has characteristic function

$$\phi(t)=e^{-|t|}.$$

Thus

$$\rho(t)=\phi(t(\alpha+\beta))$$

and ρ is the characteristic function of $(\alpha+\beta)Y$ (see (5.7.6)). By (4.7.2) the density function of $\Lambda=(\alpha+\beta)Y$ is

$$f_\Lambda(\lambda)=\frac{1}{\alpha+\beta}f_Y\left(\frac{\lambda}{\alpha+\beta}\right)$$

$$=\frac{\alpha+\beta}{\pi((\alpha+\beta)^2+\lambda^2)}, \qquad -\infty<\lambda<\infty$$

and this is the spectral density function of X. The spectrum of X is the whole real line $\mathbb{R}$. ●

(17) **Example. Autoregressive scheme.** Let $\{Z_n\}$ be uncorrelated random variables with zero means and unit variances, and define

$$X_n=\alpha X_{n-1}+Z_n, \qquad -\infty<n<\infty$$

where α is real and satisfies $|\alpha|<1$. We saw in Problem (8.6.2) that X has autocorrelation function

$$\rho(n)=\alpha^{|n|}, \qquad -\infty<n<\infty.$$

Use (12) to find the spectral density function f_X of X:

$$f_X(\lambda)=\frac{1}{2\pi}\sum_{n=-\infty}^{\infty}e^{-in\lambda}\alpha^{|n|}$$

$$=\frac{1-\alpha^2}{2\pi\,|1-\alpha e^{i\lambda}|^2}=\frac{1-\alpha^2}{2\pi(1-2\alpha\cos\lambda+\alpha^2)}, \qquad -\pi\leqslant\lambda\leqslant\pi.$$

More generally, suppose that the process Y satisfies

$$Y_n=\sum_{j=1}^{r}\alpha_j Y_{n-j}+Z_n, \qquad -\infty<n<\infty$$

where $\alpha_1,\ldots,\alpha_r$ are constants. The same techniques can be applied, though with some difficulty, to find that Y is stationary if the complex roots $\theta_1,\ldots,\theta_r$ of the polynomial

$$A(z)=z^r-\alpha_1 z^{r-1}-\ldots-\alpha_r=0$$

satisfy $|\theta_j|<1$. If this holds then the spectral density function f_Y of Y is given by

$$f_Y(\lambda)=\frac{1}{2\pi\sigma^2\,|A(e^{-i\lambda})|^2}, \qquad -\pi\leqslant\lambda\leqslant\pi$$

where $\sigma^2=\operatorname{var}(Y_0)$. ●

9.3 The spectral representation

Let $X=\{X(t):-\infty<t<\infty\}$ be a stationary process which takes values in $\mathbb{C}$, as before. In the last section we saw that the autocorrelation function ρ enjoys the representation

(1) $$\rho(t)=\int_{-\infty}^{\infty} e^{it\lambda}\,dF(\lambda)$$

as the characteristic function of some distribution function F whenever ρ is continuous at $t=0$. This spectral representation is very useful in many contexts, including for example statistical analyses of sequences of data, but it is not the full story. Equation (1) is an analytical result with little probabilistic content; of more interest to us is the process X, and (1) leads us to ask whether X itself enjoys a similar representation. The answer to this is in the affirmative, but the statement of the result is complicated and draws deeply from abstract theory. We are only able to sketch it here.

Without loss of generality we can suppose that $X(t)$ has mean 0 for all t. With each such stationary process X we can associate another process S called the 'spectral process' of X, in much the same way as the spectral distribution function F is associated with ρ.

(2) **Spectral Theorem.** *If X is a stationary process with zero means and continuous autocorrelation function, then there exists a complex-valued process $S=\{S(\lambda):-\infty<\lambda<\infty\}$ such that*

(3) $$X(t)=\int_{-\infty}^{\infty} e^{it\lambda}\,dS(\lambda).$$

S is called the ***spectral process*** *of X.*

We are not equipped to explain the integral (3) in any detail without digressing into alien territory. Let us think of it as follows. Equation (3) is a statement about random variables and asserts that each outcome $X(t;\omega)$ has an integral representation in terms of the sample paths of S. You may think of the integral in (3) as the limit of sums of the form

(4) $$\sum_{j=1}^{n} \exp(it\lambda_j)\{S(\lambda_j;\omega)-S(\lambda_{j-1};\omega)\}$$

for suitably chosen $\lambda_0<\lambda_1<\ldots<\lambda_n$ as $n\to\infty$. These sums are random variables; any rigorous treatment will include details of the modes of convergence of such limits.

The spectral representation (2) provides an alternative way of studying stationary processes. Consideration of X as a time-dependent process yields results which relate to the so-called 'time domain'; consideration of S yields results in the 'frequency domain'.

The spectral process S of X is not defined uniquely by (3), in that (3) does not specify all the continuity properties of S. We can and shall assume that S has the following important and useful properties, which are included here for reference only; move directly to the next section. We offer no justification for them.

(5) $\mathbf{E}(S(\lambda))=0$ for all λ.

(6) S has *orthogonal increments*, which is to say that

$$\mathbf{E}((S(\mu)-S(\lambda))(\bar{S}(\beta)-\bar{S}(\alpha)))=0$$

whenever $\lambda\leqslant\mu<\alpha\leqslant\beta$.

(7) S is a right-continuous process with left limits, which is to say that

$$\lim_{y\downarrow x} S(y;\omega)=S(x;\omega) \quad \text{for all } x \text{ and } \omega$$

$$\lim_{y\uparrow x} S(y;\omega) \quad \text{exists for all } x \text{ and } \omega.$$

(Why do French mathematicians call such a process *cadlag*?) Furthermore, S is *right-continuous in mean square*, which is to say that

$$\mathbf{E}(|S(y)-S(x)|^2)\to 0 \quad \text{as} \quad y\downarrow x \quad \text{for all } x.$$

The similarity between the spectral representations of X and ρ leads us to investigate the link between the spectral process S and the spectral distribution function F. We state the result here as a lemma, although the correct place for it is with the list of properties (5), (6), and (7).

(8) **Lemma.** *Whenever* $\lambda\leqslant\mu$

$$\mathbf{E}(|S(\mu)-S(\lambda)|^2)=c(0)\{F(\mu)-F(\lambda)\}$$

where $c(0)=\text{var}\,(X(0))$.

Partial proof. It is easy to see that

(9) $$\mathbf{E}(|S(\mu)-S(\lambda)|^2)=H(\mu)-H(\lambda)$$

whenever $0\leqslant\lambda\leqslant\mu$, where

$$H(\lambda)=\mathbf{E}(|S(\lambda)-S(0)|^2);$$

just expand (9) and use (6). H is monotone non-decreasing and right-continuous by (7), but H is not generally a distribution function. However, it can be shown that

$$H(\lambda)=c(0)(F(\lambda)-F(0)) \quad \text{when} \quad \lambda\geqslant 0.$$ ■

The Fourier inversion theorem enables us to find the distribution which corresponds to a given characteristic function; it also provides a way of finding the spectral process S from a knowledge of X. The relevant formula is very similar to the result of (5.9.2).

The discrete-time process $X=\{X_n:-\infty<n<\infty\}$ also has a spectral representation. The only significant difference in this case is that the domain of the spectral process is usually taken to be $(-\pi, \pi]$, in the same way as the spectral distribution of the autocorrelation function of X can be assumed to be concentrated on this interval. Thus (3) becomes

$$X_n = \int_{(-\pi,\pi]} e^{in\lambda}\, dS(\lambda)$$

if X has zero means.

9.4 The ergodic theorem

The Law of Large Numbers asserts that

(1) $$\frac{1}{n}\sum_{j=1}^{n} X_j \to \mu$$

whenever $\{X_j\}$ is an independent identically distributed sequence with mean μ; the convergence takes place almost surely. This section is devoted to a complete generalization of the Law of Large Numbers, the assumption that the X's be independent being replaced by the assumption that they form a stationary process. This generalization is called the 'Ergodic Theorem' and it has more than one form depending on the type of stationarity—weak or strong—and the required mode of convergence; recall the various corresponding forms of the Law of Large Numbers.

It is usual to state the ergodic theorem for discrete-time processes, and we conform to this habit here. Similar results hold for continuous-time processes, sums like $\sum_1^n X_j$ being replaced by integrals like $\int_0^n X(t)\,dt$.

Here is the usual form of the ergodic theorem.

(2) **Theorem. Ergodic theorem for strongly stationary processes.** *Let $X=\{X_n:n\geq 1\}$ be a strongly stationary process such that $\mathbf{E}|X_1|<\infty$. Then there exists a random variable Y with the same mean as the X's such that*

$$\frac{1}{n}\sum_{j=1}^{n} X_j \to Y \quad \textit{a.s. and in mean.}$$

The proof of this is difficult, as befits a complete generalization of the Strong Law of Large Numbers (see Problem (9.10.9)); we omit this. The following result is much easier to prove.

(3) **Theorem. Ergodic theorem for weakly stationary processes.** *If $X=\{X_n:n\geq 1\}$ is a (weakly) stationary process then there exists a random variable Y such that $\mathbf{E}Y=\mathbf{E}X_1$ and*

$$\frac{1}{n}\sum_{j=1}^{n} X_j \xrightarrow{\text{m.s.}} Y.$$

We give two proofs of this. Proof A is conceptually easy but has some technical difficulties; we show that $n^{-1}\sum_1^n X_j$ is a mean square Cauchy convergent sequence (see Problem (7.10.11)). Proof B uses the spectral representation of X; we sketch this here and show that it yields an explicit form for the limit Y as the contribution made towards X by 'oscillations of zero frequency'.

Proof A. Recall from (7.10.11) that a sequence $\{Y_n\}$ converges in mean square to some limit if and only if $\{Y_n\}$ is *mean square Cauchy convergent*, which is to say that

(4) $$\mathbf{E}(|Y_n - Y_m|^2) \to 0 \quad \text{as} \quad m, n \to \infty.$$

A similar result holds for complex-valued sequences. We shall show that the sequence $\{n^{-1}\sum_1^n X_j\}$ satisfies (4) whenever X is stationary. This is easy in concept, since it involves expressions involving the autocovariance function of X alone; the proof of the mean square version of the Law of Large Numbers was easy for the same reason. Unfortunately, the verification of (4) is not a trivial calculation.

For any complex-valued random variable Z, define

$$\|Z\| = (\mathbf{E}(|Z|^2))^{1/2};$$

the function $\|\cdot\|$ is a norm (see Section 7.2). We wish to show that

(5) $$\|\langle X\rangle_n - \langle X\rangle_m\| \to 0 \quad \text{as} \quad n, m \to \infty$$

where

$$\langle X\rangle_n = \frac{1}{n}\sum_{j=1}^{n} X_j;$$

physicists often use the notation $\langle\cdot\rangle$ to denote expectation. Set

$$\mu_N = \inf_{\boldsymbol{\lambda}} \|\lambda_1 X_1 + \lambda_2 X_2 + \ldots + \lambda_N X_N\|$$

where the infimum is calculated over all vectors $\boldsymbol{\lambda} = (\lambda_1, \ldots, \lambda_N)$ with $\lambda_i \geq 0$ and $\sum_1^N \lambda_i = 1$. Clearly $\mu_N \geq \mu_{N+1}$ and so

$$\mu = \lim_{N\to\infty} \mu_N = \inf_N \mu_N$$

exists. If $m < n$ then

$$\|\langle X\rangle_n + \langle X\rangle_m\| = 2\left\|\sum_1^n \lambda_j X_j\right\|$$

where

$$\lambda_j = \begin{cases} \dfrac{1}{2}\left(\dfrac{1}{m} + \dfrac{1}{n}\right) & \text{if} \quad 1 \leq j \leq m \\ \dfrac{1}{2n} & \text{if} \quad m < j \leq n, \end{cases}$$

and so

$$\|\langle X\rangle_n + \langle X\rangle_m\| \geq 2\mu.$$

It is not difficult to deduce (see Problem (9.10.5) for the first line here) that

$$\begin{aligned}\|\langle X\rangle_n - \langle X\rangle_m\|^2 &= 2\,\|\langle X\rangle_n\|^2 + 2\,\|\langle X\rangle_m\|^2 - \|\langle X\rangle_n + \langle X\rangle_m\|^2\\ &\leq 2\,\|\langle X\rangle_n\|^2 + 2\,\|\langle X\rangle_m\|^2 - 4\mu^2\\ &= 2\,|\,\|\langle X\rangle_n\|^2 - \mu^2| + 2\,|\,\|\langle X\rangle_m\|^2 - \mu^2|\end{aligned}$$

and (5) follows as soon as we can show that

(6) $$\|\langle X\rangle_n\| \to \mu \quad \text{as} \quad n \to \infty.$$

The remaining part of the proof is devoted to demonstrating (6).

Choose any $\epsilon > 0$ and pick N and $\boldsymbol{\lambda}$ such that

$$\|\lambda_1 X_1 + \ldots + \lambda_N X_N\| \leq \mu + \epsilon$$

where $\lambda_i \geq 0$ and $\sum_1^N \lambda_i = 1$. Define the moving average

$$Y_k = \lambda_1 X_k + \lambda_2 X_{k+1} + \ldots + \lambda_N X_{k+N-1};$$

it is not difficult to see that $Y = \{Y_k\}$ is a stationary process (see Problem (9.10.6)). We shall show that

(7) $$\|\langle Y\rangle_n - \langle X\rangle_n\| \to 0 \quad \text{as} \quad n \to \infty$$

where

$$\langle Y\rangle_n = \frac{1}{n}\sum_{j=1}^{n} Y_j.$$

Note first that, by the triangle inequality (7.1.5),

(8) $$\|\langle Y\rangle_n\| \leq \|Y_1\| \leq \mu + \epsilon \quad \text{for all } n$$

since $\|Y_n\| = \|Y_1\|$ for all n. Now

$$\langle Y\rangle_n = \lambda_1\langle X\rangle_{1,n} + \lambda_2\langle X\rangle_{2,n} + \ldots + \lambda_N\langle X\rangle_{N,n}$$

where

$$\langle X\rangle_{k,n} = \frac{1}{n}\sum_{j=k}^{k+n-1} X_j;$$

now use the facts that $\langle X\rangle_{1,n} = \langle X\rangle_n$,

$$1 - \lambda_1 = \lambda_2 + \ldots + \lambda_N,$$

and the triangle inequality to deduce that

$$\|\langle Y\rangle_n - \langle X\rangle_n\| \leq \sum_{j=2}^{N} \lambda_j\,\|\langle X\rangle_{j,n} - \langle X\rangle_{1,n}\|.$$

But, by the triangle inequality again,

$$\begin{aligned}\|\langle X\rangle_{j,n}-\langle X\rangle_{1,n}\| &= \frac{1}{n}\|(X_j+\ldots+X_{j+n-1})-(X_1+\ldots+X_n)\| \\ &= \frac{1}{n}\|(X_{n+1}+\ldots+X_{j+n-1})-(X_1+\ldots+X_{j-1})\| \\ &\leqslant \frac{2j}{n}\|X_1\|\end{aligned}$$

since $\|X_n\|=\|X_1\|$ for all n, and so

$$\|\langle Y\rangle_n-\langle X\rangle_n\| \leqslant \sum_{j=2}^{N}\lambda_j\frac{2j}{n}\|X_1\| \leqslant \frac{2N}{n}\|X_1\|;$$

let $n\to\infty$ to deduce that (7) holds. Use (8) to obtain

$$\begin{aligned}\mu \leqslant \|\langle X\rangle_n\| &\leqslant \|\langle X\rangle_n-\langle Y\rangle_n\|+\|\langle Y\rangle_n\| \\ &\leqslant \|\langle X\rangle_n-\langle Y\rangle_n\|+\mu+\epsilon \\ &\to \mu+\epsilon \quad \text{as} \quad n\to\infty.\end{aligned}$$

But ϵ was arbitrary; let $\epsilon\downarrow 0$ to see that (6) holds. See (12) for a proof that $\mathbf{E}Y=\mathbf{E}X_1$, completing the proof of (3). ■

Sketch Proof B. Suppose that $\mathbf{E}(X_n)=0$ for all n. X has a spectral representation

$$X_n = \int_{(-\pi,\pi]} e^{in\lambda}\,\mathrm{d}S(\lambda).$$

Now,

$$\text{(9)}\qquad \begin{aligned}\langle X\rangle_n = \frac{1}{n}\sum_{j=1}^{n}X_j &= \int_{(-\pi,\pi]}\frac{1}{n}\sum_{j=1}^{n}e^{ij\lambda}\,\mathrm{d}S(\lambda) \\ &= \int_{(-\pi,\pi]} g_n(\lambda)\,\mathrm{d}S(\lambda)\end{aligned}$$

where

$$\text{(10)}\qquad g_n(\lambda)=\begin{cases}1 & \text{if}\quad \lambda=0 \\ \dfrac{e^{i\lambda}}{n}\dfrac{1-e^{in\lambda}}{1-e^{i\lambda}} & \text{if}\quad \lambda\neq 0.\end{cases}$$

Now,

$$|g_n(\lambda)|\leqslant 1 \quad \text{for all } n \text{ and } \lambda,$$

and, as $n \to \infty$,

(11) $$g_n(\lambda) \to g(\lambda) = \begin{cases} 1 & \text{if} \quad \lambda = 0 \\ 0 & \text{if} \quad \lambda \neq 0. \end{cases}$$

It can be shown that

$$\int_{(-\pi,\pi]} g_n(\lambda)\, dS(\lambda) \xrightarrow{\text{m.s.}} \int_{(-\pi,\pi]} g(\lambda)\, dS(\lambda) \quad \text{as} \quad n \to \infty,$$

implying that

$$\langle X \rangle_n \xrightarrow{\text{m.s.}} \int_{(-\pi,\pi]} g(\lambda)\, dS(\lambda) = S(0) - S(0-),$$

by the right-continuity of S, where

$$S(0-) = \lim_{y \uparrow 0} S(y).$$

This shows that $\langle X \rangle_n$ converges in mean square to the random magnitude of the discontinuity of $S(\lambda)$ at $\lambda = 0$ (this quantity may be zero); in other words, $\langle X \rangle_n$ converges to the 'zero frequency' or 'infinite wavelength' contribution of the spectrum of X. This conclusion is natural and memorable, since the average of any oscillation with non-zero frequency is zero. ■

This second proof is particularly useful in that it provides an explicit representation for the limit in terms of the spectral process of X. It is easy to calculate the first two moments of this limit.

(12) **Lemma.** *If X is a stationary process with zero means and autocovariance function c then the limit variable*

$$Y = \lim_{n\to\infty} \frac{1}{n} \sum_{j=1}^{n} X_j$$

satisfies

$$\mathbf{E}(Y) = 0, \qquad \mathbf{E}(|Y|^2) = \lim_{n\to\infty} \frac{1}{n} \sum_{j=1}^{n} c(j).$$

A similar result holds for processes with non-zero means.

Proof. $\langle X \rangle_n \xrightarrow{\text{m.s.}} Y$, and so $\langle X \rangle_n \xrightarrow{1} Y$ by (7.2.3). The result of Problem (7.10.1) implies that as $n \to \infty$,

$$\mathbf{E}(\langle X \rangle_n) \to \mathbf{E}(Y);$$

but $\mathbf{E}(\langle X \rangle_n) = \mathbf{E}(X_1) = 0$ for all n.

To prove the second part, either use (7.10.1) again and expand $\mathbf{E}(\langle X \rangle_n^2)$ in terms of c, or use the method of Proof B of (3). We use the latter method. The autocovariance function c satisfies

$$\frac{1}{n}\sum_{j=1}^{n} c(j) = c(0) \int_{(-\pi,\pi]} g_n(\lambda)\,\mathrm{d}F(\lambda)$$

$$\to c(0) \int_{(-\pi,\pi]} g(\lambda)\,\mathrm{d}F(\lambda) \qquad \text{as } n \to \infty,$$

$$= c(0)\{F(0) - F(0-)\}$$

where g_n and g are given by (10) and (11), F is the spectral distribution function and

$$F(0-) = \lim_{y \uparrow 0} F(y)$$

as usual. We can now use (9.3.8) and the continuity properties of S to show that

$$c(0)\{F(0) - F(0-)\} = \mathbf{E}(|S(0) - S(0-)|^2) = \mathbf{E}(|Y|^2). \qquad \blacksquare$$

Theorems (2) and (3) generalize the Law of Large Numbers. There are similar generalizations of the Central Limit Theorem and the Law of the Iterated Logarithm, though Example (9.2.14) makes it clear that such results hold only for stationary processes which satisfy certain extra conditions. We give no details of this here, save for pointing out that these extra conditions take the form 'X_m and X_n are "nearly independent" when $|m-n|$ is large'.

Finally, here are some examples of the use of the Ergodic Theorem.

(13) **Example. Markov chains.** Let $X = \{X_n\}$ be an irreducible ergodic Markov chain with countable state space S, and let $\boldsymbol{\pi}$ be the unique stationary distribution of the chain. Suppose that $X(0)$ has distribution $\boldsymbol{\pi}$; then the argument of (8.2.4) shows that X is strongly stationary. Choose some state k and define the collection $I = \{I_n : n \geq 0\}$ of indicator functions by

$$I_n = \begin{cases} 1 & \text{if } X_n = k \\ 0 & \text{otherwise.} \end{cases}$$

Clearly I is strongly stationary. It has autocovariance function

$$c(n, n+m) = \operatorname{cov}(I_n, I_{n+m}) = \pi_k(p_{kk}(m) - \pi_k), \qquad m \geq 0,$$

where $p_{kk}(m) = \mathbf{P}(X_m = k \mid X_0 = k)$. The partial sum

$$S_n = \sum_{j=0}^{n-1} I_j$$

is the number of visits to the state k before the nth jump, and a short calculation gives

$$\frac{1}{n}\mathbf{E}(S_n) = \pi_k \quad \text{for all } n.$$

It is a consequence of the Ergodic Theorem (2) that

$$\frac{1}{n} S_n \xrightarrow{\text{a.s.}} S \quad \text{as} \quad n \to \infty,$$

where S is a random variable with mean

$$\mathbf{E}(S) = \mathbf{E}(I_0) = \pi_k.$$

Actually S is constant,

$$\mathbf{P}(S = \pi_k) = 1;$$

just note that

$$c(n, n+m) \to 0 \quad \text{as} \quad m \to \infty$$

and use the result of Problem (9.10.8). ●

(14) **Example.** Let X be uniformly distributed on $[0, 1]$. X has a binary expansion

$$X = 0 . X_1 X_2 \ldots = \sum_{j=1}^{\infty} X_j 2^{-j}$$

where $X_1, X_2, \ldots$ is a sequence of independent identically distributed random variables, each taking one of the values 0 or 1 with probability $\frac{1}{2}$ (see (7.10.4)). Define

(15) $$Y_n = 0 . X_n X_{n+1} \ldots \quad \text{for} \quad n \geq 1$$

and check for yourself that $Y = \{Y_n : n \geq 1\}$ is strongly stationary. Use (2) to see that

$$\frac{1}{n} \sum_{j=1}^{n} Y_j \xrightarrow{\text{a.s.}} \frac{1}{2} \quad \text{as} \quad n \to \infty;$$

you will need the result of (9.10.8) again here.

Generalize this example as follows. Let $g : \mathbb{R} \to \mathbb{R}$ be such that

(a) g has period 1, so that $g(x+1) = g(x)$ for all x

(b) g is uniformly continuous and integrable,

and define $Z = \{Z_n : n \geq 1\}$ by

$$Z_n = g(2^{n-1} X)$$

where X is uniform on $[0, 1]$ as before. The process Y, above, may be constructed in this way by choosing

$$g(x) = x \quad \text{modulo} \quad 1.$$

Check for yourself that Z is strongly stationary, and deduce that

$$\frac{1}{n} \sum_{j=1}^{n} g(2^{j-1} X) \xrightarrow{\text{a.s.}} \int_0^1 g(x)\, dx \quad \text{as} \quad n \to \infty.$$

Can you adapt this example to show that

$$\frac{1}{n}\sum_{j=1}^{n} g(X+(j-1)\pi) \xrightarrow{\text{a.s.}} \int_0^1 g(x)\,dx \quad \text{as} \quad n\to\infty$$

for any fixed positive irrational number π? ●

9.5 Gaussian processes

Let $X=\{X(t):-\infty<t<\infty\}$ be a real-valued stationary process with autocovariance function c; in line with (9.2.2), c is a real-valued function which satisfies

(a) $c(-t)=c(t)$
(b) c is a non-negative definite function.

It is not difficult to see that a function $c:\mathbb{R}\to\mathbb{R}$ is the autocovariance function of some real-valued stationary process if and only if c satisfies (a) and (b). Subject to these conditions on c, there is an explicit construction of a corresponding stationary process.

(1) **Theorem.** *If $c:\mathbb{R}\to\mathbb{R}$ and c satisfies (a) and (b) above then there exists a real-valued strongly stationary process X with autocovariance function c.*

Proof. We shall construct X by defining its finite-dimensional distributions and then use the Kolmogorov consistency conditions (8.5.3). For any vector $\boldsymbol{t}=(t_1,\ldots,t_n)$ of real numbers with some finite length n, let $F_{\boldsymbol{t}}$ be the multivariate normal distribution function with zero means and covariance matrix $\mathbf{V}=(v_{jk})$ with entries $v_{jk}=c(t_k-t_j)$ (see (4.7.9)). A slight complication arises when we apply the results of (4.7.9) in order to construct $F_{\boldsymbol{t}}$. For $\mathbf{V}$ may not be positive definite but merely non-negative definite; that is, there may exist a non-zero vector $\boldsymbol{x}$ such that

(2) $$\boldsymbol{x}\mathbf{V}\boldsymbol{x}'=0,$$

implying that $\mathbf{V}$ has determinant 0 and no inverse. This is resolvable roughly as follows. If $n=2$ and (2) holds for $\boldsymbol{x}=(x_1,x_2)\neq(0,0)$, then $\mathbf{V}$ is the covariance matrix of a pair $\mathbf{X}=(X(t_1),X(t_2))$ of variables, say, and (2) becomes

$$\boldsymbol{x}\mathbf{V}\boldsymbol{x}'=\boldsymbol{x}\mathbf{E}(\mathbf{X}'\mathbf{X})\boldsymbol{x}'=\mathbf{E}((\boldsymbol{x}\mathbf{X}')^2)=0;$$

thus

$$\boldsymbol{x}\mathbf{X}'=x_1X(t_1)+x_2X(t_2)=0 \quad \text{almost surely.}$$

If $X(t_1)$ is normal then so is $X(t_2)$, but they have no joint density function because, conditional on the value of $X(t_1)$, $X(t_2)$ is a constant random variable. In this case the joint distribution of $X(t_1)$ and $X(t_2)$ is called a 'singular' multivariate normal distribution. A similar construction holds for larger values of n, and we have defined a joint distribution function $F_{\mathbf{t}}$ for each $\mathbf{t}$. Now, the family $\{F_{\mathbf{t}} : \mathbf{t} \in \mathbb{R}^n, n = 1, 2, \dots\}$ satisfies the Kolmogorov consistency conditions (8.5.3) and so there exists a process X with this family of fdds. It is clear that X is strongly stationary with autocovariance function c. ■

A result similar to (1) holds for complex-valued functions $c : \mathbb{R} \to \mathbb{C}$, (a) being replaced by

(a′) $c(-t) = \overline{c(t)}$.

We do not explore this here, but choose to consider real-valued processes only. The process X which we have constructed in the foregoing proof is an example of a (real-valued) 'Gaussian process'.

(3) **Definition.** A real-valued continuous-time process X is called **Gaussian** if each finite-dimensional vector $(X(t_1), \dots, X(t_n))$ has the multivariate normal distribution $N(\boldsymbol{\mu}(\mathbf{t}), \mathbf{V}(\mathbf{t}))$ for some mean vector $\boldsymbol{\mu}$ and some covariance matrix $\mathbf{V}$ which may depend on $\mathbf{t} = (t_1, \dots, t_n)$.

As in the proof of (1), we allow the X's to have a singular multivariate normal distribution. We shall often restrict our attention to Gaussian processes with $\mathbf{E}(X(t)) = 0$ for all t; as before, similar results are easily found when this fails to hold.

A Gaussian process is not necessarily stationary.

(4) **Theorem.** *The Gaussian process X is stationary if and only if $\mathbf{E}(X(t))$ is constant for all t and the covariance matrix $\mathbf{V}(\mathbf{t})$ in Definition* (3) *satisfies*

$$\mathbf{V}(\mathbf{t}) = \mathbf{V}(\mathbf{t} + h)$$

for all $\mathbf{t}$ and $h > 0$, where $\mathbf{t} + h = (t_1 + h, \dots, t_n + h)$.

Proof. This is an easy *exercise*. ■

It is clear that a Gaussian process is strongly stationary if and only if it is weakly stationary.

Can a Gaussian process be a Markov process? The answer is in the affirmative. First, we must rephrase the Markov property (6.1.1) to deal with processes which take values in uncountable sets.

(5) **Definition.** The continuous-time process X, taking values in $\mathbb{R}$, is called a **Markov process** if

(6) $$\mathbf{P}(X(t_n) \le x \mid X(t_1), \dots, X(t_{n-1})) = \mathbf{P}(X(t_n) \le x \mid X(t_{n-1}))$$

for all x and all increasing sequences $t_1 < t_2 < \dots < t_n$ of times.

(7) **Theorem.** *The Gaussian process X is a Markov process if and only if*

(8) $$\mathbf{E}(X(t_n) \mid X(t_1), \ldots, X(t_{n-1})) = \mathbf{E}(X(t_n) \mid X(t_{n-1}))$$

for all increasing sequences $t_1 < \ldots < t_n$ of times.

Proof. This is not difficult. It is clear from (5) that (8) holds whenever X is Markov. Conversely, suppose that X is Gaussian and satisfies (8). Both the left- and right-hand sides of (6) are normal distribution functions. But any normal distribution is specified by its mean and variance, and so we need only show that the left- and right-hand sides of (6) have equal first two moments. The equality of the first moments is trivial, since this is simply the assertion of (8). Also, if $1 \leq r < n$, then

$$\mathbf{E}(YX_r) = 0$$

where

(9) $$Y = X_n - \mathbf{E}(X_n \mid X_1, \ldots, X_{n-1}) = X_n - \mathbf{E}(X_n \mid X_{n-1})$$

and we have written $X_r = X(t_r)$ for ease of notation; to see this, write

$$\begin{aligned}\mathbf{E}(YX_r) &= \mathbf{E}(X_n X_r - \mathbf{E}(X_n X_r \mid X_1, \ldots, X_{n-1}))\\ &= \mathbf{E}(X_n X_r) - \mathbf{E}(X_n X_r) = 0.\end{aligned}$$

However, Y and X_r are normally distributed and thus are independent by (4.5.9). It follows that Y is independent of the collection $X_1, X_2, \ldots, X_{n-1}$ by properties of the multivariate normal distribution. Therefore

$$\begin{aligned}\mathbf{E}(X_n^2 \mid X_1, \ldots, X_{n-1}) &= \mathbf{E}(Y^2 \mid X_1, \ldots, X_{n-1}) + \mathbf{E}(X_n \mid X_1, \ldots, X_{n-1})^2\\ &= \mathbf{E}(Y^2) + \mathbf{E}(X_n \mid X_{n-1})^2\\ &= \mathbf{E}(X_n^2 \mid X_{n-1})\end{aligned}$$

by (9). Thus the left- and right-hand sides of (6) have the same second moment also, and the result is proved. ∎

(10) **Example. A stationary Gaussian Markov process.** Suppose X is stationary, Gaussian and Markov, and has zero means. Use the result of (4.10.11) to obtain that

$$c(0)\mathbf{E}(X(s+t) \mid X(s)) = c(t)X(s) \quad \text{whenever} \quad t \geq 0,$$

where c is the autocovariance function of X. Thus, if $0 \leq s \leq s+t$ then

$$\begin{aligned}c(0)\mathbf{E}(X(0)X(s+t)) &= c(0)\mathbf{E}(\mathbf{E}\{X(0)X(s+t) \mid X(0), X(s)\})\\ &= c(0)\mathbf{E}(X(0)\mathbf{E}\{X(s+t) \mid X(s)\})\\ &= c(t)\mathbf{E}(X(0)X(s))\end{aligned}$$

by (7.7.10). Thus

(11) $$c(0)c(s+t) = c(s)c(t) \quad \text{for} \quad s, t \geq 0.$$

This is satisfied whenever

(12) $$c(t) = c(0)e^{-\alpha|t|}.$$

Following (4.10.5) we can see that (12) is the general solution to (11) subject to some condition of regularity such as that c be continuous. We shall see later (see (9.10.13)) that such a process is called a stationary *Ornstein–Uhlenbeck process.* ●

(13) **Example. The Wiener process.** Suppose that $\sigma^2 > 0$ and define

(14) $$c(s, t) = \sigma^2 \min\{s, t\} \quad \text{whenever} \quad s, t \geq 0.$$

We claim that there exists a Gaussian process $W = \{W(t) : t \geq 0\}$ with zero means such that $W(0) = 0$ and

$$\text{cov}(W(s), W(t)) = c(s, t).$$

By the argument in the proof of (1), it is sufficient to show that the matrix $\mathbf{V}(\boldsymbol{t})$ with entries (v_{jk}), where $v_{jk} = c(t_k, t_j)$, is positive definite for all $\boldsymbol{t} = (t_1, t_2, \ldots, t_n)$. To see this let $z_1, z_2, \ldots, z_n$ be complex numbers and suppose that $0 = t_0 < t_1 < \ldots < t_n$. Then it is not difficult to check that

$$\sum_{j,k=1}^{n} c(t_k, t_j) z_j \bar{z}_k = \sigma^2 \sum_{j=1}^{n} (t_j - t_{j-1}) \left| \sum_{k=j}^{n} z_k \right|^2 > 0$$

whenever one of the z's is non-zero; this guarantees the existence of W. It is called the *Wiener process*; we explore its properties in more detail in the next sections, noting only two facts here.

(15) **Lemma.** *The Wiener process W satisfies*

$$\mathbf{E}(W(t)^2) = \sigma^2 t \quad \textit{for all } t \geq 0.$$

Proof. $\mathbf{E}(W(t)^2) = \text{cov}(W(t), W(t)) = c(t, t) = \sigma^2 t.$ ■

(16) **Lemma.** *The Wiener process W has stationary independent increments, which is to say that, if $u \leq v \leq s \leq t$,*

(a) *the distribution of $W(t) - W(s)$ depends on $t - s$ alone*
(b) *$W(t) - W(s)$ and $W(v) - W(u)$ are independent.*

Proof. The increments $W(v) - W(u)$ and $W(t) - W(s)$ are jointly normally distributed; their independence follows as soon as we have shown that they are uncorrelated. However,

$$\begin{aligned}\mathbf{E}(\{W(v) - W(u)\}\{W(t) - W(s)\}) &= c(v, t) - c(v, s) + c(u, s) - c(u, t)\\ &= \sigma^2(v - v + u - u) = 0\end{aligned}$$

by (14).

Finally, $W(t) - W(s)$ is normally distributed with zero mean, and with variance

$$\begin{aligned}\mathbf{E}((W(t) - W(s))^2) &= \mathbf{E}(W(t)^2) - 2c(s, t) + \mathbf{E}(W(s)^2)\\ &= \sigma^2(t - s) \quad \text{if} \quad s \leq t.\end{aligned}$$ ■●

9.6 Brownian motion

Let us suppose that we choose to observe a container of water. When seen from a distance the water appears to be motionless, but this is an illusion. If we are able to approach the container so closely as to be able to distinguish individual molecules then we may perceive that each molecule enjoys a motion which is unceasing and without any apparent order. The disorder of this movement arises from the high density of the fluid and the frequent occasions at which the molecule is repulsed by other molecules which are nearby at the time. The first scientific experiments involving this phenomenon were performed by the botanist R. Brown around 1827; he studied the motion of pollen particles suspended in water, and lent his name to the type of erratic movement which he observed. It is a classical problem of probability theory to model this movement.

Brownian motion takes place in continuous time and continuous space. Our first attempt to model it might proceed by approximating to it by a discrete process such as a random walk. At any epoch of time the position of an observed particle is constrained to move about the points $\{(a\delta, b\delta, c\delta): a, b, c = 0, \pm 1, \pm 2, \dots\}$ of a three-dimensional 'cubic' lattice in which the distance between neighbouring points is δ; δ is a fixed positive number which is very small. Suppose further that the particle performs a symmetric random walk on this lattice (see Problem (6.13.6) for the case $\delta = 1$) so that its position $\mathbf{S}_n$ after n jumps satisfies

$$\mathbf{P}(\mathbf{S}_{n+1} = \mathbf{S}_n + \delta\boldsymbol{\epsilon}) = \tfrac{1}{6} \quad \text{if} \quad \boldsymbol{\epsilon} = (\pm 1, 0, 0), (0, \pm 1, 0), (0, 0, \pm 1).$$

Let us concentrate on the x co-ordinate of the particle, and write

$$\mathbf{S}_n = (S_n^1, S_n^2, S_n^3).$$

Then, as in Section 5.2,

$$S_n^1 - S_0^1 = \sum_{i=1}^{n} X_i$$

where $\{X_i\}$ is an independent identically distributed sequence with

$$\mathbf{P}(X_i = k\delta) = \begin{cases} \frac{1}{6} & \text{if} \quad k = -1 \\ \frac{1}{6} & \text{if} \quad k = +1 \\ \frac{2}{3} & \text{if} \quad k = 0. \end{cases}$$

We are interested in the displacement $S_n^1 - S_0^1$ when n is large; the Central Limit Theorem (5.10.4) tells us that the distribution of this displacement is approximately $N(0, \frac{1}{3}n\delta^2)$. Now suppose that the jumps of the random walk take place at time epochs $\tau, 2\tau, 3\tau, \dots$ where $\tau > 0$; τ is the time between jumps and is very small, implying that a large number of jumps occur in any large time interval. Observe the particle after some time $t(>0)$ has elapsed. By this time it has experienced

$$n = \lfloor t/\tau \rfloor$$

jumps, and so its x co-ordinate $S^1(t)$ is such that $S^1(t)-S^1(0)$ is approximately $N(0, \frac{1}{3}t\delta^2/\tau)$, which depends on δ and τ alone for any fixed t. At this stage in the analysis we let the interpoint distance δ and the interjump time τ approach zero; in so doing we hope that the discrete random walk may approach some limit whose properties have something in common with the observed features of Brownian motion. We let $\delta\downarrow 0$ and $\tau\downarrow 0$ in such a way that $\frac{1}{3}\delta^2/\tau$ remains constant, since the variance of the distribution of $S^1(t)-S^1(0)$ fails to settle down to a non-trivial limit otherwise. Set

(1) $$\tfrac{1}{3}\delta^2/\tau=\sigma^2$$

where σ^2 is a positive constant, and pass to the limit to obtain that the distribution of $S^1(t)-S^1(0)$ approaches $N(0, \sigma^2 t)$. We can apply the same argument to the y co-ordinate and the z co-ordinate of the particle to deduce that the particle's position

$$\mathbf{S}(t)=(S^1(t), S^2(t), S^3(t))$$

at time t is such that the asymptotic distribution of the co-ordinates of the displacement $\mathbf{S}(t)-\mathbf{S}(0)$ is multivariate normal whenever $\delta\downarrow 0$, $\tau\downarrow 0$, and (1) holds; furthermore, it is not too hard to see that $S^1(t)$, $S^2(t)$ and $S^3(t)$ are independent of each other.

We may guess from the asymptotic properties of this random walk that an adequate model for Brownian motion will involve a process $\mathbf{X}=\{\mathbf{X}(t): t\geq 0\}$ taking values in $\mathbb{R}^3$ with a co-ordinate representation

$$\mathbf{X}(t)=(X^1(t), X^2(t), X^3(t))$$

such that

(a) $\mathbf{X}(0)=(0,0,0)$, say
(b) X^1, X^2, and X^3 are independent and identically distributed processes
(c) $X^1(s+t)-X^1(s)$ is $N(0, \sigma^2 t)$ for any $s, t\geq 0$
(d) X^1 has *independent increments* in that $X^1(v)-X^1(u)$ and $X^1(t)-X^1(s)$ are independent whenever $u\leq v\leq s\leq t$.

We have not yet shown the existence of such a process $\mathbf{X}$; the foregoing argument only indicates certain plausible distributional properties without showing that they are attainable. However, properties (c) and (d) are not new to us and remind us of the Wiener process of Example (9.5.13); we deduce that such a process $\mathbf{X}$ indeed exists, and is given by

$$\mathbf{X}(t)=(W^1(t), W^2(t), W^3(t))$$

where W^1, W^2 and W^3 are independent Wiener processes.

This conclusion is gratifying in that it demonstrates the existence of a random process which seems to enjoy at least some of the features of Brownian motion. A more detailed and technical analysis indicates some weak points of the Wiener model. This is beyond the scope of this text, and we are able only to skim the surface of the main difficulty. For each ω

in the sample space Ω, $\{\mathbf{X}(t;\omega):t\geqslant 0\}$ is a sample path of the process along which the particle may move. It can be shown that, in some sense,

(a) almost all sample paths are continuous functions of t
(b) almost all sample paths are nowhere differentiable functions of t.

Property (a) is physically necessary, but (b) is a property which *cannot* be shared by the physical phenomenon which we are modelling, since mechanical considerations, such as Newton's Laws, imply that only particles with zero mass can move along routes which are nowhere differentiable. So, as a model for the local movement (over a short time interval) of particles, the Wiener process is poor; over longer periods of time the properties of the Wiener process are indeed very similar to experimental results.

A popular improved model for the local behaviour of Brownian paths is the so-called Ornstein–Uhlenbeck process. We close this section with a short account of this. Roughly, it is founded on the assumption that the velocity of the particle (rather than its position) undergoes a random walk; the ensuing motion is damped by the frictional resistance of the fluid. The result is a 'velocity process' with continuous sample paths; their integrals represent the sample paths of the particle itself. Think of the motion in one dimension as before, and write V_n for the velocity of the particle after the nth jump. At the next jump the change $V_{n+1}-V_n$ in the velocity is assumed to have two contributions: the frictional resistance to motion, and some random fluctuation owing to collisions with other particles. We shall assume that the former damping effect is directly proportional to V_n, so that

$$V_{n+1}=V_n+X_{n+1}$$

where

$$\mathbf{E}(X_{n+1}\mid V_n)=-\beta V_n \qquad \text{:frictional effect}$$
$$\operatorname{var}(X_{n+1}\mid V_n)=\sigma^2 \qquad \text{:collision effect,}$$

where β and σ^2 are constants. $\{V_n\}$ is no longer a random walk on some regular grid of points, but it can be shown that the distributions converge as before, after suitable passage to the limit. Furthermore, there exists a process $V=\{V(t):t\geqslant 0\}$ with the corresponding distributional properties, and whose sample paths turn out to be almost surely continuous. These sample paths do not represent possible routes of the particle, but rather describe the development of its velocity as time passes. The possible paths of the particle through the space which it inhabits are found by integrating the sample paths of V with respect to time (this is not so easy in practice as it may sound). Of course, the resulting paths are almost surely continuously differentiable functions of time.

9.7 Diffusion processes

We say that a particle is 'diffusing' about a space $\mathbb{R}^n$ whenever it experiences erratic and disordered motion through the space; for example, we may speak of radioactive particles diffusing through the atmosphere, or even of a rumour diffusing through the population. For the moment, we restrict our attention to one-dimensional diffusions, for which the position of the observed particle at any time is a point on the real line; similar arguments will hold for higher dimensions. Our first diffusion model is the Wiener process.

(1) **Definition.** A **Wiener process** $W=\{W(t):t\geqslant 0\}$, starting from $W(0)=w$, say, is a real-valued Gaussian process such that

(a) W has independent increments (see (9.5.16))
(b) $W(s+t)-W(s)$ is $N(0,\sigma^2 t)$ for all $s, t\geqslant 0$ where σ^2 is a positive constant.

Clearly (a) and (b) specify the fdds of a Wiener process W, and the argument of (9.5.1) shows that such a process exists. In agreement with (9.5.14), the autocovariance function of W is given by

$$\begin{aligned} c(s,t) &= \mathbf{E}\{(W(s)-W(0))(W(t)-W(0))\} \\ &= \mathbf{E}\{(W(s)-W(0))^2+(W(s)-W(0))(W(t)-W(s))\} \\ &= \sigma^2 s+0 \quad \text{if} \quad 0\leqslant s\leqslant t \end{aligned}$$

and so

(2) $$c(s,t)=\sigma^2\min\{s,t\} \quad \text{for all } s,t\geqslant 0.$$

W is called a *standard* Wiener process if $\sigma^2=1$. If W is non-standard, then $W_1=W/\sigma$ is standard. W is said to have 'stationary' independent increments since the distribution of $W(s+t)-W(s)$ depends on t alone. A simple application of (9.5.7) shows that W is a Markov process.

The Wiener process W can be used to model the apparently random displacement of Brownian motion in any chosen direction. For this reason, W is sometimes called 'Brownian motion'; however, *we* reserve the use of this term to describe the motivating physical phenomenon.

Roughly speaking, there are two types of statement to be made about diffusion processes in general, and the Wiener process particularly; we made a similar remark in Section 8.1. The first deals with sample path properties, and the second with distributional properties. The former occupies us only briefly since the details of any rigorous argument are much too difficult for inclusion here. We confine ourselves to the statement of one lemma, and refer the reader to Billingsley 1979, p. 467 for a concise explanation of some of the issues which it involves†.

(3) **Lemma.** *The sample paths of a Wiener process are almost surely continuous but nowhere differentiable functions of time.*

Figure 9.1 is a diagram of a typical sample path. Certain distributional

† Actually, it is possible to construct Wiener processes for which this lemma fails since (remember Example (8.5.4)) many sample path properties are not specified by the fdds, but we shall be in little danger if we overlook this possibility.

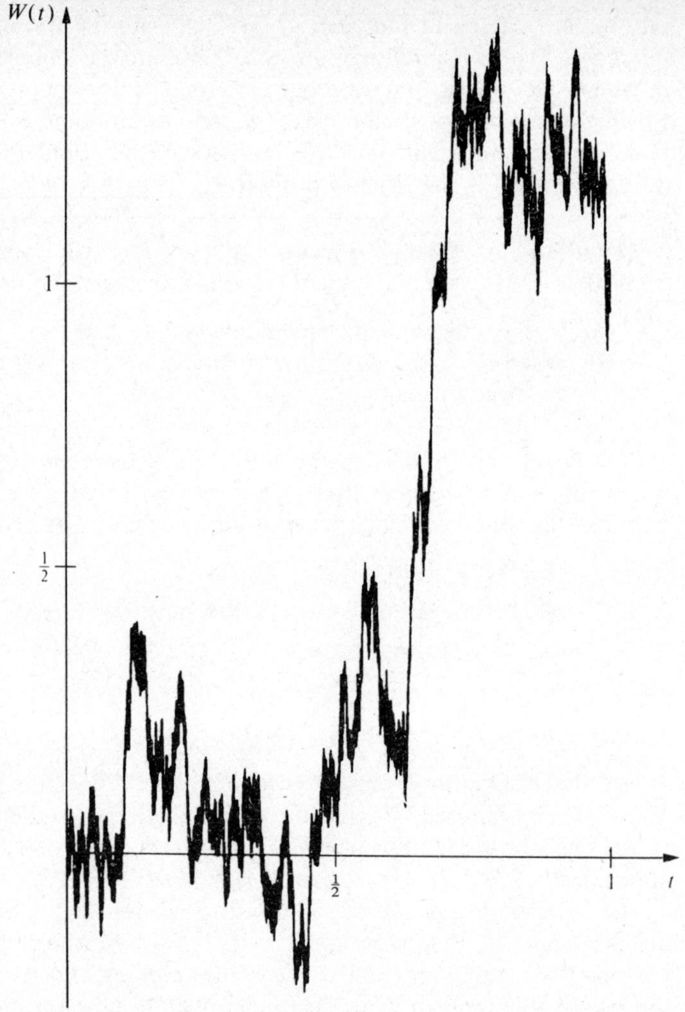

FIG. 9.1 A typical realization of a Wiener process W. This is a scale drawing of a sample path of W over the time interval $[0, 1]$. Note that the path is continuous but very spiky. This picture indicates the general features of the path only; the dense black portions indicate superimposed fluctuations which are too fine for this method of description. Tim Brown and Adrian Bowyer drew the picture, with the aid of a computer, using 100,000 steps of a symmetric random walk and the scaling method of Section 9.6.

properties of continuity are immediate. For example, W is 'continuous in mean square' in that

$$\mathbf{E}((W(s+t)-W(s))^2) \to 0 \quad \text{as} \quad t \to 0;$$

this follows easily from (2). Consequently, W is 'continuous in probability', in that

$$\mathbf{P}(|W(s+t)-W(s)|>\epsilon) \to 0 \quad \text{as} \quad t \to 0, \quad \text{for all } \epsilon>0.$$

Let us turn our attention to the distributions of a standard Wiener process W. Suppose we are given that $W(s)=x$, say, where $s \geqslant 0$ and $x \in \mathbb{R}$. Conditional on this, $W(t)$ is $N(x, t-s)$ for $t \geqslant s$, which is to say that the conditional distribution function

$$F(y, t \mid x, s) = \mathbf{P}(W(t) \leqslant y \mid W(s) = x)$$

has density function

$$f(y, t \mid x, s) = \frac{\partial}{\partial y} F(y, t \mid x, s)$$

which is given by

(4) $$f(y, t \mid x, s) = \frac{1}{\{2\pi(t-s)\}^{1/2}} \exp\left\{-\frac{(y-x)^2}{2(t-s)}\right\}, \qquad -\infty < y < \infty.$$

This is a function of four variables, but just grit your teeth. It is easy to check that f is the solution of the following differential equations.

(5) **Forward diffusion equation:** $$\frac{\partial f}{\partial t} = \frac{1}{2}\frac{\partial^2 f}{\partial y^2}.$$

(6) **Backward diffusion equation:** $$\frac{\partial f}{\partial s} = -\frac{1}{2}\frac{\partial^2 f}{\partial x^2}.$$

We ought to specify the boundary conditions for these equations, but avoid this at the moment. Subject to certain conditions, (4) is the unique density function which solves (5) or (6). There is a good reason why (5) and (6) are called the *forward* and *backward* equations. Remember that W is a Markov process, and use arguments similar to those of Sections 6.8 and 6.9. Equation (5) is obtained by conditioning $W(t+h)$ on the value of $W(t)$ and letting $h \downarrow 0$; (6) is obtained by conditioning $W(t)$ on the value of $W(s+h)$ and letting $h \downarrow 0$. You are treading in Einstein's footprints as you perform these calculations. The derivatives in (5) and (6) have coefficients which do not depend on x, y, s, t; this reflects the fact that the Wiener process is homogeneous in space and time, in that

(a) the increment $W(t) - W(s)$ is independent of $W(s)$ for all $t \geqslant s$
(b) the increments are stationary in time.

Next we turn out attention to diffusion processes which *lack* this homogeneity.

The Wiener process is a Markov process, and the Markov property provides a method for deriving the forward and backward equations. There are other Markov diffusion processes to which this method may be applied in order to obtain similar forward and backward equations; the coefficients in these equations will *not* generally be constant. The existence of such processes can be demonstrated rigorously, but here we explore their distributions only. Let $D = \{D(t) : t \geqslant 0\}$ denote a diffusion process. We need to impose some conditions on the transitions of D in order to derive its diffusion equations; these conditions take the form of specifying the mean and variance of increments $D(t+h) - D(t)$ of the process over small time intervals $(t, t+h)$. Suppose that there exist functions $a(x, t)$, $b(x, t)$ such that

$$\mathbf{P}(|D(t+h)-D(t)|>\epsilon \mid D(t)=x)=o(h) \quad \text{for all } \epsilon>0$$
$$\mathbf{E}(D(t+h)-D(t) \mid D(t)=x)=a(x, t)h+o(h)$$
$$\mathbf{E}((D(t+h)-D(t))^2 \mid D(t)=x)=b(x, t)h+o(h);$$

a and b are called the 'instantaneous mean' and 'instantaneous variance' of D respectively. Subject to certain other technical conditions (see Prabhu 1965*a*, pp. 89, 98), if $s \leq t$ then the conditional density function of $D(t)$ given $D(s)=x$,

$$f(y, t \mid x, s)=\frac{\partial}{\partial y}\mathbf{P}(D(t)\leq y \mid D(s)=x),$$

satisfies the following partial differential equations:

(7) **forward equation:** $$\frac{\partial f}{\partial t}=-\frac{\partial}{\partial y}\{a(y, t)f\}+\frac{1}{2}\frac{\partial^2}{\partial y^2}\{b(y, t)f\}$$

(8) **backward equation:** $$\frac{\partial f}{\partial s}=-a(x, s)\frac{\partial f}{\partial x}-\frac{1}{2}b(x, s)\frac{\partial^2 f}{\partial x^2}.$$

It is an extraordinary fact that the density function f is specified as soon as the instantaneous mean a and variance b are known; we need no further information about the distribution of a typical increment. This is very convenient for many applications, since a and b are often specified in a natural manner by the description of the process.

(9) **Example. The Wiener process.** If increments have zero means and constant variances then

$$a(x, t)=0, \qquad b(x, t)=\sigma^2$$

for some $\sigma^2>0$, and the diffusion equations (5) and (6) follow from (7) and (8) for processes with variance σ^2. ●

(10) **Example. The Wiener process with drift.** Suppose a particle undergoes a type of Brownian motion in one dimension, in which it experiences a drift at constant rate in some particular direction. That is to say,

$$a(x, t)=m, \qquad b(x, t)=\sigma^2$$

for some drift rate m and constant σ^2. The forward diffusion equation becomes

$$\frac{\partial f}{\partial t}=-m\frac{\partial f}{\partial y}+\frac{1}{2}\sigma^2\frac{\partial^2 f}{\partial y^2}$$

and it follows that the corresponding diffusion process D is such that

$$D(t)=W(t)+mt$$

where W is a Wiener process. ●

(11) **Example. The Ornstein–Uhlenbeck process.** Recall the discussion of this process at the end of Section 9.6. It experiences a drift towards the origin of magnitude proportional to its displacement. So

$$a(x, t) = -\beta x, \qquad b(x, t) = \sigma^2$$

and the forward equation is

$$\frac{\partial f}{\partial t} = \beta \frac{\partial}{\partial y}(yf) + \frac{1}{2}\sigma^2 \frac{\partial^2 f}{\partial y^2}.$$

See Problem (9.10.13) for the solution of this equation. ●

(12) **Example. Diffusion approximation to the branching process.** Diffusion models are sometimes useful as continuous approximations to discrete processes. In Section 9.6 we saw that the Wiener process approximates to the random walk under certain circumstances; here is another example of such an approximation. Let $\{Z_n\}$ be the branching process of Section 5.4, with $Z_0 = 1$ and such that

$$\mathbf{E}(Z_1) = \mu, \qquad \text{var}\,(Z_1) = \sigma^2.$$

A typical increment $Z_{n+1} - Z_n$ has mean and variance given by

$$\mathbf{E}(Z_{n+1} - Z_n \mid Z_n = x) = (\mu - 1)x$$
$$\text{var}\,(Z_{n+1} - Z_n \mid Z_n = x) = \sigma^2 x;$$

these are directly proportional to the size of Z_n. Now, suppose that the time intervals between successive generations become shorter and shorter, but that the means and variances of the increments retain this proportionality; of course, we need to abandon the condition that the process be integer-valued. This suggests a diffusion model as an approximation to the branching process, with instantaneous mean and variance given by

$$a(x, t) = ax, \qquad b(x, t) = bx$$

and the forward equation of such a process is

(13) $$\frac{\partial f}{\partial t} = -a\frac{\partial}{\partial y}(yf) + \frac{1}{2}b\frac{\partial^2}{\partial y^2}(yf).$$

Subject to appropriate boundary conditions, this equation has a unique solution; this may be found by taking Laplace transforms of (13) in order to find the moment generating function of the value of the diffusion process at time t. ●

(14) **Example. A branching diffusion process.** The next example is a modification of the process of (6.12.15) which modelled the distribution in space of the members of a branching process. Read the first paragraph of (6.12.15) again before proceeding with this example. It is often the case that the members of a population move around the space which they

inhabit during their lifetimes. With this in mind we introduce a modification into the process of (6.12.15). Suppose a typical individual is born at time s and at position x. We suppose that this individual moves about $\mathbb{R}$ until its lifetime T is finished, at which point it dies and divides, leaving its offspring at the position at which it dies. We suppose further that it moves as a standard Wiener process W, so that it is at position $x+W(t)$ at time $s+t$ whenever $0\leq t\leq T$. We assume that each individual moves independently of the positions of all the other individuals. We retain the notation of (6.12.15) whenever it is suitable, writing N for the number of offspring of the initial individual, W for the process describing its motion, and T for its lifetime. This individual dies at the point $W(T)$.

We no longer seek complete information about the distribution of the individuals around the space, but restrict ourselves to a less demanding task. It is natural to wonder about the rate at which members of the population move away from the place of birth of the founding member. Let $M(t)$ denote the position of the individual who is furthest right from the origin at time t. That is,

$$M(t)=\sup\{x:Z_1(x,t)>0\}$$

where $Z_1(x,t)$ is the number of living individuals at time t who are positioned at points in the interval $[x,\infty)$. We shall study the distribution function of $M(t)$

$$F(x,t)=\mathbf{P}(M(t)\leq x),$$

and proceed roughly as before, noting that

$$F(x,t)=\int_0^\infty \mathbf{P}(M(t)\leq x\mid T=s)f_T(s)\,ds. \tag{15}$$

where f_T is the density function of T. However,

$$\mathbf{P}(M(t)\leq x\mid T=s)=\mathbf{P}(W(t)\leq x)\quad\text{if}\quad s>t,$$

whilst, if $s\leq t$, use of conditional probabilities gives

$$\mathbf{P}(M(t)\leq x\mid T=s)=\sum_{n=0}^\infty\int_{w=-\infty}^\infty \mathbf{P}(M(t)\leq x\mid T=s,N=n,W(s)=w)$$
$$\times\,\mathbf{P}(N=n)f_{W(s)}(w)\,dw$$

where $f_{W(s)}$ is the density function of $W(s)$. But, if $s\leq t$, then

$$\mathbf{P}(M(t)\leq x\mid T=s,N=n,W(s)=w)=\{\mathbf{P}(M(t-s)\leq x-w)\}^n,$$

and so (15) becomes

$$F(x,t)=\int_{s=0}^{t}\int_{w=-\infty}^{\infty} G_N\{F(x-w,t-s)\}f_{W(s)}(w)f_T(s)\,dw\,ds \tag{16}$$
$$+\mathbf{P}(W(t)\leq x)\int_{s=t}^\infty f_T(s)\,ds.$$

We consider here only the Markovian case when T is exponentially distributed, so that

$$f_T(s) = \mu e^{-\mu s} \quad \text{for} \quad s \geq 0.$$

Multiply through (16) by $e^{\mu t}$, substitute $x - w = v$ and $t - s = u$ within the integral and differentiate with respect to t to obtain

$$e^{\mu t}\left(\mu F + \frac{\partial F}{\partial t}\right) = \mu \int_{v=-\infty}^{\infty} G_N(F(v, t)) f_{W(0)}(x - v) e^{\mu t}\, dv$$
$$+ \mu \int_{u=0}^{t} \int_{v=-\infty}^{\infty} G_N(F(v, u))\left(\frac{\partial}{\partial t} f_{W(t-u)}(x - v)\right) e^{\mu u}\, dv\, du$$
$$+ \frac{\partial}{\partial t} \mathbf{P}(W(t) \leq x).$$

Now differentiate the same equation twice with respect to x, remembering that $f_{W(s)}(w)$ satisfies the diffusion equations and that $\delta(v) = f_{W(0)}(x - v)$ needs to be interpreted as the Dirac δ function at the point $v = x$ to find that

(17) $$\mu F + \frac{\partial F}{\partial t} = \mu G_N(F) + \frac{1}{2}\frac{\partial^2 F}{\partial x^2}.$$

Many eminent mathematicians have studied this equation; for example, Kolmogorov and Fisher were concerned with it in connection with the distribution of gene frequencies. It is difficult to extract precise information from (17). One approach is to look for solutions of the form

$$F(x, t) = \psi(x - ct)$$

for some constant c to obtain the following second-order ordinary differential equation for ψ:

(18) $$\psi'' + 2c\psi' + 2\mu H(\psi) = 0$$

where

$$H(\psi) = G_N(\psi) - \psi.$$

Solutions to (18) yield information about the asymptotic distribution of the so-called 'advancing' wave of the members of the process. ●

9.8 First passage times

We have often been interested in the time which elapses before a Markov chain visits a specified state for the first time, and we continue this chapter with an account of some of the corresponding problems for a diffusion process.

Consider first a standard Wiener process W starting from $W(0) = 0$. W

has the property that the process W_1 given by

(1) $$W_1(t) = W(t+T) - W(T), \qquad t \geq 0$$

is a standard Wiener process for any fixed value of T and, conditional on $W(T)$, W_1 is independent of $\{W(s): s<T\}$; the Poisson process enjoys a similar property, which in (6.8.6) we called the 'Weak Markov Property'. It is a very important and useful fact that this holds even when T is a random variable, so long as T is a stopping time for W (see (7.9.1) for a definition of stopping times with respect to discrete-time processes).

(2) **Definition.** Let $\mathscr{F}(t)$ be the smallest σ-field with respect to which $W(s)$ is measurable for each $s \leq t$. T is called a *stopping time* for W if $\{T \leq t\} \in \mathscr{F}(t)$ for all t.

We say that W has the 'Strong Markov Property' in that this independence holds for all stopping times T. Why not try to prove this? We have made implicit use of such a property in the earlier chapters; see for example the proof of (5.3.5). Here, we make use of the Strong Markov Property for certain particular stopping times T.

(3) **Definition.** The **first passage time** $T(x)$ to the point $x \in \mathbb{R}$ is given by

$$T(x) = \inf\{t : W(t) = x\}.$$

This definition is not entirely satisfactory unless we have made the assumption that the sample paths of W are almost surely continuous; see the discussion concerning (9.7.3).

(4) **Lemma.** *$T(x)$ is a stopping time for W.*

(5) **Theorem.** *$T(x)$ has density function*

$$f_{T(x)}(t) = \frac{|x|}{\sqrt{(2\pi t^3)}} \exp\left(-\frac{x^2}{2t}\right), \qquad t \geq 0.$$

Clearly $T(x)$ and $T(-x)$ are identically distributed. For the case when $x=1$ we encountered this density function and its moment generating function in Problems (5.11.14) and (5.11.15); it is easy to deduce that $T(x)$ has the same distribution as Z^{-2} where Z is $N(0, x^{-2})$. Before the proof of Theorem (5), here is a result about the size of the maximum of a Wiener process.

(6) **Theorem.** *Let*

$$M(t) = \max\{W(s) : 0 \leq s \leq t\}.$$

Then $M(t)$ has the same distribution as $|W(t)|$; thus $M(t)$ has density function

$$f_{M(t)}(m) = \left(\frac{2}{\pi t}\right)^{1/2} \exp\left(-\frac{m^2}{2t}\right), \qquad m \geq 0.$$

You should draw your own diagrams to illustrate the translations and reflections used in the proofs of this section.

Proof of (6). Suppose $m>0$, and observe that

(7) $$T(m)\leq t \quad \text{if and only if } M(t)\geq m.$$

Then

$$\mathbf{P}(M(t)\geq m)=\mathbf{P}(M(t)\geq m,\ W(t)-m\geq 0)+\mathbf{P}(M(t)\geq m,\ W(t)-m<0).$$

However, by (7),

$$\begin{aligned}\mathbf{P}(M(t)&\geq m,\ W(t)-m<0)\\ &=\mathbf{P}(W(t)-W(T(m))<0 \mid T(m)\leq t)\mathbf{P}(T(m)\leq t)\\ &=\mathbf{P}(W(t)-W(T(m))\geq 0 \mid T(m)\leq t)\mathbf{P}(T(m)\leq t)\\ &=\mathbf{P}(M(t)\geq m,\ W(t)-m\geq 0)\end{aligned}$$

since $W(t)-W(T(m))$ is symmetric whenever $t\geq T(m)$ by the Strong Markov Property; we have used sample path continuity here, in that we have used the fact that

$$\mathbf{P}(W\{T(m)\}=m)=1.$$

Thus

$$\begin{aligned}\mathbf{P}(M(t)\geq m)&=2\mathbf{P}(M(t)\geq m,\ W(t)\geq m)\\ &=2\mathbf{P}(W(t)\geq m)\end{aligned}$$

since $W(t)\leq M(t)$. Hence

$$\mathbf{P}(M(t)\geq m)=\mathbf{P}(|W(t)|\geq m)$$

and the theorem is proved on noting that $|W(t)|$ is the absolute value of a $N(0, t)$ variable. ■

Proof of (5). This follows immediately from (7), since if $x>0$ then

$$\begin{aligned}\mathbf{P}(T(x)\leq t)&=\mathbf{P}(M(t)\geq x)\\ &=\mathbf{P}(|W(t)|\geq x)\\ &=\left(\frac{2}{\pi t}\right)^{1/2}\int_x^\infty \exp\left(-\frac{m^2}{2t}\right)\mathrm{d}m\\ &=\int_0^t \frac{|x|}{\sqrt{(2\pi y^3)}}\exp\left(-\frac{x^2}{2y}\right)\mathrm{d}y\end{aligned}$$

by the substitution $y=x^2t/m^2$. ■

We are now in a position to derive some famous results about the times at which W returns to its starting point, the origin. We say that 'W has a zero at time t' if $W(t)=0$.

(8) **Theorem.** *Suppose $0 \le t_0 < t_1$. The probability that a standard Wiener process W has a zero in the time interval (t_0, t_1), starting from $W(0)=0$, is*

$$\frac{2}{\pi}\cos^{-1}\left\{\left(\frac{t_0}{t_1}\right)^{1/2}\right\}.$$

Proof. If $0 \le u < v$, let $E(u, v)$ denote the event

$$E(u, v) = \{W(t) = 0 \quad \text{for some } t \in (u, v)\}.$$

Condition on $W(t_0)$ to obtain

$$\mathbf{P}(E(t_0, t_1)) = \int_{-\infty}^{\infty} \mathbf{P}(E(t_0, t_1) \mid W(t_0) = w) f_0(w)\, dw$$

$$= 2\int_{-\infty}^{0} \mathbf{P}(E(t_0, t_1) \mid W(t_0) = w) f_0(w)\, dw$$

by the symmetry of W, where f_0 is the density function of $W(t_0)$. However, if $a > 0$,

$$\mathbf{P}(E(t_0, t_1) \mid W(t_0) = -a) = \mathbf{P}(E(0, t_1 - t_0) \mid W(0) = -a)$$
$$= \mathbf{P}(T(a) < t_1 - t_0 \mid W(0) = 0)$$

by the homogeneity of W in time and space. Use (5) to obtain that

$$\mathbf{P}(E(t_0, t_1)) = 2\int_{a=0}^{\infty}\int_{t=0}^{t_1 - t_0} f_{T(a)}(t) f_0(-a)\, dt\, da$$

$$= \frac{1}{\pi\sqrt{t_0}}\int_{t=0}^{t_1 - t_0} t^{-3/2}\int_{a=0}^{\infty} a \exp\left(-\tfrac{1}{2}a^2\left(\frac{t+t_0}{tt_0}\right)\right) da\, dt$$

$$= \frac{\sqrt{t_0}}{\pi}\int_{t=0}^{t_1 - t_0} \frac{dt}{(t+t_0)\sqrt{t}}$$

$$= \frac{2}{\pi}\tan^{-1}\left\{\left(\frac{t_1}{t_0} - 1\right)^{1/2}\right\} \quad \text{by the substitution } t = t_0 s^2$$

$$= \frac{2}{\pi}\cos^{-1}\left\{\left(\frac{t_0}{t_1}\right)^{1/2}\right\} \quad \text{as required.}$$ ■

The result of (8) indicates some remarkable properties of the sample paths of W. Set $t_0 = 0$ to obtain

$$\mathbf{P}(\text{there exists a zero in } (0, t) \mid W(0) = 0) = 1 \quad \text{for all } t > 0,$$

and it follows that

$$T(0) = \inf\{t \ne 0 : W(t) = 0\}$$

satisfies $T(0)=0$ almost surely. A deeper analysis shows that, with probability one, W has infinitely many zeros in any non-empty time interval $[0, t)$; it is no wonder that W has non-differentiable sample paths! The set

$$Z=\{t: W(t)=0\}$$

of zeros of W is rather a large set; in fact it turns out that Z has Hausdorff dimension $\frac{1}{2}$ (see *Fractals: Form, Chance and Dimension* by B. Mandelbrot for a charming discussion of fractional dimensionality).

The proofs of (5), (6), and (8) have relied heavily upon certain symmetries of the Wiener process; these are similar to the symmetries of the random walk of Section 5.2. Other diffusions may not have these symmetries, and we may need other techniques for finding out about their first passage times. We illustrate this point by a glance at the Wiener process with drift (9.7.10). Let $D=\{D(t): t\geqslant 0\}$ be a diffusion process with instantaneous mean and variance given by

$$a(x, t)=m, \qquad b(x, t)=1$$

where m is a constant. It is easy to check that, if $D(0)=0$, then $D(t)$ is $N(mt, t)$. It is not so easy to find the distributions of the sizes of the maxima of D, and we take this opportunity to display the usefulness of martingales and optional stopping.

(9) **Theorem.** *Let* $U(t)=\exp\{-2mD(t)\}$. *Then* $U=\{U(t): t\geqslant 0\}$ *is a martingale.*

Our only experience to date of continuous-time martingales is contained in our solution to Problem (7.10.23).

Proof. D is a Markov process, and so U is a Markov process also. To check that the continuous martingale condition of (7.10.23) holds with U in place of S and N, it suffices to show that

(10) $$\mathbf{E}(U(t+s) \mid U(t))=U(t) \quad \text{for all } s, t\geqslant 0.$$

However,

(11) $$\begin{aligned}\mathbf{E}(U(t+s) \mid U(t)=e^{-2md}) &= \mathbf{E}(\exp\{-2mD(t+s)\} \mid D(t)=d)\\ &= \mathbf{E}(\exp[-2m\{D(t+s)-D(t)\}-2md] \mid D(t)=d)\\ &= e^{-2md}\mathbf{E}(\exp[-2m\{D(t+s)-D(t)\}])\\ &= e^{-2md}\mathbf{E}(\exp\{-2mD(s)\})\end{aligned}$$

because D is Markovian with stationary independent increments. Now,

$$\mathbf{E}(\exp\{-2mD(s)\})=M(-2m)$$

where M is the moment generating function of a $N(ms, s)$ variable; M is given by (5.8.5) as

$$M(u)=\exp(msu+\tfrac{1}{2}su^2).$$

Thus

$$\mathbf{E}(\exp\{-2mD(s)\}) = 1$$

and so (10) follows from (11). ■

We can use this martingale to find the distribution of first passage times, just as we did in (7.9.5) for the random walk. Let $x, y > 0$ and define

$$T(x, -y) = \inf\{t : D(t) = x \quad \text{or} \quad D(t) = -y\}$$

to be the first passage time of D to the set $\{x, -y\}$. It can be shown that $T(x, -y)$ is a stopping time which is almost surely finite (just adapt the relevant part of the proof of (9.9.5)).

(12) **Theorem.** $\mathbf{E}(U\{T(x, -y)\}) = 1$ *for all* $x, y > 0$.

Proof. This is just an application of the Optional Stopping Theorem (7.9.3), suitably reformulated to deal with continuous-time processes. U is a martingale and $T(x, -y)$ is a stopping time. Thus

$$\mathbf{E}(U\{T(x, -y)\}) = \mathbf{E}(U(0)) = 1. \qquad ■$$

(13) **Corollary.** *If $m < 0$ and $x > 0$ then the probability that D ever visits the point x is*

$$\mathbf{P}(D(t) = x \quad \text{for some } t) = e^{2mx}.$$

Proof. By (12),

$$1 = e^{-2mx}\mathbf{P}(D\{T(x, -y)\} = x) + e^{2my}(1 - \mathbf{P}(D\{T(x, -y)\} = x)).$$

Let $y \to \infty$ to obtain

$$\mathbf{P}(D\{T(x, -y)\} = x) \to e^{2mx}$$

so long as $m < 0$. Now complete the proof yourself. ■

The condition of (13), that the drift be negative, is natural; it is clear that if $m > 0$ then D almost surely visits all points on the positive part of the real axis. The result of (13) tells us about the size of the maximum of D also, since if $x > 0$

$$\{\max_{t \geq 0} D(t) \geq x\} = \{D(t) = x \quad \text{for some } t\}$$

and the distribution of

$$M = \max\{D(t) : t \geq 0\}$$

is easily deduced.

(14) **Corollary.** *If $m < 0$ then M is exponentially distributed with parameter $-2m$.*

9.9 Potential theory

Finally, we return to the three-dimensional Wiener process and show that the study of its sample paths is bound up with the theory of gravitational (or electrostatic) potentials and Laplace's equation.

Recall the theory of scalar potentials. Matter is distributed about regions of $\mathbb{R}^3$. According to the laws of Newtonian attraction, this matter gives rise to a function $V:\mathbb{R}^3 \to \mathbb{R}$ which assigns a potential $V(\boldsymbol{x})$ to each point $\boldsymbol{x} \in \mathbb{R}^3$. In open space V satisfies

(1) **Laplace's equation:** $\nabla^2 V = 0$,

whilst in a region containing matter of density ρ, V satisfies

(2) **Poisson's equation:** $\nabla^2 V = -4\pi\rho$

where

$$\nabla^2 V = \frac{\partial^2 V}{\partial x^2} + \frac{\partial^2 V}{\partial y^2} + \frac{\partial^2 V}{\partial z^2}.$$

The following is an application of Green's Theorem. If $\boldsymbol{\Sigma}$ is the surface of an empty sphere with radius a and centre $\boldsymbol{x}$, then the potential $V(\boldsymbol{x})$ at $\boldsymbol{x}$ can be obtained as the integral of V over the surface of $\boldsymbol{\Sigma}$, suitably normalized by the area of this surface:

(3) $$V(\boldsymbol{x}) = \int_{\boldsymbol{y} \in \boldsymbol{\Sigma}} \frac{V(\boldsymbol{y})}{4\pi a^2}\, \mathrm{d}S.$$

Furthermore, V satisfies (3) for such spheres $\boldsymbol{\Sigma}$ if and only if V is a solution to Laplace's equation (1) in the appropriate region.

Now we return to the Wiener process. Let

$$\boldsymbol{W}(t) = (X(t), Y(t), Z(t))$$

be a three-dimensional Wiener process, so that X, Y, and Z are independent Wiener processes. $\boldsymbol{W}(t)$ is a triple of random variables with joint density function

(4) $$f_{\boldsymbol{W}(t)}(\boldsymbol{r}) = (2\pi\sigma^2 t)^{-3/2} \exp\left(-\frac{1}{2\sigma^2 t}|\boldsymbol{r}-\boldsymbol{w}|^2\right), \qquad \boldsymbol{r} \in \mathbb{R}^3$$

where $\boldsymbol{W}(0) = \boldsymbol{w}$ and $|\boldsymbol{r}|^2 = x^2 + y^2 + z^2$ if $\boldsymbol{r} = (x, y, z)$.

The particle in question performs a random diffusion about $\mathbb{R}^3$. Now, suppose it starts from $\boldsymbol{W}(0) = \boldsymbol{w}$, and ask for the probability that it visits some subset G of $\mathbb{R}^3$ before it visits some other subset H, disjoint from G. A particular case of this might arise as follows. Suppose that $\boldsymbol{w}$ is a point in the interior of some closed bounded connected domain D of $\mathbb{R}^3$, and suppose that the surface ∂D which bounds D is fairly smooth (if D is a ball then ∂D is the bounding spherical surface, for example). Sooner or later the particle will leave D for the first time. If $\partial D = G \cup H$ for some disjoint sets G and H, then we may ask for the probability that the particle leaves D by way of a point in G rather than a point in H (take D to be the solid ball of radius 1 and centre $\mathbf{w}$ for example, and let G be a hemisphere of D).

(5) **Theorem.** *Let G and H be disjoint nice subsets of $\mathbb{R}^3$, and let $p(\mathbf{w}) = \mathbf{P}(\mathbf{W}$ visits G before it visits $H \mid \mathbf{W}(0) = \mathbf{w})$. Then p satisfies Laplace's equation,*

$$\nabla^2 p(\mathbf{w}) = 0$$

at all points $\mathbf{w} \notin G \cup H$, with the boundary conditions

$$p(\mathbf{w}) = \begin{cases} 0 & \text{if } \mathbf{w} \in H \\ 1 & \text{if } \mathbf{w} \in G. \end{cases}$$

We shall not explain the condition that G and H be nice.

Proof. Let $\mathbf{\Sigma}$ be a sphere with radius a and centre $\mathbf{w} \notin G \cup H$, such that no point of $\mathbf{\Sigma}$ or its interior lies in $G \cup H$; we require that $G \cup H$ be closed in order that such a sphere exists for any given $\mathbf{w}$. Let

$$T = \inf\{t : \mathbf{W}(t) \in \mathbf{\Sigma}\}$$

be the first passage time of $\mathbf{W}$ to the sphere $\mathbf{\Sigma}$, starting from $\mathbf{W}(0) = \mathbf{w}$. T is a stopping time for $\mathbf{W}$; the proof of this is omitted, since it is related to the continuity of sample paths, a taboo topic. It is not difficult to see that

$$\mathbf{P}(T < \infty) = 1.$$

For, let A_i be the event

$$A_i = \{|\mathbf{W}(i) - \mathbf{W}(i-1)| \leq 2a\}$$

and note that

$$\begin{aligned} \mathbf{P}(T > n) &\leq \mathbf{P}(A_1 \cap A_2 \cap \ldots \cap A_n) \\ &= \mathbf{P}(A_1)^n \quad \text{by independence} \\ &\to 0 \qquad\quad \text{as } n \to \infty \end{aligned}$$

because $\mathbf{P}(A_1) < 1$. Now, $\mathbf{W}(T) \in \mathbf{\Sigma}$, and the spherical symmetry of the density function (4) of $\mathbf{W}(t)$ implies that $\mathbf{W}(T)$ is uniformly distributed over the surface of $\mathbf{\Sigma}$. The subsequent path of the process is a copy of $\mathbf{W}$, but with the new starting point $\mathbf{W}(T)$; this follows from the Strong Markov Property. Thus, the probability that $\mathbf{W}$ visits G before it visits H is just $p(\mathbf{W}(T))$, and we are led to the surface integral

(6)
$$p(\mathbf{w}) = \int_{\mathbf{y} \in \mathbf{\Sigma}} \mathbf{P}(G \text{ before } H \mid \mathbf{W}(T) = \mathbf{y}) f(\mathbf{y})\, dS$$

where

$$\{G \text{ before } H\} = \{\mathbf{W} \text{ visits } G \text{ before it visits } H\}$$

and $f(\mathbf{y})$ is the conditional density function of $\mathbf{W}(T)$ given $\mathbf{W}(0)=\mathbf{w}$. However,

$$f(\mathbf{y})=\frac{1}{4\pi a^2} \quad \text{for all } \mathbf{y}\in\mathbf{\Sigma}$$

by the uniformity of $\mathbf{W}(T)$, and (6) becomes

(7) $$p(\mathbf{w})=\int_{\mathbf{y}\in\mathbf{\Sigma}} \frac{p(\mathbf{y})}{4\pi a^2}\,\mathrm{d}S.$$

This integral equation holds for any sphere $\mathbf{\Sigma}$ with centre $\mathbf{w}$ whose contents do not overlap $G\cup H$, and we recognize it as the characteristic property (3) of solutions to Laplace's equation (1). Thus p satisfies Laplace's equation. The boundary conditions are derived easily. ■

This simple observation provides us with an elegant technique for finding the probabilities that $\mathbf{W}$ visits certain subsets of $\mathbb{R}^3$. The principles of the method are simple, although some of the ensuing calculations may be lengthy (see Example (14) and Problem (9.10.19b), for instance).

(8) **Example.** The foregoing discussion holds in two dimensions also. Start a two-dimensional Wiener process $\mathbf{W}$ from a point $\mathbf{W}(0)=\mathbf{w}\in\mathbb{R}^2$. Let G be a circle, radius ϵ and centre at the origin, such that $\mathbf{w}$ does not lie within the interior of G. What is the probability that $\mathbf{W}$ visits G ever?

Solution. We shall need two boundary conditions in order to find the appropriate solution to Laplace's equation. The first arises from the case when $\mathbf{w}\in G$. To find the second, let H be a circle, radius R and centre at the origin and suppose that R is much bigger than ϵ. We shall solve Laplace's equation in polar co-ordinates

(9) $$\frac{1}{r}\frac{\partial}{\partial r}\left(r\frac{\partial p}{\partial r}\right)+\frac{1}{r^2}\frac{\partial^2 p}{\partial\theta^2}=0$$

in the region $\epsilon\leqslant r\leqslant R$, and use the boundary conditions

(10) $$p(\mathbf{w})=\begin{cases}0 & \text{if } \mathbf{w}\in H\\ 1 & \text{if } \mathbf{w}\in G\end{cases}$$

to find

$$p(\mathbf{w})=\mathbf{P}(G \text{ before } H \mid \mathbf{W}(0)=\mathbf{w}).$$

Solutions to (9) with circular symmetry take the form

$$p(\mathbf{w})=A\log r+B \quad \text{if} \quad \mathbf{w}=(r,\theta)$$

where A and B are arbitrary constants. Use (10) to obtain

$$p(\mathbf{w})=\frac{\log(r/R)}{\log(\epsilon/R)}.$$

Now let $R \to \infty$ to obtain that

$$\mathbf{P}(G \text{ before } H \mid \mathbf{W}(0) = (r, \theta)) \to 1.$$

We have shown that $\mathbf{W}$ almost surely visits any ϵ-neighbourhood of the origin regardless of its starting point. Such a process is called *persistent* (or *recurrent*) since its sample paths pass arbitrarily closely to every point in the plane with probability one. ●

(11) **Example.** Next consider a three-dimensional version of (8). Let G be the sphere with radius ϵ and centre at the origin of $\mathbb{R}^3$. Again, start a three-dimensional Wiener process $\mathbf{W}$ from some point $\mathbf{W}(0) = \mathbf{w}$ which does not lie within G. What is the probability that $\mathbf{W}$ visits G?

Solution. As before, let H be a sphere with radius R and centre at the origin, where R is much larger than ϵ. We seek a solution to Laplace's equation in spherical polar co-ordinates

$$\frac{\partial}{\partial r}\left(r^2 \frac{\partial p}{\partial r}\right) + \frac{1}{\sin\theta}\frac{\partial}{\partial\theta}\left(\sin\theta \frac{\partial p}{\partial\theta}\right) + \frac{1}{\sin^2\phi}\frac{\partial^2 p}{\partial\phi^2} = 0, \tag{12}$$

subject to the boundary conditions (10), in order to find

$$p(\mathbf{w}) = \mathbf{P}(G \text{ before } H \mid \mathbf{W}(0) = \mathbf{w}).$$

Solutions to (12), which depend on r only, take the form

$$p(\mathbf{w}) = \frac{A}{r} + B \quad \text{if} \quad \mathbf{w} = (r, \theta, \phi). \tag{13}$$

Use (10) to obtain

$$p(\mathbf{w}) = \frac{r^{-1} - R^{-1}}{\epsilon^{-1} - R^{-1}}.$$

Let $R \to \infty$ to obtain

$$\mathbf{P}(G \text{ before } H \mid \mathbf{W}(0) = (r, \theta, \phi)) \to \frac{\epsilon}{r}$$

and we have shown that $\mathbf{W}$ ultimately visits G with probability ϵ/r; is it surprising that the answer is *directly* proportional to ϵ?

We have shown that the three-dimensional Wiener process is *not* persistent, since its sample paths do not pass through every ϵ-neighbourhood with probability one. This mimics the behaviour of symmetric random walks. Recall from Problems (5.11.5) and (6.13.6) that the two-dimensional symmetric random walk is persistent whilst the three-dimensional walk is transient (see (15) also). ●

(14) **Example.** Let Σ be the unit sphere in $\mathbb{R}^3$ with centre at the origin, and let

$$G = \{(r, \theta, \phi) : r = 1, 0 \leq \theta \leq \tfrac{1}{2}\pi\}$$

be the upper hemisphere of $\boldsymbol{\Sigma}$. Start a three-dimensional Wiener process $\mathbf{W}$ from a point $\mathbf{W}(0)=\mathbf{w}$ which lies in the *interior* of $\boldsymbol{\Sigma}$. What is the probability that $\mathbf{W}$ visits G before it visits $H=\boldsymbol{\Sigma}\backslash G$, the lower hemisphere of $\boldsymbol{\Sigma}$?

Solution. Let

$$p(\mathbf{w})=\mathbf{P}(G \text{ before } H \mid \mathbf{W}(0)=\mathbf{w}).$$

p satisfies Laplace's equation (12), subject to the boundary conditions (10). Solutions to (12) which are independent of ϕ are also solutions to the simpler equation

$$\frac{\partial}{\partial r}\left(r^2\frac{\partial p}{\partial r}\right)+\frac{1}{\sin\theta}\frac{\partial}{\partial\theta}\left(\sin\theta\frac{\partial p}{\partial\theta}\right)=0.$$

We abandon the calculation at this point, leaving it to the reader to complete. Some knowledge of Legendre polynomials and the method of separation of variables may prove useful. ●

(15) **Example. Random walks revisited.** We may think of a Wiener process as a continuous space-time version of a symmetric random walk. In the light of the discussion of Brownian motion in Section 9.6, it is not surprising that Wiener processes and random walks have many properties in common. In particular, potential theory has applications to random walks; we terminate this chapter with a brief but powerful demonstration of this. For simplicity we consider a symmetric random walk on the two-dimensional square lattice $\mathbb{Z}^2$, but it will be clear that more general results are obtainable by similar arguments.

A particle moves about the points $\{(m, n): m, n=0, \pm 1, \pm 2, \ldots\}$ according to the following rule. If after n steps it is at the point (x, y), then it moves at the next step to one of the four neighbouring points $(x\pm 1, y)$, $(x, y\pm 1)$, each such point being chosen with probability $\frac{1}{4}$ independently of all previous choices. We write $\mathbf{W}_n$ for the particle's position after n steps. We are concerned with first passage probabilities. Let G and H be disjoint sets of points in $\mathbb{Z}^2$, and write

$$p(\mathbf{w})=\mathbf{P}(G \text{ before } H \mid \mathbf{W}_0=\mathbf{w})$$

for the probability that the walk $\mathbf{W}$ visits some point in G before it visits any point in H, starting from the point $\mathbf{w}$. In place of the integral equation (7), p satisfies the difference equation

(16)
$$p(\mathbf{w})=\tfrac{1}{4}\{p((w_1+1, w_2))+p((w_1-1, w_2))+p((w_1, w_2+1)) +p((w_1, w_2-1))\},$$

where $\mathbf{w}=(w_1, w_2)$, subject to the boundary conditions

(17)
$$p(\mathbf{w})=\begin{cases}0 & \text{if } \mathbf{w}\in H\\ 1 & \text{if } \mathbf{w}\in G.\end{cases}$$

Equation (16) is easily derived by conditioning on the first step of the walk.

Now think of $\mathbb{Z}^2$ as an electrical network in which each pair of neighbouring points ((0, 0) and (0, 1), for example) is joined by a conducting wire with resistance 1 ohm. Connect a battery into the network in such a way that the points in H are joined to earth and the points in G are raised to the potential 1 volt. It is physically clear that this potential difference induces a potential $V(\mathbf{w})$ at each point $\mathbf{w}$ of $\mathbb{Z}^2$, together with a current along each wire. These potentials and currents satisfy a well known collection of equations called Kirchhoff's Laws and Ohm's Law, and it is an easy consequence of these laws (*exercise*) that V satisfies (16) and (17). This equivalence between first passage probabilities and electrical potentials is the discrete analogue of Theorem (5). As a beautiful application of this equivalence, we show that the walk is persistent; you have seen two proofs of this result already (remember Problem (5.11.5)).

(18) **Theorem.** *The two-dimensional symmetric random walk is persistent.*

Proof. Let G be the origin 0 of $\mathbb{Z}^2$ and let H_n be the set of points $\{(x, \pm n), (\pm n, y) : -n \leq x, y \leq n\}$ on the edge of the square with side length $2n$ and centre at 0. Then

$$p_n(\mathbf{w}) = \mathbf{P}(0 \text{ before } H_n \mid \mathbf{W}_0 = \mathbf{w})$$

satisfies (16) and (17). If $\mathbf{W}_0 = 0$ then we may see that the probability ${}_np_{00}$, that $\mathbf{W}$ revisits 0 before hitting H_n, satisfies

(19) $${}_np_{00} = \tfrac{1}{4}\{p_n((0, 1)) + p_n((1, 0)) + p_n((0, -1)) + p_n((-1, 0))\},$$

by conditioning on the first step. Also, 0 is a persistent state if and only if ${}_np_{00} \to 1$ as $n \to \infty$.

Now think of $\mathbb{Z}^2$ as an electrical network. By (19) and the remarks preceding the theorem, $4(1 - {}_np_{00})$ equals the current which flows into the network at 0 as a result of applying 1 volt at 0 and earthing all the points in H_n. By Ohm's Law, the resistance R_n between 0 and H_n satisfies

$$R_n = \frac{1}{4(1 - {}_np_{00})},$$

and it follows that 0 is persistent if and only if $R_n \to \infty$ as $n \to \infty$. To show that this holds, construct a lower bound for R_n in the following way. For each $r \leq n$, short out all the points in H_r (draw your own diagram), and use the parallel and series resistance laws to find that

$$R_n \geq \frac{1}{4} + \frac{1}{12} + \ldots + \frac{1}{8n-4}.$$

This shows that $R_n \to \infty$ as $n \to \infty$, and the result is shown. ■

(20) **Theorem.** *The three-dimensional symmetric random walk is transient.*

Proof. This is an *exercise*. You must show that the resistance between 0 and the "points at infinity" is finite in $\mathbb{Z}^3$. See the solution of Problem (6.13.6) for another method of proof. ■●

9.10 Problems

1. Let $X=\{X_n : n \geq 1\}$ be given by

$$X_n = \cos(nU)$$

where U is uniformly distributed on $[-\pi, \pi]$. Show that X is stationary but not strictly stationary. Find the autocorrelation function of X and its spectral density function.

2. Let W be a standard Wiener process and define $X=\{X(t): t \geq 1\}$ by

$$X(t) = W(t) - W(t-1).$$

Show that X is strictly stationary and find its autocovariance function. Find the spectral density function of X.

3. Let $Z_0, Z_1, \ldots$ be uncorrelated variables, each with zero mean and unit variance.
   (a) Define the moving average process X by

$$X_n = Z_n + \alpha Z_{n-1}$$

   where α is a constant. Show that X is stationary and find its spectral density function.
   (b) More generally, let

$$Y_n = \sum_{i=0}^{r} \alpha_i Z_{n-i},$$

   where $\alpha_0 = 1$ and $\alpha_1, \ldots, \alpha_r$ are constants. Find the spectral density function of Y.

4. Show that the complex-valued stationary process $X=\{X(t): -\infty < t < \infty\}$ has a spectral density function whenever its autocorrelation function ρ is continuous and satisfies

$$\int_0^\infty |\rho(t)|\, dt < \infty.$$

5. Define the norm $\|\cdot\|$ by

$$\|Z\| = (\mathbf{E}(|Z|^2))^{1/2}$$

for any complex-valued random variable Z. Show that $\|\cdot\|$ satisfies the 'parallelogram rule'

$$\|X+Y\|^2 + \|X-Y\|^2 = 2\|X\|^2 + 2\|Y\|^2$$

for any X and Y with finite second moment.

6. Let $X=\{X_n : n \geq 1\}$ be stationary with autocovariance function c. Fix $\lambda_1, \ldots, \lambda_N$ and define $Y=\{Y_n : n \geq 1\}$ by

$$Y_k = \lambda_1 X_k + \lambda_2 X_{k+1} + \ldots + \lambda_N X_{k+N-1}.$$

Show that Y is stationary, and express its autocovariance function in terms of c and $\boldsymbol{\lambda}$.

7. Consider the ergodic theorem (9.4.3) for weakly stationary processes. Suppose

that $X=\{X_n:n\geq 1\}$ is a real-valued stationary process with zero means. Show that

$$\mathbf{E}\left(\left(\frac{1}{n}\sum_{j=1}^{n}X_j\right)^2\right)\to 0 \quad \text{as} \quad n\to\infty$$

if and only if the autocovariance function c satisfies

$$\frac{1}{n}\sum_{j=0}^{n-1}c(j)\to 0 \quad \text{as} \quad n\to\infty.$$

You have shown that this condition is necessary and sufficient for $n^{-1}\sum_{j=1}^{n}X_j$ to converge to 0 in mean square.

8. Let $X=\{X_n:n\geq 1\}$ be stationary with constant mean $\mu=\mathbf{E}(X_n)$ for all n. Use the previous question to show that

$$\frac{1}{n}\sum_{j=1}^{n}X_j \xrightarrow{\text{m.s.}} \mu$$

whenever $\operatorname{cov}(X(0),X(n))\to 0$ as $n\to\infty$.

9. (a) Use the result of (8) and the Ergodic Theorem (9.4.2) to deduce the Law of Large Numbers (7.4.3).
(b) Use the zero–one law (7.3.17) and the Ergodic Theorem (9.4.2) to deduce the Strong Law of Large Numbers (7.5.1).

10. Let $X=\{X(t):t\geq 0\}$ be a non-decreasing random process such that
(a) $X(0)=0$, X takes values in the non-negative integers
(b) X has stationary independent increments
(c) the sample paths $\{X(t,\omega):t\geq 0\}$ have only jump discontinuities of unit magnitude.
Show that X is a Poisson process.

11. Let X be a continuous-time process. Show that
(a) if X has stationary increments and $m(t)=\mathbf{E}(X(t))$ is a continuous function of t, then there exist α and β such that

$$m(t)=\alpha+\beta t$$

(b) if X has stationary independent increments and $v(t)=\operatorname{var}(X(t))$ is a continuous function of t then there exists σ^2 such that

$$\operatorname{var}(X(s+t)-X(s))=\sigma^2 t \quad \text{for all } s.$$

12. Let W be a standard Wiener process, and let α be a positive constant. Show that
(a) $\alpha W(t/\alpha^2)$ is a standard Wiener process
(b) $W(t+\alpha)-W(\alpha)$ is a standard Wiener process
(c) the process V, given by $V(t)=tW(1/t)$ for $t>0$, $V(0)=0$, is a standard Wiener process.

13 Use (9.7.11) to show that the Ornstein–Uhlenbeck process $V=\{V(t):t\geq 0\}$ is such that $V(t)$ is $N(ue^{-\beta t},\sigma^2(1-e^{-2\beta t})/(2\beta))$ where $u=V(0)$. Deduce that $V(t)$ is asymptotically $N(0,\frac{1}{2}\sigma^2/\beta)$ as $t\to\infty$, and show that V is strictly stationary if $V(0)$ is $N(0,\frac{1}{2}\sigma^2/\beta)$. Use Example (9.5.10) to show that such a process is the *only* stationary Gaussian Markov process with continuous autocovariance function, and find its spectral density function.

14. Let $X=\{X(t):t\geq 0\}$ be a Gaussian process with zero means and autocovariance

function

$$c(s, t) = u(s)v(t) \quad \text{for} \quad s \leq t$$

where u and v are continuous functions. Suppose that the ratio

$$r(t) = u(t)/v(t)$$

is continuous and strictly increasing with inverse function r^{-1}. Show that

$$W(t) = \frac{X(r^{-1}(t))}{v(r^{-1}(t))}$$

is a standard Wiener process. If

$$c(s, t) = s(1-t) \quad \text{for} \quad s \leq t < 1$$

express X in terms of W.

15. Show that

$$U(t) = e^{-\beta t} W(e^{2\beta t} - 1)$$

is an Ornstein–Uhlenbeck process if W is a standard Wiener process.

16. Let D be a Wiener process with drift m and unit variance (see (9.7.10) and Section 9.8), and suppose that $D(0) = 0$. Place an absorbing barrier at the point $b(>0)$, and show that $D(t)$ has density function

$$f_{D(t)}(y) = \frac{1}{\sqrt{(2\pi t)}} \left[\exp\left\{ -\frac{(y-mt)^2}{2t} \right\} - \exp\left\{ 2mb - \frac{(y-2b-mt)^2}{2t} \right\} \right]$$

for $y < b$.

17. Let D be a Wiener process with drift m, and again suppose that $D(0) = 0$. This time place absorbing barriers at the points $x = -a$ and $x = b$ where a and b are positive real numbers. Show that the probability p_a that the process is absorbed at $-a$ is given by

$$p_a = \frac{e^{2mb} - 1}{e^{2m(a+b)} - 1}.$$

Compare this with the result of (7.9.5).

18. Let W be a standard Wiener process and let $F(u, v)$ be the event that W has no zero in the interval (u, v).

(a) If $ab > 0$, show that $\mathbf{P}(F(0, t) \mid W(0) = a,\ W(t) = b) = 1 - \exp(-2ab/t)$.
(b) If $W(0) = 0$ and $0 < t_0 \leq t_1 \leq t_2$, show that

$$\mathbf{P}(F(t_0, t_2) \mid F(t_0, t_1)) = \frac{\sin^{-1}\{(t_0/t_2)^{1/2}\}}{\sin^{-1}\{(t_0/t_1)^{1/2}\}}.$$

(c) If $W(0) = 0$ and $0 < t_1 \leq t_2$, show that

$$\mathbf{P}(F(0, t_2) \mid F(0, t_1)) = (t_1/t_2)^{1/2}.$$

19. (a) Let $\mathbf{W}$ be a two-dimensional standard Wiener process with $\mathbf{W}(0) = \mathbf{w}$, and let F be the unit circle. What is the probability that $\mathbf{W}$ visits the upper semicircle G of F before it visits the lower semicircle H?
(b) Complete Example (9.9.14).

20. Let W_1 and W_2 be independent standard Wiener processes with $W_1(0) = W_2(0) = 0$; the pair $\mathbf{W}(t) = (W_1(t), W_2(t))$ represents the position of a particle

which is experiencing Brownian motion in the plane. Let ℓ be some straight line in $\mathbb{R}^2$, and let P be the point on ℓ which is closest to the origin O. Draw a diagram. Show that

(a) the particle visits ℓ, with probability one,

(b) if the particle hits ℓ for the first time at the point R, then the distance PR (measured as positive or negative as appropriate) has the Cauchy density function

$$f(x)=\frac{d}{\pi(d^2+x^2)}, \quad -\infty<x<\infty$$

where d is the distance OP,

(c) the angle $\mathrm{P\hat{O}R}$ is uniformly distributed on $[-\frac{1}{2}\pi, \frac{1}{2}\pi]$.

10 Renewals

10.1 The renewal equation

We saw in Section 8.3 that renewal processes provide attractive models for many natural phenomena. Recall their definition.

(1) **Definition.** A **renewal process** $N=\{N(t):t\geq 0\}$ is a process such that

$$N(t)=\max\{n:T_n\leq t\}$$

where

$$T_0=0, \qquad T_n=X_1+\ldots+X_n \quad \text{for} \quad n\geq 1$$

and $\{X_i\}$ is a sequence of independent identically distributed non-negative† random variables.

We commonly think of a renewal process $N(t)$ as representing the number of occurrences of some event in the time interval $[0, t]$; the event in question might be the arrival of a person or particle, or the failure of a light bulb. With this in mind, we shall speak of T_n as the 'time of the nth arrival' and X_n as the nth inter-arrival time'. We shall try to use the notation of (1) consistently throughout, denoting by X and T a typical inter-arrival time and a typical arrival time of the process N.

When is N an honest process (see (6.8.18) for the definition of honesty)?

(2) **Theorem.** $\mathbf{P}(N(t)<\infty)=1$ *for all t if and only if* $\mathbf{E}(X_1)>0$.

This amounts to saying that N is honest if and only if the inter-arrival times are not concentrated at zero. The proof is simple and relies upon the following important observation:

(3) $$N(t)\geq n \quad \textit{if and only if} \quad T_n\leq t.$$

We shall make repeated use of (3). It provides a link between $N(t)$ and the sum T_n of independent variables; we know a lot about such sums already.

Proof of (2). Clearly, if $\mathbf{E}(X_1)=0$ then

$$\mathbf{P}(X_i=0)=1 \quad \text{for all } i$$

since the X's are non-negative, and so

$$\mathbf{P}(N(t)=\infty)=1 \quad \text{for all } t>0.$$

† But soon we will impose the stronger condition that the X's be *strictly* positive.

Conversely, suppose that $\mathbf{E}(X_1)>0$. There exists $\epsilon>0$ such that $\mathbf{P}(X_1>\epsilon)=\delta>0$. Writing A_i for the event $\{X_i>\epsilon\}$, we see that the event $A=\{X_i>\epsilon \text{ i.o.}\}=\limsup A_i$, that infinitely many of the X's exceed ϵ, occurs with probability one, since

$$\mathbf{P}(A^c)=\mathbf{P}(X_n\leqslant\epsilon \text{ for all large } n)=\lim_{m\to\infty}(1-\delta)^m=0;$$

remember (1.8.14). Therefore, by (3),

$$\mathbf{P}(N(t)=\infty)=\mathbf{P}(T_n\leqslant t \text{ for all } n)\leqslant\mathbf{P}(A^c)=0. \qquad \blacksquare$$

Thus N is honest if and only if X_1 is *not* concentrated at 0. Henceforth we shall assume not only that $\mathbf{P}(X_1=0)<1$, but also impose the stronger condition that $\mathbf{P}(X_1=0)=0$. That is, *we consider only the case when the X's are strictly positive.*

It is easy in principle to find the distribution of $N(t)$ in terms of the distribution of a typical inter-arrival time. Let F be the distribution function of X_1, and let F_k be the distribution function of T_k.

(4) **Lemma.**† *$F_1=F$ and $F_{k+1}(x)=\int_0^x F_k(x-y)\,dF(y)$ for $k\geqslant 1$.*

Proof. Clearly $F_1=F$. Also

$$T_{k+1}=T_k+X_{k+1},$$

and (4.8.1) gives the result when suitably rewritten for independent variables of general type. $\blacksquare$

(5) **Lemma.** $\mathbf{P}(N(t)=k)=F_k(t)-F_{k+1}(t)$.

Proof. $\{N(t)=k\}=\{N(t)\geqslant k\}\backslash\{N(t)\geqslant k+1\}$. Now use (3). $\blacksquare$

We shall be interested largely in the expected value of $N(t)$.

(6) **Definition.** The **renewal function** m is given by $m(t)=\mathbf{E}(N(t))$.

Again, it is easy to find m in terms of the F's.

(7) **Lemma.** $m(t)=\sum_{k=1}^{\infty}F_k(t)$.

Proof. Define the indicator variables

$$I_k=\begin{cases}1 & \text{if } T_k\leqslant t\\ 0 & \text{otherwise.}\end{cases}$$

† Readers of Section 5.6 may notice that the statement of this lemma violates our notation for the domain of an integral. We adopt the convention that expressions like $\int_a^b g(y)\,dF(y)$ denote integrals over the half-open interval $(a, b]$, with the left endpoint excluded.

Then

$$N(t) = \sum_{k=1}^{\infty} I_k$$

and so

$$m(t) = \mathbf{E}\left(\sum_{k=1}^{\infty} I_k\right) = \sum_{k=1}^{\infty} \mathbf{E}(I_k) = \sum_{k=1}^{\infty} F_k(t). \qquad \blacksquare$$

An alternative approach to the renewal function is by way of conditional expectations and the 'renewal equation'. First note that m is the solution of a certain integral equation.

(8) **Lemma.** *The renewal function m satisfies the* ***renewal equation,***

(9) $$m(t) = F(t) + \int_0^t m(t-x)\, \mathrm{d}F(x).$$

Proof. Use conditional expectation to obtain

$$m(t) = \mathbf{E}(N(t)) = \mathbf{E}(\mathbf{E}(N(t) \mid X_1));$$

but,

$$\mathbf{E}(N(t) \mid X_1 = x) = 0 \quad \text{if} \quad t < x$$

since the first arrival occurs after time t. On the other hand,

$$\mathbf{E}(N(t) \mid X_1 = x) = 1 + \mathbf{E}(N(t-x)) \quad \text{if} \quad t \geqslant x$$

since the process of arrivals, starting from the epoch of the first arrival, is a copy of N itself. Thus

$$m(t) = \int_0^{\infty} \mathbf{E}(N(t) \mid X_1 = x)\, \mathrm{d}F(x) = \int_0^t \{1 + m(t-x)\}\, \mathrm{d}F(x)$$

as required. $\blacksquare$

We know from (7) that

$$m(t) = \sum_{k=1}^{\infty} F_k(t)$$

is a solution to the renewal equation (9). Actually, it is the unique solution to (9) which is bounded on finite intervals. This is a consequence of the next lemma. We shall encounter a more general form of (9) later, and it is appropriate to anticipate this now. The more general case involves solutions μ to the *renewal-type equation*

(10) $$\mu(t) = H(t) + \int_0^t \mu(t-x)\, \mathrm{d}F(x), \qquad t \geqslant 0$$

where H is a uniformly bounded function.

(11) **Theorem.** *The function* μ, *given by*

$$\mu(t) = H(t) + \int_0^t H(t-x)\,\mathrm{d}m(x),$$

is a solution of the renewal-type equation (10). *If* H *is bounded on finite intervals then* μ *is bounded on finite intervals and is the unique solution of* (10) *with this property*†.

We shall make repeated use of this result, the proof of which is simple.

Proof. If $h:[0,\infty)\to\mathbb{R}$, define the functions $h*m$ and $h*F$ by

$$(h*m)(t) = \int_0^t h(t-x)\,\mathrm{d}m(x)$$

$$(h*F)(t) = \int_0^t h(t-x)\,\mathrm{d}F(x)$$

whenever these integrals exist. The operation $*$ is a type of convolution; do not confuse it with the related but different convolution operator of Sections 3.8 and 4.8. It can be shown that

$$(h*m)*F = h*(m*F),$$

and so we write $h*m*F$ for this double convolution. Note also that

(12) $$m = F + m*F \quad \text{by (9)}$$

(13) $$F_{k+1} = F_k * F = F * F_k \quad \text{by (4).}$$

Using this notation, μ can be written as

$$\mu = H + H*m.$$

Convolute with F and use (12) to find that

$$\begin{aligned}\mu*F &= H*F + H*m*F\\ &= H*F + H*(m-F)\\ &= H*m = \mu - H,\end{aligned}$$

and so μ satisfies (10).

If H is bounded on finite intervals then

$$\begin{aligned}\sup_{0\le t\le T}|\mu(t)| &\le \sup_{0\le t\le T}|H(t)| + \sup_{0\le t\le T}\left|\int_0^t H(t-x)\,\mathrm{d}m(x)\right|\\ &\le (1+m(T))\sup_{0\le t\le T}|H(t)| < \infty,\end{aligned}$$

† Think of the integral in (11) as $\int H(t-x)m'(x)\,\mathrm{d}x$ if you are unhappy about its present form.

and so μ is indeed bounded on finite intervals; we have used the finiteness of m here (see Problem (10.5.1b)). To show that μ is the unique such solution of (10), suppose that μ_1 is another bounded solution and write $\delta(t)=\mu(t)-\mu_1(t)$; δ is a bounded function. Also

$$\delta=\delta * F \text{ by (10).}$$

Iterate this equation and use (13) to find that

$$\delta=\delta * F_k \quad \text{for all } k\geq 1$$

which implies that

$$|\delta(t)|\leq F_k(t) \sup_{0\leq u\leq t} |\delta(u)| \quad \text{for all } k\geq 1.$$

Let $k\to\infty$ to find that $|\delta(t)|=0$ for all t, since

$$F_k(t)=\mathbf{P}(N(t)\geq k)\to 0 \quad \text{as} \quad k\to\infty$$

by (2). The proof is complete. ■

The method of Laplace–Stieltjes transforms is often useful in renewal theory (see Definition (15) of Appendix I). For example, we can transform (10) to obtain the formula

$$\mu^*(\theta)=\frac{H^*(\theta)}{1-F^*(\theta)} \quad \text{for} \quad \theta\neq 0,$$

an equation which links the Laplace–Stieltjes transforms of μ, H, and F. In particular, setting $H=F$, we find from (8) that

(14) $$m^*(\theta)=\frac{F^*(\theta)}{1-F^*(\theta)},$$

a formula which is directly derivable from (7) and (13). Hence there is a one–one correspondence between the renewal functions m, and the distribution functions F of the inter-arrival times.

(15) **Example. Poisson process.** This is the only Markovian renewal process, and has exponentially distributed inter-arrival times with some parameter λ. The epoch T_k of the kth arrival is distributed as $\Gamma(\lambda, k)$; Lemma (7) gives that

$$m(t)=\sum_{k=1}^{\infty}\int_0^t \frac{\lambda(\lambda s)^{k-1}e^{-\lambda s}}{(k-1)!}\,ds=\int_0^t \lambda\,ds=\lambda t.$$

Alternatively, just remember that $N(t)$ is Poisson with parameter λt to obtain the same result. ●

10.2 Limit theorems

Next, we study the asymptotic behaviour of $N(t)$ and its renewal function $m(t)$ for large values of t. There are four main results here, two for each of N and m. For the renewal process N itself there is a law of large numbers and a central limit theorem; these rely upon the relation (10.1.3), which links N to the partial sums of independent variables. The two results for m deal also with first- and second-order properties. The first asserts that $m(t)$ is approximately linear in t; the second asserts that the gradient of m is asymptotically constant.

How does $N(t)$ behave when t is large? Let $\mu = \mathbf{E}(X_1)$ be the mean of a typical inter-arrival time. Henceforth we assume that $\mu < \infty$.

(1) **Theorem.** $\frac{1}{t}N(t) \xrightarrow{\text{a.s.}} \frac{1}{\mu}$ *as* $t \to \infty$.

(2) **Theorem.** *If* $\sigma^2 = \text{var}(X_1)$ *and* $0 < \sigma < \infty$, *then*

$$\frac{N(t) - t/\mu}{(t\sigma^2/\mu^3)^{1/2}} \xrightarrow{\text{D}} N(0, 1) \quad \textit{as} \quad t \to \infty.$$

It is not quite so easy to find the asymptotic behaviour of the renewal function.

(3) **Elementary Renewal Theorem.** $\frac{1}{t}m(t) \to \frac{1}{\mu}$ *as* $t \to \infty$.

The second-order properties of m are hard to find, and require a preliminary definition.

(4) **Definition.** Call a random variable X and its distribution F_X **arithmetic with span** $\lambda(>0)$ if X takes values in the set $\{m\lambda : m = 0, \pm 1, \dots\}$ with probability one, and λ is maximal with this property.

If the inter-arrival times of N are arithmetic, with span λ say, then so is T_k for each k. In this case $m(t)$ may be discontinuous at values of t which are multiples of λ, and this affects the second-order properties of m.

(5) **Renewal Theorem.** *If* X_1 *is not arithmetic then*

(6) $$m(t+h) - m(t) \to \frac{h}{\mu} \quad \textit{as} \quad t \to \infty \quad \textit{for all } h.$$

If X_1 *is arithmetic with span* λ, *then* (6) *holds whenever* h *is a multiple of* λ.

It is appropriate to make some remarks about these theorems before we set to their proofs. Theorems (1) and (2) are straightforward, and use the Law of Large Numbers and the Central Limit Theorem for partial sums of independent sequences. It is perhaps surprising that (3) is harder to demonstrate than (1) since it concerns only the mean value of $N(t)$; it has a suitably probabilistic proof which uses the method of truncation, a technique which proved useful in the proof of the Strong Law (7.5.1). On the other hand, the proof of (5) is difficult. The usual method of proof is largely an exercise in solving integral equations; it is not appropriate to include this here (see Feller 1971, p. 360). There is an alternative proof which is short, beautiful, and probabilistic, and uses 'coupling' arguments related to those in the proof of the ergodic theorem for discrete-time Markov chains. This method requires some results which appear later in this chapter, and so we defer a sketch of the argument until (10.4.21). There is an apparently more general form of (5) which is deducible from (5). It is called the 'Key Renewal Theorem' because of its many applications.

In the rest of this chapter we shall commonly assume that the interarrival times are *not* arithmetic. Similar results often hold in the arithmetic case, but they are usually more complicated to state.

(7) **Key Renewal Theorem.** *If* $g:[0,\infty)\rightarrow[0,\infty)$ *is such that*

(a) $g(t)\geqslant 0$ *for all* t

(b) $\int_0^\infty g(t)\,dt<\infty$

(c) g *is monotone non-increasing*

then

$$\int_0^t g(t-x)\,dm(x)\rightarrow\frac{1}{\mu}\int_0^\infty g(x)\,dx \quad as \quad t\rightarrow\infty$$

whenever X_1 *is not arithmetic.*

Some hints about proving this are given in Problem (10.5.3).

Proof of (1). This is easy. Just note that

(8) $T_{N(t)}\leqslant t<T_{N(t)+1}$ for all t.

Therefore, if $N(t)>0$,

$$\frac{T_{N(t)}}{N(t)}\leqslant\frac{t}{N(t)}<\frac{T_{N(t)+1}}{N(t)+1}\left\{1+\frac{1}{N(t)}\right\}.$$

As $t\rightarrow\infty$, $N(t)\xrightarrow{\text{a.s.}}\infty$, and the Strong Law of Large Numbers gives

$$\mu\leqslant\lim_{t\rightarrow\infty}\left(\frac{t}{N(t)}\right)\leqslant\mu \quad \text{almost surely.}$$ ∎

Proof of (2). This is Problem (10.5.4). ∎

We need a lemma to prepare for the proof of (3).

(9) **Lemma.** *$M = N(t)+1$ is a stopping time for $\{X_j; j \geq 1\}$ for any t, and thus*

$$\mathbf{E}(T_{N(t)+1}) = \mu(m(t)+1).$$

Proof. See (7.9.1) for the definition of a stopping time. In this case

$$\{M=n\}=\{N(t)=n-1\}=\left\{\sum_{j=1}^{n-1} X_j \leq t < \sum_{j=1}^{n} X_j\right\},$$

and so M is a stopping time. The next part of the lemma is just Wald's equation (7.9.8). ■

The assertion of (9) would fail if M were given by $M = N(t)$ instead of $M = N(t)+1$; the forthcoming Example (10.3.2) is an indication of some of the dangers here.

Proof of (3). Half of this is easy. From (8),

$$t < T_{N(t)+1};$$

take expectations of this and use (9) to obtain

$$\frac{m(t)}{t} > \frac{1}{\mu} - \frac{1}{t}.$$

Letting $t \to \infty$, we obtain

(10) $$\liminf_{t\to\infty} \frac{1}{t} m(t) \geq \frac{1}{\mu}.$$

We may be tempted to proceed as follows in order to bound $m(t)$ above. From (8)

$$T_{N(t)} \leq t$$

and so

(11) $$\begin{aligned} t \geq \mathbf{E}(T_{N(t)}) &= \mathbf{E}(T_{N(t)+1} - X_{N(t)+1}) \\ &= \mu(m(t)+1) - \mathbf{E}(X_{N(t)+1}). \end{aligned}$$

The problem is that $X_{N(t)+1}$ depends on $N(t)$, and so $\mathbf{E}(X_{N(t)+1}) \neq \mu$ in general. To cope with this, truncate the X's at some $c > 0$ to obtain a new sequence

$$X_j^c = \begin{cases} X_j & \text{if } X_j < c \\ c & \text{if } X_j \geq c. \end{cases}$$

Now consider the renewal process N^c with associated inter-arrival times $\{X_j^c\}$. Apply (11) to N^c, noting that $\mu^c = \mathbf{E}(X_j^c) \leq c$, to obtain

(12) $$t \geq \mu^c\{\mathbf{E}(N^c(t))+1\} - c.$$

However, $X_j^c \leq X_j$ for all j, and so $N^c(t) \geq N(t)$ for all t. Therefore

$$\mathbf{E}(N^c(t)) \geq \mathbf{E}(N(t)) = m(t)$$

and (12) becomes

$$\frac{m(t)}{t} \leqslant \frac{1}{\mu^c} + \frac{c-\mu^c}{\mu^c t}.$$

Let $t \to \infty$ to obtain

$$\limsup_{t\to\infty} \frac{1}{t} m(t) \leqslant \frac{1}{\mu^c};$$

now let $c \to \infty$ and use monotone convergence (5.6.12) to find that $\mu^c \to \mu$, and so

$$\limsup_{t\to\infty} \frac{1}{t} m(t) \leqslant \frac{1}{\mu}.$$

Combine this with (10) to obtain the result. ■

10.3 Excess life

Suppose that we begin to observe a renewal process N at some epoch t of time. A certain number $N(t)$ of arrivals have occurred by then, and the next arrival will be the $(N(t)+1)$th. That is to say, we have begun our observation at a point in the random interval

$$I_t = [T_{N(t)}, T_{N(t)+1}),$$

the endpoints of which are arrival times.

(1) **Definition.**

(a) The **excess lifetime** at t is $E(t) = T_{N(t)+1} - t$.
(b) The **current lifetime** (or **age**) at t is $C(t) = t - T_{N(t)}$.
(c) The **total lifetime** at t is $D(t) = E(t) + C(t) = X_{N(t)+1}$.

$E(t)$ is the time which elapses before the next arrival, $C(t)$ is the elapsed time since the last arrival (with the convention that the zeroth arrival occurs at time 0), and $D(t)$ is the length of the inter-arrival time which contains t (see Figure 8.1 for a diagram of these random variables).

(2) **Example. Waiting time paradox.** Suppose that N is a Poisson process with parameter λ. How big is $\mathbf{E}(E(t))$? Consider the two following lines of reasoning.
(A) N is a Markov chain, and so the distribution of $E(t)$ does not depend on the arrivals prior to time t. Thus $E(t)$ has the same mean as $E(0) = X_1$, and so $\mathbf{E}(E(t)) = \lambda^{-1}$.
(B) If t is fairly large, then on average it lies near the midpoint of the inter-arrival interval I_t which contains it. That is

$$\mathbf{E}(E(t)) \simeq \tfrac{1}{2}\mathbf{E}(T_{N(t)+1} - T_{N(t)}) = \tfrac{1}{2}\mathbf{E}(X_{N(t)+1}) = (2\lambda)^{-1}.$$

These arguments cannot both be correct. The reasoning of (B) is false, in that $X_{N(t)+1}$ does *not* have mean λ^{-1}; we have already observed this after

(10.2.11). In fact, $X_{N(t)+1}$ is a very special inter-arrival time; longer intervals have a higher chance of catching t in their interiors than small intervals. In Problem (10.5.6) we shall see that

$$\mathbf{E}(X_{N(t)+1})=\frac{1}{\lambda}(2-e^{-\lambda t}).$$

For this process, $E(t)$ and $C(t)$ are independent for any t; this property holds for no other renewal process with non-arithmetic inter-arrival times. ●

Now we find the distribution of $E(t)$.

(3) **Theorem.** *The distribution function of the excess life $E(t)$ is given by*

$$\mathbf{P}(E(t)\leq y)=F(t+y)-\int_0^t\{1-F(t+y-x)\}\,dm(x).$$

Proof. Condition on X_1 in the usual way to obtain

$$\mathbf{P}(E(t)>y)=\mathbf{E}(\mathbf{P}(E(t)>y\mid X_1)).$$

However, you will see after a little thought that

$$\mathbf{P}(E(t)>y\mid X_1=x)=\begin{cases}\mathbf{P}(E(t-x)>y) & \text{if } x\leq t\\ 0 & \text{if } t<x\leq t+y\\ 1 & \text{if } x>t+y\end{cases}$$

since $E(t)>y$ if and only if no arrivals occur in $(t,t+y]$. Thus

$$\mathbf{P}(E(t)>y)=\int_0^\infty \mathbf{P}(E(t)>y\mid X_1=x)\,dF(x)$$

$$=\int_0^t \mathbf{P}(E(t-x)>y)\,dF(x)+\int_{t+y}^\infty dF(x).$$

So

$$\mu(t)=\mathbf{P}(E(t)>y)$$

satisfies (10.1.10) with $H(t)=1-F(t+y)$; use (10.1.11) to see that

$$\mu(t)=1-F(t+y)+\int_0^t\{1-F(t+y-x)\}\,dm(x)$$

as required. ■

(4) **Corollary.** *The distribution of the current life $C(t)$ is given by*

$$\mathbf{P}(C(t)\geq y)=\begin{cases}0 & \textit{if } y>t\\ 1-F(t)+\displaystyle\int_0^{t-y}\{1-F(t-x)\}\,dm(x) & \textit{if } y\leq t.\end{cases}$$

Proof. $C(t) \geq y$ if and only if there are no arrivals in $(t-y, t]$. Thus

$$\mathbf{P}(C(t) \geq y) = \mathbf{P}(E(t-y) > y) \quad \text{if} \quad y \leq t$$

and the result follows from (3). ∎

Might the renewal process N have stationary increments, in that the distribution of $N(t+s)-N(t)$ depends on s alone when $s \geq 0$? This is true for the Poisson process but fails in general. The reason is simple: generally speaking, the process of arrivals after time t depends on the age t of the process to date. When t is very large, however, it is plausible that the process may forget the date of its inception, thereby settling down into a stationary existence. This turns out to be the case. To show this asymptotic stationarity we need to demonstrate that the distribution of $N(t+s)-N(t)$ converges as $t \to \infty$. It is not difficult to see that this is equivalent to the assertion that the distribution of the excess life $E(t)$ settles down as $t \to \infty$, an easy consequence of the Key Renewal Theorem (10.2.7) and (4.3.4).

(5) **Theorem.** *If X_1 is not arithmetic and $\mu = \mathbf{E}(X_1) < \infty$ then*

$$\mathbf{P}(E(t) \leq y) \to \frac{1}{\mu} \int_0^y \{1 - F(x)\}\, dx \quad \textit{as} \quad t \to \infty.$$

Some difficulties arise if X_1 is arithmetic. For example, if the X's are concentrated at the value 1 then, as $n \to \infty$,

$$\mathbf{P}(E(n+c) \leq \tfrac{1}{2}) \to \begin{cases} 1 & \text{if} \quad c = \frac{1}{2} \\ 0 & \text{if} \quad c = \frac{1}{4}. \end{cases}$$

10.4 Applications

Here are some examples of the ways in which renewal theory can be applied.

(1) **Example. Counters, and their dead periods.** In Section 6.8 we used an idealised Geiger counter which was able to register radioactive particles, irrespective of the rate of their arrival. In practice, after the detection of a particle such counters require a certain interval of time in order to complete its registration. These intervals are called 'dead periods'; during its dead periods the counter is locked and fails to register arriving particles. There are two common types of counter.

Type 1. Each detected arrival locks the counter for a period of time, possibly of random length, during which it ignores all arrivals.

Type 2. Each arrival locks the counter for a period of time, possibly of random length, irrespective of whether the counter is already locked or not. The counter registers only those arrivals that occur whilst it is unlocked.

Genuine Geiger counters are of Type 1; this case might also be used to model the process (8.3.1) of replacement of light bulbs in rented property when the landlord is either mean or lazy. We consider Type 1 counters briefly; Type 2 counters are harder to analyse, and so are left to the reader.

Suppose that arrivals occur as a renewal process N with renewal function m and inter-arrival times $X_1, X_2, \ldots$ with distribution function F. Let L_n be the length of the dead period induced by the nth detected arrival. It is customary and convenient to suppose that an additional dead period, of length L_0, begins at time $t=0$; the reason for this will soon be clear. We suppose that $\{L_n\}$ is a family of independent variables with the common distribution function F_L, where $F_L(0)=0$. Let $\tilde{N}(t)$ be the number of arrivals detected by the Type 1 counter by time t. Then $\tilde{N}$ is a stochastic process with inter-arrival times $\tilde{X}_1, \tilde{X}_2, \ldots$ where

$$\tilde{X}_{n+1} = L_n + E_n$$

and E_n is the excess life of N at the end of the nth dead period (see Figure 10.1). $\tilde{N}$ is *not* in general a renewal process, because the $\tilde{X}$'s need be neither independent nor identically distributed. In the very special case when N is a Poisson process the E's are independent exponential variables and $\tilde{N}$ is a renewal process; it is easy to construct other examples for which this conclusion fails.

It is not difficult to find the elapsed time $\tilde{X}_1$ until the first detection. Condition on L_0 to obtain

$$\mathbf{P}(\tilde{X}_1 \leq x) = \mathbf{E}(\mathbf{P}(\tilde{X}_1 \leq x \mid L_0))$$

$$= \int_0^x \mathbf{P}(L_0 + E_0 \leq x \mid L_0 = l)\, dF_L(l).$$

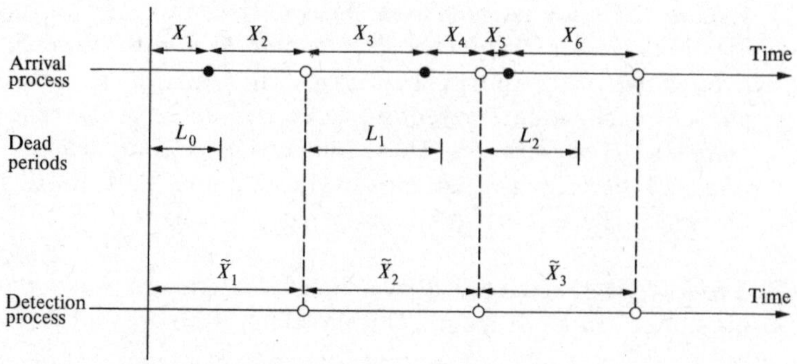

FIG. 10.1 Arrivals and detections by a Type I counter; • indicates an undetected arrival, and ○ indicates a detected arrival.

However, $E_0 = E(L_0)$, the excess lifetime of N at L_0, and so

$$\mathbf{P}(\tilde{X}_1 \leq x) = \int_0^x \mathbf{P}(E(l) \leq x - l)\, \mathrm{d}F_L(l). \tag{2}$$

Now use (10.3.3) and the integral representation

$$m(t) = F(t) + \int_0^t F(t-x)\, \mathrm{d}m(x),$$

which is derivable from (10.1.12), to find that

$$\begin{aligned} \mathbf{P}(\tilde{X}_1 \leq x) &= \int_0^x \left[\int_l^x \{1 - F(x-y)\}\, \mathrm{d}m(y) \right] \mathrm{d}F_L(l) \\ &= \int_0^x \{1 - F(x-y)\} F_L(y)\, \mathrm{d}m(y). \end{aligned} \tag{3}$$

If N is a Poisson process with intensity λ, then (2) becomes

$$\mathbf{P}(\tilde{X}_1 \leq x) = \int_0^x (1 - e^{-\lambda(x-l)})\, \mathrm{d}F_L(l).$$

$\tilde{N}$ is now a renewal process, and this equation describes the common distribution of the inter-arrival times.

If the counter is registering the arrival of radioactive particles, then we may seek an estimate $\hat{\lambda}$ of the unknown emission rate λ of the source based upon our knowledge of the mean length $\mathbf{E}(L)$ of a dead period and the counter reading $\tilde{N}(t)$. Assume that the particles arrive like a Poisson process. Let

$$\gamma = \frac{\tilde{N}(t)}{t}$$

be the density of observed particles. Then

$$\gamma \simeq \frac{1}{\mathbf{E}(\tilde{X}_1)} = \frac{1}{\mathbf{E}(L) + \lambda^{-1}} \quad \text{for large } t,$$

and so

$$\lambda \simeq \frac{\gamma}{1 - \gamma \mathbf{E}(L)}.$$

We may estimate λ by $\hat{\lambda}$, given by

$$\hat{\lambda} = \frac{\gamma}{1 - \gamma \mathbf{E}(L)}. \qquad \bullet$$

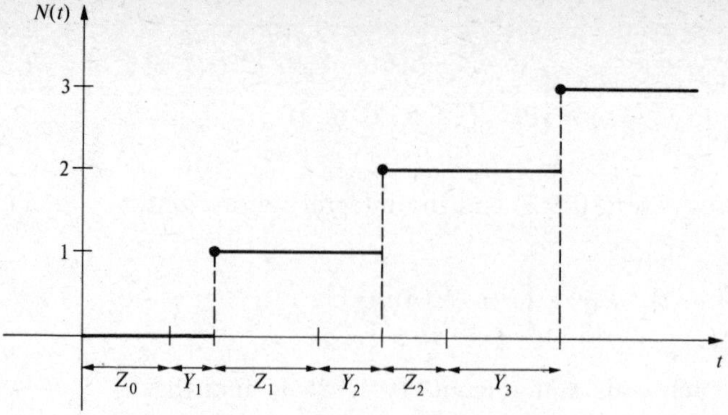

FIG. 10.2 An alternating renewal process.

(4) **Example. Alternating renewal process.** A machine breaks down repeatedly. After the nth breakdown the repairman takes a period of time, length Y_n, to repair it; subsequently the machine runs for a period of length Z_n before it breaks down for the next time. We assume that the Y's and Z's are independent of each other, the Y's having common distribution function F_Y and the Z's having common distribution function F_Z. Suppose that the machine was installed at time $t=0$. Let $N(t)$ be the number of completed repairs by time t (see Figure 10.2). N is a renewal process with inter-arrival times $X_1, X_2, \ldots$ given by

$$X_n = Z_{n-1} + Y_n$$

with distribution function

$$F(x) = \int_0^x F_Y(x-y)\,\mathrm{d}F_Z(y).$$

Let $p(t)$ be the probability that the machine is working at time t.

(5) **Lemma.**

$$p(t) = 1 - F_Z(t) + \int_0^t p(t-x)\,\mathrm{d}F(x)$$

and hence

$$p(t) = 1 - F_Z(t) + \int_0^t \{1 - F_Z(t-x)\}\,\mathrm{d}m(x)$$

where m is the renewal function of N.

Proof. The probability that the machine is on at time t satisfies

$$\begin{aligned}p(t) &= \mathbf{P}(\text{on at } t)\\ &= \mathbf{P}(Z_0 > t) + \mathbf{P}(\text{on at } t, Z_0 \leq t)\\ &= \mathbf{P}(Z_0 > t) + \mathbf{E}(\mathbf{P}(\text{on at } t, Z_0 \leq t \mid X_1))\\ &= \mathbf{P}(Z_0 > t) + \int_0^t \mathbf{P}(\text{on at } t \mid X_1 = x)\, dF(x) \qquad \text{since } \mathbf{P}(\text{on at } t, Z_0 \leq t \mid X_1 > t) = 0\\ &= \mathbf{P}(Z_0 > t) + \int_0^t p(t-x)\, dF(x).\end{aligned}$$

Now use (10.1.11). ■

(6) **Corollary.** *If X_1 is not arithmetic then*

$$p(t) \to \frac{1}{1+\rho} \quad \text{as} \quad t \to \infty$$

where $\rho = \mathbf{E}(Y)/\mathbf{E}(Z)$ is the ratio of the mean lengths of a typical repair period and a typical working period.

Proof. Use the Key Renewal Theorem (10.2.7). ■●

(7) **Example. Superposition of renewal processes.** Suppose that a room is illuminated by two lights, the bulbs of which fail independently of each other. On failure, they are replaced immediately. Let N_1 and N_2 be the renewal processes describing the occurrences of bulb failures in the first and second lights respectively, and suppose that these are independent processes with the same inter-arrival time distribution function F. Let $\tilde{N}$ be the superposition of these two processes; that is, $\tilde{N}(t) = N_1(t) + N_2(t)$ is the total number of failures by time t. In general $\tilde{N}$ is not a renewal process. Let us assume for the sake of simplicity that the inter-arrival times of N_1 and N_2 are not arithmetic.

(8) **Theorem.** *$\tilde{N}$ is a renewal process if and only if N_1 and N_2 are Poisson processes.*

Proof. It is easy to see that $\tilde{N}$ is a Poisson process with intensity 2λ whenever N_1 and N_2 are Poisson processes with intensity λ. Conversely, suppose that $\tilde{N}$ is a renewal process, and write $\{X_n(1)\}$, $\{X_n(2)\}$ and $\{\tilde{X}_n\}$ for the inter-arrival times of N_1, N_2, and $\tilde{N}$ respectively. Clearly

$$\tilde{X}_1 = \min\{X_1(1), X_1(2)\}$$

and so the distribution function $\tilde{F}$ of $\tilde{X}_1$ satisfies

(9) $$1 - \tilde{F}(y) = \{1 - F(y)\}^2.$$

Let $E_1(t)$, $E_2(t)$, and $\tilde{E}(t)$ denote the excess lifetimes of N_1, N_2, and $\tilde{N}$ respectively at time t. Clearly,

$$\tilde{E}(t) = \min\{E_1(t), E_2(t)\},$$

and so

$$\mathbf{P}(\tilde{E}(t) > y) = \mathbf{P}(E_1(t) > y)^2.$$

Let $t \to \infty$ and use (10.3.5) to obtain

(10) $$\frac{1}{\tilde{\mu}} \int_y^\infty \{1 - \tilde{F}(x)\}\, dx = \frac{1}{\mu^2} \left[\int_y^\infty \{1 - F(x)\}\, dx \right]^2$$

where $\tilde{\mu} = \mathbf{E}(\tilde{X}_1)$ and $\mu = \mathbf{E}(X_1(1))$. Differentiate (10) and use (9) to obtain

$$\frac{1}{\tilde{\mu}} \{1 - \tilde{F}(y)\} = \frac{2}{\mu^2} \{1 - F(y)\} \int_y^\infty \{1 - F(x)\}\, dx$$

$$= \frac{1}{\tilde{\mu}} \{1 - F(y)\}^2$$

(this step needs further justification if F is not continuous). Thus

$$1 - F(y) = \frac{2\tilde{\mu}}{\mu^2} \int_y^\infty \{1 - F(x)\}\, dx$$

which is an integral equation with solution

$$F(y) = 1 - \exp\left(-\frac{2\tilde{\mu}}{\mu^2} y \right).$$

■●

(11) **Example. Delayed renewal processes.** The Markov chain example (8.3.2) indicates that it is sometimes appropriate to allow the first inter-arrival time X_1 to have a distribution which differs from the shared distribution of $X_2, X_3, \ldots$.

(12) **Definition.** Let $X_1, X_2, \ldots$ be independent positive variables such that $X_2, X_3, \ldots$ have the same distribution. Let

$$T_0 = 0, \quad T_n = \sum_1^n X_i, \quad N^D(t) = \max\{n : T_n \leq t\}.$$

Then N^D is called a **delayed** (or **modified**) **renewal process.**

Another example of a delayed renewal process is provided by a variation of the Type 1 counter of (1) when particles arrive like a Poisson process. It was convenient there to assume that the life of the counter began with a dead period in order that the process $\tilde{N}$ of detections be a renewal process. In the absence of this assumption $\tilde{N}$ is a delayed renewal process. The theory of delayed renewal processes is very similar to that of ordinary renewal processes and we do not explore it in detail. The renewal equation (10.1.9) becomes

$$m^D(t) = F^D(t) + \int_0^t m(t-x)\,dF^D(x)$$

where F^D is the distribution function of X_1 and m is the renewal function of an ordinary renewal process N whose inter-arrival times are $X_2, X_3, \dots$. It is left to the reader to check that

(13) $$m^D(t) = F^D(t) + \int_0^t m^D(t-x)\,dF(x)$$

and

(14) $$m^D(t) = \sum_{k=1}^{\infty} F_k^D(t)$$

where F_k^D is the distribution function of $T_k = X_1 + \dots + X_k$ and F is the shared distribution function of $X_2, X_3, \dots$.

With our knowledge of the properties of m, it is not too hard to show that m^D satisfies the renewal theorems. Write μ for $\mathbf{E}(X_2)$.

(15) **Theorem.** $\frac{1}{t} m^D(t) \to \frac{1}{\mu}$ *as* $t \to \infty$.

If X_2 *is not arithmetic then*

(16) $$m^D(t+h) - m^D(t) \to \frac{h}{\mu} \quad \textit{as} \quad t \to \infty \quad \textit{for any} \quad h.$$

If X_2 *is arithmetic with span* λ *then* (16) *remains true whenever* h *is a multiple of* λ.

There is an important special case for the distribution function F^D.

(17) **Theorem.** N^D *has stationary increments if and only if*

(18) $$F^D(y) = \frac{1}{\mu} \int_0^y \{1 - F(x)\}\,dx.$$

If F^D is given by (18), then N^D is called a *stationary* (or *equilibrium*) *renewal process*. We should recognize (18) as the asymptotic distribution (10.3.5) of the excess lifetime of the ordinary renewal process N. So the result of (17) is no surprise since N^D starts off with this 'equilibrium' distribution. We shall see that in this case $m^D(t) = t/\mu$ for all $t \geq 0$.

Proof of (17). Suppose that N^D has stationary increments. Then

$$m^D(s+t) = \mathbf{E}\{(N^D(s+t) - N^D(s)) + N^D(s)\}$$
$$= \mathbf{E}(N^D(t)) + \mathbf{E}(N^D(s))$$
$$= m^D(t) + m^D(s).$$

By monotonicity,

$$m^D(t) = ct$$

for some $c > 0$. Substitute into (13) to obtain

$$F^D(t) = c\int_0^t \{1 - F(x)\}\, dx$$

and let $t \to \infty$ to obtain $c = \dfrac{1}{\mu}$.

Conversely, suppose that F^D is given by (18). Substitute (18) into (13) and use the method of Laplace–Stieltjes transforms to deduce that

(19) $$m^D(t) = \frac{t}{\mu}.$$

Now, N^D has stationary increments if and only if the distribution of $E^D(t)$, the excess lifetime of N^D at t, does not depend on t. But

$$\mathbf{P}(E^D(t) > y) = \sum_{k=0}^{\infty} \mathbf{P}(E^D(t) > y, N^D(t) = k)$$
$$= \mathbf{P}(E^D(t) > y, N^D(t) = 0)$$
$$+ \sum_{k=1}^{\infty} \int_0^t \mathbf{P}(E^D(t) > y, N^D(t) = k \mid T_k = x)\, dF_k^D(x)$$
$$= 1 - F^D(t+y) + \int_0^t \{1 - F(t+y-x)\}\, d\left\{\sum_{k=1}^{\infty} F_k^D(x)\right\}$$
$$= 1 - F^D(t+y) + \int_0^t \{1 - F(t+y-x)\}\, dm^D(x)$$

from (14). Now substitute (18) and (19) into this equation to obtain the result. ■●

(20) **Example. Markov chains.** Let $Y = \{Y_n : n \geq 0\}$ be a discrete-time Markov chain with countable state space S. At last we are able to prove the ergodic theorem (6.4.21) for Y, as a consequence of the renewal theorem (16). Suppose that $Y_0 = i$ and let j be an aperiodic state. We can suppose that j is persistent, since the result follows from (6.2.5) if j is transient.

Observe the sequence of visits of Y to the state j. That is, let

$$T_0 = 0, \qquad T_{n+1} = \min\{k > T_n : Y_k = j\} \quad \text{for} \quad n \geq 0.$$

T_1 may equal $+\infty$; actually $\mathbf{P}(T_1 < \infty) = f_{ij}$. Conditional on $\{T_1 < \infty\}$, the inter-visit times

$$X_n = T_n - T_{n-1} \quad \text{for} \quad n \geq 2$$

are independent and identically distributed; following (8.3.2),

$$N^D(t) = \max\{n : T_n \leq t\}$$

defines a delayed renewal process with a renewal function

$$m^D(t) = \sum_{n=1}^{t} p_{ij}(n) \quad \text{for integral } t.$$

Now, adapt (16) to deal with the possibility that the first inter-arrival time $X_1 = T_1$ equals infinity, to obtain

$$p_{ij}(n) = m^D(n) - m^D(n-1) \to \frac{f_{ij}}{\mu_j} \quad \text{as} \quad n \to \infty$$

where μ_j is the mean recurrence time of j. ●

(21) **Example. Sketch proof of the renewal theorem.** There is an elegant proof of the renewal theorem (10.2.5) which proceeds by coupling the renewal process N to an independent delayed renewal process N^D; here is a sketch of the method. Let N be a renewal process with inter-arrival times $\{X_n\}$ and inter-arrival time distribution function F with mean μ. We suppose that F is non-arithmetic; the proof in the arithmetic case is easier. Let N^D be a stationary renewal process (see (17)) with inter-arrival times $\{Y_n\}$, where Y_1 has distribution function

$$F^D(y) = \frac{1}{\mu} \int_0^y \{1 - F(x)\}\, dx$$

and $Y_2, Y_3, \ldots$ have distribution function F; suppose further that the X's are independent of the Y's. The idea of the proof is as follows.

(a) For any $\delta > 0$, there must exist an arrival time $T_a = \sum_1^a X_i$ of N and an arrival time $T_b^D = \sum_1^b Y_i$ of N^D such that

$$|T_a - T_b^D| < \delta.$$

(b) If we replace $X_{a+1}, X_{a+2}, \ldots$ by $Y_{b+1}, Y_{b+2}, \ldots$ in the construction of N, then the distributional properties of N are unchanged since all these variables are identically distributed.

(c) But the Y's are the inter-arrival times of a stationary renewal process, for which (19) holds; this implies that $m^D(t+h) - m^D(t) = h/\mu$ for all t, h. However, $m(t)$ and $m^D(t)$ are nearly the same for large t, by the previous remarks, and so

$$m(t+h) - m(t) \simeq h/\mu \quad \text{for large } t.$$

The details of the proof are slightly too difficult for inclusion here (see Lindvall 1977). ●

(22) **Example. Age-dependent branching process.** Consider the branching process $Z(t)$ of Section 5.5 in which each individual lives for a random length of time before splitting into its offspring. We have seen that the expected number

$$m(t)=\mathbf{E}(Z(t))$$

of individuals alive at time t satisfies the integral equation (5.5.3):

$$m(t)=\nu\int_0^t m(t-x)\,\mathrm{d}F_T(x)+\int_t^\infty \mathrm{d}F_T(x) \tag{23}$$

where F_T is the distribution function of a typical lifetime and ν is the mean family size; we assume that F_T is continuous for simplicity. We have changed some of the notation of (5.5.3) for obvious reasons. Equation (23) reminds us of the renewal-type equation (10.1.10) but the factor ν must be assimilated before the solution can be found using the method of (10.1.11). This presents few difficulties in the supercritical case. If $\nu>1$ then there is a unique $\beta>0$ such that

$$F_T^*(\beta)=\int_0^\infty e^{-\beta x}\,\mathrm{d}F_T(x)=\frac{1}{\nu};$$

this holds because the Laplace–Stieltjes transform $F_T^*(\theta)$ is a strictly decreasing continuous function of θ with

$$F_T^*(0)=1, \qquad F_T^*(\theta)\to 0 \quad \text{as} \quad \theta\to\infty.$$

Now, with this choice of β, define

$$\tilde{F}(t)=\nu\int_0^t e^{-\beta x}\,\mathrm{d}F_T(x)$$

$$g(t)=e^{-\beta t}m(t).$$

Multiply through (23) by $e^{-\beta t}$ to obtain

$$g(t)=h(t)+\int_0^t g(t-x)\,\mathrm{d}\tilde{F}(x) \tag{24}$$

where

$$h(t)=e^{-\beta t}\{1-F_T(t)\};$$

(24) has the same general form as (10.1.10), since our choice for β ensures that $\tilde{F}$ is the distribution function of a positive random variable.

Thus (10.1.11) provides the unique g which is bounded on finite intervals:

(25) $$g(t) = h(t) + \int_0^\infty h(t-x)\,\mathrm{d}\tilde{m}(x)$$

where $\tilde{m}$ is the renewal function of a renewal process whose inter-arrival times have distribution function $\tilde{F}$. Now h satisfies the conditions of the Key Renewal Theorem (10.2.7) and so (25) yields

$$g(t) \to \frac{\int_0^\infty h(x)\,\mathrm{d}x}{\int_0^\infty x\,\mathrm{d}\tilde{F}(x)} = \frac{\nu - 1}{\beta\nu^2 \int_0^\infty xe^{-\beta x}\,\mathrm{d}F_T(x)} = \delta, \text{ say,}$$

as $t \to \infty$. But $g(t) = e^{-\beta t}m(t)$ and we have shown that

$$m(t) \simeq \delta e^{\beta t} \quad \text{for large } t.$$

The parameter β is called the 'Malthusian rate of growth', after Malthus, who discussed the exponential growth of populations. ●

10.5 Problems

In the absence of indications to the contrary $\{X_n\}$ denotes the inter-arrival times of either a renewal process N or a delayed renewal process N^D. In either case F^D and F are the distribution functions of X_1 and X_2 respectively, though $F^D \neq F$ only if the renewal process is delayed. We denote $\mathbf{E}(X_2)$ by μ. m and m^D denote the renewal functions of N and N^D.

1. (a) Show that $\mathbf{P}(N(t) \to \infty \text{ as } t \to \infty) = 1$.
(b) Show that $m(t) < \infty$ if $\mu \neq 0$.
(c) More generally, show that

$$\mathbf{E}(N(t)^k) < \infty \quad \text{if} \quad \mu \neq 0 \quad \text{for all } k > 0.$$

2. Let $v(t) = \mathbf{E}(N(t)^2)$. Show that

$$v(t) = m(t) + 2\int_0^t m(t-s)\,\mathrm{d}m(s).$$

Find $v(t)$ when N is a Poisson process.

3. Set $g(x) = I_{[0,h]}(x)$, the indicator function of the interval $[0, h]$, to deduce in the non-arithmetic case that the Key Renewal Theorem (10.2.7) is more general than the renewal theorem (10.2.5). Conversely, students who know about increasing sequences of step functions (see Section 5.6) will be able to deduce (10.2.7) from (10.2.5). First show that (10.2.7) holds for indicator functions, then for step functions with bounded support, and finally take increasing limits of sequences of such functions to deduce the general result. You should take great care over the analytical details.

4. Prove (10.2.2) and (10.3.5).

5. Find the asymptotic distribution of the current life $C(t)$ of N as $t \to \infty$ when X_1 is not arithmetic.

6. Let N be a Poisson process with intensity λ. Show that the total life $D(t)$ at time t has distribution function

$$\mathbf{P}(D(t) \leqslant x) = 1 - (1 + \lambda \min\{t, x\})e^{-\lambda x} \quad \text{for} \quad x \geqslant 0.$$

Deduce that

$$\mathbf{E}(D(t)) = \frac{1}{\lambda}(2 - e^{-\lambda t}).$$

7. A Type 1 counter records the arrivals of radioactive particles. Suppose that the arrival process is Poisson with intensity λ and that each dead period has a fixed length T. Show that the detection process $\tilde{N}$ of (10.4.1) is a renewal process with inter-arrival time distribution

$$\tilde{F}(x) = \lambda e^{-\lambda(x-T)} \quad \text{if} \quad x \geqslant T.$$

Find $\mathbf{P}(\tilde{N}(t) \leqslant k)$.

8. Fill in the details of the derivation of the distribution function (10.4.3) of the first inter-arrival time of the detection process for a Type 1 counter.

9. (a) Show that

$$m(t) = \tfrac{1}{2}\lambda t - \tfrac{1}{4}(1 - e^{-2\lambda t})$$

if $F(x) = \lambda^2 x e^{-\lambda x}$ for $x \geqslant 0$.
(b) Radioactive particles arrive like a Poisson process, intensity λ, at a counter. This counter fails to register the nth arrival whenever n is odd but suffers no dead periods. Find the renewal function $\tilde{m}$ of the detection process $\tilde{N}$.

10. Show that the Poisson process is the only renewal process with the property that the excess lifetime $E(t)$ and the current lifetime $C(t)$ are independent for each choice of t, and which has non-arithmetic inter-arrival times.

11. Use the argument of (10.4.8) to show the following result. If N_1 is a Poisson process and N_2 is a renewal process which is independent of N_1 and has finite mean inter-arrival time, then

$$\tilde{N}(t) = N_1(t) + N_2(t)$$

is a renewal process if and only if N_2 is a Poisson process.

12. Let N be an ordinary renewal process and suppose that F is not arithmetic and that $\sigma^2 = \text{var}(X_1) < \infty$. Use (10.1.14) and the properties of the moment generating function $F^*(-\theta)$ of X_1 to deduce the formal expansion

$$m^*(\theta) = \frac{1}{\theta\mu} + \frac{(\sigma^2 - \mu^2)}{2\mu^2} + o(1) \quad \text{as} \quad \theta \to 0.$$

Invert this Laplace–Stieltjes transform formally to obtain

$$m(t) = \frac{t}{\mu} + \frac{\sigma^2 - \mu^2}{2\mu^2} + o(1) \quad \text{as} \quad t \to \infty.$$

Now, prove this rigorously in the non-arithmetic case by showing that

$$m(t) = t/\mu - F_E(t) + \int_0^t \{1 - F_E(t-x)\}\, dm(x),$$

where F_E is the asymptotic distribution function (10.3.5) of the excess life time, and applying the Key Renewal Theorem. Compare the result with the renewal theorems.

13. Show that the renewal function m^D of a delayed renewal process satisfies

$$m^D(t) = F^D(t) + \int_0^t m^D(t-x)\, dF(x).$$

Show that $v^D(t) = \mathbf{E}(N^D(t)^2)$ satisfies

$$v^D(t) = m^D(t) + 2\int_0^t m^D(t-x)\, dm(x)$$

where m is the renewal function of the renewal process with inter-arrival times $X_2, X_3, \ldots.$

14. Let $m(t)$ be the mean number of living individuals at time t in an age-dependent branching process with exponential lifetimes and mean family size $\nu > 1$. Describe the asymptotic behaviour of $m(t)$ as $t \to \infty$.

15. Consider the alternating renewal process of (10.4.4). Show that the Laplace–Stieltjes transform p^* of p satisfies

$$p^*(\theta) = \frac{1 - M_Z(-\theta)}{1 - M_Y(-\theta)M_Z(-\theta)}$$

where M_Y and M_Z denote the appropriate moment generating functions.

11 Queues

11.1 Single-server queues

We consider only the simpler queueing systems which are described in Section 8.4. With each queue we can associate two sequences $\{X_n : n \geq 1\}$ and $\{S_n : n \geq 1\}$ of independent positive random variables, the X's being inter-arrival times with common distribution function F_X and the S's being service times with common distribution function F_S. We assume that customers arrive like a renewal process with inter-arrival times $\{X_n\}$, the nth customer arriving at

$$T_n = X_1 + \ldots + X_n.$$

Each arriving customer joins the line of customers who are waiting for the attention of the *single* server. When the nth customer reaches the head of this line he is served for a period of length S_n, after which he leaves the system. Let $Q(t)$ be the number of waiting customers at time t (including any customer whose service is in progress at t); clearly $Q(0) = 0$. Then $Q = \{Q(t) : t \geq 0\}$ is a random process whose fdds are specified by the distribution functions F_X and F_S. We seek information about Q. For example, we may ask:

(a) When is Q a Markov chain, or when does Q contain an imbedded Markov chain?
(b) When is Q asymptotically stationary, in the sense that the distribution of $Q(t)$ settles down as $t \to \infty$?
(c) When does the queue length grow beyond all bounds, in that the server is not able to cope with the high density of arrivals?

The answers to these and other similar questions take the form of applying conditions to F_X and F_S; the style of the analysis may depend on the types of these distribution functions. With this in mind, it is convenient to use a notation for the queue system which incorporates information about F_X and F_S. The most common notation scheme describes each system by a triple $A/B/s$, where A describes F_X, B describes F_S, and s is the number of servers ($s = 1$ always, for us). Typically, A and B may each be one of the following:

$D(d) \equiv$ almost surely concentrated at the value d (D for 'deterministic')
$M(\lambda) \equiv$ exponential, parameter λ (M for 'Markovian')
$\Gamma(\lambda, k) \equiv$ gamma, parameters λ and k
$G \equiv$ some general distribution, fixed but unspecified.

(1) **Example.** $\boldsymbol{M(\lambda)/M(\mu)/1}$**.** Inter-arrival times are exponential with parameter λ and service times are exponential with parameter μ. Thus, customers arrive like a Poisson process with intensity λ. $Q=\{Q(t)\}$ is a continuous-time Markov chain with state space $\{0, 1, 2, \ldots\}$; this follows from the lack-of-memory property of the exponential distribution. Furthermore, such systems are the *only* systems whose queue lengths are homogeneous Markov chains. Why is this? ●

(2) **Example.** $\boldsymbol{M(\lambda)/D(1)/1}$**.** Customers arrive like a Poisson process, and each requires a service time of constant length 1. Q is not a Markov chain, but we shall see later that there exists an imbedded discrete-time Markov chain $\{Q_n : n \geq 0\}$ whose properties provide information about Q. ●

(3) **Example.** $\boldsymbol{G/G/1}$**.** In this case we have no special information about F_X or F_S. Some authors denote this system by $GI/G/1$, reserving the title $G/G/1$ to denote a more complicated system in which the inter-arrival times may not be independent. ●

The notation $M(\lambda)$ is sometimes abbreviated to M alone. Thus Example (1) becomes $M/M/1$; this rather unfortunate abbreviation does *not* imply that F_X and F_S are the same. A similar remark holds for systems described as $G/G/1$.

Broadly speaking, there are two types of statement to be made about Q:

(a) 'time-dependent' statements, which contain information about the queue for finite values of t;
(b) 'limiting' results, which discuss the asymptotic properties of the queue as $t \to \infty$. These include conditions for the queue length to grow beyond all bounds.

Statements of the former type are most easily made about $M(\lambda)/M(\mu)/1$, since this is the only Markovian system; such conclusions are more elusive for more general systems, and we shall generally content ourselves with the asymptotic properties of such queues.

In the subsequent sections we explore the systems $M/M/1$, $M/G/1$, $G/M/1$, and $G/G/1$, in that order. We present these cases roughly in order of increasing difficulty for the readers' convenience. This is not really satisfactory, since we are progressing from the specific to the general, so we should like to stress that queues with Markovian characteristics are very special systems and that their properties do not always indicate features of more general systems.

Here is a final piece of notation.

(4) **Definition.** The **traffic density** ρ of a queue is defined as

$$\rho = \frac{\mathbf{E}(S)}{\mathbf{E}(X)},$$

the ratio of the mean of a typical service time, to the mean of a typical inter-arrival time.

We assume throughout that neither $\mathbf{E}(S)$ nor $\mathbf{E}(X)$ takes the value zero or infinity.

We shall see that queues behave in qualitatively different manners depending on whether $\rho<1$ or $\rho>1$. In the latter case, service times exceed inter-arrival times, on average, and the queue length grows beyond all bounds with probability one; in the former case, the queue attains an equilibrium as $t\to\infty$. It is a remarkable conclusion that the threshold between instability and stability depends on the mean values of F_X and F_S alone.

11.2 *M/M/1*

The queue $M(\lambda)/M(\mu)/1$ is very special in that Q is a continuous-time Markov chain. Furthermore, reference to (6.11.1) reminds us that Q is a birth–death process with birth and death rates given by

$$\lambda_n = \lambda \quad \text{for all } n$$

$$\mu_n = \begin{cases} \mu & \text{if} \quad n \geq 1 \\ 0 & \text{if} \quad n = 0. \end{cases}$$

The probabilities $p_n(t)=\mathbf{P}(Q(t)=n)$ satisfy the Kolmogorov forward equations in the usual way:

(1) $$\frac{dp_n}{dt}=\lambda p_{n-1}(t)-(\lambda+\mu)p_n(t)+\mu p_{n+1}(t) \quad \text{for} \quad n\geq 1$$

(2) $$\frac{dp_0}{dt}=-\lambda p_0(t)+\mu p_1(t)$$

subject to the boundary conditions $p_n(0)=\delta_{0n}$, the Kronecker delta. It is a bit tricky to solve these equations, but routine methods provide the answer after some manipulation. There are at least two possible routes: either use generating functions or use Laplace transforms with respect to t. We proceed in the latter way here. Let

$$\hat{p}_n(\theta)=\int_0^\infty e^{-\theta t}p_n(t)\,dt$$

be the Laplace transform† of p_n.

(3) **Theorem.** *$\hat{p}_n(\theta)=\dfrac{1}{\theta}\{1-\alpha(\theta)\}\{\alpha(\theta)\}^n$ where*

(4) $$\alpha(\theta)=\frac{(\lambda+\mu+\theta)-\{(\lambda+\mu+\theta)^2-4\lambda\mu\}^{1/2}}{2\mu}.$$

† Do not confuse $\hat{p}_n$ with the Laplace–Stieltjes transform $p_n^*(\theta)=\int_0^\infty e^{-\theta t}\,dp_n(t)$.

The actual probabilities $p_n(t)$ can be deduced in terms of Bessel functions. It turns out that

$$p_n(t)=J_n(t)-J_{n+1}(t)$$

where

$$J_n(t)=\int_0^t (\lambda/\mu)^{\frac{1}{2}n} ns^{-1}e^{-s(\lambda+\mu)}I_n(2s(\lambda\mu)^{1/2})\,ds$$

and I_n is a modified Bessel function (see Feller 1971, p. 482).

Proof. Transform (1) and (2) to obtain

(5) $$\mu\hat{p}_{n+1}-(\lambda+\mu+\theta)\hat{p}_n+\lambda\hat{p}_{n-1}=0 \quad \text{for} \quad n\geq 1$$

(6) $$\mu\hat{p}_1-(\lambda+\theta)\hat{p}_0=-1$$

where we have used the fact (see equation (14) of Appendix I) that

$$\int_0^\infty e^{-\theta t}\frac{dp_n}{dt}\,dt=\theta\hat{p}_n-\delta_{0n}, \quad \text{for all} \quad n.$$

(5) is an ordinary difference equation, and standard techniques (see (5.2.5)) show that it has a unique solution which is bounded as $\theta\to\infty$ and which is given by

(7) $$\hat{p}_n(\theta)=\hat{p}_0(\theta)\{\alpha(\theta)\}^n$$

where α is given by (4). Substitute (7) into (6) to deduce that

$$\hat{p}_0(\theta)=\frac{1}{\theta}\{1-\alpha(\theta)\}$$

and the proof is complete. ■

The asymptotic behaviour of $Q(t)$ as $t\to\infty$ is deducible from (3), but more direct methods yield the answer more quickly. Remember that Q is a Markov chain.

(8) **Theorem.** *Let* $\rho=\lambda/\mu$ *be the traffic density.*
(a) *If* $\rho<1$ *then*

$$\mathbf{P}(Q(t)=n)\to(1-\rho)\rho^n=\pi_n, \quad \textit{say, for} \quad n\geq 0$$

where $\boldsymbol{\pi}$ *is the unique stationary distribution.*
(b) *If* $\rho\geq 1$ *then there is no stationary distribution, and*

$$\mathbf{P}(Q(t)=n)\to 0 \quad \textit{for all} \quad n.$$

This result is very natural. It asserts that the queue settles down into equilibrium if and only if inter-arrival times exceed service times on average. We shall see later that if $\rho > 1$ then $\mathbf{P}(Q(t) \to \infty \text{ as } t \to \infty) = 1$, whilst if $\rho = 1$ then the queue length experiences wild oscillations with no reasonable bound on their magnitudes.

Proof. Q is an irreducible chain. Let us try to find a stationary distribution. Let $t \to \infty$ in (1) and (2) to find that the mass function $\boldsymbol{\pi}$ is a stationary distribution if and only if

(9) $$\pi_{n+1} - (1+\rho)\pi_n + \rho\pi_{n-1} = 0 \quad \text{for } n \geq 1$$
$$\pi_1 - \rho\pi_0 = 0.$$

(The operation of taking limits is justifiable by (6.9.20) and the uniformity of Q.) The general solution to (9) is

$$\pi_n = \begin{cases} A + B\rho^n & \text{if } \rho \neq 1 \\ A + Bn & \text{if } \rho = 1 \end{cases}$$

where A and B are arbitrary constants. Thus the only bounded solution to (9) with bounded sum is

$$\pi_n = \begin{cases} B\rho^n & \text{if } \rho < 1 \\ 0 & \text{if } \rho \geq 1. \end{cases}$$

Hence, if $\rho < 1$,

$$\pi_n = (1-\rho)\rho^n$$

is a stationary distribution, whilst if $\rho \geq 1$ then there exists no stationary distribution. By Theorem (6.9.21), the proof is complete. ∎

There is an alternative derivation of the asymptotic behaviour (8) of Q, which has other consequences also. Let U_n be the epoch of time at which the nth change in Q occurs. That is to say

$$U_0 = 0, \qquad U_{n+1} = \inf\{t > U_n : Q(t) \neq Q(U_n+)\}.$$

Now let $Q_n = Q(U_n+)$ be the number of waiting customers immediately after the nth change in Q. Clearly $\{Q_n : n \geq 0\}$ is a random walk on the non-negative integers, with

$$Q_{n+1} = \begin{cases} Q_n + 1 & \text{with probability } \dfrac{\lambda}{\lambda+\mu} = \dfrac{\rho}{1+\rho} \\[2ex] Q_n - 1 & \text{with probability } \dfrac{\mu}{\lambda+\mu} = \dfrac{1}{1+\rho} \end{cases}$$

whenever $Q_n \geq 1$ (see paragraph A after (6.11.8) for a similar result for another birth–death process). When $Q_n = 0$ we have that

$$\mathbf{P}(Q_{n+1} = 1 \mid Q_n = 0) = 1,$$

so that the walk leaves 0 immediately after arriving there; it is only in this regard that the walk differs from the random walk (6.4.14) with a reflecting barrier. Look for stationary distributions of the walk in the usual way to find (*exercise*) that there exists such a distribution if and only if $\rho<1$, and it is given by

(10) $$\pi_0=\tfrac{1}{2}(1-\rho), \qquad \pi_n=\tfrac{1}{2}(1-\rho^2)\rho^{n-1} \quad \text{for} \quad n\geq 1.$$

Follow the argument of (6.4.14) to find that

$$\{Q_n\} \text{ is} \begin{cases} \text{non-null persistent} & \text{if} \quad \rho<1 \\ \text{null persistent} & \text{if} \quad \rho=1 \\ \text{transient} & \text{if} \quad \rho>1. \end{cases}$$

Equation (10) differs from the result of (8) because the walk $\{Q_n\}$ and the process Q behave differently at the state 0. It is possible to deduce (8) from (10) by taking account of the times which elapse between the jumps of the walk (see Ross 1970, p. 105, for details). It is clear now that $Q_n\to\infty$ almost surely as $n\to\infty$ if $\rho>1$, whilst $\{Q_n\}$ experiences large fluctuations in the symmetric case $\rho=1$.

11.3 *M/G/1*

*M/M/*1 is the only queue which is a Markov chain; the analysis of other queueing systems requires greater ingenuity. If either inter-arrival times or service times are exponentially distributed then the general theory of Markov chains still provides a method for studying the queue. For, in these two cases we may find a discrete-time Markov chain which is imbedded in the continuous-time process Q. We consider *M/G/*1 in this section, which is divided into three parts dealing with equilibrium theory, the 'waiting time' of a typical customer, and the length of a typical 'busy period' during which the server is continuously occupied.

(A) Asymptotic queue length. Consider $M(\lambda)/G/1$. Customers arrive like a Poisson process with intensity λ. Let D_n be the time of departure of the nth customer from the system, and let $Q(D_n)$ be the number of customers which he leaves behind him in the system on his departure (really, we should write $Q(D_n+)$ instead of $Q(D_n)$ to make clear that the departing customer is not included). Then $Q(D)=\{Q(D_n):n\geq 1\}$ is a sequence of random variables. What can we say about a typical increment $Q(D_{n+1})-Q(D_n)$? If $Q(D_n)>0$, then the $(n+1)$th customer begins his service time immediately at D_n; during this service time S_{n+1}, a random number, A say, of customers arrive and join the waiting line. Therefore the $(n+1)$th customer leaves $A+Q(D_n)-1$ customers behind him as he departs. That is,

(1) $$Q(D_{n+1})=A+Q(D_n)-1 \quad \text{if} \quad Q(D_n)>0.$$

If $Q(D_n)=0$ then the server must wait for the $(n+1)$th arrival before he sets to work again. When this service is complete, the $(n+1)$th customer leaves exactly A customers behind him where A is the number of arrivals during his service time, as before. That is,

(2) $$Q(D_{n+1})=A \quad \text{if} \quad Q(D_n)=0.$$

Combine (1) and (2) to obtain

(3) $$Q(D_{n+1})=A+Q(D_n)-h(Q(D_n))$$

where h is defined by

$$h(x)=\begin{cases}1 & \text{if} \quad x>0\\ 0 & \text{if} \quad x\leqslant 0.\end{cases}$$

Equation (3) holds for any queue. However, in the case of $M(\lambda)/G/1$ the random variable A depends *only* on the length of time S_{n+1} and is independent of $Q(D_n)$ because of the special properties of the Poisson process of arrivals. We conclude from (3) that $Q(D)$ is a Markov chain.

(4) **Theorem.** *$Q(D)$ is a Markov chain with transition matrix*

$$\mathbf{P}_D=\begin{pmatrix}\delta_0 & \delta_1 & \delta_2 & \cdots\\ \delta_0 & \delta_1 & \delta_2 & \cdots\\ 0 & \delta_0 & \delta_1 & \cdots\\ 0 & 0 & \delta_0 & \cdots\\ \cdot & \cdot & \cdot & \\ \cdot & \cdot & \cdot & \\ \cdot & \cdot & \cdot & \end{pmatrix}$$

where

$$\delta_j=\mathbf{E}\left(\frac{(\lambda S)^j}{j!}e^{-\lambda S}\right)$$

and S is a typical service time.

Of course, δ_j is just the probability that exactly j customers join the queue during a typical service time.

Proof. We need only show that $\mathbf{P}_D$ is the correct transition matrix. In the notation of Chapter 6,

$$\begin{aligned}p_{0j}&=\mathbf{P}(Q(D_{n+1})=j\mid Q(D_n)=0)\\ &=\mathbf{E}(\mathbf{P}(A=j\mid S))\end{aligned}$$

where $S=S_{n+1}$ is the service time of the $(n+1)$th customer. Thus

$$p_{0j}=\mathbf{E}\left(\frac{(\lambda S)^j}{j!}e^{-\lambda S}\right)=\delta_j$$

as required, since, conditional on S, A has the Poisson distribution with parameter λS. Likewise, if $i \geq 1$ then

$$p_{ij} = \mathbf{E}(\mathbf{P}(A = j-i+1 \mid S)) = \begin{cases} \delta_{j-i+1} & \text{if } j-i+1 \geq 0 \\ 0 & \text{if } j-i+1 < 0. \end{cases}$$

■

This result enables us to observe the behaviour of the process $Q = \{Q(t)\}$ by evaluating it at the time epochs $D_1, D_2, \ldots$ and using the theory of Markov chains. It is important to note that this course of action provides reliable information about the asymptotic behaviour of Q only because $D_n \to \infty$ almost surely as $n \to \infty$. The asymptotic behaviour of $Q(D)$ is described by the next theorem.

(5) **Theorem.** *Let $\rho = \lambda \mathbf{E}(S)$ be the traffic density.*

(a) *If $\rho < 1$ then $Q(D)$ is ergodic with a unique stationary distribution $\boldsymbol{\pi}$, with generating function*

$$G(s) = \sum_j \pi_j s^j = (1-\rho)(s-1)\frac{M_S(\lambda(s-1))}{s - M_S(\lambda(s-1))},$$

where M_S is the moment generating function of a typical service time.

(b) *If $\rho > 1$ then $Q(D)$ is transient.*

(c) *If $\rho = 1$ then $Q(D)$ is null persistent.*

Here are two consequences of this.

(6) **Busy period.** A *busy period* is a period of time during which the server is continuously occupied. The length B of a typical busy period behaves similarly to the time B' between successive visits of the chain $Q(D)$ to the state 0. Thus

$$\begin{array}{lll} \text{if } \rho < 1 & \text{then} & \mathbf{E}(B) < \infty \\ \text{if } \rho = 1 & \text{then} & \mathbf{E}(B) = \infty, \mathbf{P}(B = \infty) = 0 \\ \text{if } \rho > 1 & \text{then} & \mathbf{P}(B = \infty) > 0. \end{array}$$

See the forthcoming Theorems (17) and (18) for more details about B.

(7) **Stationarity of Q.** It is an immediate consequence of (5) and (6.4.16) that $Q(D)$ is asymptotically stationary whenever $\rho < 1$. In this case it can be shown that Q is asymptotically stationary also, in that

$$\mathbf{P}(Q(t) = n) \to \pi_n \quad \text{as} \quad t \to \infty.$$

Roughly speaking, this is because $Q(t)$ forgets more and more about its origins as t becomes larger.

Proof of (5). $Q(D)$ is irreducible and aperiodic. We proceed by applying (6.4.3), (6.4.9), and (6.4.12).

(a) Look for a root of the equation $\boldsymbol{\pi} = \boldsymbol{\pi} \mathbf{P}_D$. Any such $\boldsymbol{\pi}$ satisfies

(8) $$\pi_j = \pi_0 \delta_j + \sum_{i=1}^{j+1} \pi_i \delta_{j-i+1}, \quad \text{for} \quad j \geq 0.$$

First, note that if $\pi_0 (\geq 0)$ is given, then (8) has a unique solution $\boldsymbol{\pi}$. Furthermore, this solution has non-negative entries. To see this, add equations (8) for $j = 0, 1, \ldots, n$ and solve for π_{n+1} to obtain

(9) $$\pi_{n+1} \delta_0 = \pi_0 \epsilon_n + \sum_{i=1}^{n} \pi_i \epsilon_{n-i+1} \quad \text{for} \quad n \geq 0$$

where

$$\epsilon_n = 1 - \delta_0 - \delta_1 - \ldots - \delta_n > 0 \quad \text{because} \quad \sum_j \delta_j = 1.$$

From (9), $\pi_{n+1} \geq 0$ whenever $\pi_i \geq 0$ for all $i \leq n$, and so

(10) $$\pi_n \geq 0 \quad \text{for all} \quad n$$

if $\pi_0 \geq 0$, by induction. Return to (8) to see that the generating functions

$$G(s) = \sum_j \pi_j s^j, \qquad \Delta(s) = \sum_j \delta_j s^j$$

satisfy

$$G(s) = \pi_0 \Delta(s) + \frac{1}{s} \{G(s) - \pi_0\} \Delta(s)$$

and so

(11) $$G(s) = \frac{\pi_0 (s-1) \Delta(s)}{s - \Delta(s)}.$$

$\boldsymbol{\pi}$ is a stationary distribution if and only if $\pi_0 > 0$ and $\lim_{s \uparrow 1} G(s) = 1$. Apply L'Hôpital's rule to (11) to discover that

$$\pi_0 = 1 - \Delta'(1) > 0$$

is a necessary and sufficient condition for this to occur, and thus there exists a stationary distribution if and only if

(12) $$\Delta'(1) < 1.$$

However,

$$\begin{aligned} \Delta(s) &= \sum_j s^j \mathbf{E}\left(\frac{(\lambda S)^j}{j!} e^{-\lambda S}\right) \\ &= \mathbf{E}\left(e^{-\lambda S} \sum_j \frac{(\lambda s S)^j}{j!}\right) \\ &= \mathbf{E}(\exp\{\lambda S(s-1)\}) = M_S(\lambda(s-1)) \end{aligned}$$

where M_S is the moment generating function of S. Thus

(13) $$\Delta'(1)=\lambda M_S'(0)=\lambda \mathbf{E}(S)=\rho$$

and condition (12) becomes

$$\rho<1.$$

Thus $Q(D)$ is non-null persistent if and only if $\rho<1$. In this case, $G(s)$ takes the form given in (5a).

(b) Recall from (6.4.9) that $Q(D)$ is transient if and only if there is a bounded non-zero solution $\{y_j : j\geq 1\}$ to the equations

(14) $$y_1=\sum_{i=1}^{\infty} \delta_i y_i$$

(15) $$y_j=\sum_{i=0}^{\infty} \delta_i y_{j+i-1} \quad \text{for} \quad j\geq 2.$$

If $\rho>1$ then Δ satisfies

$$0<\Delta(0)<1, \qquad \Delta(1)=1, \qquad \Delta'(1)>1$$

from (13). Draw a picture to see that there exists a number $b\in(0, 1)$ such that

$$\Delta(b)=b.$$

By inspection,

$$y_j=1-b^j$$

solves (14) and (15), and (b) is shown.

(c) $Q(D)$ is transient if $\rho>1$ and non-null persistent if and only if $\rho<1$. We need only show that $Q(D)$ is persistent if $\rho=1$. But it is not difficult to see that $\{y_j : j\neq 0\}$ solves equation (6.4.13), when y_j is given by

$$y_j=j \quad \text{for} \quad j\geq 1,$$

and the result follows. ■

(B) Waiting time. When $\rho<1$ the queue length settles down into an equilibrium distribution $\boldsymbol{\pi}$. Suppose that a customer joins the queue after some large time t has elapsed. He will wait a period W of time before his service begins; W is called his *waiting time* (this definition is at odds with that used by some authors who include the customer's service time in W). The distribution of W will not vary very much with t since the system is 'nearly' in equilibrium.

(16) **Theorem.** *The waiting time W has moment generating function*

$$M_W(s)=\frac{(1-\rho)s}{\lambda+s-\lambda M_S(s)}$$

when the queue is in equilibrium.

Proof. The condition that the queue be in equilibrium amounts to the supposition that the length $Q(D)$ of the queue on the departure of a customer is distributed according to the stationary distribution $\boldsymbol{\pi}$. Suppose that a customer waits for a period of length W and then is served for a period of length S. On his departure he leaves behind him all those customers who have arrived during the period, length $W+S$, during which he was in the system. The number Q of such customers is Poisson with parameter $\lambda(W+S)$, and so

$$\begin{aligned}\mathbf{E}(s^Q) &= \mathbf{E}(\mathbf{E}(s^Q \mid W, S))\\ &= \mathbf{E}(\exp\{\lambda(W+S)(s-1)\})\\ &= \mathbf{E}(e^{\lambda W(s-1)})\mathbf{E}(e^{\lambda S(s-1)}) \text{ by independence}\\ &= M_W(\lambda(s-1))M_S(\lambda(s-1)).\end{aligned}$$

However, Q has distribution $\boldsymbol{\pi}$ given by (5a) and the result follows. ■

(C) Busy period: a branching process. Finally, put yourself in the server's shoes. He is not so interested in the waiting times of his customers as he is in the frequency of his tea breaks. Recall from (6) that a *busy period* is a period of time during which he is continuously occupied, and let B be the length of a typical busy period. That is, if the first customer arrives at time T_1 then

$$B = \inf\{t > 0 : Q(t + T_1) = 0\};$$

B is well-defined whether or not $Q(D)$ is ergodic, though it may equal $+\infty$.

(17) **Theorem.** *The moment generating function M_B of B satisfies the functional equation*

$$M_B(s) = M_S(s - \lambda + \lambda M_B(s)).$$

It can be shown that this functional equation has a unique solution which is the moment generating function of a (possibly infinite) random variable (see Feller 1971, pp. 441, 473). The server may wish to calculate the probability

$$\mathbf{P}(B < \infty) = \lim_{x\to\infty} \mathbf{P}(B \leq x)$$

that he is eventually free. It is no surprise to find the following, in agreement with (6).

(18) **Theorem.**

$$\mathbf{P}(B<\infty)\begin{cases} =1 & \textit{if } \rho \leq 1\\ <1 & \textit{if } \rho > 1.\end{cases}$$

This may remind you of a similar result for the extinction probability of a branching process. This is no coincidence; we prove (17) and (18) by methods first encountered in the study of branching processes.

Proof of (17) and (18). Here is an imbedded branching process. Call customer C_2 an 'offspring' of customer C_1 if C_2 joins the queue while C_1 is being served. Let $\{G_n : n \geq 0\}$ be disjoint sets of customers given as follows. G_0 contains the first customer only; G_{n+1} contains the set of offspring of customers in G_n. Let Z_n be the size of G_n. Then $Z = \{Z_n : n \geq 0\}$ is a branching process; this assertion relies upon the fact that customers arrive like a Poisson process so that the numbers of arrivals during different service times are independent and identically distributed. The process Z is ultimately extinct if and only if the queue is empty at some time later than the first arrival. That is,

$$\mathbf{P}(B < \infty) = \mathbf{P}(Z_n = 0 \quad \text{for some } n).$$

But, by (5.4.5),

$$\eta = \mathbf{P}(Z_n = 0 \quad \text{for some } n).$$

satisfies

$$\eta = 1 \quad \text{if and only if} \quad \mu \leq 1$$

where μ is the mean number of offspring of the first arrival. However, in the notation of the proof of (5),

$$\mu = \Delta'(1) = \rho$$

by (13), and (18) is proved.

Each individual in this branching process has a service time; B is the sum of these service times. Thus

(19) $$B = S + \sum_{j=1}^{Z_1} B_j$$

where S is the service time of the first customer and B_j is the sum of the service times of the jth member of G_1 together with all his descendants (this is similar to the argument of Problem (5.11.9)). The two terms on the right-hand side of (19) are *not* independent of each other; after all, if S is large then Z_1 is likely to be large as well. However, condition on S to obtain

$$M_B(s) = \mathbf{E}\left(\mathbf{E}\left(\exp\left\{s\left(S + \sum_{j=1}^{Z_1} B_j\right)\right\} \mid S\right)\right)$$

and remember that, conditional on Z_1, the random variables $B_1, \ldots, B_{Z_1}$ are independent with the same distribution as B to obtain

$$M_B(s) = \mathbf{E}(e^{sS} G_P\{M_B(s)\})$$

where G_P is the probability generating function of the Poisson distribution with parameter λS. Thus

$$M_B(s) = \mathbf{E}(\exp\{S(s - \lambda + \lambda M_B(s))\})$$

as required. ∎

11.4 *G/M/1*

The system $G/M(\mu)/1$ contains an imbedded discrete-time Markov chain also, and this chain provides information about the properties of $Q(t)$ for large t. This section is divided into two parts, dealing with the asymptotic behaviour of $Q(t)$ and the waiting time distribution.

(A) Asymptotic queue length. This time, consider the epoch of time at which the nth customer *joins* the queue, and let $Q(A_n)$ be the number of individuals who are ahead of him in the system at the moment of his arrival. $Q(A_n)$ includes any customer whose service is in progress; more specifically, $Q(A_n)=Q(T_n-)$ where T_n is the instant of the nth arrival. The argument of the last section shows that

(1) $$Q(A_{n+1})=Q(A_n)+1-D$$

where D is the number of departures from the system during the interval $[T_n, T_{n+1})$between the nth and $(n+1)$th arrival. This time D depends on $Q(A_n)$ since not more than $Q(A_n)+1$ individuals may depart during this interval. However, service times are exponentially distributed, and so, conditional upon $Q(A_n)$ and $X_{n+1}=T_{n+1}-T_n$, D has a truncated Poisson distribution:

(2) $$\mathbf{P}(D=d \mid Q(A_n)=q, X_{n+1}=x)=\begin{cases} \dfrac{(\mu x)^d}{d!}e^{-\mu x} & \text{if } d\leq q \\ \displaystyle\sum_{m>q}\frac{(\mu x)^m}{m!}e^{-\mu x} & \text{if } d=q+1. \end{cases}$$

Anyway, given $Q(A_n)$, D is independent of $Q(A_1), \ldots, Q(A_{n-1})$, and so $Q(A)=\{Q(A_n): n\geq 1\}$ is a Markov chain.

(3) **Theorem.** *$Q(A)$ is a Markov chain with transition matrix*

$$\mathbf{P}_A=\begin{pmatrix} 1-\alpha_0 & \alpha_0 & 0 & 0 & \cdots \\ 1-\alpha_0-\alpha_1 & \alpha_1 & \alpha_0 & 0 & \cdots \\ 1-\alpha_0-\alpha_1-\alpha_2 & \alpha_2 & \alpha_1 & \alpha_0 & \cdots \\ \vdots & \vdots & \vdots & \vdots & \end{pmatrix}$$

where

$$\alpha_j=\mathbf{E}\left(\frac{(\mu X)^j}{j!}e^{-\mu X}\right)$$

and X is a typical inter-arrival time.

Of course, α_j is just the probability that exactly j events of a Poisson process occur during a typical inter-arrival time.

Proof. This proceeds as for (11.3.4). ■

(4) **Theorem.** *Let* $\rho = \{\mu \mathbf{E}(X)\}^{-1}$ *be the traffic density.*

(a) *If* $\rho < 1$ *then* $Q(A)$ *is ergodic with a unique stationary distribution* $\boldsymbol{\pi}$ *given by*

$$\pi_j = (1-\eta)\eta^j \quad \textit{for} \quad j \geq 0$$

where η *is the smallest positive root of*

$$\eta = M_X(\mu(\eta - 1))$$

and M_X *is the moment generating function of* X.

(b) *If* $\rho > 1$ *then* $Q(A)$ *is transient.*
(c) *If* $\rho = 1$ *then* $Q(A)$ *is null persistent.*

If $\rho < 1$ then $Q(A)$ is asymptotically stationary. Unlike the case of $M/G/1$, however, the stationary distribution $\boldsymbol{\pi}$ given by (4a) need *not* be the limiting distribution of Q itself; to see an example of this, just consider $D(1)/M/1$.

Proof. Let Q_d be a $M(\mu)/G/1$ queue whose service times have the same distribution as the inter-arrival times of Q (Q_d is called the *dual* of Q, but more about that later). The traffic density ρ_d of Q_d satisfies

(5) $$\rho\rho_d = 1.$$

From the results of Section 11.3, Q_d has an imbedded Markov chain $Q_d(D)$, obtained from the values of Q_d at the epochs of time at which customers depart. We shall see that $Q(A)$ is non-null persistent (respectively transient) if and only if the imbedded chain $Q_d(D)$ of Q_d is transient (respectively non-null persistent) and the results will follow immediately from (11.3.5) and its proof.

(a) Look for non-negative solutions $\boldsymbol{\pi}$ to the equation

(6) $$\boldsymbol{\pi} = \boldsymbol{\pi}\mathbf{P}_A$$

which have sum $\boldsymbol{\pi}\mathbf{1}' = 1$. Expand (6), set

(7) $$y_j = \pi_0 + \ldots + \pi_{j-1} \quad \text{for} \quad j \geq 1,$$

and remember that $\sum_j \alpha_j = 1$ to obtain

(8) $$y_1 = \sum_{i=1}^{\infty} \alpha_i y_i$$

(9) $$y_j = \sum_{i=0}^{\infty} \alpha_i y_{j+i-1} \quad \text{for} \quad j \geq 2.$$

These are the same equations as (11.3.14) and (11.3.15) for Q_d. As in the proof of (11.3.5), it is easy to check that

(10) $$y_j = 1 - \eta^j$$

solves (8) and (9) whenever

$$A(s)=\sum_{j=0}^{\infty}\alpha_j s^j$$

satisfies

$$A'(1)>1$$

where η is the unique root in the interval (0, 1) of the equation

$$A(s)=s.$$

However, write A in terms of M_X, as before, to find that

$$A(s)=M_X(\mu(s-1))$$

giving

$$A'(1)=\rho_d=\rho^{-1}.$$

Combine (7) and (10) to find the stationary distribution for the case $\rho<1$. If $\rho\geqslant 1$ then $\rho_d\leqslant 1$ by (5), and so (8) and (9) have no bounded non-zero solution since otherwise $Q_d(D)$ would be transient, contradicting (11.3.5). Thus $Q(A)$ is non-null persistent if and only if $\rho<1$.

(b) To prove transience, we seek bounded non-zero solutions $\{y_j : j\geqslant 1\}$ to the equations

(11) $$y_j=\sum_{i=1}^{j+1} y_i\alpha_{j-i+1} \quad \text{for} \quad j\geqslant 1.$$

Suppose that $\{y_j\}$ satisfies (11), and that $y_1\geqslant 0$. Define $\boldsymbol{\pi}=\{\pi_j : j\geqslant 0\}$ as follows:

$$\pi_0=y_1\alpha_0, \qquad \pi_1=y_1(1-\alpha_0), \qquad \pi_j=y_j-y_{j-1} \quad \text{for} \quad j\geqslant 2.$$

It is an easy exercise to show that $\boldsymbol{\pi}$ satisfies (11.3.8) with the δ's replaced by the α's throughout. But (11.3.8) possesses a non-zero solution with bounded sum if and only if $\rho_d<1$, which is to say that $Q(A)$ is transient if and only if $\rho=(\rho_d)^{-1}>1$.

(c) $Q(A)$ is transient if and only if $\rho>1$ and non-null persistent if and only if $\rho<1$. If $\rho=1$ then $Q(A)$ has no choice but null persistence. ■

(B) Waiting time. An arriving customer waits for just as long as the server needs to complete the service period in which he is currently engaged and to serve the other waiting customers. That is, the nth customer waits for a length W_n of time:

$$W_n=Z_1^*+Z_2+Z_3+\ldots+Z_{Q(A_n)} \quad \text{if} \quad Q(A_n)>0$$

where Z_1^* is the *excess* (or *residual*) *service time* of the customer at the head of the queue, and $Z_2,\ldots,Z_{Q(A_n)}$ are the service times of the others. Given $Q(A_n)$, the Z's are independent, but Z_1^* does not in general have the same distribution as $Z_2, Z_3, \ldots$. In the case of $G/M(\mu)/1$, however, the lack of memory property helps us around this difficulty.

(12) **Theorem.** *The waiting time W of an arriving customer has distribution*

$$\mathbf{P}(W \leq x) = \begin{cases} 0 & \text{if } x < 0 \\ 1 - \eta e^{-\mu(1-\eta)x} & \text{if } x \geq 0 \end{cases}$$

where η is given in (4a), when the queue is in equilibrium.

Note that W has an atom of size $1-\eta$ at the origin.

Proof. By the lack of memory property, W_n is the sum of $Q(A_n)$ independent exponential variables. Use the equilibrium distribution of $Q(A)$ to find that

$$M_W(s) = (1-\eta) + \eta \frac{\mu(1-\eta)}{\mu(1-\eta) - s}$$

which we recognize as the moment generating function of a random variable which either equals zero with probability $1-\eta$, or is exponentially distributed with parameter $\mu(1-\eta)$ with probability η. ■

Finally, here is a word of caution. There is another quantity called *virtual* waiting time, which must not be confused with *actual* waiting time. The latter is the actual time spent by a customer after his arrival; the former is the time which a customer *would* spend if he were to arrive at some particular instant. The equilibrium distributions of these waiting times may differ whenever the stationary distribution of Q differs from the stationary distribution of the imbedded Markov chain $Q(A)$.

11.5 *G/G/1*

If neither inter-arrival times nor service times are exponentially distributed then the methods of the last three sections fail. This apparent setback leads us to the remarkable discovery that queueing problems are intimately related to random walk problems. This section is divided into two parts, one dealing with the equilibrium theory of $G/G/1$ and the other dealing with the imbedded random walk.

(A) Asymptotic waiting time. Let W_n be the waiting time of the nth customer. There is a useful simple relationship between W_n and W_{n+1} in terms of the service time S_n of the nth customer and the length X_{n+1} of time between the nth and the $(n+1)$th arrivals.

(1) **Theorem. Lindley's Equation.**

$$W_{n+1} = \max\{0, W_n + S_n - X_{n+1}\}.$$

Proof. The nth customer is in the system for a length $W_n + S_n$ of time. If $X_{n+1} > W_n + S_n$ then the queue is empty at the $(n+1)$th arrival, and so $W_{n+1} = 0$. If $X_{n+1} \leq W_n + S_n$ then the $(n+1)$th customer arrives while the

nth is still present, but only waits for a period of length $W_n + S_n - X_{n+1}$ before the previous customer leaves. ■

We shall see that Lindley's equation implies that the distribution functions

$$F_n(x) = \mathbf{P}(W_n \leqslant x)$$

of the W's converge as $n \to \infty$ to some limit function $F(x)$. Of course, F need not be a proper distribution function; indeed, it is intuitively clear that the queue settles down into equilibrium if and only if F is a distribution function which is not defective.

(2) **Theorem.** *Let* $F_n(x) = \mathbf{P}(W_n \leqslant x)$. *Then*

$$F_{n+1}(x) = \begin{cases} 0 & \text{if } x < 0 \\ \displaystyle\int_{-\infty}^{x} F_n(x-y)\,\mathrm{d}G(y) & \text{if } x \geqslant 0 \end{cases}$$

where G is the distribution function of $U_n = S_n - X_{n+1}$. Thus

$$F(x) = \lim_{n \to \infty} F_n(x)$$

exists.

Note that $\{U_n : n \geqslant 1\}$ is a collection of independent identically distributed random variables.

Proof. If $x \geqslant 0$ then

$$\begin{aligned} \mathbf{P}(W_{n+1} \leqslant x) &= \int_{-\infty}^{\infty} \mathbf{P}(W_n + U_n \leqslant x \mid U_n = y)\,\mathrm{d}G(y) \\ &= \int_{-\infty}^{x} \mathbf{P}(W_n \leqslant x - y)\,\mathrm{d}G(y) \quad \text{by independence,} \end{aligned}$$

and the first part is proved. We claim that

(3) $$F_{n+1}(x) \leqslant F_n(x) \quad \text{for all } x \text{ and } n.$$

If (3) holds then the second result follows immediately; we prove (3) by induction. Trivially,

$$F_2(x) \leqslant F_1(x)$$

because $F_1(x) = 1$ for all $x \geqslant 0$. Suppose that (3) holds for $n = k-1$, say. Then, for $x \geqslant 0$,

$$F_{k+1}(x) - F_k(x) = \int_{-\infty}^{x} \{F_k(x-y) - F_{k-1}(x-y)\}\,\mathrm{d}G(y) \leqslant 0$$

by the induction hypothesis. The result is complete. ■

So the distribution functions of $\{W_n\}$ converge as $n \to \infty$. It is clear, by monotone convergence, that the limit $F(x)$ satisfies the Wiener–Hopf equation

$$F(x) = \int_{-\infty}^{x} F(x-y)\, dG(y) \quad \text{for} \quad x \geq 0;$$

this is not easily solved for F in terms of G. However, it is not too difficult to find a criterion for F to be a proper distribution function.

(4) **Theorem.** *Let $\rho = \mathbf{E}(S)/\mathbf{E}(X)$ be the traffic density.*

(a) *If $\rho < 1$ then F is a non-defective distribution function.*
(b) *If $\rho > 1$ then $F(x) = 0$ for all x.*
(c) *If $\rho = 1$ and $\operatorname{var}(U) > 0$ then $F(x) = 0$ for all x.*

An explicit formula for the moment generating function of F when $\rho < 1$ is given in Theorem (14) below. Theorem (4) classifies the stability of $G/G/1$ in terms of the sign of $1 - \rho$; note that this information is obtainable from the distribution function G since

(5) $$\rho < 1 \quad \Leftrightarrow \quad \mathbf{E}(S) < \mathbf{E}(X) \quad \Leftrightarrow \quad \mathbf{E}(U) = \int_{-\infty}^{\infty} u\, dG(u) < 0$$

where U is a typical member of the U's.

The crucial step in the proof of (4) is very important in its own right. Use Lindley's equation (1) to see that

$$W_1 = 0$$
$$W_2 = \max\{0, W_1 + U_1\} = \max\{0, U_1\}$$
$$W_3 = \max\{0, W_2 + U_2\} = \max\{0, U_2, U_2 + U_1\}$$

and in general

(6) $$W_{n+1} = \max\{0, U_n, U_n + U_{n-1}, \ldots, U_n + \ldots + U_1\}$$

which expresses W_{n+1} in terms of the partial sums of a sequence of independent identically distributed variables. It is difficult to derive asymptotic properties of W_{n+1} directly from (6) since every non-zero term changes its value as n increases from the value k, say, to the value $k+1$. The following theorem is the crucial observation.

(7) **Theorem.** *W_{n+1} has the same distribution as*

$$W'_{n+1} = \max\{0, U_1, U_1 + U_2, \ldots, U_1 + \ldots + U_n\}.$$

Proof. $(U_1, \ldots, U_n)$ and $(U_n, \ldots, U_1)$ are sequences with the same joint distribution. Replace each U_i in (6) by U_{n+1-i}. ■

That is to say, W_{n+1} and W'_{n+1} are *different* random variables but they have the *same* distribution. Thus

$$F(x)=\lim_{n\to\infty} \mathbf{P}(W_n\leqslant x)=\lim_{n\to\infty} \mathbf{P}(W'_n\leqslant x).$$

Furthermore,

(8) $$W'_n\leqslant W'_{n+1} \quad \text{for all } n\geqslant 1,$$

a monotonicity property which is not shared by $\{W_n\}$. This property provides another method for deriving the existence of F in (2).

Proof of (4). From (8)

$$W'=\lim_{n\to\infty} W'_n$$

exists almost surely (and, in fact, pointwise) but may be $+\infty$. Furthermore,

(9) $$W'=\max\{0, \Sigma_1, \Sigma_2, \ldots\}$$

where

$$\Sigma_n=\sum_{j=1}^{n} U_j$$

and $F(x)=\mathbf{P}(W'\leqslant x)$. Thus

$$F(x)=\mathbf{P}(\Sigma_n\leqslant x \quad \text{for all } n) \quad \text{if} \quad x\geqslant 0,$$

and the proof proceeds by using properties of the sequence $\{\Sigma_n\}$ of partial sums, such as the Strong Law (7.5.1):

(10) $$\frac{1}{n}\Sigma_n \xrightarrow{\text{a.s.}} \mathbf{E}(U) \quad \text{as} \quad n\to\infty.$$

Suppose first that $\mathbf{E}(U)<0$. Then

$$\mathbf{P}(\Sigma_n>0 \text{ for infinitely many } n)=\mathbf{P}\left(\frac{1}{n}\Sigma_n-\mathbf{E}(U)>|\mathbf{E}(U)| \text{ i.o.}\right)$$
$$\to 0 \quad \text{as} \quad n\to\infty$$

by (10). Thus, from (9), W' is almost surely the maximum of only finitely many terms, and so

$$\mathbf{P}(W'<\infty)=1,$$

implying that F is a non-defective distribution function.

Next suppose that $\mathbf{E}(U)>0$. Pick any $x>0$ and choose N such that

$$N\geqslant\frac{2x}{\mathbf{E}(U)}.$$

Then, if $n\geqslant N$,

$$\mathbf{P}(\Sigma_n\geqslant x)=\mathbf{P}\left(\frac{1}{n}\Sigma_n-\mathbf{E}(U)\geqslant\frac{x}{n}-\mathbf{E}(U)\right)$$
$$\geqslant\mathbf{P}\left(\frac{1}{n}\Sigma_n-\mathbf{E}(U)\geqslant-\tfrac{1}{2}\mathbf{E}(U)\right).$$

Let $n \to \infty$ and use the Weak Law to find that

$$\mathbf{P}(W' \geq x) \geq \mathbf{P}(\Sigma_n \geq x) \to 1 \quad \text{for all } x.$$

Therefore W' almost surely exceeds any finite number, and so

$$\mathbf{P}(W' < \infty) = 0$$

as required.

In the case when $\mathbf{E}(U) = 0$ these crude arguments do not work and we need a more precise measure of the fluctuations of Σ_n; one way of doing this is by way of the Law of the Iterated Logarithm (7.6.1). If var $(U) > 0$ and $\mathbf{E}(U_1^2) < \infty$, then $\{\Sigma_n\}$ enjoys fluctuations of order $O((n \log \log n)^{1/2})$ in both positive and negative directions with probability one, and so

$$\mathbf{P}(\Sigma_n \geq x \quad \text{for some } n) = 1 \quad \text{for all } x.$$

There are other arguments which yield the same result. ∎

(B) Imbedded random walk. The sequence $\Sigma = \{\Sigma_n : n \geq 0\}$ given by

(11) $$\Sigma_0 = 0, \qquad \Sigma_n = \sum_{j=1}^{n} U_j \quad \text{for} \quad n \geq 1$$

describes the path of a particle which performs a random walk on $\mathbb{R}$, jumping by an amount U_n at the nth step. This simple observation leads to a wealth of conclusions about queueing systems. For example, we have just seen that the waiting time W_n of the nth customer has the same distribution as the maximum W'_n of the first n positions of the walking particle. If $\mathbf{E}(U) < 0$ then the waiting time distributions converge as $n \to \infty$, which is to say that the maximum displacement $W' = \lim W'_n$ is almost surely finite. Other properties also can be expressed in terms of this random walk, and the techniques of reflection and reversal which we discussed in Section 5.3 are useful here.

The limiting waiting time distribution is the same as the distribution of the maximum,

$$W' = \max\{0, \Sigma_1, \Sigma_2, \ldots\},$$

and so it is appropriate to study the so-called 'ladder points' of Σ. Define an increasing sequence $L(0), L(1), \ldots$ of random variables by

$$L(0) = 0, \qquad L(n+1) = \min\{m > L(n) : \Sigma_m > \Sigma_{L(n)}\};$$

that is, $L(n+1)$ is the earliest epoch m of time at which Σ_m exceeds the walk's previous maximum $\Sigma_{L(n)}$. The L's are called *ladder points*; *negative ladder points* of Σ are defined similarly as the epochs at which Σ attains new minimum values. The result of (4) amounts to the assertion that

$$\mathbf{P}(\text{there exist infinitely many ladder points}) = \begin{cases} 0 & \text{if } \mathbf{E}(U) < 0 \\ 1 & \text{if } \mathbf{E}(U) > 0. \end{cases}$$

The total number of ladder points is given by the next lemma.

(12) **Lemma.** *Let $\eta = \mathbf{P}(\Sigma_n > 0$ for some $n \geq 1)$ be the probability that at least one ladder point exists. The total number Λ of ladder points has mass function*

$$\mathbf{P}(\Lambda = l) = (1-\eta)\eta^l \quad \textit{for} \quad l \geq 0.$$

Proof. Σ is a discrete-time Markov process. Thus

$$\mathbf{P}(\Lambda \geq l+1 \mid \Lambda \geq l) = \eta$$

since the path of the walk after the lth ladder point is a copy of Σ itself. ■

Thus the queue is stable if $\eta < 1$, in which case the maximum W' of Σ is related to the height of a typical ladder point. Let

$$Y_j = \Sigma_{L(j)} - \Sigma_{L(j-1)}$$

be the difference in the displacements of the walk at the $(j-1)$th and jth ladder points. Conditional on the value of Λ, $\{Y_j : 1 \leq j \leq \Lambda\}$ is a collection of independent identically distributed variables, by the Markov property. Furthermore,

(13) $$W' = \Sigma_{L(\Lambda)} = \sum_{j=1}^{\Lambda} Y_j;$$

this leads to the next lemma, relating waiting time distribution to the distribution of a typical member Y of the Y's.

(14) **Lemma.** *If Q is stable then its equilibrium waiting time distribution has moment generating function*

$$M_W(s) = \frac{1-\eta}{1-\eta M_Y(s)}$$

where M_Y is the moment generating function of Y.

Proof. Q is stable if and only if $\eta < 1$. Use (13) and (5.1.15) to find that

$$M_W(s) = G_\Lambda(M_Y(s)).$$

Now use the result of (12). ■

Lemma (14) describes the waiting time distribution in terms of the distribution of Y. Analytical properties of Y are a little tricky to obtain, and we restrict ourselves here to an elegant description of Y which provides a curious link between pairs of 'dual' queueing systems.

The server of the queue enjoys busy periods during which he works continuously; in between busy periods he has *idle periods* during which he drinks tea. Let I be the length of his first idle period.

(15) **Lemma.** *Let $L = \min\{m > 0 : \Sigma_m < 0\}$ be the first negative ladder point of Σ. Then $I = -\Sigma_L$.*

That is, I equals the absolute value of the depth of the first negative ladder point. It is of course possible that Σ has *no* negative ladder points.

Proof. Call a customer *lucky* if he finds the queue empty as he arrives (customers who arrive at exactly the same time as the previous customer departs are deemed to be unlucky). We claim that the $(L+1)$th customer is the first lucky customer after the very first arrival. If this holds then (15) follows immediately since I is the elapsed time between the Lth departure and the $(L+1)$th arrival:

$$I=\sum_{j=1}^{L} X_{j+1}-\sum_{j=1}^{L} S_j=-\Sigma_L.$$

To verify the claim remember that

(16) $$W_n=\max\{0, V_n\} \quad\text{where}\quad V_n=\max\{U_{n-1}, U_{n-1}+U_{n-2}, \ldots, \Sigma_{n-1}\}$$

and note that the nth customer is lucky if and only if $V_n<0$. Now

$$V_n\geq\Sigma_{n-1}\geq 0 \quad\text{for}\quad 2\leq n\leq L,$$

and it remains to show that

$$V_{L+1}<0.$$

To see this, note that

$$U_L+U_{L-1}+\ldots+U_{L-k}=\Sigma_L-\Sigma_{L-k-1}\leq\Sigma_L<0$$

whenever $0\leq k<L$. Now use (16) to obtain the result. ■

Now we are ready to extract a remarkable identity which relates 'dual pairs' of queueing systems.

(17) **Definition.** If Q is a queueing process with inter-arrival time distribution F_X and service time distribution F_S, then the **dual process** Q_d of Q is a queueing process with inter-arrival time distribution F_S and service time distribution F_X.

For example, the dual of $M(\lambda)/G/1$ is $G/M(\lambda)/1$, and vice versa; we made use of this fact in the proof of (11.4.4). The traffic densities ρ and ρ_d of Q and Q_d satisfy

$$\rho\rho_d=1;$$

Q and Q_d cannot both be stable except in pathological instances when all their inter-arrival and service times almost surely take the same constant value.

(18) **Theorem.** *Let Σ and Σ_d be the random walks associated with the queue Q and its dual Q_d. Then $-\Sigma$ and Σ_d are identically distributed random walks.*

Proof. Let Q have inter-arrival times $\{X_n\}$ and service times $\{S_n\}$; Σ has jumps of size $U_n = S_n - X_{n+1}$ $(n \geq 1)$. The reflected walk $-\Sigma$, which is obtained by reflecting Σ in the x axis, has jumps of size $-U_n = X_{n+1} - S_n$ $(n \geq 1)$ (see Section 5.3 for more details of the reflection principle). Write $\{S'_n\}$ and $\{X'_n\}$ for the inter-arrival and service times of Q_d; Σ_d has jumps of size $U'_n = X'_n - S'_{n+1}$ $(n \geq 1)$, which have the same distribution as the jumps of $-\Sigma$. ■

This leads to a corollary.

(19) **Theorem.** *The height Y of the first ladder point of Σ has the same distribution as the length I_d of a typical idle period in the dual queue.*

Proof. From (15), $-I_d$ is the height of the first ladder point of $-\Sigma_d$, which by (18) is distributed like the height Y of the first ladder point of Σ. ■

Here is an example of an application of these facts.

(20) **Theorem.** *Let Q be a stable queueing process with dual process Q_d. Let W be a typical equilibrium waiting time of Q and I_d a typical idle period of Q_d. Their moment generating functions are related by*

$$M_W(s) = \frac{1-\eta}{1-\eta M_{I_d}(s)}$$

where $\eta = \mathbf{P}(W > 0)$.

Proof. Use (14) and (19). ■

An application of this result is given in Problem (11.7.12). Another application is a second derivation of the equilibrium waiting time distribution (11.4.12) of $G/M/1$; just remark that the dual of $G/M/1$ is $M/G/1$, and that idle periods of $M/G/1$ are exponentially distributed (though, of course, the server does not have many such periods if the queue is unstable).

11.6 Heavy traffic

A queue settles into equilibrium if its traffic density ρ is less than 1; it is unstable if $\rho > 1$. It is our shared personal experience that many queues (such as in doctors' waiting rooms and at airport check-in desks) have a tendency to become unstable. The reason is simple: employers do not like to see their employees idle, and so they provide only just as many servers as are necessary to cope with the arriving customers. That is, they design the queueing system so that ρ is only slightly smaller than 1; the ensuing queue is long but stable, and the server experiences 'heavy traffic'. As $\rho \uparrow 1$ the equilibrium queue length Q_ρ becomes longer and longer, and it is interesting to ask for the rate at which Q_ρ approaches infinity. Often it turns out that a suitably scaled form of Q_ρ is asymptotically exponentially distributed. We describe this here for the $M/D/1$ system, leaving it to the reader to amuse himself by finding corresponding results for other queues. In this special case, $Q_\rho \simeq Z/(1-\rho)$ as $\rho \uparrow 1$ where Z is an exponential variable.

(1) **Theorem.** *Let $\rho = \lambda d$ be the traffic density of the $M(\lambda)/D(d)/1$ queue, and let Q_ρ be a random variable with the equilibrium queue length distribution. Then $(1-\rho)Q_\rho$ converges in distribution as $\rho \uparrow 1$ to the exponential distribution with parameter $\frac{1}{2}$.*

Proof. Use (11.3.5) to see that Q_ρ has moment generating function

(2) $$M_\rho(s) = \frac{(1-\rho)(e^s-1)}{\exp\{s-\rho(e^s-1)\}-1} \quad \text{if} \quad \rho<1.$$

The moment generating function of $(1-\rho)Q_\rho$ is $M_\rho((1-\rho)s)$; make the appropriate substitution in (2). Now let $\rho \uparrow 1$ and use L'Hôpital's rule to deduce that

$$M_\rho((1-\rho)s) \to \frac{1}{1-2s}.$$ ■

11.7 Problems

1. **Finite waiting room.** Consider $M(\lambda)/M(\mu)/1$ with the constraint that arriving customers who see N customers in the line ahead of them leave and never return. Find the stationary distribution of queue length.

2. **Baulking.** Consider $M(\lambda)/M(\mu)/1$ with the constraint that if an arriving customer sees n customers in the line ahead of him, he joins the queue with probability $p(n)$ and otherwise leaves in disgust.

   (a) Find the stationary distribution of queue length if $p(n)=(n+1)^{-1}$.
   (b) Find the stationary distribution $\boldsymbol{\pi}$ of queue length if $p(n)=2^{-n}$, and show that the probability that an arriving customer joins the queue is $\mu(1-\pi_0)/\lambda$.

3. **Series.** In a Moscow supermarket customers queue at the cash desk to pay for the goods they want; then they proceed to a second line where they wait for the goods in question. If customers arrive in the shop like a Poisson process with parameter λ and all service times are independent and exponentially distributed, parameter μ_1 at the first desk and μ_2 at the second, find the stationary distributions of queue lengths, when they exist, and show that the two queue lengths are independent in equilibrium.

4. **Batch (or bulk) service.** Consider $M/G/1$, with the modification that the server may serve up to m customers simultaneously. If the queue length is less than m at the beginning of a service period then he serves everybody waiting at that time. Find an expression for the probability generating function of the stationary distribution of queue length and evaluate it explicitly for the case when $m=2$ and service times are exponentially distributed.

5. Consider $M(\lambda)/M(\mu)/1$ where $\lambda<\mu$. Find the moment generating function of the

length B of a typical busy period, and show that

$$\mathbf{E}(B)=\frac{1}{\mu-\lambda}, \qquad \text{var}(B)=\frac{\lambda+\mu}{(\mu-\lambda)^3}.$$

Show that the density function of B is

$$f_B(x)=\frac{(\mu/\lambda)^{1/2}}{x}e^{-(\lambda+\mu)x}I_1(2x(\lambda\mu)^{1/2}) \quad \text{for} \quad x>0$$

where I_1 is a modified Bessel function.

6. Consider $G/M/1$. Verify (11.4.2), that the number of departures during an inter-arrival time has a truncated Poisson distribution. Now suppose that the inter-arrival times are exponential also, and use (11.4.12) to derive the equilibrium waiting time distribution for a stable $M/M/1$ queue. Verify your answer directly using (11.2.8).

7. Consider $M(\lambda)/G/1$ in equilibrium. Square both sides of (11.3.3) to obtain an expression for the mean queue length. Show that the mean waiting time in equilibrium is $\frac{1}{2}\lambda\mathbf{E}(S^2)/(1-\rho)$ where S is a typical service time.

8. Let W be the time which a customer would have to wait in a $M(\lambda)/G/1$ queue if he were to arrive at time t. Show that the distribution function

$$F(x;t)=\mathbf{P}(W\leqslant x)$$

satisfies

$$\frac{\partial F}{\partial t}=\frac{\partial F}{\partial x}-\lambda F+\lambda\mathbf{P}(W+S\leqslant x)$$

where S is a typical service time, independent of W.

9. Use the *Wiener–Hopf equation* of Section 11.5,

$$F(x)=\int_{-\infty}^{x}F(x-y)\,dG(y) \quad \text{if} \quad x\geqslant 0$$

for the limiting waiting time distribution F of $G/G/1$, to confirm the stationary distribution (11.4.12) of waiting time in $G/M/1$.

10. Apply Theorem (11.5.20) to find yet another derivation of the stationary waiting time distribution of $G/M/1$.

11. Consider a $G/G/1$ queue in which the service times are constantly equal to 2, whilst the inter-arrival times take either of the values 1 and 4 with equal probability $\frac{1}{2}$. Find the limiting waiting time distribution.

12. Consider a stable $M/G/1$ queue with traffic density ρ and its associated random walk Σ, in the notation of Section 11.5. Apply Theorem (11.5.20) to deduce the moment generating function of the idle period of an unstable $G/M/1$ queue.

Appendix I
Foundations and notation

Here is a list of topics with which many readers will already be familiar, and which are used in the body of the text. We begin with some notation.

(A) Basic notation. The end of each example or subsection is indicated by the symbol ●; the end of each proof is indicated by ■.

The largest integer which is not larger than the real number x is denoted by $\lfloor x \rfloor$; $\lceil x \rceil$ denotes the smallest integer not smaller than x.

We use the following symbols:

$\mathbb{R} \equiv$ the real numbers $(-\infty, \infty)$
$\mathbb{Z} \equiv$ the integers $(\ldots, -2, -1, 0, 1, 2, \ldots)$
$\mathbb{C} \equiv$ the complex plane $\{x + iy : x, y \in \mathbb{R}\}$.

The symbol $\Leftrightarrow$ is interchangeable with the expression 'if and only if'.
Here are two 'delta' functions.

Kronecker δ: If i and j belong to some set S, define

$$\delta_{ij} = \begin{cases} 1 & \text{if} \quad i = j \\ 0 & \text{if} \quad i \neq j. \end{cases}$$

Dirac δ function: If $x \in \mathbb{R}$, the symbol δ_x represents a notional function with the properties

(a) $\delta_x(y) = 0 \quad \text{if} \quad y \neq x$

(b) $\displaystyle\int_{-\infty}^{\infty} g(y)\,\delta_x(y)\,dy = g(x)$ for all integrable $g : \mathbb{R} \to \mathbb{R}$.

(B) Sets and counting. In addition to the union and intersection symbols, $\cup$ and $\cap$, we employ the following notation:

set difference: $A \setminus B = \{x \in A : x \notin B\}$
symmetric difference: $A \triangle B = (A \setminus B) \cup (B \setminus A) = \{x \in A \cup B : x \notin A \cap B\}$.

The *cardinality* $|A|$ of a set A is the number of elements which A contains. The *complement* of A is denoted by A^c.

The *binomial coefficient* $\binom{n}{r}$ is the number of distinct combinations of r objects that can be drawn from a set containing n distinguishable objects.

The following texts treat this material in more detail: Halmos (1960), Ross (1976), and Rudin (1976).

(C) Vectors and matrices. The symbol $\boldsymbol{x}$ denotes the row vector $(x_1, x_2, \ldots)$ of finite or countably infinite length. The transposes of vectors $\boldsymbol{x}$ and matrices $\mathbf{V}$ are denoted by $\boldsymbol{x}'$ and $\mathbf{V}'$ respectively. The determinant of a square matrix $\mathbf{V}$ is written as $|\mathbf{V}|$.

The following books contain information about matrices, their eigenvalues and their canonical forms: Lipschutz (1974), Rudin (1976), and Cox and Miller (1965).

(D) Convergence

(1) **Limits inferior and superior.** We often use inferior and superior limits, and so we review their definitions. Given any sequence $\{x_n : n \geq 1\}$ of real numbers, define

$$g_m = \inf_{n \geq m} x_n, \qquad h_m = \sup_{n \geq m} x_n.$$

then

$$g_m \leq g_{m+1}, \qquad h_m \geq h_{m+1} \quad \text{for all } m$$

and so the sequences $\{g_m\}$ and $\{h_m\}$ converge as $m \to \infty$. Their limits

$$g = \lim_{m \to \infty} g_m, \qquad h = \lim_{m \to \infty} h_m$$

are denoted by '$\liminf_{n \to \infty} x_n$' and '$\limsup_{n \to \infty} x_n$' respectively. Clearly

$$\liminf_{n \to \infty} x_n \leq \limsup_{n \to \infty} x_n.$$

The following result is very useful.

(2) **Theorem.** *The sequence $\{x_n\}$ converges if and only if*

$$\liminf_{n \to \infty} x_n = \limsup_{n \to \infty} x_n.$$

(3) **Cauchy convergence.** The criterion of convergence (for all $\epsilon > 0$, there exists N such that $|x_n - x| < \epsilon$ if $n \geq N$) depends on knowledge of the limit x. In many practical instances it is convenient to use a criterion which does not rely on such knowledge.

(4) **Definition.** The sequence $\{x_n\}$ is called **Cauchy convergent** if, for all $\epsilon > 0$, there exists N such that

$$|x_m - x_n| < \epsilon \quad \text{whenever } m, n \geq N.$$

(5) **Theorem.** *A real sequence converges if and only if it is Cauchy convergent.*

(6) **Continuity.** Recall that the function $g : \mathbb{R} \to \mathbb{R}$ is *continuous* at the point x if

$$g(x+h) \to g(x) \quad \text{as} \quad h \to 0.$$

We often encounter functions which satisfy only part of this condition.

(7) **Definition.** The function $g : \mathbb{R} \to \mathbb{R}$ is called

(i) **right-continuous** if $g(x+h) \to g(x)$ as $h \downarrow 0$ for all x

(ii) **left-continuous** if $g(x+h) \to g(x)$ as $h \uparrow 0$ for all x.

So g is continuous if and only if g is both right- and left-continuous.

If g is monotone then it has left and right limits, $\lim_{h\uparrow 0} g(x+h)$, $\lim_{h\downarrow 0} g(x+h)$, at all points x; these may differ from $g(x)$ if g is not continuous at x. We write

$$g(x+)=\lim_{h\downarrow 0} g(x+h), \qquad g(x-)=\lim_{h\uparrow 0} g(x+h).$$

(8) **Infinite products.** We make use of the following result concerning products of real numbers.

(9) **Theorem.** *Let* $p_n=\prod_{i=1}^{n}(1+x_i)$.

(a) *If* $x_i>0$ *for all* i, *then* $p_n\to\infty$ *as* $n\to\infty$ *if and only if*

$$\sum_i x_i=\infty.$$

(b) *If* $-1<x_i\leq 0$ *for all* i, *then* $p_n\to 0$ *as* $n\to\infty$ *if and only if*

$$\sum_i |x_i|=\infty.$$

(10) **Landau's notation.** Use of the O–o notation is standard. If f and g are two functions of a real variable x, then we say that

$$f(x)=o(g(x)) \quad \text{as} \quad x\to\infty \quad \text{if} \quad \lim_{x\to\infty}\{f(x)/g(x)\}=0$$

$$f(x)=O(g(x)) \quad \text{as} \quad x\to\infty \quad \text{if} \quad |f(x)/g(x)|<C$$

for all large x and some constant C.

Similar definitions hold as $x\downarrow 0$ and for real sequences $\{f(n)\}, \{g(n)\}$ as $n\to\infty$.

For more details about the topics in this section see Apostol (1957) or Rudin (1976).

(E) Complex analysis. We make use of elementary manipulation of complex numbers, the formula

$$e^{itx}=\cos(tx)+i\sin(tx),$$

and the theory of complex integration. Readers are referred to Phillips (1957) and Nevanlinna and Paatero (1969) for further details.

(F) Transforms. An *integral transform* of the function $g:\mathbb{R}\to\mathbb{R}$ is a function $\tilde{g}$ of the form

$$\tilde{g}(\theta)=\int_{-\infty}^{\infty} K(\theta,x)g(x)\,dx;$$

such transforms are very useful in the theory of differential equations. Perhaps the most useful is the *Laplace transform*.

(11) **Definition.** The **Laplace transform** of g is defined to be

$$\hat{g}(\theta)=\int_{-\infty}^{\infty} e^{-\theta x}g(x)\,dx \quad \text{where} \quad \theta\in\mathbb{C}$$

whenever this integral exists.

As a special case of the Laplace transform of g, set $\theta = i\lambda$ for real λ to obtain the *Fourier transform*

$$G(\lambda) = \hat{g}(i\lambda) = \int_{-\infty}^{\infty} e^{-i\lambda x} g(x)\,dx.$$

Often, we are interested in functions g which are defined on the half-line $[0, \infty)$, with Laplace transform

$$\hat{g}(\theta) = \int_{0}^{\infty} e^{-\theta x} g(x)\,dx;$$

such a transform is called 'one-sided'. We often think of g as a function of a *real* variable θ.

Subject to certain conditions (such as existence and continuity) Laplace transforms have the following important properties.

(12) **Inversion.** *g can be retrieved from knowledge of $\hat{g}$ by the 'inversion formula'.*

(13) **Convolution.** *If* $k(x) = \int_{-\infty}^{\infty} g(x-y)h(y)\,dy$ then $\hat{k}(\theta) = \hat{g}(\theta)\hat{h}(\theta)$.

(14) **Differentiation.** *If* $G:[0, \infty) \to \mathbb{R}$ *and* $g = \dfrac{dG}{dx}$ *then*

$$\theta\hat{G}(\theta) = \hat{g}(\theta) + G(0).$$

It is sometimes convenient to use a variant of the Laplace transform.

(15) **Definition.** The **Laplace–Stieltjes transform** of g is defined to be

$$g^*(\theta) = \int_{-\infty}^{\infty} e^{-\theta x}\,dg(x) \quad \text{where} \quad \theta \in \mathbb{C}$$

whenever this integral exists.

We do not wish to discuss the definition of this integral (it is called a 'Lebesgue–Stieltjes' integral and is related to the integrals of Section 5.6). You may think about it in the following way. If g is differentiable then its Laplace–Stieltjes transform g^* is defined to be the Laplace transform of the derivative g' of g, since in this case

$$dg(x) = g'(x)\,dx.$$

Laplace–Stieltjes transforms g^* always receive an asterisk to distinguish them from Laplace transforms. They have properties similar to (12), (13), and (14). For example, (13) becomes

(16) **Convolution.** *If* $k(x) = \int_{-\infty}^{\infty} g(x-y)\,dh(y)$ *then* $k^*(\theta) = g^*(\theta)h^*(\theta)$.

Fourier–Stieltjes transforms are defined similarly.

More details are provided by Apostol (1957) and Hildebrand (1962).

Appendix II
Further reading

This list is not comprehensive. The bibliography lists a larger collection of titles, selected from the vast library.

Probability theory. Ross (1976) and Hoel, Port, and Stone (1971*a*) are excellent elementary texts. Even more elementary is Gray (1967). There are many fine advanced texts, including Billingsley (1979), Breiman (1968), and Chung (1974). The probability section of Kingman and Taylor (1966) provides a clear and concise introduction to the modern theory. Moran (1968) is often useful at our level.

The two volumes of Feller's treatise (Feller 1968, 1971) are essential reading for budding probabilists; the first deals largely in discrete probability, and the second is an idiosyncratic and remarkable encyclopaedia of the continuous theory.

Markov chains. There is no account of discrete-time Markov chains which is wholly satisfactory, though various treatments have attractions. Billingsley (1979) proves the ergodic theorem by the coupling argument, Çinlar (1975) and Karlin and Taylor (1975) contain many examples, and Ross (1970) is clear and to the point; do not overlook Cox and Miller (1965), Feller (1968), and Prabhu (1965*a*). Chung (1960) and Freedman (1971) are much more advanced, and include rigorous treatments of the continuous-time theory; these are difficult books. More elementary treatments are by Gray (1967) (very simple), Cox and Miller (1965), Karlin and Taylor (1975) (very clear), and Çinlar (1975).

Other random processes. Any full account of processes with continuous state spaces, and their sample path properties, is far beyond the scope of this reading list. Karlin and Taylor (1975) contains excellent chapters on the Wiener process and stationary processes. You may read Prabhu (1965*a*) and Cox and Miller (1965) for interesting discussions of the general diffusion equations.

Ross (1970) and Karlin and Taylor (1975) deal well with renewal theory. Prabhu (1965*a*) includes a proof of the renewal theorem.

Most authors do not treat queueing theory as a single topic, but prefer to consider the various systems at appropriate moments in chapters on Markov chains and renewal. Ross (1970), Çinlar (1975), Billingsley (1979), Prabhu (1965*a*), and Karlin and Taylor (1975) follow this scheme. A more consolidated, but heavily analytical, treatment is provided by Prabhu (1965*b*).

Bibliography

Apostol, T. M. (1957). *Mathematical analysis.* Addison-Wesley, Reading, Mass.

Athreya, K. B. and Ney, P. E. (1972). *Branching processes.* Springer, Berlin.

Billingsley, P. (1979). *Probability and measure.* John Wiley, New York.

Breiman, L. (1968). *Probability.* Addison-Wesley, Reading, Mass.

Chung, K. L. (1960). *Markov chains with stationary transition probabilities.* Springer, Berlin.

—— (1974). *A course in probability theory.* Academic Press, New York.

Çinlar, E. (1975). *Introduction to stochastic processes.* Prentice-Hall, Englewood Cliffs, N.J.

Clarke, L. E. (1975). *Random variables.* Longman, London.

Cox, D. R. and Miller, H. D. (1965). *The theory of stochastic processes.* Chapman and Hall, London.

—— and Smith, W. L. (1961). *Queues.* Chapman and Hall, London.

Doob, J. L. (1953). *Stochastic processes.* John Wiley, New York.

Dubins, L. and Savage, L. (1965). *How to gamble if you must.* McGraw-Hill, New York.

Feller, W. (1968). *An introduction to probability theory and its applications*, Vol. 1 (3rd edn.). John Wiley, New York.

—— (1971). *An introduction to probability theory and its applications*, Vol. 2 (2nd edn.) John Wiley, New York.

Freedman, D. (1971). *Markov chains.* Holden-Day, San Francisco.

Gray, J. R. (1967). *Probability.* Oliver and Boyd, Edinburgh.

Halmos, P. R. (1960). *Naive set theory.* Van Nostrand, Princeton, N.J.

Harris, T. E. (1963). *The theory of branching processes.* Springer, Berlin.

Hildebrand, F. B. (1962). *Advanced calculus for applications.* Prentice-Hall, Englewood Cliffs, N.J.

Hoel, P. G., Port, S. C., and Stone, C. J. (1971*a*). *Introduction to probability theory.* Houghton Mifflin, Boston.

—— (1971*b*). *Introduction to stochastic processes.* Houghton Mifflin, Boston.

Karlin, S. and Taylor, H. M. (1975). *A first course in stochastic processes* (2nd edn.). Academic Press, New York.

—— (1981). *A second course in stochastic processes.* Academic Press, New York.

Kelly, F. P. (1979). *Reversibility and stochastic networks.* John Wiley, New York.

Kingman, J. F. C. and Taylor, S. J. (1966). *Introduction to measure and probability.* Cambridge University Press, Cambridge.

Laha, R. G. and Rohatgi, V. K. (1979). *Probability theory.* John Wiley, New York.

Lindvall, T. (1977). *Ann. Probability* **5,** 482–485.

Lipschutz, S. (1974). *Linear algebra.* Schaum Outline, McGraw-Hill, New York.

Loève, M. (1977). *Probability theory*, Vol. 1 (4th edn.). Springer, Berlin.

—— (1978). *Probability theory*, Vol. 2 (4th edn.). Springer, Berlin.

Lukacs, E. (1970). *Characteristic functions* (2nd edn.). Griffin, London.

Mandelbrot, B. (1977). *Fractals: form, chance, and dimension.* Freeman, San Francisco.

Moran, P. A. P. (1968). *An introduction to probability theory*. Clarendon Press, Oxford.

Nevanlinna, R. and Paatero, V. (1969). *Introduction to complex analysis*. Addison-Wesley, Reading, Mass.

Parzen, E. (1962). *Stochastic processes*. Holden-Day, San Francisco.

Phillips, E. G. (1957). *Functions of a complex variable*. Oliver and Boyd, Edinburgh.

Prabhu, N. U. (1965*a*). *Stochastic processes*. Collier Macmillan, New York.

—— (1965*b*). *Queues and inventories*. John Wiley, New York.

Ross, S. (1970). *Applied probability models with optimization applications*. Holden-Day, San Francisco.

—— (1976). *A first course in probability*. Collier Macmillan, New York.

Rudin, W. (1976). *Principles of mathematical analysis* (3rd edn.). McGraw-Hill, New York.

Whittle, P. (1970). *Probability*. Penguin, Harmondsworth, Middlesex.

Remarks about selected problems

No experienced mathematician feels well acquainted with a subject until he has tackled some problems; through attempting and failing, we extend the boundaries of our knowledge and experience. This observation applies to students also. *It would be a big mistake to treat the remarks of this section as a solution sheet.* Many of the hints and comments will be useful only to those who have spent a half hour, say, on the problem already. The remarks vary in style and content between small hints and detailed solutions; some problems receive no comments at all (indicating, perhaps, that they are either very easy or good challenges).

Chapter 1

1. (a) $2 \cdot \frac{1}{6} \cdot \frac{5}{6}$ (b) $\frac{3}{6} \cdot \frac{3}{6}$ (c) $3 \cdot \frac{1}{36}$ (d) $12 \cdot \frac{1}{36}$.

2. (a) $(\frac{1}{2})^n$ (b) $\binom{n}{\frac{1}{2}n}(\frac{1}{2})^n$ (c) $\binom{n}{2}(\frac{1}{2})^n$ (d) $1-(\frac{1}{2})^n - n(\frac{1}{2})^n$.

3. $B \backslash A = B \cap A^c$; $\bigcap_i A_i = \left(\bigcup_i A_i^c\right)^c$.

4. (a) $\Omega = \{H, T\}^3$, $\mathcal{F} = \{0, 1\}^\Omega$, $\mathbf{P}(HHH) = p^3$, $\mathbf{P}(HHT) = p^2(1-p)$, etc., if $A \subseteq \Omega$ then $\mathbf{P}(A) = \sum_{a \in A} \mathbf{P}(a)$.

5. $A \triangle B = (A \cup B) \backslash (A \cap B)$.

7. $A^c \cap B = B \backslash (A \cap B)$.

8. $\Omega \cap \varnothing = \varnothing$. Use (1.3.1b).

9. You must show that $\mathbf{Q}$ is countably additive and $\mathbf{Q}(\Omega) = 1$. The final part shows that, in order to condition on the simultaneous occurrences of two events A and B, it suffices to condition on the individual occurrences one by one, in either order.

10. (a) To prove the induction step, argue that, by (1.3.4c),

$$\mathbf{P}\left(\bigcup_1^{n+1} A_i\right) = \mathbf{P}\left(\bigcup_1^{n} A_i\right) + \mathbf{P}(A_{n+1}) - \mathbf{P}\left(\bigcup_1^{n} (A_i \cap A_{n+1})\right)$$

and use the induction hypothesis on the first and third terms of the right-hand side.

(b) $A = \bigcup_1^n (A \cap B_i)$; now use the additivity property of $\mathbf{P}$.

11. (a) Induction. (b) Apply (a) to $A_1^c, \ldots, A_n^c$.

13. (a) Use the result of (12) with $A_j = \{N = j\}$ and $B = \{S = 4\}$ to find that $\mathbf{P}(N = 2 \mid S = 4) = \frac{1}{12} \cdot \frac{1}{4} / (\frac{1}{6} \cdot \frac{1}{2} + \ldots)$.

(b) $$\mathbf{P}(S = 4 \mid N \text{ even}) = \frac{\sum_r \mathbf{P}(S = 4 \mid N = 2r)\mathbf{P}(N = 2r)}{\mathbf{P}(N \text{ even})} = \frac{1 + 2^4 3^3}{2^8 3^3}.$$

(c) Use (12).

(d) Let $A_r = \{\text{largest} \leqslant r\} = \{\text{all dice show} \leqslant r\}$. Then

$$\mathbf{P}(A_r) = \sum_n \mathbf{P}(A_r \mid N = n)\mathbf{P}(N = n) = \frac{r}{12 - r}.$$

14. (d) $\mathbf{P}(C_n) \leqslant \mathbf{P}(A_n) \leqslant \mathbf{P}(B_n)$.

15. This is a more complicated example than (1.7.2). Each of the links in the following diagram is absent with probability p.

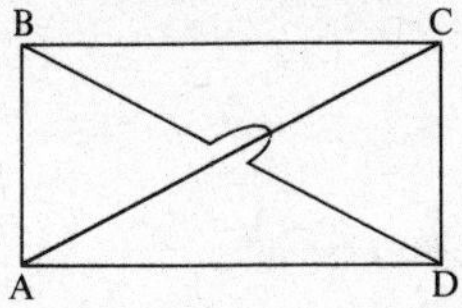

(c) $\mathbf{P}(\text{D hears it} \mid \text{B and C quarrel}) = 1 - p(1-(1-p)^2)^2$.

16. Use (1.4.4) with $A = \{\text{even number of heads after } n \text{ tosses}\}$ and $B = \{\text{first toss yields heads}\}$. Iterate the difference equation for $n = 1, 2, \ldots$, guess the general solution, and thus prove by induction that $p_n = \frac{1}{2}\{1 + (1-2p)^n\}$.

17. Use (1.4.4) with $A = \{\text{run of } r \text{ heads before run of } s \text{ tails}\}$ and $B = \{\text{first toss shows heads}\}$. Also, if $C = \{\text{first } r \text{ tosses show heads}\}$, then

$$\begin{aligned}\mathbf{P}(A \mid B) &= \mathbf{P}(A \mid B \cap C)\mathbf{P}(C \mid B) + \mathbf{P}(A \mid B \cap C^c)\mathbf{P}(C^c \mid B)\\ &= 1p^{r-1} + \mathbf{P}(A \mid B^c)(1 - p^{r-1}).\end{aligned}$$

Together with a similarly derived expression for $\mathbf{P}(A \mid B^c)$, this yields

$$\mathbf{P}(A) = \frac{p^{r-1}(1-q^s)}{p^{r-1} + q^{s-1} - p^{r-1}q^{s-1}}$$

where $p + q = 1$.

18. (a) $\frac{1}{4}$ (b) $\dfrac{2875}{3876}$.

Chapter 2

1. $\mathbf{P}(X \leqslant x) = 1 - q^{\lfloor x \rfloor}$ for $x \geqslant 0$.
2. $X = \sum_i x_i I_{A_i}$ where $A_i = \{\omega : X(\omega) = x_i\}$.
3. If $a > 0$, $\mathbf{P}(aX + b \leqslant x) = \mathbf{P}(X \leqslant a^{-1}(x - b))$. What if $a < 0$?
4. (a) $\frac{1}{2}$ (c) $\mathbf{P}(X^2 \leqslant X) = \mathbf{P}(X \leqslant 1)$ (d) $1 - 1/(4\pi)$
(e) $1/(4\pi)$ (f) $\mathbf{P}(\sqrt{X} \leqslant x) = \mathbf{P}(X \leqslant x^2)$ if $x \geqslant 0$.
5. (a) q (b) 0 (c) $\frac{1}{2}p$.
6. $\frac{1}{2}$.
9. (a) $\mathbf{P}(X^+ \leqslant x) = \begin{cases} F(x) & \text{if } x \geqslant 0 \\ 0 & \text{if } x < 0. \end{cases}$

(c) $\mathbf{P}(|X| \leqslant x) = \mathbf{P}(X \leqslant x) - \mathbf{P}(X < -x) = F(x) - \lim_{y \uparrow -x} F(y)$ if $x \geqslant 0$.

10. Use (2.1.6c) and (2.1.11c).
11. $m = \sup\{x : F(x) < \frac{1}{2}\}$ is a median.
12. If p_1 and p_2 are the mass functions of the dice then the sum S satisfies

$$\mathbf{P}(S = 2) = p_1(1)p_2(1), \qquad \mathbf{P}(S = 12) = p_1(6)p_2(6).$$

But $\mathbf{P}(S = 7) \geqslant p_1(1)p_2(6) + p_1(6)p_2(1)$.

Chapter 3

1. (a) $\{g(X) = a\} \cap \{h(Y) = b\} = \bigcup_{\substack{x \in g^{-1}(a) \\ y \in h^{-1}(b)}} (\{X = x\} \cap \{Y = y\})$.

(b) If $f_{X,Y}(x, y) = g(x)h(y)$, then $f_X(x) = g(x)\sum_y h(y)$ and $f_Y(y) = h(y)\sum_x g(x)$; but $\sum_{x,y} f_{X,Y}(x, y) = 1$, and so $\sum_x g(x) \sum_y h(y) = 1$, giving $f_{X,Y}(x, y) = f_X(x)f_Y(y)$.

2. $\operatorname{var}(X)=\sum_x \{x-\mathbf{E}(X)\}^2 f_X(x)=0$ if and only if every summand equals zero.
3. (b) $\mathbf{E}(g(X))=\sum_a a\mathbf{P}(g(X)=a)=\sum_a a \sum_{x:g(x)=a} f(x)=\sum_x g(x)f(x)$.
   (c) Use (3.2.3) and (3.3.9).
4. $U=XY$ has mass function $f_U(2)=f_U(3)=f_U(6)=\frac{1}{3}$, $f_U(u)=0$ otherwise.
$$f_{Y|Z}(2\mid 2)=\frac{\mathbf{P}(Y=2, Z=2)}{\mathbf{P}(Z=2)}=\frac{\mathbf{P}(\omega_1)}{\mathbf{P}(\omega_1\cup\omega_2)}=\tfrac{1}{2}, \quad \text{and so on.}$$
5. (a) $k=1$ (b) $\alpha<-1$, $k^{-1}=\sum n^{\alpha}=\zeta(-\alpha)$, the Riemann zeta function.
6. (a) Use (3.8.1). (b) $B\left(n, \dfrac{\lambda}{\lambda+\mu}\right)$.
7. X has the 'lack of memory' property in the sense that, if we know that X exceeds some value n, then the distribution of $X-n$ is the same as the original distribution of X. If X has this property then, for $m, n\geq 0$, $\mathbf{P}(X>m+n\mid X>n)=\mathbf{P}(X>m)$ and so $G(m)=P(X>m)$ satisfies $G(m+n)=G(m)G(n)=\{G(1)\}^{m+n}$; thus X is geometric.
8. Use (3.8.1).
10. Remember the similar limiting result of (3.5.4).
11. This hypergeometric distribution has parameters $2n$, N, and n.
12. (a) $d=(c+d)(b+d)$. (b) $d=(c+d)(b+d)$; in this case X and Y are independent if and only if they are uncorrelated.
13. (a) $\sum_{n=0}^{\infty}\sum_{m=n+1}^{\infty}\mathbf{P}(X=m)=\sum_{m=1}^{\infty}\sum_{n=0}^{m-1}\mathbf{P}(X=m)$.
   (b) An alternative to using (a) is to use a difference equation. Condition on the colour of the first chosen ball to obtain an expression relating $m(b, r)$, the mean number in question, to $m(b, r-1)$.
   (c) The following two questions are equivalent.
   (i) Begin with all the balls in urn I. Transfer them one by one to urn II until all the remaining balls in urn I have the same colour. How many are left?
   (ii) Begin with all the balls in urn II. Transfer them one by one back to urn I until the first occasion at which a chosen ball's colour differs from those picked so far. Disregarding this last ball, how many balls are in urn I?
   Following scheme (ii), condition on the colour of the first ball and use (b) to find the mean number to be
$$\frac{b}{r+1}+\frac{r}{b+1}.$$
14. Use (3.3.8) and (3.3.11).
15. $\boldsymbol{V}$ is singular if and only if there exists a vector $\boldsymbol{x}$ ($\neq\mathbf{0}$) such that $\boldsymbol{x}\boldsymbol{V}\boldsymbol{x}'=0$. But $\boldsymbol{x}\boldsymbol{V}\boldsymbol{x}'=\mathbf{E}(Y^2)$ where $Y=\sum_i x_i(X_i-\mathbf{E}X_i)$. Now use (2).

Chapter 4

1. (a) $$\left(\int_{-\infty}^{\infty} e^{-x^2}\,dx\right)^2=\int_{-\infty}^{\infty}\int_{-\infty}^{\infty}\exp\{-(x^2+y^2)\}\,dx\,dy=\int_{r=0}^{\infty}\int_{\theta=0}^{2\pi} r\exp(-r^2)\,dr\,d\theta.$$
   (b) $$\int_{-\infty}^{\infty}\frac{x}{\sqrt{(2\pi)}}\exp(-\tfrac{1}{2}x^2)\,dx=0, \qquad \int_{-\infty}^{\infty}\frac{x^2}{\sqrt{(2\pi)}}\exp(-\tfrac{1}{2}x^2)\,dx=1.$$
   (c) $(1-3y^{-4})\exp(-\frac{1}{2}y^2)\leq\exp(-\frac{1}{2}y^2)\leq(1+y^{-2})\exp(-\frac{1}{2}y^2)$.

2. (a) $0 \leqslant \alpha < \beta \leqslant 1$. (b) $6\{3(\beta^2 - \alpha^2) - 2(\beta^3 - \alpha^3)\}^{-1}$.
3. Remember (3.9.13).
4. (a) (i) If $F(y) = x$ then $\mathbf{P}(F(X) \leqslant x) = \mathbf{P}(X \leqslant y)$.
5. Remember (3.9.7). To prove the last part, suppose that $g(s+t) = g(s)g(t)$, $g(0) = 1$, and g is non-negative and right-continuous. For positive integers n, $g(n) = g(1)g(n-1) = \{g(1)\}^n$. For rationals m/n, $\{g(m/n)\}^n = g(m) = \{g(1)\}^m$, giving $g(m/n) = \{g(1)\}^{m/n}$. Now use right-continuity to deduce that $g(s) = \{g(1)\}^s$ for all $s \geqslant 0$.
6. Remember (3.9.1).
7. (a) No. $\mathbf{P}(X > 1, Y < 1) = 0$ but $\mathbf{P}(X > 1)\mathbf{P}(Y < 1) > 0$.
   (b) $f_X(x) = 2e^{-2x}$, $f_Y(y) = 2e^{-y}(1 - e^{-y})$, $x, y > 0$; $\text{cov}(X, Y) = \frac{1}{4}$.
8. Use (4.8.1) and integration by parts.
9. (b) Use (4.7.4) to deduce that $U = X + Y$ and $V = X/(X+Y)$ have joint density function

$$f_{U,V}(u, v) = \frac{\lambda^{m+n}}{\Gamma(m)\Gamma(n)} u^{m+n-1} e^{-\lambda u} v^{m-1}(1-v)^{n-1}, \qquad u, v \geqslant 0.$$

   (c) $I_m = \displaystyle\int_t^\infty \frac{\lambda^m x^{m-1}}{\Gamma(m)} e^{-\lambda x}\, dx$ satisfies $I_m = I_{m-1} + \dfrac{(\lambda t)^{m-1}}{\Gamma(m)} e^{-\lambda t}$.
11. Find the conditional density function $f_{X|Y}$.
12. Remember (4.7.6). $Z = Y/X$ has density function $f_Z(z) = \displaystyle\int_{-\infty}^{\infty} |u|\, f(u, uz)\, du$.
13. $r \exp(-r^2/2)$
14. (b) Use (4.8.1) to find the distribution function of $X + \frac{1}{2}Y$.

$$\mathbf{E}(V) = \mathbf{E}(X) + \tfrac{1}{2}\mathbf{E}(Y) = \tfrac{3}{2}, \qquad \text{var}(V) = \tfrac{5}{4}.$$

16. $f_{X_{(k)}}(x) = k\dbinom{n}{k} F(x)^{k-1}\{1 - F(x)\}^{n-k} f(x)$, where F is the distribution function of the X's.
17. In the notation of (15), $g(\mathbf{y}) = n!L(\mathbf{y})/T^n$, if $0 \leqslant y_i \leqslant T$ for all i, where $\mathbf{y} = (y_1, \ldots, y_n)$.
18. (a) Consider the function $g(t) = t^p/p + t^{-q}/q$ for $t > 0$. Show that g has a unique minimum at $t = 1$, and deduce that $g(t) \geqslant 1$ for all $t > 0$. Hence show that $0 \leqslant xy \leqslant x^p/p + y^q/q$ for all $x, y \geqslant 0$. Now replace x by $|X|\,(\mathbf{E}\,|X^p|)^{-1/p}$ and y by $|Y|\,(\mathbf{E}\,|Y^q|)^{-1/q}$ and take expectations.
   (b) Suppose $p > 1$. Use Hölder's inequality to deduce that

$$\begin{aligned}\mathbf{E}(|X+Y|^p) &\leqslant \mathbf{E}(|X|\,|X+Y|^{p-1}) + \mathbf{E}(|Y|\,|X+Y|^{p-1}) \\ &\leqslant (\mathbf{E}\,|X^p|)^{1/p}(\mathbf{E}(|X+Y|^p))^{1/q} + (\mathbf{E}\,|Y^p|)^{1/p}\mathbf{E}(|X+Y|^p)^{1/q}\end{aligned}$$

   where $p^{-1} + q^{-1} = 1$. Divide by $\mathbf{E}(|X+Y|^p)^{1/q}$.
19. Replace X and Y by $|Z|^{\frac{1}{2}(b-a)}$ and $|Z|^{\frac{1}{2}(b+a)}$ respectively, where $0 \leqslant a \leqslant b$. Thus g is convex with $g(0) = 0$, and hence $p^{-1}g(p)$ is a non-decreasing function of p.
20. Remember (4.6.5).

Chapter 5

1. Coefficient of s^{17} in $(\frac{1}{6})^{10}(1 - 10s^6 + 45s^{12} - \ldots)(1-s)^{-10}$.
2. (a) $f(0) = f(1) = f(2) = 0$, $f(3) = p^3$. There are two possible difference equations:
   (i) $f(k) = qf(k-1) + pqf(k-2) + p^2qf(k-3)$ for $k > 3$
   (ii) $f(k) = \{1 - f(0) - f(1) - \ldots - f(k-4)\}qp^3$ for $k > 3$

where $p+q=1$. Either solve (i) directly or use generating functions. Secondly,

$$\mathbf{E}(X)=q\{1+\mathbf{E}(X)\}+pq\{2+\mathbf{E}(X)\}+p^2q\{3+\mathbf{E}(X)\}+3p^3$$

and thence $\mathbf{E}(X)=p^{-3}(1+p+p^2)$.

(b) (ii) Let $\kappa=e^{2\pi i/3}$ denote a complex cube root of unity.

3. $G(s)=[ps/\{1-(1-p)s\}]^r$.

4. Remember (5.3.3). The mean number $P_0(1)=\sum_n p_0(2n)$ of visits to the origin is infinite if and only if $p=\frac{1}{2}$. Now use (5.3.1a) as before.

5. (b) There are at least two ways of finding $p_0(2n)$. The longer way is as follows:

$$p_0(2n)=\left(\frac{1}{4}\right)^n\sum_{m=0}^{n}\frac{(2n)!}{(m!)^2\{(n-m)!\}^2}=\left(\frac{1}{4}\right)^n\binom{2n}{n}\sum_{m=0}^{n}\binom{n}{m}^2=\left(\frac{1}{4}\right)^n\binom{2n}{n}^2.$$

It is no coincidence that $p_0(2n)$ is the square of the corresponding one-dimensional quantity. Project the walk $\{(X_n, Y_n)\}$ onto the diagonal lines $y=\pm x$ to obtain two projected *independent* one-dimensional walks. Finally, use Stirling's formula and the argument of (4). What happens if the walk is asymmetric? (See Example (9.9.15) for yet another way of doing this.)

6. Place an absorbing barrier at position b $(>a)$, and solve the appropriate difference equation to find that the answer is $\{\frac{1}{2}(-1+\sqrt{(1+4q/p)}\}^a$ if $p>\frac{1}{3}$ and $a>0$. What happens if $p\leq\frac{1}{3}$ or $a<0$?

7. Remember (5.3.8) and (5.3.9) for the first part.

9. Condition on the size Z_1 of the first generation to find that the total number Y_n satisfies $Y_n=1+Y(1)+Y(2)+\ldots+Y(Z_1)$ where the $Y(i)$'s are independent copies of Y_{n-1}.

10. $\mathbf{P}(Z_m=0\mid Z_n=i)=\{G_{m-n}(0)\}^i$.

11. (b) We can suppose that $H(0)<1$. If $\{H(s)\}^{1/n}$ is a probability generating function for any $n\geq1$ then $H(0)>0$, since otherwise $H^{1/n}$ cannot be a power series for all n unless $H\equiv0$. Thus $0<1-H(s)<1$ for $0\leq s<1$, and so

$$\log H(s)=\log[1-\{1-H(s)\}]=\lambda\left(-1+\sum_{1}^{\infty}a_js^j\right)=\lambda\{-1+A(s)\}$$

where $\lambda=-\log H(0)$ and $A(1)=1$. To show that $a_j\geq0$ for each j, note that

$$\frac{d^j}{ds^j}\{H(s)e^{\lambda}\}^{1/n}\bigg|_{s=0}=\frac{\lambda}{n}j!a_j+o\left(\frac{1}{n}\right)\quad\text{as}\quad n\to\infty.$$

12. Remember the result of (3).

15. (a) $\mathbf{E}(e^{itX/Y})=\mathbf{E}(\mathbf{E}(e^{itX/Y}\mid Y))=(2/\pi)^{1/2}I(1/\sqrt{2},|t|/\sqrt{2})$ in the notation of (14). Remember (5.8.4).

(b) Remember (14e).

(c) $W^{-2}=X^{-2}+Y^{-2}+Z^{-2}$, and W is symmetric.

17. $-X$ has characteristic function $\phi_X(-t)$.

18. Recall (5.7.5). Deduce from the functional equation that $\psi(t)=\phi(t)/\phi(-t)$ satisfies $\psi(t)=\{\psi(t/2^n)\}^{2^n}\to1$ as $n\to\infty$, remembering (5.7.4b). Thus $\phi(t)=\{\phi(t/2^n)\}^{4^n}\to\exp(-\frac{1}{2}t^2)$ as $n\to\infty$.

19. See Example (7.4.10).

20. (b) Remember (17).

(d) $\{2-\phi_1(t)\}^{-1}=G(\phi_1(t))$, where G is the probability generating function of a geometric variable with parameter $\frac{1}{2}$. The answer is $\sum_{i=1}^{N}X_1(i)$, where

$X_1(1), X_1(2), \ldots$ are independent with the same distribution as X_1, and N has mass function $\mathbf{P}(N=n)=(\frac{1}{2})^n$ for $n \geq 1$ and is independent of the $X_1(i)$'s.
(e) $\phi_1(ut)=\mathbf{E}(\exp(itX_1Y) \mid Y=u)$ for any random variable Y.

21. (a) This is the characteristic function of $f(x)=(1-\cos x)/(\pi x^2)$ by the Inversion Theorem (5.9.1).
(b, c) In both cases $\phi''(0)=0$. Now use (5.7.4).
(d) Let X take values ± 1 with equal probability $\frac{1}{2}$.

22. $|1-e^{ix}|^2=2(1-\cos x) \leq x^2$ for all x.

24. (a) $1-\cos x \geq \frac{1}{2}x^2-\frac{1}{24}x^4$.
(b) You may need the fact that $\sin x \leq x \sin 1$ for $x \geq 1$.

25. Remember (4.10.14).

26. (b) Do not confuse $\Gamma(1, \lambda)$ with $\Gamma(\lambda, 1)$.

27. Consider the distribution functions

$$F_n(x)=\begin{cases} 0 & \text{if} \quad x<-n \\ \frac{1}{2}(1+x/n) & \text{if} \quad -n \leq x<n \\ 1 & \text{if} \quad x \geq n. \end{cases}$$

28. $1+s+\ldots+s^{10}=(1-s^{11})/(1-s)$ cannot be factorized into the product of two polynomials of degree five with real coefficients because the complex roots of unity occur in conjugate pairs.

29. Remember (3.2.2) and (5.1.19).

Chapter 6

1. (a) $\{1, 2\}$ is irreducible ergodic, 3 is aperiodic and transient, 4 is absorbing.

2. (a) $\sum_i p_{ij}(n)=1$ for all n; now use (6.2.5) and (6.2.9).
(b) If $\boldsymbol{\pi}$ is a stationary distribution and the chain is aperiodic then $1 \geq \sum_{i \leq N} p_{ij}(n) \rightarrow N\pi_j$ as $n \rightarrow \infty$, giving $\pi_j \leq N^{-1}$ for all N.

3. Remember that $p_{ii}(m+r+n) \geq p_{ij}(m)p_{jj}(r)p_{ji}(n)$. If $d(i)=d$, $r=0$, and LHS>0, it follows that $m+n$ is a multiple of d. Now, the left-hand side equals 0 unless r is a multiple of d, and so $d(j)$ is a multiple of d.

4. (a) $d(j)=1$ and so there exist integers $n_1, \ldots, n_r$ with greatest common divisor 1 and such that $p_{jj}(n_k)>0$ for $k=1, \ldots, r$. Any sufficiently large n can be expressed as the sum $n=\sum a_k n_k$ of multiples of the n_k's, and so $p_{jj}(n)>0$. If $p_{ij}(m)>0$ then $p_{ij}(m+n) \geq p_{ij}(m)p_{jj}(n)>0$ for all large n.

6. $\sum p_{ijk}^2 \leq \max\{p_{ijk}\} \sum p_{ijk}$, giving that

$$\mathbf{P}(\mathbf{X}_{2n}=(0,0,0)) \leq \frac{(2n)!}{2^{2n}3^n n!\{\Gamma(\frac{1}{3}n+1)\}^3} \simeq Cn^{-3/2}.$$

See Example (9.9.15) for an alternative method of proof.

7. No, because the three-dimensional symmetric random walk is transient.

8. Remember Section 6.6.

9. $\pi_j=\binom{N}{j}^2 \Big/ \binom{2N}{N}$, the hypergeometric distribution, of course.

10. (a) If the probability in question is zero, then each visit to j is preceded by a return to the starting point i with probability one. By the Markov property, the chain never visits j, which is a contradiction.
(b) $1-f_{jj} \geq \alpha_{ji}(1-f_{ij})$, where α_{ji} is the probability that, starting from j, the chain visits i without revisiting j in the meantime.

11. Show that $1-F(z)$ has no zero for $|z|\leq 1$ except at $z=1$, and deduce that $(1-z)P(z)$ is analytic in the domain $|z|\leq 1+\delta$ for some $\delta>0$.

12. To prove continuity, we demonstrate the stronger inequality

$$|p_{ij}(t+h)-p_{ij}(t)|\leq 1-p_{ii}(h) \quad \text{if} \quad h>0.$$

For,

$$\begin{aligned} p_{ij}(t+h)-p_{ij}(t) &= \sum_k (p_{ik}(h)-\delta_{ik})p_{kj}(t) \\ &= (p_{ii}(h)-1)p_{ij}(t)+\sum_{k\neq i} p_{ik}(h)p_{kj}(t) \\ &\leq \sum_{k\neq i} p_{ik}(h) = 1-p_{ii}(h). \end{aligned}$$

To prove the last part, note that

$$\frac{p_{ii}(t)-1}{t}=\frac{g(t)}{t}\,\frac{p_{ii}(t)-1}{\log p_{ii}(t)}\to\lambda \quad \text{as} \quad t\downarrow 0.$$

13. Suppose $i\neq j$ and let N be the smallest value of n such that $g_{i,k_1}g_{k_1,k_2}\cdots g_{k_n,j}\neq 0$ for some $k_1,\ldots,k_n$; then $(\mathbf{G}^n)_{i,j}=0$ for $n<N$ and $(\mathbf{G}^N)_{i,j}>0$ (*strictly* positive, because the shortest sequence uses only *off-diagonal* terms of $\mathbf{G}$). Therefore $p_{ij}(t)=t^N\sum_{n\geq N}\dfrac{t^{n-N}}{n!}(\mathbf{G}^n)_{i,j}$, which is positive for small t. The converse is similar, but easier.

14. If $\{\mathbf{P}_t\}$ is uniform and $X(s)$ has distribution $\boldsymbol{\pi}$ then we claim that $X(t)$ has distribution $\boldsymbol{\pi}$ for all t. The only difficulty arises if $t<s$. Suppose $t<s$ and $X(t)$ has distribution $\boldsymbol{\mu}$. Then $\boldsymbol{\pi}=\boldsymbol{\mu}\exp(u\mathbf{G})$ for all $u\geq s-t$; such an identity must hold for all u, and, setting $u=0$, we obtain that $\boldsymbol{\mu}=\boldsymbol{\pi}$. To complete the theoretical part of the question, show that
   (i) $\pi_j(\mathbf{G}^n)_{j,i}=\pi_i(\mathbf{G}^n)_{i,j}$ for all i, j, n
   (ii) $\pi_j p_{ji}(t)=\pi_i p_{ij}(t)$ for all i, j, t
   (iii) the pairs $(X(s), X(s+t))$ and $(Y(s), Y(s+t))$ have the same joint distribution
   (iv) the collections $(X(t_1),\ldots,X(t_n))$ and $(Y(t_1),\ldots,Y(t_n))$ have the same joint distributions for all $t_1<\ldots<t_n$.

15. Suppose that $\mathbf{P}=\mathbf{P}_1$, where $\{\mathbf{P}_t\}$ is a uniform semigroup with generator

$$\mathbf{G}=\begin{pmatrix}-\beta & \beta \\ \gamma & -\gamma\end{pmatrix}.$$

From (6.10.12),

$$\mathbf{P}_t=\frac{1}{\beta+\gamma}\begin{pmatrix}\beta h(t)+\gamma & \beta\{1-h(t)\} \\ \gamma\{1-h(t)\} & \beta+\gamma h(t)\end{pmatrix}$$

where $h(t)=\exp(-t(\beta+\gamma))$. Thus $\beta=\gamma=-\frac{1}{2}\log(2\alpha-1)$.

16. The forward equations yield

$$\frac{\partial G}{\partial t}=(s-1)\left(\lambda G-\mu\frac{\partial G}{\partial s}\right), \qquad G(s,0)=s^I.$$

17. If $N(0)=0$ then $\mathbf{E}(s^{N(t)})=\exp\left\{(s-1)\int_0^t \lambda(u)\,du\right\}$.

18. $F_t(x)=\mathbf{P}(N^*(t)\leq x)$ satisfies

$$\frac{\partial}{\partial t}F_t(x)=-\lambda F_t(x)+\lambda\int_{-\infty}^{\infty}F_t(x-y)\,\mathrm{d}F_Y(y).$$

Thus $\phi_t(u)=\mathbf{E}(\exp\{iuN^*(t)\})$ satisfies

$$\frac{\partial}{\partial t}\phi_t(u)=-\lambda\phi_t(u)+\lambda\phi_t(u)\phi_Y(u)$$

with solution $\phi_t(u)=\exp[\lambda t\{\phi_Y(u)-1\}]$. Remember (5.11.11).

19. $\mathbf{E}(N(t))=\frac{1}{2}t(\lambda_1+\lambda_2)$.

20. Use (6.9.20) to find that $\pi_j=A\nu_j$ is a stationary distribution if and only if $A=(\sum\nu_j)^{-1}>0$. To solve the difference equation for the η's, write $\zeta_j=\eta_{j+1}-\eta_j$, to find that

$$\eta_{n+1}=\eta_1+(\eta_1-1)\sum_{i=1}^{n}e_i.$$

21. Suppose that $X(0)=0$, say. Let $T_n=\inf\{t:X(t)\geq n\}$ be the earliest time at which $X(t)$ exceeds $n-1$, and let $X_{n+1}=T_{n+1}-T_n$. Show that $\lambda_n\mathbf{E}(X_{n+1})=1+\mu_n\mathbf{E}(X_n)$, for $n\geq 0$, and deduce that X is dishonest if $\mathbf{E}(T_\infty)=\sum\epsilon_i<\infty$, where

$$\epsilon_i=\frac{1}{\lambda_i}+\frac{\mu_i}{\lambda_i\lambda_{i-1}}+\dots+\frac{\mu_i\mu_{i-1}\dots\mu_1}{\lambda_i\lambda_{i-1}\dots\lambda_0}.$$

A poor sufficient condition for X to be honest is that $\sum\lambda_i^{-1}=\infty$; can you see how to find a better condition?

22. T has the gamma distribution.

23. Use either the lack of memory property or (4.7.4).

24. Use (4.10.4a(i)), (23), and (4.10.4a(ii)) in that order.

25. $1-x\leq e^{-x}$ for $x\geq 0$. Monotonic series may be approximated by integrals.

Chapter 7

1. If $\|\cdot\|$ is a norm, then $|\|X_n\|-\|X\||\leq\|X_n-X\|$.

2. (c) $\{|U+V|>\epsilon\}\subseteq\{|U|>\frac{1}{2}\epsilon\}\cup\{|V|>\frac{1}{2}\epsilon\}$.

(d) Set $Y_n=-X_n$ in (7.2.2).

(e) This result does not hold for convergence in rth mean or convergence in distribution (*you* should provide counter-examples) but remember (7.2.14) in the latter case. To prove convergence in probability, note first that

$$\mathbf{P}(|(X_n-X)Y|>\epsilon)\leq\mathbf{P}(|X_n-X|>\epsilon/y)+\mathbf{P}(|Y|>y)$$

for any $\epsilon, y>0$; now let $n\to\infty$ and $y\to\infty$ to find that $(X_n-X)Y\xrightarrow{P}0$. Together with other similar results and the identity $X_nY_n-XY=(X_n-X)(Y_n-Y)+(X_n-X)Y+(Y_n-Y)X$, this yields the conclusion.

3. (a) For $\delta>0$, pick M such that $\mathbf{P}(|X|\geq M)<\delta$. On the interval $[-M,M]$, g is uniformly continuous; thus, given $\epsilon>0$ there exists $\eta>0$ such that

$$|g(x)-g(y)|<\epsilon \text{ if } |x-y|<\eta \text{ and } |y|\leq M.$$

Hence $\mathbf{P}(|g(X_n)-g(X)|<\epsilon, |X|\leq M)\geq\mathbf{P}(|X_n-X|<\eta, |X|\leq M)\geq\mathbf{P}(|X_n-X|<\eta)-\mathbf{P}(|X|>M)$.

(b) This is an extension of the Helly–Bray Theorem (see Moran 1968, p. 254, or Laha and Rohatgi 1979, p. 137). The classical proof is very dull; it is much better to use the method of (7.2.18).

4. Use (5.9.5).

5. (b) $\text{cov}(N(s), N(t)) = \lambda \min\{s, t\}$.
(d) $N(t)$ is *differentiable in probability* with derivative $N'(t)$ if, for all $\epsilon > 0$,

$$\mathbf{P}\left(\left|\frac{N(t+h)-N(t)}{h} - N'(t)\right| > \epsilon\right) \to 0 \quad \text{as} \quad h \to 0.$$

But, if $\epsilon h < 1$,

$$\mathbf{P}\left(\left|\frac{N(t+h)-N(t)}{h}\right| > \epsilon\right) = \lambda h + o(h)$$

and so N has derivative zero in probability. However,

$$\mathbf{E}\left(\left|\frac{N(t+h)-N(t)}{h}\right|^2\right) = \frac{\lambda}{h} + \lambda^2, \quad \text{if} \quad h > 0.$$

6. You need (7.2.10b) together with (7.3.4) with $g(x) = x^4$.

7. Use (7.2.10b) and (7.3.4) again.

8. Either argue directly, by way of distribution functions, or use characteristic functions. (7.2.18) provides a sledgehammer method.

9. Either use Chebyshov's inequality to bound $\mathbf{P}(X + c \geq t + c)$ or notice that $t = \mathbf{E}(t - X) \leq \mathbf{E}((t - X)I_A)$, where $A = \{X < t\}$, and use the Cauchy–Schwarz inequality.

10. $|x| > \epsilon$ if and only if $\dfrac{|x|}{1+|x|} > \dfrac{\epsilon}{1+\epsilon}$ for $\epsilon > 0$.

11. If $X_n \xrightarrow{\text{m.s.}} X$ then $\{X_n\}$ is m.s. Cauchy convergent; just use the triangle inequality (7.1.5). The converse is harder. If $\{X_n\}$ is m.s. Cauchy convergent, then it is Cauchy convergent in probability, in that $\mathbf{P}(|X_n - X_m| > \epsilon) \to 0$ as $m, n \to \infty$ for all $\epsilon > 0$. Hence there exists a subsequence $X_{n_1}, X_{n_2}, \ldots$ which converges almost surely to some X. Now

$$\begin{aligned}\mathbf{E}((X_n - X)^2) &= \mathbf{E}\left(\liminf_{k\to\infty} (X_n - X_{n_k})^2\right) \\ &\leq \liminf_{k\to\infty} \mathbf{E}((X_n - X_{n_k})^2) \to 0 \quad \text{as} \quad n \to \infty;\end{aligned}$$

we have used Fatou's lemma (see Clarke 1975, p. 90, or Moran 1968, p. 205). The corresponding result holds for convergence in probability, almost surely and in rth mean.

12. As in the proof of (7.4.3). The point is that the Law of Large Numbers holds in this case even though the X's may not be independent.

15. (a) You need to show that $\mathbf{E}(R_{n+1} \mid R_n) = \dfrac{n+3}{n+2} R_n$.
(b) By (7.8.1), $R_n/(n+2) \xrightarrow{\text{a.s.}} R$, $G_n/(n+2) \xrightarrow{\text{a.s.}} 1 - R$ for some R. Thus $R_n/G_n \xrightarrow{\text{a.s.}} R/(1-R)$. Actually R has the beta distribution with parameters 1, 1 (see Karlin and Taylor 1975, p. 290).
(c) Use the Optional Stopping Theorem, noting that $G_{T-1} = 1$.

16. Remember (7.9.9).

17. $Y_n = Y_0 + X_1 + \ldots + X_n$, where $X_i = P - C_i$. Choose t such that $M_X(t) = 1$, and use the Optional Stopping Theorem applied to the martingale $Z_n = \exp(tY_n)$, as for (16).

20. The proof of (7.8.1) requires only slight adaptation.

21. Choose $t_0>0$ such that $\phi_S(t)\neq 0$ if $|t|\leq t_0$. Then $\phi_n(t)\neq 0$ for all large n and $|t|\leq t_0$. It is now easy to show that $\{Z_n\}$ is a uniformly bounded martingale whenever $|t|\leq t_0$. The final observation, that sums which converge in distribution converge almost surely as well, follows by the following steps:
(a) for almost every $\omega\in\Omega$, there exists $T_\omega\subseteq T=[-t_0,t_0]$ such that $T\backslash T_\omega$ has Lebesgue measure 0 and $\lim_{n\to\infty}\exp(itS_n(\omega))$ exists for $t\in T_\omega$ (remember that $\phi_n(t)\to\phi_S(t)$ as $n\to\infty$);
(b) if s_n is real and $\exp(its_n)$ converges to a limit for each $t\in T$, then s_n converges to a finite limit. (See Chung 1974, pp. 176, 248, 347, for some more details.)

22. $S_{n+1}=\mathbf{E}(S_{n+1}\mid S_{n+1})=\sum_{i=1}^{n+1}\mathbf{E}(X_i\mid S_{n+1})=(n+1)\mathbf{E}(X_{n+1}\mid S_{n+1})$ by symmetry. Thus,

$$\mathbf{E}(S_n\mid S_{n+1})=\left(1-\frac{1}{n+1}\right)S_{n+1}.$$

24. $S_T=T-p^{-3}(1+p+p^2)$. Use (7.9.3). The answer to the last part is $p^{-1}+(p^2q)^{-1}$. Note that these two mean values are different if $p=q=\frac{1}{2}$, even though HHH and HTH are equally likely to occur in any sequence of three tosses.

25. The event $A=\lim_{r\to\infty}\{|X_n-X_m|>r^{-1}\text{ i.o.}\}$ satisfies $\mathbf{P}(A)=0$. Use Cauchy convergence at each $\omega\in A$.

Chapter 8

1. If $m\geq 0$, $c(m)=\sum_{i=0}^{r-m}\alpha_i\alpha_{m+i}$.

2. Note that $Y_n=\sum_{j=0}^{\infty}\alpha^jZ_{n-j}$, where the limit of the partial sums exists in mean square and almost surely (use the stationarity of Y to bound the mean square difference, or use (7.8.1)). If $m>0$ then

$$c(m)=\mathbf{E}(Y_nY_{n-m})=\mathbf{E}((\alpha Y_{n-1}+Z_n)Y_{n-m})=\alpha c(m-1).$$

3. $N(t)$ has a negative binomial distribution. For integral $t\leq k$, $\mathbf{P}(N(t)=k)=\binom{k}{t}p^{t+1}(1-p)^{k-t}$.

4. This is the immigration–death process of (6.11.3) and (6.13.16).

Chapter 9

1. $c(m)=0$ $(m\neq 0)$, $c(0)=\frac{1}{2}$. $\mathbf{E}(\cos(nU)\cos\{(n+m)U\}\cos\{(n+m+r)U\})$ depends on n. Remember (9.2.13).

2. Remember (9.5.4). $c(h)=1-|h|$ if $|h|<1$; now use (5.11.21a).

3. (a) Use (9.2.12) to find that $f(\lambda)=\dfrac{1}{2\pi}\left(1+\dfrac{2\alpha\cos\lambda}{(1+\alpha^2)}\right)$, $|\lambda|\leq\pi$.
(b) $f(\lambda)=\dfrac{1}{2\pi\sigma^2}|A(e^{i\lambda})|^2$, where $\sigma^2=\sum\alpha_j^2$ and $A(z)=\sum_{j=0}^{r}\alpha_jz^{r-j}$. Compare with the result of (9.2.17).

4. Recall Problem (5.11.16).

5. Expand.

6. If $\mathbf{E}(X_k)=0$ for all k then $\mathbf{E}(Y_k\bar{Y}_{k+m})=\sum_{i,j}\lambda_i\lambda_jc(m+j-i)$.

7. $n^{-1}\sum_{j=0}^{n-1}c(j)=\mathbf{E}(X_1\langle X\rangle_n)$ is the covariance of X_1 and $\langle X\rangle_n$. Use the Cauchy–Schwarz inequality to prove that the first limit implies the second. Conversely, expand the

quadratic to find that

$$\mathbf{E}(\langle X\rangle_n^2)=\frac{1}{n^2}\left\{2\sum_{i=1}^{n}\sum_{j=0}^{i-1}c(j)-nc(0)\right\}.$$

Given $\epsilon>0$, pick N such that $\left|n^{-1}\sum_{j=0}^{n-1}c(j)\right|<\epsilon$ for all $n\geq N$. Then

$$\left|\frac{1}{n^2}\sum_{i=1}^{n}\sum_{j=0}^{i-1}c(j)\right|\leq\left|\frac{1}{n^2}\sum_{i=1}^{N-1}\sum_{j=0}^{i-1}c(j)\right|+\left|\frac{1}{n^2}\sum_{i=N}^{n}i\cdot\left(\frac{1}{i}\sum_{j=0}^{i-1}c(j)\right)\right|\leq\frac{A}{n^2}+\epsilon.$$

9. (b) You may need (7.10.1).

10. You should prove that there exists $\lambda\geq 0$ such that
(a) $\mathbf{P}(X(t)=0)=e^{-\lambda t}$
(b) $t^{-1}\mathbf{P}(X(t)\geq 2)\to 0$ as $t\downarrow 0$
(c) $t^{-1}\mathbf{P}(X(t)=1)\to\lambda$ as $t\downarrow 0$.
It is easy to deduce that $X(t)$ has the Poisson distribution. Merely show that $G_t(s)=\mathbf{E}(s^{X(t)})$ satisfies $G_{t_1+t_2}=G_{t_1}G_{t_2}$ (see Çinlar 1975, pp. 71–75, for more details).

11. (a) $X(s+t)=(X(s+t)-X(s))+X(s)$. Remember the hint in (4.10.5).

12. Check the conditions of (9.7.1).

13. Either use transforms (see Prabhu 1965*a*, p. 97) or change the variables in (9.7.11) from (y,t) to (x,τ) by $x=ye^{\beta t}$, $\tau=(1-e^{-2\beta t})/(2\beta)$ to obtain the forward diffusion equation for a Wiener process. Recall (9.2.15) for the last part.

14. Find the autocorrelation function of W. $X(t)=(1-t)W(t/(1-t))$ for $0\leq t<1$.

15. This transformation arises from (14) if $u(s)=e^{\beta s}-e^{-\beta s}$ and $v(t)=e^{-\beta t}$. Show that U is Gaussian and has stationary independent increments with the correct distributions.

16. We seek a solution $f(y,t)$ to the diffusion equation of (9.7.10) which satisfies the boundary condition $f(b,t)=0$ for all t (think of the random walk analogy). Let $f(y,t\mid x,0)$ be the density function of $D(t)$ in the absence of the absorbing barrier, starting from $D(0)=x$; f is the $N(x+mt,t)$ density function. By the method of images (or inspection)

$$f(y,t)=f(y,t\mid 0,0)-e^{2mb}f(y,t\mid 2b,0)$$

is the required solution.

17. Recall the proof of (9.8.13).

18. (a) If $a>0$, $b>0$ then $p_t(b\mid a)=\mathbf{P}(W(t)>b,F(0,t)\mid W(t)=a)$ satisfies (by the reflection principle: draw a diagram)

$$\begin{aligned}p_t(b\mid a)&=\mathbf{P}(W(t)>b\mid W(0)=a)-\mathbf{P}(W(t)<-b\mid W(0)=a)\\&=\mathbf{P}(b-a<W(t)<b+a\mid W(0)=0).\end{aligned}$$

But $\mathbf{P}(F(0,t)\mid W(0)=a,W(t)=b)=-\left(\frac{\partial}{\partial b}p_t(b\mid a)\right)\Big/f(b,t\mid a)$ for some appropriate conditional density function f.
(b) Use (9.8.8). (c) Let $t_0\downarrow 0$ in (b).

19. (a) Separate the variables in (9.9.9) to find solutions of the form $p(\mathbf{w})=\sum_{n\geq 0}r^n\{a_n\sin(n\theta)+b_n\cos(n\theta)\}$, if $\mathbf{w}=(r,\theta)$ where $r<1$. By the theory of Fourier series applied to the appropriate boundary condition, $a_n=(1-\cos(n\pi))/(n\pi)$, and so on. The same argument works for $r>1$ by replacing r^n by r^{-n}.

20. (a) Project $\mathbf{W}$ onto the direction of OP to obtain a one-dimensional process.
(b) Take ℓ to be parallel to the y axis and let $T(d)$ be the first passage time of W_1 to ℓ. Find the characteristic function of $W_2(T(d))$ by conditioning on $T(d)$ and using (9.8.5) and (5.11.14e).
(c) Remember (4.10.4b).

Chapter 10

1. (a) Use (10.1.3).
(b) There exists r such that $F_r(t)<1$, since if $F(t_0)<1$ then $F_n(nt_0)<1$. But, if $n=mr+s$ then $F_n(t)\leqslant\{F_r(t)\}^m$. Now use (10.1.7).
2. Condition on X_1 as for (10.1.9), and either follow the proof of (10.1.11) or use Lebesgue–Stieltjes transforms.
4. (a) For fixed x, let $t\to\infty$ and $n\to\infty$ in such a way that $(t-n\mu)(\sigma^2 n)^{-1/2}=-x$. Then

$$\lim_{t\to\infty}\mathbf{P}\left(\frac{N(t)-t/\mu}{\sqrt{(t\sigma^2/\mu^3)}}<x\right)=\lim_{\substack{t\to\infty\\ n\to\infty}}\mathbf{P}(S_n>t).$$

Now use the Central Limit Theorem.
5. Apply the Key Renewal Theorem to the result of (10.3.4).
6. $D(t)=C(t)+E(t)$, where $C(t)$ is truncated exponential and $E(t)$ is exponential.
7. $\mathbf{P}(\tilde{N}(t)\leqslant k)=\mathbf{P}(Z>t-(k+1)T)$ where Z is $\Gamma(\lambda, k+1)$.
9. (a) Remember that $x+x^3/3!+\ldots=\frac{1}{2}(e^x-e^{-x})$.
(b) The sum of independent identically distributed exponential variables has the gamma distribution.
10. $\mathbf{P}(E(t)\geqslant x, C(t)\geqslant y)=\mathbf{P}(E(t-y)\geqslant x+y)$. Use (10.3.5).
11. If $\tilde{N}$ is a renewal process then its inter-arrival times are not arithmetic.
12. $F^*(\theta)=1-\theta\mu+\frac{1}{2}\theta^2(\sigma^2+\mu^2)+o(\theta^2)$ as $\theta\to 0$; remember that

$$g^*(\theta)=1\quad\text{if}\quad g(t)=\begin{cases}1 & \text{for } t\geqslant 0\\ 0 & \text{for } t<0.\end{cases}$$

To establish the integral equation note that

$$m^D(t)=F_E(t)+\int_0^t F_E(t-x)\,dm(x)$$

where m^D is the renewal function of the stationary delayed renewal process whose first inter-arrival time has distribution function F_E; now use (10.4.19). In applying the Key Renewal Theorem to $g(t)=1-F_E(t)$, you may need to change the order of integration.
13. Either follow the proof of (10.1.11) or use Laplace–Stieltjes transforms together with (10.1.14), (10.4.13), and the result of (2).
14. $m(t)\simeq(\nu-1)(\lambda/\beta)e^{\lambda t(\nu-1)}$ where $\lambda^{-1}=\mathbf{E}(T)$.
15. Use (10.4.5) and (10.1.14), remembering the appropriate part of the hint for (12).

Chapter 11

1. $\boldsymbol{\pi}$ satisfies $\sum\pi_i=1$, $\mu\pi_1-\lambda\pi_0=0$, and $\mu\pi_{n+1}-\pi_n(\lambda+\mu)+\lambda\pi_{n-1}=0$ for $1\leqslant n\leqslant N-1$. Thus $\pi_n=\rho^n(1-\rho)/(1-\rho^{N+1})$.
2. (a) The equilibrium queue length has a Poisson distribution.
3. Writing $\pi(i,j)=\mathbf{P}(Q_1=i, Q_2=j)$, in the obvious notation, we obtain equations of the form

$$\mu_2\pi(i,j+1)+\mu_1\pi(i+1,j-1)-\pi(i,j)(\lambda+\mu_1+\mu_2)+\lambda\pi(i-1,j)=0$$

for appropriate i and j. Substitute $\pi(i, j) = A\theta^i\psi^j$ in this bivariate difference equation to obtain $\theta = \lambda/\mu_1$, $\psi = \lambda/\mu_2$, and thus $\pi(i, j) = (1-\theta)(1-\psi)\theta^i\psi^j$ if $\theta, \psi < 1$.

4. The number $Q(D_n)$ of waiting customers at the end of the nth service period (excluding those just served) satisfies $Q(D_{n+1}) = A + Q(D_n) - h(Q(D_n))$ where A is the number of arrivals during a typical service period and $h(x) = \min\{x, m\}$. Thus the generating function $G(s) = \mathbf{E}(s^Q)$ of the equilibrium queue length Q satisfies

$$G(s) = \mathbf{E}(s^A)\mathbf{E}(s^{Q-h(Q)})$$

giving

$$G(s) = \frac{\sum_{i<m} \pi_i(s^m - s^i)}{\{s^m/M_S(\lambda(s-1))\} - 1}$$

where $\pi_i = \mathbf{P}(Q = i)$. The π's are found by the condition that, inside the unit circle $|s| < 1$ in the complex plane, the numerator vanishes whenever the denominator vanishes (see Cox and Smith 1961, p. 170, but correct the obvious misprint).

5. To find $M_B(s)$, either use (11.3.17) or, more elegantly, the random walk method from the end of Section 11.2 together with (5.3.5), to find that

$$M_B(s) = (\mu/\lambda)^{1/2}\{h(s) - (h(s)^2 - 1)^{1/2}\}$$

where $h(s) = (\lambda + \mu - s)(4\lambda\mu)^{-1/2}$. For the final part, remember the discussion after (11.2.3) and see Feller 1971, pp. 437, 482.

6. For $M(\lambda)/M(\mu)/1$, you will find that $\eta = \rho$. To do the last part, note that, in the obvious notation,

$$\mathbf{P}(W \leqslant x) = \mathbf{P}(S_1 + \ldots + S_{Q(A)} \leqslant x),$$

and remember the gamma distribution.

7. $\mathbf{E}(Q(D)) = \rho + \frac{1}{2}\lambda^2\mathbf{E}(S^2)/(1-\rho)$. Using the method of (11.3.16), $\mathbf{E}(Q(D)) = \lambda\mathbf{E}(W+S)$.

8. Find an expression for $F(x; t+dt)$ by conditioning on the event that a customer arrives in $(t, t+dt)$. For a solution of this differential equation see Prabhu 1965*b*, p. 48.

9. To derive (11.4.12) from the integral equation, follow Cox and Smith 1961, p. 119. Otherwise, merely check that the result of (11.4.12) satisfies the integral equation. To see this, you may need the following observations.
(a) If $y \geqslant 0$ then $G(y) = 1 - \alpha e^{-\mu y}$, for some $\alpha \geqslant 0$, where μ is the parameter of an exponential service time. For,

$$1 - G(y) = \mathbf{P}(S - X > y) = \int_0^\infty e^{-\mu(x+y)}\,dF_X(x).$$

(b) $$\int_{-\infty}^{x} e^{ty}\,dG(y) = \int_{-\infty}^{\infty} e^{ty}\,dG(y) - \int_{x}^{\infty} e^{ty}\,dG(y) = \frac{\mu}{\mu - t}\{M_X(-t) - \alpha e^{-(\mu-t)x}\}$$

for $x \geqslant 0$, $0 < t < \mu$.

10. Use the hint after (11.5.20).

11. Use the Wiener–Hopf equation of (9) to deduce that

$$F(r) = 1 - \left(\frac{-1+\sqrt{5}}{2}\right)^{r+1}, \qquad r = 0, 1, \ldots$$

12. Note first that $\eta = \mathbf{P}(\Sigma$ has a ladder point) satisfies $\eta = \rho$. For, let $s \to -\infty$ in the result of (11.3.16) to find that $\mathbf{P}(W > 0) = \rho$. Now substitute $M_W(s)$ into (11.5.20) to find that I_d has moment generating function $(M_X(s) - 1)/(s\mathbf{E}(X))$, where X is an inter-arrival time of the $G/M/1$ queue.

List of notation

a, b, c, d	constants
$c(n), c(t)$	autocovariances
$\text{cov}(X, Y)$	covariance
f, f_j, f_{ij}	probabilities
$f(x), f_X(.)$	mass or density functions
$f_{Y\mid X}(y \mid x)$	conditional density
$f_{X,Y}(x, y)$	joint density
$g(.), h(.)$	nice functions
i	$\sqrt{(-1)}$
i, j, k, l, m, n, r, s	indices
$m(.), m^D(.)$	mean functions
max, min	maximum, minimum
$p, p_i, p_{ij}, p(t), p_i(t)$	probabilities
$\text{var}(X)$	variance
$B(a, b)$	beta function
$B(n, p)$	binomial distribution
$C(t), D(t), E(t)$	current, total, excess life
$\mathbf{E}$	expectation
$F(r, s)$	F distribution
$F(x), F_X(x)$	distribution functions
$F_{Y\mid X}(y \mid x)$	conditional distribution
$F_{X,Y}(x, y)$	joint distribution
$G(s), G_X(s)$	generating functions
H, T	head, tail
I_A	indicator of the event A
J	Jacobian
$M(t)$	moment generating function
$N(\mu, \sigma^2)$	Normal distribution
$N(t)$	Poisson process
$\mathbf{P}(.), \mathbf{Q}(.)$	probability measures
$Q(t)$	queue length
$X, Y, Z, X(\omega)$	random variables
$\mathbf{X}, \mathbf{Y}, \mathbf{W}$	random vectors
$\mathbf{V}(\mathbf{X})$	covariance matrix
$W(t), \mathbf{W}(t)$	Wiener processes
W, W_n	waiting times

$\mathcal{A}, \mathcal{B}, \mathcal{F}, \mathcal{G}, \mathcal{H}, \mathcal{I}$	σ-fields
$\mathcal{B}$	Borel σ-field
δ_{ij}	Kronecker delta
$\delta(t)$	Dirac delta
η	probability of extinction
$\chi^2(.)$	chi-squared distribution
$\phi(t)$	characteristic function
$\psi(X)$	conditional expectation
μ	mean
μ_i	mean recurrence time
$\boldsymbol{\pi}$	stationary distribution
${}_0\pi_j$	taboo probability
σ	standard deviation
$\rho(n)$	autocorrelation
ω	elementary event
$\rho(X, Y)$	correlation between X and Y
$\Gamma(n)$	gamma function
$\Gamma(\lambda, t)$	gamma distribution
Ω	sample space
$\Phi(x)$	normal distribution
$\mathbb{C}$	complex plane
$\mathbb{R}$	real numbers
$\mathbb{Z}$	integers
$\varnothing$	empty set
$f * g$	convolution
$\hat{g}$	Laplace transform
g^*	Laplace–Stieltjes transform
$\lVert\cdot\rVert$	norm
$\lvert A\rvert$	cardinality of A
$\mathbf{A}'$	transpose of $\mathbf{A}$
$\lvert\mathbf{V}\rvert$	determinant of $\mathbf{V}$
$f'(t)$	derivative of f
$\mathbf{A}'$	matrix with entries $a'_{ij}(t)$

Index

Abbreviations used in this index: c.f. characteristic function; p.g.f. probability generating function; r.v. random variable; r.w. random walk